Romans

Romans

The Divine Marriage

A Biblical Theological Commentary

TOM HOLLAND

PICKWICK *Publications* · Eugene, Oregon

ROMANS
The Divine Marriage—A Biblical Theological Commentary

Pickwick Publications
An Imprint of Wipf and Stock Publishers
199 W. 8th Ave., Suite 3
Eugene, OR 97401

www.wipfandstock.com

ISBN 13: 978-1-60899-809-8

Cataloging-in-Publication data:

Holland, Tom.

    Romans : the divine marriage—a biblical theological commentary / Tom Holland.

    xiv + 544 p. ; 23 cm. Includes bibliographical references and indexes.

    ISBN 13: 978-1-60899-809-8

    1. Bible. N.T. Romans—Commentaries. I. Title.

BS2665.3 H75 2011

Manufactured in the U.S.A.

Dedicated to

Eryl Davies,

a man of vision and grace,
and a Barnabas of our time.

Contents

Preface

WHY SUBTITLE A COMMENTARY on Romans *The Divine Marriage*? Mainly because the central message of the Bible has to do with the drama of God seeking out a people for himself. The Old Testament described Israel as God's bride because she was called to a unique, personal relationship with her God.

However, Paul's contention is that national Israel's exclusive claim to be the bride no longer stands. The apostle's message is that God has created a new covenant with those who believe in his Son, and that believing Jews and Gentiles have now become the true bride of God. The Jewish remnant and believing Gentiles both draw from the same divinely-appointed stock as they share the promises given by God to Abraham.

The theme of the divine marriage (which is the culmination of the new exodus) shaped and guided the letters that Paul wrote. This is especially true for the letter to the Romans, the letter of the divine marriage.

Acknowledgments

THE WRITING OF ANY commentary is far from a solitary task. Although authors hope that they bring a unique contribution to its understanding, all recognize that their thinking has been stimulated and aided by the writings of hundreds, if not thousands, of theologians they have read along the way. In the bibliography, I acknowledge those debating partners who have stimulated my thinking—and I do so with gratitude.

There have been others, whose aid has been as crucial as that of any debating partner. Their encouragement and support have made possible the long process of study and writing. Many individuals deserve mention, but I must limit myself to a few.

I gladly acknowledge the debt I owe to Dr. Eryl Davies, the former principal of The Evangelical Theological College of Wales (now called Wales Evangelical School of Theology [WEST]). He appointed me to a teaching post in the school twenty years ago—a position I continue to hold. Eryl Davies is a Barnabas of our time. His patience, godly example, and support have been humbling to observe and experience. As he watched on, my research must have caused him much concern; but he allowed me the vital space to question and struggle with well-established interpretations of the text of Romans. His support and patience have been crucial to the completion of the research and the writing of this commentary.

I am also grateful to Jonathan Stephen, the present principal of WEST. He has encouraged me to persevere, and has done everything possible to bring this book to publication.

I am also very thankful for a multitude of friends, who have kindly read sections of the text, making valuable suggestions as to how the reading experience could be improved. It is appropriate that I thank especially Colin Hammer, Howard Jones, Bernard Lewis, Anna Coplin, Elsie Marshall, Bill and Ann Weaver, Desmond Cartwright, Digby James, Peter Wilkinson, Gareth Williams, Kevin Green, Iwan Rhys Jones, John Kendall, Tom Gledhill, Toby Cowton, and Barbara, my wife, for the time they gave to this task.

And, of course, how can I not acknowledge the patience and love of Barbara, who has allowed me to spend my life in the service of the Savior.

Tom Holland
WEST (Wales Evangelical School of Theology)

An Open Invitation to the Reader

THIS COMMENTARY SEEKS TO correct the faulty reading that results from placing the individual at the center of the message of Romans. One of the repercussions of such individualism is that almost all hymns speak of individual Christian experience instead of the corporate people of God.

To help pastors provide better hymns for their congregations to sing, you are invited to contribute to a new listing of songs called "Hymns for the People of God." The collection corrects older hymns that are out of copyright and invites song writers to submit their own work. Revision of more recent songs can only be accepted with the copyright holder's permission. The hymns are about God's saving love for his covenant people.

To view and add to the hymn list, please visit
www.hymnsforthetwentyfirstcenturychurch.com

To see reviews and comments on *Romans: The Divine Marriage*, visit
www.romansthedivinemarriage.com

For exploring new exodus theology and for further resources visit
www.exploringnewexodustheology.com

Abbreviations

AffCr	*Affirmation & Critique* (Anaheim, Calif)
ALW	*Archiv fur Liturgiewissenschaft* (Regensburg)
AnaBib	*Analecta Biblica*
AnaBru	*Analecta Bruxellensia*
ATI	*American Theological Inquiry*
AusBR	*Australian Biblical Review*
Bib	*Biblica*
BibToday	*Bible Today*
BR	*Biblical Research*
BSac	*Bibliotheca Sacra*
BT	*Bible Translator*
BTB	*Biblical Theological Bulletin*
CBQ	*Catholic Biblical Quarterly*
Di	*Dialog*
DPL	*Dictionary of Paul and His Letters*
DS	*Daughters of Sarah*
EGT	*Eglise er théologie*
Enc	*Encounter*
EstBib	*Estudios Biblicos*
EvQ	*Evangelical Quarterly*
EvT	*Evangelische Theologie*
ExAud	*Ex Auditu*
ExpTim	*Expository Times*
HeyJ	*Heythrop Journal*
HTR	*Harvard Theological Review*
HvTSt	*Hervormde Teologiese Studies*
IBS	*Irish Biblical Studies*
Int	*Interpretation*
JBL	*Journal of Biblical Literature*
JETS	*Journal of the Evangelical Theological Society*
JJS	*Journal of Jewish Studies*
JPS	*Journal of Pentecostal Studies*
JSJ	*Journal for the Study of Judaism*
JSNT	*Journal for the Study of the New Testament*

JTS	Journal of Theological Studies
Jud	Judaica (Basil)
KEK	H. A. W. Meyer, Kritisch—exegetischer Kommentar über das Neue Tesament
Neot	Neotestamentica
NestTheolRev	Near East School of Theology Theological Review (Beirut)
NICNT	New International Commentary of the New Testament
NovT	Novum Testamentum
NTS	New Testament Studies
PCB	Peaks Commenatry on the Bible
RTR	Reformed Theological Review
ResQuart	Restoration Quarterly
RevExp	Review and Expositor
RBB	Revista biblica brasileira
SBET	Scottish Bulletin of Evangelical Theology
SBL	Society of Biblical Literature
SBLDS	SBL Dissertation Series
SBT	Studies in Biblical Theology
SE	Studia Evangelica
SID	Studies in Interreligious Dialogue
SJT	Scottish Journal of Theology
ST	Studia Theologica
TDNT	Theological Dictionary of the New Testament
Them	Themelios
TheolBeitr	Theologische Beiträge (Wuppertal)
TJ	Trinity Journal
TLZ	Theologische Literaturzeitung
TRu	Theologische Rundschau
TToday	Theology Today
TynBul	Tyndale Bulletin
USQR	Union Seminary Quarterly Review
VE	Verbum et Ecclesia
WTJ	Westminster Theological Journal
ZNW	Zeitschrift für die neutestamentliche Wissenschaft

Introduction

GETTING INTO ROMANS

IT IS UNDERSTANDABLE IF you are tempted to skip the introduction.. You might not be interested in technical details about the letter but in what the letter says. Despite this, I hope you will read this section because it is important and it will help you to understand what is going on in Paul's letter to the Romans.

In the introduction, I am not going to discuss topics usually found at the opening of commentaries on Romans such as the dating of the letter, where it was written, to whom it was written, whether the last chapter was part of the original letter etc. There are plenty of commentaries which deal with such matters and I can add nothing to what has been said. In this commentary, I wish to keep to the message of the letter. For anyone who wants answers to the above, there are numerous books that can be consulted.[1]

FACING THE PROBLEMS

Reading any part of the New Testament provides us with great challenges. First, the New Testament was mostly written by Jews. (Luke was an exception, but it can be shown that he had become heavily influenced by his Jewish companions.) In writing their accounts of Jesus and his teaching, the history of the Jewish people was crucial to their plots. However, there is an added complication. They wrote for Gentiles as well as Jews, and this could have influenced the cultural settings of their writings. Was the setting Jewish or Greek, or did the writers slide between the two cultures in an unconscious way just as Europeans slide between American culture and their own?

Second, the New Testament documents were written almost two thousand years ago and we know that ideas and language can change even within a generation. Today, the cultural gap between older and younger generations is partly because the young are living in a rapidly advancing technological age in which the meaning and significance of familiar words, symbols, and stories have changed. As a result, the older generation feels uncomfortable. If such alterations can take place in one generation and within the same people group, how much greater are the changes that have happened over two thousand years and between people of different cultures? The western reader especially has huge cultural hurdles to overcome when reading the Bible.

---

1. See e.g., Dunn, *Romans*; Fitzmyer, *Romans*; Witherington *Romans*, and the extended bibliographies they provide.

HISTORICAL RECONSTRUCTION

These obstacles to understanding the message of the New Testament are not new. Scholars have been aware for a long time that different variations of thought existed in the NT and most modern scholars have assumed that the early church was willing to sacrifice its Jewish inheritance in order to communicate its message effectively to the Gentile world. Until recently, it was widely assumed the early church had been swamped by Greek thinking.

Most scholars claim this process of Hellenization (that is, the domination of Greco-Roman culture) can be seen in the three layers of tradition in the New Testament documents, especially the Gospels. The first layer is seen to be Jewish, coming from the life and teaching of Jesus in Palestine. After the first Easter, when the church took its message to the Jews who were scattered throughout the Roman Empire (the Diaspora), the message was simplified for them because they lacked the background of Palestinian Judaism. To help them understand the teaching of Jesus, his message was rewritten. So, for example, imagery was dropped that would have been understood in Palestine but was meaningless in their cultures. In its place, imagery familiar to the Diaspora Jews was used. Hence, a second layer of tradition emerged.

The third layer of tradition appeared when the church began to explain its message to the Gentiles. These knew even less of the Palestinian background of Jesus' life and teaching. It is argued they lacked the knowledge of the Old Testament that the Diaspora Jews shared with the Palestinian Jews. Many scholars believe the original Jewish message was all but abandoned by the church as it attempted to communicate its message in a Hellenistic context to the Gentiles.[2] Imagery familiar to them was used to explain the message concerning Jesus. An example of imagery thought to have been adopted at this stage was slave purchase which was likened to redemption. This evolution of the message of Christ is still assumed by many scholars to be the historical development of the New Testament writings.[3]

2. So e.g., Chadwick, "All Things," 273, says: "The eschatological and apocalyptic character of the primitive Palestinian Gospel was a grave liability in preaching the Gospel of Christ to an audience of Hellenistic intellectuals, he boldly reinterpreted the Gospel so as to put into the background the concept of the end of the world, and interpreted the supremacy of Jesus Christ in terms of Cosmic Wisdom, the agent of God in creation." Hengel, *The Atonement*, 4, says: "Any historical investigation which is to do justice to the New Testament cannot be content with stressing the tradition of the Old Testament and Judaism, important though that may be; it must also pay very close attention to the Greco-Roman world, where the problems become particularly interesting to the point where Jewish and Greek conceptions have already become fused in the pre-Christian period." Engberg-Pedersen, *Stoics*, argues that Paul cannot be understood without the help of the stoic philosophers. See also Ashton, *Religion*; Klijn, "Study"; Boers, "Jesus"; Kee, "Christology," 232; Kummel, *Theology*, 105ff. and 118ff.; Marshall, "Palestinian," 283; Davies, *Rabbinic*, 105; Sanders, *Paul*, 555; Strom, *Reframing*; and Sampley, "Roman." Contra Munck, "Jewish," 103–16; Dunn, "Identity," 175; Nanos, *Romans* 8; Wright, "Faith," 77.

3. In recent years, it has been increasingly recognized that the NT is essentially a collection of Jewish writings (See Nanos, *Mystery*, 8), and that the above outline has been mistaken. Nevertheless, it is still assumed to be true by some academics, and its assumptions guide the arguments that are found in many books. Even though there has been this growing recognition of the NT texts being Jewish, it is my claim that they are still read with Hellenistic predispositions. This applies even to those scholars who are recognized as having identified this hiatus of culture and thought.

PRACTICAL IMPLICATIONS

If this is a true account of how the New Testament writings developed, then the apostles have left an example for future generations of Christians. Whenever we take the Gospel into a new culture, we are at liberty to discard from its message anything offensive or obscure. Indeed, it is our duty (just as it was for the early church) to rewrite the Gospel using culturally acceptable symbols that would help the people we are seeking to evangelize. The legitimacy of this contextualization is so widely assumed that it is hardly commented upon.

KEY QUESTIONS

However, the observation above raises two very important questions. The first is: "How can we know the meaning of the New Testament documents if we do not know the culture against which they should be read?" The second question is: "Should we preserve the details of these documents in their apostolic form or is it our responsibility to copy the early church's apparent example in reinterpreting their message in a way that speaks to people today?" If the answer to the latter question is affirmative, then the outcome is the collapse of objective biblical truth because truth would change according to the context in which it is being read or heard. This is at the core of much modern thinking, leading many to abandon hope that there is such a thing as objective biblical truth.

The dilemma of preserving the meaning of a set of beliefs while taking it into another culture is not just historical, it is modern and immediately relevant to the mission of the church. It exists on all five continents as Christian evangelists take the Gospel into new cultures. How should they fulfil their task? Do they follow the apostles' supposed model of contextualization, allowing, for example, the Indians of South America to adopt Christ and surround him with all the paraphernalia of their cultural and religious understanding? This is the dilemma and heartache of many Christian missionaries as they see the Gospel distorted and effectively abandoned when it absorbs alien traditions. Would not the same loss have happened in the early church if this process had been pursued by the apostles in their evangelism of the Gentiles?

The belief that Hellenization controlled the emergence of New Testament documents applied to most documents but not all. Those that are normally exempt are the letters of James, Jude, and the writer to the Hebrews. All are commonly seen to be written to Jewish Christian communities and so underwent little contextualization.

CHANGES IN UNDERSTANDING

If the assumption is correct that Paul and the other apostles Hellenized the Gospel,[4] it follows there were significant Greek influences on the theological understanding of the early church. In other words, God had not finally revealed himself through the words and writings of the prophets of the Old Testament and Jesus. His final message came through philosophical debate, as well as intellectual and spiritual syncretism. From this

---

4. See e.g., Blauw, "Pioneer," 66–75.

perspective, it ought to be clear why liberal theology has been so devastating for the life and witness of the church. Its teaching has resulted in the Bible being abandoned in favor of a much more "certain truth"—the speculations of man.

But things are changing in scholarly understanding.[5] The assumptions outlined above are now being seriously challenged. The evidence suggests this process never took place when the New Testament was being written.[6] The original teaching of Jesus and the apostles was not Hellenized, and the teaching of the church remained faithful to its Jewish origin. This Greek influence did not begin to pervade the thinking of the church until the second century AD—too late to have any influence on the early church.

The Hellenization of the church was due to two momentous events. The first was the division that took place between the Gentile church and the Jewish mother church in the latter part of the first century. The second was the rise of Gentile leadership within the emerging Gentile church. These men brought with them the baggage of their Hellenistic training and unwittingly read it into the Greek text of the Hebrew scriptures and the New Testament writings. In other words, the Hellenization of the Christian Gospel was later than scholars have assumed—it was not in the apostolic age but in the time of the church fathers. The outcome was that Gentile Christians lost touch with the Jewish roots of their scriptures.

The appreciation that the New Testament is essentially Jewish is partly the fruit of studies done on the Dead Sea Scrolls which were discovered in 1947. These pristine Jewish documents, totally unaffected by Hellenistic influences, used much of the same language and imagery that had been assumed to be Hellenistic in origin. Previously, the presence of this language in the New Testament was understood to be proof that its documents had absorbed Hellenistic teachings, but here was crucial evidence in authentic Jewish writings that showed that language which had been supposed to be Hellenistic was not unique to Hellenism. In other words, the liberal argument which held that the Christian message and the church's understanding of the person of Christ evolved "from Jewish prophet to Gentile God" crumbled.[7] No evidence existed to support such a theory.

A DIFFERENT UNDERSTANDING

It is now being realized that there is a much better way to explain how the Gospel of Jesus was communicated. Instead of the message being adapted to the culture of the people that were hearing it for the first time, they were taught the Jewish history and culture from which the Gospel originated. The Jewish scriptures (the Christian Old Testament) dominated this, of course. Through their newly acquired understanding, converts were helped to understand the significance of the life and teaching of Jesus against his Jewish

---

5. See, e.g., Dunn, "Identity," 174–93, where he argues that Paul was anchored in the historic, religious heritage of his people but was adapting to the demands of the fresh revelation of fulfillment that had come in Jesus Christ.

6. Skarsaune, *Shadow*, argues for a much longer continuance of the Jewish influence on the Christian church than is normally recognized.

7. Casey, *Gentile*, 253–77.

background. The responsibility of the Christian teachers was to apply the principles of this Jewish message to the life of the churches which were made up of Jews and Gentiles.

The following scenario is what probably happened. The first missionaries were Jews who went to the synagogues with their message. In the synagogues, Jews shared their culture with God-fearers. These were Gentiles who were disgusted with the corruption and teaching of their religions and had turned to the God of the Jewish people, attracted by the moral standards of Judaism. Despite attending the synagogue services, few God-fearers became Jews because of the initiation ceremony of circumcision. Most Gentiles found this an immense obstacle to converting to Judaism.

The good news about Jesus was first taken to these Jews and God-fearing Gentiles in the synagogue. They had knowledge of the Old Testament and did not need to be taught Israel's history and culture. After a short period of instruction, they were able to understand the message of Jesus almost in its entirety. Furthermore, they were soon capable of teaching others who came to faith in the Messiah.

Often the apostles were driven out of the communities they had preached to, leaving behind a handful of believers who were young in the faith (Acts 13:40—14:7) but who were able to grow because they had the Old Testament. These scriptures formed the cultural base of Judaism and taught the believers all that God was going to do. The scriptures gave them a framework to understand their past and hope to face their future.

What sort of things guided a Jew in his thinking in the first century of the Christian calendar? To understand this, we need to know something of the history of the Jewish people because for individuals, as well as nations, it is our past that moulds our self-awareness, our present and our future.

THE INFLUENCE OF HELLENISM ON POST ENLIGHTENMENT NEW TESTAMENT STUDIES.

For many decades, the New Testament has been interpreted by relying on Greek secular texts. They appeared to be the source of many New Testament ideas. This reliance on Greek texts, and hence Greek culture, has been reinforced by the academic preparation for studying theology. Since the New Testament documents were written in the common Greek that pervaded every level of the Hellenistic world, it was understandable that a thorough grounding in the Greek classics was thought to be the most appropriate preparation for studying theology.

As a result, New Testament scholars of previous generations followed this well-trodden and little-questioned route into the discipline. Those who had this classical education were considered to be eminently suited to the task of New Testament exegesis. They were able make use of their classical training by applying it to the interpretation of New Testament documents. They had the advantage of their broad knowledge of the Hellenistic world with its culture, thought patterns and vocabulary. They were supremely equipped, it was thought, to interpret the texts.

Few saw the flaw in the method. While the vocabulary of the New Testament could be found throughout the Hellenistic world, it did not have the same meaning when used in a religious sense within the Jewish community. Here, the language had imbibed its own theological meaning as a result of translating the Hebrew Bible into Greek two hundred years or so before Christ. The Hebrew meaning had been poured into the text of the Greek translation to produce a language that had its own particular meaning. Its alphabet and vocabulary were Greek, but its mindset and essential meaning were Hebraic.[8] This is the language Judaism bequeathed to the infant church as she interpreted and proclaimed the message of the prophets.

Seen from this perspective, the classical methodology of training for theological study was fundamentally flawed. The writers of the New Testament had drawn their ideas from Jerusalem, not Athens. Much of the theological literature that exists demonstrates this confusion. Even those who hold to the New Testament's dependence on the Old Testament invariably turn to the classics for help in unraveling ideas or words. It is not unusual to find them referring to Hellenistic culture and literature from which they suppose ideas in the text were drawn. Until this dependence on Hellenism was exposed, there was little chance of identifying the Old Testament origins of New Testament thought and of appreciating the importance of the old exodus paradigm, a subject which will soon be discussed.

Thankfully, this misplaced dependency is increasingly being rectified with more New Testament scholars seeing its documents as Jewish literature. However, even those who are attempting to rectify the previous error still fall into the trap which ensnared former generations and naturally turn to Greek sources to unravel exegetical problems. It is extremely difficult to change a default mental position and the practice of reading the NT as a collection of Greek texts still controls the minds of many scholars. Equally important, the task is not one that scholars alone need to attend to; it is crucial for the church and its teachers to learn to do this.

REDEMPTIVE HISTORY—THE KEY TO THE MINDSET
OF THE EARLY CHURCH

Jews boast that they have a unique history. Their great ancestor, Abraham, lived in Ur, the remains of which are located in modern Iraq. God called him to leave the security of his home and journey to a land that he was promised he would be given (Gen 12:1–9). This is modern Israel. God made a promise to Abraham regarding his descendants. This promise, or covenant, is the basis of all that was to happen to Abraham's offspring (Gen 15:1–21, 17:1–27).

After many trials and setbacks, Abraham and his household eventually settled in the land of Canaan and his descendants prospered. As with most families, there were difficult times. A major setback came almost two hundred years later when descendants moved to Egypt to survive a famine that had ravaged Canaan. They settled in Goshen and enjoyed a time of plenty. As time went by, the government of the land changed and took a hard line against them. The Hebrews became the object of ferocious persecution

---

8. See Hill, *Meanings*; Zeisler, *Righteousness*; Wright, *People*; Hays, *Echoes*; and Beale, "Preach," 89–96.

and were forced into slavery. Their situation worsened and the Pharaoh commanded that their male babies be put to death at birth (Exod 1:8–22).

At this point, another great Hebrew figure came on to the scene of Jewish history. As a baby, Moses' life was spared when an Egyptian princess found him (after his mother, to save his life, had hidden him amongst the reeds at the edge of the river) and adopted him into the royal family (Exod 2:1–10). Eventually, as an adult, he transferred his allegiance to his own people, the Hebrews. He led them out of slavery in Egypt into the wilderness to begin a journey back to their promised land.

The events surrounding this exodus tell of how God protected his people when Pharaoh, the Egyptian ruler, did everything possible to stop them from leaving (Exod 5:1—11:10). Moses warned the king that if he did not let the Hebrews go, his firstborn son would be stricken dead as would those of all the other Egyptian families. This warning was ignored. The Jews, however, obeyed what they were told to do. They took the blood of slain lambs and smeared it on the doorposts of their homes (Exod 12:21–24). That night, the LORD went through the land of Egypt.[9] Wherever he saw the blood, he passed over the dwelling. Where no blood was found, the LORD destroyed the firstborn male child. This was the night of the Passover. Still celebrated by the Jews to this day, it is the greatest event in Jewish history for it precipitated their exodus from Egypt.

The Jews eventually settled once more in the promised land and their subsequent history had its highs and lows. The nation became a monarchy, believing this would change its fortunes. In fact, the nation already had a king whom it would not obey. The king was, of course, God. Their first anointed king was Saul (1 Sam 10:20–24) and he was succeeded by another important figure in Jewish history, King David.

The Bible records that David was a man of integrity who mostly strove to do what he knew God wanted of him. Under his leadership, the nation was made secure and prospered, but he was denied the one thing he wanted. David desired to build a temple in which God could dwell. God would not allow him to do this because as a military commander, he had shed much blood. But he was pleased with David's desire and pledged that rather than having him build a house for God, God would build a house for him. The family of David would become the Jewish royal dynasty and David was promised that one of his descendants would always rule over the chosen people (2 Sam 7:1–17). This promise made by Yahweh to David is known as the Davidic covenant.

THE FAILURE OF THE SON OF PROMISE

Tragically, David's son Solomon was not the king the nation needed. Although known for his wisdom in dealing with Israel's problems, he could not apply this same wisdom to his own life. He demanded too much tax from the people to fund expensive building programs and abandoned God's clear instruction not to marry foreign wives. This was commanded to prevent the gods of the other nations gaining a foothold in the affections of the nation. However, this is exactly what happened. Solomon's foreign wives

---

9. On the night of the Passover, it was "the LORD" who passed through the land (Exod 12:23). Before and after the Passover, the term "angel of the Lord" is used (Exod 3:2; 14:19; 23:20, etc.).

brought their entourages with them and soon not only were thousands of aliens living in Jerusalem as part of the extended royal family but their gods were being worshipped also. The monotheism of Israel's ancestors was being abandoned and paganism, which they had suffered so much to overcome, was being practiced.

With the worship of these foreign gods came the lifestyles of the surrounding nations. The Jewish people imitated them and in so doing broke the moral commands that God had given them. This act of flirting with the gods of the surrounding nations was described as "adultery" (Ezek 16:15ff.; Hos 3:1), for Israel's God was described as a husband and Israel was depicted as his bride. When the Israelites left Egypt under Moses' leadership, they entered into a solemn agreement—a covenant (Exod 24:8). They promised to be faithful to their God, and in return, he promised that he would be faithful to them as a nation. Included in the covenant agreement was a strong warning that God would not tolerate Israel sharing her life with other gods. If she did, God would put Israel away (Deut 30:17–19).

As her national life declined, God sent prophets to warn Israel of her sins and the consequences of not turning back to him. The nation became divided under two kings (1 Kgs 12:1ff.). Both leaders rejected the messages of the prophets and the divided nation declined further into moral chaos. Eventually, God acted against his people. The breakaway northern kingdom was invaded by the Assyrians in BC 721, resulting in deportation. Its cities were destroyed and its people were taken into exile (2 Kgs 17:1–20). Later, the Babylonians came against Judah, who had stayed faithful to the house of David, and destroyed its towns and villages. They laid siege to Jerusalem, its capital, and eventually overthrew it in BC 586 (Jer 39; 2 Kgs 25:1ff.), destroying the entire city including the sacred temple. Members of the royal family were either put to death or taken into captivity along with most of the population (2 Kgs 25:1ff.). It was the beginning of one of the darkest periods of ancient Israel's history.

THE PROMISES OF RESTORATION

Understandably, the morale of the nation collapsed. The people never thought God would allow this to happen to them. They saw the exile as punishment for their sins and found great difficulty in thinking that there could be a new start. But this is the very thing the prophets had promised them. In spite of the collapse of the royal family, they predicted that a descendant of David would be raised up (Isa 11:1; 55:3–4; Jer 33:14–17) who would lead the people from their captivity back to the promised land (Isa 11:11; 48:20–21; 52:1–12; Ezek 36:24). He would be anointed with the Spirit of the Lord for this task (Isa 61:1–2) and would lead the people through the wilderness (Hos 2:14; 12:9). It would be like when the Hebrews left Egypt—it would be a second exodus.

The pilgrimage through this new desert would be under the protection of the Holy Spirit (Isa 44:3; 59:21; 61:1–3; Ezek 36:24–28; 37:1–4), just as the pilgrimage from Egypt had been. There would be miracles (Mic 7:15) as there were when they came out of Egypt, and the desert would be transformed as nature shared in the re-creation of the nation (Isa 55:13). The exiles would return, telling of the salvation of God (Isa 52:7–10) and a new covenant would be established which would center on the Davidic prince (Isa 9:6–7; 11:1; 55:3–4; Jer 33:14–17). Unlike the exodus from Egypt when flesh was circumcised, the hearts of the people would be circumcised (Jer 31:31–34; Ezek 36:26–27).

Once the people arrived back in Jerusalem, they would build a magnificent temple which the descendant of David would dedicate (Ezek 44–45). Into this temple, all the nations would come to worship Israel's God (Isa 2:1–5; 9:1–7; 19:23–25; 49:6–7; 49:22–23; 56:3; 60:3, 10). The Lord would come into his temple (Mal 3:1) and the marriage between God and his people would be celebrated with a great cosmic banquet (Isa 54:1–8; 61:10; 62:4–5; Hos 2:16, 19).

The promises contained in the three paragraphs above are so important for understanding the NT that they are worth committing to memory. These are the promises we find throughout the New Testament, the claim of its writers being that Jesus has, or will, fulfil them all (2 Cor 1:20).

We find the history of the return of the Jews from exile in Babylon in the books of Ezra, Nehemiah and the Minor Prophets such as Haggai, Zechariah and Malachi. What these books show is that while the people attempted to rebuild a temple in Jerusalem (Ezra 3:7ff.; Neh 4:1ff.), it was a pathetic attempt compared with the one which had been destroyed by the Babylonians (Hag 2:3–9). They constantly looked for the coming of the descendant of King David (Hag 1:13–14; Zech 3:8–9), but he did not appear. For four hundred years they groaned in their sense of failure, guilt and disappointment.

CONTINUING PAIN

The next four hundred years saw no significant change for the Jews. They were always under the control of another nation. Their exile seemed to continue and they longed for its end. They had returned to their own land but were as far from God as they had ever been, for despite a brief period during the days of the Maccabees, they never had their own independence; for them, God had not yet fulfilled his promises. Not until they had complete freedom could they accept that their punishment was over. The literature of the Jews during this period—known as the Intertestamental or Second Temple period—shows the faith they continued to have. They clung to the hope that God would fulfil the promises he had made to them through the prophets. The Scriptures surveyed above became their light throughout the long dark years of shame under the domination of Rome.[10] They longed for the promised deliverance from their helplessness and the degradation of enslavement. These promises, though interpreted differently, seem to have been the source of hope for all Jewish groups.

This brief survey indicates the degree to which the expectation of a new exodus had saturated the nation at the time of the Baptist's ministry. To ignore this expectation in any attempt to understand the development of the Christian message would be folly. What is abundantly clear is that the hope that these promises would one day be fulfilled did not die. In all the Jewish literature of the period, there is clear evidence that this hope

---

10. For evidence, see Holland, *Contours*, chapter 1.

was what sustained the nation. The people waited for the day when these promises would be fulfilled.

THE NEW TESTAMENT AND THE NEW EXODUS

God's response to this cry for deliverance resonates throughout the pages of the New Testament. Its message is that God has acted decisively in the death of Jesus, his own Son, to bring about salvation, not from physical or political bondage, but from spiritual slavery.[11]

The main references to the old exodus in the New Testament (there are also numerous allusions and parallels) are in Acts 26:17–18; Gal 1:3–4; Col 1:12–14 and Rev 1:5–6. Luke 1–2 tells of the expectations of a group of devout Jews at the time of the birth of Jesus who would have been in touch with traditions reflected in literature from the intertestamental period. The fact that both John the Baptist and Jesus began their ministries by quoting Isa 40:3–5 (Luke 3:4–6) and Isa 61:1–2 (Luke 4:18–19) respectively is very significant as both passages are old exodus based. By citing these texts, they were declaring that the eschatological (end of time) salvation which Isaiah predicted had at long last broken into human history. Also, when John sent his disciples to Jesus to ask if he was the Christ, Jesus replied by pointing to the signs of Isaiah (Luke 7:21–22). He also commended John in saying that he fulfilled the prophecy of the one sent before the Lord to prepare his way (Luke 7:27), recalling the text in Isa 40:3–5 where the prophet spoke of the announcement of the deliverance from Babylon. The Egyptian exodus was accompanied by miraculous happenings (Exod 7:3), and a repetition of this was predicted by Isaiah (Isa 35:6; 42:7) for the deliverance from Babylon. Jesus said his miracles bore witness to who he was because they were the signs that God's salvation—God's delivering activity for his people—was about to happen at last. Clearly, both John the Baptist and Jesus set their ministries in the context of the Isaianic predictions of the new exodus.[12]

THE NEW MOSES

Among the expectations commonly held in relation to the new exodus was a belief in the identity of the new Moses who would lead the Jews out of captivity. He was not to be of the tribe of Levi, like Moses, but of the tribe of Judah. He was to be none other than the promised descendant of David who Yahweh had declared would have an everlasting throne (Isa 9:7). The identification of Jesus with the promises relating to the Davidic de-

---

11. Ballentine, "Exodus," 27–41; Song & Rand, "Story," 337.

12. For an example of how Mark configured this, see Watts, *Mark*. Luke followed the same reading of the Gospel story; see Strauss, *Davidic*. For a less detailed account of the presence of the new exodus in the understanding of Jesus, see Wright, *Victory*. An on-going collaborative research project, under my supervision, demonstrates that the same understanding is embedded in John's Gospel. Two of the four contributors to the first part of the project (John 1–10) have been awarded PhDs from the University of Wales and their work awaits publication, see Ra, "John," and Coxon, "John." For the theme's presence in Hebrews, see Shin, "Hebrews." A PhD thesis of another student (Richard Cozart) is soon to be examined demonstrating the presence of the theme in Ephesians. Other research on specialized themes within the new exodus motif has also been done which has further identified the motifs widespread presence in Biblical literature.

liverer is crucial for appreciating how the early church understood the person and work of her Savior. It is no coincidence that the evidence brought against Jesus, which secured his crucifixion, related to his claims to kingship. Nor is it less of a coincidence that Jesus denied claims to an earthly kingdom while asserting his claim to a spiritual one.

The significance of this would be clear to any Jewish believer when he heard that Jesus had died with the inscription above his head: "THIS IS THE KING OF THE JEWS" (Luke 23:38). The king was establishing the kingdom in which his followers were to be subjects. If we bypass the eighth century prophets and merely link the significance of Jesus' Davidic descent with the promise to David of an eternal throne, we miss the new exodus motif lurking beneath the surface of the title. Not only is this seen in the Gospel narratives, where Jesus is continually honored as the long-awaited descendant of David, but also in the preaching of the early church as recorded in Acts. The reference to the raising again of the tent of David (Acts 15:16–17) is particularly significant since it demonstrates that the early church saw Jesus to be the promised Davidic king and that all the blessings of the Davidic covenant were fulfilled through him. The title "Son of David" is coupled with the title "the Christ" and used regularly throughout the New Testament. It means "the anointed one" and carries with it all the Messianic associations of the Son of David. In other words, the Davidic king is the Christ.

The New Testament emphasis on Jesus being the promised Son of David must not be missed. Its writers did not need to keep using the term Son of David because they could choose from a range of related titles which, to the first-century believer, meant exactly the same. Many scholars say that Matthew's Gospel (recognized by most as written for the Jews) shows Jesus as the second Moses. But this misses the fact that Moses is only mentioned as a person twice in the Gospel (Matt 17:3, 4)—all other references are about injunctions commanded by him—whereas Jesus is repeatedly called the "son of David" (Matt 1:6, 17, 20; 9:27; 12:23; 15:22; 20:30, 31; 21:15; 22:42, 43, 45). While Matthew's Gospel clearly has an exodus structure, it is not Moses who brings about this deliverance but the Son of David as the prophets had foretold. This fact will be very important for our exposition of the letter to the Romans.

THE MESSIAH AND HIS WORK

For most readers, the name "Jesus Christ" reads like a forename and a family name as is normal in the west. This is unfortunate as the term "Christ" is crucially important. In the Old Testament, the Hebrew *Messiah* meant "the anointed one," and that is the same meaning behind the Greek term *Christos* used in the New Testament.

In the Old Testament, there were many messiahs. Anyone who was anointed was a messiah. So the priests, kings, judges, and prophets were all messiahs. They were anointed with oil when they were set apart for the work God called them to do. The anointing was a symbol of the provision of the Holy Spirit (1 Sam 10:1; 16:13; Isa 61:1–3). While there is nothing unusual in Old Testament terms about someone being called a messiah or Christ, the Jews came to expect that God would send a special one, *the* Messiah, *the* one anointed to deliver Israel from her captivity. So, when Jesus is called "the Christ" (Matt 16:16), Peter is confessing his faith that Jesus is the King whom Yahweh had promised.

We could go through Romans and refer to Jesus as the Messiah or the King, but to reinforce Old Testament roots I have decided to use the term "the Messiah king." This is deliberately done with the hope that the reader will reflect on the roles that the Messiah would fulfill. These have been briefly noted in the section, *The Promises of Restoration*, found on page viii of this commentary. The entire letter is about the Messiah king and how he has completed the work that Yahweh promised he would do for his people.

The centrality of the Messianic theme of the letter is normally overlooked. This has largely been due to the fact that the letter has been read within a Hellenistic framework which has filtered out the significance of *Christos* from its argument. More recent commentators have alerted their readers to its importance but, in my judgment, not sufficiently.[13] While they have acknowledged the importance of the title, they have not driven its significance through the letter.

All four Gospels begin with the theme of the kingship of Jesus, expressed in the terms kingdom/king/*Messiah*/*Christos* and indicating that it was a key theme for the early church. The importance of this theme is further reflected in the use of *Christos* in Romans where Paul uses the title sixty times. (On the other hand, Matthew uses *Christos* only sixteen times, despite the Gospel being twice the length of the Epistle and written for the Jewish church.)[14] As the Roman church appears to have had a large Gentile membership (some thinking that it had become mostly Gentile as a result of the edict of Claudius), the saturation of the letter to the Romans with the term *Christos* has huge significance. It emphasizes the importance of the theme of Jesus being the fulfilment of the Scriptures.

COMMON THEMES

Other new exodus themes are widely dispersed throughout the New Testament. The new covenant (2 Cor 3:6; 5:17; 6:16–18; Heb 8:8–13), circumcision of the heart (Rom 2:28–29; Phil 3:3; Col 2:11), gift of the Spirit (Rom 8:9–27; Gal 4:6–7; 2 Cor 3:16–17; Eph 1:13–14), pilgrimage[15] (Gal 5:18, 25; 2 Cor 5:1–5; Eph 6:13–17; Phil 3:12–14; Heb 3:7—4:11; 12:1–3; 18–28), the eschatological temple (1 Cor 6:19; 2 Cor 6:16; Eph 2:19–22; Rev 21:1–4), the conversion of the nations (Rom 10:12; 15:12–16; Acts 9:15; 15:13–21; Eph 2:11–21), the inclusion of the nations in the covenant community (Rom 2:28–29; Gal 6:15; Eph 3:6) and the eschatological marriage (Rom 7:1–4; 2 Cor 11:2; Eph 5:25ff.; Rev 19:6–8) are further examples of Old Testament expectations overflowing into the aspirations and understanding of the early church.[16]

The above list demonstrates how the New Testament writers relied on and developed the promises of the Old Testament Scriptures. Note how NT arguments of fulfilment dovetail into the list of predictions of what would happen when the new exodus

13. So e.g., Dunn, *Romans;* and Wright, "Romans."

14. The fact that Matthew uses the title "Son of David" seventeen times whereas Romans uses the title three times hardly alters the facts of the emphasis.

15. The NIV effectively hides the pilgrimage motif by translating "walk" (*peripateite*) as "lives."

16. We will discover that other key doctrines have their roots in this model, so topics such as the person of Christ (Christology), justification, sanctification, union with Christ and resurrection.

came to pass as given by the prophets (see pages 6–9). It is vitally important that the significance of this list is appreciated. The New Testament writers continually showed these OT predictions to be fulfilled in the birth, life, death, resurrection and ascension of Jesus of Nazareth, establishing the fact that the infant church was not groping for understanding. She had inherited a theological framework from the Jewish "mother" church which had been taught by her Savior. They knew how to read these key texts. These Scriptures spoke of him, and this realization changed the hearts of people as they entered into the new creation. Once the ministry of Jesus, the true Son of David, was placed at the center of these predictions, the meaning and significance of his person and work broke out with such energy, power, and meaning that it drove the early church on to achieve incredible things for her master.

In addition to the widely recognized themes in these passages, a whole substructure of allusions is lit up with a clarity that is compelling. Much of this material requires detailed exegesis.

This then is the background to the New Testament. Each Gospel begins with John the Baptist announcing that he was the voice of one crying in the desert that the way of the Lord should be prepared (Matt 3:3; Mark 1:3; Luke 3:4; John 1:23). The importance of this text is clear in that it is one of the few events recorded in all four Gospels. John was taking his words from the prophecy of Isaiah which announced the coming of the descendant of David who would fulfil God's promises. When the Lord Jesus stood up in the synagogue and said the Spirit of the Lord was upon him to preach the good news to the poor (Luke 4:18–19), he was claiming to be the one who had come to bring freedom from captivity. He was announcing that he was the Son of David.

PAUL AND ISAIAH

The influence of Isaiah's prophecy on the thinking of Judaism inevitably meant that it also influenced the apostle Paul. Isaiah is not only quoted by Paul more times than the sum of all the other prophets put together, but he (Paul) used his (Isaiah's) writings as the skeleton of his gospel. He arranged citations from Isaiah in such a way as to outline the history of salvation from the fall of Man to the eventual establishment of the Messianic kingdom. Around these quotations, Paul built his argument which frames the letter to the Romans. The full import of this fact is only appreciated when the quotations are listed in the order in which they appear in the letter and read in that same sequence. If we can imagine the original letter being laid out as a continuous papyrus with the citations being raised out of the text and suspended at their point of use, the texts summarize the history of salvation. Such a pattern is mathematically highly improbable and their sequential use can be nothing but intentional:

> As it is written, "God's name is blasphemed among the Gentiles because of you."
> (Rom 2:24; Isa 52:5; LXX)

> As it is written, "Their feet are swift to shed blood; ruin and misery mark their ways, and the way of peace they do not know." (Rom 3:15–17; Isa 59:7–8)

Isaiah cries out concerning Israel: "Though the number of the Israelites be like the sand by the sea, only the remnant will be saved. For the Lord will carry out his sentence on earth with speed and finality." It is just as Isaiah had said previously. (Rom 9:27–28; Isa 10:22–23; LXX)

It is just as Isaiah said previously, "Unless the Lord Almighty had left us descendants, we would have become like Sodom, we would have been like Gomorrah." (Rom 9:29; Isa 1:9; LXX)

As it is written, "See, I lay in Zion a stone that causes men to stumble and a rock that makes them fall." (Rom 9:33a; Isa 8:14)

And "the one who trusts in him will never be put to shame." (Rom 9:33b; Isa 28:16; LXX)

As the Scripture says, "Anyone who trusts in him will never be put to shame." (Rom 10:11; Isa 28:16; LXX)

As it is written, "How beautiful are the feet of those who bring good news!" (Rom 10:15; Isa 52:7)

For Isaiah says, "Lord, who has believed our message?"

But there would be the same response of unbelief to the Gospel message (Rom 10:16; Isa 53:1).

Even so, the electing purposes of God would not be overturned by the sinfulness of humanity. What he purposes, he will achieve (Rom 10:21; Isa 65: 2; Rom 11:8; Isa 29:10).

God's plan will be fulfilled and all Israel, as Paul has already defined her (Rom 4:11–12), will be saved (Rom 11:26–27; Isa 59:20–21; 27:9).

All of this is beyond humanity's ability to conceive; it is of God alone (Rom 11:33–34; Isa 40:13).

The salvation promised through Abraham, in which the nations share in the covenantal blessings, will finally be fulfilled. Those who were never part of the people of God have come into the eschatological community (Rom 15:21; Isa 52:15).

This dependency upon Isaiah must not obscure the fact that the new exodus theme was not -used only by "the evangelical prophet." Pre-exilic, exilic, and post-exilic prophets shared it widely. Because of this, themes that are prominent in the writings of other prophets could be interwoven into the material received from Isaiah, without altering the perspective of the new exodus.

We can see from the above analysis of Romans that the use of Isaiah's writings was not haphazard.[17] The mathematics of chance excludes any possibility that the order of these texts could be an accident. In other words, Paul did not only use the prophecy of Isaiah, he lived by it. It formed the framework of his world view. His reasoning and exposition of the good news of Jesus were arranged around this structure because Jesus,

17. For other ways that Paul depends on Isaiah, see Wagner, *Heralds*, 336–40. For other studies on the importance of Isaiah in early theology, see Punt, "Hermeneutics," 377–425; Wagner, *Romans*, 117–32. For a fuller discussion on Paul's use of Scripture, see Holland, *Contours*, chapter 2.

the Son of David and deliverer of his people, is the fulfilment of all that the prophets had been saying.[18] Paul does not merely use the texts,[19] he is driven by their message. Indeed, it could be said they control him![20] Their meaning forms the foundation of Paul's argument throughout his letter to the Romans.[21]

THE REASON FOR THE LETTER

There are many possible reasons why Paul wrote to the Romans. It could be argued that he wanted to prepare for his trip to Spain (Rom 15:20) and hoped that his letter would generate support to make this mission possible. While he may have hoped to get help from the church, it is difficult to think this would be the reason for his greatest work. A more personal letter would have been far more appropriate for such a task.

It is a fact there were pastoral problems in Rome that needed to be addressed. These problems had their roots in theological confusion. Once they had been unraveled, the pastoral difficulties would begin to be resolved. But what were these problems? Is there evidence that Paul knew any existed? If he did, there is another question that needs to be asked. How did Paul become aware of these problems if it was true that he had never visited the church?

While the themes of the letter have been carefully examined and traces of conflict searched for, we would be guessing about the pastoral and theological misunderstandings of the Roman church if we limited ourselves to this one NT letter. This speculation is part of the reason why so many views are offered. It would be sensible to consider letters

18. Stanley, *Quotations*, 138, says: "Paul seems to have crafted his quotation in such a way that the readers with very little biblical knowledge could grasp his essential point."

19. Contra Laato, "Considerations," 354.

20. Thus Vleugels, "Scriptures," 156–63, is wrong to argue that Paul's ultimate criterion for divine authority lies in God's direct revelation to him, not in Scripture.

21. Molland, *Euangelion*, 33, cited by Käsemann, *Romans*, says that Jesus understood his own mission in terms of Deutero Isaiah. Käsemann accepts the presence of Isaianic influence, but rejects Molland's claim that it formed part of the core of original Jewish Christianity saying the tradition was not widely used in the NT period. Käsemann demonstrates that he misses the thrust of the new exodus theme in Paul when he says: "the Deutero Isaiah tradition was relatively unimportant," 8, [contra Bruce, *Romans*, 72, and Hays, "Believed," 47]. He fails to discern Paul's repeated interplay with the two exoduses of the old covenant. The two have to be played off against each other for the former, while it had an element of promise (Gen 15:7ff.), was not as strong as the promise of the new exodus in the writings of the prophets with its attention on the Davidic prince who would bring it about. Interplay between the two produced the required composite type of the new exodus which is inaugurated by a Passover in which the beloved Son (i.e., the Davidic king) dies as a fulfillment of all that the law and the prophets had pointed to. See Schaefer, "Relationship," 384. If the claim is correct that the new exodus theme is the basis of the Gospels and the Pauline letters, then Bornkamm, *Paul*, 110, is wrong to say that Paul never makes the slightest effort to expound the teaching of the historical Jesus, for Jesus both introduced and interpreted his own ministry in the light of the new exodus promises, cf. Luke 4:14–21 and John 1:23. Fuller, *Foundations*, 189, notes: "This means that the Davidic sonship is now not merely the qualification for the end time messianic office, but has a positive significance for the whole of Jesus' earthly ministry." Thus, the common interpretative factor that harmonizes Jesus and Paul is the new exodus. This hermeneutic model resolves the tensions that many scholars have seen to exist between their teachings. See also Wright, *Victory*, who, despite basing his exegesis of the Gospels on the new exodus model, still thinks that Paul's interpretation of atonement differs from that of Jesus. I will argue that they are mutually consistent and that they draw on common OT concepts.

to the wider church to see if problems that are identifiable in different congregations match remedies prescribed in the Roman letter.[22]

COMMON PROBLEMS

The main problem experienced by Gentile Christianity emanated from the believing Jews. There were many sincere Jewish believers in Christ who could not accept Gentiles into the covenant unless they went through the initiation of circumcision. This affected virtually every church mainly because Judaizers were roaming the empire in an effort to persuade Paul's converts to take the final step of circumcision so they could be brought into the full grace of the covenant.[23]

The issue of circumcision was threatening to split the young church, separating the Gentile church from its "Jewish Christian" mother. For Paul, this would have been disastrous as there was one body and one Lord who dealt with all people on the same grounds of grace. Not only do Paul's letters show him struggling to maintain the relationship between the two communities—a relationship that was costly in the extreme for Paul to advocate—but the writer of the Acts of the Apostles records the lengths he went to in order to keep the doors of communication and fellowship open. His two time-consuming visits to Jerusalem are evidence of the importance of the relationship (Acts 15:1–2; 21:17–26). His first visit was to allow the apostles to examine his ministry and the second was to take a gift from the Gentile churches to the poor in the Jerusalem church. Some scholars see this substantial gift as Paul's attempt to remove Jewish Christian suspicion of the Gentile churches while others contend that he wanted to lead a gift-bearing Gentile team into Jerusalem as fulfilment of prophecy (Isa 60:8–14).

In churches with no evidence of Judaizing subversion, there were other issues that divided. A common problem concerned meat which was offered to idols and then sold in the street market (Rom 14:14–17; 1 Cor 8:4; 10:20, 25–32; Col 2:16). For the converted Jews, eating such meat was not a problem. With their strong background of monotheism, they knew the idols did not exist (1 Cor 8:4–7) and were the product of the darkened imaginations of men. When a person became a believer, he understood there were no other gods. This knowledge was not from some esoteric insight but gained directly from Old Testament teaching.

When we bring these two problems (that is, circumcision and the eating of meat offered to idols) to the letter to the Romans, we find a remarkable fit with the theology and practice advocated by Paul.[24] We shall see that its first eleven chapters are essentially

---

22. So also Karris, "Occasion," 65–84, and Fitzmyer, *Romans*, 638.

23. See Miller, *Obedience*, who argues that Paul's letter to the Romans was a pre-emptive strike against the opposition that Paul expected would arrive in Rome before he did.

24. Longenecker, "Prolegomena," 152, correctly notes: "how one understands an author's purpose has a profound effect on how one understands the character and content of what is written." Lemico, "Unifying," 13, says: "amid the unquestionable pluralism of the New Testament, there lies a unifying kerygmatic centre. It is formal and specific rather than abstract and general, internal and native rather than external and artificial. Furthermore, among the several trajectories along which development of thought can be discerned, there remains a complementary stability."

about the way God has dealt with the Jews. Early in the letter, in chapters 2 and 4, Paul argues they were uncircumcised when God accepted them in Abraham. In other words, the Gentiles were being brought into the covenant in exactly the same way as the Jews. Paul regularly makes the point that the redemption from Egypt was only a type or picture of the salvation that was going to be accomplished in the last days (Acts 26:15-18; Rom 3:21ff.; 8:1–3; 1 Cor 2:9–10; 5:7–8; Gal 1:3; Col 1:13–14), a salvation that would include Gentile as well as Jewish believers (Rom 9:30–33; 11:25–27).

Paul's reference to the eating of meat offered to idols is dealt with in the section below.

SECOND CLASS CITIZENS

Being treated as second-class citizens of the kingdom[25] provoked the Gentile believers to respond to the Jews. Some goaded the Jews by saying they had displaced them, God no longer having any purpose for his ancient people in his redemptive plans.[26] The evidence in support of their argument was all around them. The increasing numbers of Gentiles coming into the church was shifting the balance of its congregation, with Gentile believers far outnumbering Jewish believers. Such tensions had to be resolved, not least because both Jewish and Gentile believers were members of the one body and belonged to the same Lord.

In the midst of the theological debates over priority, the Gentiles were faced with a very practical problem. Before their conversion, they had worshipped in the temples of the local gods. Often these temples were centers of social activity and the gods were seen as patrons of the various trade guilds. When a man was converted, he stopped attending the temple and could no longer be involved in the guild under which his trade operated. His conversion threatened his livelihood.

Furthermore, even though he no longer visited the temple, he continued to feel its influence. After the temple sacrifices had been made, the meat was sold to local butchers for resale to the public. For the Jewish Christian, this was no problem. They did not believe in the existence of the gods that were worshipped in the temple so why shouldn't they eat the meat, providing it was kosher? The fact that it had been offered to a god that didn't exist meant that the problem didn't exist either. In practice, few Jews would want or need to eat this meat. They would have continued to eat their kosher meat which was probably beyond what most Gentile Christians could afford.

But such indifference to the meat's origin was a real problem for those who had lived for many years in fear of the gods to which it had been sacrificed. While the Gentile converts knew that there was only one God, they could not forget the things that had so deeply affected them. In reality, the sacrifices had been about involvement in something evil and satanic. Even if the deities did not exist, they knew that behind all of these ceremonies was Satan who exploited their ignorance and fear. For the Gentile converts, there was a real concern of being associated with anything that happened in the pagan

---

25. So also Anderson, "Solution," 2–40.

26. For an example of this line of thinking, see Nanos, "Audience," 283–304.

temples. They feared that eating the meat would be a compromise and the means by which Satan would control their lives again. This concern produced so much distress that some Gentile Christians were won over to the Jewish argument that meat offered to "non-gods" could be eaten without fear or compromise. They embraced Judaism, no doubt with all of its rituals and sacrifices, boasting in their newfound superior knowledge. Probably, they were financially supported by their Judaizing friends who made sure that they could afford kosher meat. Such success by the Judaizers was costly to the church as other Gentile believers were overtaken with confusion and their faith was wrecked. We get insights of this happening in Corinth (1 Cor 8:9–13) and Colossae (Col 2:16–19), as well as in the Asian churches (Rev 2:2, 20–22).

A PASTORAL LETTER

These problems were common in the Jewish/Gentile churches. Indeed, because of the intense loyalty of the Jewish community to the Law of Moses, it was inevitable these problems would arise wherever the two communities coexisted. The letter to the Romans was not an attempt to guess at their problems nor was it merely an opportunity for Paul to explain his gospel. The letter was an attempt to keep the two communities in Rome together so that they could bear a common witness of the Lord who had saved them. The letter demonstrates Paul's keen theological and pastoral awareness. He writes meaningfully, addressing the Jewish/Gentile relationship frankly. He is acutely aware of the pastoral problems caused by the integration of the two communities. The removal of the dividing wall of hostility (Eph 2:14) was yet to be worked out in the life of the believing community in Rome. They might be one new man in Christ (Eph 2:15; Col 3:10), but the new man was a man at war within himself.[27]

It was only from a united Roman church that Paul could effectively embark on his mission to Spain. He was aware that divisions in his supporting churches would distract him from the task of evangelism. The Gospel was not about casting the Jews off in favor of the Gentiles, but about bringing both into the eschatological covenantal community.[28] The nations would take note of what God was doing in Christ only as they accepted each other and lived as the "new man." The reconciliation of enemies to each other remains the most powerful witness to the saving ability of Christ. Their unity was vital to Paul's mission to Spain.

THE CORPORATE SETTING OF THE LETTER

In attempting to explore Paul's Jewish mindset, we need to ensure that he is not isolated from the corporate outlook of the Old Testament. It is easy to forget that Paul was a devout Jew before he responded to the claim of Jesus to be the Messiah. Even after conversion he did not reject his heritage. One of the features of that heritage was the public

---

27. Wood, "Purpose," 211–19, argues that while Paul's immediate purpose in writing was to prepare the Christians of Rome for his projected visit to their city, his ultimate purpose was to check antinomian and separatist tendencies within the church.

28. See Campbell, *Identity*.

reading of the Scriptures to congregations in their synagogues. These gatherings were an essential part of Paul's experience from the earliest years of childhood until his house arrest in Rome when he was denied access to its synagogue (Acts 28:30).

The significance of the synagogue experience was that it controlled the way Paul heard the Jewish Scriptures. Hearing them corporately was not a distorting influence, for the messages of the prophets were delivered to the people of the covenant collectively and rarely to individuals (Isa 44:1; 48:1; Jer 19:3; Ezek 2:3–5; Hos 4:1; Amos 3:1). The gathered synagogue congregation was, therefore, the ideal setting in which another generation of the covenant people could hear the same word being delivered. The reference to the blessing of the readers of the book of Revelation (Rev 1:3) is clear evidence of the role that corporate readings of texts had in the early church.

This principle of the gathered Roman congregation hearing Paul's letter is found in other churches that received letters from him. He expects believers to meet for this purpose and composed his letters with congregations in mind. In other words, the practice of interpreting the letters as though they were to individuals is misguided. The letters are not about what God has done or is doing *for a Christian*, they are what God has done or is doing *for his covenant people*, the church. It is not permissible—despite widespread practice—to read the details as though they describe the experience of the individual believer. Such practice not only makes much of the individual, it makes little of the covenant community. The privilege of an individual owning his own copy of the Scriptures for private reading is a recent blessing. Our private possession of the Scriptures is only possible due to recent technological advance and increased private wealth.

If it is argued this loses the perspective of the New Testament addressing individuals, the reply must be made "what do you mean by that?" Western individualism is not the same as biblical individualism. That there is responsibility in both the Old Testament and the New Testament for individuals to apply the Word of God to their lives goes without saying (Lev 19:3ff.; 18:6ff.; 20:3ff.; Job 19:11; 31:1–40; Ps 31:1–5; Prov 3:21–26; Matt 5:21–48; 18:15–17; 19:16–22; Luke 3:10ff.; 8:12; John 14:15–21; Acts 2:40–41; 1 Cor 10:6–14, etc.), but this is not the individualism of modern understanding. The biblical perspective is that every person is a member of a community and that membership determines his identity. The individual believer is addressed through the message that is given to the people of God and its primary reference is to the collective group. While its immediate application is to the church, there is another level where the individual is called to fulfil his obligations to the covenant. Just as the Old Testament prophets reminded Israel of her unique relationship with Yahweh, calling her (and, by implication, each individual Jew) to live it out, so Paul constantly reminds the church of her calling (Rom 1:7; 1 Cor 10:3ff.; Eph 1:13–14; 2:11—3:13; Col 1:12–14; 1 Thess 1:12–14) and appeals to her to live as the covenant community in the world (Rom 12:1ff.; Eph 5:1; Phil 2:1ff.; Col 3:2ff.).

At times, Paul applies his exhortations to specific groups of people (1 Cor 7:25–28; Eph 5:22–25; 6:1–9), spelling out the ramifications of what he has said for their daily lives. While very occasionally he addresses individuals (Rom 16:1ff.; Phil 4:2; Col 4:17), the undoubted thrust of his letters is to the church. If this is lost sight of, his letters become texts that wrongfully endorse all manner of unbiblical individualistic behavior and understanding.

By insisting that the letters are to the church, I am not saying anything new. Most commentators say the same thing. However, despite acknowledging the corporate dimension of the letters, they are not consistent in their corporate interpretation of them. Some commentators do identify sections of the letters to be about corporate experience, but lapse into individualism when interpreting the remainder of the text. My intent is to keep this corporate perspective to the fore of my thinking as I interpret the letter to the Romans. I shall seek to interpret it as a corporate document unless there is clear evidence that Paul is directing his teaching to a particular individual or group of people within the church.

COMMUNITY AND INITIATION

If my claim concerning the corporate nature of the letter is correct, it inevitably raises the question of initiation into the Christian life. This is unavoidable because passages which have been seen to refer to the individual's entrance into the covenant community will, with this refocusing, be seen to refer to the historical creation of the covenant with the covenant community. The question that must, therefore, be answered is this: where does the individual believer fit into this scheme of reading?

The question is an important one. There are those who view salvation as applying to the whole of mankind and who would accept the corporate reading with enthusiasm. Such euphoria is not well-founded. It will become clear that Paul insists there is a fundamental division in the human race. There are those who are in Adam (Rom 5:12; 1 Cor 15:22) and those who are in Christ (2 Cor 5:17; Eph 1:2; Phil 1:1; Col 1:2; 1 Thess 1:1; 4:16). To ignore this fundamental premise of Pauline theology is to destroy the very basis of his argument. Regardless of the doctrine of salvation that one accepts, it does not correspond to the apostle's teaching if this fundamental division is ignored.

However, one thing is clear–the early church saw the need for personal repentance and faith (Matt 3:1–6; Acts 2:38–41; 8:34–38; Rom 10:9). While there is no suggestion that man automatically benefits from Christ's death, God calls all men everywhere to repent and believe (Rom 10:9–15). Any argument arising from the corporate nature of the letters must respect this clear basic tenet of the early apostolic church's thought, expressed so clearly in her evangelistic ministry.

To suggest solutions to this problem of initiation at this stage is to anticipate the arguments that need to be made. It will not make sense to offer a solution until the relevant texts have been considered and a case made for their corporate perspective.

COMMUNITY AND IDENTITY

How does Paul view the congregation in Rome? It would be natural to say it is a local church. Understandable as that reply is, there is an unexpected silence concerning this theme in the letter. Throughout the body of the letter to the Romans (Paul's *magnum opus*), he does not refer to "the church."[29] It is not until we get to the end of the letter that the term "church" appears and it is not in a significant theological sense but in the context of the fellowship of believers. In Rom 16:1, Paul writes: "I commend to you our sister Phoebe, a servant of the church in Cenchrea." In Rom 16:3, 5a, he writes: "Greet Priscilla and Aquila, my fellow workers in Christ Jesus. . . . Greet also the church that meets at their house." Finally, in Rom 16:23a, Paul writes: "Gaius, whose hospitality I and the whole church here enjoy, sends you his greetings." Clearly, none of these references to churches are in any sense theological. Even in his private letter to Philemon, Paul begins by greeting the church that meets in his house (Phlm 1:2). It will be noticed in his letters to the Ephesians and to the Colossians that, despite not greeting the believers as churches, the theology of the church pulsates within their teaching. In Romans, this does not happen. Indeed, when he greeted the Roman believers at the opening of his letter, he did not greet them as "the church that is in Rome" as was occasionally his practice (1 Cor 1:2; 1 Thess 1:1; 2 Thess 1:1).

The fact that the redeemed community is not referred to as "the church" in the theological section of Romans (nor in any part of the letter to the Galatians) could be significant. Both are dealing with the identity of the Gentiles and their right to be included in the covenants of promise. The argument of both letters is highly dependent on Old Testament exegesis–far more than any other New Testament letter. It is possible that Paul's concern is to debate these issues in clear Old Testament imagery, emphasizing that the Gentiles are fully part of the promised new covenant community. They are not to be shunted off by the Jews into a second division called "the church." To do so might suggest that the church was a mere stepping stone toward final inclusion into the true people of God. The believing Gentiles are bona fide children of Abraham and not part of an entity that waits for admission.

While it would be a fascinating study to see what determines the language Paul uses in his different letters, this is not the purpose of the present work. I am interested in seeing how Paul speaks of the Christian community in this pivotal letter and the reason for the language he selects.

In Rom 14:17, Paul writes: "For the kingdom of God is not a matter of eating and drinking, but of righteousness, peace and joy in the Holy Spirit." As this is the only reference to the kingdom in the entire letter, the kingdom of God is not a major theme.[30]

What we do find is language and imagery which stress continuity with the Old Testament. The members of the believing community are those who are circumcised in the heart, not in the flesh (Rom 2:28–29). They have been redeemed through the true Paschal sacrifice (Rom 3:21 25) and are now on pilgrimage (Rom 5:3–5; 8:25–39). They

---

29. Noted by Jewett, "Ecumenical," 94, whose explanation is that there was no central body but many house churches in Rome. This fails to convince as the same pattern probably operated in other cities to whose churches Paul wrote, addressing them as such, e.g., 1 Cor 1:2; Gal 1:2.

30. Of course, the imagery of the church and the kingdom are both rooted in the OT and can be claimed to reflect the continuity that is noted. The point is that such key terms are marked by their infrequent use in the letter. When they are used, it is not with the theological significance that is given to them in the Gospels ("kingdom") or in Ephesians and Colossians ("church").

belong to the community which has been grafted into the Abrahamic root with all of its promise. They are described as priestly people (Rom 12:1–2) and are responsible for completing Israel's failed mission (Rom 11:11–24).

It would seem from the above that Paul wants to identify the believers in Rome with the pilgrim community which has been redeemed and showered "with every spiritual blessing in Christ" (Eph 1:3b). He is deliberately using language that makes this connection clear and is reluctant to use any vocabulary that might, for whatever reason, obscure the extraordinary calling the church has as the Israel of God (Gal 6:16).

COVENANT AND THE THEOLOGY OF ROMANS

It will be evident that the perspective I am taking in interpreting Romans presupposes a covenantal framework for Paul's thinking. Like the issue of initiation, it would be tempting to justify this framework at the beginning of the exposition. However, this task must wait until there has been an examination of the text and the theological substructure upholding its arguments. For this reason, justification for using a covenantal framework for interpreting the letter will have to come from the evidence of the letter as a whole. What can be said is that if Paul is dependent on the new exodus model outlined earlier then the heart of his thinking is the fulfilment by God of his promises (his covenants) to Abraham and David. The new exodus theme is a very important subsection of the Old and New Testament themes of covenant and fulfilment.

The letter to the Romans begins by introducing Jesus as the Christ who was born of the seed of David according to the flesh (Rom 1:3). The theme of salvation, promised by the prophets (Rom 1:2), is heavily covenantal in that the promises were all part of the covenant. Clear echoes of the theme of righteousness as found in Isaiah come through in Rom 1:17. This righteousness, or saving response from Yahweh toward his people, was the hallmark of the prophet.

In chapter 2, there is discussion about the true Jew. While he was not circumcised in the flesh but in the heart (Rom 2:28–29), circumcision was at the "heart" of the Old Testament covenant and without it no one could claim to be a member of the covenant community.

Chapter 3 has distinct echoes of the Passover event (Rom 3:21–25) which inaugurated Israel as the people of God under the Mosaic covenant.

Chapter 4 returns to covenant community membership. We will see that the passage has a significant corporate perspective, dealing with the status of Gentiles in relation to the law and its demands. Whatever position is taken, it is beyond dispute that the covenant is embedded in the argument to such an extent that the chapter cannot make sense without the recognition of its significance, purpose, and role.

The same is true of chapter 5. The argument for two communities—one in Adam and one in Christ—can only be made in the light of federal headship and covenant.

We find covenantal themes in chapter 6 with the church being baptized into Christ's death and sharing his life through being raised with him. Some have recognized the exodus imagery which throbs behind the letter's teaching, and with that imagery all the ideas of covenant flood into the passage.

Chapter 7, with its presentation of someone who is battling with the law, does not exclude the fact that the law for any Jew is covenant law. This is confirmed in the opening verses where the imagery speaks of being married to the law. Marriage is nothing if it is not covenantal.

Chapter 8 is about the community's experience of the Spirit and, again, its reading requires a covenantal context. The Spirit's presence was one of the distinctive blessings promised to the new covenant community by the prophets.

Chapters 9, 10, and 11 are so widely recognized as being about the issue of covenant membership that their reliance on covenant assumptions does not need to be defended.

This brief overview of the theological section of Paul's letter to the Romans suggests that it should be read in a covenantal framework. Its covenantal argument will be worked out in detail as we engage with its text.

THE EXTRA-CANONICAL WRITINGS

While the mistakes of previous generations of scholars are slowly being rectified, the present generation is falling into its own trap. The mushrooming of intertestamental studies as a result of the discoveries of the Dead Sea Scrolls at Qumran has produced another method for training theologians. The Jewish literature of the period immediately prior to and contemporary with the New Testament writings have become key texts for deciphering their message. It is argued that the literature provides a vital understanding of first century Jewish thought, the New Testament writers in particular. There is no doubt these documents give fascinating insight into this period of Judaism, but their relevance for the New Testament message must be questioned.

As we have seen, the mistake of the past was to assume the Greek of the New Testament was the same as that used in secular society. Many New Testament scholars today are making this same assumption but in another guise. They assume there is a strict equivalence in terminology and themes found in these writings and in the New Testament. They use the intertestamental texts as the key for understanding the New Testament texts. This presupposes they share the same theological outlook and their meanings are transposable. However, this understanding is flawed.

There are many theologies in Judaism. Those who specialize in the intertestamental literature are fond of saying: "We cannot speak of Judaism but of Judaisms." The documents represent various Jewish perspectives, many of which are distinctively different. They cannot be used safely until those distinctions are understood and their compatibility with the New Testament writings established. Unloading these texts mindlessly into footnotes or the main text of commentaries in order to give a sense of scholarly respectability achieves the very opposite.[31] To argue for a uniform Jewish intertestamental

---

31. An example of this can be seen in the way that Paul and the Qumran community used the term "flesh" (*sarks*). Murphey, "Literature," 74, argues that while flesh (*sarks*) in Qumran: "is a relatively pale and negative concept . . . Paul's notion of *sarks* as a power, as a creditor, is completely absent." Thus to ignore the differences in how the many different communities used the same terminologies is to introduce serious flaws into the interpretation of the New Testament documents.

understanding is to disregard the important fact that there was not a single Jewish view, but rather a broad agreement as to which beliefs were essential for one to be considered as part of the Jewish fold. Even so, some of the writings we have would have been uncomfortable reading for the majority of Jews in the time of the writing of the New Testament and would never be held to represent mainstream Judaism.[32]

Even if it was possible to demonstrate theological equivalence between the New Testament texts and those of the Pseudepigrapha,[33] what does it prove? How widely were the writings of Qumran known? How far had their message penetrated Judaism? How can we know that we have correctly identified a reference, or an echo, from the Jewish Pseudepigrapha or later rabbinic traditions? How many members of the early church had even heard of the Psalms of Solomon, let alone knew what the document contained?[34] When claims are made that echoes of books like Maccabees are found in the New Testament, what evidence is there that they would have been recognized by the early church? This approach assumes these writings represent a common mindset in intertestamental Judaism and, therefore, should determine how the New Testament documents are read. For example, the Qumran documents were far from representative of Judaism. Indeed, they were a protest against it and the product of a minority grouping. Many critical issues need to be addressed before they can be used to understand Judiasm.[35]

It is more than likely these pseudepigraphal writers, while sharing a common source with the New Testament writers, i.e., the Old Testament, interpreted the source very differently. There are plenty of texts which demonstrate that different groups used the same Old Testament passage to make a case which supported their own viewpoints. Common ideas cannot be assumed because common terminology is found.[36]

The following example illustrates the concern I am expressing. A student seeks to understand the meaning of "baptism." He enquires at his local Anglican church, a Methodist church, and a Baptist church, and finds that despite common vocabulary, bap-

---

32. Another source of literature from this period is the collection of rabbinical traditions. Their possible influence on the NT writers has been widely discussed. However, some scholars point out that since these oral traditions were not recorded until the end of the third century, their trustworthiness must be suspect. Other scholars reject this skepticism and treat the rabbinical writings as accurately preserving the traditions of the rabbis who are quoted. This latter group have no problem in using the rabbinical texts as keys to unlock the meaning of the NT. A representative of those who are skeptical about the use of the rabbinical material is Davies, "Dating," 59–67, while one who advocates its use is Brewer, "Sources," 281–98.

33. This is a classification of Jewish writings that are claimed to be authored by revered figures of Jewish history. The true authors' intention was that by using revered names the writings would be given a status they otherwise would not have had. For this reason they are called Pseude (false) grapha (writings). They are part of the collection of the intertestamental writings.

34. For a recent examination of the provenance of the Pseudepigrapha, see Davila, *Provance*, 10–73. His conclusions are that caution needs to be exercised when allowing the Pseudepigrapha to inform NT studies.

35. For an example of how different the Qumran community was in its use of Isaiah as compared with that of the early church, see Shum, *Isaiah*, 170–72.

36. For a discussion of problems relating to the use of the Pseudepigrapha, see Sandmel, "Parallelomania," and Davila, "Background," 53–57. See also discussion in Holland, *Contours*, chapter 3.

tism means very different things to each denomination. However, he amalgamates all that he has learned into an essay explaining what Christians believe about baptism and returns to the churches for their approval of his work, asking the clergy to endorse his essay with their signatures. However, on reading his work, they find their own distinctive understanding has been lost in the quest for a common meaning with the result that none of the clergy are able to give approval to the proposed understanding of baptism.

This illustration reflects the conduct of much contemporary New Testament research. In the hands of scholars, the same terminology can often be used to convey different meanings.[37]

TEXTUAL CERTAINTIES

But these observations are not meant to suggest that we languish in ignorance concerning the mindset of the early church. Our earlier discussion on Paul's use of the prophets has shown the dependence of the early church on their writings. Indeed, we know the whole of Judaism fed off these Scriptures, drinking in from their streams of comfort, encouragement and hope as they gathered to hear them read and taught, and as they used its psalms to express their worship to God. These writings saturate the New Testament, and any understanding which that fails to see them as the key for New Testament interpretation must be rejected as fundamentally flawed. The only allusions or echoes we can safely consider are those which reflect the Old Testament literature, for it was this set of writings alone that was nationally known. Indeed, it is the only set of writings that were known beyond the borders of Israel. To rely on texts which are the product of minority groups is dangerous. In fact, this literature may not represent national thinking at all. We have no idea what was destroyed in the various national disasters following the birth of Christianity. We only have the Qumran documents because the members of the community had the foresight to store their treasures in the caves before the Romans arrived. Thus, to say that we know what Israel believed in the intertestamental period is a dangerous claim since most of the evidence has been destroyed and what remains may be massively misrepresentative.

However, what we do know is that the Old Testament Scriptures were influential, not only throughout every form of Judaism within the promised land, but in every synagogue throughout the Roman Empire. We also know we have accurate copies of this literature and that these texts were universally the basis of Israel's faith. Paul explicitly states it is these writings which are fulfilled in the person and work of Jesus, the Son of David (Rom 1:3; 3:21ff.; 1 Cor 15:3). It is true the different sects of Judaism read these Scriptures in different ways, but that serves to make the point that the way the Christians read the Old Testament was decisive for their understanding of its message. To introduce the reading of the Old Testament that other groups adopted—even if they could be recovered—would have little or no significance for the Christian church. If Baptists pay so little attention as to how Anglicans read New Testament texts today, how much less

---

37. For further discussion, see Piper, *Future*, 133–44. See also Sandmel, "Parallelomania," 1–13, for a discussion on the danger of linking common vocabulary and the building of arguments from its results.

will the early church have been interested in the readings of communities such as the one at Qumran!

In the early church (as in that of the twenty-first century), there were many translations of the Hebrew Scriptures available for the Jews and those who believed in Jesus to study. Nevertheless, the overwhelming evidence is that there was one dominant translation in use and this determined the theological mindset of Jews and the followers of Jesus. This was the Greek Septuagint version (LXX), which was used by the majority of Jews throughout the Roman Empire. This translation was destined to make an immense contribution to the early church's theological understanding. It served its members well as a commonly accepted translation for use in debate with Jews and in the teaching of converts. The Septuagint translated the Hebrew Scriptures in such a way as to mostly preserve Hebrew ideas for future non-Hebrew speaking members of the community to access. This made the translation massively important. Here was a Greek translation that was not tied to the classical meaning of the Greek world, but carried the theological concepts of the Old Testament revelation of God to his people. Rather than intertestamental literature being the key for interpreting the New Testament, the theological concepts poured into the vocabulary of the Greek Old Testament should be the authoritative Rosetta stone.

CONCLUSION

Paul was a Jew who lived in the full flow of Old Testament promises and expectations. In order to read him correctly, we have to immerse all his arguments back into the Old Testament, allowing its themes and patterns of thought to control how we read his writings. Only when we have exhausted the Old Testament's theology should we look at the possibility that the apostle was writing outside of the thought-patterns of his own upbringing. Of course, there are others who agree with this and have sought to follow such a principle. But this commentary goes further than merely recognizing Paul's dependence on the Old Testament. It is this author's conviction that Hellenistic models continue to be embedded in most New Testament exegesis and that most commentators fail to appreciate the influence of these hermeneutic assumptions. The claim of this work is that the Old Testament, with its promises and expectations (particularly of a new exodus), provides all the material that we need to rightly understand Paul's, as well as the rest of the NT church's understanding of the divine marriage as the conclusion of the Gospel's message, which was at the heart of Israel's hope.

ROMANS 1

THE MESSIAH KING AND HIS SERVANT

Paul, a servant of Christ Jesus, called to be an apostle and set apart for the gospel of God—the gospel he promised beforehand through his prophets in the Holy Scriptures regarding his Son, who as to his human nature was a descendant of David, and who through the Spirit of holiness was declared with power to be the Son of God by his resurrection from the dead: Jesus Christ our Lord. (Rom 1:1–4)

INTRODUCTION

Like any introduction, the opening of Paul's letter to the church in Rome is intended to help the reader and those who hear the document read out to them understand what the letter is about and prepare them for its unfolding content. Because of this it is hugely significant that the letter, written to a largely Gentile community, begins with a statement about a Jewish king who had lived a thousand years or so before.

It is what God had promised this king and the people he ruled that is crucial for understanding how and why the believers at Rome exist in the first place. These promises, and how they were fulfilled, define the faith of the community that was meeting in the name of Jesus.

Interestingly, there is nothing else said in the opening chapter about any other Jew (other than Paul's reference to himself). Instead, Paul weighs in to describe the condition of humanity and explain the nature of God's solution to his devastating critique. Admittedly the order is to introduce the achievement of Jesus the Son of David and the nature of the salvation he has brought and then to explain why it is so desperately needed.

The letter will go on to explore this majestic topic and instruct the believers in Rome how this salvation relates to their own lives and confession.

1:1 Paul, a servant of Christ Jesus, called to be an apostle and set apart for the gospel of God. The opening section of the letter (the salutation) contains important theological information which gives Paul the opportunity to establish how he wants the letter's recipients to engage with its central message.[1] We shall see as the commentary

---

1. Most commentators consider that the first sixteen verses of the letter form its introduction. However, such an assumption does not explain Paul's use of the conjunction γάρ (*gar*) "for" in v.16 which links the text that follows with the preceding passage. For this reason, I assume that vss. 1–15 are integral to the main body of the letter and the key to its interpretation.

unfolds that Paul develops the themes of these opening verses. He tells how the Son of God, who came through the line of David, has fulfilled his Father's mission, bringing to completion the promises made throughout the Old Testament to Israel.

Paul introduces himself with a greeting typical of letters written at that time. He then states his position and his purpose in writing to the church in Rome.

The term Paul uses to describe himself is δοῦλος (*doulos*) "servant." This term has been the cause of a great deal of confusion. In classical Greek, it means "slave" and many commentators have assumed that Paul intended to describe himself as one who, without any rights of his own, was owned by Christ.[2] We can begin to identify the confusion when we realize that the term was very important in the LXX. It was used to translate the Hebrew word *ebed*. An examination of the Old Testament Hebrew text, particularly that of Isaiah, shows that *ebed* was a title applied to a wide range of people. There were no alternative titles available for the Old Testament writers, so the variation in meaning had to be derived from the context in which the individual word was used. So for example, *ebed* was used for kings (Isa 37:24), prophets (Isa 20:3), the nation of Israel (Isa 41:8–9), the Messiah (Isa 42:1), and even ordinary Israelites (Isa 65:13–15). What can be said of *ebed* is that it spoke of someone who was subordinate either to God or to man. However, *ebed* (translated *doulos*) was also used in the LXX for the person who was a slave—often one who was taken by the force of an alien power.

In other words, in the Greek Old Testament *doulos* described a relationship within the covenant that God had made with Israel (unless the context makes it clear that it was otherwise). This is also the case in the New Testament, where the context normally shows it to describe a relationship within the new covenant which God has established through Christ. This covenantal use does not speak of someone who has no rights but of someone who is showered with honor and privilege as a result of being a servant of the living God.[3]

Paul could not think of himself apart from his relationship to his Savior, and this relationship had cost him dearly. At one time he had hated Jesus Christ, doing everything to silence all who claimed to be his followers. He had been a fanatical Pharisee, and in his attempt to guard the purity of Judaism he had travelled far beyond the borders of his country to bring the followers of Jesus before the Jewish court. He would not tolerate the suggestion that Israel's Messiah had been crucified because the law said that anyone who hangs on a tree is cursed by God (Deut 21:22–23).

Paul had been convinced that Jesus was an impostor. He knew that the followers of Jesus claimed that he had been raised from the dead following his crucifixion by the Romans. This was further evidence to him of the lie of the movement. However, on the way to Damascus to arrest some of Jesus' disciples, Paul experienced a life-transforming

---

2. See also Barrett, *Romans*,15; Nygren, *Commentary*, 44; Kay, *Structure*, 84. This Hellenistic context led to such confusion that Petersen, *Rediscovering*, 24ff., says that Paul saw slavery to be the present state and sonship the future state when Christ returned.

3. See also Lane, "Covenant," 3ff.; Hays, *Echoes*, 14; Court, "Pattern," 37–60. For a full discussion see Holland, *Contours*, chapter 4. There are some uses of *doulos* as slave in the NT, but the context makes it clear that it is the intended meaning.

encounter with Jesus and could no longer deny that he had been raised from the dead. He became a member of the community he had tried to destroy and, accepting that Jesus was the Son of God, became his servant.

Paul states that he is an ἀπόστολος (*apostolos*) "apostle," or "one who is sent." He had been sent by Christ as an ambassador to make known the good news of salvation to the Gentiles (Acts 9:15).

His life was now dedicated to spreading far and wide the good news that Jesus Christ had fulfilled the Scriptures (v.2), and this is one of the purposes of his letter. Paul sets out to show that Jesus is the one for whom the Jewish people had been waiting. All the promises that they had waited for hundreds of years to come to completion were now being fulfilled through him. Paul's message is not only for believing Jews but also for believing Gentiles in Rome. The promises that the Gentiles would be brought into the covenant community as a result of the coming of the Messiah are now being fulfilled, and Paul is anxious that the Jews and Gentiles in the Roman church he is writing to have a clear understanding of this.

Paul is not an apostle because he chose to be one. His apostleship was "by the will of God," reflecting God's call on men in the Old Testament such as Abraham, Moses, David, Isaiah and Ezekiel. In the Old Testament, God called individuals to roles of service (such as prophet or deliverer) rather than to salvation (Gen 12:1; Exod 3:10; Judg 13:2–5; 1 Sam 3:4; 16:12), choosing to save the nation of Israel to be his people (Isa 42:1; 45:4; Rom 9:11). In New Testament times, we find that individuals like Paul were chosen to fulfil tasks that God had prepared for them, reflecting his dealings in the OT (John 15:16; Acts 13:2; Gal 1:15–17). Similarly, we find passages in the NT reflecting the OT—God choosing to save the church, rather than individuals, to be his people (Eph 1:4; 1 Thess 1:4; 1 Pet 2:9). However, there are some texts in the NT which do not fit either category; they refer to people being chosen for salvation (John 6:37; Acts 18:10; 13:48; 1 Cor 1:26–29). This said, the number of texts which speak about individuals being chosen for this purpose is relatively small compared to the number that refer to communities chosen by God to be his elect people. One must take care not to confuse the two as this can lead to doctrinal imbalance.

Paul is "a servant of Christ Jesus, called to be an apostle," locating his message in Jewish history. Jesus of Nazareth was none other than the long-expected Messiah. The use of the term Χριστός (*Christos*) "Christ" is important as it translates the Hebrew מָשִׁיחַ (*māšiaḥ*) "Messiah." Some scholars claim that the title had lost its Messianic significance and that when Paul used the term it had no greater importance than a family name or surname. This claim has been examined, however, with the result that many now believe that the Messianic significance of the term had not been lost and that whenever Paul speaks of Jesus Christ, he is saying: "Jesus, who is the Christ (or the Messiah)." This brings to the fore the Jewish nature of Paul's message that Jesus is the long-awaited Messiah who has come to bring salvation to the whole of humankind. We will soon come across a specific reference to Jesus being the "Son of David" (Rom 1:3). The use of this title is another way of saying that Jesus is the Christ. Once this is appreciated, it becomes clear that the whole thrust of Paul's proclamation about Jesus is that he is the one who has fulfilled all of the promises of God.

Paul says that he was ἀφωρισμένος (*aphōrismenos*) "set apart." The use of this term is significant for it appears in the LXX ristCspecifically in a cultic context (i.e., for a ministry to do with the sacrificial system of the temple). It spoke of priestly service and of Israel's service to God (cf. Num 8:11; Lev 20:24–26). Its use here suggests that Paul sees his ministry to be in some way priestly. This understanding is confirmed by Paul when he writes in Rom 15:16 that he has: "the priestly duty of proclaiming the gospel of God." Paul is not implying that this priestly ministry is in any way exclusive because he extends it to all the believers in the Roman church he is writing to (Rom 12:1–2).

Paul was set apart for the "gospel of God." The term εὐαγγέλιον (*euangelion*) "gospel" means good news. It was characteristic of the message of Isaiah who declared that Yahweh was about to deliver his people from their exile in Babylon (Isa 52:7). This was the good news. It was to be a deliverance achieved under the leadership of a descendant of David whom Yahweh would raise up to bring about this promised salvation (Isa 9:7; 11:1–5; 22:22; 55:3).

Paul is interacting with the promises of Isaiah by saying that Jesus is the long-promised Son of David whom God has raised up to deliver his people. "Gospel" is part of the technical terminology of Isaiah's message of salvation from Babylon. The purpose of Israel's salvation was that she could renew her priestly ministry by making God known to the nations. Paul says that he and the church fulfil this same ministry as they advance the good news of God's salvation (Rom 12:1–2 [see commentary notes];15:16). His message is that the deliverance from the greatest exile has begun and both Jews and Gentiles are being called to leave their alienation from God and to be reconciled to him.[4] This is possible because Jesus, the Son of David, has dealt with the cause of separation and exile—the sin of man. Paul will develop this theme in chapter 3.

1:2 The gospel he promised beforehand through his prophets in the Holy Scriptures Paul is an apostle and his message is about the "Gospel"—the good news concerning Jesus Christ. The good news is that God has acted through Jesus to fulfil the promises he made to the Jewish people hundreds of years earlier. While it is legitimate to look for specific prophecies in the OT to see how they have been fulfilled in Christ, this predictive approach is not to the fore in Paul's thinking. Rather, he sees the many prophecies about the ending of Israel's shame in exile and her deliverance through the coming of the Son of David to be fulfilled in Jesus. This is why you were asked to remember the OT prophecies on [x-ref]. They gird the gospel. As we continue to explore the letter, we shall see that Paul's understanding of the fulfilment of the scriptures is at the level of typology. In this method of interpretation, corresponding features of OT events are

---

4. "[T]here is abundant evidence in Paul's letters that he read Isaiah 40–55 as a coherent prophetic vision foretelling and authorizing Paul's own apostolic activity. The surprising disclosure of God's righteousness, the proclaiming of the word to the nations, the unbelief of Israel, the apostle's commission to announce the good news of salvation—all these themes are richly suggested by the passages in Isaiah that Paul quotes and echoes" (Hays, "Believed," 58).

identified in God's dealings with the NT church and it is from the resulting parallels that lessons are drawn (Rom 15:4; 1 Cor 10:1–13).

1:3 Regarding his Son, who as to his human nature was a descendant of David, The good news concerns Jesus, who is God's Son. It could be that he is God's son because he was born of the seed (family) of David and is the one who the prophets promised would lead God's people out of bondage. However, this is an understanding that I will reject shortly (see comments on page 34). Many scholars see vv. 3–4 to be a statement from an existing confession of faith—probably one that was used in the early church at baptisms (Paul was in the habit of quoting from confessions and hymns, possibly assuring the recipients of his letters that he was in agreement with the message which the apostles had received from Jesus [Phil 2:5–8, Col 1:13–20]). Scholars believe that Paul did not compose this confession as it contains a number of words and expressions which are not found elsewhere in his writings and because the finely-honed description was typical of the early church's fastidiously-worked confessional statements.

The expression "as to his human nature" translates the phrase κατὰ σάρκα (*kata sarka*), which means, literally "according to the flesh." For the ancient Greeks, all flesh was evil but all spiritual things were good, so they believed that the spirit of man was imprisoned in his evil (physical) body.

These ideas opposed Jewish understanding. Because of the creation account in Genesis, a Jew saw that all of God's creation was good, and this applied even to the human body, the flesh. He knew that the body was capable of great evil but that, of itself, it was not evil. As a result of Adam's sin (commonly known as the "fall"), the whole of creation was fundamentally flawed including the physical condition of man. This "spoiling" did not make human flesh (man's body) sinful but it did make it weak. As we will demonstrate,[5] the term "flesh" has many meanings; it is, therefore, extremely important to read the context of the passage in which the word is used to get some idea of its particular meaning.

In this verse, "human nature" ("flesh") refers to the human condition as weak and vulnerable. The verse is saying that, according to natural descent, Jesus was of the line of King David. He was truly man and shared all the weakness of the human condition. Because he shared in the whole range of human experience and entered into our weakness (apart from our sinful status) he can be our faithful high priest, understanding our needs and sympathizing with us in our frailty (Heb 2:17–18). One could argue that being born into the royal family brought Jesus privilege—but that misreads the plot. The Son of David was not destined to privilege but to suffering and death. Isaiah identified the Suffering Servant (Isa 52:13—53:12) with the descendant of David (Isa 55:3) whose sufferings would bring about Israel's release from Babylon, and Paul clearly makes the same connection. This is indicated in the following verse, where the mention of the resurrection of the Son of David implies prior death—a death which redeemed his people (Rom 3:21–25; Gal 4:3; Col 1:13–14). In this verse, we have the reference to "his Son," that is, the "Son of God." This is a description which has two layers of meaning. The first is one with

5. See "Excursus F: Sin in the Theology of Paul," pages 203–25.

which both Jews and Christians can identify,[6] but the second layer is unique to Christian understanding.

The first meaning comes from the OT where some of the leaders are called "sons of God." The term was a description given to judges (Ps 82:6), kings (Ps 2:7) and angels (Job 1:6 NAS, RSV). It referred to those chosen to represent God. In the case of the kings, the Holy Spirit was given to empower them to fulfil the tasks to which they were called (1 Sam 10:10; Ps 51:11). The whole nation of Israel was also called "the son of God" (Exod 4:23; Hos 11:1) because she was called by God to represent him to other nations. To enable her to fulfil her task, she was also given the Spirit (Isa 42:1; 44:3; 59:19–21; 61:1; Ezek 36:27; 37:10–14). It is clear that this OT usage did not convey the idea that the giving of the Spirit made the recipient divine. Thus in the OT the term "son of God" did not denote divinity.

When we come into the NT, we find that Christians are also called sons of God (Rom 8:15–17). Their status means that they are heirs of all that God has (Rom 8:17; Eph 3:6), just as the kings were Yahweh's heirs in the OT (Ps 2:8). Their responsibility is to represent him to an unbelieving world (2 Cor 5:20; Eph 6:20) and, to enable them to do this, they have also been given the Holy Spirit (Rom 8:9). Furthermore, the universal church—the Israel of God—is called "the son of God" (Rom 8:14, 19; 2 Cor 6:18; Phil 2:15). She has been called to do the work that Israel failed to do in taking the good news of Yahweh's mercy to the nations (Phil 1:27). Again, she has received the Holy Spirit to empower her for this work (Luke 24:48–49; John 15:26; 16:13; 1 Cor 2:4; 12:7–13; 2 Cor 3:18; Gal 3:2; 4:6).

But the term is not only used in the NT for Christians or for the church, it is also used of Christ himself. Without any implication of deity, Jesus is regularly called the "Son of God" (Matt 16:16; 27:54). In the OT sense, this title means nothing more than that Jesus is the promised king, the descendant of David (albeit with a ministry which excels that of other representatives of Yahweh). He is the one the prophets had predicted would come to sit on the throne of his father David (2 Sam 7:5–16; Jer 33:15–16; Amos 9:11–12; Zech 6:12–14). When the disciples used this term in the Gospels, it is likely that they did so with this restricted Jewish understanding.

It was not until after the resurrection that the disciples began to realize who Jesus really was and to appreciate the significance of the term "Son of God." Their understand-

---

6. See also Carson, "Ambiguities," 112; Hengel, *Son*, 124–25; Cullmann, *Christology*, 273–74. Wright, *Messiah*, 11, says: "The use of Christ is OT and related to the Davidic King and stays titular more than most recognize rather than a proper name. This widespread assumption is at the root of many problems. . . . When Paul wrote *Christos* he regularly meant the true Davidic King (in that he gave the word the meaning which it would most naturally have in his day)." Others who see the Messianic significance of the title include de Lacey, "Image," 4 n. 3; Davies, "Paul," 4–39; Dunn, "Understanding," 130; Caird, *Theology*, 169; Grech, "Source," 42; contra, Moule, "Circumstances," 260; Marshall, "Origins," 92; Casey, "Earliest," 258. De Jonge, "Suggestions," 321–22; Whitsett, "Son," 661–81; Morris, *Romans*, 37; Keck, "Renewal," 369, are not correct to say the title had become of little importance to Paul and had become nothing more than a proper name. The title was the vital link with the appointed representative of Yahweh who would bring about the new exodus. Jesus is being introduced to the Roman readers as the promised Davidic leader of the new exodus who "was promised beforehand through his prophets in the Holy Scriptures" (v. 2). The primitive nature of Rom 1:2–3 is upheld by Bornkamm, *Paul*, 248, who cites support.

ing of him as the eternal Son of God came from the realization that what he had achieved through his death could not be achieved by any human agent. They came to see that God alone could do those things which the prophets had said would happen as a consequence of the coming of the Messiah.

The disciples came to see Jesus in a unique way. They understood that he was the Son of David who had come to bring his people salvation as predicted by the prophets. The Jews had expected the resurrection of the righteous at the end of history but here, at the resurrection, they were faced with the reality that Jesus had been raised from the dead. They would have known that accompanying the prediction of the redemption of Israel from Babylon was the promise of the redemption of creation itself (Isa 55:13). If Jesus had fulfilled the prophets' predictions, the redemption of creation had, at least in principle, taken place. The apostles were discovering not only what Jesus had accomplished but also who he was. The OT is clear that only God, the Creator, could redeem his creation. The prophets predicted that God would bring his people back from exile and restore creation to its state of perfection. This twofold act of redemption was inseparably linked with and was at the heart of the new exodus promises proclaimed by the OT prophets.

Jesus is the fulfiller and fulfilment of these new exodus promises that make OT categories of "son of God" inadequate to properly describe him. What the Son of God achieved, the redemption of creation, is beyond what any earthly king can do, no matter how exceptionally endowed he is with the Spirit. This achievement puts this Son of God into an altogether different category that Yahweh alone can fulfil.

This evidence for the divinity of Jesus is based on what he has accomplished—in other words, "functional Christology" helps us to understand who Jesus is through what he has achieved. Paul will argue from "functional Christology" in chapter 8, linking Jesus' redeeming death (Rom 8:3) with the redemption of the entire created order (Rom 8:19–25). In chapter 8, he describes Jesus as the "firstborn of many brothers" (Rom 8:29). This is significant imagery which he also uses in his letter to the Colossians, describing Jesus as the "firstborn over ('of' RSV) all creation" (Col 1:15).

What is the significance of this term "firstborn"? We can recall that on the night of the Passover, the firstborn male of each Egyptian family died on its behalf (as its representative). His death meant that the remaining members of his family were spared judgment at the hand of God. But the death of Jesus, the firstborn of the human family, has much more significance than this. His death delivered his people from the kingdom of darkness into the kingdom of God and restored the whole of creation to God's reign (Col 1:13–14, 19–20; 1 Cor 15:26–28). Interestingly, in the OT the king was called God's firstborn (Ps 89:27) and, of course, the Gospels make clear that it was King Jesus (the Son of David, the firstborn over the kings of the earth, and the Son of God) who died as the Passover sacrifice to redeem the entire creation.[7]

This Christological development was not wild speculation. It was the inevitable logic of the resurrection. Growing confidence in the eternal Sonship of Jesus led the in-

---

7. For further discussion, see Holland, *Contours*, chapters 11 and 12.

fant church to give expression to her increasing understanding that her Savior was more than the promised descendant of David—he was himself God. The church chose to use the term "Son of God" to describe Jesus. This was fitting, for Jesus himself used the term in a way that made him equal with God and not merely his Messiah (Matt 28:19; John 10:33–39). The early Christians, therefore, adopted this specific usage when they wanted to speak of Jesus' divinity.[8]

In summary, the term "S/son of God" has two levels of meaning in the understanding of the early church: the Jewish meaning which applies equally to Christ, the church, and her members, and the eternal (ontological) meaning which uniquely applies to Jesus. We have to examine every use of "S/son of God" with care in order to decide how they are being used in the passages read.

So, what is the meaning of the statement "his Son" in this verse? I would suggest that it is specifically ontological in meaning.[9] Paul is constructing a chiasm, a well established literary technique used throughout the ancient world. The device compared truths around a central fact. So A'—B—A where A' and A are the corresponding truths. In this chiasm A' represents the eternal Son before his incarnation, who became the son of David (B) and then returned to his pre-incarnate Sonship following the resurrection (A). In a chiasm the central position is the important truth that is being served by the corresponding statements and in this chiasm it is no less a feature. It is only because he was the eternal Son that as the son of David he could redeem creation. His status as son of David allows Jesus to gather all of the promises of redemption together so as to fulfil them, and this includes the promised redemption of creation.

Thus in this chiasm Paul is presenting the one who is "his Son" and who became the Davidic son (the son of God) and following his resurrection is recognized to be what no one in his earthly life recognized: that he is the eternal Son of God. Paul states that the declaration of Jesus' eternal Sonship was made through his resurrection. He had been declared to be the Messiah by the disciples and the crowds and, most significantly, by the Father at his baptism (Matt 3:17). The only declaration of sonship therefore that needed to take place was his eternal Sonship, and this was done through his resurrection. The resurrection was the evidence that the work of redemption had been completed. In a new exodus context, that meant the redemption of creation was also completed. Therefore, the resurrection attests Christ's divinity, for only Yahweh could redeem his creation.

This understanding has hitherto been missed because the creedal statement has been read outside of the new exodus context that the stress on Jesus as the son of David undoubtedly points to. We will see that not only is the letter to the Romans about this eschatological salvation, but that the hymns of the NT repeatedly recall it. Examination

---

8. It would be impossible for Paul, an orthodox Jew, to speak of himself putting faith in anyone other than Yahweh. Yet, in Gal 2:20, he says: "I have been crucified with Christ and I no longer live, but Christ lives in me. The life I live in the body, I live by faith in the Son of God, who loved me and gave himself for me." Texts which indicate that Paul taught the deity of Christ include 2 Cor 4:4 and Col 1:15–19. For an explanation of how the Colossian text supports the deity of Christ, see Holland, *Contours*, chapter 12.

9. Contra Wright, *Romans*, 417 and Jewett, *Romans*, 104–5 who argue that the confession is the product of an evolving Christology that evidences the progression from a primitive Christology to an Hellenistic one.

of these hymns show that they glory in Jesus, the son of David, who is the true Passover offering, the firstborn whose death has restored creation to its Creator (see Col 1:13–20; Heb 1:1–4; Rev 1:5–8).

Nevertheless, while the confession drives the reader towards a high Christology, the reference to Jesus being a "descendant of David" is crucial. If the theme of Jesus being the promised Messiah (the Son of David, who has come for his bride) does not control the exegesis, then there will be a serious misreading of the letter. Paul is saying that this good news is how God fulfilled his promises. He has sent his Son who has come as the promised Davidic king (Rom 3:21; 16:25–26; 2 Cor 1:20). No Jew would have expected that the longed-for King was the eternal Son of God, nor would he have anticipated what the Son of David would do once he had come. Jesus' choice to submit himself to death at the hands of the Roman overlords was unthinkable. The scandal of the cross (1 Cor 1:23) was an insurmountable problem for any Jew who had not faced the reality of the resurrection and experienced the work of Christ's Spirit (1 Cor 2:14; 2 Cor 3:13–16).

1:4 And who through the Spirit of holiness was declared with power to be the Son of God, by his resurrection from the dead. It was beyond question that Jesus was the promised deliverer and not an impostor. He had been given "the Spirit of holiness" who had raised him from the dead. This expression (the Spirit of holiness) was used in the OT to speak of the perfection required for an animal sacrifice to be acceptable to God.[10] Paul is saying that the sacrifice which Jesus made (Rom 3:21ff.; 8:3) was unique. His death has been accepted by God as the means by which he could forgive his people their sins and give them new life. Paul explains this more fully later in the letter.

Being "declared with power to be the Son of God" is a deliberate echo of God's saving activities in the OT. On each of those great occasions—the deliverance from Egypt and then from Babylon—God showed his power (Ps 106:8–10; Exod 9:16; 32:11; Deut 4:37; Isa 40:26; 66:1–2; Jer 16:21). Paul is saying in this verse that another major saving event has happened in the death and resurrection of Jesus. We shall see that this event was unique and achieved what no previous saving activity of God ever did.

The statement that Jesus was declared with power to be the Son of God is also significant. In the OT the power of God was manifest supremely in God's creative activity (Ps 65:6; Isa 40:26; Jer 10:12; 27:5) and then in his activity in saving his people (Exod 15:16; 32:11; Num 14:13; Deut 8:17; 9:26; Isa 40:10; Ps 78:42). The resurrection exemplifies the same themes, for in it God brings about the new creation and it is the climax of his redeeming his people from exile.

The term ὁρισθέντος (*horisthentos*) can be "appointed," "established," or "declared." Some say that it means Paul had an adoptionist Christology—that Jesus became the Son of God following his resurrection, God adopting him as a reward for his faithfulness. Such an understanding fails to recognize that there are two ways of speaking of Jesus as

10. See also Käsemann, *Romans*, 11. Bruce, *Romans*, 73 and Zeisler, *Romans*, 63, acknowledge the Semitic origin of the term but do not identify the source. If the expression is a reference to cultic holiness then its use could serve to prepare the church for the declaration that the eschatological sacrifice was offered in the person of the Son (Rom 3:21–22; 8:3). Isaiah (61:1) promised the Spirit to the Servant in order to help him accomplish the task given him by Yahweh.

the Son of God, as we have seen in the previous verse. The first way could be used by Jews since it speaks of Jesus as the Messiah, with no suggestion of eternal deity. If this is the way that Paul is using the title, it follows that his concern at this point is not to establish the deity of Jesus, but to establish that Jesus has fulfilled the Scriptures (v.2).

However, the resurrection was the decisive event for the understanding of the disciples. They began to appreciate how the Scriptures had been fulfilled in Jesus and to see that those same Scriptures testified that he was more than the Davidic King. They came to see that Jesus was the eternal Son of God. This ontological understanding is present in embryo in this text and becomes increasingly clear in other NT passages (John 1:1–2; Col 2:9; Heb 1:3). Finally, it is expressly stated in the Trinitarian creeds of the early church.

Resurrection from the dead has OT roots. When Israel was in exile, Ezekiel likened her return to the promised land (under the leadership of the Davidic King) to resurrection (Ezek 37:1–14; Hos 13:14). While this was a symbolic resurrection, the typological fulfilment of Jesus—the descendant of David, the King of the Jews, and the true representative of his people—had been literal. His real and historical resurrection was deliverance from bondage and exile. It was his exodus, and through it he brought with him his own people from bondage (1 Cor 10:1–4).

THE MESSIAH KING AND HIS PEOPLE

THROUGH HIM AND for his name's sake, we received grace and apostleship to call people from among all the Gentiles to the obedience that comes from faith. And you also are among those who are called to belong to Jesus Christ. To all in Rome who are loved by God and called to be saints: Grace and peace to you from God our Father and from the Lord Jesus Christ. (Romans 1:5–7)

1:5 Through him and for his name's sake, we received grace and apostleship to call people from among all the Gentiles to the obedience that comes from faith. Paul is saying that, because of Jesus' resurrection, it was possible to call Gentiles into the covenant that God made with his people. The prophets had said that the Gentiles would be allowed to come into the covenant relationship with God on an equal footing with the Jews (Isa 19:19–25; 42:6–7; 56:6–7). They declared that this would be possible after the new exodus, an event which they saw as Israel's resurrection when the New Israel (the church) would be brought out of exile by the resurrection of her Savior (Gal 1:4.; Col 1:13–14).

Paul's former companions in the cause of Judaism were horrified for he now argued that, in this new covenant, the Gentiles were accepted by God without circumcision. They saw him as a betrayer of Israel's law and of the covenant. For them, it was unforgivable to say that God had abrogated the requirements of the law, and they planned the apostle's death on several occasions. Paul develops this theme of the termination of the requirements of the law later in the letter.

Paul describes himself as a herald of this message. Some scholars have sought to trace the progression of Paul's thinking from that of nationalistic Jew to Christian missionary to the Gentiles, suggesting that this metamorphosis was the cause of much distress for him.[11] But this ministry did not cause Paul any theological problems. Even before he became a believer he knew that the coming of the Messiah would mean the calling of the Gentiles. Once he had accepted Jesus as Messiah it was inevitable that the consequence would be their evangelization.

The Gentiles are not only called to faith but to "obedience that comes from faith." The NT knows nothing of a faith that does not obey. The Apostle James said that "faith without works is dead" (Jas 2:26), and another apostle, John, said that if we see our brother in need and refuse to help him, our claim that the love of God dwells in us is meaningless (1 John 3:16–24). For Paul, obedience meant taking up the challenge of reaching the Gentiles with the message of salvation so that they could bring glory to God for the mercy he had shown them.[12]

1:6-7 And you also are among those who are called to belong to Jesus Christ. To all in Rome who are loved by God and called to be saints: Grace and peace to you from God our Father and from the Lord Jesus Christ. It is little short of miraculous that Paul could write these words to a congregation that was mainly made up of Gentile believers. He describes the Gentiles as God's beloved people: "To *all* in Rome who are loved by God" (emphasis added). This change of status was only possible because all of God's blessings had been brought to man through the resurrection of Jesus from the dead. The OT promises had all been fulfilled in Jesus (2 Cor 1:20), including the acceptance of believing Gentiles as the people of God. This fact was not easy for the believing Jews of Paul's day to accept. Because the apostle saw the full implication of the Gentiles being accepted by God, he strenuously defended them from the attempts of zealous Jews to bring them into Judaism via circumcision. Paul could not countenance this for one moment as he saw that it would ultimately betray the essential message of the Gospel. On account of his concern to shield the Gentiles from being entangled in the requirements of Jewish initiation ceremonies, he became the object of intense hatred. Paul deals with the initiation issues later in the letter.

When Paul says that his readers are "loved by God and called to be saints," he uses distinctive OT vocabulary which was used to describe Israel's relationship with Yahweh (2 Chr 6:42; Ps 37:28; Dan 7:18). Once again Paul expresses his conviction that the church has inherited the calling and mission of Israel. This is a view that he expresses regularly in his letters, giving evidence that the church is the fulfilment of the covenant promises (Gal 2:2–5; Eph 2:18–22). This does not imply that God is no longer concerned for the Jews but that, in terms of the Gospel, they have no priority over Gentiles believers. Together, with all believers, they form the new community of God's people (Gal 3:26–29).

In using the greetings χάρις (*charis*) "grace" and εἰρήνη (*eirēnē*) "peace"—echoing the Hebrew חֶסֶד (*ḥesed*) and שׁלוֹם (*šālôm*)—Paul uses salutations that the believers in Rome would have heard regularly in their gatherings. While the citizens of that city

11. See Dodd, *Essays.*

12. 2 Cor 9:12: "This service that you perform is not only supplying the needs of God's people but is also overflowing in many expressions of thanks to God."

looked to the emperor to show them grace and kindness, the believing community looked to God the Father and the Lord Jesus Christ for their salvation and peace. The terms "grace" and "peace" are saturated with OT meaning (Num 6:26; Judg 6:23; Ps 85:8; Zech 12:10) and are greetings that feature extensively in Paul's letters (e.g., 1 Cor 1:3; 2 Cor 1:2; Gal 1:3; Eph 1:2; Phil 1:2; Col 1:2).

THE MESSIAH KING AND HIS PEOPLE'S NEEDS

FIRST, I THANK my God through Jesus Christ for all of you, because your faith is being reported all over the world. God, whom I serve with my whole heart in preaching the gospel of his Son, is my witness how constantly I remember you in my prayers at all times; and I pray that now at last by God's will the way may be opened for me to come to you. I long to see you so that I may impart to you some spiritual gift to make you strong—that is, that you and I may be mutually encouraged by each other's faith. I do not want you to be unaware, brothers, that I planned many times to come to you (but have been prevented from doing so until now) in order that I might have a harvest among you, just as I have had among the other Gentiles. I am bound both to Greeks and non-Greeks, both to the wise and the foolish. That is why I am so eager to preach the gospel also to you who are at Rome. (Romans 1:8–15)

1:8–10 First, I thank my God through Jesus Christ for all of you, because your faith is being reported all over the world. God, whom I serve with my whole heart in preaching the gospel of his Son, is my witness how constantly I remember you in my prayers at all times; and I pray that now at last by God's will the way may be opened for me to come to you. Paul now informs the Roman believers of his prayers for them. He encourages them with the good reports that he has heard concerning their faith and assures them that he shares their faith and concern for the lost as his whole life is spent in preaching the same Gospel that had brought them peace with God.

Paul writes that he serves God with his "whole heart." The term for "serve" is latreu,w (*latreuō*) and it refers to cultic activity. When the term has a divine being as its object (as it does here), it often means "worship." As we have noted, Paul speaks of his proclamation of the Gospel as being priestly (Rom 15:16) and urges the believers to fulfill their priestly ministry (Rom 12:1).

Paul does not give any details of his prayers but we can get an idea of what they would have been by reading the prayers in his letters to other churches (1 Cor 1:4–6; Eph 1:15–23; 2:14–21; Phil 1:3–11; Col 1:3–14; Phlm 4–7). From these prayers we can see that his concern was not for happiness or comfort in the lives of his congregations but for the kingdom of God being advanced through them. This might bring suffering, but Paul prayed for faithfulness and spiritual growth in the believers.

He states that he prays constantly for the Roman believers (thought, by most, to be people he had never met). Clearly, he had a sense of the oneness of God's people as he could not think of them without finding that he prayed for them. They shared the same task of making Christ known to a world that was under condemnation and in need of the salvation that God had secured through the death of his Son. Moreover, the Roman believers were in a crucial geographical location at the heart of the empire and would have a strategic role to play in fulfilling God's purposes. However, Paul did not put them above other believers as it is clear from his prayers in other letters that he valued equally all believers and their witness to Christ.

Paul longs to visit the church in Rome. He prays that this will come about if it is God's will (Rom 15:32). He distinguishes between what he wants to do—even though it is for God's glory—and what God might allow him to do (Acts 18:21). Paul sees that in all he does God is sovereign and that his plans will only be achieved if God promotes them.

1:11–12 I long to see you so that I may impart to you some spiritual gift to make you strong—that is, that you and I may be mutually encouraged by each other's faith. Paul knew how important fellowship and mutual encouragement were (Acts 20:2; 2 Cor 7:13; Eph 6:22; Col 4:8). While he had no sense of superiority over other believers, he knew that he had a God-given task to encourage the church in Rome. However, Paul opens his heart. He needs encouragement and support too, and longs for the believers to refresh his weary spirit. He looks forward to his visit for the blessing he will receive as much as for the blessing he can give. Encouragement is something that all can give, and its effects and benefits are immense. Paul demonstrates how even exceptional leaders, and therefore all believers, need this kind of support and love.

1:13–14 I do not want you to be unaware, brothers, that I planned many times to come to you (but have been prevented from doing so until now) in order that I might have a harvest among you, just as I have had among the other Gentiles. I am bound both to Greeks and non-Greeks, both to the wise and the foolish. There had been some misunderstanding about Paul's desire to visit the church in Rome. Perhaps he had made known his intention to visit at some earlier date and his plans had not materialized. The pressures on him must have been immense and demands from many quarters would have meant that his responses would have to be prioritized. Sometimes he felt that a church was about to succumb to the seductions of skilful infiltrators who were teaching things that destroyed the Christian Gospel (Acts 15:1–2; 20:26–35; 2 Cor 11:13–15; Gal 1:6–9). In the face of such a threat, Paul probably abandoned prior engagements in order to rescue believers from confusion. He knew that heresy would lead to the collapse of the testimony that he had sacrificed himself to establish. The book of the Acts of the Apostles and the letters Paul wrote give us some insight into the ongoing demands upon him.

To assure the Romans that he had not deliberately ignored them, Paul emphasizes that he had no other desire than to reach all men with the Gospel. By saying that he was obligated "both to the Greeks and non-Greeks, both to the wise and the foolish," he encompasses all people. For Paul, there was no niche market for his message. He did not select a particular social class or religious grouping for his evangelism. His understanding of the Gospel would have been incompatible with modern sophisticated marketing techniques which target some while ignoring others.

When such techniques are applied to evangelism, what sort of church is produced? Does it reflect the church that Christ has died to create (Col 3:10–14), where there is no ageism, or racial and social distinctions? While specialized ministries may be necessary, they must not obscure the responsibility that churches have to ensure that all people in their local communities hear the Gospel. If the message being preached does not make demands on those who believe to take up this task of evangelizing *all* people, it can be nothing other than a distortion of the Gospel of Jesus. In describing the Gospel's relevance as being for the Greeks and non-Greeks, both to the "wise and the foolish, Paul spells out its limitless relevance for everyone. He has total confidence in its origin. It is the Gospel of God, and he is eager to continue his ministry by preaching it in Rome.

The Roman Christians probably had no idea of the pressures upon Paul. What mattered to them was that he had not come, and they may well have communicated this disappointment. To assure them of his concern, he tries to explain that his desire to be among them is much more than just to meet them—it is to fulfil Christ's commission. He wants to see Christ's promise fulfilled that he would bear witness to the emperor himself (Acts 9:15), for only then would he consider that his work was complete.

1:15 That is why I am so eager to preach the gospel also to you who are at Rome. Why should Paul, a Jew, have such concern for the Gentiles? It was not an insipid sympathy that created this energy and concern but rather his understanding of the OT Scriptures. Even before his conversion he knew that the climax of the purposes of God was that the Gentiles would be brought into the covenant community. They were to be inheritors of the promise God had made to Abraham that the nations would be blessed through the seed of Isaac, and of the later promises he had made through the prophets that the nations would turn to Israel's God and worship him (Gen 22:17ff.; Isa 2:1–5; 19:23–25; 42:5–7; 56:3–8). This motivated Paul's evangelistic work. The promises of God had to be fulfilled. His motivation was not only his concern for the lost but also his awareness that, unless the Gospel went to the furthest parts of the world, the promise of God would not be completed. Not until that happened could the great celebration of the salvation of God take place. Indeed, not until then could God be justified before all humankind, as only then would it be seen that God had kept his covenant. In other words, Paul was motivated not only by concern for the lost but supremely by covenantal obligation and his passion for the glory of God.

THE MESSIAH KING AND HIS MISSION

I AM NOT ashamed of the gospel, because it is the power of God for the salvation of everyone who believes: first for the Jew, then for the Gentile. For in the gospel a righteousness from God is revealed, a righteousness that is by faith from first to last, just as it is written: "The righteous will live by faith." (Romans 1:16–17)

1:16 I am not ashamed of the gospel, because it is the power of God for the salvation of everyone who believes: first for the Jew, then for the Gentile. Why is Paul not ashamed of the Gospel? Because it is "the power of God for the salvation of everyone who believes." He does not speak of this from a mere academic/theoretical position. It had transformed his life, and he is confident that it will do the same for others when they are brought into a right relationship with God. He believes the Gospel to be authoritative, being in accord with the law and the prophets (Rom 3:21) and being authenticated by the resurrection of Jesus from the dead (Rom 1:4).

The term "Gospel" (good news), is saturated with echoes from the book of Isaiah.[13] The reference to Paul "not being ashamed" is a further Isaianic echo. Isa 28:16 states that those who put their trust in the one who is called "the stone" will never be put to shame. This "stone" passage is the most quoted OT passage in the NT (Matt 21:44; Mark 12:10; Luke 20:17; Acts 4:11; 1 Pet 2:6–8), so the Roman believers would immediately associate Paul's statement of "not being ashamed" with faith in the promised Messiah: "See, I lay a stone in Zion, a tested stone, a precious cornerstone for a sure foundation; the one who trusts will never be dismayed" (Isa 28:16). In fact, Paul quotes from this passage himself (Rom 9:33). The one who is called "the stone" is the promised Son of David, and in the book of Isaiah, as elsewhere in the prophetic writings, he is the one promised who would bring the Jews out of exile and lead them back to Jerusalem (Isa 11:1; 48:20–21; 52:1–12).

"Ashamed" is a key term. In Isaiah Israel and the nations are constantly ashamed for refusing to obey Yahweh (Isa 1:29; 23:4; 24:23; 29:22; 33:9). In the NT the time has arrived when faith is "not ashamed" because the believers' trust is responded to. Paul says that he is not ashamed of "the Gospel." The message that God was acting to deliver his people was the Gospel—the good news—to the poor (Ps 9:18; 34:6; 35:10; Isa 29:19; Matt 5:3; 11:5; Luke 4:18; 14:13). Paul uses this theme in chapter 10 where he quotes from Isaiah: "how beautiful are the feet of those who bring good news" (Isa 52:7). His use of the phrase "power of God," which will be the key to his description of the resurrection in chapter 6, is again from the OT. Biblical scholars widely acknowledge that the two major occasions when the power of God was displayed in the OT was when he brought the Jews out of bondage from Egypt and then from Babylon. These two deliverances

---

13. Hays, *Echoes*, 37, sees Rom 1:16–17 to be an echo of Ps 92:2, and claims that v.3 of the Psalm echoes the theological framework of Rom 1:16–17. Hays says: "The hope of the Psalmist is that God's eschatological vindication of Israel will serve as a demonstration to the whole world of the power and the faithfulness of Israel's God, a demonstration that will bring even Gentiles to acknowledge him." Hays also hears echoes of Isa 51:4–5 and 52:10 behind the declaration of confidence given by Paul. The significant thing about this identification is the context of these sources. Hays has missed this context because he does not see the power of the new exodus motif in Paul's writing. Ps 92 is, in fact, a psalm of lament over the condition of Israel during her exile. The cry for the power of God to be displayed and his faithfulness to be demonstrated is, like the passages identified in Isaiah, new exodus material. In other words, Paul takes Scriptures which relate to the historical condition of Israel's shame, humiliation, and punishment and brings them into a global perspective. The issue Paul is dealing with is no longer the separation of Israel from her God, but of humankind from its Creator. Hays notes that Paul's declaration about not being ashamed of the Gospel reflects Ps 43:10 (LXX), where the Psalmist is not ashamed of Yahweh's covenant. It also echoes Isa 28:16 (LXX), to which Paul will later appeal (Rom 9:33). Again, both passages are closely linked with the exile and the expectation that Yahweh would intervene on behalf of his people. As if to reinforce this, Paul quotes from the much discussed passage in Hab 2:4. However he intends his adaptation to be understood, there can be no doubt that he is turning to an exilic context for his citation. Habakkuk refers to the faithful community which is languishing in despair because its expectations have not been fulfilled. He urges the people to wait in hope for the display of God's righteousness, that is, his salvation. Once again, the theme of the second exodus is utilized to provide the theological framework for Paul's statement concerning the Gospel.

are repeatedly spoken of as God saving his people, and the technical term "salvation" (Hebrew יְשׁוּעָה *yĕšûʿâ*, Greek σωτηρία *sōtēria*. See Exod 14:13; 15:2; Isa 49:6; 52:10; 56:1) is, again, one that Paul uses here.

So, Paul is embracing the technical vocabulary of Isaiah. However, it is not just the prophet's vocabulary that he adopts. He uses the historical situation of the Jews in exile as his model, for he sees the event as a type of humanity. He says that humankind is in bondage, alienated from God, and in a desperate situation. Indeed, Man's situation is far worse than that of the Jews in exile—an exile that resulted from their disobedience to God's word. Paul sees that the whole of humanity is cut off from its Creator and under the control of Satan. Humankind is bound as a captive in the kingdom of darkness (Acts 26:17–18; Col 1:13–14); there is no way out, and the situation is dire. The judgment that will come upon Satan will also come upon the human family, for it has foolishly accepted his lies about God and has become part of Satan's rebellion. The outcome is that mankind is at enmity with God (Eph 2:1–3, 11–13).

Paul states that this salvation is for all who will believe—it is for Jews and Gentiles. Indeed, the universality of God's love was constantly proclaimed throughout the OT (Gen 12:3; Jonah 3:10; Ps 98:1–6; 100:1–5). While the Jews were the elect people of the OT, Paul—one of their most fanatical members before his conversion—now insists that the good news is for all people. The calling of the Gentiles was so fundamental for him that he not only devoted himself to their evangelization, but constantly risked his life as a result of the bitter hatred of those who thought he was compromising the integrity of Judaism (Acts 9:23; 23:12; Gal 5:11).

Those Jews who hated Paul were not objecting to Gentile evangelism. They would have been delighted if Paul had led the Gentiles into Judaism as converts who submitted to the law. But Paul could not do this. He knew that the law had not brought salvation to the Jews. They had to put away their dependence on the law because, although it was good and holy, it was never given as a means of salvation but as an expression of the covenant that God had graciously established between himself and Israel.

In fact, Judaism was divided over the significance of the law. While some saw keeping it as a way of pleasing God and attaining salvation, others saw the law as evidence that they had nothing else to receive from God. It's very possession was evidence that the Lord had accepted them, and, as far as they were concerned, any who would be accepted by Yahweh had to come under the yoke of this sacred gift. This was the point that Paul, the disciple of Jesus, could no longer accept. While he had previously rejoiced in the law (Phil 3:1–6), he now realized that he had made it a substitute for Christ (Phil 3:7–11). For many devout Jews, there was nothing beyond the law. The Torah was the vital evidence that they had been accepted by Yahweh and therefore were saved.

Why are there these two different positions in Judaism? The giving of the law was certainly intended to bless the covenant community, but Paul's experience on the Damascus road caused him to review his understanding of salvation history. He came to see how his ancestors had broken the covenant at Sinai by committing adultery (Exod 32:1–8). This happened on Israel's wedding night (the prophets' description of the Sinai event [Hos 2:14–23]), after her "marriage" to Yahweh, her God. Israel broke the marriage covenant when she worshipped the golden calf and so came under the covenantal curses. The law was intended to bring life, but because of her disobedience and unfaithfulness it became a ministry of death to Israel (2 Cor 3:9). Paul came to see that his adulterous nation needed the same salvation promised to the Gentiles—a salvation that was entirely of grace. It was such Jews, who had lost confidence in the law's ability to save, who cried out for mercy and forgiveness.

But now the good news promised by the prophets had arrived. National privilege was terminated; the promised Messiah had come. Jews were not excluded, but they were not given favor denied to the Gentiles. What had previously been the differing status of Jews and Gentiles counted for nothing under the new covenant (Col 3:10–11). All had to accept their need of God's free grace through his Son's life, death, and resurrection.

The loss of privilege caused the Jewish community huge distress. The Jews wanted Gentiles to be brought into Judaism. They knew that when their Messiah came, the Gentiles would acknowledge God and turn to him. But what the Jews could not accept was that this would come via the death of their Messiah. For most Jews, the cross was a scandal with which they could not come to terms (1 Cor 1:23). They found immense difficulty in accepting a Messiah who had been put to death by their arch-enemies, the Romans. Furthermore, it was these same Gentiles who were now, claimed Paul, freely invited into the covenant community.

Despite Paul's insistence on the equality of believing Jews and believing Gentiles, he still recognized the priority of the Jews in hearing the Gospel, for it was through them that the message was to go into the entire world. For this reason, the Gospel is for the Jew first. In giving the Jews the first opportunity to hear, God fulfils his promise to Abraham that he would respond to their cry for help, allowing them to fulfil their calling to be a light to the nations (Gen 15:13–14; Isa 49:6).

1:17 For in the gospel a righteousness from God is revealed, a righteousness that is by faith from first to last, just as it is written. The righteous will live by faith. Paul's use of Hab 2:4: "The righteous will live by faith," suggests that he follows/holds the perspective/view of the promised new exodus. In the original context the statement was addressed to those about to go into exile. They were tempted to reject the prophets, who had warned them not to strive to overthrow their captors. The way of faith entailed submission both to the judgment and the promise of Yahweh. The righteous do not seek to achieve their own freedom or deliverance, but recognize the justice of the judgment that they are under and wait for God to fulfil his word and bring them salvation (Ezek 34:1–16).[14]

Again, Paul borrows a key term from Isaiah, the prophets, and the psalms. "Righteousness" is the term used to describe God's acts of doing right (of keeping his

14. Campbell, "Interpretation," 265–85, sees this verse as crucial for understanding Paul's meaning of "faith in Christ." He says: "The eschatological saving righteousness of God is being revealed in the gospel by means of faithfulness (namely, the faithfulness of Christ), with the goal of the faith/fullness (in the Christian)." Zorn, "Messianic," 213–30, argues that the "messianic" interpretation of Hab 2:4 helps us to see that Paul is contrasting human righteousness with God's righteousness and covenantal fidelity in Rom 1:17.

promises). In the prophecy of Isaiah God acted to save his people from their exile. He had promised them that he would not abandon them, even though they deserved rejection. This righteousness (covenant faithfulness worked out in his saving activity) included God restoring the Jews to be the people they should have been. The Jews could not think of being in a right relationship with God without worshipping him, and this necessitated their return to the temple in Jerusalem. For God to bring them there from their place of exile meant that he had to deliver them and accept their worship. In other words, he had to forgive their sins.

However, Paul is saying that it is not from Babylon that believers have been rescued but from the kingdom of darkness. It is not in the earthly Jerusalem that they will worship but in heaven itself. Of course, we are able to worship God now, as the Spirit enables us (John 4:23–24; Phil 3:3); but any worship that we offer here is only a taste of what it will be like in heaven when we are totally free from sin (1 Cor 2:9). Paul says that this astonishing salvation is not something we earn by impressing God with our sincerity or zeal—it is given to us simply because we put our faith (our total confidence) in the God who never fails to keep his promises.

The statement "by faith from first to last" has been much analyzed. The most natural meaning is "from God's faithfulness to human faithfulness."[15]

---

15. See also Dunn, *Romans*; Wright, *Romans*, 425.

THE MESSIAH KING AND THE REBELLION OF MAN

THE WRATH OF God is being revealed from heaven against all the godlessness and wickedness of men who suppress the truth by their wickedness, since what may be known about God is plain to them, because God has made it plain to them. For since the creation of the world God's invisible qualities—his eternal power and divine nature—have been clearly seen, being understood from what has been made, so that men are without excuse. For although they knew God, they neither glorified him as God nor gave thanks to him, but their thinking became futile and their foolish hearts were darkened. Although they claimed to be wise, they became fools and exchanged the glory of the immortal God for images made to look like mortal man and birds and animals and reptiles. Therefore God gave them over in the sinful desires of their hearts to sexual impurity for the degrading of their bodies with one another. They exchanged the truth of God for a lie, and worshipped and served created things rather than the Creator—who is forever praised. Amen. Because of this, God gave them over to shameful lusts. Even their women exchanged natural relations for unnatural ones. In the same way the men also abandoned natural relations with women and were inflamed with lust for one another. Men committed indecent acts with other men, and received in themselves the due penalty for their perversion. Furthermore, since they did not think it worthwhile to retain the knowledge of God, he gave them over to a depraved mind, to do what ought not to be done. They have become filled with every kind of wickedness, evil, greed and depravity. They are full of envy, murder, strife, deceit and malice. They are gossips, slanderers, God-haters, insolent, arrogant and boastful; they invent ways of doing evil; they disobey their parents; they are senseless, faithless, heartless, ruthless. Although they know God's righteous decree that those who do such things deserve death, they not only continue to do these very things but also approve of those who practise them. (Rom 1:18–32)

1:18 The wrath of God is being revealed from heaven against all the godlessness and wickedness of men who suppress the truth by their wickedness. Paul says that man is under the sentence of the wrath of God. He is not saying that God is angry in some uncontrollable way but rather that he cannot be indifferent to those who break his laws. In the same way, it would be utterly shameful if a judge excused a murderer, or if a society was indifferent to its pedophiles. God cannot be both holy and at the same time indifferent to humanity's sin.

Paul is about to argue that sin destroys humankinds ability to think in a way that reflects his position as a creature obligated to his Creator. Sin causes man to seek to usurp the authority of God and to excuse his actions and attitudes as mature, liberal, and enlightened. Sin is rebellion, no matter how culturally acceptable and reasonable it may appear to be. God can have only one attitude towards it—one of hostility. Any other attitude would mean that he had surrendered to Satan. He would be helpless and unable to deal with the tyranny of man. For God to be just and holy, he has to judge sin. In doing that, he must judge humankind.

Paul says: "the wrath of God is being revealed from heaven against all the godlessness and wickedness of men who suppress the truth." The wrath of God is a present reality for it is "being" revealed. It will come to its climax on the day of judgment, when he will sentence those who have rejected his rightful authority (Rom 2:5, 16; 14:10). Paul is again faithful to OT teaching. The great act of judgment on Israel for her sin was giving the nation over to her enemies–the Babylonians taking her into exile. Paul says that God has given rebellious man over to sin, and the sentence brought upon him is imprisonment in the kingdom of darkness–exiled from the God who created and loved him (Acts 26:18; Gal 1:4; Col 1:13–14).

The "wrath of God" is seen by many as an outmoded way of speaking of God's reaction to sin. It has been argued that this expression suggests that he is angry and not in control of his emotions–a description inconsistent with the God of love of the NT. However, such an argument does not do justice to the biblical evidence, not least because the NT regularly proclaims the wrath of God (Matt 3:7; John 3:36; Eph 2:3; 1 Thess 2:16; 2 Thess 1:5–10). The NT speaks of the same God as is found in the OT—a God who never ceases to be angry at sin. To remove God's wrath from the description of his character would be to create a god in our own image. He would be an idol. How shocking is the thought that Christian worship can so easily become idolatrous.

The wrath of God is being revealed "against all godlessness and wickedness of men." Our sin will find us out, and its consequence is not temporal separation from God as in the OT, but eternal exile. This exile is based on the OT model. In the Garden, Adam preferred the voice of the serpent to the voice of God and was consequently exiled. Israel, a nation created for God to be his people, rejected his rightful claims and was eventually exiled also. While the language of hell in the Gospels is vivid and awful, we must not lose sight of the fact that this language was used in the OT to speak of God's judgment on faithless Israel. Expressions about the soul being cast into a lake of fire[16] and the sinner being "cut off" must be kept in the OT framework of judgment.[17] The imagery is not literal but powerfully symbolic of separation from God in exile. A symbol is always a faint reflection of the reality it is used to convey. If the lake of fire is only a symbol, what is the reality? No wonder the writer of the letter to the Hebrews said: "It is a dreadful thing to fall into the hands of the living God" (Heb 10:31).

Paul says that God's wrath is coming on those who "suppress the truth." This is a frightening statement and conflicts with modern opinion. We live in an age when truth is seen as nothing more than private opinion. It is claimed that what is true for one person may not be true for another. "Truth" it is claimed is not absolute, each person has their own version of truth which is as valid as any other version. This understanding, which is the fruit of postmodernism, is promoted within universities and through media—it permeates society, determining private and public morality.

Moral confusion is the inevitable result of denying the existence of God. If there is no God, then right and wrong are mere reflections of the preferences of humans and societies. Any claim for a moral principle being true is nothing more than saying: "in

---

16. Isa 66:24: "And they will go out and look upon the dead bodies of those who rebelled against me; their worm will not die, nor will their fire be quenched, and they will be loathsome to all mankind."

17. Ps 37:9: "For evil men will be cut off, but those who hope in the LORD will inherit the land." Isa 48:19: "Your descendants would have been like the sand, your children like its numberless grains; their name would never be cut off nor destroyed from before me."

my opinion, it is 'true.'" The powerful argument that there are no absolute truths has profoundly shaped modern society. However, when this product of postmodernism is subjected to its own definition, it emerges as one opinion in over six billion opinions and is worth no more than any other! In other words, there is no more truth in the belief that there are no absolutes than in the belief that there are. Thus "postmodernism," like all other "isms" contains the seed of its self destruction within its own argument. Likewise, the claim that there is no God is itself only an opinion. It is of no more value than the other six billion opinions which are in the marketplace of ideas! To get to this position the evidence has been carefully selected and Atheism's "unassailable" claims constructed. The fact is that even the most ardent atheist instinctively ponders the reason for his existence, and he can only make sense of his being once he acknowledges the existence of God.

If we argue that Paul's opinions are worth no more than any others, we must remember from whom his message came. It was not the result of his imagination or reflection, but of an unmistakable encounter with the Son of God who had been crucified and raised from the dead. Paul's message was not speculation; it was based on revelation. The Christian Gospel is not a record of man's searching after God, but a record of God's saving initiative to save humankind from a desperate situation.

Paul says that the truth is suppressed by the wickedness of those who reject it. Rejection of the truth does not happen by chance—it is the direct result of humankind's sinfulness. It is "the suppression of the truth by their wickedness" (2 Tim 3:1-8). Such an analysis would have been as repugnant in Paul's day as it is to modern man, and he was rejected as much then as he is now. He would have been tempted to change his message in order to make it more acceptable, but he could not. Paul was not giving his opinion, but was bringing the message given by God. His message was nothing other than the message of Moses and the prophets who announced God's will to both Jews and Gentiles.

1:19–20 Since what may be known about God is plain to them, because God has made it plain to them. For since the creation of the world God's invisible qualities—his eternal power and divine nature—have been clearly seen, being understood from what has been made, so that men are without excuse. Paul is aware that people claim innocence because of ignorance. For the Gentiles, ignorance was their defense. Paul responds to this plea by saying that nature (the creative work of God) bears witness to God's existence. Theologians call this "natural theology"; it is knowledge about God that can be deduced from creation. Consideration of nature suggests design which points to a superior intelligence. The vastness of the universe points not only to design but to majesty and power. While nature does not give humanity knowledge of God which leads to salvation, it does testify to a Creator God who deserves worship. This can be the first step in the search for God who reveals himself through his Son. However, despite this observable evidence, man suppresses the truth and argues that no case can be made for the claims of God upon his life.

1:21 For although they knew God, they neither glorified him as God nor gave thanks to him, but their thinking became futile and their foolish hearts were darkened. At this point in his argument, Paul goes back to the creation narrative in the book of Genesis where the story of the fall is recorded. He describes the process of depravity that was its consequence.[18] Adam was a crucial figure in the message of the early church and this spoke of the human predicament of guilt, darkness and fear as the result of his sin. This will become clearer when we consider chapter 5. However, it is helpful at this point to appreciate that the theme of many of the hymns quoted in the NT is of Jesus being the last Adam, saving his people from the tragedy of the disobedience of the first (Rom 1:3–4,[19] 3:21–26; Col 1:13–12; Phil 2:5–11; Heb 1:1–14; 2:6–13; Rev 1:4–8).

We know that Paul visits the account of the fall in this verse because he writes: "although they knew God." For Paul, a Jew, there is only one man and one woman who have known God in the intimate way he describes. Adam and his wife had perfect fellowship with God. They had been created for this unique relationship. Despite this extraordinary privilege, they rejected his love and friendship and believed the lie that Satan presented. They accepted that, if they asserted their independence, they would be as gods who knew the difference between good and evil (Gen 3:5). They were neither thankful to God nor did they glorify him.

This description was not only true of Adam and Eve but of all their descendants. God is accused of imposing his power, making men into religious robots who are deprived of fulfilment and self-realization. In reality, the situation is reversed. It is God who delights in the development and growth of man, but it is Satan who seeks to make him into a mindless being with no freedom. The god of this world has darkened the minds of those who do not believe (2 Cor 4:4; Eph 4:18).

The outcome of this sin is that humankind is warped in its thinking. Despite great scientific and cultural advancement, sin distorts their ability to reflect on the consequences of its actions and attitudes. To achieve goals such as self-satisfaction, power, and economic success, ends justify means and personal morality is interpreted through the lens of personal happiness. While such moral bankruptcy exists, the human heart becomes ever darker.

1:22 Although they claimed to be wise, they became fools. Paul underlines the depravity of humanity's condition—for they have no real appreciation of their predicament. Although their heart is in darkness, they claim to be wise and have as a consequence become fools. But in whose eyes have they become a fool? The policies and values Paul challenges are upheld by many powerful and educated people. They can accommodate God as long as his presence justifies their agenda, but when his claims are taken seriously by an individual, the follower of Christ is accused of being fanatical. A person's reaction to this allegation marks them out as a true believer. The approval of others is not impor-

---

18. For scholars who see Paul to be unfolding the story of Adam in the latter part of the chapter, see Barrett, *First*, 17–19; Hooker, "Adam," 301ff., and "Further," 297–306; Dunn, *Romans*, 1:53, and *Making*, 101; Wright, "Adam," 359–89.

19. Note how the language and imagery of Rom 5:12ff. is anticipated in this creedal statement.

tant, for their values are not those of the kingdom that controls humanity. What matters is the approval of the King who has saved them from darkness and death.

1:23 And exchanged the glory of the immortal God for images made to look like mortal man and birds and animals and reptiles. The darkness and ignorance of unbelieving men resulted in them creating their own gods. The reference to their exchanging the glory of God for images echoes Ps 106:20, which references Israel's sin in making the golden calf.[20] In other words, even though Israel experienced the mighty saving power of God in bringing her out of Egypt, she still behaved like the people from whom she had been rescued.

While Paul was limited in his knowledge of the ancient Mediterranean, his analysis is not weakened by modern social theories. His description of man's decline into depravity as he seeks a god that he finds acceptable is equally true of twenty-first century man. Humans have made gods that they think they can control. However, it is not long before these gods take control of their "creators." The claim that the living God has limited their freedom soon turns on its head as the gods which people have made become their masters, engendering fear by their merciless rule. However, this is not a psychological bondage. Elsewhere Paul shows that behind the idols is Satan, the prince of darkness and ruler of this fallen world (1 Cor 10:19–22).

1:24 Therefore God gave them over in the sinful desires of their hearts to sexual impurity for the degrading of their bodies with one another. In saying, "God gave them over," Paul alludes to Ps 81. In this Psalm of Asaph, the following words of God are recorded: "Hear, O my people, and I will warn you—if you would but listen to me, O Israel! You shall have no foreign god among you; you shall not bow down to an alien god. I am the LORD your God, who brought you up out of Egypt. Open wide your mouth and I will fill it. But my people would not listen to me; Israel would not submit to me. So I gave them over to their stubborn hearts to follow their own devices" (Ps 81:8–12).[21] In alluding to this text and to Ps 106:20 in v. 23, Paul seems to be preparing for his debate with the Jewish community which he will open up in chapter 2. By using OT allusions—

---

20. Hooker, "Adam," helpfully points out that Paul has imported the word "image" into the quotation of the psalm. As this term is always linked with the Genesis account in Paul, Hooker argues that Paul intends to take the reader back to the fall. She reasons that the rest of the chapter is about the fall and not a discussion on the rejection of natural revelation. Her argument is most helpful, but the phrase "they disobey their parents" (Rom 1:30) can hardly apply to Adam and Eve. It would be better, in my judgment, to see Hebraic fluidity as found in the Psalms and the Servant Songs. In these texts the writers move between the figurehead or the representative and the represented with such naturalness that it is almost impossible to follow who is being spoken about at any particular point in the narrative. In other words, accepting that the text is earthed in the fall does not preclude some of the history of Adam's descendants and their rejection of God. For further discussion, see chapter 7.

21. Wright, *Romans*, 433, when referring to Paul's use of Ps 81:12 notes: "This Psalm is itself a hymnic telling of the exodus narrative, warning of idolatry, bemoaning the fact that Israel has not heeded the warning, and appealing for the people to return to Yahweh. Thus, again, Paul's surface text describes paganism, but the subtext quietly includes Israel in the indictment." Thus, the new exodus theme is embedded in Paul's theology of the fall. The fall led to humanity's exile from God's presence and the Gospel is about how God has made this exile to end.

which refer to Israel's idolatry—Paul indicates that humanity's sinfulness is universal, encompassing even the covenant community.

Paul exposes the truth of man's condition by describing him as an idolater. The values he lives by are not the commandments of the living God but the uncontrolled wishes of his foolish and darkened heart. He lives without considering his Maker, his own gods controlling and sanctioning his behavior. A feature of man's rejection of God is the rejection of sexual purity. It is no accident that this sin is often referred to as evidence of man's depravity (Matt 15:19–20; 1 Cor 6:9–10; Gal 5:19–21; Rev 18:2–3). When man is left to the imaginations of his heart with no conscience restraining him, he becomes like one of the animals. In so doing, he destroys his unique dignity. Man without God is a creation without purpose, meaning, and morality.

Sexual immorality is never seen in the Bible as unforgivable, but it is a sin with an unforgettable effect. Millions live with the fear that AIDS is the silent guest in their bodies and many victims suffer through no fault of their own. Many live with the insecurity of not knowing their fathers, and countless children live day by day in the turmoil of marriage breakdowns due to the unfaithfulness of a parent. Sex is vitally important, and the consequences of infidelity and promiscuity are awful and unchanging.

1:25 They exchanged the truth of God for a lie, and worshipped and served created things rather than the Creator—who is forever praised. Amen. Paul underlines the basis of this behaviour. He repeats that man has devised a system of values with no authority other than what his darkened heart approves. This opens the door to every form of perversion and corruption and, because he has substituted the truth of God for a lie, there is no sense of guilt. There is an arrogant denial of evil, and no limit to what he will do as he asserts his rights.

But man's rejection of God is far from the last word. Paul indicates this by saying: "the Creator–who is forever praised." Paul uses the doxology as a way of distancing himself from worship that does not recognize that all blessings come from the Creator.[22] Man, the pinnacle of God's creation, is nothing more than a twisted, self-deceiving creature upon whom his majestic, powerful Creator looks in pain.

1:26-27 Because of this, God gave them over to shameful lusts. Even their women exchanged natural relations for unnatural ones. In the same way the men also abandoned natural relations with women and were inflamed with lust for one another. Men committed indecent acts with other men, and received in themselves the due penalty for their perversion. Because man excluded God from his thinking, he has been given over to the consequences of his self-created darkness.[23] This results in the practice of every sexual perversion. All forms of homosexuality are clearly condemned.[24] This

22. See also Dunn, *Romans*, 1:64.

23. Käsemann, *Romans*, 47, notes: "Paul paradoxically reverses the cause and the consequence: Moral perversion is the result of God's wrath, not the reason for it."

24. Malick, "Condemnation," 327–40, notes that Paul did not impose Jewish customs and rules on his readers. Instead, he addressed same-sex relations from the transcultural perspective of God's created order.

does not deny that there may be genetic orientation,[25] but this cannot be the excuse for behavior which is contrary to the commands of God.

The argument heard many times is "God has made me like I am. He accepts me, why can't you?" This plea misses one vital element crucial to biblical understanding. Humanity is no longer how it was created. Sin, or the fall, has radically changed its very being. The image of God in human society[26] is not only marred, it has left humanity as the prisoner of Satan. God does not accept us as we are. He calls us to repentance of all sin (not just a particular one), and without this repentance we remain alienated from him forever.

Paul is quite clear: the consequence of men abandoning the commandments of God is that "they receive in themselves the due penalty for their perversion."[27] The present tense is used, suggesting that Paul sees the process of judgment as having begun. In exchanging the truth of God for a lie, man has devalued himself and is no longer the noble being that God intended him to be. Instead, he has become a prisoner of Sin.[28]

1:28-32 Furthermore, since they did not think it worthwhile to retain the knowledge of God, he gave them over to a depraved mind, to do what ought not to be done. They have become filled with every kind of wickedness, evil, greed and depravity. They are full of envy, murder, strife, deceit and malice. They are gossips, slanderers, God-haters, insolent, arrogant and boastful; they invent ways of doing evil; they disobey their parents; they are senseless, faithless, heartless, ruthless. Although they know God's righteous decree that those who do such things deserve death, they not only continue to do these very things but also approve of those who practise them. Paul continues his analysis of the condition of man. Again, he asserts that God has given man over to a depraved mind. There is one other place in the Bible where the phrase "given up" occurs. Num 21:29 says: "Woe to you, O Moab! You are destroyed, O people of Chemosh! He has given up his sons as fugitives and his daughters as captives to Sihon king of the Amorites." Moab's children have been given over to the enemy who will "destroy" them. If this reference is behind Paul's usage (and there are parallels with God giving up his people to the enemy) then the meaning Paul might have is that God no longer defends man from Satan's attacks. This is the consequence of rejecting him.

Abandonment to a depraved mind opens the floodgates to evil and the saturation of human personality with obsession for the vile. It could be argued that Paul has been excessive in describing man in such horrific terms and that few sink to such depths of depravity. However, such responses miss the perspective that Paul has as he describes the condition of man. He paints the picture at the corporate level, where nations, busi-

---

25. Paul's reference to homosexuality not being according to nature is not a reference to the nature of man but, following Jewish custom, to the natural order that God has intended. See Moo, *Encountering*, 60.

26. As we will eventually see, Paul's anthropological terms are almost always corporate.

27. Fitzmyer, *Romans*, 285, notes: "Having exchanged a true God for a false one (1:25), pagans inevitably exchange their true natural functions for perverted ones."

28. In the exegesis of chapter 6, I will argue that Paul's use of the singular "sin" does not refer to violations of the law but to Satan.

nesses, communities, and families assert their "rights" and use whatever is necessary to secure them.[29]

While moral rules are usually followed within immediate social units, it is outside of them that the true heart of the community is exposed. It may not be that individuals demonstrate perversity in their own lives, but they support those who represent them and become guilty through association. For example, in the modern world such ruthless behavior might emanate from multinational banks and companies. They crush nations with debt and rob the poor of their resources in order to inflate profits and bonuses. These institutions represent millions of people who are prepared to let hard-nosed businessmen represent them in their dealings without questioning the morality of the organization of which they are part.

The reason for the terrifying state of affairs that Paul expounds is found in the book of Genesis. The beginning of humankind was one of joy and happiness, when God created Adam for the purpose of perfect fellowship with himself. This unique relationship was thrown away when Satan's lie was believed (Gen 3:4), and humankind became part of the kingdom of darkness. This darkness has penetrated every part of human existence. It results in humanity's ongoing rejection of God with blatant attempts to overthrow his rule.

This understanding is supported by the recognition of many scholars that the description Paul used to outline the condition of man follows the events that ensued as a result of the fall (Gen 3). Humankind is in a frightening dilemma. Instead of being the pinnacle of creation, it is its destroyer. Instead of living in moral, intellectual, and spiritual purity, it lives in darkness and defilement. It was promised that it would become like God; but it has become the very opposite and is under condemnation. In its condition of exile, humanity needs a Savior. Paul is going to explain how God, whose love has been rejected, has provided such a person.

CONCLUSION OF ROMANS 1

Paul has introduced the subject of his Gospel as the Son of David—the one who Isaiah spoke about as the agent of God's salvation for his people. By his use of the Isaianic theme of "the righteousness of God" in vv. 16–17, Paul has rooted the account of his Gospel in the theological expectations of the prophet's message. In Isaiah, the revelation of the righteousness of God was the coming of God in salvation, bringing deliverance to Israel.

---

29. Jewett, *Romans*, 177, says: "the popular application of the modern concept of the individual sexual orientation based on biological differences is anachronistic. Such exegesis misreads Paul's argument as dealing with individual sins rather than the corporate distortion of the human race since Adam's fall."

ROMANS 2

THE MESSIAH KING AND HIS PATIENCE

You, THEREFORE, HAVE no excuse, you who pass judgment on someone else, for at whatever point you judge the other, you are condemning yourself, because you who pass judgment do the same things. Now we know that God's judgment against those who do such things is based on truth. So when you, a mere man, pass judgment on them and yet do the same things, do you think you will escape God's judgment? Or do you show contempt for the riches of his kindness, tolerance and patience, not realizing that God's kindness leads you towards repentance?

But because of your stubbornness and your unrepentant heart, you are storing up wrath against yourself for the day of God's wrath, when his righteous judgment will be revealed. God "will give to each person according to what he has done." To those who by persistence in doing good seek glory, honor and immortality, and follow evil, there will be wrath and anger. There will be trouble and distress for every human being who does evil: first for the Jew, then for the Gentile; but glory, honor and peace for everyone who does good: first for the Jew, then for the Gentile. For God does not show favoritism.

All who sin apart from the law will also perish apart from the law, and all who sin under the law will be judged by the law. For it is not those who hear the law who are righteous in God's sight, but it is those who obey the law who will be declared righteous. (Indeed, when Gentiles, who do not have the law, do by nature things required by the law, they are a law for themselves, even though they do not have the law. They show that the requirements of the law are written on their hearts, their consciences also bearing witness, and their thoughts sometimes accusing them and at other times even defending them.) This will take place on the day when God judges people's secrets through Jesus Christ, as my gospel declares.

Now you, if you call yourself a Jew; if you rely on the law and brag about your relationship to God; if you know his will and approve of what is superior because it will give eternal life. But for those who are self-seeking and who reject the truth you are instructed by the law; if you are convinced that you are a guide for the blind, a light for those who are in the dark, an instructor of the foolish, a teacher of infants, because you have in the law the embodiment of knowledge and truth—you, then, who teach others, do you not teach yourself? You who preach against stealing, do you steal? You who say that people should not commit adultery, do you commit adultery? You who abhor idols, do you rob temples? You who brag about the law, do you dishonor God by breaking the law? As it is written: "God's name is blasphemed among the Gentiles because of you." Circumcision has value if you observe the law, but if you break the law, you have become as though you had not been circumcised. If those who are not circumcised keep the law's requirements, will they not be regarded as though they were circumcised? The one who is not circumcised physically and yet obeys the law will condemn you who, even though you have the written code and circumcision, are a law-breaker. A man is not a Jew if he is only one outwardly, nor is circumcision merely outward and physical. No, a man is a Jew if he is one inwardly; and circumcision is cir- cumcision of the heart, by the Spirit, not by the written code. Such a man's praise is not from men, but from God. (Rom 2:1–29)

INTRODUCTION

HAVING PAINTED THE CONDITION of humanity in the preceding chapter, Paul focuses on the Jewish community and the claims it makes. He has no difficulty in constructing his argument because he had once been part of this select group who knew that they had shunned the very things that characterized the lives of the Gentiles.

To get his point across, Paul creates a diatribe, a situation in which he debates with an imaginary representative of the chosen people. We will find exegetical problems in the text that have caused commentators difficulties, because Paul seems to contradict his own understanding of justification that he will teach latter in the letter. If the apparent contradiction is so obvious to twenty-first century people it will have been no less obvious to those first hearing the letter. So what is going on in this passage on this crucially vital subject?

I will suggest that like many other points of confusion, the difficulties were neither in Paul's mind nor the minds of the original recipients. This was for one simple reason— they would have read/heard the argument in its corporate setting without even having to try to adjust their understanding, because it was their natural way of thinking. Read in this corporate way the argument sounds quite different.

2:1 You, therefore, have no excuse, you who pass judgment on someone else, for at whatever point you judge the other, you are condemning yourself, because you who pass judgment do the same things. Paul has already made his argument regarding the depravity of man—painting a horrific picture of him clothed in cultural respectability while being more dangerous than any other creature on earth.

In applying his analysis to ordinary people, Paul stands in the line of OT prophets who were condemned for their pessimism. History proved them right, however, and Paul is confident that his analysis is correct also. Indeed, his life story provides reliable evidence for his argument. He had been among the respected of Israel, and had taken pride in his achievements (Phil 3:4–6). As a young man, he would have been appalled to think that he was accused of not loving God, but he had now come to realize that his motives were not pure but driven by pride, arrogance and ambition.

Paul's discovery of the perversity of his heart was how he also discovered the darkness and hopelessness of the human condition. It was not just Gentiles who lived in opposition to God, but Jews as well. He came to understand the painful truth of the Scriptures that all people live in active rebellion against the one who has made them. There is, therefore, no place for self-righteous judgment on others when they fail. Indeed, such condemning judgment rebounds on the ones making it. He is not cautioning against exercising discernment when it comes to people who may harm others, nor is he appealing for naivety, rather, he is dealing with those who cruelly scrutinize other people's lives.

God's judgment is based on truth, for, unlike humans, he is no respecter of persons (Deut 16:19). We excuse people with whom we are sympathetic—our professed concern for truth being polluted through nepotism. God's judgment is not so. He will not be bribed by anyone and is never influenced by the status of the one he is judging. This is a vitally important teaching of the OT because it sets the God of Israel apart from all other gods. They are the product of man's darkened mind and have no concern for righteousness.

2:2 Now we know that God's judgment against those who do such things is based on truth. Human beings pass judgment on people continually. At best, our judgment is flawed; at worst, it is malicious. This is not so with God. His judgment is based on truth for he is omniscient, knowing all things. He does not rely on the testimony of others as he sees all that they do and knows all that is in their hearts (Gen 16:13; Ps 33:13–15).

2:3 So when you, a mere man, pass judgment on them and yet do the same things, do you think you will escape God's judgment? Paul continues to warn the believers in Rome against self-righteousness. He asks them whether they think they are beyond God's judgment. The fact is they are not, and the longer they continue to behave in the way they are, the greater will be the number of offenses brought to judgment on the day of reckoning.

The OT records some of God's judgments (Deut 32:22; 2 Chr 36:16; Ps 7:11; Isa 51:17), as does the NT (John 3:36; Rom 2:8; Eph 5:6). The warnings of punishment apply to the Jews as much as to the Gentiles. The exile demonstrated beyond any doubt that the covenant did not excuse or protect Israel from judgment. Indeed, the covenant increased her responsibility to live a life that was worthy of the God who had rescued her from slavery (Lev 18:1–5;19:2; Amos 3:2).

2:4 Or do you show contempt for the riches of his kindness, tolerance and patience, not realizing that God's kindness leads you towards repentance? Paul challenges the Roman believers by asking them if they hold God in contempt because he is delaying judgment. This has been the history of man's relationship with him throughout the ages. Scripture is full of examples of nations and individuals who thought that his delay in acting in judgment indicated his inability or unwillingness to act (2 Pet 2:4–18; 3:3–5). They viewed him as a parent who had lost control of his child and was too sentimental to take the child in hand with some firm discipline. Such a view of God totally misunderstands the Bible's teaching,[1] for it is out of love that he holds back his anger—giving man the opportunity to repent before acting in judgment on those who have despised his grace and kindness (Acts 17:30–31; Rom 2:8; 1 Thess 2:14–16; 2 Thess 1:5–10; Rev 6:16).

---

1. The patience of God was widely understood in first century Judaism. See *Wis,*11:23; 12:10; 15:1; *2 Apoc Bar* 59:6; *4 Ezra,* 7:74.

2:5 But because of your stubbornness and your unrepentant heart, you are storing up wrath against yourself for when his righteous judgment will be revealed. Moses could have addressed this statement to Pharaoh. Indeed, there is a clear reference to Pharaoh and the hardening of his heart later in the letter (Rom 9:17). In that passage, Paul takes what was said of Pharaoh and applies it to the Jews. It would seem that Pharaoh could be taken as a type of all those who choose to reject God and resist his will. Indeed, there is a distinct echo of Stephen's criticism of his murderers in this text also (Acts 7:51–53; cf. also Acts 28:25–28).

2:6 God "will give to each person according to what he has done." Although Paul is reasoning at the corporate level, he cannot avoid making this categorical statement about the responsibility of the individual before God.

The Jews of Jeremiah's day had tried to argue that they could not be held responsible for the things that their fathers had done and for which they were being threatened with punishment. Their favorite excuse was to recite the proverb: "the fathers had eaten sour grapes and the children's teeth had, as a result, been set on edge." Jeremiah told them they were not being punished for the sins of others but for their own (Jer 31:29). In the same way, Paul is not prepared to allow any in Rome think he or she can avoid responsibility by appealing to circumstance or heritage. Individuals will not be punished for the sins of others—but will be held accountable for their own.

2:7 To those who by persistence in doing good seek glory, honour and immortality, he will give eternal life. This statement may seem to imply that man is able to achieve acceptance by God through good works. The key to understanding this verse is to appreciate what is being sought. These people are seeking God's glory and honor. They are seeking the God who alone grants immortality (1 Tim 6:16; Titus 2:11–14). They are not seeking their own righteousness but the God who can make them righteous. The present active participle, "seeking," is marked out by its commitment and carries the idea of pursuance or continuance in seeking. The word, "persistence," comes from the Greek ὑπομονή (*hypomonē*) and means "continuance" or "endurance," conveying the idea of consistency.[2]

The statement reflects what Paul has said in Rom 1:5, where he speaks of "the obedience that comes from faith." Such seeking is an expression of faith in a God to be found, even though of itself it is not the source of salvation. Paul does not suggest that men seek God through contemplation but through works which reflect his character. Of course, such works can never save, but they can be evidence that a person is sincerely seeking and should not be despised (Luke 7:1–10; John 3:1–2; Acts 10:17–23; 16:14–15).

Paul's use of "eternal life" in this verse is often interpreted in the light of John's use (e.g., John 3:16, 36; 5:24; 6:40; 10:28; 17:3). The terms that Paul normally uses for being right with God are "reconciled" (Rom 5:10; 2 Cor 5:18, 20; Col 1:22) and "justified" (e.g., Rom 3:24; 5:9; 8:30; Gal 3:24), and these are terms which are not found in John's writings.

---

2. Morris, *Romans*, 116, says that *hypomonē* denotes an active manly fortitude. He says it is used of the soldier who, "in the thick of a hard battle, gives as much as he gets; he is not dismayed by the blows he receives, but fights on to the end."

To read "eternal life" in this passage in the Johannine way probably misses the mark. For John, eternal life is very much about being in the kingdom of God (John 3:1–8). (This is not the anticipated earthly kingdom of the OT, where Israel's return from exile as a restored covenant community was seen as her resurrection to eternal life [Dan 12:3].)

Jews expected—or hoped—to receive eternal life. However, this was not the "eternal life" of the NT, for the "kingdoms" in the OT and the NT were very different. We can see the distinctively Pauline use of "kingdom" language in Acts 14:22 where the apostle encourages the believers in Antioch to remain true to the faith. He tells them that he and they "must go through many hardships to enter the kingdom of God." In Eph 5:5, Paul writes about the kingdom "of Christ and of God" and in 1 Cor 15:24–25 he recounts: "then the end will come, when he (Christ) hands over the kingdom to God the Father, after he has destroyed all dominion, authority and power. For he must reign until he has put all his enemies under his feet." These Pauline texts suggest that Paul views two "kingdom" stages. Believers are already members of the kingdom of Christ, and here they will suffer as they make their pilgrimage to the heavenly Zion. They will enter the kingdom of God at "the end," when Christ will deliver the kingdom to God the Father.

John does not seem to know of such a progression. He views eternal life as the eschatological gift that is enjoyed here and now, using the term "kingdom of God" to describe the present and future inheritance of the believer. There is no fundamental difference between the understanding of John and Paul. John's use of "kingdom" language reflects "realized eschatology" where the future is already present.

The question posed by the rich young ruler: "what must I do to inherit eternal life?" (Luke 18:18) is concerned with the kingdom of the Messiah. Most likely, he was not referring to "heaven" as suggested by John but to the kingdom as used in Daniel. This OT understanding is the setting for Paul's statement in this verse. This becomes clear when it is appreciated that Paul is explaining to his Jewish readers that God has always left the door open for those who strive to enter the Messianic kingdom. His use of OT/Jewish language would have resonated immediately in every Jewish mind.

If the question is asked as to whether Paul's readers could be expected to differentiate between these two meanings of "eternal life," the answer must be an unreserved "Yes!" You will remember that Paul uses the term "Son of God" with its OT echo of the descendant of David, the appointed king and with its distinctively ontological Christian meaning.[3] This is evidence that the NT church had no difficulty in discerning the various shades of a word's meaning. In doing this, they were not displaying exceptional ability but a universal characteristic of the human brain to process information.

The above discussion on the possibility of two kingdom stages would seem to go against the teaching of the Gospels which appear to speak of only one kingdom—the kingdom of God. However, the traditional understanding of this has recently come under scrutiny with scholars coming to a new conclusion. Previously, most argued that the "kingdom of heaven" in Matthew's Gospel[4] was another way of saying the "kingdom of

---

3. See notes on Rom 1:3.

4. It has recently been argued that Matthew's Gospel was widely known among the churches. See Laurer, *Writing*.

God" as used by the other gospel writers. It was argued that Matthew chose the term to avoid speaking of God in a way that would offend the Jews for whom his Gospel was written. However, this explanation was never fully satisfactory as it did not explain why Matthew, having avoided "kingdom of God" in his parallel passages, still occasionally used the term he is supposed to have abandoned.[5] A number of scholars[6] have researched this anomaly and have challenged the traditional understanding of Matthew's use of the term, "kingdom of heaven." They have concluded that for Matthew, the "kingdom of heaven" and "kingdom of God" are two stages of the same kingdom—God's kingdom. Gospel studies have moved towards the explanation of the kingdoms of Christ and of God given above, lending weight to the argument being made.

2:8 But for those who are self-seeking and who reject the truth and follow evil, there will be wrath and anger. The term Paul uses for "evil" is ἀδικία (*adikia*) which means "unrighteousness" or "wickedness." This is the same word he used in Rom 1:18 to contrast with God's righteousness. Rejection of God's truth exhibits itself in "self-seeking" ἐριθεία (*eritheia*), a term meaning "selfishness" or "selfish ambition." Paul explained in Rom 1:18ff. that such behavior leads to wrath and anger.

Such a statement as v.8 is a dreadful warning to modern man, who sees himself as autonomous and answerable to no one for the standards he sets in his life. This is very different from what Paul and the other writers of Scripture proclaim. They say that man cannot escape the day when he will stand in God's awesome presence. To be found guilty of excluding God from his life means that a man will be eternally separated from him. If men choose to live without God, they will certainly die without him and be in eternity without him.

It might be thought that religious people are excluded from the description of those who "reject the truth and follow evil." Evil can have many "acceptable" faces—even one of religious devotion. Regardless of how cultural, religious, humane or noble a man is, if he is without God he is in darkness and is a prisoner of Sin.

Obviously, such an evaluation is bound to be offensive. In social terms, Paul would be supportive of a system which acknowledges and promotes stability and wellbeing (Rom 13:1–7). However, he says—as does the rest of scripture—that these qualities will have a different significance on the day of judgment if they have been used as arguments for rejecting the saving activity of God. For this reason, Paul raises this issue in the section of his letter which describes the condition of the Jews.

---

5. See Matt 12:28; 21:31, 43.

6. Pamment, "Kingdom," 232, argues that the kingdom of God is a present reality, preparing individuals for the kingdom of heaven, which, in Matthew, refers to an eschatological and futuristic kingdom. She describes this future kingdom as a "wholly future reality which is imminent but other-worldly in the sense that the world as it is experienced now will no longer exist." This is a similar conclusion to that reached by Albright and Mann, *Matthew*, 155, 233. However, Albright and Mann argue that the kingdom of heaven exists with Jesus until the final judgment whereas the kingdom of God will be established at the final judgment. What is clear is that Pamment reverses the significance of the two kingdoms as seen by Albright and Mann. Regardless of this strange difference, they both see a distinction between the two kingdoms. For a summary of the evidence relating to the use of the term "kingdom" in the Gospels, see Udoeyop, *New People*, 109–12.

Finally, note that in v.7 Paul said that God "will give eternal life" but here he writes that "there will be wrath and anger"[7] for self-seekers. He does not say God will give these, but that "there will be." It is possible that Paul seeks to emphasize that only God gives eternal life but that wrath is the due desert of man.

2:9 There will be trouble and distress for every human being who does evil: first for the Jew, then for the Gentile. "Trouble" in Greek is θλῖψις (*thlipsis*), means "pressure to the point of breaking." The term is used to describe the force put on grapes when they are pressed. It speaks of acute suffering. The term στενοχωρία (*stenochōria*) "distress" conveys the idea of being cramped for space from which comes the idea of extreme affliction. Together, the two terms emphasize the anguish that will fall upon the ungodly.

Paul stresses that this judgment is not only for Gentiles but also for Jews who reject God's salvation. This was very difficult for Jews to come to terms with. They saw themselves as different from the Gentiles who, they thought, deserved God's judgment for their obvious sins. The Jew was religious and devout. He had a religious tradition that went all the way back to his ancestor Abraham to whom God had made unique promises. He could point back to the exodus and say: "this is when God saved us." As a result, the Jew saw himself as being in a right relationship with God. However, Paul says this is not the case. Wrath and anger will be experienced in trouble and distress, and the Jews will be the first to be brought to judgment: "first for the Jew, then for the Gentile." Because the Jews had religious privileges above the Gentiles they have no excuse before God for their disobedience. They were appointed to be the first who heard (Rom 1:17); now they are appointed the first to be judged.

Too often, religious people think they have certain advantages before God that non-religious people do not have—as though God was pleased with the effort they made. Paul is saying this is not how God views it. People who have been taught what God requires should know they cannot negotiate with him to ignore parts of the law's demands. Everyone—Jew or Gentile—needs to acknowledge there is no excuse for sinning and that all need to be forgiven by coming to God through Jesus.

When Paul writes to his Jewish readers that God gives eternal life to those who persist in "doing good" (v. 7), he is not denying the Gospel of salvation through faith. He is saying nothing more than faithful Jews are promised membership of the Messianic kingdom. For them, this kingdom was going to be an earthly one in which they gloried in their privileged relationship with the God of Abraham. This is still short of the salvation which Paul is going to describe—one in which believers have become incorporated into the person of the Messiah and into his death.

2:10 But glory, honor and peace for everyone who does good: first for the Jew, then for the Gentile. For those who seek God, the end is so very different than for those who reject him. For the true seeker, there is glory, honor, and peace. When Paul speaks of glory, he is not speaking of the glory of success but about a dimension familiar to the Jew.

---

7. For a discussion on the significance of wrath and anger, see Büchsel, *TDNT*, III, 168; Morris, *Apostolic*, chapters 4 and 5.

Man had been created for the glory (praise) of God, having been bestowed with a dignity that made him unique. He was made in the image of God, with characteristics that set him apart from the rest of creation. Being made with such unique qualities meant that he reflected the very qualities of God.

However, this glory was lost when Adam sinned (Rom 3:23). He was deprived of his position as one stripped of rank in the army, and put out of service. From then on, man ceased to rule on God's behalf and ruled with his own interests on the agenda. Paul's reference to "honor" reflects this background and the status that was lost through the fall.

He writes that peace will be granted to those who seek God. How different for those who disobey and experience wrath, trouble, and distress (vv. 5, 9). There is no exemption from this judgment that God makes on such people—not even the Jews can escape it. Indeed, Paul says it is the Jews who are the first to come under God's judgment, for they have had the greatest privileges of all the nations. This is not a new notion. The prophet Amos spoke God's word to Israel, saying: "You only have I known of all the peoples of the earth, therefore I will punish you" (Amos 3:2). Paul drives home the truth of God's impartiality in judgment in the following verse.

2:11 For God does not show favouritism. This statement is at the heart of the Mosaic law. The judges of Israel were not allowed to show favoritism or accept bribes (Exod 23:1–9) because they represented God in their solemn work. To pervert the course of justice was to implicate God in unrighteousness and corruption.

The Jews perceived that they were objects of God's favor, but Paul insisted this perception was founded on a wrong reading of the OT. They were, indeed, a privileged people—called and blessed by God (Rom 9:1–5). However, these were not signs of unconditional favor but rather the means by which Yahweh's grace would be made known to the Gentile nations.

This understanding of the reason for Israel's blessing is found in many of the parables of Jesus. Often they are read as teaching for the church, and while there is obviously instruction in them, they were not intended or delivered in that way. The parables were essentially critical assessments of Israel's failure to be the true servant of Yahweh. So, for example, the "talents" of Jesus' parable recorded in Matt 25:14–15 are not natural abilities but money or treasure. They were symbolic of the treasure of the knowledge of God that Israel was to share with the Gentiles. The severity of God's judgment is the measure of how signally Israel failed in her task. The treasure was to be taken from Israel and given to another, the church, for her to share with the world. The application for the church is that when any Christian community sees itself in the light of its blessings and not in the light of its responsibilities, it is in grave danger of discovering that the blessings have been withdrawn. What was true of Israel can also be true of a national or even a local church.

This OT teaching on God's impartiality in his dealings with man is found throughout the NT. Jesus warned of the danger of being over-impressed with the rich and the powerful (Luke 6:24–26), and his message was repeated regularly to warn of the danger of respecting status (Jas 2:1–7; 1 John 3:17). A Christian church should not be a place where the wealthy and successful are adulated and men elevated to positions of responsibility because of their natural abilities. The church's values should cause her to identify the grace of God at work in the lives of all people and to be concerned equally for those who have not succeeded materially as well as those who have.

2:12 All who sin apart from the law will also perish apart from the law, and all who sin under the law will be judged by the law. Paul now turns to consider the condition of the Gentiles. They have not had the same privileges as the Jews, so they will be judged against a different standard. Because they have not had the law, the law will not judge them. All who have sinned under the law,[8] that is, the Jews, will be judged by the law. In stating this, Paul repeats his argument of v.10, thereby closing off any way of escape for those who think they can avoid the issue of guilt. The statement, in so far as it refers to those not under the law, was not unique to Paul.[9] The judgment he refers to is the day of judgment, when all Jews and Gentiles, Christian and non-Christians, will be judged. In the case of the Christians who have put their trust in the redemption that Christ has secured and have accepted his lordship, the sentence has already been carried out as far as their eternal destiny is concerned (Rom 3:21–26; Gal 3:13; 2 Cor 5:21). However, they will be judged on their work as believers (1 Cor 3:8; 2 Cor 5:10).

2:13 For it is not those who hear the law who are righteous in God's sight, but it is those who obey the law who will be declared righteous. Paul expounds the issue of the Jews' culpability. This is possibly because he is acutely aware of the way he had excused himself before becoming a follower of Christ. He had been comfortably satisfied with his religious achievements (Phil 3:4–6), even though he knew that he had not kept the whole law. In taking this attitude, he had been like most Jews. While he was aware of God's holiness and his perfect standards, he saw himself as belonging to a nation that had been especially and graciously chosen by God and forgiven. This forgiveness was secured by the death of sacrificial animals. This was the means God had appointed to remove the defilement of sin and make Israel acceptable. With such a solution to sin in place, Paul, like most of his fellow Jews, saw the problem of Israel's sin as having been dealt with. In his mind, it was only the Gentiles who were outside of this special relationship with God and who needed to fear.

However, Paul now attacks this Jewish concept of spiritual security. It is not those who know the law who are saved, but those who obey it.[10] This obedience was about keeping all of the law's demands. Elsewhere in the letter, Paul states that breaking one

---

8. For a discussion on the meaning of "under the law," see Morris, *Romans*, 143ff., and, more importantly, Wilder, *Echoes*, 75–107.

9. See, e.g., *2 Bar* 48:40, 70.

10. Edwards, *Romans*, 72, points out that the early rabbinic tradition agreed with Paul over the importance of keeping the law. Edwards points out it was not until about AD 135 (following the Hadrian decree) that those caught studying the Torah were to be executed. However, at the Council of Lydda, the rabbis decreed that under no circumstances could the study of the Torah be neglected. This resulted in the study of the law taking precedence over the keeping of the law. Following this, the emphasis on the knowledge of the Torah rather than its practice became characteristic of rabbinic Judaism.

commandment brought spiritual death (Rom 5:12ff.; cf. Jas 2:10). This is not dismissing the fact that it is better to keep nine of the ten commandments than break all ten, but, in terms of God's ultimate dealings with man, the purposeful breaking of one part of the law is evidence of the same guilt as is found in the hearts of those who openly defy the whole law. It is, therefore, only those who obey the whole law who will be declared righteous.[11]

Paul argues that the plight of all men—not just the Jews—is critical. He values the law given by God on Mount Sinai. He knows that it inspired and motivated men to higher standards than what they would have achieved without it. He also knows that it has constrained many from actions that they would have done without its threats and warnings. However, since becoming a believer, Paul has come to see that the law did not change the heart of man. It merely put a safety fence around the people of Israel to keep them from the danger of their sinfulness.

Paul will explain what sin is in detail in chapter 5. We will see that it is far bigger than our wrong doings—it is opposition towards God himself. An illustration may help. When the Prime Minister of Great Britain declared war on Germany and its allies in 1939, millions of people were plunged into a state of hostility. Chamberlain was the nation's representative, and his actions took the nation into war. On the larger canvas of human history, Adam was the head of the human family, and its representative. His actions in the Garden of Eden plunged all of his descendants into a state of hostility. This hostility was not towards another nation but towards God. It is a condition in which we are all bound and from which we cannot escape. How can man be released from this condition where he is controlled by Sin?[12] It is this very question that Paul is preparing to answer, but, before giving his response, he clarifies the issue. His diagnosis is devastating.

Paul makes an important "throw-away comment" when he uses the phrase: "those who hear the law,"[13] reminding us of the corporate nature of Israel's religion. The Jews' knowledge of the law depended on hearing it read, and we have already noticed how they gathered regularly for such readings. Few private copies of the Scriptures were available in Paul's day and so worshippers would hear the Torah but not read it. This comment reminds us that the NT writings would have been read to believing communities when they gathered for worship. The apostles, aware of this obvious fact, directed their messages to the communities that heard them rather than to individuals. This realization ought to direct us to read the texts as written to *communities* about *their* experiences of the grace of God. In other words, the long-held practice of reading the Roman letter as a

---

11. Schreiner, "Justification," 131–55, argues the reference to the need of works in this passage does not contradict Paul's statements that salvation is through faith and without works. Schreiner argues these works that Paul refers to can only be done by Christians and, therefore, are the fruit of salvation, not its grounds. See also Wright, *Romans*. Contra, Edwards, *Romans*, 70, who says: "His whole argument depends on the premise that apart from Christ, Jews and Gentiles deserve God's wrath. Paul is contending for an innate moral sense in humanity, to whose voice Gentiles are bound as are Jews to the Torah."

12. Writing "Sin" in this way is deliberate. It is a pseudonym for Satan and is personal/relational rather than legal.

13. The term "law" νόμος (*nomos*), lacks the definite article. It is possible that Paul is referring to law in general, including the Mosaic law.

description of the salvation of the individual believer is, I would argue, not in harmony with the letter's historical and theological facts.

Paul's statement that "it is those who obey the law who will be declared righteous" suggests an understanding of justification that is different from that which came out of the Reformation. Such an observation is certainly right, but what Paul is arguing here is not the doctrine that he will go on to thrash out later in the letter. At this point Paul is solely discussing the Jewish understanding of being right with God, and this understanding is not the same as what he constructs in the following chapters. Here he is dealing exclusively with Jewish claims and allows them to glory in the law, eventually turning it back on them by pointing out that this law will ultimately condemn them. When he eventually raised the matter of the Gentiles and the law, his concern is not about their forgiveness, for he knows they have been forgiven. His concern is over what the Jewish church requires in order to accept the Gentiles into full covenantal membership and stand in the line of Abraham with all of the OT promises that come to his offspring. Thus his debate with the Jews over circumcision is honed differently when the Gentiles are in the frame. For his countrymen it is: "do not reject what you have been promised, and to receive what you have been promised you will have to welcome believing Gentiles as your brothers." For the Gentiles it is "all your efforts to appease God are ended; you are to walk in faith knowing that God has accepted and forgiven you."

2:14 (Indeed, when Gentiles, who do not have the law, do by nature things required by the law, they are a law for themselves, even though they do not have the law. Paul is acutely aware there are many Gentiles who are more righteous in their lives than his fellow Jews.[14] He states that some Gentiles are living to a higher moral standard than some Jews, showing that there is another law in operation which brings about this behavior. This is why he writes: "they are a law for themselves." This does not mean the Gentiles are lawless. Paul is about to explain that God has put an unwritten law into the hearts of all people which nullifies any claim of innocence on the grounds of ignorance. This law is the law of conscience which Paul has already discussed in chapter 1.[15] There, he argued that nature bears witness to man of his Creator and that this is apparent to all who do not harden their hearts. Cornelius (Acts 10:22), Lydia (Acts 16:14), and many other God-fearers were such Gentiles.

---

14. Wright, *Romans*, argues that Paul's perspective is that only someone with the Spirit can keep the law. Therefore, this argument is not about moral Gentiles but Gentile believers who, because of the Spirit in their lives, keep the law. Cranfield, *Shorter*, 51, supports the view that it speaks of Gentile believers, yet says: "it would not be accurate to describe Gentile Christians as not possessing the law, since as Christians they of course would have some knowledge of the Old Testament law, whereas to describe them as not possessing the law by nature, that is by their birth, would be appropriate." See also Gathercole, "Revisited," 27–49. This position lacks wider support as Cornelius (without the Spirit) was commended for keeping the law, as indeed was Paul himself. This wider understanding is supported by Zeisler, *Romans*, 86, and Käsemann, *Romans*, 64, who says: "everything depends on the fact that the Gentiles also experience the transcendent claim of the divine will and thus become, not the law or a law, but law to themselves."

15. For a detailed study of the biblical view of conscience, see Pierce, *Conscience*.

2:15 Since they show that the requirements of the law are written on their hearts, their consciences also bearing witness, and their thoughts now accusing, now even defending them.) In writing this, Paul is not referring to man's conscience, for he is about to write that this law is acknowledged by the conscience. He goes even further, saying that "their thoughts" accuse and even defend them. Paul seems to be dividing the self-consciousness of man into various parts: conscience, heart and thought. He is not a modern psychoanalyst. Paul is describing man's spiritual and moral existence in terms that would have been familiar to people of his day. Part of the difficulty of interpreting Paul is the uncertainty of knowing whether he describes man according to Jewish or Greek understanding.[16] The perspective favored will inevitably affect the way Paul's argument is understood. In this commentary, I have taken the position that Paul stays within his Jewish heritage and that his readers are Jews and Gentiles who have sought God · within a Jewish/Christian community where they have learned the OT perspective of man's make up. In this context, Paul would not think of man as existing in three separate parts—body, soul and spirit—but as one physical and spiritual being, described as body and soul.[17]

One difficulty presented by this verse is that Paul does not say concerning what the Gentiles' consciences bear witness. Scholarly opinions range from the law to morality. I would see it as a reference to the law which Paul has said is written on the heart of man.

2:16 This will take place on the day when God will judge men's secrets through Jesus Christ, as my gospel declares. Paul says that the final judgment will be through Jesus Christ. He declared the same message to the people of Athens, when he said: "he has set a day when he will judge the world with justice by the man he has appointed" (Acts 17:31), and, because Jesus "has been tempted in every way, just as we are—yet without sin" (Heb 4:15b), no mitigating excuses can be brought to the judgment seat of God.

Paul makes the frightening statement that God's judgment will not be based on conformation to a set of rules but on the deep, hidden motives of the heart. A person may live up to acceptable standards of behavior, and yet harbor wrong attitudes such as pride, selfishness, or jealousy. Reality can be so very different in the sight of God (Ps 33:12–15), and he is a God who will expose and judge men's secrets on the day of judgment.

2:17 Now you, if you call yourself a Jew; if you rely on the law and brag about your relationship to God; Paul has been dealing with the condition of the religiously

16. Aune, "Nature," 291–97, warns of the danger of generalizing. Both Judaism and Hellenism had many conflicting positions of understanding within their own systems.

17. The exception to this seems to be 1 Thess 5:23. Schweizer, "πνεῦμα," 435, suggests that Paul is merely reflecting popular Hellenistic anthropology in the trichonomy of spirit, soul, and body and thinks that because of the liturgical setting of the statement it should not be taken as a precise description of the constitutive parts of human nature, see also Best, *Thessalonians*, 243f.; Wanamaker, *Thessalonians*, 206; Malherbe, *Thessalonians*, 339, and Green, *Thessalonians*, 268. The point on which all these authorities agree is that while Paul uses familiar terminology in 1 Thess 5:23, and even uses the understanding of Greeks, he does not thereby endorse their understanding but emphasizes that his prayer is for their complete protection. Other texts, such as 1 Cor 7:34 which is arguing theologically, demonstrates his Hebraic position. For an alternative Hebraic reading see p. 213 n. 19.

self-righteous. As he builds his case for their bankrupt religion, he begins to address an imaginary fellow Jew. By using the method of diatribe to penetrate the hypocrisy of his kinsmen, he lessens the damage to the already weak relationship that a direct attack would cause. He writes to this representative Jew in what appears to be a confrontational manner: "Now you, if you call yourself a Jew." By this stinging address, Paul attempts to shake the Jews out of their complacency. He wants them to realize that true Jews are Jews inwardly, with hearts that are circumcised (Rom 2:28–29). Paul seeks to show them that their bragging is without foundation, for while they are proud of their supposed status as God's covenant people and qualification to judge others, they continue to condemn themselves by doing the same things (Rom 2:1–3).[18]

In his letters to the Corinthians, Paul also addresses misplaced confidence in believers. At the opening of his first letter, he quotes the prophet, Jeremiah: "Let him who boasts boast in the Lord" (1 Cor 1:31). The passage from which Paul took his quote is very applicable to the boastful, circumcised Jews in Rome who claimed to know God and understand his ways:

> This is what the LORD says: "Let not the wise man boast of his wisdom or the strong man boast of his strength or the rich man boast of his riches, but let him who boasts boast about this: that he understands and knows me, that I am the LORD who exercises kindness, justice and righteousness on the earth, for in these I delight," declares the LORD. "The days are coming," declares the LORD, "when I will punish all who are circumcised only in the flesh—Egypt, Judah, Edom, Ammon, Moab and all who live in the desert in distant places. For all these nations are really uncircumcised, and even the whole house of Israel is uncircumcised in heart." (Jer 9:23–26)

2:18–19 if you know his will and approve of what is superior because you are instructed by the law; if you are convinced that you are a guide for the blind, a light for those who are in the dark, Paul prefaces statements to this representative Jew with the conjunction "if." He knows the claims that the Jews in Rome would have been boasting about as once he had made these claims himself. But now it was time for evaluation. The irony is palpable. Paul is not afraid of offending those who pervert the truth about themselves and rob God of glory.

He challenges his beloved kinsmen where they are most sensitive—their relationship with God and their possession of the law. He teases their representative that, because he has been taught the law, he is an authority on God's will. He can discern, while others without the law cannot, and can give assent, therefore, to things that are in line with the law. The term translated "superior" is found in Phil 1:10, where it is better translated "what is best."

With his vast knowledge of the law, the Jew should be listened to as a guide and a light to unfortunate Gentiles who are in darkness. Paul is implying that the Jews see themselves as the privileged ones who can bring the knowledge of God to the nations.

---

18. Berkley, *Broken*, evaluates the claim that Pauline intertextual exegesis of OT texts (Gen 17; Deut 29–30; Jer 7:2–1; 9:23–26; Ezek 36:16–27) provides the basis for his conclusions on Rom 2:17–29. Berkley concludes that Paul's themes come from these texts and provide him with the basis of his argument.

This, indeed, was their calling, but it was a calling they did not fulfill and which has been rescinded.

Paul uses the word "convinced" because he knew the certainty the Jews had about their status. It was formed from hundreds of years of history, when God had repeatedly intervened in the most hopeless situations to save his people. Their instruction in the law contributed to their certainty. It was taught to them from their earliest years and reinforced by the rituals the community kept.

2:20 An instructor of the foolish, a teacher of infants, because you have in the law the embodiment of knowledge and truth. It is probable that Paul continues the point he has just made, employing the same irony to describe the Jews as "instructors" and "teachers," and the Gentiles—as the Jews would perceive—as foolish and infantile. Irony is not something that Paul is averse to using in his letters when he wants to drive a point home (2 Cor 11:1).

The reference to the "instructor of the foolish" may imply Jewish dedication to helping God's people lead upright lives that are worthy of the covenant, and not the teaching of Gentiles. Moreover, the reference to the teaching of infants may be exactly that, as teaching children is a noble task in Judaism, preparing them to become upright, God-fearing citizens of the covenant community when they come of age.

Whichever interpretation is correct—and I would favor the former—Paul is not against instruction and teaching. He may have been involved in such activities himself when, in his zeal to please God, he strove to be perfect before the law (Phil 3:4–6). No doubt he concluded that the Jews who followed Jesus were foolish, and sought to correct their understanding and bring them in line with the teaching of Judaism. But now his concern is that the Jews are foolish. They see everyone else's needs and how the law addresses them, without hearing what that same law[19] has been saying to them as a nation for hundreds of years. They have been deaf to the voice of God.

The statement: "you have in the law the embodiment of knowledge and truth" indicates the esteem in which Paul, along with all other devout Jews, holds the law. We know from rabbinical records that the Jews saw the purpose of creation to be enjoyment of the law. The Torah was seen as having an eternal existence. It was the manifestation of God's wisdom, and devout Jews meditated on it, finding joy and delight in its teachings (Ps 119:16, 151–52, 158–60, 162, 167).

2:21 You, then, who teach others, do you not teach yourself? You who preach against stealing, do you steal? The questions Paul asks the Jews in Rome do not concern their social morality but their spiritual reality. He asks them to face up to the fact that they are not living out the demands of the law. They can teach it to others, guiding, instructing, and explaining all matters contained within, but their ears are closed to their own teaching, and their own needs are not met.

---

19. Paul is not averse to leaving out the definite article (the anarthrous form), but here he uses the article probably to emphasize that the law is the embodiment of knowledge and truth.

"You who preach against stealing, do you steal?" Such a question would receive the answer, "Certainly not!" from any reasonable Jew, never mind a devout one. However, when seen in the light of the Jew's God-given responsibility to serve him by taking the message of his love to the nations, the answer would have to be: "Yes." They have stolen glory from God and hope from the nations to whom they should have been ambassadors.

2:22 You who say that people should not commit adultery, do you commit adultery? You who abhor idols, do you rob temples? If Paul is suggesting to the Jews that their suitability to be guides, lights, instructors and teachers to the Gentiles is unfounded, then what they are teaching is not being worked out in their lives—they have been circumcised outwardly, but not inwardly. The questions that he is about to pose them would highlight their behavior and their awful willingness to leave the Gentiles in darkness and under the control and power of Sin (Satan).

In querying adultery in the representative's life, Paul is delivering a wounding blow to the Jews. They have been teaching from the law that adultery is condemned, yet, as a nation, they have committed adultery against God by going after other gods. They have failed to fulfill their God-given role to take the good news about him to the Gentile nations who, as a result, have continued to live in the darkness of alienation from him. God longs for the salvation of the lost—Gentiles as well as Jews—but, like the elder son in the parable of the prodigal son, Israel does not. The elder son despised his father for the joy the father had in his brother's return from the far country. Likewise, the Jews despise the heart of God for his willingness to welcome "Gentile sinners" (Gal 2:15) into the covenant.

The Jews have become spiritual adulterers in that the god they love is not the God of their own Scriptures but another—one made in their own image.[20] Like their ancestors of whom Hosea speaks, they have substituted an image for the one true God and have committed spiritual adultery (Hos 5:3).

What does Paul mean by "do you rob temples?" There is not one recorded example in history of Jews robbing heathen temples.[21] As a minority community in Rome, they would have put themselves in serious danger by attempting such a thing. What is Paul's point?[22] What is he saying? To take his question literally is to have him construct an ar-

---

20. They are of their father, the devil, and they bear the image of the one who has begat them.

21. Contra Käsemann, *Romans*, 71, who cites Philo, *De confusione, linguarum*, 163, which has the same combination of stealing, adultery, and robbing temples; while Corpus, *Hereticum*, XII:5, has the last two (BAGD, 373b). Käsemann also points to CD 4:15ff. This speaks of the "three nets of Belial" which he thinks have some connection with what Paul is saying in this text. The evidence offered by Wright, "Romans," 447, for this practice is unconvincing. Having acknowledged that it was very rare, he cites evidence from Josephus, *Against Apion*, 1.310–11, that the name "Jerusalem" was a pun on the word "temple-robber." For such a pun to be appreciated, the practice would need to be widespread or the point of the pun would be missed. Also, his suggestion that Acts 19:37 shows the charge was likely to be levied against Jews in the pagan world is reading too much into the text.

22. Derrett, "Abominate," 558–71, thinks that Paul's appeal is that his Jewish readers should cease from doing such things if they were involved in any way—even indirectly—as they were a crime against the Torah. They damaged the reputation of the Jewish community and hence the attractiveness of the Hebrew religion and the reputation of her God. However, such an indecisive exhortation as "in case you are doing this, stop it," would hardly assist Paul's argument.

gument with no power. This was not how Jews behaved. His opponents would no doubt respond that he was out of touch with reality and not worth hearing. By his supposed argument, he would have attacked his own case.

However, in answer to this particular question, Paul may well have wanted to hear the believers answer, "Yes!" The church is the temple of the living God, and the Gentile community was seen to be the very opposite—the dwelling place of evil.[23] To evangelize people is to claim them for Christ's rule. Paul urged people to leave the control of Satan and come under Christ's headship. He "robbed Satan"—the very thing the Jews should have been doing themselves.

This explanation is a possible solution to why he posed the question in v. 22b. Another explanation is that Paul was actually accusing the Jews of robbing their own Temple. We have seen that the actions and teaching of Jesus in the Temple as recorded in John 2:13–22 might have been guiding Paul in the earlier section of the chapter. The term ἱεροσυλέω (*hierosuleō*) "to rob a temple"[24] can be translated "to desecrate a temple." By turning the Court of the Gentiles in the Temple over to trade, the Jewish priests had effectively prevented Gentiles from seeking God. As a result, Israel had become a nation of temple desecrators.[25]

As noted elsewhere,[26] it is possible that the Roman church had access to the Gospel of Matthew. It is significant that in Matthew's account of the cleansing of the Temple (Matt 21:12–13), Jesus condemns the officials for "making it a den of robbers." The subsequent narrative (Matt 21:18–20) is about the curse of the fig tree, which is a picture of Israel in danger of judgment (Matt 24:32–45). The theme in Matthew has strong similarities to the passage we are considering.

2:23–24 You who brag about the law, do you dishonor God by breaking the law? As it is written: "God's name is blasphemed among the Gentiles because of you." Paul's question does not probe their fulfillment of orthodox Jewry, but of the obligation the law laid upon them as God's appointed vehicle of revelation. Their rejection of this mission is the most serious form of Law breaking, for they not only disobeyed the command they were given but left the Gentiles in ignorance of God's character. The Gentiles could understandably conclude that God had no interest in them, causing them to blaspheme his

---

23. For examples of Paul's use of such ideas, see notes on Rom 6:6.

24. Acts 19:37 records that Paul and his companions are exonerated from being "sacrilegious" (RSV), where the Greek word is the related adjective ἱερόσυλος. See Wright, *Romans*, 447, and Zeisler, *Romans*, 91. But this evidence is thin. Why should the people of Ephesus suspect that Jews would be temple-robbers? There is no record that a Jewish community had ever been involved in such activity. The charge is about the dishonor Paul's message has brought to Diana in that people are turning from her worship. The charge is not about Jews who were plundering temples, but a charge made up by the guildsmen to have Paul and his co-workers silenced so that their message would not affect their wealth. In fact, Deut 7:25 clearly forbids theft from pagan temples. There is a record of embezzlement of the funds given as contributions to the temple in Jerusalem but such an action falls short of robbing temples. Josephus, *Antiquities*, XVIII.

25. A figurative interpretation finds support from Barrett, *Romans*, 56–57. See also Cranfield, *Shorter*, 56, who presumes that Paul is thinking not only of behavior which is obviously sacrilegious, but also of less obvious and more subtle forms of sacrilege.

26. Laurer, *Writing*. See also the comparative study of Matt 5–7 and Rom 12:9–21 (p. 411).

name. Behind the statement in v. 24 there is an echo of Ezek 36:20–23, where the prophet says that the Jews' exilic condition brought dishonor to God. This exilic condition still exists in Paul's mind for, though Israel had been redeemed from Babylon, members of the nation still formed part of the kingdom of darkness.

The quotation in v. 24 is from Isaiah, although Paul has changed the focus of the original text (Isa 52:5). The prophet had said that Israel's suffering in exile caused the name of Yahweh to be blasphemed among the Gentiles. Paul changes the focus of the statement to say that it is Israel's spiritual exile which causes God's name to be shamed. This is not abusing the text, as Israel's suffering and exile were a result of her behavior.

2:25 Circumcision has value if you observe the law, but if you break the law, you have become as though you had not been circumcised. This important principle was not unique to Paul's thought. Jeremiah had told the Jews about the importance of having a circumcised heart (Jer 4:4), and the same sense is found in the earlier writings of Deuteronomy: "Circumcise your hearts, therefore, and do not be stiff-necked any longer" (Deut 10:16). In Paul's day, the Jews of the Diaspora stressed this was more important than physical circumcision[27] and he uses this understanding to chastise his Jewish readers in Rome. He warns them that their physical circumcision is of little importance if the law is not kept. Indeed, their guilt renders them as though they had not been circumcised and bestows on them the same status as the Gentiles whom they despise so much.

2:26 If those who are not circumcised keep the law's requirements, will they not be regarded as though they were circumcised? Paul argues that Gentiles who keep the law are regarded as though they are circumcised. The point Paul is making is that ritual or ceremony does not make someone right with God. What is important is the truth behind the ritual. The question that arises from this verse is: "who are these non-circumcised who keep the law?"

Scripture recognizes there are people outside of the covenant community who do good, but Paul does not seem to be referring to these socially responsible unbelievers who, as he can testify, are still excluded from the redeemed community.[28] The fact that Paul argues they will be treated as if circumcised must be on the basis that their hearts have been circumcised. In other words, they are Gentile believers in the Messiah and his work of salvation.[29]

Some see this description of Gentiles who keep the law to apply to Gentile "Christians." It is argued that Paul could not conceive of anyone being able to keep the law other than by the Spirit. This argument ignores "general grace" in the lives of unbelievers such as Cornelius. He is an example of an upright Gentile who had not yet believed on Christ, and the testimony about him is a genuine appreciation of the quality of his life (Acts 10:1–2, 22). Of course, in saying some Gentiles keep the law does not

---

27. See Schreiner, *Entrée*.

28. Such would no doubt include Cornelius (Acts 10:41), Lydia (Acts 16:14) and Paul himself (Phil 3:6).

29. See Wright, *Romans*, 441.

mean they are able to earn salvation. It is one thing to keep the law in a commendable and exemplary manner, but it is another to keep the law perfectly. Besides, to argue that Paul could not conceive of an unbeliever keeping the law is to tie Paul into a view of sin that is essentially dualistic. We will discuss this issue later in the commentary.[30] However, the fact that Paul says they will be treated as circumcised suggests he is not speaking about moral people but genuinely spiritual people—those, who though not circumcised, are seeking Israel's God. Such people—who demonstrate by the lives they live that they are earnest about seeking God—conform to Israel's law. Although they may be ignorant of the fullness of the revelation that has come in Christ, nevertheless, they trust in God's mercy to deal adequately with their sin, and are treated as circumcised.

2:27 The one who is not circumcised physically and yet obeys the law will condemn you who, even though you have the written code and circumcision, are a lawbreaker. Paul goes even further. He argues that Gentiles who live according to the light they have will actually judge the Jews for failing to conform to the law's commands. Such a statement was an astounding challenge to opinionated Jews. If Paul is challenging his countrymen at the level of their covenantal responsibilities, he is doing the same thing that Jesus did in many of his parables.

Jesus constantly warned that the kingdom (represented as a vineyard [Matt 21:33–46] and a wedding banquet [Matt 22:1–14]) was about to be taken from those who had it and given to another. The same message was behind the parables of the workers in the vineyard (Matt 20:1–16), the two sons (Matt 21:28–32), and the prodigal son. In this last parable, the elder son represents self-righteous Israel. As has been mentioned, he despised the love his father showered on his younger, wayward brother. The younger brother represents the Gentiles. This is hinted at in the setting of the parable, which was told in response to the Pharisees who criticized Jesus for welcoming Jewish sinners and tax collectors. Such Jews were no better than the Gentiles in the eyes of the self-righteous (Luke 15:11–32).

God's intent to bring the Gentiles into the kingdom had been hinted at in many of the other sayings and incidents in Jesus' life such as the healing of the Canaanite's daughter (Matt 15:21–28), the healing of the centurion's servant in Capernaum (Luke 7:1–10), and his regular acceptance of the outsiders within Judaism who were reckoned as being no better than the Gentiles. More importantly, there were numerous promises regarding the inclusion of the Gentiles given in the OT.

2:28 A man is not a Jew if he is only one outwardly, nor is circumcision merely outward and physical. In making this statement, Paul is encroaching on one of the most important points of Judaism. While it was acknowledged that circumcision did not make a man right with God, it was seen, nevertheless, as the indispensable evidence that he sought to live within the requirements of the covenant. Paul was raising an issue that was going to bring him into unavoidable conflict with many of the believers in Rome. Being Jews, or Gentiles who had embraced Judaism, they could not conceive of the covenant

---

30. See Excursus F: "Sin in the Theology of Paul," p. 203.

without circumcision—to reject circumcision was to reject the law itself. A rejection of the law meant a rejection of the covenant and the relationship it had established between God and his people.[31]

2:29 No, a man is a Jew if he is one inwardly; and circumcision is circumcision of the heart, by the Spirit, not by the written code. Paul lays down the principle of true righteousness. It is not outward, no matter how pure the religious pedigree. What matters is that the outward rite is matched by an inward reality. The absence of physical circumcision does not render the inward reality void, but the absence of the inward reality makes the outward symbol valueless.

Circumcision was intended to remind the Jews of their special relationship with God, but, while continuing to observe this religious ritual, they turned from the commandments that he gave them and followed the ways of their pagan neighbors. The prophets emphasized that the mark of a true Jew was not the circumcision of the flesh but of the heart (Jer 31:31–34). A change of heart meant a change of life—the true fulfillment of circumcision. Without this, the prophets warned that God would judge such Jews for their sins.

Their conquest by the Babylonian armies and subsequent deportation brought this about. The prophets promised that, when the Jews were brought back from exile, God would make a new covenant with them. They would not be circumcised in the flesh, as were their ancestors, but in their hearts. As a result, they would love God and want to obey him (Jer 31:33; Ezek 36:26).

The importance of circumcision is that it was the means of entry into the covenant community. While non-circumcised people were allowed to live with the Jews on condition that they accepted their law (Lev 19:33–34), they were not allowed to eat the Passover meal, which celebrated God's redemption of his people (Num 9:13–14). It is of great significance that, whenever the NT mentions the death of Jesus, there are normally strong Paschal themes. As we will see, the Passover is crucial to the NT understanding of what the death of Jesus achieved[32] and that alongside these texts, there is almost always a reference to the importance of the circumcision of the heart and not the flesh (Rom 2:28, 29; [cf. Rom 3:21–26]; Gal 3:13–14; [cf. Gal 5:16]; Eph 1:7; 2:13; 5:25–27; [cf. Eph 2:11]; Col 1:13; [cf. Col 2:11]; Phil 3:10–11; [cf. Phil 3:3]).

I will argue that in the letter to the Romans, Jesus' death is seen as the fulfillment of the Passover. If this is so, then the NT, not just Paul, is saying that in order for an individual to benefit from Jesus' death and be delivered from the kingdom of darkness, there has to be circumcision. Corporate circumcision of believers took place when Jesus underwent physical circumcision–the tearing away of his flesh—in his death by crucifixion (Col 2:11). Despite this awesome, corporate, historic reality, the heart of each seeking person has to be circumcised, so that he may receive the benefit of this glorious salvation.

---

31. Barclay, "Circumcision," 536–56, made a comparison between Philo, (*Spec. Leg.*, 1:1–11; *Migr. Abr.* 89–93) and Paul (Rom 2:25–29), and concluded that Paul's hermeneutic revolution matched anything found in Second Temple Judaism.

32. See notes on Rom 3:21–26.

This reflects the situation for each Jew, who, though baptized into Moses in the exodus, entered into the covenant community as an individual through his own circumcision.

We are going to see how the themes of circumcision and Passover are united in Paul's explanation of the death of Jesus. Only those who have been circumcised in their hearts can benefit from his death and share in his Passover sacrifice. This means that the covenant people enter this freedom as a result of Jesus' death, and continually benefit from the achievements of his sacrifice as they feed on the living Passover (1 Cor 5:7–8; John 6:32–70).

CONCLUSION OF ROMANS 2

Paul has confronted his countrymen with truth they would not want to hear: Jews stand in need of the same grace of God as do the Gentiles.

Despite addressing an individual in the diatribe he constructs, Paul is not arguing at an individualistic level but at that of the nation. Because of his understanding of the solidarity of people groups, he is able to see that individual Jews are bound up with the obedience and disobedience of the wider community and with its fate. He observes that many of his fellow Jews assume their circumcision assures them of membership of the OT covenant community and has sealed their acceptance by God, guaranteeing their acquittal on the day of judgment. Paul has done everything he can to dissuade his kinsmen of this delusion. It was this false belief that had driven him to persecute the Christian community before he met the ascended Christ, and he understands the mindset that it produces.

Throughout the chapter, Semitic ideas—with constant quotes from the OT—drive the argument forward. Israel displays all the characteristics of a people alienated from God and, just like the Gentiles, in exile from his presence. She needs to be saved from the awaiting judgment also, and Paul uses new exodus material from the OT to describe her condition.

He will build on this foundation in coming chapters to explain how God has made a way of salvation for all people. However, Paul has hinted that the status of Israel as the bride in the divine marriage drama is seriously at risk.

ROMANS 3

THE MESSIAH KING AND HIS RIGHTEOUS JUDGMENT

WHAT ADVANTAGE, THEN, is there in being a Jew, or what value is there in circumcision? Much in every way! First of all, they have been entrusted with the very words of God. What if some did not have faith? Will their lack of faith nullify God's faithfulness? Not at all! Let God be true, and every man a liar. As it is written: "So that you may be proved right when you speak and prevail when you judge." But if our unrighteousness brings out God's righteousness more clearly, what shall we say? That God is unjust in bringing his wrath on us? (I am using a human argument.) Certainly not! If that were so, how could God judge the world? Someone might argue, "If my falsehood enhances God's truthfulness and so increases his glory, why am I still condemned as a sinner?" Why not say—as we are being slanderously reported as saying and as some claim that we say—"Let us do evil that good may result"? Their condemnation is deserved.

What shall we conclude then? Are we any better? Not at all! We have already made the charge that Jews and Gentiles alike are all under sin. As it is written: "There is no one righteous, not even one; there is no one who understands, no one who seeks God. All have turned away, they have together become worthless; there is no one who does good, not even one." "Their throats are open graves; their tongues practice deceit." "The poison of vipers is on their lips." "Their mouths are full of cursing and bitterness." "Their feet are swift to shed blood; ruin and misery mark their ways, and the way of peace they do not know." "There is no fear of God before their eyes."

Now we know that whatever the law says, it says to those who are under the law, so that every mouth may be silenced and the whole world held accountable to God. Therefore no one will be declared righteous in his sight by observing the law; rather, through the law we become conscious of sin. (Rom 3:1–20)

INTRODUCTION

In this passage, Paul continues to answer his opponents' claim that the Jews had a special status and were therefore exempt from God's judgment. Some believe Paul has constructed a diatribe,[1] in which he acknowledges the privileges and blessings of the Jewish people (Rom 3:2). However, in a subtle move, he quotes from David's psalm of penitence (Ps 51:3–6). Even David, the chosen of the Lord and the one with whom the everlasting covenant was made, had come under Yahweh's judgment. David did not question

---

1. For example, see Stowers, "Dialogue," especially 715. However, Hall, "Reconsidered," 183–97, rejects this understanding, pointing out that Paul gives too much detail for and against the argument. He considers that such detail was uncharacteristic of a diatribe.

Yahweh's verdict, acknowledging him to be righteous (Rom 3:4). If David did not escape the righteous judgment of God, what hope of deliverance did the people of Israel have?

Aware of the deviousness of the human heart to seek its own justification, Paul responds to those who accept their guilt but claim, in mitigation, that their sin is for God's glory. They would argue that God should not be angry, since sin puts his holiness into clearer focus and so glorifies him (Rom 3:5–8).

Paul drives home his argument about the righteousness of God and the guilt of man by citing a series of texts from the psalms, along with a passage from Isaiah (Isa 59:7–8). The first citation in Rom 3:12 is: "There is no one who does good, not even one." This is from Ps 14:1–3, or possibly Ps 53:1–3—both psalms being attributed to David. Whatever the origin of the citation and the circumstance of its composition, an exilic theme is its backcloth.[2] Both psalms speak of the people being devoured, crying out to God for deliverance and restoration to their former blessings.

The citation of Ps 5:9 in Rom 3:13a is of wider significance when examined in its context. David, longing to return to the house of the Lord in order to worship him writes:

> Lead me, O Lord, in your righteousness because of my enemies—make straight your way before me. Not a word from their mouth can be trusted; their heart is filled with destruction. Their throat is an open grave; with their tongue they speak deceit. Declare them guilty, O God! Let their intrigues be their downfall. Banish them for their many sins, for they have rebelled against you. (Ps 5:8–10)

Again, the theme of God's righteousness is present. This is an appropriate text for Paul to use as he introduces the subject of the eschatological revelation of God's righteousness (Rom 3:21). Once more, there is an echo of the exile as the psalmist appeals to Yahweh to deliver him from the ungodly who seek his death.

The use of Ps 140:3[3] (Rom 3:13b) in the suggested exilic theme may seem surprising, until it is remembered that Israel could adopt the prayers of David as her own due to the covenantal/representative relationship that existed. As the nation's head, he spoke on her behalf. His fear of destruction, as expressed in Ps 140:1–5, would naturally be adopted by Israel to express her fear in times of national crisis. Such a psalm would have echoed throughout Babylon during the exilic period.

In Rom 3:14, Paul quotes from Ps 10.[4] This psalm speaks of David's enemies pursuing, sitting in ambush, murdering, watching, lurking, seizing and crushing. It resonates with the awful anticipation of a future invasion, when a ruthless army would take away members of the covenant community into exile.

---

2. Psalm 14:7 says, "Oh, that salvation for Israel would come out of Zion! When the Lord restores the fortunes of his people, let Jacob rejoice and Israel be glad!" and Ps 53:6 says, "Oh, that salvation for Israel would come out of Zion! When God restores the fortunes of his people, let Jacob rejoice and Israel be glad!"

3. Ps 140:3: "They make their tongues as sharp as a serpent's; the poison of vipers is on their lips. Selah."

4. Ps 10:7: "His mouth is full of curses and lies and threats; trouble and evil are under his tongue."

Isa 59:7–8,[5] cited in Rom 3:17 speaks of Israel's condition which merited the judgment of exile. Isaiah states there was no one who could intercede on Israel's behalf. The chapter concludes with Yahweh putting on his armor to come forward as her Redeemer (Isa 59:16–20).

The final citation (Rom 3:18) in this catena of texts is from Ps 36:1,[6] where the psalmist writes that he has an oracle in his heart concerning the condition of the wicked who have no fear of God. The psalm then goes on to contrast the wickedness of man with the faithfulness of Yahweh:

> Your love, O Lord, reaches to the heavens, your faithfulness to the skies. Your righteousness is like the mighty mountains, your justice like the great deep. O Lord, you preserve both man and beast. How priceless is your unfailing love! Both high and low among men find refuge in the shadow of your wings. They feast on the abundance of your house; you give them drink from your river of delights. For with you is the fountain of life; in your light we see light. (Ps 36:5–9)

There could not be a more fitting introduction to the subject of the redemption in Christ (Rom 3:21) than this extract from Ps 36. The sinfulness of man is declared (v. 1) and, in awesome contrast, the love (v. 5), faithfulness (v. 5), righteousness (v. 6), and justice (v. 6) of Yahweh are proclaimed.

If it is correct that Paul's chosen texts support these themes, then there is no disputing the fact that this collection of texts speaks about the universal sinfulness of man and the condition of exile into which that sinfulness has brought him. It is an exile through which the righteousness of God will be displayed as he saves those who call upon him.

The sting for the Jews is how Paul uses these texts. He does not apply them to Israel's oppressors but to those in the nation who are uncircumcised in heart. The ones who thought of themselves as examples of righteousness were in fact godless. They opposed the work of Yahweh to bring salvation through the fulfillment of the new exodus promises, and thus kept the true people of the covenant from their inheritance. Paul will argue this more directly in chapter 10.

The new exodus theme is the background to the description of Jesus' death as a redemptive sacrifice. In Rom 3:23, Paul sates that: "all have sinned and fall short of the glory of God." The glory of God is often seen to refer to the state of Adam before the fall, but the same expression is used elsewhere with new exodus significance. God says of Israel: "whom I created for my glory" (Isa 43:7). Yahweh laments that through Israel's exile he is disgraced, and he promises to restore his people back to her role of bringing glory to him. To do this, she must be delivered and returned to the promised land. Paul takes this statement about Israel in her exile, and applies it to the whole of humankind. For man to glorify his Creator, he must first experience the redemption that is in Christ Jesus.

---

5. Isa 59:7–8: "Their feet rush into sin; they are swift to shed innocent blood. Their thoughts are evil thoughts; ruin and destruction mark their ways. The way of peace they do not know; there is no justice in their paths. They have turned them into crooked roads; no-one who walks in them will know peace."

6. Ps 36:1: "An oracle is within my heart concerning the sinfulness of the wicked: There is no fear of God before his eyes."

3:1 **What advantage, then, is there in being a Jew, or what value is there in circumcision?** Paul is aware that the argument he has given could be misunderstood. He does not want his readers to conclude that he sees no value in the law for the Jewish people. While the law did not bestow salvation, it had a vitally important role in preparing for it. The importance of the OT as preparation for the coming of the Gospel is evident throughout Paul's writings, particularly the letter to the Romans. The fact that the OT is regularly quoted in letters that were written to essentially Gentile congregations in Rome, Corinth and Galatia is evidence that the Gentile church needed to know its teaching in order to understand the message of the Gospel. Without the teaching of the OT, the Gospel's foundation would be like sand. Alas, all too many Christians tend to disregard the OT, and see it as a collection of writings the church has outgrown. Such an understanding is perilous. To ignore the OT is to fail to put a firm foundation in place, which is indispensable for a healthy and vital faith.

3:2 **Much in every way! First of all, they have been entrusted with the very words of God.** Paul is decisive in answering the question of v. 1: "what advantage, then, is there in being a Jew?" If the OT had not prepared God's people for the coming of the Messiah, it would have had little value. But it had been preparing them to appreciate what God was doing in human history, and especially in Jewish history. For this reason, Paul replies: "Much in every way! First of all, they have been entrusted with the very words of God."

The dedication shown by the Jews to the teaching and understanding of their Scriptures is an example to Christian communities. If the living God has spoken (and the Jewish/Christian Scriptures testify that he has), then these writings are indispensable for understanding human existence. Their neglect will lead to a false view of man and to idolatry.

Paul argues the Jewish privilege is that she was given the gift of God's revelation ("the very words of God"). The Scriptures are the best gift any child could be given by his parents. To be taught them—through formal instruction and by example—is to be given the greatest treasure anyone can receive. In the words of the moderator of the Scottish Presbyterian church as he presents the Bible to the new monarch during the British coronation ceremony: "Here are the oracles of God."

The importance of the OT for the early church cannot be over-emphasized. Since the NT documents did not exist as a collection of writings during the early years of the church, it is obvious that its Scriptures would have been the Jewish Bible—the OT. The apostles saw it to be the key to understanding what had happened in the life, death and resurrection of their Lord.

The OT not only helped them understand things about Jesus, but also the experience and responsibilities of the Christian community. The Spirit compelled the church to face important issues like the evangelization of the Gentiles (Acts 11:11–18), and confirmed the sense of God's guidance (Acts 15:12–18). To understand these and many other issues, the early Christians went back to the OT (e.g., Acts 15:15–21) where they knew that God had spoken through the prophets about the days in which they were now living (2 Tim 3:14–17).

⟶ **3:3 What if some did not have faith? Will their lack of faith nullify God's faithfulness?** The fact that not everyone believes is no reason to abandon the responsibility of sharing the message of God's love. Paul asserts that man's lack of faith will not nullify[7] God's faithfulness. He will fulfill his promise to Abraham by saving those who are of the same faith as the patriarch.

The Greek word Ἀπιστία (*apistia*) "unbelief" can also be translated "unfaithfulness," implying that they have lost the faith they once had. This is probably the way that Paul saw the people of Israel, for he was sure that despite many claiming to be faithful to the Scriptures, they had departed from them. They had become unfaithful. Jesus indicated this in the parable of the Good Samaritan where the Priest and Levite, refusing to demonstrate God's compassion towards the robbed and injured man, showed that the law had not affected their lives (Luke 10:31–32).

⟶ **3:4 Not at all! Let God be true, and every man a liar. As it is written: "So that you may be proved right when you speak and prevail when you judge."** Paul writes that ultimately, God will be seen to be true, and every man will be shown to be a liar. In support, he quotes Ps 51:3–6. It is a subtle and decisive move. By quoting David's penitential psalm, Paul gives an example of a Jew who had been elected and who stood in a covenant relationship with Yahweh. By doing this, he was able to show there is no exception. Even the one in whom God had delighted, and on whom his love was set, came under the divine sentence of righteous judgment when he sinned. If David had not escaped the judgment of God, what hope did the rest of Israel have?

⟶ **3:5 But if our unrighteousness brings out God's righteousness more clearly, what shall we say? That God is unjust in bringing his wrath on us? (I am using a human argument.)** The comment that I have made at the end of chapter 2, regarding the importance of circumcision of the heart, will need to be kept in mind until we reach the end of this chapter. Paul will speak about the way Jesus' death sets his people free from the judgment they would have otherwise suffered had he not borne the wrath of God and rescued them from the kingdom of darkness.

Before we get to that point in his argument, we see Paul continuing to consider man's condition. He has already described this in chapters 1 and 2, but is aware that his case is not yet complete. Like a skilful lawyer arguing his case to a jury, Paul wants all the evidence to be clearly understood before he progresses to the next part of his defense of the Gospel. He raises the objection that might be in the believers' minds: if man's sinfulness magnifies the righteousness of God, it is unjust to condemn man for his sin. Such an objection does not show the unreasonableness of the case but the darkness of their hearts.

⟶ **3:6 Certainly not! If that were so, how could God judge the world?** Paul responds emphatically that God is not unjust. He argues that if God compromised himself by treating sin lightly in order to magnify his grace, the inevitable outcome would be that he

---

7. Morris, *Romans*, 155 n. 1, found eighty ways in which reputable versions have rendered the word καταργέω (*katargeō*). He opts for "nullify."

could not judge at all—his righteousness would be in shreds. Paul responds instinctively as a Jew, for it was evident that God is fitted to be the judge of man. The answer given to Abraham when he asked Yahweh to spare Lot and his family was: "will not the judge of all the earth do right?" (Gen 18:25. Cf. also Deut 32:4; Job 8:3; 34:10ff.). The righteous judgment of God is foundational to his OT revelation.

3:7 Someone might argue, "If my falsehood enhances God's truthfulness and so increases his glory, why am I still condemned as a sinner?" Paul repeats the argument, but this time he puts it into the mouth of an adversary rather than posing the question himself.[8] In v.5, Paul writes of unrighteousness glorifying God, but here the adversary substitutes "falsehood" for "unrighteousness." There is no indication as to why the change was made, but it may have made Paul's defense more specific. The same basic question is asked: "if my falsehood enhances God's truthfulness and so increases his glory, why am I still condemned as a sinner?" A parallel to Rom 3:7 would be a convicted criminal claiming that he should be compensated for giving the police an opportunity to practice the technique of arrest! Paul will not hear of any such defense, arguing that God is true and never responsible for the sin of man. This is not to say that God does not cause the sinfulness of man to serve him (Ps 76:10), but nevertheless, he is not the author of evil (Jas 1:13–18).

3:8 Why not say—as we are being slanderously reported as saying and as some claim that we say—"Let us do evil that good may result"? Their condemnation is deserved. Paul states the inevitable logic of the argument he has been attacking. It will lead to anarchy, with people saying: "Let us do evil that good may result." Paul is aware that he has been accused of saying such things himself. He is deeply alarmed that he and his colleagues have been spoken of in this way. Such a rumor could do untold damage to the Gospel's progress in Europe. His Spanish mission was one of the reasons for Paul writing to the Romans as he hoped that they would make that mission possible (Rom 15:23–24).

Rom 3:8 should challenge our use of the tongue and our response to damaging slander. Paul did not ignore the accusation or seek to bear it meekly. He chose to raise it publicly in his letter. He knew that, should his response reach the ears of those who had wronged him; further accusation would follow in an attempt to justify what had been said. Despite this possibility, he felt that bringing it into the open was a risk worth taking. His defense is not about protecting his reputation. He would be content in the knowledge that in time, judgment would come on such slanderers as the OT principle of not slandering still stood (Lev 19:16). From Paul's distressing experience of being slandered, the believers in Rome could learn that confrontation is necessary when the Gospel is at stake.

---

8. The NAB gives "But if God's truth redounds to his glory through my falsehood, why am I still being condemned as a sinner?" There is nothing in the Greek to justify the NIV's reading, but most agree that Paul is not stating his own opinion—he is citing an objection that might be used against it. The uncertainty is because of textual variations in the opening of the verse.

3:9 What shall we conclude then? Are we any better? Not at all! We have already made the charge that Jews and Gentiles alike are all under sin. The argument that began in Rom 3:1 was concerned with the advantages that the Jews have over the Gentiles. Paul now asks the rhetorical question: "Are we any better?" His answer is "Not at all!" because both Jews and Gentiles are "under sin." This description of being "under sin" is a key expression for Paul, and its significance will be explained as his letter unfolds.

The Jews knew what it was to be "under" an authority other than God. They had been "under" Pharaoh and then "under" Nebuchadnezzar, as prisoners under the power of those who enslaved them. In this condition, they were not only socially and economically abused but stripped of all identity. When a nation was conquered in antiquity, it was seen to come under the gods of the victorious nation. This was inevitable, as its deities (so it seemed) had given the conquering nation the victory, reducing the conquered nation to a state of servitude and humiliation.

Paul is saying that both Jews and Gentiles are "under sin." Such an expression is surprising. To have said they were under the condemnation of the law would seem to make better sense, and is the way that the expression is normally understood. As Paul develops his argument in chapters 5 and 6, we will see that when he speaks of sin, he is actually speaking of Satan. The statement in Rom 3:9 is saying that all people—Jews and Gentiles—are in bondage to Satan. This is the result of the cosmic conquest which Paul will describe in chapter 5, when Adam was taken as Satan's willing prisoner. The whole human family, of which Adam is the head, was taken with him. Of course, saying that people are "under sin" (Satan) does not deny they are under the sentence of the law and so will be judged.

3:10 As it is written: "There is no one righteous, not even one; Paul begins a series of quotations from the Hebrew Scriptures in order to demonstrate the state of man. Each text is related to the condition that led Israel into exile and the sufferings she subsequently experienced.

The collection of proof texts has to be viewed from the perspective of someone who has witnessed this happening to his people. The texts reflect the fact that Israel's exile was deserved because the warnings of the prophets had been ignored. The quotations in vv. 10–12 are taken from either Ps 14:1–2 or 53:1–3. Both psalms are attributed to David.

3:11 There is no one who understands, no one who seeks God. Such a statement would anger and offend the religious Jew. He would accept it as a description of the Gentiles but not of the Jews. However, Paul is not saying anything that has not already been said in the OT. When Isaiah spoke of Yahweh's distress at the condition of the nation and her inevitable exile, he said Yahweh looked for a righteous representative saying, "I looked, but there was no one to help, I was appalled that no one gave support" (Isa 63:5). Isaiah also said, "All our righteous acts are like filthy rags" (Isa 64:6). Both statements were directed to the Jews and were about their failure.

3:12 **All have turned away, they have together become worthless; there is no one who does good, not even one."** The description of the nation as "worthless" is highlighted with the statement that there is not one individual among the people of God who "does good." This indicates the seriousness of their condition. The people, who had been the apple of God's eye and his inheritance, could not be described in a more stark way. The OT passage quoted is Ps 14:1–3. It speaks of those who devour God's people (Ps14:4), and ends with a prayer that salvation would come for Israel out of Zion (Ps 14:7; cf. Isa 59:20; see notes on Rom 11:26–27). The psalm echoes the exile perfectly.

3:13 **"Their throats are open graves; their tongues practice deceit." "The poison of vipers is on their lips."** This verse, which uses parts of Ps 5:9 and Ps 140:3, emphasizes the underhanded nature of evil by using the term "deceit," and its open display by using the expression, "The poison of vipers is on their lips." These sinful actions come to fruition in the breakdown of human relationships.

The citation of these verses follows Paul's description of man's decline in Rom 1:18–32. The consequence of rejecting God is man's rejection of his fellow man. This is evident in the history of the nations of the earth. Men scheme and plot against those they are called to respect and with whom they are to live in harmony. This description does not deny there are exemplary human beings who live for the well-being of others, but it is true of the solidarities that Paul writes about. To describe a nation as sick to the core does not mean that every citizen is equally evil.

3:14 **"Their mouths are full of cursing and bitterness."** Paul paints the picture of Israel's depravity more strikingly. Such a description does not typify her whole history, but does match the sort of evil the eighth-century prophets preached against when they predicted her exile if she did not repent and seek Yahweh's forgiveness (Hos 5:13–15).

The cited passage is from Ps 10:7, where evildoers afflict the weak. While Paul has applied the description to Israel, it originally referred to her enemies, whose raiding parties afflicted the scattered Jewish communities. In other words, the psalm speaks of external oppressors who have no respect for the God of Israel. They foreshadowed the invading Babylonian armies who brought about Israel's exile. Again, Paul takes texts which speak of the sin of the Gentiles and applies them to Israel.

3:15 **"Their feet are swift to shed blood;**" Paul's description of Israel has touched on her rejection of God's word (vv. 10–11), her search for worthless pleasure (v. 12), and her evil speaking and vilification of others (vv. 13–14).

Now Paul says that "their feet are swift to shed blood." The people are searching for the opportunity for violence towards those they hate, and they pursue it with excitement and pleasure. This verse, along with the following two verses, is a citation from Isa 59:7–8, which is part of Yahweh's indictment against Israel and his justification for sending her into exile. The source of the passage lends support to the claim that the catena of quotations describes the condition of Israel which brought about her exile.[9]

---

9. If this reference is seen to be about the fall of humanity, then it refers to the reproach brought upon Yahweh through the alienation of his creation. This would explain the following quote from Isaiah: "that

Throughout the NT, we find Jewish leaders who rejected God's word and turned on those who accepted it. Their involvement in the death of Jesus, Stephen (Acts 7:54–60), and James (Acts 12:1–3) bears witness to this rejection. Indeed, in the book of Revelation, God speaks of the church's persecution in Smyrna by the "synagogue of Satan" (Rev 2:9). With these facts in mind, it is understandable why Paul painted such an horrific picture of his own people.

3:16 Ruin and misery mark their ways, The people of God, who were called to be a light to the nations, live in the same darkness as the Gentiles. The nation of Israel, which boasted that the glory of God dwelt in her midst, lived in a condition of sin that mirrored the nations around her. This was so distressing to Yahweh that he called Israel "a harlot" (Jer 23:10; Ezek 23:29–31; Hos 6:10) because she had given herself to the gods of the surrounding nations.

3:17 And the way of peace they do not know." Instead of being characterized by the peace of God, Israel was noted for its absence. How tragic that the nation chosen for such blessing had sold her heritage for the favors of gods with whom she had flirted. Her children should have known joy and happiness, but experienced fear and terror. Her elderly should have been valued and respected, but were insulted and abused. Her women should have been held in honor and treated with dignity, but were treated as valueless—objects of violence and exploitation.

The covenant people were as vile and depraved as the Gentiles—norms of decency were overthrown, and life was lived for self advancement and satisfaction.

3:18 "There is no fear of God before their eyes." Like the Gentiles (Rom 1:29–31), the Jews had lost their capacity to be ashamed.[10] They argued God was not displeased and they had done nothing to offend him. They remonstrated that the prophets were negative and should have spoken about the good things their religion gave the people rather than about a God whom they should fear.

The quotation is from Ps 36:1. While the psalm could refer to David's personal experience, it makes better sense to see the affliction as national.

3:19 Now we know that whatever the law says, it says to those who are under the law, so that every mouth may be silenced and the whole world held accountable to God. Paul has spoken previously about being "under sin" (v. 9), but here he speaks about being "under the law." For Paul, the two terms "sin" and "law" were synonymous. Such an understanding is unexpected of one who valued the law as the holy gift of God to his people. Indeed, recent NT studies have focused on the positive attitude the Jews of the NT period had towards the law. It is argued they did not see it as threatening, but

---

their feet are swift to shed blood." It would refer to the next step in the descent of humankind—the slaying of Cain by Abel. (I owe this observation to Rev. Alvin Lewis of Calgary, Canada.)

10. Kirkpatrick, *Psalms*, 184, points out that the Hebrew for "fear" in the original text denotes terror inspired by God and not reverence for God.

ennobling and a means of blessing. Indeed, Paul himself speaks of the law as "holy" (Rom 7:12).

Israel was sent into exile (Ezek 13:19) because she disobeyed the law given to her through Moses. Thus, she was "under the law," serving the sentence the law passed on her as a result of sinful disobedience. Paul therefore, can speak of being "under sin" as being "under the law." If I am right in saying that "sin" is to be read as "Satan" in Paul's writings, then being "under sin" means being under the authority of Satan. Being "under the law" refers to being under its sentence, which is alienation from God. Such a view of the law does not mean that Paul sees it as sinful (he deals with such an objection in chapter 7) but as the instrument for upholding righteousness by judging sin(s).[11]

Paul's view of man's condition is that he is in bondage to Satan and held captive in the kingdom of darkness (Acts 26:17–18; Gal 1:4; Col 1:13–14). In other words, Israel's historical exile was a picture (or type) of humankind's condition in Sin. It is because Israel had been promised a Davidic deliverer who would lead her out of bondage in Babylon (just as Moses had led her earlier deliverance out of Egypt) that Paul is able to relocate the promises made to Israel. He applies them to the deliverance of man from bondage to Satan by the true Son of David. In transposing these promises, he keeps true to their original context, using them to show how Israel's history had been typological (1 Cor 10:1–6; Rom 15:4). They are a picture of man's condition and the response of God.

Paul has reached a climatic conclusion to his argument when he says that, because all of mankind is in spiritual exile from God, "every mouth will be silenced and the whole world held accountable to God." This is the inevitable outcome of humanity being in Adam, a theme which he will develop in chapter 5.

3:20 Therefore no one will be declared righteous in his sight by observing the law; rather, through the law we become conscious of sin. In stating that no one will be declared righteous in God's sight by observing the law, Paul cuts right across the path of Jewish expectation. Whether he refers to the legal fulfillment of the moral code or the acceptance of the boundary markers that identify Jews, the result is still the same: fulfilling the law's requirements does not lead to salvation.

This statement is all inclusive; the preceding argument makes it clear that it applies to all Jews and Gentiles. It cuts into the very heart of the Jewish sense of privilege which went beyond the intended purpose of the giving of the law. The nation claimed something that had never been her right (Rom 9:4; 10:1–4; 1 Cor 4:6). Indeed, the concluding statement makes it clear that the role of the law was never intended to achieve salvation but to alert man to his need of it, for the law brings consciousness of sin.

The Greek for "declared righteous" is δικαιόω (*dikaioō*), a relational word referring to being brought into a right relationship with God.[12] In the Greek which Paul uses, the

---

11. We will repeatedly find difficulty in deciding what the term "sin" means in texts Paul writes. It can mean "Satan" (so should be written "Sin") or it can be a reference to man's disobedience. Unfortunately, the Greek cannot help us to decide as the upper case was not used in the NT documents.

12. Louw and Nida comment on *dikaioô, dikiôsis* and *dikaiosunç*: "to cause someone to be in a proper or right relation with someone else, to put right with, to cause to be in a right relationship with." They say

phrase πᾶσα σάρξ (*pasa sarx*) translates as "all flesh" shall not be justified.[13] The flow of the argument requires that we translate "*pasa sarx*" as "all humanity." Thus, Paul is adamant that no one can be brought into a right relationship with God by observing the law. By using the term "all flesh," Paul is stressing this applies to Jews as well as to Gentiles. The use of this Greek term echoes Ps 143:2 (142:2 LXX), which says: "Do not bring your servant into judgment, for no one living is righteous before you."

THE MESSIAH KING AND HIS WORK OF REDEMPTION

BUT NOW A righteousness from God, apart from law, has been made known, to which the Law and the Prophets testify. This righteousness from God comes through faith in Jesus Christ to all who believe. There is no difference, for all have sinned and fall short of the glory of God, and are justified freely by his grace through the redemption that came by Christ Jesus. God presented him as a sacrifice of atonement, through faith in his blood. He did this to demonstrate his justice, because in his forbearance he had left the sins committed beforehand unpunished—he did it to demonstrate his justice at the present time, so as to be just and the one who justifies those who have faith in Jesus. (Rom 3:21–26)[14]

EXCURSUS A: PAUL'S USE OF "RIGHTEOUS"

If Paul is following the theme of the new exodus, his main source materials would be from the law and the writings of the prophets. The law (the Pentateuch) deals with the exodus from Egypt, and the writings of the prophets predict a second exodus from Babylon, following the exile. Indeed, Paul has been explicit on this matter, for he has claimed that the Gospel is according to the law and the prophets (Rom 1:2; 3:21). A crucial contributor in this connection was Isaiah, and we shall see that Paul draws extensively on his prophecy. Paul was not the only NT writer who was influenced in his understanding of the Passover and the exodus (and other themes) by Isaiah's prophecy. The prophet's influence is throughout most NT books, but especially the Gospels.[15]

---

that some scholars interpret *dikaioô, dikiôsis* and *dikaiosunç* as meaning "forensic righteousness," i.e., the act of being declared righteous on the basis of Christ's atoning ministry. They go on to say: "but it would seem more probable that Paul uses these expressions in the context of the covenant relation rather than in the context of legal procedures." Louw and Nida, 1:452.

Ridderbos, *Outline*, 175, comments: "The justification of the ungodly is a justification 'in Christ,' that is to say, not only on the grounds of his atoning death and resurrection, but also by virtue of the corporate inclusion in him of his own."

13. οὐ δικαιωθήσεται πᾶσα σάρξ (*ou dikaiôthēsetai pasa sarx*). There has been a debate over whether Paul actually composed the paragraph. Bultmann, *Theology*, 1.46, supported by Käsemann, *Exegetische*, 1.96–100, argued that it was non-Pauline and adapted by him to make the argument he was seeking to give. Others, on both sides of the Atlantic, have followed this argument; in the USA, see Talbert, "Fragment," 287–96, and, in the UK, Zeisler, *Righteousness*, 209–10. However, Young, "Compose," 25 n. 7, has rejected the hypothesis, claiming the passage is genuinely Pauline. Either way, it is clear what Paul intends to convey.

14. Cranfield, *Romans*, 199, says that Rom 3:21–26 is "the centre and heart of the whole of Romans."

15. See Watts, *Mark*; Mánek, *Luke*; Ra, *John*; Coxon, *John*; Cozart, *Ephesians*; Wright, *Romans*; Keesmaat, *Galatians*.

God's righteousness is more than moral perfection, and being righteous before him is more than being declared innocent. Both understandings are certainly part of biblical understanding, but they are not the full picture. The term also describes God's mercy toward his people (Ps 71:15; 85:13; 98:2) and speaks of his saving activity in redeeming them (Isa 45:13; 56:1).

Righteousness is a key OT concept and links into Israel's return from exile. Isaiah said that Israel was made righteous as a result of her return from exile (Isa 54:14; 62:1–2). The prophet's view of righteousness was not only one of forgiveness but also of the nation's restoration to her inheritance (Isa 51:5–11; 61:3).

This OT background has increasingly led scholars to appreciate that Paul's concept of the "righteousness of God" is rooted in the understanding of the eighth century BC prophets and the psalms, and that it has to do with Israel's restoration to a right relationship with God. Cut off from the temple and exiled in Babylon (where her broken relationship was displayed to the nations), Israel needed to experience the saving righteousness of God. She had experienced the judgment of his righteousness by which he had threatened to enact the covenantal curses (Deut 32:1–35). After many appeals from the prophets and the most awful, ruthless destruction of her capital city and supporting network of communities, the nation had been swept away into exile. But after many years, the righteousness of God was shown and experienced yet again when he delivered and restored his people to their inheritance.

We have also seen that Paul's use of the OT is not arbitrary, but is guided by clear principles.[16] He sees the promises of the prophets to be fulfilled in Jesus; the prediction that the Jews would be released from bondage in Babylon having now been fulfilled in Christ. Thus, Paul continues to use the term "righteousness" in this OT way. This is made clear when he says that the righteousness of God, as revealed in the saving death of Jesus, has been testified to in the Law and the Prophets (3:21). It is unwise to go outside of the Scriptures to find Paul's meaning of "righteousness." Traditionally many commentators used the Roman legal model to define the meaning of this key term, but by so doing limited their understanding to an exclusively forensic and moral one. Paul's constant appeal to OT texts strongly suggests that his source of understanding for this vital concept is not the Roman legal system but the OT. Indeed, we will find as our exegesis develops that for Paul there is a crucial context for much of his justification language that has been largely missed—that of the new exodus and the theme of the divine marriage.[17]

EXCURSUS B: THE INFLUENCE OF THE PROPHET EZEKIEL ON PAUL'S THEOLOGY

As we have seen, the letter to the Romans is full of OT quotations and allusions. Paul not only knew the OT Scriptures, he was saturated in them and driven by their message. He

---

16. See pages 6–15.

17. See comments on Rom 6:6–7 and 7:1–6. The imagery has been noted by Campbell, *Deliverance*, 663, who failed to see its new exodus and divine marriage context and as a result emphasized solely the theme of deliverance. For further discussion on "righteousness" language, see Excursus D: "Justification in the language of Paul" on pages 107–30.

clearly expected the believers in Rome to also be familiar with them. The church at this stage in her history had no Scriptures other than the OT.

Most of the Roman believers were Gentiles who would know there were two great annual religious celebrations spoken of in the OT. Both centered on animal sacrifice. These were the Day of Atonement (Lev 16) and the Passover (Exod 12). Traditionally, Rom 3:21–25 has been seen to compare Jesus' death to the sacrifice on the Day of Atonement—a sacrifice that brought forgiveness and acceptance by God. This is an understandable conclusion, because Paul uses the word ἱλαστήριον (hilastērion), which is translated by some as "expiation" (covering or cleansing)[18] and by others as "propitiation" (making atonement or appeasing).[19] "Propitiation" is recognized by most scholars to be the meaning of the term hilastērion and that it was the purpose of the sacrifice on the Day of Atonement.

However, since the middle of the twentieth century, scholars have been uncertain whether this feast was the setting in Paul's mind. This is because, while the term hilastērion has clear links with the Day of Atonement, the rest of the imagery in the passage points away from it. The reference to προτίθημι (protithēmi), the "public display" of the sacrifice (v. 25), stands in stark contrast to the complete solitude of the Most Holy Place (the Holy of Holies). On the Day of Atonement, the sacrificial blood was presented to Yahweh in this inner room (Lev 16). Indeed, the act itself was even hidden from the high priest as the cover above the testimony (mercy seat lid), where the atonement was made, lay hidden in a cloud of smoke from the burning incense (Lev 16:13–14).

Because of this difficulty, an increasing number of modern scholars have suggested the reference to the hilastērion links the death of Jesus with the death of the Maccabean martyrs, who prayed that their sacrifice would be an hilastērion for the nation's sins.[20] This resonated with Jewish teaching about the offering of Isaac (Gen 22:1–19), the prototype of all martyrs, that was an integral part of the extensive rabbinical theological structure of atonement. This teaching claimed the "offering" of Isaac in Gen 22 had been accepted by Yahweh as atonement for Israel's sins. Known as the Aqedah, this doctrine went so far as to argue that all the sacrifices of the temple were mere remembrances of the "offering" of Isaac, and it was his willingness to die for his offspring that gave the temple sacrifices their efficacy. One problem with adopting the Aqedah[21] doctrine as Paul's paradigm relates to the ongoing controversy regarding the dating of the various rabbinic authorities. Claims that link Paul's understanding with this Aqedah teaching are likely to be rejected on the basis of inadmissible evidence because there is no certainty Paul knew the texts

---

18. See Dodd, "Meaning," 33ff., supported by Moule, Sacrifice, 46. Hill, Words, 24, says that Dodd's failure was to omit all discussion of the contexts of passages he relied on from his study, thereby depriving himself of an important guide to understanding the texts. Young, "Hilaskesthai," 67ff., says that Dodd oversimplified the issues and granted the LXX translators too great a freedom in supposedly radically modifying the use of (ex)ilaskomai.

19. Black, Romans, 68; Kidner, "Metaphors," 124, and Morris, "Meaning," 33ff.

20. Seifrid, "Romans," 619; Barrett, Romans, 1:217–18; Morris, Atonement, 168; "Meaning," 42; Romans, 253. Also, see Downing, Martyrdom, 242. Morris eventually came to favor the Maccabean interpretation, before reverting to the Day of Atonement setting.

21. Meaning "the binding," so-called because Isaac was bound on the altar (Gen 22:9).

that form the basis of the argument.[22] However, the books of Maccabees (which contain the story of the death of the Maccabean martyrs and which are held by most scholars to be pre-Pauline) can stand in their own right without depending on rabbinical material. But to what extent the traditions of the Maccabean martyrs were known in Rome cannot be verified. Without this knowledge, the believers in Rome could not make the supposed connection. Moreover, by resorting to these Maccabean texts, motifs in Rom 3:21–25, which cannot be contained in martyrdom theology, are silenced.[23] "Righteousness," "justification," and "redemption" (terms found in vv. 21–25) are absent from the martyr texts but are at home in the new exodus framework. Added to this, Paul repeats his claim that the law and the prophets bore witness to this redemption (v. 21). If we are to understand his mindset, it is imperative that we look to these OT writings for his model.

There is only one cultic event in the entire OT (and in Jewish literature in general) in which redemption is celebrated. It is the Passover. Given the significance of this pivotal occasion in Israel's national life, the idea that Paul relied on this motif makes good sense. First, it is the one cultic event that could be celebrated away from the temple. More importantly, this is the only feast Jesus used to interpret his death. Furthermore, it was the one festival about which Jews and God-fearers would have had detailed knowledge as it was celebrated in homes across the Roman Empire. This background against which the atoning significance of the death of Jesus could be interpreted was probably overlooked because the offering was described as an *hilastērion* and most interpreters believed there was no propitiatory value in the Passover. Although an atoning content could be supported by appealing to a range of authorities, such an exercise would merely illustrate the confusion which exists over the nature of the festival. Even those who see propitiatory value in the Passover as practiced in the Mosaic period or in the NT do not see a connection between the Feast and Rom 3:21–25. However, there is evidence which has not been considered hitherto and which is important for our study.

We can see the influence of Ezekiel on Paul in many ways. Ezekiel, like Isaiah, saw the importance of a Davidic prince who would rise up and lead the remnant out of Babylon (Isa 11:1ff.; 55:3–4; Jer 23:1–8; 33:4–17). The prince—Ezekiel's designation of the Son of David—would be the shepherd-king that Israel longed for (Ezek 34:23–31; 37:24–25). He saw that the prince's main function was to provide sacrifices to atone for the sins of the covenant community. In Ezek 45:21–25, the prophet tells how, having built the eschatological temple, the prince will offer an abundance of sin offerings for the sins of the people. The passage says:

> In the first month on the fourteenth day you are to observe the Passover, a feast lasting seven days, during which you shall eat bread made without yeast. On that day the prince is to provide a bull as a sin offering for himself and for all the people of the land. Every day during the seven days of the Feast he is to provide seven bulls and seven rams without defect as a burnt offering to the LORD, and a male goat for a sin offering. He is to provide as a grain offering an ephah for each bull and an ephah for each ram, along with a hin of oil for each ephah. During the seven days

22. For a fuller discussion of the debate, see Holland, *Contours*, 256ff.

23. Dunn, *Romans*, vol. 1.

of the Feast, which begins in the seventh month on the fifteenth day, he is to make the same provision for sin offerings, burnt offerings, grain offerings and oil. (Ezek 45:21–25)

What is significant is that these sacrifices are not made on the Day of Atonement as would be expected. Indeed, Ezekiel never mentions the Day of Atonement in the context of the eschatological temple. What he does say is that these sacrifices will be offered to celebrate the Passover. This is of great importance for understanding Paul. Ezekiel—a priest who preached against the sin of tampering with the laws of Yahweh—does the unthinkable by changing the instructions of the Torah relating to the sacrificial system. He can be doing only one thing—he is emphasizing the importance of the Passover for dealing with the sins of the people!

It is also significant that Ezekiel had the Davidic prince making these Paschal-atoning sacrifices, and that Paul has introduced Jesus as the Davidic descendant in the opening of the letter (Rom 1:3).[24] By his use of the cultic expression, "the Spirit of holiness,"[25] Paul indicates that it is the Son of David, the Son of God, who achieves his people's redemption through his own death (Rom 1:3–4; 3:21–26). Further evidence that this is how the early church followed the narrative is that it matches what Jesus taught his disciples. He had instructed them on the purpose of his death, making it clear that it was to atone for their sins and to renew their relationship with God ("This cup is the new covenant in my blood," Luke 22:20). Moreover, this sacrifice was offered at Passover! Indeed, the Gospels mention no other sacrificial feast.

A further influence that is clearly flowing from Ezekiel is Paul's teaching on the resurrection. Ezekiel 37 tells of the vision of the valley of dry bones. Yahweh tells the prophet to prophecy to the bones, and eventually, a mighty army is formed that returns to Zion. This passage is widely seen to be the source of Paul's teaching on the resurrection, when the church will be raised to inherit the heavenly city.

Another major theme that Paul draws from Ezekiel is his doctrine of baptism. We shall see later that the key influence from the OT on the doctrine of baptism is the passage in Ezek 16. The passage speaks of Yahweh finding Israel, who is likened to a bleeding and abandoned newborn baby. The Lord cares for her, and in time he covenants himself to her, washing her with water and cherishing her as a much-loved bride. Paul makes use of similar imagery in 1 Cor 6:11 and in Eph 5:25–27, where he has Christ cleansing the church "by the washing with water through the word."[26] Such a crucial contribution to yet another major theme reinforced the impact Ezekiel had on NT thinking.

Furthermore, in tracing Ezekiel's influence, we find that the expression "Spirit of Holiness" (Rom 1:3) is also significant because it has been identified as an OT term.

---

24. The importance of the Davidic king for the atonement of Israel's sins has been noted by Johnson, *Kingship*, 13–14, who says: "The king is not only found leading his people with the offering of sacrifices and prayer on important occasions in the life of the nation, but throughout the four hundred years of the Davidic Dynasty, from the time of David's active concern for the Ark to that of Josiah's thorough-going reform, he himself superintends the organization of the cultus in all its aspects."

25. The term denotes an animal that meets the requirements for sacrifice. See Käsemann, *Romans*.

26. See Holland, *Contours*, 208.

It describes the criteria for accepting animal sacrifices in the Jewish Temple.[27] Paul is introducing the king, whose death will be a sacrifice to redeem his people and atone for their sins. Obviously, the redemptive death of the Davidic prince is not something that Ezekiel ever anticipated.

We have already noted that the theme of the circumcised heart in chapter 2 would have been familiar to God-fearers before Paul's instruction. This is because Ezek 44:7, 9 (verses dealing with the circumcised heart) was emphasized in the Hellenistic synagogues and would have been familiar to Jewish congregations at the time of John the Baptist. Circumcision was a requirement for partaking in the Passover and not to submit to it led to exclusion from the covenant (Ex 12:44–48). The rabbis developed the significance of this rite of passage and linked it to the celebration of the Passover in their writings. It is no coincidence that the circumcision of the heart is repeatedly linked with the Paschal death of Jesus throughout Paul's writings (Rom 2:28; 3:21ff.; Gal 3:13; 6:15; Eph 2:11–18; 1:7; 5:25; Col 1:13–15; 2:11). Without experiencing such circumcision, a person cannot partake in "Christ our Passover" and share in the benefits of his saving Paschal death.

Further Influences of Ezekiel on Paul's Thought

It is not only significant that Ezekiel merged atonement with redemption, but also that the translators of the LXX chose the preposition ὑπέρ (*hyper*) "on behalf of" when the text spoke of a sacrifice offered in place of the guilty party. This term is used throughout the Pauline cultic passages. Indeed, it became the standard expression of the apostles to describe the substitutive death of Christ.[28] Such clear dependence, either direct or indirect, underlines the importance of Ezekiel's understanding of cultic arrangements and the use that the early church made of them.

Ezekiel is also seen to be the source of Paul's view of the church as the temple of the living God.[29] The image of the Davidic leader making sacrifices to cleanse the temple and the people would naturally suggest to Paul the greater sacrifice of Israel's true king. This brought into existence the spiritual Temple of the living God where Yahweh dwelt with his people. This was all part of the testimony of the law and the prophets.

A further link is made by some between Ezekiel's use of the "Son of Man" motif and Paul's Adamic Christology. For these scholars, the two themes merge, the theological content of one enriching the other so that the "Son of Man" is the "Last Adam." This informs the argument of Rom 3:21ff.,[30] which many see to have an Adamic theme embedded within it.

---

27. Käsemann, *Romans*.

28. See Riesenfeld, "ὑπέρ" 512. Also, Moule, *Idiom*, 64; Driver, *Understanding*, 135; Davies, "Place," 7–8. Cousar, "Death," 40, says that *hyper* is the key to Paul's soteriology.

29. See McKelvey, *Temple*; McKay, "Ezekiel," 4–16.

30. See Carson, "Ambiguities," 97ff. See also Richardson, *Introduction*, 145–46; Schweizer, "Son," 127; Bowker, "Man," 23; Black, "Literature," 11; Emerton, "Imagery," 231; Wifall, "Man," 337–38; Maddox, "Function," 192–93 and "According," 56; McKay, "Ezekiel," 4ff. Bultmann, "Hermeneutischer," saw 3:21ff. to reflect Adamic theology. See also Stuhlmacher, *Righteousness*, 104. This suggests that the theme continues from the earlier chapters, where the fall of Man was very much in view. Thus, the thrust of the argument

Ezekiel's influence in Romans is seen by some to be in the statement: "peace with God" (Rom 5:1). It is linked with Ezek 37:26: "I will make with them a covenant of peace."[31] It has been demonstrated that Ezek 37 is present in 1 Cor 15.[32] The argument of Rom 8, which relates to the resurrection, is a summary of that found in 1 Cor 15. Indeed, the resurrection of the people of God in Ezek 37 could well be an important influence on Paul's thinking in Rom 6:1–4, where he speaks of the resurrection of the church with Christ. It is, of course, well known that Ezek 37 was read at the Passover celebration. This would add support to echoes of Ezekiel's promises of atonement in the argument Paul constructs.

Lastly, we have seen that some identify Ezekiel as the source of the term *hilastērion*. This is the word used in Heb 9:5 for the "atonement cover." Some claim it has been borrowed from Ezekiel where it is similarly used. Furthermore, certain scholars[33] claim the reference to the *hilastērion* in Rom 3:25 comes from the word used to describe the covering of the ark of the covenant in the eschatological temple of Ezekiel's vision (Ezek 43:14, 17, 20).

Thus, it would seem reasonable that Ezekiel has been a major influence on Paul's thinking and on the argument he is making in Romans. If this is so, it would be sensible to suggest that the significance of the Davidic king's Paschal offering—the sacrifice he made to cleanse the temple and make his people fit for service as shown in Ezek 45:21–25—would have been appreciated by the first century church.

However, it must not be overlooked that there is another possible source for the interpretation of Christ's death as atonement in the Passover setting. This comes from Jesus himself. Clearly, he regarded his death as an atonement. It is equally clear that the timing of his death was deeply significant for himself and the early church.[34] Jesus is probably drawing on Ezekiel as he interprets his death, deliberately bringing about his betrayal and death at Passover. Previously, as the Son of David, he had accepted the acclamation of the crowds when entering Jerusalem on the foal of a donkey, thereby activating another favorite Davidic text: "Rejoice greatly, O Daughter of Zion! Shout, Daughter of Jerusalem! See, your king comes to you, righteous and having salvation, gentle and riding on a donkey, on a colt, the foal of a donkey." (Zech 9:9; Matt 21:1–9). Thus, the Paschal tradition and its reinterpretation did not need to wait for the emergence of a thinker of Paul's calibre—it was in place well before his conversion. There is, therefore, no dis-

---

is that Christ's death is the act of redemption that rescues man from bondage and spiritual exile resulting from the fall. This will be upheld by the argument in chapter 5, and the way that Paul continues to thread Adamic imagery into the plight of man and the role of Christ as the last Adam. Casey, "Earliest," 273, says that Rom 3:25 is a midrashic symbolism in the Pauline manner, but is more allusive and less developed than in other instances. See also Skehan, "Cultic," 163. In addition to the above, Ezekiel's influence in chapter 5 is evident, the "peace with God" in Rom 5:1 reflecting Ezek 37:26a: "I will make a covenant of peace with them." It has also been demonstrated that Ezek 37 is present in 1 Cor 15. This is of interest in this commentary because the argument of Rom 8, which relates to the resurrection, parallels 1 Cor 15.

31. See Dunn, *Romans*, 1, 429.

32. See Schneider, "Corporate," 156–59. See also Davies, "People," 16.

33. See Cranfield, *Romans*, 1.214–18; Moo, *Romans*, 231–36.

34. Wright, *Victory*.

agreement between Jesus' understanding of the purpose of his death and the explanation found in Paul's letters.

Ezekiel's Wider Influence on NT Writers.

Ezekiel's influence has been detected in the statement John the Baptist made about Jesus, when he cried: "Look, the Lamb of God, who takes away the sin of the world!" (John 1:29). As we have noted, redemption by the death of the Paschal lamb and atonement made on the Day of Atonement do not go together in the understanding of most scholars. However, the fusion of Passover and the Day of Atonement in Ezek 45:25 has persuaded some that the Baptist saw an atoning significance in the Passover sacrifice.[35] They argue that the merger by Ezekiel had been understood in Judaism, and that the hearers of the Baptist would have understood his point. If it is right to make this link between atonement and Passover, then John's hearers would have understood his meaning. It follows that there must have been widespread appreciation of the origin of the idea behind the Baptist's cry, and this was key to understanding the achievements of the death of Christ. It is surprising that neither of the scholars who made this link in John 1:29[36] went on to bring this association into the Rom 3:21ff. passage. If they had done so, they would have identified the Passover as the setting of the passage long ago. Thus, Paul was not creating a Paschal/atonement link; the link already existed.

Ezekiel's influence on the cultic imagery of other NT writers has been identified by a number of scholars.[37] It has been appreciated that the tabernacle imagery, used in the letter to the Hebrews, is not Platonic (as was thought) but based on the eschatological temple described by Ezekiel. If this is so, it explains how the writer could speak of Christ having "obtained eternal redemption" (Heb 9:12). "Redemption" is not part of the Day of Atonement language, but it is an essential part of Passover. While, in other places, the writer of Hebrews uses concepts which are clearly drawn from the atoning sacrificial system of the Day of Atonement, here, and without explaining why, he also ties them to Paschal liturgy. In other words, Hebrews seems to be following the pattern in Ezekiel by pulling the sacrifices of the Day of Atonement into the orbit of Passover celebration. If this is so, it suggests that this approach was basic to the early church's cultic thinking, for the material is handled in Hebrews in such a way that the convergence is regarded as understood. Thus, Ezekiel's influence on the writer to the Hebrews and on Paul seems

---

35. Dunn, "Understanding," 132–33; Howard, "Eucharist," 331–32. Noted also by Morris, "Meaning," 92.

36. Dodd, *John*, argued that the Lamb of God referred to the lamb of the Apocalypse (Rev 6:16–17), whose wrath purges away the sin of the world. Thus, he claims, the Baptist did not refer to an atoning sacrifice but to the coming eschatological judgment. This suggestion is certainly interesting. It explains why the Baptist was confused (Luke 7:18–23) as to whether Jesus was the Messiah since he was not exercising a ministry of judgment. However, it does not remain focused on the fact that the overall theme of John's Gospel is Christ as the Paschal offering. What Dodd's suggestion does have in its favor is that the king was to take away Israel's sin through an atoning Paschal offering (see note on Rom 1:4).

37. McKelvey, *Temple*.

evident. Indeed, a comparison of the themes in Rom 3:24–26 and Heb 9:1–10 shows them to be the same.[38]

The widespread influence of Ezekiel in the early church is attested to by scholars who also see his shadow in the description of the eschatological temple in Revelation.[39] Interestingly, the cultic language of Revelation concentrates exclusively on the Passover.[40]

It is significant that the temple imagery of Ezekiel certainly had a profound influence on the Qumran community, and there is no mention of the Day of Atonement in either the Dead Sea Scrolls or in Jubilees. If this interpretation of the NT cultic language is correct, then it would appear to be in keeping with other strands of Judaism.

EXCURSUS C: PASSOVER THEMES IN PAUL'S THEOLOGY

The presence of this Passover model is supported by the reference to πάρεσις (paresis) the "passing over" ("forbearance" [NIV], "passing over" [KJV]) of sins previously committed (Rom 3:25). Here, there is a clear echo of the LORD passing over the Jewish homes on the night of the Passover, but visiting Egyptian homes in order to strike the firstborn sons in judgment on behalf of their families. On the night of the eschatological Passover (1 Cor 5:7), God "passed over" the family of mankind but visited Calvary, where he struck his beloved Son—his firstborn, and our elder brother (Rom 8:17, 29). Jesus is the Redeemer (Rom 3:21), the gōēl of his people. There is not only an allusion to the Passover in the use of paresis but also to the way it was used by the translators of Isaiah, who, in a second exodus context, used the same term to speak of Yahweh keeping back his anger from Israel (Isa 64:10–12; 42:14 [LXX]; 63:15 [LXX]).

"Justification" (Rom 3:24) is also a new exodus term. When Israel was brought out of exile in Babylon, she was said to have been justified (Isa 50:8; 53:11). The expression spoke of being removed from one kingdom and placed in another. While held in exile, Israel was defiled and shaped by the people who had taken her captive.[41] The return to her own land sanctified her, for she was cleansed from all that polluted her and enabled to live in the ways that God wanted.

Additionally, the suggested link between atonement and Passover is upheld by the reference to the display of God's righteousness (Rom 3:21–22) and justification (Rom 3:24, 26). These are motifs of the new exodus, especially as provided by Isaiah. Yahweh's act of redemption will not only justify his people but will justify to the nations his character as the covenant-keeping God. His righteousness refers to "his right acts" in being faithful to his promises. Yahweh—who promised to act to secure deliverance for Israel through his servant David—had now fulfilled his promises (Gen 15:13–14; Isa 55:1–13). His righteousness was universally displayed and his covenant faithfulness blazed abroad

---

38. See Moo, *Romans*, 246. However, Moo did not notice absorption of the Day of Atonement sacrifices into the Passover.

39. Beale, *Revelation*.

40. Shepherd, *Paschal*.

41. Bornkamm, *Damascus*, 102; Reumann, "Righteousnes," 445; Casey, "Earliest," 274; Käsemann, *Romans*, 41; Stuhlmacher, *Reconciliation*, 81.

when his own Son was given up to death. The Davidic Prince was not merely to provide sacrifices for the eschatological Passover—he *was* the eschatological Passover. As the king and Yahweh's firstborn over the kings of the earth (Ps 89:27), he was "put forward" (publicly displayed), and, as the king of the Jews, suffered death for his people in the midst of the Passover.

In addition to the above themes of public display, passing over, justification, and God's righteousness, there is the undisputable Paschal language of redemption (Rom 3:24) that came by Christ Jesus. The language of redemption is uniquely paschal—redemption and cannot be housed in any event other than the Passover. It is about how Yahweh delivered his people, which is the indisputable theme of the Passover. The mention of blood (Rom 3:25) reinforces this claim. The Passover was, therefore, about redemption secured through the shedding of blood.

Further support for the claim that Rom 3:24–25 is based on the Passover is provided by scholars who have attempted to identify the source of the text. It is generally agreed that the passage reflects a liturgical formula, which was used either as a baptismal or Eucharistic confession. Whichever it may be, both themes are strongly linked with the death of Christ and its setting in the context of the Passover.

The claim that the passage has an Adamic content[42] also fits the picture of the eschatological Passover. The redemption that Paul describes reverses the catastrophic effects of the fall, bringing man out of the spiritual bondage in which he has been incarcerated since the covenant with Yahweh was violated by Adam. It is a salvation that comes through faith in Christ Jesus. Paul concludes the section (Rom 3:26–28) by insisting that the law is fulfilled in the redemption which is in Christ. The Law and the Prophets, i.e., the whole of Scripture, had looked forward to this eschatological event of atonement and redemption. This salvation is not for the Jews alone but for all who will have faith in the character and saving work of God. It is available to all who are willing to submit to God's Spirit, having their hearts circumcised so that they can share in the Lord's Pesach (Passover).

If we go beyond the passage under consideration, we find further evidence of the influence that Paschal language and imagery had on Paul. Some studies have identified the Passover as formative in the composition of imagery used in Rom 5:1ff.,[43] while others have identified the same imagery behind the "dying and rising with Christ" in Rom 6:1ff.[44]

Significant support for the primacy of the Passover in Paul's thinking can be found in the Corinthian Epistles.[45] In 1 Cor 5:7b, Paul writes: "For Christ, our Passover lamb,

---

42. That is, the passage is framed around an argument about undoing the disastrous outcome of Adam's sin.

43. Whiteley, *Theology*, and "Atonement," 250, notes that the reference to being "justified by his blood" in Rom 5:9 reflects the Passover.

44. See footnotes on Rom 6:1 for details.

45. Contra Witherington, *Romans*, 92, who commenting on Rom 3:21–31 says: "It is telling that when Paul chooses to tell the story of Christ's atoning sacrifice in 3:21–31, with further development in ch.5, there are no OT quotations or really any convincing allusions to exodus discussions of sacrifice and liberation."

has been sacrificed."[46] If we acknowledge consistency in the apostle's thinking, his second letter will help to consolidate our understanding of his convictions. In 2 Cor 5:21, the death of Christ is described in terms suggesting a sin offering. This description should not be isolated from an earlier passage in the Epistle as if it was a different strand of tradition, for 2 Cor 5:21 follows a statement which is clearly a reference to the new exodus. The declaration: "Therefore, if anyone is in Christ he is a new creation" (2 Cor 5:17) is a distinct echo of the Isaianic promise of a new creation (Isa 65:17), which was part of the new exodus promise. Indeed, 2 Cor 5:1ff. deals with the temporal nature of the believers' earthly journey—a theme which depicts the church as the new exodus pilgrim community. If there is any doubt about this, Paul's use of the Isaianic servant material in the opening of 2 Cor 6 ought to allay our fears. The emergence of Israel from her shame and exile was the setting of the Servant Songs, the imagery being used by Paul to describe his ministry to a wayward section of the new Israel.

Further support is found for the link between atonement and Passover in the letter to the Galatians. Gal 1:3 is overtly new exodus material. The cultic event, describing the means of deliverance from wrath, is clearly presented in terms of a sin offering and is in a new exodus context (Gal 3:13).

Col 1:12–14 is the introduction to a hymn which also uses new exodus language. It describes how the Colossians were delivered from the kingdom of darkness and brought into the kingdom of Christ. The hymn concludes in v. 20, where it uses atonement imagery to describe what the sacrifice of redemption has achieved: "and through him to reconcile to himself all things, whether things on earth or things in heaven, by making peace through his blood, shed on the cross" (Col 1:20). Christ's sacrifice has achieved nothing less than the reconciliation to himself of "all things." We have noted the Paschal significance of the phrase in v. 15: "firstborn of/over all creation."[47] In v. 20, we find the merger of Passover and Day of Atonement imagery with no hint of an explanation. The text is clearly influenced by the merger of these feasts in Ezek 45:21–25. Indeed, John 1:29 reflects this tradition also—the Baptist's proclamation indicating that it was well

---

46. Note that Paul does not use the word "lamb." He simply says that "Christ, our Passover, has been sacrificed for us." The addition of "lamb" has resulted in the loss of Paul's emphasis that Christ is the Paschal sacrifice because he is the Lord's firstborn, the appointed offering for atonement. See Holland, *Contours*, 237–74.

47. The NIV opts for the phrase: "over all creation," reflecting its translators' preference for a hierarchical meaning. The more natural Greek translation is: "of all creation." This reading is much more suited to the theme of the immediate context, where there has been a rescue from the kingdom of darkness. The language of sacrifice in this passage points to an important Paschal theme, which opens doors to a greater understanding of Christian teaching. Paul never refers to Christ as "the Lamb of God." 1 Cor 5:7b is not an exception. No Greek text has "lamb," but reads: "Christ, our Passover, has been sacrificed." Although Paul never uses the term "lamb" to describe Christ, he regularly uses the term, "the Son of God" (Rom 5:10; 8:3, 32; Gal 4:4; Col 1:13). This answers the question of Christ being designated "the firstborn of all creation" in Col 1:15. There again, in the context of the second exodus motif (Col 1:12–14), Paul describes Christ in soteriological, not ontological, terms. It can be shown that the early church dropped the title "Redeemer" in favor of the more important and cultic-focused term, "firstborn." Such reasoning can be explained by an examination of the significance of the status and role of the firstborn in Hebrew thought and cult, particularly in relation to the Passover. See Holland, *Contours*, 237–73.

known in Judaism as well as in the early church:[48] "The next day John saw Jesus coming toward him and said, 'Look, the Lamb of God, who takes away the sin of the world!'"

The "washing" in Eph 5:26 is a corporate event.[49] It is the church's baptism, and widely acknowledged to be based on Ezek 16:9–14. In this OT text, Yahweh tells how he chose Israel, redeeming and washing her. He made her clean through his word in order that she might be his bride. This being so, it would be natural to see Eph 5:25 as referencing the Passover sacrifice because the first Passover was recognized as the marriage between Yahweh and Israel. It is natural, therefore, that the eschatological Passover should become the occasion of the Messiah's marriage to his bride. Indeed, in Eph 1:7, the sacrifice has already been described in Paschal language as "redemption through his blood." It is significant that the Jews read from the Song of Solomon during the Passover Feast, for the feast and the Song celebrate Yahweh's love for his people. They both look forward to the eschatological divine marriage.

Ongoing Paschal/Exodus Themes in the Bible

The exodus affected the social and religious lives of Israel for all time. All Israel's ethical decisions would be based on the fact that Yahweh had redeemed her. Because of this redemption, the Israelites had to treat aliens in their land with the respect which they had craved in Egypt (Ex 22:21). As a nation, Israel's identity was determined by the covenant her ancestor Abraham had entered into with Yahweh, and the redemption God had wrought in delivering her from Egypt. She was the nation with whom God was in covenant and towards whom he had acted in saving mercy.

While insight into Israel's social life is well documented, aspects of her religious life are not so well known. One example is God's taking of the Levites in place of the firstborn sons in Israel who were spared in the Passover (Num 8:18). Immediately after the Passover event, God told Moses to consecrate to him the firstborn in Israel, including men and of animals (Exod 13:1–2). The intention was for these firstborn to be given over to God when the Israelites entered Canaan. The two exceptions to the consecration of the firstborn was the firstborn of the families of Israel and the firstborn of the donkey. The first was because the whole purpose of the Passover was to spare Israel's sons and the latter because of the practical value the donkeys had for the Jewish economy (Exod 13:11–15). Three months after leaving Egypt, Israel camped at the foot of Mount Sinai. While Moses was in the mountain, the Israelites demanded that Aaron the priest make gods for their protection. Aaron complied, crafting a golden calf. Many of God's firstborn were among the Israelites who worshipped the idol.

In response to God's anger at the nation's unfaithfulness, men of the tribe of Levi volunteered to obey God's command. They went up and down the camp, putting idol worshippers to death (Exod 32:27–28). Because of their obedience, God substituted them, man for man, for his firstborn (Num 3:12, 44–45) and set the tribe of Levi apart to become his possession. The two hundred and seventy-three firstborn without cor-

---

48. See Dunn, "Understanding," 125–41.

49. See Best, *Ephesians*, 543; Hoehver, *Ephesians*, 756.

responding Levites had to be redeemed with money—five shekels of silver each (Num 3:40–51). The Levites were officially consecrated as belonging to God and as part of the ceremony Aaron presented them as a wave offering to the Lord (Num 8:5–14). This account actually supplements an earlier account, for Yahweh had claimed the firstborn, designating them to priestly service because he spared their lives in the Passover by accepting lambs as a substitutionary atonement (Num 3:42–49; 8:17–23).

The function of the Levites was two-fold. First, they were given as gifts to Aaron and his sons (the priests), to assist them (under their supervision) in the Tent of Meeting. They would do the work of the tabernacle on behalf of the Israelites (Num 3:5–9; 8:22). Second, they were to atone for the Israelites lest they be judged. As reward for their work, the Levites would receive the tithes that the Israelites presented "as an offering to the LORD" (Num 18:24).

This Levitical arrangement makes a valuable contribution when considering the atoning significance of the Passover. The vicarious nature of the death of the firstborn is reflected in the atonement the Levites made on behalf of the Israelites: "Of all the Israelites, I have given the Levites as gifts to Aaron and his sons to do the work at the Tent of Meeting on behalf of the Israelites and to make atonement for them so that no plague will strike the Israelites when they go near the sanctuary" (Num 8:19).

The unexpected statement "to make atonement" cannot be a reference to making sacrifices, for the Levites were excluded from such service on pain of death (Num 18:1–7). Num 8:19 suggests that in some way, their very presence performed a propitiatory act by turning the wrath of Yahweh from the people when they approached the sanctuary. This protection is commented on earlier in the book of Numbers, where instructions are given for the locations of the different tribes in relation to the tabernacle when Israel set up camp. Num 1:53a says: "The Levites, however, are to set up their tents around the tabernacle of the Testimony so that wrath will not fall on the Israelite community." The LXX has substituted ἁμάρτημα "sin" for the Hebrew קֶצֶף (qeṣep) "wrath." The translators of the NIV have correctly followed the Hebrew with: "so that wrath will not fall," anticipating the Num 8:19 text. Thus, the Levites, who were substituted for the firstborn, continue their propitiatory function. This takes place outside of the tabernacle, endorsing the earlier suggestion that it had nothing to do with the offering of sacrifices for the nation. Just as the slain lambs saved the firstborn from wrath on the night of the Passover, so the substitutes for the firstborn, the Levites, continued to perform this same function in keeping God's wrath away from the people when they went near the sanctuary.

Obviously, it could be claimed that the Levites prevented wrath coming upon the nation by fulfilling cultic requirements. If they failed to fulfill the duties allotted to them, then wrath would come upon the people. But this interpretation does not do justice to the strong statement: "make atonement for the Israelites." The statement is emphatic. The Levites are there "to make atonement" for the people so that the plague would not come upon them when they come to the tent of meeting. The statement is not about averting wrath by fulfilling cultic regulations. In their ministry of atonement, the Levites paralleled the ministry of the firstborn. On the night of the Passover, each firstborn was designated to protect his family; now, the Levites provide an ongoing protection for the nation.

This interpretation finds support in the passage's rabbinical interpretation, atonement being restricted to the firstborn. However: "This prerogative was then conferred upon the tribe of Levi who, moreover, dedicating themselves, man for man, to the service of the Lord, served as an atonement for the firstborn, that they might not be destroyed as they deserved."[50]

From this discussion, we can see how the propitiatory nature of the Passover was upheld by the Levitical arrangements that flowed from it—arrangements that were essentially about an ongoing propitiation of God's wrath.

3:21 But now a righteousness from God, apart from the law, has been made known, to which the Law and the Prophets testify. The righteousness[51] that has been secured through the death of Jesus is apart from the law. It cannot annul the law as though it did not matter, because God could not accept any arrangement that was unjust. This righteousness, though apart from the law, had to satisfy the justice that it demanded. This is not a scheme that has been devised as a last attempt to solve the problem of sin—it is one "to which the Law and the Prophets testify."[52]

3:22 This righteousness from God comes through faith in Jesus Christ to all who believe. There is no difference. This is a different righteousness from that known by the returning exiles, to which the law and the prophets testified. In their case, the righteous-

---

50. Ginzberg, *Legends,* 3:226; North, *Numbers,* 69, says: "it remains quite obscure what in fact is meant by this." Gray, *Numbers,* 81, says the Levites screened the people from the anger that would be evoked if the service of the firstborn or their substitutes was withheld. This, however, is not following the sense of the text. Noordtzij, *Numbers,* 80, also sees the passage referring to the danger of committing cultic errors. A similar view is given by McNeile, *Numbers,* 46. Budd, *Numbers,* 93, cites Péter who says the laying-on of hands in the consecration of the Levites (v.16) is not a reference to consecration, but is an act of substitution or identification. This would favor our proposed exegesis, as does Dunn's suggestion, "Understanding," 135, that the significance of the laying-on of hands in order to consecrate the Levites is linked with the laying-on of hands on the blasphemer before execution (Num 8:10; Lev 24:14). The Levite's consecration is part of the judgment of Passover; see Ginzberg, *Legends,* 3:226. Herrmann, *TDNT,* 3: 301–10, points out that Ps 79:8–9 says: "Do not hold against us the sins of our fathers." He points out that the ministry of the Levites is intended to atone, and appeals to Num 8:8–32 (especially v.19; cf. Num 1:53; 18:5). Kidner, "Metaphors," 119ff., says that, in Num 8:10ff., the Levites had hands laid on them and were offered as living sacrifices to the Lord. Procksch, *TDNT,* 4:328–35, points to Num 18:16 and Ps 49:8 for the redemption of the firstborn. There is, in some way, an atoning significance in the very presence of the Levites—a presence which substitutes for the firstborn; see also Garnet, "Constructions," 147.

51. It is theologically impossible that this phrase should mean "a righteousness from God." A better translation is, "God's saving justice" (NJB). See Wright, *Romans,* 465. For further discussion, see Excursus D: Justification in the theology of Paul, pages 107–30. Linguistically, the NIV is technically beyond dispute but theologically questionable.

52. Meyer, "Formula," 198–208; Wilckens, *Übersetzt,* 1:199, says that Rom 3:21–26 is the basis of Romans, the rest of the letter being an expansion. Käsemann, *Romans,* 38, says Rom 3:21–26 is obscure because Paul has not identified the tradition he has used, and has interpreted it by additions. Knox, "Romans," 431, says of Rom 3:24–26 that while it is one of the most important passages in the letter, it is unclear what Paul is trying to say. I would suggest that the Paschal context and interpretation removes uncertainty over the passage's origin and subject matter.

ness of God had been displayed in his faithfulness to the covenant. He had not spared his people from suffering but delivered them over to the Babylonians, thus fulfilling the covenantal curses of Deut 11:26. Righteousness (deliverance) came when God was satisfied that his people had paid the price for their sins through their sufferings in Babylon (Isa 40:2). The Israelites had served the sentence that the law demanded, and now they were returning home!

However, their return home was a prelude to the final salvation. This great act of salvation, which the prophets had foretold, would deal with sin in a different way from the Babylonian deliverance. Sin would be dealt with once and for all; there would be no more sacrificial offerings. Indeed, this restoration would not be geographical or political, as the Jews would have wanted; it would be a restoration to God's eternal presence, where no sin would be tolerated and no evil would gain entrance. To provide a lesser salvation would be a denial of God's holiness. For this righteousness to be accepted by God, it had to put away sin and cleanse his people completely.

In saying this righteousness comes through faith in Jesus Christ, the NIV (like many other translations) has sidestepped the conclusions of much recent scholarly work. Many scholars accept that the expression should be translated: "by the faithfulness of Jesus Christ."[53] This rendering, apart from its linguistic merits, has the great advantage in removing salvation from dependency on a person's faith. The sensitive soul will always ask the question: "Do I have enough or the right kind of faith?" Paul's statement speaks of Christ's faithfulness as the grounds of salvation. Of course this does not remove the need for faith, as the rest of the NT makes clear, but it lays a much firmer foundation. We are saved by God because of the faithfulness of his Son, who achieved—through obedience and death—the great work of salvation.

In the phrase: "There is no difference," Paul again stresses the culpability of Jews and Gentiles. However, while the proclamation of the Gospel is all inclusive, salvation is only for those who embrace it.

3:23 For all have sinned and fall short of the glory of God. When the Jews in Rome heard this statement, they would have known it reflected part of their painful history. Not only did it refer to the head of the human family sinning and bringing all of his offspring into a state of rebellion against God, but it also alluded to Israel in exile. God had said of the nation: "I have created you for my glory" (Isa 43:7); but in exile, she was a picture of shame and sinfulness. Paul's kinsmen could acknowledge these ancestral sins, but could not accept they were in a state of exile too. This exile was far worse than being in Egypt or Babylon, for like the Gentiles they were dwelling in the kingdom of darkness (Acts 7:51–58).

3:24 And are justified freely by his grace through the redemption that came by Christ Jesus. This final act of justification is not the result of the community being punished for her sin, but of her representative taking the guilt of his fellow men. Paul says

---

53. Hays, ΠΙΣΤΙΣ, 7114–49; Campbell, *Debate*, 265–85. Contra Moo, *Romans*, 224. For the most recent discussions see Bird, *Faith*.

this justification has been achieved by Christ Jesus. By deliberately putting "Christ" first in the title, "Christ Jesus," Paul emphasizes that Jesus is the Messiah—the promised one who would deliver his people from bondage (see commentary on Rom 1:3). Because Jesus is the Son of David (who the Scriptures had promised would be raised up for his people), all that he does is according to the Scriptures.

Paul states that the church was justified freely by God's grace "through the redemption that came by Christ Jesus." The Jews had been justified when God delivered them from the control of their oppressors. They had claimed to be the people of God—a claim that seemed ridiculous in light of their condition (Ps 80). But it was a valid claim, which God justified when he delivered them from exile. Later in the letter, Paul writes that Jesus was "delivered over to death for our sins and was raised to life for our justification" (Rom 4:25), meaning that God delivered, or justified, his people when he raised up his Son, the promised seed of David. When he did this, he also redeemed his people.[54]

This act of redemption exceeds anything that God achieved for his people in Egypt or Babylon. On the night of the Passover, the sacrificial lambs served as substitutes for the Hebrew firstborn. Each Jewish family slew a lamb, smearing its blood on the lintel and doorposts. When the LORD came through Egypt, he saw the blood and passed over their homes. Thus, the blood of the Passover lambs redeemed the Jews. Their deliverance from Babylon was also an act of redemption (Isa 52:9; 54:5–6; 59:20; 62:12). However there was no vicarious sacrifice provided;[55] the Jewish people themselves were punished for the sins that caused their exile (Is 40:2). Nevertheless, Israel's deliverance was an act of redemption, for she was released by God from bondage; Yahweh raised up the Persians to conquer the Babylonians so that the Jews could return home. The price of Israel's redemption was the overthrow of the Babylonians, which the sovereign God of history used to fulfill his word to his people.

The redemption that has come by Christ Jesus, however, is totally different. It is one in which the covenant community is justified freely, not as the result of its own suffering but through the shedding of the blood of Christ Jesus. The first point is important, because this redemption is as a result of the grace of God. We do not get what we deserve, but the Jews, when sent into exile, fully got what they deserved. Once the suffering that God considered appropriate had been completed (Isa 51:17–23), he delivered/redeemed them. Paul, however, is not talking about a temporary exile, where it is possible to be punished and the past put behind. He is talking about an eternal exile from the presence of God. This is a totally different situation from anything depicted in Israel's history. This exile in the kingdom of darkness came about when man became bound to Satan in a covenant relationship, enslaving him in hopeless and, humanly speaking, inescapable bondage.

---

54. Campbell, "Atonement," 237–50, rejects the business model as the basis of Rom 4:25 and advocates a biblical theological one.

55. The Suffering Servant (Isa 53) must be commented upon briefly. From Yahweh's perspective, his death was essential for Israel's deliverance, but for Israel, there was no way that she would acknowledge a suffering Messiah. Of course, the early church had no such difficulty, and saw the passage as speaking about her Messiah—the one Israel had rejected.

Because he was the representative of humankind and the appointed caretaker for God's world, when Adam disobeyed and entered into an unholy alliance with Satan the whole of creation became a victim of his sin. In that fatal act of rebellion, Adam discharged himself from the love of his Creator by embracing the lies and false hope of the prince of darkness. As a result, all that Yahweh had created became enslaved to Sin/Satan and exiled from his presence.[56] Here, it must suffice to say that the nature of the exile with which the death of Jesus deals is of a different dimension and order than any other in human history. It requires an act of cosmic redemption—a redemption that the offender can in no way achieve—and an act of atonement, which no creature in the whole of creation could offer.

The redemption that Paul writes about "came by Christ Jesus." At first glance, his is not a surprising statement, for the redemption of the Jews from Egypt was by Moses, and the redemption from Babylon was by a Persian king (Isa 45:1–4). It becomes startling, however, when we read Paul's next clause. He describes the work of Christ as, "justified freely by his grace through the redemption." This is unusual because justification has nothing to do with redemption in OT terms unless we appreciate the merger noted earlier, when Ezekiel brought the Day of Atonement sacrifices into the orb of the Passover—the feast which the prophet saw as a great act of redemption.

3:25a God presented him as a sacrifice of atonement, through faith in his blood. The redemption achieved by Christ is unique. It is the result of God giving up to death the Messiah (Christ Jesus), who is the king, the Son of God (Ps 2:7; Rom 1:3–4). It is a redemption that exceeds any other, causing one hymn writer to pen: "Who is a pardoning God like Thee, and who has grace so rich and free?"[57] God has provided for atonement and redemption through the sacrifice of his own Son. In chapter 8, Paul will explain the cosmic dimension of this redemption—a marvelous truth that he has dealt with elsewhere (cf. Col 1:15–19).[58]

The word προτίθημι (protithēmi) "presented" means "publicly displayed" or "set forth." Here, we have another hint that Paul is describing Jesus as the Passover victim. Of all the sacrifices the Levitical law legislated for, the Passover sacrifices were the only ones that were displayed for all to see. While the Passover lambs' blood was daubed on the doorposts and lintels of Hebrew houses, the blood of all other sacrifices was offered to God within the temple. The cultic significance of *protithēmi* is supported by the fact that it was a technical term for the presenting of a sacrifice.[59]

---

56. This concept will be dealt with later. See excursus D: Justification in the theology of Paul, pages 107–30.

57. Samuel Davies, 1723–61.

58. The connection between Rom 3:25 and Col 1:14 is supported by Käsemann, *Romans*, 96, who says that *apolutrōsis* is not a reference to the sacral manumission of slaves as claimed by Deissmann, Lietzmann, Althaus, etc, but is a liturgical expression, similar to those used in 1 Cor 1:30; Col 1:14; Eph 1:7, which emphasizes the eschatological event. The formula points to the mediator of salvation, a view supported by the author's discussion of 1 Cor 6:20 in Holland, *Contours*, chapter 6.

59. See Zeisler, *Romans*, 115. Longenecker, "Neglected," 478–80, argues that the phrase διὰ "τῆς πίστεως in Rom 3:25a should be regarded as an original part of a quoted formula, and should not be

The term (*hilastērion*) "sacrifice of atonement" has already been examined. This term was traditionally translated "propitiation"—a translation which I have argued should be retained. This meaning has been largely rejected because the text does not support a Day of Atonement setting in which propitiation was considered to belong. In the minds of the majority of scholars, there was no propitiatory value in the blood of the Passover lamb, and therefore, it was not given the consideration it deserved. However, once it is appreciated there are good reasons to say that the early church, through the influence of the Ezek 45:25 text, saw the Passover to be a sacrifice of propitiation, the natural setting for the passage becomes obvious.[60]

The Greek has διὰ [τῆς] πίστεως ἐν τῷ αὐτοῦ αἵματι (*dia [tēs] pisteōs, en tō autou haimati*). This is better translated with the RSV: "by his blood, to be received by faith," rather than linking faith with propitiation/expiation. Thus, the relationship is not restored through faith but through the shedding of blood. Of course, this salvation is received by personal faith, but this is not the theme in this particular text.

Just as the Jews in Egypt had to put their faith in the efficacy of the blood of the Passover lambs on that eventful night, so all those who are threatened with judgment since Calvary must place their faith in the blood of Christ (the Christian Passover victim). The ones who trust in Christ's sacrifice believe they will escape the last judgment and be in his presence for evermore because of what God has done through his Son's death.

3:25b He did this to demonstrate his justice, because in his forbearance he had left the sins committed beforehand unpunished. The death of Jesus satisfies the dilemma of how a holy God can appear to deal so lightly with sin. There have been many times in human history when it seemed that he did not act justly and ignored man's wrongdoing. However, Paul is adamant that this was never the case. God chose not to take immediate action because he had a plan to rescue man from his condition of exile and judgment. In this saving act, he demonstrated that he took sin seriously—so seriously that it necessitated giving his beloved Son up to death in a demonstration of justice and love. Indeed, it was not merely a demonstration, it was an absolute necessity. Without Christ's death and resurrection, there could be no hope for humankind.

Paul says that God, in his forbearance (*paresis*), had left "sins committed beforehand unpunished." The term *paresis*, which means "passing over," is only found in Rom 3:25, so we are dependent on its context to understand its meaning. Once again, we find a distinct echo of the Passover in the passage, for on that night, the LORD "passed over" the sins of the Jewish people, leaving them unpunished (Exod 12:27). Paul is saying the reason

viewed as an insertion made by Paul. If this is correct, then Rom 3:25 reads: "whom God put forward as an atoning sacrifice, through (Jesus') faithfulness by means of his blood." Thus, the faithfulness of Christ is the basis through which covenant relationship with God is established. This view is supported by the emphasis that is given in Rom 5 on the importance of the obedience of Christ for the salvation of his people. See Garlington, "Obedience," 87–112.

60. Note Hays, "Believed" 66, "Paul's use of Old Testament texts suggests that his 'implied reader' not only knows scripture but also appreciates allusive subtlety. Whether the reader accepts the compliment or not, the apostle still delights in intertextual play."

God dealt so patiently with sin throughout history was not that he was indifferent but that, in his foreknowledge, he had a plan to address it. This plan was far beyond human imagination and only possible because of his prodigious love. The atonement, which was brought about by the death of Jesus, the Son of God, dealt with all the sins of God's people—past, present and future. Conversely, just as the Paschal lamb did not protect any who disregarded the word of Yahweh and who did not partake in the lambs' death by eating the Passover, Christ's death does not avail for unbelievers.

3.26 He did it to demonstrate his justice at the present time, so as to be just and the one who justifies those who have faith in Jesus. Paul returns to the theme of God's justice once more. There had been a question over how this would be settled from the time of the fall but now, through the death of Jesus, it has been settled. No one can ever question God's commitment to justice. He has dealt with sin by giving up his beloved Son to death, making him the Passover victim. He has demonstrated beyond doubt his love and justice, silencing forever any who would question his character.

By giving up Jesus to death, God is just and the one who justifies those who have faith in Jesus. When God justified Israel, she was in exile in Babylon and he rescued her. In doing this, he was justifying her claim to be his covenant people. Such a claim made by the Jews to their Babylonian captors would have been the source of much ridicule. But when God brought Israel back to her inheritance, he justified the claims she had made. She was shown to be the people of the covenant-keeping God to the whole world.

Paul is saying that God has now justified his people, i.e., those who have faith in Jesus. As we have seen previously, the word "justified" in the OT is used to speak of deliverance from exile. The thrust of Paul's argument (which comes to a climax in Rom 5:12ff.) is that God has delivered his people from the exile into which the first Adam took them.

THE MESSIAH KING AND HIS MERCY

WHERE, THEN, IS boasting? It is excluded. On what principle? On that of observing the law? No, but on that of faith. For we maintain that a man is justified by faith apart from observing the law. Is God the God of Jews only? Is he not the God of Gentiles too? Yes, of Gentiles too, since there is only One God, who will justify the circumcised by faith and the uncircumcised through that same faith. Do we, then, nullify the law by this faith? Not at all! Rather, we uphold the law. (Rom 3:27–31)

3:27 Where, then, is boasting? It is excluded. On what principle? On that of observing the law? No, but on that of faith. In commenting on boasting (Rom 2:17; 2:23), Paul echoes the warning of Jeremiah: "let him who boasts boast about this: that he understands and knows me, that I am the LORD" (Jer 9:24). The prophet was warning the exiles that in their temptation to take matters into their own hands, they were not trusting God. Jeremiah was warning the exiles not to seek deliverance from their enemies by attempting a rebellion. They were to accept that their condition was God's judgment upon them, and were not to plan their own salvation but to wait in faith for

God to fulfill his promise. Habakkuk addressed the same exiles saying, "the just shall live by faith" (Hab 2:4). Paul has already used this quotation in Rom 1:17, where he appeals for the same submission and faith.

Here, Paul urges the believers in Rome not to even think of boasting, for they would be bragging about their own accomplishments and understanding of the law. Such pride indicates they were seeing their own achievements to be the source of their salvation. However, their salvation was not on the basis of the works of the law[61] but on the basis of faith in God's intervention on their behalf. How appropriate for Paul to bring forward these quotations from the two prophets and apply them to the law boasting community in Rome!

3:28 For we maintain that a man is justified by faith apart from observing the law. Paul repeats himself. The issue is too important for there to be any confusion. Deliverance from Sin's domain[62] is not a human achievement but the result of God's saving activity. Again, he uses the term "justified" with its prophetic/covenantal meaning, rather than the forensic meaning with which it is so often credited. The framework of this OT setting does not exclude the features of the forensic model but goes beyond its restricted horizon. The OT's framework is deliverance, and here, in Rom 3:28, it is about the deliverance of the people of God from Satan's control. This is made clear by the term's association with redemption in v. 24. We shall consider this further in Rom 4:3. Paul is rejecting the deliverances of the OT in which the Jews boasted. These acts of salvation upon which had once depended and in which he had boasted continued to be his countrymen's hope and they were based on keeping the law. The apostle is appealing to his countrymen to put all their hope in the Messiah, whose death is the foundation for the eschatological deliverance and acceptance. This vital deliverance, which Jews and Gentiles all had to appropriate, was apart from observing the law.

3:29–30 Is God the God of Jews only? Is he not the God of Gentiles too? Yes, of Gentiles too, since there is only one God, who will justify the circumcised by faith and the uncircumcised through that same faith. In v. 30, the NIV translators have weakened Paul's argument by omitting εἴπερ (eiper) "if indeed." Instead, they translate it: "since there is only." If the Greek text is retained, the reading of the ASV should be followed: "Or is God the God of Jews only?" Paul, therefore, is saying: "Is he not the God of the Gentiles also? Yes, of the Gentiles also." The statement does not introduce a new argument, but brings the earlier argument to its conclusion.

Paul has returned to his earlier theme of God dealing with all people through faith (Rom 2:25–29). In asking if God is the God of the Jews alone, he answers his question by appealing to the law and the prophets who said that God was concerned for the Gentiles as well as the Jews. The covenant with Abraham (Gen 17:4–5; 22:18; 26:4) promised that all the nations of the earth would be blessed through his offspring, and the prophets

---

61. Contra, Wright, *Romans*, 480, and Cranfield, *Romans*, 219–20. Both say that *nomos* (law) refers to a principle.

62. The higher case is deliberately used as Paul makes clear in chapters 5–8 that sin, the singular, is a metonym for Satan.

repeatedly pointed to the time when the Gentiles would be accepted on an equal footing with the Jews (Isa 19:23–25; Hos 1:10). Both needed to know the salvation of God and be rescued from exile in Sin. To deny that God was the God of the Gentiles was to deny monotheism itself, and such a denial would sound the death knell of Israel's faith.

3:31 Do we, then, nullify the law by this faith? Not at all! Rather, we uphold the law. Paul was aware that the ultimate test for the Jewish believers in Rome was whether the matter discussed was according to the law. If he could not demonstrate this, he had no chance of convincing them that the Gospel he was preaching was from God. In saying the Gospel upholds the law, Paul is stressing that the law looked forward to God sending a deliverer who would bring salvation and the final revelation of himself. The law also looked to the time when Israel's bondage to sin would be over. The Gospel, therefore, fulfills the law.[63] The law was nothing less than a chaperone[64] to bring Jews and Gentiles to Christ. Thus, the law is not overruled, but fulfilled.

CONCLUSION OF ROMANS 3

Paul corrects any suggestion that Israel's history and calling count for nothing and discounts the suggestion that sin serves the purposes of God by magnifying his grace. Paul emphasizes that Jews and Gentiles share the same fallen condition—both are in danger of judgment. Once again, he brings together his OT evidence from material which principally relates to Israel's exile. His point is that Israel, like the Gentiles, is alienated from God.

He then tells of the salvation that God has brought about for all men (vv. 21–26). He relies heavily on atonement (propitiatory) vocabulary and redemption imagery drawn from the Egyptian exodus, and supplements this with such a range of second exodus promises from the prophets that they become the dominant and controlling structures of his ongoing theology. This new exodus, which has been underway since Calvary,[65] is possible only because God has put forward his Son as a propitiation for his people's sin.

We have seen how Paul has linked into the widely anticipated and longed for second exodus promises and how he has integrated these with the model of the Egyptian exodus to form the new exodus paradigm. This was not unique to him for it had been predicted by Ezekiel, whose writings had a widespread influence on the early church. Paul brings nothing essentially new to the theology of the early church, his contribution was to develop an already existing model and to help build a theological system that was especially supportive of allowing the Gentiles to be part of the new exodus community without conversion to Judaism. Paul explored this new exodus model to build a doctrine of justification that remained true to the OT understanding and that was again able to embrace the Gentiles without the need of circumcision.

63. For a summary of these OT predications and expectations see pages 8–9.

64. For the significance of the term "chaperone" rather than "schoolmaster," "prison warden," or "guard," see Holland, *Contours*, 211–12 and Holland, *Paul: Law, Spirit and the People of God*, forthcoming.

65. Because in the death of Christ the new covenant community were united with him sharing his exodus, see Luke 9:21 and Excursus E: Baptism into Christ, pages 168–77.

Paul concludes that Jews no longer have anything to boast about. God is now dealing with them on the same basis as the Gentiles. The implication is that Israel's special status is over, and the bride of the new covenant will not be the same as the one at the centre of the old. This will become clearer as the argument develops in the following chapters. Like the redemption from Egypt and Babylon was intended to be, the conclusion of this glorious redemption is the divine marriage. It is a marriage in which the bride will include both Jews and Gentiles who have been delivered from the kingdom of darkness and brought into the kingdom of God's Son.

ROMANS 4

THE MESSIAH KING AND THE PRINCIPLE OF HIS KINGDOM

WHAT THEN SHALL we say that Abraham, our forefather, discovered in this matter? If, in fact, Abraham was justified by works, he had something to boast about—but not before God. What does the Scripture say? "Abraham believed God, and it was credited to him as righteousness." Now when a man works, his wages are not credited to him as a gift, but as an obligation. However, to the man who does not work but trusts God who justifies the wicked, his faith is credited as righteousness. David says the same thing when he speaks of the blessedness of the man to whom God credits righteousness apart from works: "Blessed are they whose transgressions are forgiven, whose sins are covered. Blessed is the man whose sin the Lord will never count against him." Is this blessedness only for the circumcised, or also for the uncircumcised? We have been saying that Abraham's faith was credited to him as righteousness. Under what circumstances was it credited? Was it after he was circumcised, or before? It was not after, but before! And he received the sign of circumcision, a seal of the righteousness that he had by faith while he was still uncircumcised. So then, he is the father of all who believe but have not been circumcised, in order that righteousness might be credited to them. And he is also the father of the circumcised who not only are circumcised but who also walk in the footsteps of the faith that our father Abraham had before he was circumcised. It was not through law that Abraham and his offspring received the promise that he would be heir of the world, but through the righteousness that comes by faith. For if those who live by law are heirs, faith has no value and the promise is worthless, because law brings wrath. And where there is no law there is no transgression. Therefore, the promise comes by faith, so that it may be by grace and may be guaranteed to all Abraham's offspring—not only to those who are of the law but also to those who are of the faith of Abraham. He is the father of us all. As it is written: "I have made you a father of many nations." He is our father in the sight of God, in whom he believed—the God who gives life to the dead and calls things that are not as though they were. Against all hope, Abraham in hope believed and so became the father of many nations, just as it had been said to him, "So shall your offspring be." Without weakening in his faith, he faced the fact that his body was as good as dead—since he was about a hundred years old—and that Sarah's womb was also dead. Yet he did not waver through unbelief regarding the promise of God, but was strengthened in his faith and gave glory to God, being fully persuaded that God had power to do what he had promised. This is why "it was credited to him as righteousness." The words "it was credited to him" were written not for him alone, but also for us, to whom God will credit righteousness—for us who believe in him who raised Jesus our Lord from the dead. He was delivered over to death for our sins and was raised to life for our justification. (Rom 4:1–25)

INTRODUCTION

Chapter 4 of Romans provides a critical contribution to the doctrine of justification. Much of the doctrine's evolution and present-day application are rooted in how we have interpreted Paul's words to the Roman church.

Central to this has been a general understanding of Abraham's[1] justification recounted in Genesis 15, and Paul's subsequent use of the event in describing the justification that came to God's new covenant people through Christ. Pivotal to both is Gen 15:6 that speaks of God crediting righteousness to Abraham—that is, justifying him—because of his faith. Paul references Abraham's justification in Gen 15:6 throughout Rom 4, either by directly quoting the OT verse, or by alluding to the event in other parts of the chapter. It is foundational to Paul's understanding of justification.

Gen 15:6 is the only occasion where the writer of Genesis recorded that God credited righteousness to Abraham. However, despite this, most scholars[2] understand Paul's reference to Abraham's righteousness in Rom 4:22 as another occasion where God credited righteousness to the patriarch distinct from Gen 15:6, this time with the birth of Isaac. Additionally, many scholars believe both the Genesis narratives of the birth of Isaac (Gen 17:17; 18:1–15; 21:1–7) and the offering of Isaac as a sacrifice (Gen 22:15–17) show additional occasions of Abraham's justification.

Underlying all of this are the meanings of words: commonly accepted meanings associated with the justification language of Paul and other writers in both the New and Old Testaments. Because of tradition, culture or other factors, accepted meanings for particular words or phrases become part of a collective mindset such that there may be little thought given to alternatives or the writer's original intent when making application to a particular passage in Scripture. This is particularly evident when considering Paul's use of Gen 15:6 in Rom 4.

I believe a substantial case can be made there has been a widespread misunderstanding of Abraham's justification in Genesis 15:6, and Paul's subsequent use of it, by both Reformed and New Perspective theologians, and that this in turn has led to a misunderstanding of how Paul read and applied OT Scripture regarding justification. Additionally, there has been a like misunderstanding of Isaac's birth and the offering of him in sacrifice as additional occasions of Abraham's justification.

The following exegesis of Rom 4 will challenge the accepted understanding of the doctrine of justification in the following ways:

1. It will suggest the term "to credit righteousness" (to justify) has more meanings than are generally recognized.

2. It will examine how Genesis 15:6 uses the term, and will claim it means covenant making.

3. It will hold that Paul is in complete harmony with what Genesis says about justi-

---

1. References to the patriarchal couple will use their divinely given names.

2. Cranfield, *Shorter*, 93; Moo, *Romans*, 282; Morris, *Romans*, 211–12; Käsemann, *Romans*, 624; Stowers, *Reading*, 247; Fitzmyer, *Romans*, 386; Jewett, *Romans*, 335.

fication as making covenant; that he has not misread the OT text but followed its argument accurately.

4. Contrary to widespread opinion, it will attempt to show the Genesis account does not present either the birth of Isaac or the offering of him in sacrifice as occasions when Abraham was justified, but rather are records of covenant ratification ceremonies that make no mention of Abraham being credited righteousness because of their enactment.

5. Finally, in keeping with the Genesis account, it will argue Paul did not see the birth of Isaac to be an act of justification, as many understand him to say.

EXCURSUS D: JUSTIFICATION IN THE THEOLOGY OF PAUL

Prior to our verse-by-verse examination of Rom 4, however it will be helpful to explore several key issues surrounding the use of justification in Scripture, including its language and meanings, its place in salvation history, covenant making, Paul's writings, circumcision, and the law. We will also explore justification as a corporate event and as the foundation of covenantal relationship. We shall see that to one degree or another each has played a part in the origin of the justification doctrine, as well as its evolution and present-day application (or misapplication as the case may be).

The Language and Meanings of Justification

Justification language has its own semantic domain wherein reside all the words and phrases commonly associated with the doctrine, each with its own meaning that contributes to the doctrine's overall form and substance. Dominant among these meanings are "acquittal" and "imputation," which are drawn from legal and accounting usage. During the emergence of the Protestant Reformation in the sixteenth century, it was these two meanings that the Reformers focused upon, believing they framed Paul's understanding of justification. They understood that when Paul spoke of Christ's death and resurrection "justifying" men and women, he was saying that God was acquitting them of their sin, not counting them guilty. The Reformers also believed that it was because of this acquittal the redeemed would stand innocent before their judge, for God had imputed (credited) the righteousness of Christ to their accounts, so making them right before him.

Most Reformed theologians have embraced these two meanings, i.e. acquittal or being declared not guilty, and having Christ's righteousness imputed to believers, for interpreting Paul in Rom 4:3, 5, 6, 9, 11, 22, 24 and other key texts. Despite the importance of these two key meanings for Reformed understanding, they do not exhaust the semantic domain of justification. As we shall see, alternative meanings have been overlooked. These require evaluation for their influence on Paul's understanding of justification.

The New Perspective View

In recent years, the work of an Oxford scholar and subsequent debate has challenged this widely held Protestant understanding of justification. After studying the characteristics of Jewish religion at the time of Jesus and Paul, the scholar concluded the Jews of the period (known as Second Temple Judaism) had a different understanding of the purpose and value of the law from the one the Reformers believed that Paul held.[3] (As will be pointed out again in this commentary's review of Rom 5, for a Jew, the law mostly means the Mosaic law given at Sinai.) Instead of the Jews fearing the law, a position held by the Reformers, evidence suggested first century Judaism took positive delight in it, seeing it as Israel's greatest privilege and blessing. The scholar contended the law was not her accuser and enemy, as the Reformers thought, but her friend and guide.

As NT theologians considered the Oxford scholar's work, it gave rise to a stream of thought known as the New Perspective, which has come to represent a diversity of opinion with some common threads. Chief among them is a view that justification had more to do with Jewish-Gentile issues than with questions of the individual's status before God. This led to a desire to look afresh at the writings of Paul in the context of first century Judaism rather than the Reformation debates of the sixteenth century to see if greater clarification could be established.[4]

Understandably for some New Perspective theologians, this new approach to Paul, Judaism, and the law called into question the traditional view of Paul's doctrine of justification with its emphasis on the forensic legal and accounting framework of justification which supported meanings of acquittal and imputation. After all, if traditional understanding is correct—that Paul associated both meanings with the restoration of those whom the law had found guilty and condemned—how, then, could it also be true the Jews did not fear the law, but rather took delight in that which condemned them?

Attempting to resolve an apparent Pauline contradiction, some theologians concluded Paul had misrepresented the Jewish position on the law. However, another group of New Perspective theologians, who agreed with some of the Oxford scholar's conclusions on the one hand, were also of the firm conviction that Paul was a Jew who always rejoiced in his heritage. As such, he had not only represented the law correctly, but was also consistent with the OT in his belief that the law found its fulfillment in the coming of the Messiah, Jesus, who completed God's plan of salvation for his covenant people.[5]

These New Perspective theologians believe instead that it was the Reformers who had misunderstood Paul. This, they claim led the Reformers to a mistaken understanding of Paul's doctrine of justification. These New Perspective theologians argue that the misunderstanding arose because the Reformers were engaged in a heated debate with the Roman Catholic church over legalism, and they had assumed Paul was engaged in the same debate with Judaism. The Protestant Reformers were concerned with the way the church of Rome abused the law, teaching her members they could buy, or rather, earn salvation with good works, in this case through the purchase of indulgences, and so be justified (clear themselves of guilt) before God. Knowing that her adherents could not

---

3. Sanders, *Palestinian*.

4. For a helpful summary see Mattison "Introduction and Summary." Online at: http://www.thepaul page.com/new-perspective/introduction-and-summary/. The "Paul Page" provides extensive articles and book reviews concerning the development and positions of the New Perspective on Paul.

5. The two leading New Perspective scholars are J. D. G. Dunn and N. T. Wright.

keep the law's demands, the church of Rome had offered indulgences as an alternative way of salvation for those who had not committed mortal sin. By buying indulgences, the people could reduce some of the horrors of purgatory. Many, despite being extremely poor, eagerly embraced this "salvation," with the result that vast sums of money poured into the church's coffers.[6]

The Reformers protested against this practice, and argued against the possibility of securing salvation by works of any sought. They based their case on Paul's argument that Gentiles could not become members of the covenant community (i.e., become saved), by doing the works of the law. They argued from this that buying indulgences could not make them right with God because we can do nothing to make ourselves right with our judge. By confusing purchase of indulgences with seeking covenant membership through such initiatory rights as circumcision, the Reformers lost the framework of Paul's argument. Nevertheless, by proclaiming people could not earn their salvation, that God's justification was a gift of grace made possible by the acquittal of sin and imputation of righteous provided through Christ and not by the works of men, they were definitely true to the message of Paul. Thus, the New Perspective leaders claim that the true meaning of justification was lost as a result of the Reformers debate over indulgences. This misunderstood led to confusion over Paul's language of justification.

The New Perspective theologians had rightly identified that Paul's debate with the Judaizers was not one about grace versus legalism, in the sense that man must keep the moral law to be saved, but it was about God's acceptance of the Gentiles without circumcision (without works). This new understanding effectively challenged the common Protestant understanding of the doctrine of justification by moving the focus of justification away from the Reformers' legal and accounting framework and placing the imagery in the arena of covenant membership. This changed the reading of many NT texts. One of the movement's leaders went so far as to claim the Reformation had been a mistake,[7] arguing the biblical doctrine of justification was not about God making people right with him–that is, acquitted from sin and imputed or credited with righteousness—but rather that it referred to God declaring people to be in a right relationship with himself. In this understanding, justification was not about soteriology (how to be saved), but about ecclesiology (how membership of the church is defined). They are related, but as the focal point for justification, they are not the same.

The emergence of this view on justification has prompted endless debate. Many—especially those not trained in biblical theology—have found New Perspective arguments attractive, fascinating, and persuasive. Others have fought for a Reformed understanding, seeking to defend what they consider a vital component of biblical truth.[8]

The following discussion seeks to work through this debate while exploring Paul's use of justification language in Rom 4. While acknowledging the contribution these New Perspective theologians have made, I believe they are wrong in rejecting the Reformers'

---

6. The wealth accrued from the sale of these indulgences paid for the building of St. Peters in Rome.

7. See Wright, *What*.

8. See Carson, *Variegated*; Gathercole, *Boasting*; Westerholm, *Perspectives*; Piper, *Future*.

understanding of justification. I wish to make the case that the New Perspective scholars have correctly identified the Gentile debate as the context for much of the justification language in Romans and Galatians, but that their fuller argument only holds together when certain texts contrary to its position are ignored. I want to also go further, and say justification is even more glorious than the truth the Reformers themselves grasped. My only complaint with the Reformers' thinking is they did not see the larger biblical picture, which would have made their argument watertight and convincing. Such a complaint, however, is tendered with the awareness of their massive strides in the understanding of biblical truth. The Reformers came from a place of great spiritual darkness to discover the liberating doctrine of justification. For this, we need to be forever grateful.

Additional Meanings of Justification

As already mentioned the two commonly identified meanings of justification have their roots in legal and accounting languages. However, recent scholarship has shown acquittal and imputation are not the only semantic domains of justification.[9] For example, when Paul writes about justification in Rom 3:26, it is evident he was using another OT meaning employed by Isaiah. The prophet spoke of Israel being "justified" when she was delivered from Babylon and returned to Jerusalem and to the promised land.[10] In this case, justification was not the salvation of individual Jews from guilt, but related to salvation history and Israel's experience of God's faithfulness. Before we look at this and other examples of justification in detail, we shall focus on Paul's introduction to Rom 4 (vv. 1–6), where he appeals to two OT texts: one we have already introduced—Gen 15:6 concerning Abraham—and Ps 32:2 concerning David. These, along with Paul's language in Rom 4:1–6, are the linchpins of the Reformed doctrine of justification. Therefore, before considering additional meanings for justification, it is *vital* we understand what is going on in these passages.

Justification and Salvation History

Reformed understanding of Gen 15:6 is that the Hebrew phrase וַיַּחְשְׁבֶהָ לּוֹ צְדָקָה:, "he credited it to him as righteousness," speaks of Abraham's acquittal from sin.[11] The declaration follows Abraham hearing and believing God would give him a son. Reformed scholars believe God credited righteousness to Abraham in the legal sense because of this act of faith; that God acquitted him of guilt, declaring him innocent and so made him acceptable in his sight. Their argument, however, raises two questions: if legal acquittal from the guilt of sin is an outcome of God crediting righteousness, why is there no mention of sin in Gen 15? Second, what has the promise of a son to do with Abraham's justification?

---

9. See Zeisler, *Righteousness*; Hill, *Words*.

10. But in the LORD all the descendants of Israel will be found righteous and will exult. (Isa 45:25 NIV) בַּיהוָה יִצְדְּקוּ וְיִתְהַלְלוּ כָּל־זֶרַע יִשְׂרָאֵל: (Isa 45:25 WTT). After the suffering of his soul, he will see the light *of life* and be satisfied; by his knowledge my righteous servant will justify many, and he will bear their iniquities (Isa 53:11 NIV). מֵעֲמַל נַפְשׁוֹ יִרְאֶה יִשְׂבָּע בְּדַעְתּוֹ יַצְדִּיק צַדִּיק עַבְדִּי לָרַבִּים וַעֲוֹנֹתָם הוּא יִסְבֹּל: (Isa 53:11 WTT).

11. See Murray, *Romans*, 1.131.

To the first question, the narrative of Gen 15 and its key ideas contain no evidence to uphold the traditional use of legal or accounting language in order to understand the phrase "he credited it to him as righteousness" in Gen 15:6. Admittedly, it can seem Paul reads it this way when in Rom 4:6 he quotes Ps 32:2, which is about the acquittal of David's sin and his "being credited righteousness apart from works." The presence of a reference to Ps 32:2 alongside a reference to Gen 15:6 have suggested they are speaking about the same thing. Because Ps 32:2 clearly speaks of David's acquittal from his sin, the Reformed view has assumed Gen 15:6 carries this meaning also.

Thus the problem of this interpretation assumes Paul means the same when speaking of both Abraham's and David's justification. Even though the justification of these men is vital to Paul's argument regarding the reconciliation of man to God, one should consider each OT use of the term on its own merit. Justification (crediting righteousness) in Gen 15 may mean something different from justification in Ps 32, with the differing meanings augmenting each other, yielding a larger, composite meaning of the term. If Ps 32:2 speaks of the acquittal of David's sin, than what does Gen 15:6 say about justification?

As there is no mention of sin in Gen 15:6 (there most definitely is in Ps 32!), we must search its context carefully for clues as to how the writer used the expression: "he credited it to him as righteousness." We shall see the justification of Abraham in Gen 15:6 is essentially covenantal, with God committing himself to delivering (saving) his people, i.e., Abraham and his descendants, and that this understanding compliments other key passages in which justification language occurs.

God foretold his plan of salvation in Gen 3:15 as the enmity he would place between Satan and the seed of the woman. He then revealed that plan in Gen 15:4–6 with the promise of a son to Abraham, and that from this son would come many descendants. This puts the patriarch's justification at the heart of salvation history. However, it was not Abraham, but God's people—the offspring of the child of promise—who are the focal point of that promise. This understanding becomes clearer in Gen 17:1–8 when Yahweh, committing to deliver Abraham and his seed from slavery and oppression, widens his promise to include the entire human race. It is, therefore, a covenantal promise of a collective, corporate salvation that God will justify a people.

We will note later how this corporate understanding of justification is also at the heart of NT teaching. For example, Paul uses the full import of a corporate covenantal meaning of justification when he reasons the seed who is to bless the whole world is, in fact, Christ (Gal 3:16). He is "the seed to whom the promise referred" (Gal 3:19), and it is he who brings justification to God's people as he saves them from their sins. This supports the suggestion that the justification found in Gen 15 is foremost covenantal in nature.

In making this claim, we are not challenging the vitally important doctrine of justification as taught by the Reformers, but making the point that the legal and accounting elements of justification can be located in more appropriate texts than Genesis 15. If the meaning of the phrase: "he credited it to him as righteousness" in Gen 15:6 is covenantal, in that its focus is the fulfillment of the promise foretold in Gen 3:15, then we should not import meanings of justification such as acquittal and imputation that came in later through NT teaching into Gen 15:6. Our task must first be to hear the use of the term in its historical context, and understand its meaning and significance at that particular moment of redemption history. As stated, there is nothing in Gen 15:6 to suggest it is about the forgiveness of Abraham's sin.

What we also cannot to do is to merge the meanings found in the justification's semantic domain to form a one-size-fits-all meaning, which we then impose on all texts containing justification language.[12] To do so would spread linguistic naivety and confusion throughout the teaching of Scripture. We must consider each occurrence of justification language in its own context, with the appropriate meaning selected from within the semantic domain.[13] Furthermore, we must be aware it is possible for a new meaning of a term to emerge, and for this to come to dominate the semantic domain. The danger of such domination is its imposition by translators and exegetes on texts that alter the intent of the original voices. In this matter, the New Perspective theologians who seek to define the justification doctrine in primarily ecclesiological terms are experts, imposing a blanket meaning of justification on texts where it is not appropriate.

Additionally, in seeking to understand what Paul means by his use of the Gen 15:6 phrase "it was credited to him as righteousness" in Rom 4:3, we have to proceed just as carefully. We must ascertain if he takes the meaning of the phrase as found in Ps 32:2 regarding David's sin to be the same as found in Gen 15:6 regarding Abraham's faith. If the evidence supports this, then we must accept he has read Gen 15:6 in the light of Ps 32:2, and seek to understand why the separate meanings just discussed have been lost. However, if we find there are other meanings in Gen 15:6 and Ps 32:2, which scholars have not yet identified, we have to establish whether Paul was aware of them and used them. To make exegesis even more demanding, we must also recognize the apostles did give new or wider meanings to OT texts.[14] As far as biblical theology is concerned, we need to know how and why such development happened. However, even when an apostolic expansion of meaning has occurred, we must not thoughtlessly read this into all texts using the term, particularly those written earlier than the identified development.

To sum up the reasoning thus far, if there is a difference between the meanings of "he credited it to him as righteousness" in Gen 15:6 (covenant making) and Ps 32:2 (acquittal from sin), we need to decide if Paul was aware of it and ascertain whether he retained it in his respective quotes in Rom 4. If he did, then we have to decide how this affects the reading of Rom 4:1–25, and in particular his doctrine of justification.

12. This is what both Dunn and Wright do.

13. We have noted earlier that we have to do this with δουλος. In Rom 8, we shall see that we have to do this with σαρχ. Alexandra, "After Death," 42, makes the same case for understanding the Hebrew *sheol*. All of these cases are standard linguistic practices to understand how a word is used in a particular context, and it is not unusual to say the meaning of a word is to be controlled by its context.

14. For example, see commentary on Rom 11:26.

Covenant Making and Justification

While the use of justification when used in a covenant-making context has within it a legal dimension in that there is a contractual agreement or obligation, there are other uses of the term that have other meanings. Because of Scripture's use of justification in making covenant, it follows that when God justifies his people, he is establishing a covenant with them, and this use of the term is relational in nature. The end-point of making covenant is the ensuring, maintaining, or restoring (as the case may be) of a relationship between both God and his people, and between individuals one to another within his covenant community.

That said, returning to Paul's use in Rom 4:3 of Gen 15:6 "What does the scripture say? 'Abraham believed God, and it was credited to him as righteousness,'" while the promise in Gen 15:6 is building on that which was foretold in Gen 3:15, the immediate background is found in Gen 14 where Abraham risked his life to save his nephew Lot who had been taken captive by a raiding party (Gen 14:1–16). Following this heroic act, the king of Sodom went out to meet Abraham to thank him for his intervention. With the king of Sodom was Melchizedek, king of Salem, to whom Abraham paid respect by giving a tithe. The priestly king responded by blessing Abraham in the name of "God Most High" (Gen 14:18–20). Following this exchange, the king of Sodom expressed his desire to pay Abraham tribute for intervening on behalf of the alliance of kings. He asked Abraham to keep the plunder for himself but to hand over the people he had freed (Gen 14:21). Abraham rejected the offer of plunder, declaring he did not want anyone to say the king of Sodom had made him rich.

Note there is nothing in this background narrative to suggest Abraham had done anything wrong for which he needed forgiveness. On the contrary, he had kept himself from compromise by rejecting the opportunity to make himself wealthy. Indeed, his actions had been exemplary in offering tithes to Melchizedek who, in response, blessed Abraham in the name of God Most High.

Yet, these were the events leading to the vision and discourse with God in Gen 15 and the justification statement in v.6. There is nothing in the Gen 15 text to suggest Abraham's faith regarding the forgiveness of his sins. Instead, God's response to Abraham's integrity in his dealings with the two kings in the Valley of Shaveh was the blessing of his family (Gen 15:4–5). God then ratified his covenant with Abraham (Gen 15:6–18).

Fast forward to years later when God promised Abraham that Sarah, though almost ninety, would have a son (Gen 17:16). This was the second occasion when God ratified his covenant with Abraham and very different from the first. In Gen 17, there is no mention that Abraham believed God and, because of this, was credited righteousness, as is found in Gen 15:6. The key statement of Gen 17 is v. 19: "your wife Sarah will bear you a son, and you will call him Isaac. I will establish my covenant with him as an everlasting covenant for his descendants after him." For the first time, Scripture identifies Sarah as the designated mother of the child of promise.[15]

---

15. What is present in Gen 17 is a recollection of the covenant made in Gen 15, but with no reiteration of the justification of Abraham. This is not to deny that justification language comes up later in Rom 4:19–24, and that most scholars see the passage to refer to Isaac's conception, but we must consider that

If this understanding is correct, then neither the writer of Genesis nor Paul (if he is following the meaning of the original text) saw the primary concern of crediting righteousness in Gen 15:6 to be Abraham's forgiveness and acceptance by God. Rather, it was God's commitment to Abraham in covenant to make him the father of a great nation that, in turn, would bless other nations (Gen 18:18). It was about how God acted righteously towards him, keeping faith with his promise, and the faith Abraham expressed was in response to the promise Yahweh had given him.[16] Because of his response, Yahweh dealt with Abraham in righteousness and he became the object of the covenant's promises. This understanding is in agreement with the righteousness language in the book of Isaiah, which testifies to God's faithfulness (righteousness) to the covenant he had sworn to Abraham (Isa 29:22; 41:8; 51:2; 63:16).

Thus, Gen 15 is about God entering into a covenant with Abraham, to whom he promises seed as numerous as the stars in the sky (Gen 15:5). The patriarch believed God, and it was "credited to him as righteousness." Immediately, God told Abraham he would give him the land. To Abraham's question, "how can I know that I shall take possession of it?" (Gen 15:7), Yahweh responded by formally inaugurating the covenant implicitly in existence since Abraham heeded Yahweh's call to leave the land of his fathers (Gen 12:1–9). Through it all, Yahweh took responsibility for the covenant into which he had called Abraham. Scripture brings out clearly in the inaugural ceremony that God was unconditionally bearing responsibility for the covenant he instituted with Abraham:

> Abram believed the Lord, and he credited it to him as righteousness. He also said to him, "I am the Lord, who brought you out of Ur of the Chaldeans to give you this land to take possession of it." But Abram said, "O Sovereign Lord, how can I know that I shall gain possession of it?" So the Lord said to him, "Bring me a heifer, a goat and a ram, each three years old, along with a dove and a young pigeon." Abram brought all these to him, cut them in two and arranged the halves opposite each other; the birds, however, he did not cut in half. Then birds of prey came down on the carcasses, but Abram drove them away. As the sun was setting, Abram fell into a deep sleep, and a thick and dreadful darkness came over him. Then the Lord said to him, "Know for certain that your descendants will be strangers in a country not their own, and they will be enslaved and ill-treated four hundred years. But I will punish the nation they serve as slaves, and afterwards they will come out with great possessions. You, however, will go to your fathers in peace and be buried at a good old age. In the fourth generation your descendants will come back here, for the sin of the Amorites has not yet reached its full measure." When the sun had set and darkness had fallen, a smoking fire pot with a blazing torch appeared and passed between the pieces. On that day the Lord made a covenant with Abram and said, "To your descendants I give this land, from the river of Egypt to the great river, the Euphrates." (Gen 15:6–18)

---

text very carefully to see what Paul is saying. I will suggest that his statement in Rom 4:19–24, widely understood to refer to Isaac's birth, has been routinely read into the Gen 17 text by theologians and others with little thought given to its appropriateness, thus creating a misunderstanding. It follows that if Paul is not saying what he is widely thought to be saying in Rom 4:19–24, this has serious implications for our reading of both Gen 17:19 and Rom 4:19–24.

16. Kidner, *Genesis*, 124, notes that in both Gen 15 and Rom 4, faith is presented "not as a crowning merit but as readiness to accept what God promises."

There are two important points to notice in this account. First, the covenant is essentially about the promise to deliver Abraham's descendants from bondage and exile. This is at the heart of the covenant, and should be considered a possible meaning of "crediting righteousness." The prophets support this meaning. As we shall discuss in more detail, they saw Yahweh's deliverance of Israel from her exile in Babylon to be her justification.[17]

The second point to notice is the absence of Abraham's active involvement in the covenant making ceremony. The laying out of the pieces of the animals was part of the ancient contractual process. Normally, the two parties making a contract would walk together between the pieces, effectively saying to one another: "If I fail to keep my part of the agreement, let me be like these animals which we pass between." Here, in the covenant made with Abraham, Yahweh does not call on him to take responsibility, as it is something Abraham is unable to bear. Yahweh walks alone, taking full responsibility for maintaining the covenant. If it is broken, Yahweh will be the one to receive its curse.[18]

In this way, the entire covenantal relationship established between God and Abraham was of grace. Abraham contributed only his assent; that is, his faith. In saying "he believed God," the writer of Genesis effectively says Abraham's faith was his agreement to be the beneficiary of this extraordinary grace. Of course, the bigger and more glorious picture is that God remained committed to his people, even when they broke the terms of the covenant. He took sole responsibility for this, bearing the curse through the death of his Son. He did this so the true seed of Abraham could be redeemed (Gal 3:13) and brought out of the kingdom of darkness to be partakers of the heavenly kingdom (Col 1:12–13).

Justification and the Writings of Paul

While we have argued for the covenantal setting of Gen 15, we must be aware this is also the setting for the argument of Rom 4. The chapter begins with, "What shall we say that Abraham, our forefather, discovered in this matter?" (Rom 4:3). The "matter" referred to is the argument thrashed out at the close of chapter 3 in vv. 21–31 and, at its heart, contends "a righteousness from God, apart from the law, has been made known, to which the Law and the Prophets testify" (Rom 3:21). This verse is the last mention of the term "righteousness" before its re-emergence in Rom 4:3. There would have to be a very good reason for severing the "righteousness" of Rom 4:3 from its earlier use and the context controlling it. As we have seen, the imagery of covenant, the new exodus and the Paschal sacrifice saturates that context, so it would be only natural for Paul to carry it forward into Rom 4.

In the latter part of chapter 3, Paul reasoned the Mosaic covenant had not given the Jews any greater privilege than the Gentiles had. The passage, which was concerned with the covenant status of a people, prepared the Roman believers for the story of Abraham's acceptance by God. Recent scholarship has clarified that when Paul writes about "the

---

17. "Justification" or "justified" is an alternative rendering of the Hebrew term that means "crediting as righteousness."

18. The following are references to being cut off, which relate to covenantal unfaithfulness (Exod 30:13; 31:14; Lev 7:21; Num 19:20; Isa 48:9; 53:8; Jer 51:13; Ezek 37:11).

righteousness of God," he is referring to God's saving activity,[19] as were the writers of the OT (Ps 35:24; 65:5; 85:13; 98:2; 103:6; 111:3; Isa 32:17; 45:8; 46:13; 51:5; 56:1; 58:8; 60:17; 62:2). The fulfilling of God's covenant promises to save his people from the dangers they face certainly includes salvation from the penalty of sin, but also from satanic activity and control.[20] It is in this covenantal context we need to read Rom 4. To dissociate what Paul is trying to convey in this part of his letter from what he has already written in the first three chapters is to leave us vulnerable to misinterpreting his theology.

There is further evidence to support the interpretation that when Paul writes "he credited it to him as righteousness," he is referring to Yahweh bringing Abraham into covenant with him. The only other NT text that references Gen 15:6 is Gal 3:6, where Paul says, "Consider Abraham. He believed God, and it was credited to him as righteousness." This passage concerns the Galatians who, much to Paul's astonishment, were leaving the true Gospel. He acknowledges how easy it is to be won by the arguments of the Judaizers, recounting how he had been forced to publicly rebuke Peter because the apostle had withdrawn from table fellowship with Gentiles when the Judaizers arrived in Antioch (Gal 2:11–14). In this letter, Paul insists that the Galatian believers must not yield to the pressure of Judaizers who argue that circumcision is a requirement for full covenantal membership. He reminds them justification is by faith in Jesus Christ, not by observation of the law in matters such as circumcision (Gal 2:15–16). Moreover, he takes the opportunity to raise the matter of how the law had uncovered their sinfulness. Paul asks if this makes Christ responsible for promoting sin, and immediately rejects his own question (Gal 2:17–21). For those so comfortable with the law prior to their conversion, the discovery that it condemned them must have been deeply disturbing.[21]

The argument Paul used in Galatians is a condensed version of the same argument in Rom 6-7: that death has fully satisfied the demands of the law. When Paul writes about "death," he refers to the death of Christ in which all believers have shared (Rom 5:12—6:4). This was not a theoretical concept. Its reality brought Paul into a new relationship with God (Gal 2:20–21). His argument is that the new covenant, centered on the death of Jesus, achieved what the law had been unable to achieve.

In Gal 3, Paul asks the believers if they came into the covenant through works or by faith. What is surprising is he does not ask if they received God's forgiveness by keeping the law. Instead, and significantly, he asks if they had received the Spirit (the prophesied blessing of the new covenant [Ezek 36:27]) by observing the law or by faith (Gal 3:1–5). This is the very question introducing the text, "Consider Abraham: 'He believed God, and it was credited to him as righteousness.' Understand, then, that those who believe are children of Abraham" (Gal 3:6). The evidence they are accepted is that God has given them the Spirit. He is the promised gift of God and the marriage dowry to the redeemed community. In Gal 3:14, Paul says, "He redeemed us in order that the blessing given to Abraham might come to the Gentiles through Jesus Christ, so that by faith we might

---

19. See notes on 1:16–17.

20. For a fuller description of the significance of this assertion, see Holland, *Contours,* chapter 5.

21. For a discussion of Paul's discovery in this matter see pages 123–25.

receive the promise of the Spirit." One of the promised blessings of the Abrahamic covenant is the birth of a community given the Spirit. Its members are the true children of Abraham. This is the very point raised by Peter at the Council of Jerusalem:

> Brothers, you know that some time ago God made a choice among you that the Gentiles might hear from my lips the message of the gospel and believe. God, who knows the heart, showed that he accepted them by giving the Holy Spirit to them, just as he did to us. He made no distinction between us and them, for he purified their hearts by faith. Now then, why do you try to test God by putting on the necks of the disciples a yoke that neither we nor our fathers have been able to bear? No! We believe it is through the grace of our Lord Jesus that we are saved, just as they are. (Acts 15:7–11)

It is clear Peter's concern is identical to what Paul discussed in his letter to the Galatians. The evidence God had accepted the Gentiles is that he had given them the Spirit, and this is linked with their hearts being purified by faith. It is also clear the focus of the debate in the Council of Jerusalem was not the acceptance of an individual Gentile, but the believing Gentiles as an entirety.[22] In other words, we are finding the same corporate argument made at the Jerusalem synod as Paul presents throughout Romans. It did not originate with Paul—he simply expounded the law and the prophets concerning the justification (acceptance into the covenant) of the Gentiles. Indeed, the events Peter witnessed forced the position on the early church. It is wrong, therefore, to see justification, as some have, as being a doctrine created by Paul.[23]

From the above discussion, I would suggest the meaning of being "credited righteousness" in Gen 15:6 is quite different from the meaning found in Ps 32:2. David's use of the term clearly refers to his acquittal from sin, while Gen 15:6 focuses on the creation of a covenant between Yahweh and Abraham. It is likely that Paul, aware of the difference, deliberately chose the texts in Rom 4 because they served his purposes perfectly.

Gen 15:6 gave him the perfect foil in his debate with those who demanded the Gentiles must be circumcised to have full covenantal status and so take part in God's justification of his people. He was able to show God's acceptance of the Jews, in the person of their father Abraham, had been in Abraham's uncircumcised state. God had created a covenant with Abraham, and through him with his offspring. This covenant was the basis of all Jewish hope. However, the patriarch was a Gentile and not circumcised when Yahweh made his covenant with him! Therefore, the demands the Judaizers were now making on the Gentiles in the Galatian and Roman churches were not demands from God but from men. It was the Judaizers' way of controlling access to God within the church. Access would be on Jewish terms and not on God's terms. This was the final thrust of Paul's argument found at the end of chapter 3: "Is God the God of Jews only? Is he not the God of Gentiles too? Yes, of Gentiles too, since there is only one God, who will

---

22. Dunn, *Galatians*. This corporate dimension is supported further if our exegesis of Gal 3:26–29 is correct. See Excursus E: Baptism into Christ, pages 168–77.

23. "Paul did not discover the basic principles of justification by faith, it was at the heart of Israel's own faith . . . the language of Paul's thought, the currency of his theology, remained Hebraic through and through," Dunn, *Theology*, 718.

justify the circumcised by faith and the uncircumcised through that same faith" (Rom 3:29–30). It is not by coincidence Paul quotes Gen 15:6 in Rom 4:3 immediately following this question. Rather, it is the proof that establishes his case.

Having thus established that God justified Abraham because of his faith, not his works (Rom 4:3–5), Paul then references Ps 32:2 beginning with Rom 4:6 as a full rebuttal of the Judaizers who, while demanding circumcision of the Gentiles, denied it was necessary for Jews to be made right with God as they believed they were already made so. They claimed Jews shared in their nation's deliverance under Moses, and this historic even—a fulfillment of the Abrahamic covenant—continued to be the grounds for their salvation and hope of acceptance. Paul's response to them was along these lines: "You say you have salvation through Abraham and Moses. Well, remember, David did too! But even he, the king of Israel—the one with whom God entered into a covenant—was brought to the place where he acknowledged his deep need of justification, of forgiveness, and acceptance by the God against whom he had sinned. Now, if King David needed this reconciliation with God (even though having the promise his family would occupy the throne of Israel forever), don't you think you need it, too?"

This argument was the second arm of Paul's pincer movement, forcing his opponents into a defensive position. How could they demand circumcision of the Gentiles when God had accepted them in Abraham, an uncircumcised Gentile; and how could they say they were beyond the need of repentance and mercy when the nation's greatest king acknowledged his need of personal forgiveness because of sin? They were in need of acquittal just as much as was David.

Earlier we suggested the legal and accounting aspects of justification taught by the Reformers can be located in more appropriate texts than Genesis 15. Ps 32:2 and Paul's application in Rom 4:6–8 is an example, with Israel in need of receiving both forgiveness (acquittal) for her "lawless deeds" (Rom 4:7) and "righteousness apart from works" (imputation, Rom 4:6). These meanings at the heart of the Protestant doctrine of justification are as ever true. However, if we are to avoid imposing a singular meaning of justification as a blanket over every instance where Scripture speaks of justification, then it becomes necessary to distinguish when the discussion relates to God dealing with sin and when the discussion relates to God creating covenant relationships.

When considering Paul's use of the forensic aspects of justification in relation to law keeping, it is preferable to do so within the OT legal setting of the law and the prophets, rather than within what has been until recently their traditional home in the secular Roman legal setting. The growing appreciation among scholars that Paul stayed within the framework of OT covenant theology, developing it in the light of the Christ-event which brought to completion the covenant's promises, suggests this refocusing is vital for the correct understanding of his justification language. The OT law and the prophets spoke from a legal mindset that existed within the larger framework of God's covenant. When the terms of the covenant were broken, there was only one way back into fellowship with God, and that was on the basis of satisfying the law's (the Torah's) demands. It is in this context the forensic and accounting aspects of justification must be discussed, not in that of the secular law court. This Hellenistic arena, which evolved into Roman law and, eventually, into much of the current understanding of law in Western Europe, has nothing to say about the covenantal aspects of justification so central to Paul's understanding: that is, the promises of Yahweh to redeem and adopt his people and his legitimate claim upon them as their loving, righteous Creator.

Thus, when the Reformers countered the church of Rome's abuse in offering indulgences as a means of salvation with a doctrine of justification based primarily on acquittal and imputation, they were essentially fighting with one hand tied behind their backs. While they were correct in presenting acquittal and imputation as aspects of justification, they were missing the covenant making aspect that sets the keeping of God's law apart from the secular legal system and so missed the context that clarifies its reason and purpose. Paul correctly understood this in Rom 4 when he laid "crediting righteousness" as covenantal (Gen 15:6, Rom 4:3) side-by-side with "crediting righteousness" as acquittal (Ps 32:2, Rom 4:6). Each served to compliment and enhance the other, thereby giving strength to both.

Another passage where covenant and acquittal run concurrently within justification is 2 Cor 5:19, where Paul argues sin is not counted against believers because of the death of Christ. He writes, "God was reconciling the world to himself in Christ, not counting men's sins against them. And he has committed to us the message of reconciliation." In this passage, Paul echoes David in Ps 32:2 regarding God not counting sin, but focuses on the fact God does not exclude the believing community from the covenant because of sin, for her guilt has been borne by Christ. Her sin, therefore, is not counted against her. Although there is the aspect of acquittal, the passage at heart is covenantal in its setting, as is made clear by the structure of the earlier introduction where Paul compared the covenant under Moses with the covenant under Christ (2 Cor 3:7ff.). Indeed, 2 Cor 3:7—6:18 has been shown to be based on the themes of the new exodus[24] and Adamic Christology,[25] the whole section being saturated with theological concepts of covenant. Also, the new covenant context of the argument is abundantly clear in the way Paul has echoed Isa 65:17: "Behold, I will create new heavens and a new earth. The former things will not be remembered, nor will they come to mind." (Isa 65:17 NIV) in 2 Cor 5:17: "Therefore, if anyone is in Christ, he is a new creation; the old has gone, the new has come!" With the citation of this OT text and the intercontexualization that Paul so often employs comes the new covenant fulfillment that Isaiah has proclaimed.

2 Corinthians 5:19 is therefore covenantal as is Rom 4:3, where the focus is the bringing of Abraham into a covenant relationship with Yahweh. Paul has introduced a propitiatory need that was not in the original Gen 15 account. This need and provision is embedded in the justification language of redemption, atonement and acceptance in the Paschal sacrifice that has been made in Rom 3:21–26. In the Corinthian letter, the theme is also about God creating a way by which he rescues people from covenantal exclusion—all who believe being reconciled to him because of the death of his Son. Like Rom 3:21—4:9, 2 Cor 5:17–21 also speaks of acceptance because Christ has paid the

24. Webb, *Returning.*

25. Pate, *Substructure.*

penalty for sin: "God made him who had no sin to be sin for us." Thus as with Rom 4, these two aspects of justification, acquittal and imputation work together, but the overriding theme is covenant. Justification as acquittal and imputation cannot exist outside of God making covenant. This is not to say justification follows the creation of the covenant alone, even though covenant is at its heart. Justification is the covenant's beginning, its continuation, and its end. Covenant gives all other aspects of justification their purpose and meaning.

Justification and Circumcision

Regarding Paul's discussion of Jewish circumcision versus Gentile non circumcision, a point needs to be cleared. This is not to say circumcision has no part to play in justification. On the contrary, there is a significant relationship. Throughout the OT, justification and circumcision ran side-by-side and were both closely linked to the theme of Passover.[26] As we will see, this has continued into the NT as themes of the new covenant.

In Exodus, we read about the Passover event when Israel was justified; being brought out of Egypt to become God's covenant community. However, to be included in the justified community, each male member (Hebrew, slave or alien) had to be circumcised. The story of Moses and his family shows the importance of circumcision in the justification of Israel. He was married to Zipporah, a Midianite, and had two sons, at least one of whom had not been circumcised. When traveling to Egypt to lead the Hebrews out of bondage, the Lord met the family in a terrifying way. It is unclear whether God was set to slay Moses or his son, but only the son's circumcision would appease God's wrath. Zipporah, who carried out the circumcision, touched Moses' feet with the foreskin, saying to him: "Surely you are a bridegroom of blood to me" (Exod 4:24–26). Scholars see in this statement echoes of an ancient Jewish marriage requirement of circumcision.

There is possibly a greater significance to the circumcision of Moses' son than is immediately apparent. The Hebrews had probably abandoned the practice of circumcision begun when God made covenant with Abraham (Gen 17:10). Ezek 20:1–7 makes it clear that by the time Moses led Israel out of captivity, they had become as corrupt as were their Egyptian masters. It is possibly why they had to undergo national circumcision before entering the promised land (Josh 5:2–9).[27] Circumcision was a vital requirement for covenant membership (Exod 12:48). Indeed, it was a requirement for eating the Passover (Josh 5:7–10), and not partaking of this meal meant a negligent person was put out of the

---

26. None could partake of the Passover unless they were circumcised and circumcision was essential to be a member of the covenant community.

27. Following the circumcision of the people who came out of the desert, it says, "Then the LORD said to Joshua, 'Today I have rolled away the reproach of Egypt from you.' So the place has been called Gilgal to this day" (Jos 5:9). This implies that the nation had not been circumcised while in Egypt. Circumcision was not practiced by the generation who died in the wilderness, for their children were left uncircumcised (Josh 5:5). But this text clearly says that all who came out of Egypt had been circumcised. As no event is recorded when such a mass circumcision would have taken place, it possibly refers to Israel being circumcised in her representative, Moses' son. This representative circumcision seems to have remained effective until the nation reached the safety of the promised land.

community, and so lost the justification that came with membership in God's covenant community.

The themes of circumcision, covenant membership and divine marriage also run through the writings of the prophets (Jer 4:4; 31:31–34; Ezek 16:59–60; Hos 11:9–11). The new covenant was part of the second exodus promises.[28] It pledged that the hearts of the community's members would be circumcised. Among these themes was the promise of the eschatological marriage—the new people of God being made fit to marry the divine husband because their hearts were circumcised. They would be able to share the eschatological Passover—Yahweh's promised redemption of his people. This Passover was to inaugurate the (eschatological) divine marriage as had been intended at Sinai.

These themes are very much part of Paul's thinking. He teaches that Gentiles, along with Jewish believers, are now able to partake of Christ (i.e., be justified by him) because Christ underwent circumcision on their behalf. Paul writes to the Colossians:

> In him you were also circumcised, in the putting off of the sinful nature, not with a circumcision done by the hands of men but with the circumcision done by Christ, having been buried with him in baptism and raised with him through your faith in the power of God, who raised him from the dead. When you were dead in your sins and in the uncircumcision of your sinful nature, God made you alive with Christ. (Col 2:11–13a)

In other words, the corporate act of baptism we shall discuss in chapter 6 was also the occasion of a corporate act of circumcision; the great ontological event that makes the people of God acceptable to their Creator, allowing the new covenant community to become the bride of the divine groom. This is the framework found in Ephesians; circumcision, Passover, and marriage.[29] Christ has redeemed his people (Eph 1:7). This is paschal language. Gentiles have undergone spiritual circumcision (Eph 2:11–13) to form one new covenant community with Jewish believers (Eph 2:14–22). It is this community Christ takes as his bride (Eph 5:25–27), a truth that Paul describes as a "profound mystery" (Eph 5:32). However, circumcision is not only for the community (the church) but also for her individual members. Without heart-circumcision, they cannot share membership with the redeemed people of God and, therefore, cannot share in the Lord's Passover or play a part in the divine marriage.

In Galatians, there are distinct echoes of the same themes. The believers are redeemed (Gal 1:4; 3:13), share in the new heart which circumcision symbolizes (Gal 5:6; 6:14–15), and are part of the community that will be the bride of the divine marriage (Gal 3:26–29; 4:21–31).

The Passover theme is clearly linked with justification and circumcision in Pauline thought. This link is further found in Colossians where, as in the paschal passage in Rom 3:21–26, Paul speaks of the public spectacle of Christ's death: "He forgave us all our sins, having cancelled the written code, with its regulations, that was against us and that

---

28. I deliberately use "second exodus" to identify the expectations of the prophets, but use "new exodus" to speak of the fulfillment of these promises in the NT through the work of Christ.

29. See Cozart, *Ephesians*.

stood opposed to us; he took it away, nailing it to the cross. And having disarmed the powers and authorities, he made a public spectacle of them, triumphing over them by the cross" (Col 2:13b–15). This is a clear echo of the public blood daubing of the Hebrews' doorframes on the night of Israel's Passover (Exod 12:7). They also have experienced circumcision, through the circumcision of Christ (Col 2:11). The statement: "he is the head of the body, the church; he is the beginning and the firstborn from among the dead, so that in everything he might have the supremacy" (Col 1:18) carries marriage imagery.

Justification and the Law

Another issue needs clarification in order to follow Paul's argument on justification. As we have seen, leading New Perspective theologians have challenged the Reformed understanding of justification and the law. They say intertestamental literature shows the Jews did not fear the law, but lived under it with joy and gratitude. This picture is in stark contrast to the Lutheran understanding of the law as that which "hunts man down as a sinner in order to drive him to Christ.[30] More recently, commentators have challenged this view and argued the law leads the seeker to Christ,[31] a less aggressive imagery that has led to a re-examination and reinterpretation by Reformed theologians concerning Paul's understanding of the law.

As New Perspective theologians correctly point out, it is clear Paul delighted in the law before his conversion. He seems to have been like many in Judaism who saw and experienced the law in a very positive way (Phil 3:3–6). In challenging the New Perspective understanding of the law's purpose and function, I do not intend to appeal to Rom 7, as do other opponents of the position. I believe the chapter, like the whole of Romans, is meant to be interpreted within a corporate perspective. Consequently, it is difficult to identify with any certainty at what point Paul's own story enters the narrative. Even so, Rom 7 makes it clear the law was high jacked and made to serve the purposes of Sin (Rom 7:10). This hardly fits the New Perspective position, as these theologians do not recognize such a negative view of the law's function.

Paul makes significant statements elsewhere about the law that also do not fit the New Perspective model.[32] In Rom 4:15, Paul says, "for the law brings wrath," and in Gal 3:19, he says, "What then was the purpose of the law? It was added because of transgressions until the Seed to whom the promise referred had come." Further, he says, "the Scripture declared that the whole world is a prisoner of sin" (Gal 3:22). The inclusive terms, "whole world" and "all have" make it clear that Paul, as he has done elsewhere, understands the law to condemn Jews as well as Gentiles; that Jews are included in this state of condemnation (Rom 3:23). This does not match the New Perspective's covenantal nomist view of Paul's treatment of the law. Indeed, he preached the following to the Jews in the synagogue at Pisidian Antioch:

---

30. The understanding of Calvin differed from that of Luther on the role of the law. Calvin stressed the OT references in the Psalms which spoke of the law being he believer's delight.

31. Betz, *Galatians*, 177; Dunn, *Galatians*, 198; Witherington, *Galatia*, 262.

32. For a study of materials found in the Gospels that do not fit the New Perspective pattern, see Gathercole, *Boasting*.

Therefore, my brothers, I want you to know that through Jesus the forgiveness of sins is proclaimed to you. Through him everyone who believes *is justified from everything you could not be justified from by the law of Moses.* Take care that what the prophets have said does not happen to you: "Look, you scoffers, wonder and perish, for I am going to do something in your days that you would never believe, even if someone told you." (Acts 13:38–41; emphasis added)

Such preaching cannot possibly fit the model presented by New Perspective theologians. Paul's reference to "everything you could not be justified from" by the works of the law cannot refer to circumcision, Sabbath-keeping, food law observation, and the like. Few, if any, of the Jews in the synagogue are likely to have been failing on such fundamental Jewish requirements. Then, as now, works cannot produce justification, and even though they might do the works, they remained condemned. Rather, the meaning of justification is clear: Paul is preaching that, because the Jews have not fulfilled the moral requirements of the law, they must believe, repent, and be forgiven in order to be justified, i.e., to be right with God.

In addition, Paul discusses the role of the law in Rom 5, where he says: "The law was added so that the trespass might increase" (Rom 5:20), and "sin is not taken into account when there is no law" (Rom 5:13). The law referred to is the Mosaic law given to Israel at Sinai. These concepts of the law's function cannot fit the New Perspective model of the law that sees it as a blessing to the people of Israel. Paul's argument is corporate, its focus being on what the law does to the *community* that is in Adam, not to the individual in Adam. They speak of a law that did not bring the peace and well-being New Perspective theologians claim. Instead, according to these key Pauline texts, the law brought condemnation and terror to the covenant community itself. Although it was intended for Israel's blessing, in the end it clarified the nature of her rebellion, and quite opposite from a blessing, the law became a curse (Gal 3:10–13).

There is yet another Pauline text that puts the New Perspective under serious scrutiny. In 2 Cor 3:7–11, Paul writes:

Now if the ministry that brought death, which was engraved in letters on stone, came with glory, so that the Israelites could not look steadily at the face of Moses because of its glory, fading though it was, will not the ministry of the Spirit be even more glorious? If the ministry that condemns men is glorious, how much more glorious is the ministry that brings righteousness! For what was glorious has no glory now in comparison with the surpassing glory. And if what was fading away came with glory, how much greater is the glory of that which lasts!

The New Perspective model cannot possibly accommodate this statement, as Paul writes of the giving of the law as a ministry of "death" which brings "condemnation." However, this creates a problem for Phil 3:3–6 suggests Paul was a contented Jew living under the law (Phil 3:6). But in 2 Cor 3:7–11 Paul says this law, since the time of its appearing, has condemned Israel to death![33]

33. The above interpretation of 2 Cor 5:19—which is clearly part of Paul's argument since, at least, 2 Cor 3—raises a question over Wright's interpretation of 2 Cor 5:21. I agree the theme of the servant is fundamental to the passage, but it must not displace or control key statements Paul makes. The servant

However, what may suggest a contradiction disappears when considering Paul's personal history. I would suggest that the apostle did share the understanding of covenantal nomism until his conversion. Before his transforming encounter with Christ, like the rest of Israel he perceived himself as blameless according to the law, excelling in righteousness above his peers (Phil 3:3–6). However, following his conversion, Paul was forced to reflect on the purpose of the law. He then realized that, while given to bless Israel, the intention had never been achieved. Indeed, on the night God gave the law to Moses (the occasion Jews were later to see as the marriage of Yahweh to Israel), the very people who had experienced God's salvation from Egypt turned to the idols of their captivity (Ex 32:1–6). This fact could mean only one thing. On the night of her marriage, Israel played the harlot. Clearly, this understanding does not reflect Second Temple Judaism, when Israel basked in the law as though her unfaithfulness had never happened. Admittedly, she had been spared judgment by Moses' intercession and the covenant making ceremony which followed (Exod 33:12–17; 34:1–10),[34] but, despite being given time, Israel never repented and never returned to God.

---

of the Lord is called to proclamation how God has made it possible to remove the sentence of death that the law has placed on humanity. The crucial event for removing that judgment is stated in 2 Cor 5:19–21: "God was reconciling the world to himself in Christ, not counting men's sins against them. And he has committed to us the message of reconciliation. We are Christ's ambassadors, as though God were making his appeal through us. We implore you on Christ's behalf: Be reconciled to God. God made him who had no sin to be sin for us, so that in him we might become the righteousness of God." It is natural to read the statement: "made the righteousness of God" in the light of the sin-judged condition that Paul has been speaking about, with Christ being made sin for the believer. This reading is more natural than allowing the theme of the servant (which does run through the narrative) to take control of the reading, having Paul merely saying that he sees himself as an agent of righteousness. He is this because he is proclaiming the message of the crucified Christ, whose death has paid the penalty of sin. To remove the message of the crucified Messiah dying for his people is to do an injustice to the argument. It has not been about how sin has damaged creation (although, of course, he does say this elsewhere) but that man's condemnation is a result of breaking the law.

34. Note God makes the "renewed covenant" with Moses and not with Israel. However, Israel is spared judgment as a result of it: "Now leave me alone so that my anger may burn against them and that I may destroy them. Then I will make you into a great nation" (Exod 32:10). The intercession and ceremony merely delayed the inevitable. The Lord replied to Moses, "Whoever has sinned against me I will blot out of my book and my angel will go before you. However, when the time comes for me to punish, I will punish them for their sin" (Exod 32:33–34). Durham, *Exodus*, 429, notes: "The implication of this statement is, of course, that he tempered but did not altogether waive his judgment, and this implication is confirmed in the continuation of the narrative, at both Exod 32:34 and 35 and also at 33:17 and 34:6–7." Mackay, *Exodus*, 547, thinks the statement: "when the time comes for me to punish, I will punish them for their sin" (Exod 32:34) refers to the fact none of that generation would see the land (Deut 1:35); but, of course, some did! Better to see the reference to "the passing over of sins previously committed" (KJV), "because in his divine forbearance" (NIV) in Rom 3:25, as a glance back to the exodus event, supported by the repeated exodus echoes in the text, when judgment was stayed for a later day. Even though the judgment was withheld, the relationship had been irreparably damaged. Fretheim, *Exodus*, 308–9, acknowledges that the word "create" in Exod 34:10 ("I am making a covenant with you. Before all your people I will do wonders never before done in any nation in all the world. The people you live among will see how awesome is the work that I, the LORD, will do for you"), is the same word as that used in Gen 1:1. Fretheim further notes the covenant with Moses is a new act of creation which only creation language can adequately describe. He goes on to comment that Exod 34:10 "does *not*, strictly speaking, refer to a renewal of the covenant of chapters 19–24" (emphasis: Fretheim's). In other words, the covenant is with Moses. It is totally new—something which Fretheim does not identify.

The principle of protection from wrath by means of intercession, such as that of Moses at Sinai, is not without parallel in the OT. In Gen 18:16–33, Abraham interceded for Lot and his family. He structured his prayer carefully, asking God if he would spare the city of Sodom if fifty righteous citizens lived there. God agreed. Abraham repeated the prayer several times and, on each occasion, he decreased the number of righteous people necessary for God to spare the city. Eventually, Yahweh agreed to spare Sodom if he could find only ten righteous people. Through Abraham's intercession God withheld judgment until the righteous were made safe; then, judgment fell. The parallel with Moses is obvious. It was his intercession for Israel that saved her from coming under the curse of the law; but it was not a permanent repeal, for judgment was being stored up for the day of wrath (Rom 2:5; 3:25; Rev 6:7).

The theme of Israel as condemned is also evident in the message of Hosea, a public enactment of the story of Yahweh and Israel. Hosea's marriage to wayward Gomer was dead and divorce formalities were underway. It was the same for Yahweh and unfaithful Israel. Having broken the covenant by going after other gods on her wedding night, Israel put herself under the covenantal curses (Deut 32–33) and the marriage was over. The intended relationship was never re-established, as Israel's heart did not change despite the pleas of God. Her condition was like that of Gomer, who never really wanted to go back to Hosea. Taking advantage of a "new start" was never part of Israel's thinking or desire. She wanted the benefits and protection of the family home, but not the relationship her divine husband sought.

The book of Hosea provided Paul with key texts from which he constructed his understanding of sin, judgment, and mercy (Rom 9:25–26; 1 Cor 15:55).[35] One wonders how the self-righteous Saul had failed to see in his pre-conversion days how its storyline applied so tragically to Israel. It seems, along with all Israel, he had assumed her misdemeanors had been brushed under the carpet when, in reality, they had not.

It is this reality Paul discovered in his post-conversion days as a consequence of working though the implications of what Israel had done to her Messiah. He abandoned the position he once held and acknowledged that, like the Gentiles, the Jews were in Adam and so under the same judgment as the Gentiles. The Jews lived thinking their sin at Sinai had never mattered, and that the law showered the covenant blessing on them as intended. In reality, the law now played a very different role. It condemned Israel to death, i.e., to eternal separation from God.

Justification as a Corporate Event

As we have seen, justification language was used to describe Yahweh's rescue of Israel from judgment in exile (Isa 45:25; 54:14; 58:8; 62:1; with יִצְדְּקוּ being the Hebrew equivalent of "justify"). In other words, when Yahweh acted in righteousness towards Israel, he justified her.

---

35. The influence of Hosea is far greater than the number of direct quotations would suggest. Dodd, *According*, says that analysis of the influence of OT books on NT writers, Hosea is one of the most influential OT books after Deuteronomy, Psalms, and Isaiah.

This meaning is an important component of how Paul understands justification. The law had warned Israel that God would send her into exile if she broke the covenant, and the prophets and the historical writings recorded the outworking of the covenantal curses. Israel was, in the end, taken into exile, with the temple and entire city of Jerusalem left in ruins. Paul echoed this setting twice in his letter to the Romans when he wrote his Gospel was according to the law and the prophets (Rom 1:2; 3:21). This connection ought to give us confidence in Paul's typological exegesis—a form of exegesis exhibited most clearly in his statements in Rom 5:12ff. and 1 Cor 10:1–20.[36]

Looking ahead to Rom 5, the emphasis is on Christ, the last Adam, who undoes the work of the first Adam by restoring his people to God. Justification language is repeatedly used in Rom 5:1, 9, 16, and 18; in fact, it is used more times in Rom 5 than in any other section of Scripture. At the very least, justification ought to be seen as a rescue from a condition of condemnation to an experience of covenantal relationship with God. What is also significant is that the argument of chapter 5 is thoroughly corporate. It is about Christ recovering a people for himself, paralleling the saving event of the Jewish people when Yahweh recovered them from exile in Babylon and restored them to their inheritance and fellowship with himself. Thus, the exile of Israel from the promised land is a micro-version of the spiritual exile of humanity from their Creator's presence that was the fruit of the fall. Because of this relationship, concepts that belong to Israel's recovery from exile are readily transferable to Christ's recovery of God's people.

These corporate observations not only uphold the truths the Reformers identified and preached but also enhance them. However, it was the community God justified, the time of the collective act of justification being the moment of Christ's death (Rom 5:18–19; 6:7; 7:4). Paul thrashes out a corporate application of this truth in Romans regarding the covenantal status of the Gentile believers. He holds they do not have to submit to circumcision to have acceptance, and this is the same issue he deals with in Galatians.[37]

This argument does not deny individuals must be justified, but suggests each individual will become part of the justified community when, by the Spirit's work, he believes. At conversion, the individual catches up experientially with what Christ has already done for all of his people. (See chapter 6 for discussion on the significance of baptism into Christ.) Nor does it deny the individual Gentile had to respond in faith to share in this salvation (Luke 3:7–8; 9:62; 12:21; John 3:16; Acts 2:40–41; 8:34–38; 17:34; Rom 10:12–18), as faith and repentance are required before one can inherit the covenant's blessings. These blessings include forgiveness, reconciliation, inheritance and all the other riches which are part of the good news of Jesus Christ. However, as we read the text of Romans (and other letters of Paul), we must keep this important element to the fore: that justification language is often, but not exclusively, corporate. This demands that we pay careful attention to the context of each use of the term in Scripture.

---

36. These are not isolated examples of typological exegesis; the method was foundational for Paul's theology. For studies in typology see Ninow, *Indicators, and* Goppelt, *Typos*.

37. For a discussion on the importance of circumcision in OT and rabbinical thought, and for the way Paul develops it in his new exodus paradigm, see Holland, *Contours*, 21, 36, 153, 175, 179, 184, 189, 196, 213, 225, 285.

Justification and Covenantal Relationship

I have argued that Gen 15:6 is about the creation of a covenant and that this must govern how we understand the passage. Thus, as we have seen, the phrase "credited it to him as righteousness" in this particular context has nothing to do with acquittal of Abraham's sin.

However, this argument concerning the covenantal meaning of justify does not stand on Gen 15:6 alone, as another passage gives powerful support to this interpretation. Ps 106 tells of Phinehas the priest, who took action against his fellow countrymen for indulging in sexual immorality. Ps 106:31 states: "This was credited to him as righteousness for endless generations to come." The original account in Num 25:10–13 clarifies the meaning of "credited as righteousness":

> The LORD said to Moses, "Phinehas son of Eleazar, the son of Aaron, the priest, has turned my anger away from the Israelites; for he was as zealous as I am for my honour among them, so that in my zeal I did not put an end to them. Therefore tell him I am making my covenant of peace with him. He and his descendants will have a covenant of a lasting priesthood, because he was zealous for the honour of his God and made atonement for the Israelites."

The meaning of "credited as righteousness" could not be clearer. It means Phinehas was brought into a covenant relationship with Yahweh. Thus, the justification language in Ps 106:31 and Gen 15:6 is covenant making; and, while the covenants are made with individuals, they both have corporate implications for their descendants. Gen 15:18 says, "On that day the LORD made a covenant with Abraham and said '*To your descendants I give this land*, from the river of Egypt to the great river, the Euphrates,'" and Num 25:13 says, "He (Phinehas) *and his descendants* will have a covenant of a lasting priesthood" (Num 25:13).

The meaning of "credited to him as righteousness" in Ps 106, recounting events in Num 25, is crucial for understanding what happened in Gen 15. Comparison between the two incidents reveals common important features: both speak of making covenants and of changing the status of the men involved. Being credited righteousness was for Abraham and Phinehas the beginning of a new relationship with God.

In light of this OT usage, and Israel's corporate justification when Yahweh brought her back to the promised land into the new covenant he promised he would make with her, we can say that being "credited righteousness"—that is, justification—has, at its heart, reconciliation with God. This is something the New Perspective theologians have denied. Justification is not only a declaration of being in the covenant but it is also the creation of a new relationship.

As we have seen, the exilic prophets viewed Israel's release from exile as a display of God's righteousness. After suffering for her sins, the law had been satisfied: "Speak tenderly to Jerusalem, and proclaim to her that her hard service has been completed, that her sin has been paid for, that she has received from the LORD's hand double for all her sins" (Isa 40:2). We have seen evidence of Paul's interaction with the writings of the prophets, developing their themes in the light of the Christ-event but changing their rationale. Thus, in this case, it was not the delivered people of God who paid the price for breaking the law but the Son of God himself—the Paschal victim (Rom 3:21–25; Gal 3:13; Col 1:13–20).

A result of her release from exile was Israel's acquittal (God declaring her righteous) because she had no outstanding matter for which to account before his law. In acquitting her, God had not overlooked Israel's sins. She had paid the price for breaking the conditions of the covenant throughout her time in exile. He could justify her now, upholding her claim to be his covenant people. God did this by leading the remnant back to the promised land to retake possession of their inheritance, particularly the city of Jerusalem.

Additionally, Israel's justification was an act of corporate salvation in the sight of the nations. This was the proof to the nations she was the covenant people of God. Importantly, in bringing her back to Jerusalem, God was also justified. He justified himself before the nations that he really was the Creator God who had revealed himself to Abraham and kept covenant with his people. Paul echoes this double meaning in Rom 3:26: "to demonstrate his justice at the present time, so as to be just and the one who justifies those who have faith in Jesus."

At the heart of this second exodus was a new covenant, a new relationship. It was a covenant-making event when Israel was to be justified, counted righteous, given covenantal status, and made right with the God she had offended. This is significant, as it means Israel's justification was not only about her being declared to be in the covenant, but also, and primarily, it was about her being brought into the promised new one.

So it is also for the Gentiles of faith—the "many nations" Paul references in Rom 4:17—whom God has brought from darkness into this same new covenant, and declared righteous as part of the new exodus in Christ. Indeed, like the Jewish believers, they too are acquitted from sin through the blood of the Paschal sacrifice; their transgressions forgiven, their sin covered, never to be counted against them (Rom 4:7–8). However, as we have seen, Paul is not dealing with the acquittal of the sinner when he links Gen 15:6 with Rom 4, but rather with the acceptance of the Gentiles into this covenant community as they join, by faith, the "offspring" of Abraham (Gen 15:5). With their acceptance flow all the blessings of being justified! Note the corporate statements in Rom 8:28–39 and Eph 1:3–14, such as: "And we know that in all things God works for the good of those who love him, who have been called according to his purpose . . . those he called, he also justified; those he justified, he also glorified" (Rom 8:28, 30b).

It is here I differ from the New Perspective view of justification discussed at the outset: that justification is primarily about how membership of the church is defined (ecclesiology), and not about how God saves his people (soteriology). In examining Gen 15:6 and Paul's use of it in discussion of Abraham's justification we have seen that it has to do with both, but that the starting point for justification is God rescuing his people—that is, saving them—from the place of their captivity so that he can bring his people into a new covenantal relationship with him. Only then does his church, his covenant people, become the "new creation" Paul speaks of 2 Cor 5:17 and Gal 6:5, and the "one new man" of Eph 2:15. We will explore further this pilgrimage from captivity into covenant when we look at Rom 5.

Conclusion

In summary, by now it should be clear that justification language is more extensive than the legal and accounting metaphors of traditional understanding. We have seen it is not a one-size-fits-all doctrine and that attempts to make it so result in losing the richness of its various hues, and how one applies the various meanings to any one Scripture depends upon the context and argument of the passage under review.

Many meanings fall under justification's semantic domain. At times, it is about acquittal and imputation as taught by the Reformers, as in Paul's use of Ps 32:2 regarding David's sin; the same sin for which God gave Israel the Mosaic law so that, in its keeping, she might be forgiven of her sin and made righteousness. However this was a work she failed to do, and instead of being a blessing, the law brought condemnation and guilt, and in the end became a curse from which only Christ could deliver them (Gal 3:10–13). We have also seen circumcision plays a part in justification: for Israel, in its national circumcision as a prerequisite for sharing in the Passover, and for the new covenant community, in its spiritual circumcision through the circumcision of Christ, i.e., the ripping of his flesh in crucifixion (Col 2:11–12), through which she has been prepared to be his bride.

We have also seen within justification the theme of salvation: God delivering his people from captivity as in the first exodus when Moses led Israel out of Egypt, returning his people from exile as in the second exodus when he brought them into a new covenant, and redeeming his people from sin as in the new exodus in Christ. This latter Paul builds upon in Rom 5. Within each of these moments in salvation history, there exists the theme of justification largely as a corporate event, with God not simply declaring his people to be in a covenant, but with him taking the step of bringing his collective, corporate community into a new relationship with him. While there remains a place for individual justification, we have seen this is only accomplished through the individual's participation in the corporate righteousness which has come to God's entire community of the faithful—the descendants of the faith of Abraham whose number is as the stars in the sky (Gen 15:5).

Finally, there is justification as God making covenant. This is the basis of his dealings with Abraham in Genesis 15 when the patriarch was justified—credited righteousness—and promised descendants beyond his imagining solely because of his faith. We found that Gen 15:6, so central to the Reformers' doctrine of justification and generally understood in relation to God's acquittal of sin, is not at all about sin, but rather about God making covenant—initiating a new relationship, which is entirely his to uphold. In similar manner, Ps 106:31 speaks of God justifying—crediting as righteous—Phinehas and his descendants by bringing them into a covenant because of his reaction to Israel's sin, not the acquittal of his own sin. Covenant making is also at the heart of Paul's correct use of Gen 15:6 in Rom 4 and elsewhere when he speaks of those—Jew and Gentile alike—who are brought by God into a covenantal relationship with him and declared members of his covenant community in Christ.

All of these means live within the doctrine of justification, with each meaning or theme having its own part to play, at times on its own, and at times in partnership with one or the other. Running throughout from start to finish, seemly as a thread binding them all together, is justification as God making covenant in order to reconcile "the world to himself" (2 Cor 5:19), to restore that which was broken in the fall of Adam. Justification as an all-encompassing doctrine cannot singularly be about any one of these meanings, but working together, each compliments or enriches the other depending upon the context in which each is used. Paul understood this perfectly, as will be seen as we explore Rom 4.

4:1 What then shall we say that Abraham, our forefather, discovered in this matter? Paul continues to anticipate the difficulties that the Jewish members of the Roman church will have as they listen to his letter. If he can demonstrate that the law was not instrumental in Abraham's acceptance, they might come to see that being justified by God does not depend on law keeping. If Paul can establish this truth, he will have delivered a decisive blow to their objection to his all-inclusive Gospel. It is necessary, therefore, to explain Abraham's relationship to the law so that his Jewish brethren may be convinced that the Gospel of Christ was not a challenge to God's covenant with Abraham but its fulfillment![38]

All Jews held Abraham in the highest regard. Since they considered his words decisive in matters of faith, it was vital for them to know of any judgment he had made. Abraham was not only their national ancestor and father, but also a friend of God (Jas 2:23) and the one with whom Yahweh had made the sacred covenant (Gen 15:1–20). They all would have known the story of his life of faith (Gen 12–25) from their earliest years, particularly his remarkable act of obedience on Mount Moriah, when he was set to slay his promised son in response to Yahweh's command. Paul, therefore, asks them the question: "What then shall we say that Abraham, our forefather, discovered in this matter?" The question he poses is concerned with Abraham's experience and findings as to how the law relates to justification, circumcision, and boasting. Paul had raised these subjects in the closing verses of the previous chapter (Rom 3:27–32).

---

38. Hays, "Abraham," 76–98, argues that the issue is whether Gentiles have to become ethnic Jews, converting to Judaism in order to become true children of Abraham. Wright, *Romans*, 736, correctly says that there is no question in Romans of erstwhile pagans believing that they had to become full Jews in order to be a part of the family of Abraham. Wright says, "The whole emphasis of the letter runs the other way, that the Roman Christians were tempted to look down on non-Christian Jews (chapters 9–11) and now on Christians, who whether or not because of their Jewish origins, wanted to maintain some of the food taboos and other cultural markers." The "weak" might be condemning the "strong," but the main problem seems to be that the "strong" are looking down on the "weak." Tobin, "Abraham," 193–98, notes that the seed of Abraham, in Galatians, is used as a singular noun, excluding the Jews from being the seed; whereas, in Rom 4, it is interpreted as a collective noun. Thus Paul sought to bring out the continuity of his positions about justification and the place of the Gentiles.

4:2 If, in fact, Abraham was justified by works, he had something to boast about—but not before God. Paul begins to answer the question he has just posed by considering Abraham's justification. Initially, he teases his Jewish brethren by leading them in the direction of their own argument. However, at the point where they would have endorsed his words, Paul turns the argument around by adding: "but not before God." The point that he seeks to make is this: even if Abraham *had* kept the law of conscience (there being no law in Sinai-terms at this point), and so deserving the praise and admiration of men, God knew the truth of his heart. Jews should have known this, as the narrative in Genesis does not gloss over Abraham's weaknesses and failings. It presents him as a flawed man who rose to be a great example of faith. God did not justify Abraham because he kept the law, but rather conferred on him a new status because of grace.

If we examine the Genesis passage, which speaks of the justification of Abraham (Gen 15), we find it does not suggest, or even infer, that Abraham's sin was the issue. The declaration of justification (of being credited righteousness) was in response to his belief that God would give him a son.

The question, then, has to be "what has the belief God would give Abraham a son to do with his justification?" If we believe justification refers solely to acquittal from sin (the normal understanding of Protestant theology), the answer has to be "Very little;" however, if justification is to do with God delivering his people from a condition that they cannot change, then it has to be "Very much!"

Promising the birth of this child of this child was the beginning of the outworking of God's plan of salvation. This promise included Yahweh's commitment to deliver not only Abraham and his seed from slavery and oppression but the entire human race (Gen 15:13–14). Paul sees the full import of this when he reasons the seed that is to bless the whole world is, in fact, Christ himself (Gal 3:16). He is "the seed to whom the promises referred" (Gal 3:19). He is the one who brings justification to God's people because he saves them from their sins, which have separated them from God.

4:3 What does the scripture say? "Abraham believed God, and it was credited to him as righteousness." As noted, we must ensure we understand the use of being "credited righteousness" (justified) in the story of Abraham.[39] We have considered the different meanings of the term in the excursus (D), where we noted that the term has a larger semantic domain than is normally realized.

We noted Abraham's justification in Gen 15:6 spoke of his being brought into the covenant inaugurated by God. While Reformed teaching interprets the act of being de-

---

39. Fitzmyer, *Romans*, 373, notes that: "The quotation comes not from the MT ('Abram believed Yahweh, and he credited it to him as righteousness,' where one cannot tell in the ambiguous Hebrew form who is crediting uprightness to whom), but from the LXX (with the ass. Vb. and the prep. phrase *eis dikaiosynēn*). Abraham believed in Yahweh's promise of numerous progeny, and this faith was 'booked to his credit' as uprightness (*ṣĕdāqāh*)." Nevertheless, while Fitzmyer warns us of the danger of misreading the text, he imposes on it an accounting and forensic meaning, and does not follow the covenantal context which would yield a different reading. What Paul is saying is that Abraham believed that God would give him a son, and that this heir would become the first of millions of offspring. Effectively, he believed that God would be faithful to the promise he had made. God responded by declaring him righteous, i.e., he credited him with the headship of a redeemed community.

clared righteous as the acquittal of sin, we saw that, although a valid meaning elsewhere, did not apply to Gen 15:6, or to all texts employing justification language. We also noted those who accused the Reformers of error have themselves misunderstood Paul. Too often, they have focused on one meaning of the term (a declaration that an individual, or a people, is in the covenant), and have imposed it on texts containing justification terminology irrespective of context.

4:4 Now when a man works, his wages are not credited to him as a gift, but as an obligation. Paul tries to explain the significance of the statement that Abraham's faith was credited to him as righteousness. We can use the modern example of a bank account. For most people, what they earn is the result of their employment–their employers being obliged to credit their accounts accordingly. However, if money is put into someone's account as a gift, it is still credited to him, although not earned by him. In a similar way, Paul is saying there are two ways someone can be credited: because of his own effort, or as a gift.

The covenant Yahweh made with Abraham (where God gifted him with righteousness) made no demands on the patriarch other than the demand of faith. Since Paul says faith is the gift of God (Eph 2:8), we can see that the justification of Abraham was all of grace!

4:5 However, to the man who does not work but trusts God who justifies the wicked, his faith is credited as righteousness. If we adopt the traditional legal meaning for "justified" in this verse, we have Paul saying God does the very thing he has said he will not do—acquit the guilty (Exod 23:7). The practice of justifying the wicked was something Yahweh abhorred. He demanded it not be tolerated.

The only way the conflict in this verse can be resolved is by appreciating that here Paul used the term "wicked" in a particular, covenantal context. Those outside the covenant were called "the wicked" ("ungodly" in KJV).[40] If we are to avoid imposing "acquits" on "justifies," for fear of having Yahweh doing what he prohibits and so accusing him of duplicity, then we must choose the alternative meaning for the word that comes from the psalms and the prophets.[41] There, the term speaks of God rescuing his ungodly people from their condition in exile, and restoring them to their inheritance (Isa 32:1; 54:14; 62:1–2).

In spiritual terms, Paul is saying that unconverted man is outside of any relationship with God because of his condition in Adam. He is ungodly, and, therefore, unable to meet the perfect demands of God (Rom 3:23). His acceptance is possible solely because God delivers those who have faith in him.

---

40. Kreuzer, "Abrahambild," 208–19, argues that Paul's statement in Rom 4:5 that Abraham trusted "him who justifies the ungodly" suggests that Abraham is being classified among the "ungodly." Kreuzer considers early Jewish traditions regarding Abraham's stay in Mesopotamia (see Gen 15:13–16), and notes that, before his call, Abraham was "ungodly"—not in the sense of being immoral but rather as a "heathen," living in a heathen milieu.

41. See Zeisler, *Righteousness*; Hill, *Words*.

When a man is gifted with faith that God is trustworthy and has made a covenant into which he is called, God responds by crediting (gifting) him with righteousness.[42] In other words, God brings him into a covenant relationship. He is accepted as though he had kept the whole law and had done nothing to offend. He is removed from the kingdom of darkness and made to share in all the promises of God's mercy and grace. Such a hope for one who has been troubled by his wrongdoing is the most amazing message.

The statement is worthy of repetition: being credited righteousness in response to faith is *much greater* than just being treated as innocent. It speaks about being the recipient of covenant promises and blessings. Also, it must be remembered that, while the discussion is rooted in how God justified Abraham, Paul's argument is not about individual salvation but the salvation of the Gentiles. It is about how they have come into the covenant with God. In other words, Paul's is a corporate argument. However, it is clear individuals must respond, like Abraham, in faith to be brought into the covenant.

It could easily go unnoticed that the description ἀσεβής *asebēs* "ungodly" (KJV) is applied to Abraham as well as to the Gentiles. While the word is used in the LXX to speak of wickedness in general, it really denotes a wrong attitude towards God rather than actual sinful actions. Abraham, according to Gen 17,[43] was not circumcised until he was ninety-nine years old. In other words, when God justified him when he was less than eighty-five, Abraham was a Gentile. He was ungodly!

4:6 David says the same thing when he speaks of the blessedness of the man to whom God credits righteousness apart from works. Paul now turns to the justification of David, referencing David's thoughts in Ps 32:2. Apart from Abraham, he is the key figure in Jewish history and, as with Abraham, God made a covenant with him (2 Sam 7:11–17)—a covenant the Jews still look to be fulfilled. In introducing both Abraham and David, Paul plays a masterstroke. He can now put a case before his Jewish hearers they will not be able to answer.

Abraham and David are the two giants of the OT seen by Jews as great examples of men who pleased God; Abraham as a Gentile, David as a fallen Jew. If these great men needed to be credited righteousness by God, there was no way an "ordinary" Jew could be exempt. Paul focuses on the extraordinary joy which floods into a forgiven person when he says David "speaks of the blessedness." This word is μακαρισμον (*makarismon*) and has the same root as the word "blessed" used by Jesus in the Beatitudes.

The danger we face when reading the text is to think that Abraham's need was identical to that of David. However, the problem Israel's king had was his sin, and there is no direct suggestion this was so with Abraham. It is a presumption to assume a forensic meaning for "being justified" in both cases. Another difference between Abraham and David is that, while Abraham was brought into a covenant relationship with Yahweh, David was already sharing in that relationship as part of the covenant community.

---

42. This digression into individual response in no way weakens the corporate argument in the passage. Paul is defending the Gentile believers from Jewish insistence that they must accept circumcision in order to be full members of the covenant.

43. And to rabbinic tradition: *Mekita,* Exod 22:20.

The Reformed understanding of the passage (Ps 32:2) is that it speaks of sinful David's justification, or acceptance, by God, an interpretation which is then used to support the need of justification for a sinner. This has a problem, however. It misses the fact that, in OT terms, David already had that relationship with him. In NT terms, David is not seeking initial acceptance (which is what the doctrine of justification traditionally expounds), but is longing for the return of fellowship which has been spoiled by sin. If we are prepared to disregard distinct theological concepts and ignore the meanings of the words their contexts dictate, we can make the Bible teach almost anything our minds can imagine. Our task must be to respect contexts, to treat seriously the theological frameworks of the Scriptures, and to do everything in our power to avoid restricting what the text of Scripture is trying to say.

What is identical between Abraham and David is that they are both men in need of the saving activity of God: Abraham as a Gentile, David as a fallen Jew. We need to remember that Paul is addressing Jewish objections to the Gospel, and we would be failing in our exegetical task if we assumed the argument is identical for both Jews and Gentiles. To take that step of application, without reflecting more carefully on the subject of the original statement and David's status concerning the covenant, will cause us to lose the thrust of the argument. We must understand the meaning of the statements in their original settings before we look for legitimate extensions of their application. In other words, Paul is demonstrating the necessity of God's grace for those within the covenant as much as for those being brought into it. God's grace maintains the covenant as much as it has created it.

Thus, in Ps 32:1–2 LXX, David speaks of the blessedness of the man "whose transgressions are forgiven, whose sins are covered." Many would have observed David and said God blessed him because of his immense power and prestige. Having been born into a humble home, he progressed from shepherd boy to great military leader, and then became the king of Israel. This progression was not the result of burning ambition, but the result of God fulfilling his promise to him. This is clear in the way he exercised mercy toward Saul (1 Sam 26:9–11). Most would have seen David's elevation to kingship as the pinnacle of blessing and happiness–but not David. For him, the blessed person was the one who had certainty about being right with God, not because he had slavishly obeyed religious regulations, but because he knew the experience of God's forgiveness in his life.

The story of his fall is astonishing and painful. He descended from lust to adultery and, finally, to murder (2 Sam 11:1–27). Through a series of attempts at self-protection, David sank deeper and deeper into sin and guilt. The one who had been the joy of thousands became nothing but a twisted liar trying to avoid shameful exposure. He records his depression as he sinks into hopeless self-condemnation. He could not sleep and his health declined as he felt overwhelming guilt giving way to a creeping death (Ps 32:3–4). His whole world, with its achievements and prestige, collapsed in ruins around his feet, because he had thought himself to be exempt from the law of God.

It is in this setting that we need to understand the relief that flooded David's heart when he wrote of the blessedness of those whose sins are forgiven. It was out of his personal experience that he wrote. What is surprising is the absence of clear reference to sacrificial ritual in the psalm. There could be echoes of it in the statement "whose sins are covered," but the emphasis is clearly the gracious response of Yahweh to David's guilt and sin.

4:7–8 Blessed are they whose transgressions are forgiven, whose sins are covered. Blessed is the man whose sin the Lord will not count against him. Paul quotes the Psalm of David for two reasons:

First, it describes the stark contrast between guilt and forgiveness, contrasting men who are guilty before God with those who, having experienced forgiveness, have a new start in life where guilt and sin do not count against them. By using Ps 32, Paul is able to drive home the seriousness and enormity of the sinful condition.

(Here Paul uses two words from the semantic domain relating to sin. The first word is ἀνομίαι *anomiai*.[44] This term speaks of lawlessness [Rom 6:19a; 1 John 3:4], producing lawless deeds [Matt 13:41; Rom 6:19b; Heb 10:17]. The term describes man's disobedience as he disregards the commands of God and does what he pleases. The second Greek word is ἁμαρτίαν '*amartiai;*45 a term normally employed in the singular that denotes sin as a principle.)

Second, Paul quotes the psalm because King David composed it, lending weight to his argument. Jews saw David, as well as Abraham, as having a unique relationship with God and, like Abraham, God had made a covenant with him. These two figures are not only important for Jews but for Christians as well, the NT writers continually stressing how the respective covenants made with these men have been fulfilled in Jesus. They are perfect examples of how God deals with Jews by maintaining the covenant with David, the circumcised; and Gentiles by bringing Abraham, the uncircumcised, into the covenant). Contrary to popular and scholarly opinion, Moses has little significance in the NT. While the covenant made with Israel at Sinai was important, it was only temporary (Gal 3:24); and while it was not made personally with Moses, he acted as mediator between Yahweh and Israel.

By putting Abraham and David before his readers, Paul delivers a blow to all in Rome who dared think they were special, having all they needed within their religion. He seeks to use these men to show the absolute necessity for everyone to be made right with God. God dealt with Abraham from outside of the covenant and David from within. If such pillars of Israel needed to be credited righteousness, it would be presumptuous in the extreme for anyone in Rome to deny his need also.

---

44. "ἀνομία, ας *f:* to behave with complete disregard for the laws or regulations of a society—'to live lawlessly, lawlessness, lawless living.' συλλέξουσιν ἐκ τῆς βασιλείας αὐτοῦ πάντα τὰ σκάνδαλα καὶ τοὺς ποιοῦντας τὴν ἀνομίαν 'they will gather up out of his kingdom all who cause people to sin and those who live in lawlessness' Matt 13.41. In some languages one may translate ἀνομία in Matt 13.41 as 'to live as though there were no laws,' 'to refuse completely to obey the laws,' or 'to live as one who despises all laws.'" Louw-Nida 88.139.

45. "ἁμαρτία *a failure, fault, sin,* Aesch., etc.; ἁμ. τινός *a fault committed by* one, Id.; ἁμ. δόξης *fault* of judgment, Thuc. 2. generally, *guilt, sin,* Plat., Arist." N. T. Louw-Nida 2124.

4:9 Is this blessedness only for the circumcised, or also for the uncircumcised? We have noted that Abraham's faith was credited to him as righteousness and that Paul referred to the uncircumcised Abraham and the circumcised David in support of his argument.[46]

However, the danger remained that some of Paul's fellow Jews in Rome, while agreeing Abraham and David were made right with God through faith in his promises, still thought these men were Jews. They could reason, therefore, that any who would know God's mercy must also become a Jew.

Paul was extremely anxious the Roman church should resist this line of argument because, if Gentiles thought they had to become Jews to be made right with God, the Gospel was at risk. It would mean that people did not become right with God through faith in the work of Christ but through religious initiation. For Gentiles, circumcision would mean adding to the completed salvation God had given them through Jesus' death and resurrection (Rom 4:25). If God had acquitted them of their guilt, what more could they do? Trying to add anything was tantamount to saying that Christ's saving act was insufficient.

4:10 Under what circumstances was it credited? Was it after he was circumcised, or before? It was not after, but before! To ward off the line of thinking the Gentiles had to be circumcised, Paul puts before his readers the circumstances of Abraham's circumcision. He presses his readers to appreciate that, when God declared Abraham righteous, he was not circumcised. As noted earlier, he was not a Jew but a Gentile! Furthermore, he continued to be uncircumcised for many years while in covenant relationship and fellowship with God.

4:11 And he received the sign of circumcision, a seal of the righteousness that he had by faith while he was still uncircumcised. So then, he is the father of all who believe but have not been circumcised, in order that righteousness might be credited to them. Paul's argument must have struck at the hearts of those Jews in Rome who had not appreciated that the Gentiles had equal status with them before God. Their belief in the uniqueness and privilege of Israel had preserved them and their ancestors throughout the nation's long history of suffering. This conviction of privilege was now being stripped away by one who had been its very champion.

---

46. The rabbis put great emphasis on the importance of circumcision, as the following texts show: "And every one that is born, the flesh of whose foreskin is not circumcised on the eighth day, belongs not to the children of the covenant which the Lord made with Abraham, but to the children of destruction; nor is there, moreover, any sign on him that he is the Lord's" (*Book of Jubilees* 15.26). Rabbi (i.e., Judah the Patriarch, 2nd century AD) said: "Great is circumcision, for despite all the righteous duties which Abraham our father fulfilled, he was not called 'perfect' until he was circumcised" (*Nedarim* 3.11). Another is reported as saying: "But for circumcision God would not have created the world. It was laid down that: Unless the seal of Abraham is inscribed on your flesh, you cannot taste the Passover (*Exod R.* xix.5). Again: "No Israelite man who is circumcised will go down to Gehinnom. What then of the few wicked in Israel who deserve Gehinnom? They cannot go down to that place of doom circumcised, so God sends an angel who stretches their foreskin and then they descend to Gehinnom" (*Exod R.*xix.4). Cited from Morris, *Romans*, 201 n. 36.

It is difficult for Gentiles to understand what this argument must have meant, and still does, to Jews who hold to the election of Israel as God's special people. However, it had not been an election to the exclusion of other nations, but with the purpose that, through Israel's witness to them as the servant of the Lord, the nations of the earth would also seek Yahweh and become his people (Gen 12:3; Isa 19:19–25; 42:1–4). Abraham was as much the father of the believing Gentiles as he was of the believing Jews. Indeed, the point Paul is subtly, yet powerfully, making is that when God made his covenant with Abraham, he was making it with a man who was a Gentile; with one who was not circumcised.[47]

In this text, Paul speaks of circumcision as a seal of the righteousness Abraham had by faith. Some have sought to say this is grounds for linking baptism with circumcision,[48] because the early church fathers spoke of baptism as being a seal. This association, which is widely held, overlooks an important fact. Paul says the NT completion of the symbol of the circumcised body is the circumcised heart.[49] If we miss this typological fulfillment–whatever our view of baptism–we miss a vitally important part of the evidence of initiation theology. Because this circumcision is the work of God's Spirit, it is not of the will of man but of God (John 1:13).

4:12 And he is also the father of the circumcised who not only are circumcised but who also walk in the footsteps of the faith that our father Abraham had before he was circumcised. The new covenant, established in Christ, does not exclude Jews. Paul's argument is that it includes all who share the faith of Abraham. What he cannot accept is the idea of his countrymen claiming they had advantages over the Gentiles, and trying to exempt themselves from God's salvation through the death of his Son. Paul is more than willing to concede the Jews had immense privileges (Rom 9:1–5), but these were given in order that they may be prepared for the coming of the Messiah. Indeed, these privileges made them more responsible and in greater danger of judgment than the Gentiles (Amos 3:2). The Jews were given the law and could not claim ignorance of what God required. Paul, of course, has already countered any possibility of the Gentiles claiming ignorance of the law, writing that they had the law of their own consciences as had Abraham—a law they failed to follow (Rom 2:14–16).

4:13 It was not through law that Abraham and his offspring received the promise that he would be heir of the world, but through the righteousness that comes by faith. The Jews believed their future inheritance was the consequence of having the covenant, and this, in turn, was the consequence of being circumcised. However, this sequence of events reversed the progression of the OT, where the promise of the land was given

---

47. Bailey, "Territorial," 59–69, argued that Paul widened the promises to the Gentiles due to influences in Judaism. These had led some intertestamental literature writers to argue that the land was universalized and spiritualized. Such a suggestion is not only speculative but also unnecessary. The OT had repeatedly predicted that the new covenant community would incorporate people from all nations.

48. See Käsemann, *Romans*, 117.

49. For a fuller discussion, see Holland, *Contours*, chapter 7.

to Abraham *before* he was circumcised (Gen 12:7; 17:11), as was his justification (Gen 15:6).

The Reformers understood the phrase: "through the righteousness that is through faith" to mean a legal standing of innocence. There are passages where it does mean this (e.g., Rom 5:17–19) but, in this verse, Paul is correctly following the meaning of Gen 15:6 with its emphasis on covenant-making, just as he did in Rom 4:2 where he argued being credited righteousness was about Yahweh making a covenant with Abraham. If he echoes the same meaning here, then Paul is speaking of a relationship created solely because of God's mercy.

Thus, the gift of righteousness and the promise of the inheritance of the land of Canaan were independent of Abraham's circumcision, which God instituted as a sign and a seal that he had sworn an oath to him (Gen 17:1–14). This oath had been made many years earlier, when Abraham was promised he would be the father of a mighty nation. The Jews, however, made a subtle but devastating change when applying this order of events to themselves: that they had the covenant and had inherited the promises because of their circumcision, and for no other reason.

However, Paul goes beyond the original promise of inheriting the land of Canaan (Gen 17:8) to inheriting the earth. This understanding had been slowly emerging in the OT, as seen in the promise to the Davidic royal family at their coronation: "ask of me, I will make the nations your inheritance, the ends of the earth your possession" (Ps 2:8). Eventually, it was understood that, because God was the God of the whole earth (Neh 9:6; Ps 24:1–2; 96:1–5), his people's inheritance extended way beyond the original promise of Canaan to Abraham. Perhaps Paul is deliberately adopting this latter understanding because it served his purpose well. For Paul, the good news is for all the peoples of the earth: that Abraham's children of faith are being found throughout the nations. They are the inheritance of Jesus, the Son of David. They will inherit the earth and reign with Christ (Matt 5:5; 1 Cor 6:2).

4:14–15 For if those who live by law are heirs, faith has no value and the promise is worthless, because law brings wrath. And where there is no law there is no transgression. Paul continues his argument by making two important points.

First, if the Jews believe the keeping of the law exempts them from the requirement of faith, their understanding of its purpose is erroneous. We have seen that scholarship has clarified how the unconverted Paul, along with most Jews, did not see the law as a constant threat. Most saw it as the instrument God had given to maintain the covenant into which he had brought them through his free grace. In the Jewish mind, the law was about maintaining salvation and not about obtaining it. It had been true the law maintained Israel's unique relationship with God throughout the OT, but now Paul is saying its task is completed. The promise has been fulfilled, for what the law pointed to has now arrived (Gal 3:24)! The promised new covenant, which would welcome Gentiles on an equal footing with Jews, has been established.

Now, if the Jews insisted on maintaining a covenant that had served its purpose, they were rejecting God's plan for their lives. Paul challenges them to face the consequences of their understanding of the law's purpose. The claims of the Judaizers were turning the law into a means of salvation—something never intended. They had developed arguments about the need to keep it in order to control the Gentile believers. By insisting on circumcision, the Judaizers thought that they could determine who was admitted into the covenant. They had no problem in Gentiles converting to Judaism and becoming people of the covenant, but what horrified the Jews was the thought that admission could happen apart from circumcision, i.e., outside of Judaism.[50] Paul points out that, if they want the law to play this role, they are removing themselves from the grace of the covenant made with Abraham because, as their illustrious ancestor had not come into a covenant relationship with God through circumcision, they were no longer operating in the Abrahamic covenant. They had exchanged works for grace. Now, if this was so, they had put themselves *outside* of the covenant and, to their horror, into the same condition as the Gentiles.

There are a number of logical consequences to this legalistic understanding of the law. The Jews are not only reconstructing its purpose, but also reinterpreting the covenant made with Abraham. If law keeping is the condition of entrance, then the Abrahamic covenant is of no value (something no orthodox Jew could contemplate), faith has no value, and the promise is of no value. In other words, Paul is saying the Jewish understanding of Israel as the elect nation is a misguided illusion because it makes Abraham's faith worthless, the covenant wrongly administered, and Israel outside of it. And why is this so? It is because Abraham was counted righteous when he was not circumcised!

The ultimate outcome of Israel's national righteousness is God's wrath. By removing herself from the principle of faith, she invites judgment by the law, which she knows brings wrath.[51]

Second, Paul raises another consequence of their argument in saying, "where there is no law there is no transgression." Responding to the Jewish claim that the Gentiles were not under the law, he will show in the next section (from a line of argument familiar to Jewish thought) that guilt is only attributable when there is full knowledge of the law (Rom 5:13). "So," Paul says, "you are putting the Gentile believers outside of the law. Well, if you are going to be consistent, you are declaring them guiltless!"

The logic is devastating. Their argument against the universality of the Gospel caused the Jews to put themselves outside of the grace they claimed was the essence of the covenant with Abraham while, at the same time, assigning the Gentiles, whom they were seeking to control, to the place where they could be heirs of the Abrahamic

---

50. This is not the same as saying that Saul (Paul) persecuted the early Jewish believers because they were admitting uncircumcised Gentiles into the covenant, as argued by Dunn, *Theology*, and Wright, *What*. There was no Gentile mission until Peter was compelled to preach to Gentiles in Acts 10, so the persecution was about some other issue. It was, in fact, because Saul's fellow Jews, who had become followers of Jesus of Nazareth, were preaching that the Messiah had been crucified. That was, and remains, abhorrent to any Jew who has not been challenged by the resurrection (1 Cor 1: 23).

51. Hodge, *Romans*, 316, notes: It is probable, therefore, that the judicial abandonment of men "to a reprobate mind," a punitive withdrawing of the influences of his Holy Spirit, and the giving them up to the uncountereracted operation of the hardening or perverting influences by which they are surrounded, are all expressed by the language fo the apostle.

139

blessings. This was because Abraham was without the Jewish law when he was declared righteous, as it had not yet been given.

4:16 Therefore, the promise comes by faith, so that it may be by grace and may be guaranteed to all Abraham's offspring—not only to those who are of the law but also to those who are of the faith of Abraham. He is the father of us all. Having demonstrated the fault in their logic, that salvation is through the keeping of the law, Paul reminds the Jews: "the promise comes by faith." This need not threaten them, as the promise embraces the Jews as well as the Gentiles. However, it does demand they stop seeing themselves as the only race that God loves, and start accepting that the love of God extends to members of all races who are brought into the covenant on the same condition of faith as Abraham.

Paul's closing statement, "(Abraham) is the father of us all," would have been bitter medicine for the converted Jews in Rome to take, but take it they must. If Jews wanted to continue to insist God was only their father and deny the OT message (Isa 2:1–5), they cannot enter into the salvation the prophets had long predicted. They must remain outside of the covenant, for at its heart was the blessing of the nations (Gen 12:2–3).

4:17 As it is written: "I have made you a father of many nations." He is our father in the sight of God, in whom he believed—the God who gives life to the dead and calls things that are not as though they were. Paul seals his argument by quoting the very Scriptures the Jews professed to be defending. He quotes from Gen 17:5, showing there is nothing in his argument about the inclusion of the Gentiles contrary to the law. Indeed, the law demands their acceptance. In writing "he is our father in the sight of God," Paul tactfully hints it is not what the Jews make of Abraham that matters, but what God made of him. For God declared in Gen 17:5, "No longer will you be called Abram (exalted father); your name will be Abraham (father of many), for I have made you the father of many nations."[52]

In referring to God as the God who gives life to the dead and overturns death itself, Paul coins a pithy statement that sums up the OT's testimony of God. The statement helps to pave the way for the argument about Abraham's faith. In effect, Paul is saying, "It doesn't matter what you think. You will not stop God. Remember, he is used to making things out of nothing and giving life to the dead (Gen 1:1–31; Gen 2:7; Heb 11:2, 17–19; Ezek 37:1–14; Hos 13:14). What God is doing with the Gentiles is nothing new for him. If you are a true child of Abraham—if you really share his faith—then you will accept that God's grace is always achieving what man considers to be impossible."

4:18 Against all hope, Abraham in hope believed and so became the father of many nations, just as it had been said to him, "So shall your offspring be." The patriarch accepted that God would do what he had promised in giving him an heir (Gen 15:2–4). He also accepted that he would have countless descendants: "He (the LORD) took him

---

52. Most Jews recognized that the Gentiles would benefit from the fulfillment of God's promises to Abraham. However, they strictly maintained the division between Jew and Gentile in the Messianic kingdom. See Donaldson, *Remapping*, 98.

outside and said, 'Look up at the heavens and count the stars—if indeed you can count them.' Then he said to him, 'So shall your offspring be'" (Gen 15:5). Abraham's quiet acceptance of this amazing news suggests blind, simple faith (Gen 15:6). The text records no reaction to this announcement, other than his believing God. We know that he was not stunned into silence, because he swiftly articulated his anxiety to know how he would gain possession of the land God had promised him (Gen 15:8).

Why did Abraham "in hope" believe so readily God would give him a son when his ageing wife had a long history of barrenness? Perhaps the answer lies in the next chapter, where Scripture reveals Abraham was not averse to taking another wife (Gen 16:1–4a). Perhaps he could accept that God would give him a son if he embraced the convention of the day and took an unmarried woman to bear his children, so building a family for Sarah through her. It is clear Abraham did not expect Sarah would be the mother of the promised son from his reaction to the news in Gen 17: "(God said to Abraham), 'I will bless her (Sarah) and will give you a son by her. I will bless her so that she will be the mother of nations; kings of peoples will come from her.' Abraham fell face down; he laughed and said to himself, 'Will a son be born to a man a hundred years old? Will Sarah bear a child at the age of ninety?'" (Gen 17:16–18).

Paul's statement that Abraham would become "the father of many nations" was part of the prophetic promise God gave Abraham in Gen 17, describing him twice in this way (Gen 17:4–5). God gave Abraham this promise when he instituted circumcision and made the announcement Sarah was to be the mother of the promised son and of nations (Gen 17:4–5, 16).

Abraham did not question the LORD in the covenant-making and ratification ceremonies. However, when he allowed his reason to control his faith, Abraham took matters into his own hands, and laid the foundations for conflict for generations to come (Gen 16:1–16; 21:1–20; Gal 4:21–31). In like fashion, the Jews were acting like "faithless" Abraham[53] in trying to manage the promises of God as well as in providing their own heir–Judaism–as inheritor of the promises. Nevertheless, their faithlessness will not deflect God from fulfilling his promise that the Gentiles will be heirs of the covenants of promise (Eph 2:11—3:13; 1 Thess 2:14–16). Abraham's offspring will be from all nations. The fulfillment of the promise is certain, for he is the God who calls those things that are not as though they were and who gives life to the dead. What an incredible source of encouragement that must have been for Paul during the sufferings he experienced in being a midwife at the birth of the Gentile churches (Gal 4:19). It ought to be a similar source of encouragement for the church of the twenty-first century, for she can labor for the evangelisation of unbelievers with the certain knowledge that, regardless of how difficult and impossible the task might appear, God brings life out of death.

4:19–20 Without weakening in his faith, he faced the fact that his body was as good as dead—since he was about a hundred years old—and that Sarah's womb was also dead. Yet he did not waver through unbelief regarding the promise of God, but was

---

53. Of course, the text stresses the faith of Abraham. It will be shown that this description does not relate to Isaac's birth, but to another event in the patriarch's life.

strengthened in his faith and gave glory to God. The reference to Abraham's steadfast faith is clearly linked to the statement about the frailty of his body and the barrenness of Sarah's womb. It is understandable why this verse has traditionally been identified with Isaac's conception, but we need to ask if this is what Paul had in mind. Could there be another event when the reference to the condition of their bodies and steadfastness of Abraham's faith would be equally, if not more, appropriate?[54]

Indeed, such an alternative would be helpful, for it is not easy to defend the claim that Abraham's faith did not waver through unbelief at the time of his son's conception.[55] He had laughed, as had Sarah, at the promise of a child being born to them because of their advanced years and her barrenness (Gen 17:17). Furthermore, immediately after receiving the promise of Isaac's birth, Abraham acted in an astonishing way.

In his hundredth year there was famine in the land, Abraham again moved his household down into the region of the Negev where he had traveled some twenty-five years earlier when he first came to the promised land. Now, upon entering Egypt, he feared for his life because of the beauty of his wife. She agreed to say that she was his sister, with the result that she was taken into the palace to be Pharaoh's wife (causing him, in ignorance, to commit adultery). The truth of her marital state was eventually exposed, and Abraham and his household were expelled from Egypt (Gen 12:10–20).

Tragically, he repeats this scenario. The now justified and circumcised Abraham, having received the promise of the birth of Isaac, traveled to and settled in Gerar. He told King Abimelech that Sarah was his sister as, once more, he feared for his life should the king desire her. Again, Sarah was taken as the king's new wife and the plan of salvation was in jeopardy. As happened in Egypt, the truth of Abraham's sin came to light and he was reprimanded by a distraught king who restored Sarah to her husband (Gen 20). This was not a failure of the moment for Abraham had done this on other occasions as well, such as on entering the promised land when he said to Sarah, "This is how you can show your love to me: Everywhere we go, say of me, 'He is my brother'"(Gen 20:13).

It is to this narrative, at the time when Isaac was conceived, that traditional understanding applies Rom 4:19–20 as testifying of Abraham's faith that did not weaken and

---

54. The following interpretation does not deny the miraculous nature of Isaac's birth, but the miracle is not about the manner of conception nor even on a special form of faith needed for the conception, but it is that Yahweh, in fulfilment of his promise, caused Sarah to be fertile when she had previously been barren.

55. There is also the difficulty of describing the conception in such glowing terms. Murray, *Romans*, 1.150–52, falls into this absurdity when he says, "it is not unreasonable, however, to regard the faith referred to here as instrumental after the pattern of the unbelief in the preceding clause and thus to understand the clause to mean that Abraham was strengthened; that is, empowered, *by* his faith. The sense would then be that the strength by which Abraham was able to perform the procreative act in begetting Isaac was ministered through the instrumentality of faith." Morris, *Romans*, 212, makes a similar claim that is out of touch with reality: "it was not possible for the couple to have a child in the normal manner." Abraham fathered other children after the birth of Isaac with no suggestion of divine help (see Gen 25:1–4, where he has six children by Keturah), and fathering and bearing children in old age was not uncommon in OT days. These facts make it difficult to uphold the claim the birth of Isaac came about in an abnormal manner with Abraham having to be given divine strength to achieve procreation. Moo, *Romans*, 285, says: "we might also stress the meaning of the word διακρίνω as we have brought it out above and suggest that Paul is not denying the presence of some doubt in Abraham's faith (for after all, he was a sinful human) but is focusing on the heart's attitude of Abraham towards God's promise."

belief that did not waver from the promise he and Sarah would conceive a son in their old age. However, Abraham's behavior in surrendering Sarah to Abimelech at the time of Isaac's conception challenges this judgment. I am not challenging the fact that Abraham was emerging as a man of faith. He believed the promise regarding the birth of Isaac. Clearly, Heb 11:11 states Isaac's birth was the fruit of Abraham's faith, but—like Rom 4:19–20—the reference is to something other than Isaac's conception. In Heb 11, faith is faithfulness to Yahweh in the midst of the trials of life, not the special capacity to believe in such a way that the miraculous happens. At this point in his story, Abraham's faith cannot be described as steadfast and unwavering.[56]

However, there is an event when Abraham did exercise such faith, and in a way that can only be described as remarkable. That event was the offering of his son, Isaac, on Mount Moriah. How many years after the birth of Isaac this event took place, we cannot be certain. The boy, Isaac, had been weaned, and was old enough to carry wood upon his back and articulate his concern for the animal to be sacrificed (Gen 22:6–8). Perhaps Abraham was about one hundred and five years old. Paul describes him as being "about one hundred years old." He cannot be definite as the Genesis text only hints at Abraham's age at the time of this event, despite being specific at other key events in his life. These include setting out from Haran (seventy five), the birth of Ishmael (eighty six), circumcision (ninety nine), the birth of Isaac (one hundred), the death of Sarah (one hundred and thirty seven), the marriage of Isaac (one hundred and forty) and his own death (one hundred and seventy five). However, the physical condition of Abraham and Sarah at the time of Isaac's sacrifice would have matched Paul's description of their physical weakness mentioned in Rom 4:19–20. While the description would have applied at the time of Isaac's conception as well, it would apply even more so at the later time of Abraham's testing.

This test was a challenge that demanded an amazingly strong and unwavering faith. Having been given Isaac, his heir, Abraham was asked to sacrifice him as a burnt offering (Gen 22:1–2). All the promises of the covenant God had made with Abraham rested in Isaac's fathering of a family. Nevertheless, Abraham set about obeying the command immediately, and left Beersheba for Moriah in the early hours of the following day (Gen 22:3).

Such unquestioning obedience could only be displayed by a man of living faith–a man who believed God could bring life from the dead, something both he and Sarah had experienced firsthand with the conception of Isaac. It is in this context, after Isaac's conception, that Paul's description of Abraham's faith as unwavering is entirely appropriate. Having seen God bring life to his and Sarah's "dead" bodies, Abraham had to believe that, when God asked for the life of Isaac—the heir of the promise—he would raise him from the dead to fulfill his covenant promises (Gen 22:5). Paul's glowing description of

---

56. Additionally, Gal 4:23 says Isaac "was born as the result of a promise," but does not refer to Abraham's faith. The emphasis is on God's faithfulness in giving Abraham and Sarah a child. Indeed, the context of this statement is that Abraham had two sons, one born "in the ordinary way" (Gal 4:23), the other "born as the result of a promise." What is emphasized is how the weakness of Abraham's faith did not hinder God. The use of Abraham as a model of faith does not relate to the birth of Isaac, but to the faith that believed God and through which righteousness was credited (Gal 3:6–9).

Abraham as "having not weakened in his faith" cannot be about the time of Isaac's conception. Such a statement, however, is entirely appropriate for him when he was about to offer his son to God.

Is Paul reflecting upon this incident in Rom 4:19–20? Is he reminding his Jewish opponents of Abraham's amazing act of faith and obedience? The sacrifice of Isaac shows him to have become the man of faith that Paul presents him to be. All the failures that marred his earlier life have paled into insignificance. He has become the God-fearing man he aspired to be in his younger years—doing what God asked of him, regardless of the cost.

He began this journey of faith when he obeyed God's call to leave Ur. He exercised faith when he believed God would give him an heir and countless descendants; a faith that resulted in the birth of Isaac. However, one could argue Abraham's acts of faith, while praiseworthy, had less than pure motives. With each exercise of faith, there was gain for Abraham and obedience was a "sensible" choice. However, Moriah was different! Abraham soared to the highest heights of faith when he took the knife to slay Isaac. He believed God would give life to the dead. Nothing can be attributed to the patriarch to cast a shadow of doubt over his motives. He was putting *himself* to death in the sacrifice of his son. In this act of faith and obedience, Abraham showed he believed God in a way he had never shown before.

This is the occasion of Paul's description of Abraham's faith. When God challenged Abraham to make a sacrifice of Isaac, he unflinchingly obeyed.[57] Indeed, the rabbinic teachers pointed to this event when they wanted to demonstrate Abraham's faith. In their earliest texts, they were reluctant to speak of the sacrificial nature of Abraham's actions,[58] stressing instead the obedience of Isaac. However, probably due to pressure from the early church's preaching of the liberating death of Jesus for those who believed, they moved their emphasis from the obedience of Isaac to the faith of Abraham. In this way, they were able to show that the Jews also had a sacrifice, their own beloved firstborn son, who had "died" for Israel.[59]

The offering of Isaac as the focus of Rom 4:19–20 is further supported by the letter to the Hebrews which reflects Second Temple Jewish understanding of Abraham's faith (Heb 11:17–19). It says Abraham's response to the command to sacrifice his son was to believe that, if God wanted Isaac—the one he had promised was going to be the heir—then God would raise him from the dead. This step of faith flies higher than that required

---

57. The sacrifice of Isaac, known as the *Aqedah* (meaning "the binding," because Isaac was bound in preparation for his death), became a major theme of rabbinical Judaism. Some have argued that it influenced the church's understanding of the significance of the death of Jesus. Meissner, "Soteriologie," 33–49, claims that the model had little influence on the church's teaching. I agree, and consider that the influence was in reverse, the preaching of the church causing the rabbinic development. See Holland, *Contours*, 256ff.

58. Because of the clear implication of human sacrifice that was absolutely forbidden in the law.

59. The rabbinics claimed that, although Isaac did not die, Yahweh accepted his willingness as spilt blood. They claimed, therefore, they had their own sacrifice. Indeed, they then regarded this event to be the "sacrifice" that gave the Passover its efficacy. This was further developed by the rabbinics, who claimed that all sacrifices made in the temple were to remind Yahweh of the "sacrifice" of Isaac who had made atonement for Israel's sins.

for a seemingly impossible birth to an elderly couple. It is the act of faith the Jewish Rabbis emphasize when they discuss the righteousness and the consequent merits of Abraham.

There are other reasons for following this reading of Rom 4:19–20. Throughout this chapter, Paul has presented Abraham as the father of those who have faith (Rom 4:16). In his obedient departure from Ur and then Haran, he was certainly an example to follow, just as the new exodus community followed her deliverer, the Son of David, out of the realm of darkness. In what way, then, is Abraham's faith in Isaac's conception also an example? One could argue he sets an example of waiting patiently for God to fulfill his promise; but the reality, as we have seen, is he did not do this. Abraham wavered. However, on Moriah, we see him obeying in faith by preparing to sacrifice the son of the promise. It is *this* event, and the faith exhibited within it, that Paul urges his readers to follow, for it is an amazing example to his seed and the pinnacle of his faith.

Can the text support this reading? I believe it can in two ways. First, Paul's argument is moving towards its concluding statement, which is the glorious affirmation: "The words 'it was credited to him' were not written for him alone, but also for us, to whom God will credit righteousness—for us who believe in him who raised Jesus our Lord from the dead" (Rom 4:23–24). In believing the Lord Jesus Christ has been raised from the dead, the Roman believers and Paul are true sons of Abraham because they share with him—admittedly, after the event–the same faith in a resurrecting God. Second, scholars who support this reading see the following statement: "He was delivered over to death for our sins and was raised to life for our justification" (Rom 4:25) as an echo of the sacrifice of Isaac. Others see a strong allusion to the *Aqedah*—the binding of Isaac—in Paul's later statement in Rom 8:32: "He who did not spare his own Son, but gave him up for us all—how will he not also, along with him, graciously give us all things?"[60] If the scholars who make these suggestions are right, they lend evidence to Paul's focus on the "sacrifice" of Isaac.

It is clear Abraham's faith grew from its wavering beginnings in Gen 12 to its climax in Gen 22, about which Paul could write that Abraham gave glory to God. What is Paul referring to in this statement? Perhaps he is implying that Abraham had a right understanding of God and was able to trust him implicitly. Abraham had not elected himself, for it was God's plan and initiative to call and covenant with him. God was responsible from beginning to end, and Abraham gave him glory by trusting him on this darkest of days. Alternatively, Paul may have believed Abraham gave God glory in the way he named the mount on which he sacrificed the ram in Isaac's place: "So Abraham called that place The LORD Will Provide. And to this day it is said, 'On the mountain of the LORD it will be provided'" (Gen 22:14). This name, which persisted for centuries, speaks only of God and his faithfulness. It is on this mount that David sacrificed and Solomon

---

60. Dahl, "Atonement," 27, has pointed out the significance of Abraham's faith in these words: "There existed a specifically Jewish-Christian 'doctrine of the atonement,' more explicit than has often been assumed on the basis of Acts. The death of Jesus upon the cross was interpreted as fulfilling what God had promised to Abraham by oath. Abraham had not withheld his son, so God did not spare His own Son, but gave him up for Isaac's descendants. As the sacrifice provided by God, he expiated their former sins."

built the temple (2 Chron 3:1). Abraham made no mention of himself as part of the mountain's name, for it focuses on God's faithfulness alone. Perhaps it was because of this that Paul can say Abraham "gave (undivided) glory to God."

4:21 Being fully persuaded that God had power to do what he had promised. Abraham was fully persuaded God would keep his promise because he was God—Creator, sustainer, and deliverer. While there is no suggestion there was a shadow of doubt in Abraham's heart, the quality of his faith is not what is being emphasized, but the power of God to do what he had promised. Abraham took God at his word and treated the accomplishment of the promises as certain. His confidence lay in his knowledge that God would not go back on a covenant he had made and promised to fulfill.

4:22 This is why "it was credited to him as righteousness." The theme of man made righteous in the sight of God is fundamental to Paul's understanding of the Gospel of Jesus Christ. As we have seen, it has become clear the crediting of righteousness in this chapter is not exclusively, or essentially, about God imparting or even imputing his righteousness to man. It is about his saving activity, by which he honors his covenantal promise made to the patriarchs. This does not remove the important truth of man being made acceptable by God, but it places his acceptance in the much bigger framework of OT covenantal theology.

The statement "it was credited to him as righteousness," emphasizes, through Abraham's faith, the covenant promise of Yahweh was accepted and confirmed as binding. In writing "it was credited to him as righteousness," Paul highlights the nature of true saving faith. It is a faith that trusts God in the very darkest of trials. It emphasizes that God was going to be responsible for Abraham and his seed (see Rom 4:3). This would impinge on every aspect of their lives, especially their spiritual needs. In this area, Yahweh had effectively promised to deliver the progeny of Abraham from guilt and sinfulness, restoring them to himself when they failed and broke the terms of the covenant. This salvation was an expression of God's righteousness in fulfilling his covenantal promises, as well as his faithfulness in bearing its curses should the covenant be broken.

The deliverance from Egypt, with the subsequent giving of the Mosaic covenant, was one of the steps in this divine plan. Another step was the deliverance from Babylon. However, the greatest, and ultimate, act of crediting righteousness was the vicarious death of Jesus on the cross. By this saving activity, God fulfilled the promise he made to Abraham. He bore responsibility for the sinfulness of man in that his Son was treated as guilty and put to death. Through his sacrifice, he released the true seed of Abraham from bondage to Sin and Death. Paul discusses this issue further as the letter unfolds. In writing "it was credited to him as righteousness," Paul is not suggesting that Abraham had accrued personal merit from which his descendants could draw, but that his acceptance of God's promise meant God would always direct his saving activity towards his offspring. The righteousness we are focusing upon is not that of Abraham, but of God—Abraham's faith being an instrument in the covenant's ratification.

God saved Abraham because he had chosen him, and because his faith had ratified the covenant, bringing him into the orbit of God's grace. Faith does not produce righteousness. It is the "Amen" to God's offer of saving work, and without such faith it is impossible to please him.

It is strange that the traditional understanding of being credited righteousness (the bedrock of Protestant theology) is at the heart of doctrines in some branches of Christian and Jewish theology such as the merits of the saints. This doctrine holds that God accepts believers if they draw from the surplus righteousness of certain "pious" people. It presupposes the saints, themselves sinners, have surplus transferable merits from which the faithful can draw. While the Bible gives no support for such a doctrine, it certainly teaches that God transfers only Christ's righteousness or merits to those who believe.[61] Christ, the Son of God, is the only one who has "surplus" merit in God's eyes, and it was he God appointed to represent his people in death to bring them salvation. Their deliverance and transfer into the kingdom of God brings them into the realm of Christ's kingdom, where they share in all that he is and all that he has achieved.[62]

4:23–24 The words "it was credited to him" were written not for him alone, but also for us, to whom God will credit righteousness—for us who believe in him who raised Jesus our Lord from the dead. The story of Abraham is the story of all who believe. The covenantal transaction between God and the patriarch is the same as that carried out between God and his new covenant people. They believe in the God who promised, if they call on him, he will answer in saving grace (Acts 2:38–41; Rom 10:12–13). The significance of faith in the covenant promises is the same for the believer in Christ as it was for Abraham. It has no meritorious value; it is simply a faith that accepts God as the Redeemer who acts in righteousness to bring salvation to his people. The comparison is clear. The birth of Isaac and the promise to raise him from the dead (implied in the story of his offering) is the same as the story of the birth of the church with its Jewish and Gentile children. The Jews and the Gentiles are not two separate entities, but one body in Christ—once both dead in trespasses and sins, and now raised to life in and through Christ. Together, they share the promise of partaking in the resurrection of the people of God on the last day.

As noted in the comments on vv. 19–20, the focus of Abraham's crediting of righteousness has moved from the covenant-making occasion of Gen 15:6 (cited in Rom 4:3) to the mount Moriah event. In recognizing this shift, we find Paul stands on the same ground regarding justification as does James (Jas 2:21–23). A man who is justified by faith is one who can do no other than obey the command of the one who has called him. The works Paul and James speak of in their understanding of the doctrine of justification

---

61. This will be explored in detail in chapter 5.

62. For a fuller discussion on this theme, see Holland, *Contours*, chapter 10. Paul will argue for the transfer of Christ's merit in the following chapter (Rom 5:18, 19). This is the most important NT text in support of the Reformers' teaching, and is a major challenge to the New Perspective teaching on justification argued for by Dunn and Wright.

are not the works of the law, but the works of the law of faith. They believe on him who raises the dead.

The remarkable way Paul follows the story of Abraham and the stages of Yahweh's dealings with him is a testament to his lifetime engagement with the Scriptures of his people. It is also a salutary lesson to those of us who specialize in NT studies and assume the OT text is only of limited value for our sphere of specialization.

4:25 He was delivered over to death for our sins and was raised to life for our justification. Many see that there is a clear echo here of Abraham's willingness to obey God in offering Isaac as a sacrifice (Gen 22:1–19).[63] However, this is not the only echo in this text. Paul has already written about the sacrifice of Jesus (Rom 3:21ff.) where we found pointers to the death of Jesus being the eschatological Passover. While these ideas are not unrelated,[64] i.e., the binding of Isaac and the Passover, the most dominant model for Paul is of Christ being our Passover (1 Cor 5:7).[65] The idea of justification expands in this new exodus setting.[66]

In the original Passover, the lambs' death spared the Hebrew firstborn from judgment.[67] When the Hebrews were brought out of Egypt to begin their pilgrimage to the promised land, both God and the Hebrews were justified—God was justified by the public fulfillment of his promises to his people, and the people's faith in the God of their fathers was justified by their public exodus.

By his Passover, Christ protected his people from judgment and secured their redemption. When Jesus was brought out of the tomb, having been delivered from the bonds of death, both he and his people were justified. Christ was justified by the public fulfillment of his promises to his disciples, and they were justified by their exodus from the kingdom of darkness because they had been made one with him in his death (Rom 6:1–4) and now shared his resurrection (Eph 2:6). His justification, therefore, became their justification, and they followed in the train of his victory over the forces of evil. God is just, and the justifier of those who believe in Jesus (Rom 3:26). It is significant that, as we move into chapter 5, we discover clear allusions to the Passover and the death of Jesus (Rom 5:9); allusions that continue into chapters 6–8.

---

63. See Käsemann, *Romans*, 39; Schillebeeckx, "Experiment," 292. Ridderbos, "Earliest," 78, sees the text to be an allusion to Isa 53; as does Perrin, *Pilgrimage*, 101–12, who goes on to say that the usage goes back to a stage of theological reflection which precedes Mark 10:45. Taylor, *Atonement*, 95, says that Paul avoided using Isa 53 because he could not bring himself to call his Lord a *doulos*—an argument that is entirely Hellenistic, see Holland, *Contours*, chapter 4 for a refutation. Schoeps, *Paul*, 46, sees the passage as an allusion to Gen 22; while Wilckens, *Römer*, 1:280, considers the allusion to be to the Passion tradition (cf. 1 Cor 11:23). Monte, "Place," 75, says that Rom 4:25 occurs in the same context as Rom 3:21–26, and concludes that Paul is using an extended illustration from Abraham, which shows that the righteousness of God is not confined to national boundaries.

64. See Holland, *Contours*, 254ff.

65. In preference to the use of Isa 53:5, 12, as Wright, *Romans*, 503. For the reason the apostles chose to avoid using Isa 53, see Holland, *Contours*, chapter 4.

66. See comments on Rom 3:21–26.

67. For details of how the firstborn substituted for their families and were destined to die as atoning sacrifices to protect parents and siblings, see Holland, *Contours*, 207–36.

CONCLUSION OF ROMANS 4

Paul has continued to urge his Jewish brethren to recognize circumcision is not the basis of acceptance by God. He has shown that Abraham received circumcision long after God declared him righteous.

Paul appeals to David as inheritor of the promise of continued divine protection who also needed to be justified by God. David's testimony was that of a man who was not only one of Israel's greatest figures, but also one who was circumcised.

Throughout the chapter, Paul has argued it is not covenant works that make a person right with God, but grace that comes through faith in the substitutive death of Jesus for his people.

Paul has argued all Jews and Gentiles who have the same faith as Abraham—a faith in a gracious forgiving God who commits himself to saving his people—are true sons of Abraham and part of the covenant community that has been saved through the atoning death of Jesus. He has stressed that the Gentiles are not to succumb to the pressure the Judaizers put upon them to convert to Judaism.

Finally, in the concluding verse there is an echo of the second exodus theme, when Jesus, our firstborn paschal sacrifice, our justification, rescues his people from judgment. This ought not to surprise us, for the original covenant with Abraham was that Yahweh would save his people from oppression. A far greater firstborn than Abraham's has been provided to atone for the sins of his people and his resurrection has added to the promise that Abraham had believed, so that the followers of the lamb have no cause to doubt, not for one moment!

ROMANS 5

THE MESSIAH KING AND THE PILGRIMAGE OF HIS PEOPLE

THEREFORE, SINCE WE have been justified through faith, we have peace with God through our Lord Jesus Christ, through whom we have gained access by faith into this grace in which we now stand. And we rejoice in the hope of the glory of God. Not only so, but we also rejoice in our sufferings, because we know that suffering produces perseverance; perseverance, character; and character, hope. And hope does not disappoint us, because God has poured out his love into our hearts by the Holy Spirit, whom he has given us. You see, at just the right time, when we were still powerless, Christ died for the ungodly. Very rarely will anyone die for a righteous man, though for a good man someone might possibly dare to die. But God demonstrates his own love for us in this: while we were still sinners, Christ died for us. Since we have now been justified by his blood, how much more shall we be saved from God's wrath through him! For if, when we were God's enemies, we were reconciled to him through the death of his Son, how much more, having been reconciled, shall we be saved through his life! Not only is this so, but we also rejoice in God through our Lord Jesus Christ, through whom we have now received reconciliation. (Rom 5:1–11)

INTRODUCTION

AS WE COME INTO chapter 5, we find themes of chapter 4 being picked up and applied to the church–the true children of Abraham (Rom 4:18). Like Abraham, the church is justified (Rom 4:9; 5:1) and experiences God's glory (Rom 4:20; 5:2). Moreover, like Abraham, the church's deliverance came when she was totally weak (Rom 4:19; 5:6) and she lives in hope.

Pilgrimage is a thread running through the OT into the NT.[1] Abraham was on constant pilgrimage and his OT descendants are regularly described as being on pilgrimage, (Gen 42:13; Exod 15:22; Josh 1:2; 2 Kings 25:18–20; Ezra 2:1). This theme of pilgrimage unfolds in chapter 5 with the recounting of the story of Adam and his disobedience leading to the exile of him and his offspring. The mission of redemption is about the reconciliation of man to God and his pilgrimage back into God's presence in the New Creation.

Just as the Jews journeyed back from exile in Egypt or Babylon, believers have a journey to endure before they arrive at the goal of their salvation, for their inheritance is

---

1. For a study of the pilgrim motif in Scripture, see Lee, *Journey.*

stored up for them in heaven.[2] Paul sees the deliverance of believers to be the first step in their eschatological pilgrimage. The journey will inevitably involve suffering and discouragement, but these will not deter them because the Spirit is with them and the hope of God's glory lies before them. Both the giving of the Spirit (Isa 42:1–4; 44:3; 59:21) and the promise of sharing in God's glory (Isa 45:25; 58:8; 60:1–2, 13; Jer 9:23–24; Ezek 43:4) are new exodus expectations in which this new pilgrim community now shares.

As seen in Exodus 12, the first deliverance from Egypt centered on the death of the firstborn sons, with sacrificial lambs substituting for the Hebrew firstborn. The church's deliverance centers on Jesus, God's only Son, delivered up to death to bring about his people's salvation (Rom 5:6–8). The new exodus theme continues in the statement: "how much more shall we be saved from God's wrath through him" (Rom 5:9).

Paul reflects on the reason why this salvation is necessary. He explains the solidarity of humankind, and how its representative—or federal—head, Adam, brought it into a state of alienation towards God through disobedience. In contrast, Paul calls Jesus the "last Adam," (1 Cor 15:54) who, as representative head of the new covenant community, reconciles his people to God through obedience and suffering. Representative or federal headship refers to one who represents a group bound by a common cause or agreement, such as those in a covenant or federation; not only as its spokesperson, but as one whose decisions are binding on the larger group by virtue of the individual's role as federal or representative head.

We must take care not to impose our understanding on Paul's use of justification language. If this happens, we will miss important points that Paul is making. We have noted his understanding comes from the Law and the Prophets rather than the Roman legal system. It is not only that believers have been declared innocent (although this is an important part of his understanding), but also that God has rescued them from a hopeless situation, fulfilling his covenant promises. God did this when he reversed Abraham's impossible situation by giving a son to Sarah in old age, and when he rescued Israel from exile and King David from guilt.

Justification is the outcome of Jesus' death and resurrection: "he was delivered over to death for our sins and was raised for our justification" (Rom 4:25). God has been faithful to his promise to Abraham in delivering his spiritual descendants from the realm of darkness and bondage (Gen 15:13–14). The kingdom of darkness in the NT is equivalent to Egypt or Babylon in the OT where Israel was held in captivity. It is a condition, or realm, where Satan rules and man is cut off from fellowship with God. In the OT, justification was especially to do with Yahweh delivering his people from their captivity (Isa 50:9–10; 53:11), and Paul is keeping to this theological perspective as he develops his argument (see also Col 1:13–15).

Paul says this justification results from the achievements of the Lord Jesus Christ, as explained in Rom 3:21ff. (especially, v. 24) and Rom 4:25 (where the setting is the death of Jesus). He has described Jesus' death as the Passover sacrifice that delivered the people of God from captivity to Sin. Just as Israel's deliverance from Egypt was her justification,

---

2. See 1 Cor. 2:9, which cites Isa 65:4—a text addressed to the pilgrim community coming out of Babylon (cf. also Rom 8:17; 1 Pet 1:4, both texts also having strong Paschal new exodus backgrounds).

so Christ's redemptive work is his people's justification. God has put away all matters that kept him from accepting sinners into his presence, and he is now able to welcome them without any charge that would compromise his holiness. Justification is as much about the declaration of God's innocence of complicity in the sin of man as about his deliverance of them from the guilt that condemns (Rom 3:23).[3]

The NIV (like most translations) has, as an outcome of this justification, "we have peace" (Rom 5:1). This translates the Greek ἔχομεν (echomen). There is a possibility Paul never used this word. There are many ancient texts of the letter that do not have ἔχομεν (echomen), but have ἔχωμεν (echōmen) "let us have peace."[4] Scholars divide over this.[5] The oldest texts support echōmen, and, strictly, this should be followed. However, this would mean Paul is appealing to his readers to be active in establishing peace with God. The argument of the preceding chapters is that Jesus has made peace between God and man. Because of this, peace is an established reality that the people of God are to enjoy. This is reason most translators follow echomen "we have peace." Nevertheless, the strongest textual evidence does not support this translation, but rather it supports "let us have peace with God." There is thus clear tension between the theology that Paul has just thrashed out, and what he says here!

However, if Paul is following the exodus paradigm, it makes sense to stay with the older and better-attested echōmen "let us have peace." The Jews, delivered from their miserable condition of slavery in Egypt, must have found the unfolding experience of the pilgrimage daunting. Even though God had judged sin in the Passover sacrifice and redeemed the Jews from Egypt through the blood of the lambs, the knowledge they had to journey to Sinai to appear before God must have caused grave misgivings. They had seen what he had done to the Egyptians, and must have feared what he would do to them. One can almost hear the plea of Moses that they should put their confidence in their deliverer.[6] We shall see Paul envisages a similar setting when he writes in Rom 5:9: "Since we have now been justified by his blood, how much more shall we be saved from God's wrath through him!" It is clear Paul sensed a need to encourage the Roman believers to be confident that God, having redeemed them from captivity, was not going to abandon them on their pilgrimage, leaving them as victims of Satan.

This is similar to the setting of 1 Cor 10:1ff., where Paul warns the Corinthians of the danger of coming under God's chastening even though they are his covenant people. In this warning, he turns to the texts I am suggesting should guide us in the unraveling of Rom 5. He explores the typology of the exodus, and shows how the Jews fell in the wilderness because of hardened hearts. Having peace with God, therefore, is something

---

3. See comments on 6:7 and 7:1–6.

4. Ἔχωμεν (echōmen) is supported by ℵ*, A, B*, C, D, K, L, 33, 81, 1175. The weaker ἔχομεν (echomen) is supported by ¹ℵ B², F, G, P, Ψ, 0220ᵛⁱᵈ.

5. Käsemann, *Romans*, 132–33, cites Foerster, *TDNT*, II, 415, who claims the text is different from Paul's intention, because Paul dictated his letter and his scribe could not distinguish the indicative from the subjunctive. So also, Zeisler, *Romans*, 137. Of course, the argument suffers from being pure speculation, even if plausible.

6. This same theme is in Heb 12:22 where the Israelites approached the holy mountain with great fear.

Paul is anxious for the believers to actively embrace and enjoy, for it has been secured through the death of Jesus.

5:1 Therefore, since we have been justified through faith, we have peace with God through our Lord Jesus Christ Despite the dispute over the phrase "we have peace with God," there is no question about what the death of Christ has achieved. The Roman believers have been brought into this grace in which they now stand as a result of Jesus' death and resurrection. Just as Israel could stand before Mount Sinai to worship God because of the Passover, so the Roman church can stand in the grace into which she has been brought as a result of her Passover, Christ Jesus (Rom 4:25).

5:2 through whom we have gained access by faith into this grace in which we now stand. And we rejoice in the hope of the glory of God. The NIV translates Καυχώμεθα (*kauchōmetha*) as "rejoice," but it is much stronger than that. It has the strength of "exult." In the OT, God revealed his glory in a series of major events. These included creation, with the climax being God revealing his glory in the creation of man. Man lost the glory of God because of the fall, but it was revealed again when God established his covenant with Abraham (Gen 15:18). It was revealed yet again when the Jewish people were delivered from slavery (Exod 14:17–18), when the law was given at Sinai (Exod 19:7–9), when the temple was dedicated under Solomon (2 Chr 5:11–14; 7:1–3), and when the exiles returned from Babylon (Isa 40:1–5; 58:8; 59:19).

For the Christian community, the glory of God has been displayed in the death and resurrection of Jesus (John 12:2–23; Rom 6:4) and in the outpouring of the Spirit on his church (Acts 2:1–4). The final revelation of God's glory will be when the church has completed her eschatological pilgrimage (1 Cor 15:42–55; Rom 8:9–11). Then, as the "new man," she will be the pinnacle of the completed new creation, when God will dwell with her and his covenant promises towards her will have been completed. Paul describes this future experience as "the hope of the glory of God." As the people of God have suffered throughout the ages, they have been encouraged by the promise that they will see their Lord—the one whose death made their deliverance possible. No wonder Paul tells them to "exult"!

To return to the Sinai setting of the verse when the Israelites stood before Sinai as the redeemed community of the living God, Yahweh was taking Israel to be his bride.[7] While it is impossible to imagine how the redeemed people felt, Paul is saying the exodus deliverance is a shadow of the redemption God has now accomplished in Christ. The people of God have been delivered from eternal condemnation and their subservience to Sin (Satan) has been brought to an end (Sin is used by Paul in chapters 5–6 as the personification of Satan, a linkage explained in the introduction to v. 12). There has been an exodus of the people of God from the kingdom of darkness,[8] because those who were

---

7. Hos 2:14–20; Ezek 16:6–14.

8. See Maartens, "Relevance," 75–108, who claims that socio-semiotic analysis identifies the historical conditions of the readers as "returning exiles" in the aftermath of "banning orders" and the suffering inflicted on them in the Rome of 49–54 AD. If correct, then the theme of return from exile in the new exodus would resonate strongly with their own experience.

once slaves to Sin (Satan) are now free and are children of the living God. What greater grace could they experience? The church is the new covenant community called out of the kingdom of darkness to be the bride of the living God.[9] It could be Paul's use of the term "access" reflects the idea found in the OT that the bride had "access" to her husband.[10] If this is so, then Paul intended the term to be about Yahweh redeeming a people to be his bride, further enriching the exodus imagery. If this is correct, it underscores that the text is meant to be read corporately–something few expositors do.[11]

In Rom 1:3, we have seen the importance of Jesus being the priestly Son of David. In the OT, the high priest was commanded to marry a virgin (Lev 21:14). We shall see marriage imagery lies at the heart of Paul's Gospel (see comments on Rom 6:7; 7:1–4). The letter to the Ephesians tells us Christ died to wash his church from every blemish so he might present her to his Father in heaven as a spotless bride (Eph 5:25–27). In addressing the church in Ephesus, Paul makes use of strong priestly language and imagery (Eph 2:18, 21), presenting Christ as the Son of David (Eph 1:20), which most scholars recognize an echo in the text to Ps 110:1, and as the Priest King who marries a virgin (Eph 5:25–27).[12]

We have here a similar teaching that is made much clearer in the letter to the Hebrews where the writer describes Jesus as a great high priest. Indeed, he is not an ordinary high priest for he did not belong to the priestly tribe of Levi, but a priest "after the order of Melchizedek" (Heb 5:1–5). In the letter to the Hebrews, Jesus is shown to have offered a sacrifice that is unique. He has made the perfect sacrifice of his sinless life and, in so doing, has made his people clean in God's sight (Heb 9:11–14). The letter to the Hebrews also tells us Jesus prays for his people just as the OT priests did (Heb 5:7–10), and that he is the one who goes before his people to bring them into their inheritance in the promised land (Heb 12:1–17).

This high priestly picture seems to be in Romans also. Jesus is the Son of David (Rom 1:3) who is the Melchizedek priest (Ps 110:1–4). He has sacrificed his life to secure redemption for his people (Rom 3:21–25; 8:3, 32), and is now leading them on their pilgrimage to the promised land into the very presence of God himself. Pilgrimage imagery is part of the language Paul and the writer to the Hebrews use in their letters (Rom 8:34–39; Heb 3:12—4:11). Thus, for "Melchizedek" in Hebrews, we can read "Son of David" in Romans. Both figures lead their people, pray for them, and offer themselves for them in sacrifice (cf. Rom 8:14; 8:3, 34 with Heb 4:14–16; 9:14; 7:25).

5:3–4 Not only so, but we also rejoice in our sufferings, because we know that suffering produces perseverance; perseverance, character; and character, hope. The pilgrim community of the new exodus experiences difficulties, but these problems are

---

9. For a study of the divine marriage theme, see Smolarz, "Covenant."

10. Esth 1:14. Note the use of the term in Eph 2:18, with its very strong link to the marital theme seen in Eph 5:25.

11. For a corporate argument for Paul's understanding of justification, see Sandnes, "Outdated," 127–46.

12. For further work on the divine marriage theme in Paul's thinking, see Holland, *Contours,* chapter 6.

not to be viewed negatively, as though they had no purpose. God's grace is learned in the discovery of human frailties (Ps 131).

Paul's appeal that "we rejoice (or 'glory') in our sufferings" is not a Christian version of Stoicism. Sufferings serve God's purposes, making the Roman believers—and Paul—focus on their inheritance which is not of this world (Phil 3:20–21). Suffering was part of God's purpose for Jesus in order for him to become a faithful high priest who could sympathize with his people's needs (Heb 2:17–18). This is not a Pauline view alone, but is shared by other apostles and reflected the understanding of the early church (Matt 5:10–12; Acts 4:23–31; 1 Pet 1:6–7; Jas 1:2–4).

Perhaps we might have expected Paul to write that suffering merely produces hope without interjecting perseverance and character. The reality is hope that concentrates on the cessation of suffering can be very self-centered, failing to see the bigger issues with which God is concerned. Paul highlights the process of coming to true Christian hope because it is different from the "hope" many have of a better tomorrow. It is a hope for the vindication of God in his creation. Thus, the hope of the Christian is pure and centered on the glory of God. Paul supports this understanding with his comments on the last Adam's recovery of the glory of God for his people in Rom 5:12–19.

5:5 And hope does not disappoint us, because God has poured out his love into our hearts by the Holy Spirit, whom he has given us. The Holy Spirit led and protected the Jewish community on its pilgrimage (Isa 42:1–13; 61:1–11; 63:11–19). Paul is saying God has given the same Holy Spirit to the church in all of his fullness.[13] The Spirit's presence means the church continually experiences the love of God. The Greek can mean either God's love for us (subjective genitive) or our love for God (objective genitive). The NRSV and NIV prefer the former, because God's love for his people is the major theme of vv. 6–10. In addition, it is better to see hope as grounded in truth about God rather than ourselves. However, the OT makes it clear the Spirit leads people to love God and fulfill the requirements of the Torah (Ps 104:30–34; Isa 11:2–4; 42:1; 59:21; Ezek 36:26–27).

Perhaps there is no need to choose between the two meanings. If there are alternatives, it must have been the same for the believers in Rome for whom Greek was their first language. In other words, Paul speaks not only of the love poured into the heart of the community by the Spirit, but also of the love for God that comes from the hearts of his people—a love put there by God himself. In this way, the Shema (Israel's great monotheistic confession found in Deut 6:4) has been fulfilled in a way that goes beyond man struggling to love God, for love for him is poured into his people.[14]

The Greek verb ἐκχέω (ekcheō) "pour out" is used in the Septuagint version of Joel 2:28–29; Acts 2:17–18, 33; 10:45; Titus 3:6, where it speaks of God giving the Holy Spirit to men. This suggests the pouring out of the Holy Spirit is not an individualistic experi-

13. The gift of the Spirit is the sign of the new age (Isa 32:15–18; 60:17). He was also the promised helper for the returning exiles in the second exodus (Isa 59:21; Zech 4:6). For the Spirit's part in the Egyptian and Babylonian deliverances, see Klijn, "Origins," 25. Hooker, "Paul," 5, and Davies, *Rabbinic*, 211, point out that the Shekkinah in the wilderness was the Spirit.

14. Wright, "Theology," 45. Thielman, "Story," 173, notes that: "many interpreters of Romans have too readily assumed that the content of chapters 5–8 has little to do with the history of Israel."

ence but God's gift of himself to the church at its inception. His pouring out fulfills the prophecy of Joel that, in the last days, God would pour out his Spirit on all flesh. Such an understanding supports the corporate reading of the text. This does not deny the indwelling of the Spirit in the individual believer, but it puts that indwelling into its proper context. It is as members of the covenantal Spirit-indwelt community that believers experience the Spirit in their lives, and his presence is the guarantee that they will be brought to glory. He equips the church by comforting and encouraging believers in times of satanic onslaught. To use Isaiah's words: "When the enemy comes in like a flood, the Spirit of the LORD will put him to flight" (Isa 59:19, NIV margin).

The hope the Christian believers in Rome have is not a vague wish for something better. It is the certainty of knowing God will fulfill his purposes. He is the God in whom they have trusted, who keeps his promises, and who gave up his Son to death in order to save them. He is the God who raises the dead, and he is not going to leave his saving work in Rome incomplete.

5:6 You see, at just the right time, when we were still powerless, Christ died for the ungodly. In his letter to the Galatians, Paul refers to the first coming of Christ and his subsequent death as being "at just the right time," or "in the fullness of time" (Gal 4:4–5). Some have argued it was the right time because the Roman Empire had created conditions vital for the spread of the Gospel. This is hardly likely to be the reason, as the Gospel has spread as fast at other times in history without the facilitation of social, political or transport infrastructures. It is more likely the "right time" refers to the time when man's inability to keep God's law was fully displayed, having exhausted any efforts to keep it.[15]

Paul reminds his readers their salvation was not the result of their attainments but because of the free love of God in giving his Son. His concern is to emphasize the Christian life, from its beginning to its end, is a work of the grace of God. Just as no one can claim he deserved forgiveness, no one will be able to claim he accomplished his pilgrimage in his own strength. The OT covenant communities in Egypt and Babylon were powerless until Yahweh intervened. Likewise, the NT covenant community was powerless in the kingdom of darkness, and in a condition only the coming of Christ, the Son of David, could reverse. The deliverance from Egypt was at the right time (Exod 2:23; Ps 69:13; Isa 42:13–14; 49:8), as was the deliverance from Babylon (Jer 51:7). For at these times, the people acknowledged their need and their dependence on God. Now, writes Paul, the time was right, and God sent his own beloved Son.

5:7 Very rarely will anyone die for a righteous man, though for a good man someone might possibly dare to die. Paul encourages the believers to reflect on the death of Christ. He reasons from human experience. He points out that for someone to be willing to die for another is a rare quality. He does not say it never happens but, when it does, the motive is love or admiration. When Paul writes about God demonstrating his love, he is going to the very heart of the Gospel. The Gospel is not about a philosophy or

---

15. Of course, within a few years of writing this letter, the Roman war drove the Jews from the land. This destroyed the national records that established Jesus' descent from David. Thus, the fullness of time was more significant than Paul could have imagined.

a religion—it is about the saving activity of a loving God toward undeserving mankind in his need.

5:8 But God demonstrates his own love for us in this: while we were still sinners, Christ died for us. This is the unique characteristic of God's love. He loves his enemies and pays the ultimate sacrifice for their benefit and blessing. The corporate dimension of Paul's argument is clear, for he does not say, "while you were still a sinner" but "while we were still sinners" Christ died for the community, the old man.[16] Paul uses the present tense in the opening phrase of the verse, indicating the benefits of the death of Jesus are a present reality.[17]

5:9 Since we have now been justified by his blood, how much more shall we be saved from God's wrath through him! Paul's reasoning is straightforward. If the death of Jesus has saved (i.e., justified) us, delivered and brought us into covenant with God through his blood, how much more will the life of Jesus save us! It is not that Paul is arguing that the life or example of Jesus has saving effect. He has made it clear that Jesus had to die for the salvation of his people (Rom 3:21ff.).

The life Paul is referring to is Jesus' resurrection life in heaven where he serves as the mediator, or high priest, of his people. He can represent believers in this way because he made the necessary sacrifice for his people's sins. Paul is reasoning that, because the death of Jesus turned away the wrath of God when we were his enemies, the presentation of the evidence of that death in heaven will turn God's wrath away from his people when they stumble and fall on their pilgrimage.

The image of Jesus, the high priest defending his people from God's wrath echoes the imagery of the exodus narrative from Egypt. As we have seen, the Levites, who had been substituted for the firstborn, were positioned between the tabernacle and the people when the nation struck camp, so that God's wrath did not fall on the other tribes (Num 1:53). The Levites functioned as a living propitiation, protecting the people against the wrath of God.

5:10 For if, when we were God's enemies, we were reconciled to him through the death of his Son, how much more, having been reconciled, shall we be saved through his life! Paul repeats what he has been saying but in a slightly different way to emphasize his point. The repetition helps us to see how he uses his theological vocabulary: "being reconciled" means "being justified," and "being saved" means "being delivered from God's wrath." It is easy to imagine that Moses would have urged the Jews to appreciate they did not need to live in fear of God, as his love and concern were evident in that he had delivered them from Egypt.

They had no need to fear, therefore, that they would be consumed when the glory of God was revealed at Mount Sinai. Such fear was unfounded because God had demonstrated his love in redeeming them from their captivity in Egypt. This is the point Paul is

---

16. For the meaning of this term, see comments on 6:6.

17. Note Morris, *Epistle*, 224 n. 27: "The cross is an event in the past but it keeps showing the love of God."

making—but with one exception: this redemption was not at the cost of the life of a lamb, but at the cost of the life of God's beloved Son. He supports the parallel with Moses by the mention of blood in v. 9. It is the first recurrence of the subject since it was mentioned in Rom 3:21ff., where it was clearly Passover blood that was being discussed.[18]

5:11 Not only is this so, but we also rejoice in God through our Lord Jesus Christ, through whom we have now received reconciliation. Rather than fear God, Paul rejoiced in him: "Our relationship with him should not be one of fear" (2 Tim 1:7). When the Roman believers appreciate what God has done for them through the death of his Son, they could not but be amazed and worship. Their worship would not be a cold recognition of God's greatness but an overwhelming appreciation of his personal love for each one of his people.

Paul does not write that he is hoping that the Roman believers will be made right with God on a future day, for their reconciliation is a present reality. God does not put new believers on probation to see how they get on as Christians before accepting them! He accepts all of his people as repentant sinners because his Son's death has satisfied his holiness.

THE MESSIAH KING AND HIS MISSION OF RECOVERY

THEREFORE, JUST AS sin entered the world through one man, and death through sin, and in this way death came to all men, because all sinned—for before the law was given, sin was in the world. But sin is not taken into account when there is no law. Nevertheless, death reigned from the time of Adam to the time of Moses, even over those who did not sin by breaking a command, as did Adam, who was a pattern of the one to come. But the gift is not like the trespass. For if the many died by the trespass of the one man, how much more did God's grace and the gift that came by the grace of the one man, Jesus Christ, overflow to the many! Again, the gift of God is not like the result of the one man's sin: The judgment followed one sin and brought condemnation, but the gift followed many trespasses and brought justification. For if, by the trespass of the one man, death reigned through that one man, how much more will those who receive God's abundant provision of grace and of the gift of righteousness reign in life through the one man, Jesus Christ. Consequently, just as the result of one trespass was condemnation for all men, so also the result of one act of righteousness was justification that brings life for all men. For just as through the disobedience of the one man the many were made sinners, so also through the obedience of the one man the many will be made righteous. The law was added so that the trespass might increase. But where sin increased, grace increased all the more, so that, just as sin reigned in death, so also grace might reign through righteousness to bring eternal life through Jesus Christ our Lord. (Rom 5:12–21)

---

18. Whiteley, "Atonement," 250, specifically identifies the reference to blood in this verse as Paschal blood. Beet, *Corinthians*, 95, says, "If we are saved from death by the death of Christ, then Christ is to us what the lamb was to the firstborn, who but for its sacrificial death would have died." In the Christian Passover, there is, of course, no substitute for the firstborn. He—the beloved Son—had to die. Contrary to the view I am proposing, Schoeps, "Theology," 146, says the reference is to the *Aqedah*. So also is Rosenberg, "Jesus," 388; Zeller, *Römer*; Vermes, "Redemption," 218.

It might seem Paul is introducing a new subject without preparing his readers for it, but this is not so. As we have already seen, the typical western mind approaches the letters of Paul from an individualistic perspective, interpreting all the descriptions about the work of God in the light of individual Christian experience. This was not the way that the early church understood Paul's writings. The letters were to churches about the work of God for his people, and the arguments they contained were inevitably corporate. The change of perspective most detect once we get to v. 12 is not Paul's but ours—and it is false. In the West, our cultural conditioning derives largely from Greek culture, and it teaches us to think at an individualistic level.

Having argued for the security of believers (or, better, the church) in Rom 5:1–11, Paul now considers what God achieved by the death of Jesus. Paul uses an illustration with which Jews were familiar. Adam (meaning man) was the first man. He is, therefore, the father of the human race. His status makes him unique in that he is the representative or federal head of the entire human family. However, this has had dreadful consequences for, when Adam "fell" in Eden, God's judgment fell upon him and all his descendants because of his decision to disobey God, and in doing effectively join himself with Satan (Sin). History is full of prominent individuals whose actions as a federal head have affected the lives of the peoples and nations they represent. For example, when the Prime Minister of Britain, Edward Heath, signed the Treaty of Accession to the European Community in 1971, he brought every member of the British nation, and their descendents, into a legal membership and union with the rest of the European community. That one signature was as effective as though all the British people had signed the document personally. It bound every British person by a new set of laws from which no one was exempt because the Prime Minister signed the document on everyone's behalf as the nation's leader. No Briton can argue he is not under the community's laws because he had not signed personally or been consulted. He is bound in legal union with Prime Minister Heath, and all personal protestations and claims to independence are overruled. The same sort of argument applies to the American constitution and every other great national founding decree. We are all part of such covenant communities. If we are not, we are nationless.

This is the argument Paul is now making. Adam represents the human race. He is the father of mankind with an all-embracing headship. When he sinned and broke off his relationship with God, he took all of his offspring with him into darkness. Not only was Adam cut off from God, but so too was every one of his descendants. In biblical terms, the doctrine of original sin has nothing to do with an inherited, inherent distorted nature, but is about being in a condition of enmity towards God because of the sin of our father, Adam.[19] Being born in sin is to be born into the rebellious human race. It is about being part of the kingdom of darkness that Adam's rejection of God has established. As children of Adam, all humankind shares in that same sin and, in so doing, has choosing to reject God. The root of Paul's doctrine of the sin of all mankind is rooted in Adam's disobedience and the covenantal relationship with Satan (Sin) that he, Adam, established. To be in sin is to be in Adam, and through him, to be in a covenant relationship with Sin (Satan).

19. See Rapinchuk, "Salvation," 427–41.

As we read this section, we must be careful not to read into the text something Paul has not written. He does not say that *sins* have entered into the world. He says that *sin* has entered into the world. This is not splitting hairs. When Paul speaks of sin in chapters 5–6, he does not refer to wrongdoing but to Satan (Sin), the one responsible for all wrongdoing.[20] We will see in chapter 6 Paul continually compares Sin (Satan) with God. They are opponents, and God calls man to obey him and not Satan. The reason Paul uses Sin to denote Satan may be because the Jews sought to avoid using Satan's name lest it contaminate them. When they did have to use his name, they would spit afterwards in an attempt to clean their mouths of the perceived defilement.

Paul is saying that, through the sin of Adam, something catastrophic took place. Not only did man lose the fellowship with God for which he was created, but also Satan (Sin) stepped into that broken relationship. He entered the world and took control, leaving man a helpless victim. From then on, man's destiny was bound up in covenant with the purposes of Satan. This is a dramatic reversal of all God intended for man and makes sense of his subsequent history. Paul states that death itself is the consequence of Sin coming into the world.

However, there is another side to the fall not generally recognized. In the writing of Hosea, Yahweh comments on Israel's unfaithfulness to him, saying, "Like Adam, they have broken the covenant—they were unfaithful to me there . . . I have seen a horrible thing in the house of Israel. There Ephraim is given to prostitution and Israel is defiled" (Hos 6:7, 10). Israel's sin at Sinai, which involved the rejection of Yahweh in favor of other gods, is repeating the same sin as Adam committed. The Israelites' behavior in worshipping the golden calf is a repetition of what happened in the Garden of Eden.[21]

This introduces another dimension into our thinking on the fall. When Adam disobeyed, he took another as his god. He deliberately put himself under the control and protection of Satan. Satan took the place of Yahweh and became the husband. Thus, the fall was an act of spiritual adultery for which Adam was judged, being expelled from the Garden and the presence of God in the same way Israel was to suffer expulsion from the promised land and the presence of Yahweh. Both man and nation had turned their backs on their Creator, taking other gods in his place.

The absence of this covenantal perspective of the fall has produced great difficulties in interpreting Paul's writings, with many resorting to changing his text in order to fit within an individualistic mindset, and so make him appear to say what he did not write.[22] In contrast, the corporate covenantal approach taken here becomes a key that enables us to unlock Paul's intended meaning of the next two chapters.[23] In saying all sinned in Adam, Paul is emphasizing people groups rather than individuals. He is cutting across any Jew who might have thought he was exempt from having to receive the same salvation as the Gentiles.

---

20. I use the higher case in "Sin" to denote Satan.

21. For theological objections to linking Hosea 6:7 with the Garden of Eden, see Macintosh, *Hosea*, 236–39. I answer these objections in the Excursus F: Sin in the Theology of Paul, page 213.

22. For examples of this, see comments on Rom 6:7 and 7:1–6.

23. For the influence of Hosea on the NT, see Dodd, *According*.

5:12 Therefore, just as sin entered the world through one man, and death through sin, and in this way death came to all men, because all sinned—Rather than giving the opening of the verse as "therefore," a better translation would be "so it comes about."[24] Paul now describes the disintegration of the first family recorded in the Genesis account and the emergence of idolatry with all of its consequences. For the first time in the letter, Paul introduces Adam, although we have seen his shadow since the opening chapter, where the decline of human morality was outlined (Rom 1:18–32).[25] The story of Adam is important in Paul's theological system.[26] Because of Adam's rebellion, his family (mankind) became truly dysfunctional, no longer loving or obeying its Creator. This ancestral rebellion, brought about by its representative head, is the basis of Paul's doctrine of sin as well as his explanation of the way Christ has brought about redemption. The story is found within key passages about the work of Christ, such as 1 Cor 15:20–28; Phil 2:4–11; Col 1:12–21. Adamic Christology is also a crucial part of Paul's teaching concerning the identity and status of Jesus.

5:13 for before the law was given, sin was in the world. But sin is not taken into account when there is no law. Paul reflects on the history of man as recorded in the book of Genesis. For a Jew, the law means the Mosaic law, that is, the law given through Moses when Israel assembled at Mount Sinai after her release from Egypt (Exod 19–20). In reality, God had given his law to Adam when he commanded him not to eat of the tree of the knowledge of good and evil (Gen 2:16–17). The breaking of that law ruptured the relationship between God and man, allowing Satan's control of the human race.

Paul says that in the absence of law, sins (personal wrongdoing) are not held to account. He has already spoken about a law of the conscience by which God will judge the Gentiles (Rom 2:12–16). This inward law obviously operated during the period from Adam to Moses, and for the Gentiles after Moses, but Paul seems willing to accept that this law does not have the same authority as the objective written Law of Moses. No Jew would want to concede that the law of the conscience would stand comparison with the Mosaic Law for authority and privilege. This latter law was the sole property of the Jewish people and evidence of the covenant that bound her as a nation to Yahweh (Rom 9:1–5).

Even though there was no law in the Jewish sense of the term, people throughout the world died. For Paul, this was clear evidence of the universality of sin, as death was its consequence and all, except Enoch and Elijah, died,[27] proving that all sinned in Adam. This is an inevitable consequence of his logic, for he has said God does not count sin in

---

24. As Wright, *Romans*, 523, who, despite the suggestion, does not read the earlier passage corporately, nor any of chapters 2–8 other than Rom 5:12–21 which, of course, cannot be missed. See also Fitzmyer, "Constructive," 321–39.

25. For further discussion on the doctrine of sin, see Excursus F: Sin in the Theology of Paul, pages 202–24.

26. See Hooker, "Adam," 297–306; Scroggs, *Adam*; Wright, "Adam," 359–89; Sahlin, "Adam," 11–32; Wedderburn, *Investigation*; Pate, *Substructure*; Hays, "Adam."

27. Clearly, Paul would consider that God had spared these men death but, like all others, they were under its sentence.

the absence of the law. Therefore, the sin that caused death before the giving of the law cannot refer to the sins of the descendants of Adam, but to the sin of Adam himself. His act of disobedience opened the door to the reign of Satan, bringing into existence the covenant relationship with Satan (Sin) into which every human being has been born.

Such a line of argument may be hard to accept by people not used to thinking corporately, however it is a thought pattern familiar to Jews and many other nations. In the West, we are increasingly learning other cultures are more attuned to the Hebraic/Biblical worldview. The emphasis on community and corporatism, lost by the materialistic, atheistic outlook of the rational West, was at the centre of many pre-Enlightenment cultures. This is not suggesting these non-Western cultures and their religions are authoritative, but they are often more sensitive to the deep-rooted relationships that underlie human existence. Those who hold to these worldviews would have less difficulty with the argument Paul is making here than we do in the West.

For Paul, Adam's sin is the sin of the entire human family. Adolf Hitler illustrates this concept. As the country's representative head, when he declared war, he caught up every member of the German race in its awful consequences, drawing decent, family loving, honest people into a state of alienation from other nations, whether or not it was their desire. While this happens in international relationships, it also happens in spiritual ones. When Adam rebelled against God and accepted the prize with which Satan seduced him, his whole progeny was plunged into spiritual chaos and alienation. The evidence for this all-inclusive alienation is that humankind dies. An individual's guilt affects not only the individual, but has consequences for the community to which he or she belongs. For this reason, the issue is not whether one is a good moral citizen, but whether one is in Adam or in Christ. In Adam, men and women belong to Satan by virtue of Adam's headship; in Christ, they belong to God by virtue of Christ's headship. For Paul, this is the reality that all unbelievers need to be confronted with. They are members of the family of Satan from which there is no escape unless they call on the crucified and risen Lord.

5:14 Nevertheless, death reigned from the time of Adam to the time of Moses, even over those who did not sin by breaking a command, as did Adam, who was a pattern of the one to come. When Paul speaks of death having reigned, he means that it had absolute rule (with, as noted above, Enoch and Elijah being God-sanctioned exceptions). For Paul, this is the conclusive evidence that all share in the sin of Adam.

The absence of the Jewish law (not given until Sinai) meant individuals did not suffer death for the sins they had committed, and Paul has already conceded sin is not reckoned when there is no law. The sin that brought about the death of all who lived before Moses is Adam's sin.

Naturally, many complain at being punished for the sin of Adam. However, representation is a fact of human existence that objection will not change. It is the principle behind nations and governments, vast corporations and sporting events. To be human is to be part of such relationships and the solidarities they represent.

This becomes clearer when it is realized the solidarity that has brought judgment on all mankind is also the mechanism of salvation for everyone who would be freed from separation and judgment. Paul indicates this when he writes of Adam as "a pattern of the one to come." Because of man's solidarity with Adam, judgment has come on all; but the same principle of solidarity will become the means by which man can become righteous. This is because another representative head, the second (or better, the last) Adam,[28] was waiting in the wings to come on to the stage of human conflict.

5:15 But the gift is not like the trespass. For if the many died by the trespass of the one man, how much more did God's grace and the gift that came by the grace of the one man, Jesus Christ, overflow to the many! Paul wants to show how the coming of Jesus reversed the catastrophic effects of Adam's sin. While his sin brought "death" to all men, Jesus' obedience brought life to many. Despite the difference in their achievements, the same principle of federal, or representative, headship applies. Jesus is head of a new humanity, doing for his people what they are unable to do for themselves in bringing about salvation from the curse of sin and death.

Paul describes the distribution of God's grace as περισσεύω (perisseuō) "overflowing," suggesting its immediate availability. Paul also emphasizes that the gift is the product of "God's grace" and "the grace of the one man." What happened on the cross was not a conflict between the Father and his beloved Son, but the perfect and gracious outworking of their loving concern for lost mankind. Indeed, as we shall see in chapter 8, this reversal of Adam's sin not only benefits man, but also the whole of the cursed creation (Gen 3:14–19).

5:16 Again, the gift of God is not like the result of the one man's sin: The judgment followed one sin and brought condemnation, but the gift followed many trespasses and brought justification. In this verse, Paul develops the difference between the sin of Adam and the obedience of Christ. The work of Jesus is far greater than the failure of Adam. Adam's one act of disobedience brought devastation on all mankind, but Jesus, the gift of God, reverses the guilt of all who call for mercy. A recent, though weak, parallel would be the nuclear disaster at Chernobyl. The incompetence that caused such a disaster does not compare with the skill, sacrifice, and dedication needed to reverse its effects. Similarly, it required someone of far greater significance than Adam to undo his sin. Jesus had to be more than just a perfect man. Indeed, he had to be God himself. OT thinking supports this, teaching that only God could redeem his creation.

---

28. Some see a close tie between Jesus' use of the Son of Man title and Paul's use of Adamic imagery. See Cullmann, *Baptism*, 144–45; Muilenburg, "Ethiopic," 203; Manson, *Teaching*, 232–34; Schweizer, *Lordship*, 123; Colpe, *TDNT*, 8:476; Ridderbos, *Outline*, 85. Black, "Adam," 175, says, "The Second Adam doctrine provides St Paul with the scaffolding, if not the basic structure, for his redemption and resurrection Christology." Davies, *Rabbinic*, 53, thinks the concept of the second Adam played a far more important part in Paul's thought than the scanty references in Romans and 1 Corinthians suggest (although he notes Paul never calls Jesus the second Adam but the last Adam). Lambrecht, "Use," 516, says Paul probably originated Adam typology; while Bultmann, "Neueste," 18, claims the Adam/Christ imagery in Romans 5 is Gnostic. Dunn, "1 Corinthians," 140, says that Jesus became the last Adam at his resurrection (rejected by Fee, *Empowering*). Dunn, *Making*, 127, says that in Rom 5:15–19 Paul is not talking about the last Adam but the earthly Jesus, patterned according to the archetype of Adam (Rom 5:14). See Holland, *Contours*, chapter 9, for further discussion on the Son of Man/Firstborn relationship.

When Paul says the gift of Christ "brought justification," he means more than acquittal from guilt. As seen in the discussion of Rom 4, the prophets spoke of Israel being justified when God released her from a condition of slavery and returned her to a land where she could enjoy the inheritance her covenantal relationship with God had bequeathed. Paul has previously insisted the Gospel is the fulfillment of the law and the prophets (Rom 1:2; 3:21). As a corollary, he claims the death of Jesus rescues those who call on the name of the Lord, for they receive the same gift of mercy that rescued Israel from her condemnation. As with Israel, God brought the Roman believers out of an alien community into a new one whose head is the last Adam. What Jesus achieved is the recovery of what was lost through the fall, just as God recovered for Israel what she had lost in her exile. By his death, Christ has rescued the elect from the kingdom of darkness and has brought them into the kingdom of light (Col 1:13–14).

In writing that "the gift followed many trespasses and brought justification," Paul is saying "the gift brought righteousness." Justification and righteousness are the same, and refer to God's saving activity for his people, bringing them back into the relationship they had with him before the fall.

5:17 For if, by the trespass of the one man, death reigned through that one man, how much more will those who receive God's abundant provision of grace and of the gift of righteousness reign in life through the one man, Jesus Christ. Paul cannot allow his readers to misunderstand the significance of Jesus' obedience and death. Once again—though in a slightly different way—he states the consequences of the good news of Jesus. Paul takes his readers systematically through the saving event in order to clarify the significance of the cross and the atonement Christ secured.[29]

He begins by writing that death reigned through one man. In v. 12, he wrote about Sin entering the world through one man's sin. In other words, Sin took control. Sin and Death are regularly linked throughout the Scriptures. They are expressions of the same enemy who has deceived man into rebelling against God. As mentioned, the one who is called Sin and Death is Satan. So here, Paul is not thinking of Death in an abstract way. Death is nothing less than Satan's rule over man—a rule from which, of his own, he cannot escape.

When Paul speaks of "the gift of righteousness," he has in mind the state of innocence people have before God when he forgives them because of Jesus' death. When God looks upon those he has saved through the death of his Son, he sees nothing but the perfect obedience of Jesus. In other words, God declares his people righteous, innocent, and sinless, with all traces of the effects of the fall eradicated. While this alone is incredible, it is possible Paul has even more in mind.

In the OT, the term "the righteousness of God" refers to the fact God acts righteously (Isa 48:18; 56:1; 59:17), in accordance with his character and in keeping with his covenant promises. Thus, when his people were disobedient, God punished them, and this was done within the terms of the covenant (Deut 11:26–28). Equally, when they had gone through this process of correction, God delivered them from the hands of their

---

29. Stowers, *Reading*, 206–13, challenges the claim that the passage is about blood atonement.

oppressors as he had promised. If God had not done this he would not be righteous, for he would have failed to be true to his covenant promises. Thus, God's righteousness is seen in three ways: his perfect character, the upholding of his own standards, and the fulfillment of his promises to those with whom he had a covenant relationship.

It is this last aspect of righteousness that is probably behind the term in this verse: "the gift of righteousness." If it is, then Paul's meaning of "the gift of righteousness" is that God has acted to deliver his people from the rule of Satan. He not only delivers his people from Sin's reign through the death of Jesus, but also maintains that freedom. If God did not involve himself in protecting his people he would not be righteous–a suggestion the Scriptures could never countenance. This aspect of the righteousness of God is at the heart of the church's security. God is committed to saving and protecting his people, i.e., those who have believed on his Son and he has saved.

This direct involvement of God in the salvation of his people is the result of "God's abundant provision of grace." The point Paul is making is that God's people cannot enter into a situation where there is not sufficient grace to meet their need. The word χάρις (*charis*) "grace" is more than ἀγάπη (*agapē*) "love." It speaks of love within a covenantal relationship. A couple may love each other, but within marriage, the term "love" is inadequate. There, it is *charis*—covenant love: a love unreservedly committed, staying faithful until death to the one who is loved. God has covenantal love for his people because they belong to him through Christ. He loves his people in a way he does not love the world and, because of his covenantal love, makes demands on those who are its objects (Amos 3:2). God expects, and demands, the love of their hearts in glad response (Jas 4:5; Heb 10:29–31; 1 Pet 4:17).

When Paul says "how much more," he is referring to what has yet to happen. Believers are to "reign in life through the one man, Jesus Christ." What does Paul mean by reigning in life? It is possible he intended it as a contrast to their condition in Adam when they were dead and ruled by Sin. Now, in Christ, they reign! This is certainly the idea expressed in Eph 2:2–8, and we shall see that it forms part of the thinking behind the opening of Rom 6. It could also refer to the future kingdom, when believers will rule on Christ's behalf (1 Cor 6:1–2). It is not impossible that both meanings are included in the phrase.

5:18 Consequently, just as the result of one trespass was condemnation for all men, so also the result of one act of righteousness was justification that brings life for all men. Paul is anxious that his readers do not miss the scope of the redemption achieved through Christ. As all were condemned through the sin of Adam, so all will enter into life through the obedience of Jesus. This does not mean that all those who have been condemned now have life.[30] Such a view is known as universalism, which holds that God will grant everyone life, even those who have committed hideous crimes against humanity and have never faced up to their guilt.

Such an argument misses the comparisons Paul is making. He is not arguing that all will be saved, but all who are of a certain status. In other words, God has made righteous

---

30. Contra Bell, "Universal," 417–32.

and will save all who were once under the representative headship of Adam, but have now come under the representative headship of Jesus. To argue for any other position would be to ignore Paul's letters and the Scriptures as a whole (Rom 1:16–18; 1 Thess 2:9–16; Eph 2:3; Heb 2:1–3; 9:24–27). Therefore, Paul is saying God will save all who belong to Christ, just as all who belong to Satan will be lost.

5:19 For just as through the disobedience of the one man the many were made sinners, so also through the obedience of the one man the many will be made righteous. As we draw near the end of this section, we cannot escape the fact Paul has continually repeated himself—albeit with slight changes of emphasis. The only sensible conclusion one can come to is that he was exceedingly anxious to be clearly understood on this matter, which is the crux of the Christian Gospel. The failure to appreciate the truth of man's sin in Adam, and its undoing by Jesus, is at the heart of much misunderstanding in the Christian church. If the church does not get it right, what chance is there of the world properly understanding the Gospel?

Paul is presenting a far bigger picture of Jesus than as man's sin-bearer. He is presenting Jesus as the last Adam. This image is the basis for much of how Paul understands the significance of Jesus and his death. The ancient hymns found scattered throughout the NT documents clearly show the importance of this imagery for the early church. They are based on the understanding of Jesus being the last Adam (Col 1:3–21; Phil 2:6–10; Heb 1:1–6), and summarize the early church's doctrine in the same way modern hymns reflect the doctrine of the church today. Adamic Christology was foundational for the apostles' thinking. It stressed, among other things, that the exile from God, brought about through Adam's sin, has been ended by the obedience and suffering of the last Adam, Jesus Christ.

5:20 The law was added so that the trespass might increase. But where sin increased, grace increased all the more The seriousness of man's condition demands that it is seen for what it is. Paul says the giving of the law to the Jews at Mount Sinai was for this purpose. It acted as a mirror for the chosen people, enabling them to see their wretched condition and understand there had to be a sin offering to remove their guilt. Under the Law of Moses,[31] an elaborate sacrificial system was established so the Jews could approach God and seek his forgiveness (Heb 9:13). In ultimate terms, these sacrifices were never intended to remove Israel's sins (Heb 9:9), but to teach her a price had to be paid when the law was broken (Heb 9:22). The law's purpose, with its sacrifices, was to point the way to a perfect representative or champion who could remove sin. It was God's intention to be the champion of his people—to remove their sin and guilt and restore them to innocence and unspeakable blessing. For this reason, Paul can say, "where sin increased, grace increased all the more."

---

31. The Greek text lacks the definite article, so Paul speaks of law being "added." This leaves it open to the possibility that he thinks wider than the Mosaic law; although, of course, it would have been the main point of the statement.

5:21 so that, just as sin reigned in death, so also grace might reign through righteousness to bring eternal life through Jesus Christ our Lord. Here, Paul writes that Sin and Death are co-regents ruling over man. Paul has sought to describe this condition of bondage. He has dealt with this, not as an aside, but as an integral part of his main argument. Up until now, he has been developing his argument about the condition of mankind. This was the thrust of his argument in Rom 1:17—3:20. In Rom 3:21–26, Paul showed that a sacrifice had been made similar to, but greater than, the Passover when Jesus, the Passover victim, delivered his people from bondage resulting from the sin of Adam. In chapter 4, Paul argued Jews had the same need as Gentiles, that they had misplaced their confidence, as it was not through circumcision that God accepted Abraham or David. At the opening of chapter 5, he described the Christian community as one released from the sentence of death to begin its pilgrimage.

Since Rom 5:12, Paul has been discussing the fall of man in Adam. This is not a digression; he wants to show there is no other way of escape from the reign of Sin and Death. Those who reject Christ as their Passover sacrifice, and refuse to be part of the eschatological community (1 Cor 5:7; Rev 1:5–6), have no other way of escaping condemnation. They are left behind in Adam to bear all of the dreadful consequences of the fall. In so doing, he has laid the groundwork he will continue to build upon in chapter 6—that there exist two separate, and very distinct, corporate communities: one in Adam with Satan (Sin) as its head, and one in Christ with Jesus as its head, and that this is equally true for both Jew and Gentile. Applied individually, a person is a member of either one community or the other, but never both: either in Adam or in Christ, and on this relationship depends one's eternal wellbeing.

CONCLUSION OF ROMANS 5

Paul uses the language of pilgrimage and acceptance as he continues to present his theology of salvation. As those who are in Christ, the new covenant community must strive, like Israel of old, against all the forces that would bar her way as she responds to the gracious invitation of her God. Paul assures the Roman believers that all of the experiences of their pilgrimage will be the grounds of their character building, preparing them for the glory to which God is calling them. Even though the testing is severe, the gift of the Spirit and the love he pours out into the life of the community are evidence of God's love.

Paul then discusses the solidarity of man in Adam versus the redeemed in Christ. Like all of his arguments, he builds this one on Semitic concepts of solidarity. Without that understanding, the argument goes nowhere. Throughout the chapter, there are repeated allusions to the OT themes of sin and redemption. This, again, reinforces the claim that Paul is to be understood in the light of his OT heritage. The powerful message of the outpouring of God's love is another indicator that the argument of the divine marriage is moving to its climax.

ROMANS 6

INTRODUCTION

Paul has been presenting a history of the human race, explaining the dire consequences of the fall and how the Jews are not exempt from the need of salvation, despite having been chosen in Abraham and delivered from slavery through Moses. He has made it clear in the preceding chapter that all men are either 'in Adam' or 'in Christ'. These two men are the key representatives of human history who determine, as heads of two separate communities, the destinies of their members. It is clear how people came to be 'in Adam', for that is their natural condition as his descendents. But how do people come to be represented by Christ, and how did this new community come into existence?

This is what Paul answers in the sixth chapter of his letter to the Romans. He tells how the Spirit of God brought a new covenant community into existence through its participation in the death of Christ. The first Adam strove after position and recognition; the last Adam let go of his position and recognition in heaven in order to save the cursed sons of disobedient Adam.

EXCURSUS E: BAPTISM INTO CHRIST

The background of Romans 6 is found in chapter 5,[1] where Paul discusses the existence of two communities: one in Adam and the other in Christ. The apostle describes how the members of these communities share in the transgression (add "against") or obedience of their respective heads. Between the exposition in chapter 5, with its concept of solidarity in the two kingdoms, and the statement in Rom 6:6 regarding the body of sin, there is a description of the baptism that the Romans have experienced (Rom 6:1–4).

I will argue that the expression: the body of sin (Rom 6:6), is a corporate description referring to the kingdom of darkness. It is the unredeemed community which has Adam as its head. If this community argument is accepted for "the body of sin," then the description of baptism in Rom 6:1–4 lies between two corporate arguments. I will argue that this baptism also has a corporate dimension rather than the commonly held individualistic one. If this is so, then baptism in chapter 6 continues the corporate dimension of chapter 5, and leads into the corporate understanding of "the body of sin."

---

1. Surprisingly Seifrid, "Romans," 631, whose work is specifically to identify OT dependence, does not find one OT link in the entire chapter. Agersnap, *Baptism*, sees Rom 5 as the foundation of Rom 6. See also Peterson, "Understanding," 3–28. Boers, "Structure," 664–82, argues that Paul's argument in Rom 6:1–14 has nothing to do with justification by faith or baptism per se, but with the theme of death to sin and life in Christ. Thus, Paul focuses on the concrete issue of liberation from sin.

Baptism has divided the church for many centuries. To this day, opinions differ as to the significance of the ordinance. While the view that baptism was derived from the "mystery" religions has declined in popularity,[2] there is still no clear consensus as to the origin and significance of the rite.[3]

What is generally agreed is that baptism is closely associated with the death of Christ, and that Paul used the exodus of the Jews from Egypt as a type in his exposition of its significance (1 Cor 10:1–4). There is also some agreement that there are texts where the emphasis is more on believers' inclusion into Christ's baptism into suffering than baptism in water. In these texts water is not present as a medium of baptism; all that is present is a historic recounting of what happened at Calvary.

Interpretations of Rom 6:1–4 include regeneration via baptism, water baptism as a symbol of regeneration, the Spirit's baptism of the believer into the body of Christ at conversion, and water baptism as a symbol of having died with Christ at his Passion. Those who hold the latter view are divided into two groups: the first see water baptism as the occasion when the Spirit is given and the benefits of Calvary are imparted to the believer, whereas the second group believes that the Spirit is given before baptism, with baptism being no more than the means of confession rather than the occasion of regeneration.

The problem with understanding water baptism as a symbol is that it requires "water" to be introduced into the text[4] when there is no mention of it in the entire letter. One must take care, for there are various kinds of baptisms in the NT, and most do not involve water. Types of baptism include baptism into or unto repentance (Matt 3:6; Acts 2:38), baptism in the Holy Spirit (Luke 3:16; 1 Cor 12:13), baptism into suffering (Luke 12:50; Mark 10:38), baptism into Moses (1 Cor 10:2), and baptism in water (Acts 8:36). Clearly, one needs to be careful not to assume that the right concept has been chosen until all others have been considered to see if any make better sense of the passage.

What is common to all the interpretations of Rom 6:1–4 is that the experience of the individual believer is read into the passage. However, the biblical evidence allows for another possibility. This alternative view is based on the type used by Paul in 1 Cor 10:1ff. It speaks of Israel's baptism into Moses in which the whole community shared at the same decisive moment. It is not about water baptism, although water baptism bears witness to it, nor is it about the individual being united with Christ at conversion.

2. Betz, "Transferring," 118, says that: "Paul's letters reveal that he accepted the transferral of the ritual but considered its interpretation to be inadequate." Betz argues that Paul made use of the mystery religions to develop a doctrine of baptism that best suited the Gentile churches. Thiselton, *Paul*, 120, considers that on the grounds of the corporate argument being made here, any ground for appealing to the Mysteries to understand the NT teaching of baptism has been removed. For a fuller treatment see Holland, *Contours*, chapter 6.

3. See Peterson, "Understanding," 3–28, for expressions of unease about the dominant approaches to the study of Pauline baptismal theology. See also DeMaris, "Funerals," 23–34, for a recent attempt to establish dependency on pagan culture and practices.

4. Bligh, "Transformation," 371–81, exemplifies some of the problems of this approach, pointing out that what Paul anticipates will be the consequences of baptism were never achieved. Bligh argues that Paul exaggerated the power of baptism to transform the Gentile world, leading him to make mistaken predictions about the future of Israel. He argues that Paul failed to deal with the remedy for post-baptismal sin and to spell out any liturgical obligations incurred by the baptized.

What this baptism refers to is the major, redemptive event which happened long before the work of regeneration in the individual took place. This baptism is the ground upon which the Spirit does his work in the church or in the individual believer. I will try to explain this further as I proceed with the exegesis of key texts. Before doing this, we need to note that all recognize the typological exegesis that has been the basis of virtually all interpretations of Rom 5:12–21. All I am proposing is that this methodology continues as we move on through the letter, unless Paul gives clear indication that he has changed his perspective.

These observations point again in a new exodus direction for understanding Paul's thinking on baptism. What cannot be missed is the link between the death of Christ and the Passover, with all of its associations with the exodus.[5] The exodus was seen in the OT as the event when the glory and power of Yahweh were publicly and supremely displayed (note the statement "raised by the glory of the Father" in Rom 6:4). The second exodus from Babylon was seen as bringing the Son of God (Israel) from the dead (Ezek 37:13; Hos 13:14). This naturally links the exodus with the death and resurrection of the Son of God, when the power and glory of God (Exod 16:7; 40:34; Num 16:19, 42; Isa 40:5; 58:8) were supremely displayed (Exod 15:6; 32:11; Deut 4:37; Isa 40:29; Jer 32:17).[6]

Those who take the alternative approach to understanding this baptism normally point to a passage like 1 Cor 12:13, where Paul writes about being baptized into one body. It is argued that the baptism spoken of in chapter 6 is the baptism of 1 Cor 12:13—the baptism of the Spirit when he baptizes a person into Christ (into his body) at conversion. For those who hold this view, the reference to baptism in this passage has nothing to do with water baptism but rather the reality to which it points.

Now, while this latter understanding has not imported water into the passage, it has still made a choice from the range of meanings of baptism. How can we be sure that the right meaning has been chosen? To make sure, we must look at the various options carefully. We must recognize that OT theology is the foundation of all that Paul is saying,

---

5. See, especially, Warnack, "Heilsgeschehen," 259ff., and "Römerbriefes," 274ff., in which he argues that Rom 6 is based on the Jewish cultic system, the Passover being specifically identified as the source. Supporters of an exodus background to Rom 6 include Nixon, *Exodus*, 24; Knox, *Gentiles*, 91; Cullmann, *Baptism*, 45, 53, 67; Marsh, *Fullness*, 137ff.; Thielman, Story, 185. Monte, "Place," 88, says that the expression "the glory of God" is a circumlocution for God's power or possibly *pneuma*. Both concepts are clearly part of the exodus event, when the power of God was displayed in a way found nowhere else in the OT and when he accomplished his redemptive purpose by the work of his Spirit. Sahlin, "Exodus," 87, says: "What event, however, is to be regarded as the starting point of this new exodus and the counterpart of the actual departure from Egypt? The answer can only be the death and resurrection of Christ. This is obvious from Rom 6:3ff." Leaney, "1 Peter," 244, says: "In the NT, as we have seen, the new era is brought about by the exodus of the Lord in Jerusalem (Luke 18:31), inaugurated by a Passover, consummated by Pentecost when those days have 'fully come' (Acts 2), and entered by means of the covenant of baptism." If it is claimed that the argument being put forward is for a corporate redemption, i.e., the church, and that Passover was essentially individually appropriated and therefore individualistic, then Morris's comment, "Passover," 67, that the Passover was not an individual ordinance and that there is a Mishna forbidding the slaughter of a Passover sacrifice for a single individual, ought to correct the misunderstanding.

6. Note Wright's statement, *Romans*, 534, "Exodus is not a distant echo here." I would argue that it is the main theme, being the exodus of Christ. It is about the Messiah bringing his people out of exile and judgment.

and to work within this framework is to discover the treasures that false methodologies have hidden.

Paul's first letter to the Corinthians is crucial in helping us to understand what is going on in chapter 6 of the letter to the Romans. There are several reasons for saying this. First, the two letters were written at approximately the same time. Second, the contents of the letters are similar. Both have a section on the church as the pilgrim community (Rom 5:1–11; 8:35–39; 10:14–15; 1 Cor 10:1–13), both refer to Jesus as the Passover offering (Rom 3:21–26; 1 Cor 5:7), and most importantly, both have a section dealing with baptism (Rom 6:1ff.; 1 Cor 6:11; 10:1–4; 12:13) closely linked to becoming sons of God (Rom 8:15–17 and 1 Cor 6:2 refer to the function of Messianic sonship). In 1 Cor 10:1–4 Paul writes about the church having been baptized into Christ. In this passage, he warns his readers not to think that they are safe because of their baptism. He points out that the Jews also experienced baptism (a baptism "into Moses"), yet came under judgment in the wilderness.

The phrase "baptized into Moses" is important for understanding at least one aspect of Paul's teaching on baptism.[7] This baptism into/unto Moses (the Greek carries both meanings) was nothing like the baptism that was practiced by the early church, when the converts confessed their faith in the name of the Father, Son, and Holy Spirit (Matt 28:19). The baptism into Moses occurred as the people left Egypt. It was part of their exodus experience, although the Israelites were unaware that it was happening. At that time, the Jewish people were brought into a covenantal relationship with Moses who became their representative before God. This was not a baptism into water, but it was the creation of a community with Moses as its spokesman or, better, its divinely-appointed representative. This was covenantal; for God took Israel as his people and put them under the leadership, or headship, of Moses. All of God's dealings with Israel were now going to be done through Moses. Israel had been baptized unto or into him, and it was a baptism that God accomplished for the purpose of uniting Moses and Israel. Through this baptism, Moses became the representative of the Jewish people.[8]

We can get some idea of the Jewish understanding of this event when we read the account of the celebration of the Passover meal.[9] The eldest son asks the father: "What does this ceremony mean?" (Exod 12:26). Each generation of fathers then teaches the family, saying: "I do this because of what the Lord did for me when I came out of Egypt" (Exod 13:8). In Jewish understanding, the entire nation was present as Israel came out of bondage, and not just the generation which had been enslaved in Egypt. All generations—past, present, and future—shared in the exodus. Such is the power of the solidarity of the Jewish people with Moses, their chief representative before God.

As we saw in our consideration of chapter 5, the concept of a federal head representing and acting for whole populations is not just an ancient understanding that has no relevance to the twenty-first century. It is fundamental to humanity's existence. The fact

7. Ridderbos, *Outline*, 405, says that 1 Cor 10:1ff. is the key to Paul's understanding of baptism into Christ.

8. Contra Badke, "Baptised," 23–29, who sees baptism into Moses and Christ to be about allegiance.

9. Leaney, "1 Peter," 51, links Rom 6:1–11 with 1 Pet, which he says is based on a Paschal liturgy.

that the West has neglected the important implications of the solidarity of peoples and nations does not make the concept irrelevant. Its neglect results in social, moral, legal, and spiritual problems for future generations.

So for Paul, there are two great solidarities governing mankind. They are not based on class, nationality, or gender. Rather, they concern whether a person is in Adam or in Christ. Since all are in Adam at birth, how is solidarity with Christ established? This is what Paul seeks to expound—basing his explanation on the parallel solidarity established between the Jewish people and Moses as they left Egypt. Paul says that when Jesus was experiencing his exodus (cf. Luke 9:31, which is actually "his coming exodus" ἔλεγον τὴν ἔξοδον αὐτοῦ) on leaving the realm of sin, his people were united with him so that he became their head. When did this baptism into Christ take place? It took place at the point of his death, for "all of us who were baptized into Christ Jesus were baptized into his death" (Rom 6:4).

This concept is not only in 1 Cor 10:1–4, it is found elsewhere in Paul's letters.[10] Few would dispute what has been said about the passage in Corinthians but they fail to see that the same event is spoken about in other passages of Paul's letters. In these passages, the tendency is to read "water" into the texts. By doing this, the door has been closed to the meaning of the texts for they have become isolated from the corporate argument that is embedded within them.

In Eph 5:25–26, Paul says: "Husbands love your wives, just as Christ loved the church and gave himself up for her to make her holy, cleansing her by the washing with water through the word."[11] As we have seen, cleansing is baptismal language, the picture being based on Ezek 16:1–14 where the prophet recounts the history of Israel. Ezekiel reminds the nation that, before God chose her for himself, she had no hope or future. She did not exist as a nation. She was like a baby who had been born without anyone to care for her—thrown by the side of the road and still covered in the blood of birth. Ezekiel said that Yahweh came by and, seeing her in her state of certain death, had mercy on her. He took her to himself and washed her as he spoke his Word to her.

This is the parallel that Paul draws in the letter to the Ephesians. The church is God's creation. There is nothing about which she can boast other than the grace of God, for she was dead in trespasses and sins (Eph 2:1–10). In the letter, Paul tells how this transformation has come about. Christ has cleansed his people from their defilement, reflecting the words of Yahweh to Israel: "I bathed you with water and washed the blood from you" (Ezek 16:9). As Christ died, the church was made clean.[12] This is what the death of

---

10. Powers, *Participation*, seeks to demonstrate the prevailing nature that corporate unity or solidarity occupies within early Christian thinking and to investigate the traditional-historical roots of this notion of unity wherever it has soteriological relevance. Powers concludes that the corporate understanding of Christian believers being united with Christ is one of the essential foundations of the earliest believers' concept of salvation.

11. Despite the mention of water in this passage, the fact that the verse echoes Ezek 16 with its historical background shows that it is also speaking of the same corporate event of washing; see also 1 Cor 6:11.

12. It is this event that Paul speaks about in 1 Cor 5:9–11: "ἢ οὐκ οἴδατε ὅτι ἄδικοι θεοῦ βασιλείαν οὐ κληρονομήσουσιν μὴ πλανᾶσθε· οὔτε πόρνοι οὔτε εἰδωλολάτραι οὔτε μοιχοὶ οὔτε μαλακοὶ οὔτε ἀρσενοκοῖται οὔτε κλέπται οὔτε πλεονέκται οὐ μέθυσοι οὐ λοίδοροι οὐχ ἅρπαγες βασιλείαν θεοῦ κληρονομήσουσιν. καὶ

Jesus achieved for the people of God. They were made clean and pure so that they could become his bride. What ought to be clear is that Ezekiel and Paul are ultimately talking about the same thing. Ezekiel is describing Israel being taken as the bride of Yahweh and Paul (in Ephesians) is describing the church being taken as the bride of Christ. The two washings are two baptisms and both are corporate. Israel was baptized into Moses in the exodus from Egypt and the church was baptized into Christ in his death.

This corporate baptism makes sense of Eph 4:4–6, where Paul says: "There is one body and one Spirit—just as you were called to one hope when you were called—one Lord, one faith, one baptism; one God and Father of all, who is over all and through all and in all." Baptism's place in this list of foundational realities should signal to us that something other than water baptism was in Paul's mind. In the light of our consideration of Eph 5:25–26, we can see that Paul is speaking of our baptism into Christ—that great ontological reality which is the basis of all God's saving activities.[13]

Another famous baptism text of Paul is found in Gal 3:26–29, where we read: "You are all sons of God through faith in Christ Jesus, for all of you who were baptized into Christ have been clothed with Christ. There is neither Jew nor Greek, slave nor free, male nor female, for you are all one in Christ Jesus. If you belong to Christ, then you are Abraham's seed, and heirs according to the promise." The passage causes a problem for grammarians when they persist in thinking of water baptism.[14] The Greek suggests that the baptism was one event. In other words, all believing Galatians—even those who were converted after Paul left Galatia—were immersed into the water at precisely the same time. But there is no mention of water in the entire letter. What we do find in the passage is a reference to the Christians being the children of Abraham—the true people of God. We also find echoes of the exodus in the letter (Gal 1:3; 3:14; 4:1–7). In other words, it seems that this reference to the baptism of the Galatians is similar to that found in Ephesians and 1 Cor 10:2. It refers to the event when the Galatians were united with Christ in his death. Indeed, it was not only they who underwent this baptism. They

---

ταῦτά τινες ἦτε· ἀλλὰ ἀπελούσασθε ἀλλὰ ἡγιάσθητε ἀλλὰ ἐδικαιώθητε ἐν τῷ ὀνόματι τοῦ κυρίου [ἡμῶν] Ἰησοῦ Χριστοῦ καὶ ἐν τῷ πνεύματι τοῦ θεοῦ ἡμῶν "Do you not know that the wicked will not inherit the kingdom of God? Do not be deceived: Neither the sexually immoral nor idolaters nor adulterers nor male prostitutes nor homosexual offenders nor thieves nor the greedy nor drunkards nor slanderers nor swindlers will inherit the kingdom of God. And that is what some of you were. But you were washed, you were sanctified, you were justified in the name of the Lord Jesus Christ and by the Spirit of our God."

13. Keck, "What," 19, notes: "if Paul could emphasize baptismal participation in Christ's death (Rom 6:3–11), would it not have been easy at least to allude also to participatory eating and drinking (1 Cor 10:16)?" The answer, of course, is that he could; but in none of the passages Keck quotes is there a participation of the sort he assumes.

14. Schnackenburg, *Baptism*, 24, says: "It would be possible to interpret the whole baptismal event as a unity in which the baptised are plunged; it represents Christ as a Pneuma-sphere into which they are removed. All (πάντες v.26, ὅσοι v.27a, πάντες v.28b) are immersed into Jesus Christ, without respect to national, social and sexual distinctions. But this exposition causes misgivings. The imagery would attain its complete effect only under the presupposition that all were immersed unitedly into the baptismal water, but that is hardly possible." Earlier, Schnackenburg, op. cit. 21, had spoken of Gal 3:27b as "describing a profound ontological event."

were in fellowship with the whole church of God—past, present, and future—just as the baptism unto Moses had involved all generations of Israelites.

Another difficult passage for those who see baptism as the moment when the new believer is brought into the church, the body of Christ, is 1 Cor 12:13: "For we were all baptised by one Spirit into one body—whether Jews or Greeks, slave or free—and we were all given the one Spirit to drink." There are two points which suggest that the meaning is otherwise. The first is grammatical. The way that Paul constructs the sentence (εἰς plus the accusative) would normally mean that what was done was to achieve an end or goal.[15] If this is accepted, then the correct translation would be "we have all been baptized to form one body." The problem with this translation is that it would mean that the church does not exist until all the baptisms are completed. Such imagery is at odds with the fact that the church not only exists now but existed in Paul's day (e.g., Acts 20:28; Rom 16:5,16; 1 Cor 1:2; 2 Cor 8:1; Phil 3:6; Col 4:15). It is understandable why almost all translators opt for the less difficult rendering: "into one body."

However, this is not a problem with the corporate baptism of 1 Corinthians, Galatians and Ephesians. This corporate baptism by the Spirit not only brought the church into existence, it was a baptism at which all members were present and in which they shared. Another advantage of this corporate understanding is that Paul has already used this imagery in his other reference to baptism in 1 Cor 10:2. In other words, 1 Cor 12:13 is a statement about the same event as found in 1 Cor 10:4, i.e., both are speaking about the creation of the Christian community which took place as a result of the baptism of its members into the death of Christ. Furthermore, this interpretation leaves Paul saying what he has actually said, that we have all been baptized "to form one body." The Corinthian passage is saying the same sort of thing as is found in Gal 3:26–29, where all—whether Jew or Gentile, male or female, free or slave—have shared in this baptism. It is not like the baptism unto Moses, which was limited to the Jewish community. This baptism is part of Paul's great theme that everyone who believes in Christ shares in the free grace of God on exactly the same grounds.

And so we come to chapter 6 of the letter to the Romans. If there is consistency in the argument outlined, it suggests that Paul is not writing about individual baptism—either in water or by the Spirit—but about the great act of salvation that took place in the death of Christ. This was Jesus' exodus; and, in his dying and resurrection, he brought his people (of all generations) out with himself, because they had been baptised by the Spirit into union with him. What took place in Christ's death and resurrection was the transfer of the whole Christian community from the realm of the kingdom of darkness into the kingdom of Light (Gal 1:3; Col 1:13).

Linguistic analysis has highlighted the fact that Paul deliberately designated prepositions to convey the condition of the church at different stages of her development. When describing the experience of the church as she shares in Christ's death and resurrection, Paul uses the phrase "with σύν (syn) Christ," but he speaks of the life lived in fellowship

---

15. For details of the argument made here, see Holland, *Contours*, chapter 7.

with Christ as being "in ἐν (*en*) Christ."[16] This observation needs further clarification. On closer examination of the texts, we find a pattern emerging. There is no mention of being baptized together, but rather of being raised together and seated together. The fulcrum for this change from an individualistic to a corporate dimension is the death of Christ. Believers were baptized into Christ's death collectively, and were raised together to share in the blessings of the eschatological community. The question that must be posed is this: "When did the baptism into his death take place, and what was its nature?"

Scholars are aware of the need to emphasize that the raising up of believers with Christ is a historic fact. It took place at the same time as Jesus rose from the dead. They were raised and seated with him at the same time as he himself was raised and seated, and they all shared in that one historic exaltation (see Rom 6:1–4; Gal 3:27; Eph 2:4–10; Col 2:11–13). The Greek makes it clear that there have not been countless millions of risings and exaltations, but only one in which all have shared. What is never asked is how this exaltation could take place without prior union. In other words, the logic of Paul's thinking requires that the union of Christ and his people be established long before water baptism is administered—even before the experience of conversion and the reception of the Spirit. Indeed, if all believers have been raised with him, then the unity has to have been in existence even before Christ left the tomb!

This problem is overcome when one realizes that behind the "baptism into Christ" was an OT type—the baptism of the Israelites into Moses during their exodus. According to Gamaliel the Second, the grandson of Paul's teacher, all Jews of preceding and subsequent generations were present in "the coming out," and shared in the baptism that made Moses their leader. It was then that Israel became the son of God, and the gift of the Spirit was given to lead her through her wilderness journey.[17] However, we do not need to rely on rabbinical understanding to support this perspective, for the rabbis' views come directly from Scripture" (Exod 13:8).

This explains why Paul has been so decisive in his use of the preposition *syn*. There is no unity of believers, either with each other or with Christ, until they have been united together through baptism. Paul has been careful to define this baptism in terms of its occasion—it was baptism into Christ's death. Just as Moses was united with the people of God through baptism and took the Jews out of Egypt, so in his exodus Christ took those who were baptized into union with him from the realm of Sin and Death. At the same historic moment, all believers experienced the one baptism into his death and were by it feed from Satan's control (Gal 1:4; Col 1:13–14).

There was no union between believers or with Christ until this baptism had been performed by the Spirit. It was this baptism that brought the covenant community into existence. Therefore, if one is asked: "When did the church historically come into existence?" the answer is: "At the moment of Christ's death; for it was then that the Spirit baptized all members of the covenant community into union with their Lord and Savior." However, it is acceptable to see the cross as the church's conception and the Day of

---

16. See Best, *Body*.

17. While Israel is called the son of God, the key covenantal imagery relates to Israel as the bride of Yahweh.

Pentecost as her birth, thus recognizing the understanding of most systematic theologians. Once this union had been established, Paul was free to use the preposition ἐν (*en*) "in," which speaks of the fellowship of believers "in Christ." From then on, in terms of ultimate reality, no believer could experience anything apart from all other believers.

What is being argued here is that the baptism passages are not speaking about water baptism, or Christ's baptism into his sufferings (even though these are important, related themes). They are speaking about a baptism which reflects the baptism of Israel into Moses, when Israel came into a covenant relationship with Yahweh through the representative he had appointed. In Rom 6 (and in 1 Cor 12:13; Gal 3:25ff.; Eph 4:6; 5:25ff.), Paul demonstrates how the old order has been brought to an end and the new eschatological order has come into existence because believers have shared in the death of Christ. The consequence of this baptism is that they have died to the covenantal demands of the old relationship which bound them mercilessly to Sin and Death (Satan).[18] They are now free to live lives unto God, who has made them his own through Christ his Son. This new relationship will be unpacked as the divine marriage in Rom 7:1–6.

Paul's teachings in Rom 6:1–4; 1 Cor 10:2; 12:3; Gal 3:27; Eph 5:25ff. are united in their concept of corporate baptism, and in each passage sonship is part of the setting. Chapter 6 of Romans is the basis of the sonship of Rom 8:14 ff., and in 1 Cor 10, sonship is clearly part of the type. It was through the exodus that Israel became Yahweh's son (Exod 4:23; Hos 11:1). Being fundamental to Israel's experience, sonship must be part of the church's experience, i.e., she must become the son(s) of God, and 1 Cor 6:1ff. supports this claim. Here, Paul urges the Corinthians to exercise their Messianic authority which is their authority as sons of God.

The Galatians passage (Gal 3:27–28) could not be more explicit in expounding the relationship between baptism and sonship. The Eph 5:25ff. passage assumes the adoption of the Ephesian believers as God's sons through Jesus Christ (Eph 1:5). In the OT, Israel is both Yahweh's son (which is a present reality) and is designated to be his bride in the eschatological marriage.

Moreover, in each of the four letters there is the claim that the distinction between Jew and Gentile has been ended. In Romans, this is expressed in Rom 4:11–12, where Paul argues that all believers—Jews and Gentiles—are children of Abraham. In 1 Cor 12:13 and Gal 3:27, it is expressed more explicitly, when Paul says: "There is neither Jew nor Greek, bond nor free, male nor female, for you are all one in Christ Jesus." Eph 2:11–19 makes it clear that, for those who are in Christ, the division between Jew and Gentile has ended as far as God is concerned. Just as the baptism into Moses at the exodus established a covenant community in which all had equal standing, so baptism into Christ creates a community in which all distinctions are abolished.

My argument for the interpretation of Rom 6 is supported by the passage in Col 2:11–13:

---

18. At the risk of being accused of repetition, for sake of any who have missed the connection, I will use the higher cases Sin and Death to denote Satan.

In him you were also circumcised, in the putting off of the sinful nature, not with a circumcision done by the hands of men but with the circumcision done by Christ, having been buried συνταφέντες (*syntaphentes*) with him in (ἐν) baptism and raised συνηγέρθητε (*synēgerthēte*) with him through your faith in the power of God, who has raised him from the dead. When you were dead in your sins and in the uncircumcision of your sinful nature, God made you alive with Christ. He forgave us all our sins.

Here is confirmation of what we have already noted: the raising/quickening is corporate–the preposition "with" σύν (*syn*) being used to convey this. It might be thought that "having been buried with him in baptism" συνταφέντες αὐτῷ ἐν τῷ βαπτισμῷ (*syntaphentes autō en tō baptismō*).renders the claims I have made suspect because it suggests the emergence of a convert from the baptismal water. However, Paul is not saying that we have been buried with Christ in baptism but that we have been buried with him by, or because of, "the" baptism. Here again, Paul has used the definite article with baptism (v. 12) τῷ βαπτισμῷ (*tō baptismō*). For a correct understanding of "in" ἐν (*en*) in this phrase, I appeal to the immediate use Paul has made of it in the passage we are considering, showing that it can have the meaning "by" as well as "in." Thus, the passage is saying the same as Rom 6:3–4: "by baptism (accomplished by the Spirit or the baptism of the Spirit), we have been united with Christ in his death and, because of this union, we have been buried together with Christ along with all other members of the eschatological community, and have been raised with him."

This exegesis points the way to understanding the meaning of the circumcision of Christ. In the OT, circumcision was the condition of entrance into the covenant which separated Israel from the nations. In Col 2:11, it is spiritual circumcision which, while done on the representative head in his suffering, is applied to the church in her regeneration as a corporate experience. The church's members are given circumcised hearts—the requirement of entry into the covenant community—when individuals put their faith in the risen Christ and his saving work. This, again, follows the OT type, where the community exists through its baptism unto Moses—individual Jews only entering existentially into what they ontologically belong to through circumcision. For the Christian community, membership and all of its blessings is conditional on the circumcision of the heart.

THE MESSIAH KING AND HIS PEOPLE'S DELIVERANCE

> WHAT SHALL WE say, then? Shall we go on sinning, so that grace may increase? By no means! We died to sin; how can we live in it any longer? Or don't you know that all of us who were baptized into Christ Jesus were baptized into his death? We were therefore buried with him through baptism into death in order that, just as Christ was raised from the dead through the glory of the Father, we too may live a new life. If we have been united with him like this in his death, we will certainly also be united with him in his resurrection. For we know that our old self was crucified with him so that the body of sin might be done away with, that we should no longer be slaves to sin—because anyone who has died has been freed from sin. Now if we died with Christ, we believe that we will also live with him. For we know that since Christ was raised from the dead, he cannot die again; death no longer has mastery over him. The death he died, he died to sin once for all; but the life he lives, he lives to God. (Rom 6:1–10)

6:1 What shall we say, then? Shall we go on sinning, so that grace may increase? Paul has been discussing the status of man. Men are either in Adam or in Christ. Those in Adam are in the kingdom his rebellion has created, and they share in the condemnation his disobedience brings. Those in Christ are in the kingdom his obedience has inaugurated, and they are blessed with the riches that come from the relationship that he has re-established for his people with God.

In the last verse of chapter 5, Paul speaks of grace reigning through Christ. He is aware of how his ancestors abused the redemption that they had experienced when delivered from Egypt. They used it as a license to live recklessly (1 Cor 10:1–10). Paul raises the question as to what receiving eternal life (Rom 5:20) should mean for the believer. He is aware that some might argue that, if they sinned, God would be given more opportunity to forgive. There is no evidence that Paul knew of this being argued in Rome, but it was the type of argument that had been used by his ancestors with terrible consequences (Amos 5:14–27). He raises the possibility of such an abuse of Christian freedom to ensure that such reasoning is robbed of its appeal.

If Paul had been alive in the days of Moses, he would have addressed the pilgrim community with a similar argument: "You say that you have been redeemed from Egypt, then why are you living as though you were still there?" In other words, their lives should have been lived in the presence and for the glory of God who had delivered them from their misery.

There is no greater motive than love. This is implicit in all that Paul teaches and it continues throughout this section of his letter. It was God's love for the Roman believers that meant that he gave up his own Son unto death (Rom 5:8). It was God's love that had been poured into their hearts by the Holy Spirit (Rom 5:5), and it was God's grace (love) that had overflowed to the many (Rom 5:15). To use John's words: "We love because he first loved us" (1 John 4:19). If Paul is reflecting what the prophets have said about the coming new exodus, then the church has been redeemed from the bondage of Sin to be the bride of Christ just as Israel had been in the OT. The church is called to live as one who anticipates her marriage–anxious to be beautiful for her husband (Eph 5:25ff.). Sin is to be shunned because it mars the very work of redemption that the death of Christ has brought about. We will find that this theological framework will clarify several problems not resolved by traditional interpretations in chapters 6–7. Most other models of interpretation finish up with a series of unanswered questions. We will see these questions emerging as we continue to read the letter to the Romans.

In conclusion, the suggestion that Christians can deliberately sin so that God will be glorified is something that Paul could not countenance. They had not been redeemed for sin but from Sin. They had been redeemed to be the bride of Christ, and his bride was to be without spot or blemish.

6:2 By no means! We died to sin; how can we live in it any longer? What does Paul mean by the phrase "We have died to Sin"? When the Jews left Egypt, they died to the way of life that had been dictated by Pharaoh. Because of the exodus, they were free to serve and worship God. While it can be argued that the Jews died to Egypt when they passed through the Red Sea, it was only a symbolic death. Neither the Jews—nor Egypt—actually died. This is not what Paul is arguing here. He says, emphatically, that the church has died to Sin.[19] This is confirmed in the way that Paul continually links the experience of the church with the death of Jesus. What Paul is saying here is of vital importance, yet it is often missed.

We have seen that Paul has argued that, through the sin of Adam, man died to God. He came under the control of Satan (Sin) and as a result, became his servant. It is important to realize that when Paul speaks of Sin (sing.) in Rom 5–8, he is speaking of Satan. The NT makes it clear that there are parallel relationships between the church and the world. Christians are children of God; unbelievers are children of the devil (John 8:44). Believers are citizens of the kingdom of Light (Col 1:14); unbelievers are citizens of the kingdom of darkness (Eph 2:1–3). These texts suggest that the relationship the church has with Christ/God is the same in nature as the one that the world has with Sin/Satan.

The covenant that exists between God and his people would, therefore, be paralleled by a similar covenant between Satan and his community. This suggests that unredeemed man is in a covenantal relationship with Sin (Satan). This ought not to surprise us because the argument of Rom 5:12ff. compares the parallel consequences of the disobedience of Adam with the obedience of Christ. While Christ's obedience is the basis of the covenant between his people and God, the disobedience of Adam would bring about a similar relationship between his people and Satan (Sin). Both Adam and Christ represent their own people; they are representatives of human groupings and are bound to them. The inevitable logic of this comparison is that there is a covenantal relationship between

---

19. Zeisler, *Romans*, 156, comments on the term "died" in v. 2: "'Died' (*apethanomen*) is an aorist verb, indicating that it refers to a definite event. This is reinforced almost at once by the talk about baptism, also a definite event. Those who have become Christians and have been baptised have died to sin. 'To sin' may indicate possession, so that 'died to sin' means release from possession by sin. In any case, there is complete separation." Ziesler comes very close to what is being argued in this commentary, but misses the fact that the baptism Paul speaks about is not the individual's confession but the uniting of the community with Christ in his death (hence, the aorist). This is an event in which the entire Roman church has shared as part of the universal church's experience.

Adam and his people and this is the basis of man's sin. This is a reasonable conclusion because the basis of Christian righteousness is the covenantal relationship between Christ and his people.

Such ideas would be part of Paul's thinking. The Jews saw themselves as being in covenant with God and the Gentiles to be in covenant with their gods (Exod 23:32). The inevitable next step in logic is to realize that the Gentiles' covenantal relationship was not with their gods but with Satan (1 Cor 8:4). This understanding is behind what Paul says about the worship of demons. He says that demons are nothing, but then warns that what is behind them is dangerous for they are agents through which Satan works. Paul's concern in 1 Cor 10:18–22 (see also Rev 2:20–25) is that the Corinthians could enter into fellowship with demons as they partook in a covenant meal at the table of demons.

All this suggests that Paul saw man in his federal union with Adam to be bound to Satan through a covenantal relationship. This will help us to understand a number of details which we will encounter in this chapter. But this condition of being in covenant with Sin creates a problem that seems insurmountable. If man is related to Satan in this way, it follows that he is the bride of Satan just as the church is the bride of Christ. Any attempt by humanity to free itself from this relationship, in order to be united with Christ, can mean only one thing: an adulterous relationship would exist. This becomes all the worse because the new relationship involves Christ himself.

The biblical understanding of marriage is that it is permanent. The marriage bond (or covenant) terminates on the death of one of the partners. To terminate the covenant humankind has with Sin would demand the death of one of the parties, humanity or Satan. However, this is not a solution to the dilemma, for after death there is judgment. So, rather than death bringing freedom, it would confirm forever the union between humankind and Satan. As Satan cannot die—death being the experience of mortals—there seems no way out of this dire situation. Humanity, it would appear, is eternally locked into a covenantal relationship with Satan.

This desperate situation is one that no human being can reverse. Through union with Adam, all people are under this sentence of death. They are servants of Sin, and bound in a relationship of covenant and solidarity that is of a different order than people being sinners because they sin. The individual's personal accountability is but a tiny part of the whole picture of humanities plight in Adam. Unless there is another who can die on his behalf, and through that representative death bring an end to this relationship, the entire human race is in an impossible situation.

This is the point that Paul is arguing. It might be claimed that images are being introduced that are not in the text. It is true that they are not in the immediate text, but Rom 7:2–4 is the summation of the argument of chapters 5–6. In that summary is the very situation I have outlined:

> By law a married woman is bound to her husband as long as he is alive, but if her husband dies, she is released from the law of marriage. So then, if she marries another man while her husband is still alive, she is called an adulteress. But if her husband dies, she is released from that law and is not an adulteress, even though she marries another man. So, my brothers, you also died to the law through the body of

Christ, that you might belong to another, to him who was raised from the dead, in order that we might bear fruit to God. (Rom 7:2–4)

Not only are the ideas of a covenantal relationship in the summary of the argument, it is only by accepting its presence throughout chapter 6 that it is possible to resolve long-standing exegetical conundrums which we will soon meet in the text. Furthermore, if the opening of the chapter reflects the deliverance of the Jews from Egypt (as some argue), we have exodus imagery in the text. Part of that imagery is that Yahweh took Israel as his bride. In other words, if the new exodus was the theological mindset of the early church, which it is increasingly recognized to be,[20] then the letter's first recipients—guided by the church's Jewish teachers—would understand the letter in the context of the new exodus.

What Paul is saying is that the death of Christ is not "just" about the propitiation of God's wrath towards the sinner; it is about the ending of the relationship with Sin. This condition of man in Adam underlines the impossibility of people being able to make themselves acceptable before God. For God to accept them without the covenant-annulling death of Christ would implicate God in adultery! For this reason, Paul stresses that the Roman believers have shared in the death of Christ. This was not achieved through some act of will on their part. Indeed, they had no knowledge of being involved in the event, for it happened in history—in the death of Jesus himself.

Thus, the relationship with Sin is over—the death of Jesus has ended it! The death of the One for the many has had the reverse effect of the disobedience of the first Adam, whose sin brought his offspring into this terrible condition in the first place. When Paul says that we have died to Sin (not sins!), he is asserting that the relationship with Satan is terminated. Satan has no legal rights, through covenant, to claim us. Our death in Christ has brought about this amazing reversal.

The termination of covenantal relationships through death is natural to a Jewish mind. When God established a covenant with Abraham (Gen 15:12–18), the ceremony, in part, followed ancient tradition. This entailed both parties walking together through dismembered animals that had been offered in sacrifice. The practice indicated that each party was saying that if he failed to keep the terms of the covenant being made, the same would be done to him as had been done to the animals laid out on either side. The remarkable point of the covenant Yahweh made with Abraham was that Abraham did not walk between the pieces—Yahweh walked alone. In so doing, he indicated that he was taking full responsibility if the terms of the covenant were broken. The death of Jesus is God keeping righteousness, fulfilling his covenantal oath.

The same thought is behind the cutting off of offenders from the Jewish community (Exod 22:20). This was not so much for punishment but for preserving the holiness of the community (see Deut 7:26, where the property was destroyed because it was defiled and not fit for the covenant functions). This notion is expanded in the OT where Israel

---

20. Davies, *Rabbinic*, 104–7, says: "It is highly significant that in several places in the Epistles, once explicitly, and elsewhere by implication, the apostle compares the Christian life to the Passover festival; he obviously regards the great deliverance of the exodus and its accompaniments as a prototype of the mighty act of God in Christ."

was cut off from her inheritance and exiled in Babylon, an event which was viewed as her death (Ezek 37:12–13; Hos 13:14). The reason for the exile was to enable the covenant Israel had with God to be terminated. However, God was not casting her off forever, because there was the promise of a new covenant for repentant Israel and a resurrection of the nation (Isa 9:7; 55:3; Jer 31:31–34; 33:14–18; Ezek 16:59–63; 36:24–38; Amos 9:11). This same idea is found in the NT, where Paul and Jesus, in order to preserve the purity of the larger community (1 Cor 5:5; Rev 2:22–23), warn members of the danger of being handed over to Satan.

In the NT, the Sadducees tested Jesus over the resurrection (Matt 22:23–33). They told the story of a woman who married. Her husband subsequently died, leaving her a childless widow. According to the Jewish law of the levirate, the dead man's eldest brother had to take her as his wife and have children by her on his brother's behalf, keeping his name alive. The woman married the second brother, but he too died. This was repeated with the third brother and so on until all seven brothers had married her, but then died before giving her a child. Finally, she also died. "So then," the Sadducees asked Jesus, "Whose wife will she be in the resurrection?" Jesus responded that they neither knew the Scriptures nor the power of God. They did not know the power of God to raise the dead and they did not know the scriptural teaching that covenants, even marital ones, did not survive death. In the resurrection, she would be the wife of none of them. In heaven, there is neither marrying nor giving in marriage, for they "will be like the angels in heaven (Mark 12:25). Thus, Paul's understanding of the significance of death as the terminator of covenants has theological and legal bases.

Clearly, what has been said transforms the status of the believer. However, it has no bearing on the unbeliever. The community that remains in Adam continues its relationship with Satan, and the condemnation that the fall brought will finally be meted out to its members on the day of God's wrath (Rom 5:21; 6:23).

It is impossible for a believer to continue in his relationship to Sin. It would be a return to the very relationship that Christ died to end. Paul's argument is clear: having died to that relationship, it is impossible to return to it. It would be the equivalent of re-establishing the covenant with Sin that had been destroyed, and that in turn would mean the destruction of the new relationship that had been established through the death of Christ for his people. In other words, it is yet again a betrayal of the covenant love of God. This was something of deep concern to Paul. He had warned the Corinthians of this very danger, articulating it as clearly as he could. He warned that idolatry, sexual immorality, and speaking evil of God had been the cause of Yahweh's judgment on Israel in her wilderness wanderings (1 Cor 10:1–10). Earlier, Paul had spelt out the consequences of such behavior for the individual (1 Cor 6:9–11) and for the church (1 Cor 5:3–8).

6:3 Or don't you know that all of us who were baptized into Christ Jesus were baptized into his death? Paul emphasizes the grounds on which the believers' relationship with Sin has ended. He asks them, in a tone of incredulity, "Could it be possible that you don't know this?" This was at the heart of the early church's proclamation (1 Cor 15:3). The possibility that it had not been part of the message that the Romans received is beyond Paul's ability to believe. That Christ has set his people free through his death was not on the periphery of the proclaimed message but at its heart. Indeed, it is the Gospel.

In saying we were baptized into his death, Paul is not saying that we have shared in Jesus' death through water baptism.[21] His argument does not relate to water baptism at all but to the Spirit's inclusion into Christ of all of his people[22] As this took place in the moment of Jesus' death, it was a baptism into Christ's death. This sharing in the death of the last Adam makes deliverance from the kingdom of darkness possible, for death was the means by which Satan's authority was terminated and deliverance secured for those whom God foreknew. This does not deny the importance of water baptism for the early church. It was the appointed way of making a personal confession of sin, repentance, and faith in Christ; but it is not the subject of this passage.

6:4 We were therefore buried with him through baptism into death in order that, just as Christ was raised from the dead through the glory of the Father, we too may live a new life. The verse can be paraphrased as follows: "Because we have been baptized into his death, we have been raised from the dead with Christ. This was done through the power of God that we should live new live a new life. Because of our union with Christ, we have experienced all that happened to him. We have shared in his death as a result of the baptism (that is, the union of Christ and his people by the Holy Spirit) which has taken place. However, this shared experience was not limited to his death. It continued beyond, as we were raised with Christ when the Father raised him from the dead (Eph 2:4–10)![23] This is firm evidence that the baptism spoken about here is not individual and confessional. If, as most concede, the reference to being raised with Christ refers to being part of the actual resurrection event and not to some later re-enactment, the union that the passage speaks about must have happened before Christ was raised from the dead in order for the church to have been included in the Easter resurrection. Thus, the baptizing (the means of inclusion into the experience of the death of Christ) must have preceded the resurrection. Paul has made this fact clear, for it was a baptism into Christ's death.

Paul is anxious to clarify that in the case of Christ and the church, the union does not dissolve with death as other unions do (Rom 14:9; 2 Cor 5:14–15). This is probably the reason for the baptism being described as a baptism into his death. It is a union that is made in the process of death and one that death cannot break. All other unions are forged before death, and death severs them. The earlier illustration of Prime Minister Heath taking Britain into the Common Market (see page 159) may help us to appreciate how Jesus Christ's death has brought all of his people out of the kingdom of darkness and into the kingdom of Light. In the case of Jesus, the transfer was not through a signature but through his death, which undid the work and power of Satan.

21. Peterson, "Light," 3–28, claims that a ritualistic-theoretical approach to interpreting Rom 6 avoids some interpretative and epistemological problems current in Protestant studies of Pauline baptismal theology.

22. See Holland, *Contours*, chapter 6.

23. I find that all the reasons for rejecting Ephesians and Colossians as non-Pauline rest on the faulty hermeneutic of reading the letters as speaking about individual experience. When read corporately, most of the issues that challenge Pauline authorship cannot be upheld.

The union of Christ with his people survives death for unlike other relationships, that union is actually dependent on (his) death. His people have been united with the Lord of Life who is the conqueror of death; they have been raised with him and are now seated with him in the heavenly places (Eph 2:4–10). Thus, they share in his resurrection and his exaltation in his new life. They are not physically raised and exalted, but their position in Christ is such that God deals with them as though they were. Just as God dealt with the Jewish nation as though everyone experienced the exodus,[24] so God deals with every believer as though they have been raised and seated with the risen Christ. This acceptance can mean only one thing for believers: they are to live out the status that they now have in newness of life.

All that was achieved was "through the glory of the Father." "The glory of God" is another way of saying "God's power and might." As we have seen in the OT, the power of God was displayed supremely on two occasions—when he saved Israel from Egypt and when he saved her from Babylon (Exod 14:31; Deut 9:29; Isa 40:5). In the NT, the power and the glory of God were supremely displayed in the death and resurrection of Jesus. Paul says that the Easter event is the fulfillment of the OT type, the exodus. Indeed, as we have seen, he has linked baptism with Israel's coming out of Egypt under Moses in 1 Cor 10:4. This understanding is not limited to Paul as the Gospels also support this interpretation (Luke 9:31, where ἔξοδος "departure" ought to be "exodus" [AV]). Also, the four gospels emphasize the fact that Jesus interpreted the significance of his death in light of the Passover meal. The importance of this should not be missed as there is no other Jewish sacrifice mentioned, or even alluded to, in any of the four gospels. Clearly, Jesus wanted the Passover/exodus to be the key to interpreting the purpose of his death for his people.

6:5 If we have been united with him like this in his death, we will certainly also be united with him in his resurrection. Paul writes in the plural: "if we have . . . we will," reminding us that Paul is not dealing with the experience of the individual but of the church—the community of people whom God has redeemed through the death of his Son. It not only suggests that dying with Christ is a corporate experience but that being raised with him is one also. While we talk of the resurrection of the individual believer, we must be aware that this is not the perspective of the Scriptures.

The great OT passage of resurrection concerns the vision of the valley of dry bones in Ezek 37, where the exiled nation of Israel is revealed to be dead. Ezekiel is told to prophesy and, by the word of God, the dry bones are transformed into a mighty, living army. Many scholars see Ezekiel's vision to be behind what Paul says in 1 Cor 15, where he discusses the resurrection. Indeed, it can be shown that 1 Cor 15 is molded by exodus imagery.[25] In this passage in Romans, the exodus is very much part of the backcloth.

---

24. Note the answer to be given to the enquiring son on the night of the Passover, when he asks: "What do these things mean?" His father is to tell him "I do this because of what the LORD did for me when I came out of Egypt" (Exod 13:6). According to Gamaliel 11, all Jews were present on that night.

25. See Holland, *Contours*, 145–46.

Thus, the scriptural understanding focuses on the resurrection of the church rather than of the individual.

While the church looks forward to the coming of Christ and to the resurrection (1 Thess 4:16; Phil 3:20–21), these are not the focus here. Paul speaks of the past historical reality of the resurrection of Christ. It is in that resurrection which the church has already shared. It is because the church has shared in Christ's historical resurrection that she is able to live with him and be like him. She is called to take on Christ's mantle of service which inevitably involves suffering.

6:6 For we know that our old self was crucified with him so that the body of sin might be done away with, that we should no longer be slaves to sin. At first glance, it seems that Paul has reverted to considering the individual. But this apparent reversal cannot be maintained.

Although the "old self" and "the body of sin" are seen by many scholars to refer to the modes of existence of believers, there has been sustained debate over the way that Paul uses the expression "body" σῶμα (*sōma*).

The term ὁ παλαιὸς ἡμῶν ἄνθρωπος (*ho palaios hēmōn anthrōpos*) "our old self" is translated "old man" in the AV. Normally, it is assumed that the term speaks of the old life that was lived in Adam. *Anthrōpos*, it is said, refers to the ungodly life that the Romans lived before their conversion. To help the modern reader, the translators of the NIV translate *anthrōpos* as "old self." The trouble is that this translation causes the reader to envision the individual's old life. Such a translation closes the door to other shades of meaning.[26]

We must check to see if this is the correct understanding of "old man." The term is used elsewhere in a way which suggests that the individual understanding is not the one Paul had in mind. In Eph 2:15, Paul speaks of God taking the Jews and Gentiles and making out of them one new man, *anthrōpos*. This is a clear reference to the church being made up of Jews and Gentiles. The term is corporate, the church being called the "new man." In Col 3:9–12, Paul writes,

> Do not lie to each other, since you have taken off your old self (*anthrōpos*) with its practices and have put on the new self (*anthrōpos*), which is being renewed in knowledge in the image of its Creator. Here there is no Greek or Jew, circumcised or uncircumcised, barbarian, Scythian, slave or free, but Christ is all, and is in all. Therefore, as God's chosen people, holy and dearly loved, clothe yourselves with compassion.

In this passage, it is clear that the new self (the new man) refers to a community: "Here (in this community) there is neither Greek nor Jew." The only way this can be read is that the new man is the church, as it is in Eph 2:15. It follows that the corresponding

---

26. In doing this, the NIV has been directed by the most common understanding that prevails in the church. Schreiner, *Romans*, 315, correctly notes that "old man" is a redemptive-historical designation of humanity in the old era.

reality to the new man—the old man—is also corporate. This is the community that lives independently of God. It is the world or unredeemed humanity.[27]

The old man to whom the Romans have died is their relationship with the world. They are no longer part of the Adamic community. They have been released as a result of the death of Christ and their own acceptance of him as their representative head. They are no longer in Adam and no longer part of the rebellion against God and his rule. They have died to the solidarity of Sin and are now alive in a new solidarity which has Christ as its head. This new solidarity is one of righteousness.

Paul also speaks in this verse of "the body of sin" being done away with. Most expositors follow the individualistic interpretation and say that "the body of sin" is the human body under the control of sin. The problem with this understanding is that it suggests that the body is in some way sinful. Also, it suggests that the only authentic Christian experience is victory over sin i.e., moral perfection. Such claims can have devastating pastoral implications for sensitive souls who struggle with their failings. It casts them into darkness and turmoil—a self doubt and loathing that brings them to question their faith and experience of Christ's salvation. Whether the term is held to be about the principle of sin that dwells in humankind, or the body under the rule of sin, both interpretations come perilously close to dualism. Almost all commentators are aware of such an implication, and arguments are mounted to avoid slipping into such an abyss. Even after these caveats have been given, the distinct impression remains that the body is in some way intrinsically sinful. But we know that Paul, as a Jew, could never accept anything that came close to a dualistic understanding.[28]

The corporate interpretation, however, does not have this danger. The fact is that Paul's expression "the body of sin" occurs nowhere else in the whole of Scripture. Because we find no help from outside of the passage, its meaning must be decided from within. All that we have to help us decipher its meaning is the flow of the argument that is being made. This suggests, as we shall see, that it is a corporate term.

Paul has been arguing about the plight of humanity in Adam and how this condition has been reversed for those who call on Christ to be their head. Elsewhere, Paul calls the community that is in Christ "the body of Christ" (1 Cor 12:12, 27; Eph 2:16; 3:6; 5:23). Could not "the body of sin" be the community that is in Adam? There has been much serious debate over the meaning of *sōma* "body" as used by Paul. A growing number of scholars see a Hebraic background to the way he uses the term. As would be expected, the Jews (with their strong sense of solidarity of family and nation) normally use the term *sōma* "body" when referring to a corporate reality.

This line of thinking certainly fits the covenantal setting which was argued for in the opening of the chapter.[29] We have seen that the OT background suggests that the

27. For scholarly support, see Holland, *Contours*, chapter 5.

28. For a discussion on Paul's understanding of sin, see Excursus F: Sin in the Theology of Paul, pages 202–24.

29. Schrange, *Korinthens*, 2:22, rejects the solely physical meaning of *sōma*, pointing out that the physical is nevertheless important because it is the place where man experiences life and death. *Sōma* means man himself as a person. So also, Leenhardt, *Romans*, 92; Maillot, *Romains*, 224. The corporate exposition

death of Christ to Sin has annulled a covenant (as will be argued in Rom 7:1–4). We are coming very close to the idea that the body of Sin is the body that is in covenantal relationship with Sin just as the body of Christ is the body that is in covenantal relationship with Christ.

One could argue that "body of Sin" is not an appropriate expression for such a corporate understanding. If the communities are parallel, the corresponding term to "the body of Christ" ought to be "the body of Adam," for Sin parallels God in the argument that has been given and Adam parallels Christ. Is there a rationale for Paul avoiding "the body of Adam" term? The rabbis were familiar with it.[30] They used it to speak of the human race. But for Paul, Adam's mediatory work was over. He had no further function to fulfill. Indeed, Satan could argue that he now owned the kingdoms of this world (Luke 4:5–6). There is no future event that will bring the work of Adam to completion. It has been completed. So the community he has represented is no longer his body but Sin's. Satan has control, and the significance of Adam as representative head has ended. To put it another way, there is no mediatory work left for Adam to fulfill for his people.

But the kingdom of Christ has not yet reached its end. Paul says that Christ has yet to yield up the kingdom to God the Father, "after he has destroyed all dominion, authority and power" (1 Cor 15:24). Elsewhere, it is clear that Paul sees a distinct difference between the kingdom of Christ and the kingdom of God (Eph 5:5) into which believers are yet to enter (Acts 14:22).

All this evidence supports the conclusion that Paul and other NT writers see that Christ's work has yet to be completed. When that final event takes place, it will no longer be appropriate to think of the kingdom of Christ or the body of Christ, for he will have handed over the kingdom to the Father and his redemptive work will be completed. He will no longer be head of the people he has redeemed; they will finally and victoriously be restored to their previous calling and God will be their all in all.

We saw earlier that Paul was heavily dependent on the prophecy of Isaiah. The most quoted OT text in the NT is the stone passage (Isa 28:16), which is at the center of many NT descriptions of Christ (Matt 21:42; Mark 10:12; Luke 20:17; Acts 4:11; Rom 9:32–33; 1 Pet 2:4–6). In this Isaianic passage, there is also reference to a judgment that was coming on Israel (Isa 28:11–13). Isaiah said that the predicted judgment would be imminent when Israel heard people speaking in tongues that they could not understand (that is, Babylonian). Finally, in this short passage between Isa 28:11–13 and 16, there is a reference to Israel making a "covenant with death" (Isa 28:14–15). Isa 28:11–13, 16 was known to the NT church, evidenced by the fact that the passage is used in the NT without introduction or explanation, and was the most quoted OT text in the NT (For Isa 28:11–13, see 1 Cor 14:11 and for Isa 28:16, see Rom 9:33; Matt 21:42; Mark 12:10;

---

that has been given so far is supported by Lagrange, *Romains*, 146, who says: "Le but à atteindre, ce qui fait l'object de toute la péricope, c'est que nous ne servions plus le péché, considere comme une personne. Lui vit donc toujours; ce n'est donc pas lui qui a été detruit en personne ou crucifié, c'est notre corps à nous . . . The goal that we are aiming for, the whole point of the statement, *is that we would no longer serve sin, (which is) regarded as a person.* That is still alive then; sin therefore has been in itself destroyed or crucified, rather it is our own. (Emphasis added.)

30. See Scroggs, *Adam*, 15; Davies, *Rabbinic*, 57. Note the warning given by Best, *Body*, 92.

Luke 20:17; Acts 4:11; 1 Pet 2:7). It is reasonable to claim that the reference to a "covenant with death" could be recalled by the early church if only because of its location between two known proof texts.[31]

It is this reference to Israel's covenant with death that is the key to understanding Paul's "body of sin." In the original context the term referred to the Jews' alliance with the Egyptians. They were afraid of invasion, and the best way to avoid this was to enter into a pact with a stronger nation who would guarantee their security. However, to forge this alliance, Israel had to accept the patronage of the god of the Egyptians–Môt, god of death. Israel was, therefore, entering into a covenant with Death.

This idea of covenants existing between nations and their gods was common in the ancient east (Exod 23:32). Because other nations saw their gods to be their divine husbands,[32] Israel was condemned for whoredom by Yahweh, her own husband, when she worshipped the gods of the surrounding nations.

For Paul, there is no difficulty in transposing the relationships of the OT into the universal picture of the NT. Instead of humanity being divided into Jews and Gentiles, it is now divided into those who are "in Christ" and those who are "in Adam." Instead of Israel being the bride of Yahweh, the church is the bride of Christ. Those who are in Adam are in a covenant relationship with the god of this world, Satan. The concepts simply redefine OT categories so that they are no longer nationalistic but apply to the two great divisions of mankind—those in light and those in darkness, i.e., those in Christ and those in Adam.

Satan's power over humanity is through the covenant that has been created. Like a ruthless husband—demanding from his wife the loyalty of the covenant—Satan binds and abuses the human race that is in Adam. Humankinds desire to be free can be no more than a longing, for the law of the husband binds his wife to him as long as they both live (Rom 7:1–6).

However, for the church, all this has changed! She has died to this relationship with Satan by the death of her Savior who becomes her new representative—her new husband. It is through the representative, or substitutive, death of the last Adam (Jesus) that her death has taken place. As a result of this, the redeemed community has been removed from the body of Sin. She has been elected to become the body of Christ, and set apart,

---

31. To the average Western reader, the likelihood of the Roman church being able to follow this way of reading is doubtful. However, I can testify that other mindsets pick this up this way of reasoning almost immediately. In the late 1980s I conducted a series of seminars in Cluj, Romania. The attending pastors had no Christian books—only Bibles—taking strenuous measures to ensure that these were never found by the secret police when their homes were searched. These men knew their Bibles from cover to cover. On one occasion, I began to speak to them saying that I wanted to talk about the covenant with death. I referred to no Bible passage yet every pastor spontaneously opened his Bible at Isa 28:18. Immediately, a heated debate in Romanian began. After about five minutes the noise abated, and I told the translator: "What I want to tell them is . . ." but he interjected: "Oh, that's OK. They've just discussed that." Just the mention of key terms caused them to identify the appropriate text and their imaginations raced ahead of the intended exposition, arriving at the understanding that was going to be given on their own. This was a living example of intercontextualization.

32. Smolarz, "*Covenant.*"

or sanctified (1 Cor 6:11), so that she might marry her Lord and Savior, Christ Jesus.[33] In this way the authority of Sin has been broken and rendered powerless. It is powerless because Sin has no law to which it can appeal. Death has brought an end to the order that once existed. A new order, or relationship, now exists and it is a legitimate one. There can be no charge of adultery laid at the feet of the ones who once were in covenant with Satan. The believing community should not live as though still bound to Sin. The power of Sin has been brought to an end and the church is to live in the service of the one who has redeemed her. It is now to him that she is pledged in marriage.

So, I would argue that the terms "old man" and "body of Sin" are corporate concepts in Paul's thinking.[34] Their use by him confirms that it is right to argue that the letter

33. Indeed, I would argue that the language of 1 Cor 6 is about this eschatological marriage. See Holland, "Mistaken," 5–69.

34. The argument I have made for understanding the body of sin as a corporate entity has been theologically based. Others, normally through linguistic rather than theological studies, have come to conclusions that support the case that I have made. I provide their observations as a supplement to the argument I have made. First, we note the exposition of Ridderbos "the concrete mode of existence of sinful man, can sometimes be identified with sin as the 'body of sin' (Rom. 6:6.), the 'body of flesh' (Col. 2:11), the 'body of death' (Rom. 7:24). Accordingly, the life from Christ by the Holy Spirit can be typified as a 'doing away with the body of sin,' 'putting off of the body of the flesh,' 'putting to death the earthly members,' 'deliverance from the body of this death' (Rom. 6:6; Col. 2:11; 3:5; Rom. 7:24). . . . All these expressions are obviously not intended of the body itself, but of the sinful mode of existence of man." (Ridderbos, *Outline*, 229f.) Ridderbos also says "What is intended by this body of sin is, as we have already been able to determine in another context, the present human mode of existence ruled by sin. Of this bondage to sin the cross and the death of Christ have made an end." (op cit, 208). . . . "That sin, as it were, lays hold of the body 'from without' and thus subjects the entire man to itself as a slave. . . . All sorts of expressions and pronouncements in Paul's epistles give evidence of this 'direct' connection: 'Sin-body' that must be done away with, so that 'we' no longer serve sin. Here the body, in its being ruled by sin" (op cit, 194).

Torrance is even more explicit in his understanding of "the body of Sin." He says: "in his death, the many who inhered in him died too, and indeed the whole body of sin, the whole company of sinners into which he incorporated himself to make their guilt and their judgement his own, that through his death he might destroy the body of sin, redeem them from the power of guilt and death, and through his resurrection raise them up as the new Israel" (Torrance, *Reconstruction*, 203).

This corporate view of *the body of Sin* is also shared by Bruce who said: "This 'body of sin' is more than an individual affair, it is rather that old solidarity of sin and death which all share 'in Adam', but which has been broken by the death of Christ with a view to the creation of the new solidarity of righteousness and life of which believers are made part 'in Christ'" (Bruce, *Romans*, 38).

It is perhaps Manson who came closest to the thesis being worked out here. He questioned the traditional assumption that in the phrase "body of Sin" the term "of Sin" is a genitive of quality; he argued that it: "does not yield a very good sense." He took it to be a possessive genitive, and said: "It is perhaps better to regard 'the body of sin' as the opposite of 'the body of Christ.' It is the mass of unredeemed humanity in bondage to the evil power. Every conversion means that the body of sin loses a member and the body of Christ gains one" (Manson, "Romans," 945).

Manson is supported by Nygren says of Rom 6:6: "There is another body that must die. Paul speaks of it expressively as the 'body of sin'. . . . it is this body to which man formerly belonged when he was under the dominion of sin and death." (Nygren, *Romans*, 234). Because he saw the earlier part of Rom 6 to refer to water baptism, was not able to go beyond the conclusions of others.

Nygren, commenting on Romans chapter five says: "If we begin with such sociological alternatives as 'individual or collectivity,' we shall not arrive at what Paul has in mind. The only way to understand him is to take him seriously, on the one hand, the idea of the body of sin and of death of which we are by nature ('in Adam') members, and on the other hand, the body of Christ into which we are incorporated by faith and baptism" (opt cit).

must be read as the account of the church's experience rather than that of the individual believer. I believe that this is true for all of the letters written to the NT churches, and that the failure to appreciate this corporate perspective causes confusion over a number of crucially important doctrines.

6:7 because anyone who has died has been freed from sin. This verse causes most commentators considerable difficulty[35] because Paul does not actually write "freed" from sin (Sin) but δεδικαίωται ἀπὸ τῆς ἁμαρτίας (*dedikaiōtai apo tēs hamartias*) "justified" from sin (Sin). Paul's use of "justified" is totally unexpected in this context because it seems to go against his doctrine of justification as it is traditionally understood. It is widely accepted by scholars that Paul uses "justified" to speak of being accepted by God through Christ. Once this declaration of innocence has been made, the sinner (the emphasis being on the individual believer) begins to experience the blessings of God and the Christian life.

However, what is clear is that if Paul meant to use "justified," he has reversed his theology. He would be saying: "As a result of a man dying with Christ, he is justified." In other words, Paul would have reversed the *ordo salutis*, the order of salvation, making Christian experience the source of justification. This difficulty has led scholars of almost every theological persuasion to believe that Paul's intention was to say that "he who has died is *freed* from sin," (as most translations give). Indeed, Young, in his concordance, does not even list this text under his entry of *dedikaiōtai* (justified).

"Freed" is used in this way for theological reasons alone, so that it harmonizes with what is thought to be Paul's teaching on justification. However, no Greek manuscript of Romans supports this reading. Every other time Paul uses the verb δικαιόω *dikaioō* in his letter (Rom 2:13; 3:4; 3:20; 3:24; 3:26; 3:28; 3:30; 4:2; 4:5; 5:1; 5:9; 8:30; 8:33), he means "justified," and it is translated as such. What, then, could Paul have been intending to say if we allow him to mean what he says when he wrote: "Anyone that has died has been *freed* from sin"?[36]

The most common explanation is that Paul is quoting a rabbinical maxim. The rabbis argued that there was no point in taking a man to court if he had died. Death had discharged him of all responsibilities and debts to the law. His death had released him

---

Although not stressing the corporate, Keck's remarks fit the picture that we are noting. He says: "The Adamic situation is deeper than being wrongly related to God and so needs more than a rectified relationship. Sin entails also participation in a domain marked by Sin's enslaving power, whose consequence is death. Thus, the exposition of Adam in 5:12–21 prepares for 6:1—7:6, where Paul argues that freedom from this yoked tyranny of sin and death is through participation in an alternative domain—Christ's death and resurrection" (Keck, "Romans," 2).

35. Commenting on the tension between vv. 6–7, Schreiner, *Romans*, 318, says: "It is quite difficult to discern the relationship between the two verses."

36. Zeisler, *Romans*, 160, says: "In the context we might have expected deliverance language, but instead there is the language of acquittal/acceptance. We must therefore allow of the possibility that more is being said than when we are dead we are free from sin's power." Note also Käsemann's observation, *Romans*, 170: "Paul's concern is not with guilt but with the power of sin." See also more recently Campbell, *Deliverance*, 663, who identifies the justification as being about deliverance from imprisonment but has no understanding of the covenantal dimension of the bondage that humanity is bound in.

from the legal system and the law was powerless to exact its punishment. It is argued, therefore, that Paul is saying there is no charge to be answered and the believer is free through sharing in the death of Christ.

One problem with this understanding is that it ignores the fact that the term *hamartia* "sin" is a theological term. Men are not taken to court for sins but for crimes. If Paul had wanted to be understood in the way suggested, he would have used the term αἴτιον (*aition*) "criminal charge." In other words, Paul would have said that death frees from αἴτιον (*aition*) "crime." Another difficulty is that death does not discharge any man from the responsibility of his sins, and Paul clearly anticipated some sort of eschatological judgment (Rom 14:11–12; 2 Cor 5:10). Those who use the rabbinic maxim to explain the meaning of the text have not realized that the illustration has to be put back into its theological framework. If the explanation cannot fit back into its original setting, then it has pronounced its own judgment regarding its validity. To have any possibility of carrying the suggested meaning, we not only have to change the text as far as "justified" is concerned but we also have to change it so that it is not referring to sin, *hamartia*. The increasing required number of adjustments make the suggestion ever more unlikely.

So, what is Paul saying by writing "justified from sin"? If we follow the flow of the argument that has been made so far, its meaning becomes clear. We have noted the presence of exodus and Paschal language in the earlier part of the letter. It is, therefore, reasonable to suggest that Paul is dealing with the problem of how Christ can take a sinful people—even worse, a people who are the property, the bride, of Satan—as his bride. This perspective is supported by the opening of chapter 7, which struggles with this same issue. Under the old covenant, Israel had committed spiritual adultery by going after other gods. She belonged exclusively to Yahweh but had committed whoredom and taken another husband. The same is true in reverse. If Christ was to take a people for himself who belonged to another, i.e., Satan, there would rightly be a charge of adultery laid at his door.

But such a charge cannot be made, for the one who was once part of the bride of Satan has died with Christ, and the former relationship has been terminated. There is no adultery in the new marriage. There is no charge that can be laid at the feet of the parties in this new relationship. They are "justified" before the civil law and the law of God. Paul is right to use the term "justified" (or acquitted), and any who change this meaning are departing from what he intended to say. The preference for translating *dedikaiōtai* as "freed" results from the failure to appreciate the theological and corporate framework of the argument.[37] What is true of the community is not necessarily true of the individual. So, for example, the church—not the individual believer—is the bride of Christ. Paul's argument cannot be directly applied to the experience of the individual.

6:8 Now if we died with Christ, we believe that we will also live with him. The new life of the believing community is bound up with having experienced death in her representative. There is no way into the covenant community other than through the

---

37. Morris, *Romans*, 253, is one of the few scholars who thinks "justified" should be retained in the English translation, but he does not seek to deal with the problems it presents.

covenant-annulling experience of the death of Christ. Having participated in this historically, and then having appropriated its benefits by faith, the life of fellowship with Christ has become a living reality. But Paul is not concentrating on the life of the church in its earthly existence; he is raising the eyes of the Roman church to her final destiny, where she will one day reign with Christ (Rom 8:13–25; 1 Cor 6:1–3). This glorious fact ought to be to the fore of the Christian's values and hopes (Col 3:1).

6:9 For we know that since Christ was raised from the dead, he cannot die again; death no longer has mastery over him. Paul stresses the finality of the victory of Christ's death in order to prepare for his appeal to the church that she lives her life for the glory of God. Paul has said in the previous verse that believers will live with Christ. Here, he says that Christ is the absolute victor over Satan. These two facts, coupled with the reality that the church has died with Christ, are the reason why the church is to live her life for him. The fact that he is the victor over Satan dispels any lingering fear that the former husband might catch up with his "deceased wife" and renew his former authority and demands. While Satan may certainly do harm to the church in this life, he cannot overturn the new relationship and re-establish the old.

In saying that death no longer has mastery over Christ, Paul focuses on Christ's death when it seemed that Satan had won. What greater victory could Satan have than to put to death the Son of God? It was this that the Jews found so difficult to accept, i.e., the crucifixion of the Messiah. It was the great stumbling block that hindered faith (1 Cor 1:23). This was Paul's position until he met with the risen Christ. Christ's resurrection transformed the meaning and significance of the cross, for Jesus was not the victim but the victor!

6:10 The death he died, he died to sin once for all; but the life he lives, he lives to God. The NIV translators have omitted the word γάρ (gar) "for" at the beginning of this verse, which would have read: "for the death that he died." This is unfortunate, as the passage continues to develop the argument. Paul underlines the finality of Jesus' death with "once for all."[38] This finality is shared by other NT writers (Mark 10:45; John 10:11; Acts 4:10; Heb 9:24–28; Rev 1:18), and it was a truth that clearly made a great impression on the early church. Being Jewish, or saturated in Jewish theological thought, the believers understood that there was no finality about the OT sacrificial system. Sin was never absolved in such a way that it no longer threatened the assurance of the one who had offered the sacrifice.

The impact of the truth that Sin had been defeated is difficult for us to imagine in the twenty-first century. We have diluted the concept of Sin to such a mediocrity that it does not press upon us with the seriousness that it ought. As the church assembled in Rome to hear Paul's letter, there would have been many who had known great fears, guilt, and anxiety over their sin, and they believed that these would come to fruition beyond the grave. As they listened to the letter, they heard what Christ had done in order to res-

---

38. The word used by Paul is ἐφάπαξ which Stählin, *TDNT*, 1.383, considers to be a technical term defining the definiteness and the uniqueness of the death of Christ in its relation to redemption.

cue them. His decisive victory over Sin and Death had brought them into the kingdom of Christ in all of its glorious, unspeakable fullness, and their fears for all that lay ahead were over.

When Paul writes that Christ lives to God, he means more than Christ has been raised and is now seated in heaven. First, he means that God has accepted what Christ has done. This is another way of saying what Paul has already said in Rom 4:25: "He was raised for our justification." The fact that Christ is in heaven is the seal of God's acceptance. All who come through him to the Father are welcome! Second, it means that God will never deal with us as sinners. There, perpetually in heaven, is the evidence that our sin has been dealt with. Christ is fulfilling the office of the Jewish high priest, who went into the presence of God in the Temple's Most Holy Place, the place where no other person could enter. He presented the evidence that the sacrifice for sin had been made (Heb 9:1–7). Here, in Romans, we have the same idea. The theme of Jesus being the believers' high priest is not limited to the letter to the Hebrews as some think.[39] It is present throughout the Gospels and the rest of the NT.

THE MESSIAH KING AND HIS PEOPLE'S OBEDIENCE

In the same way, count yourselves dead to sin but alive to God in Christ Jesus. Therefore do not let sin reign in your mortal body so that you obey its evil desires. Do not offer the parts of your body to sin, as instruments of wickedness, but rather offer yourselves to God, as those who have been brought from death to life; and offer the parts of your body to him as instruments of righteousness. For sin shall not be your master, because you are not under law, but under grace. What then? Shall we sin because we are not under law but under grace? By no means! Don't you know that when you offer yourselves to someone to obey him as slaves, you are slaves to the one whom you obey—whether you are slaves to sin, which leads to death, or to obedience, which leads to righteousness. But thanks be to God that, though you used to be slaves to sin, you wholeheartedly obeyed the form of teaching to which you were entrusted. You have been set free from sin and have become slaves to righteousness. I put this in human terms because you are weak in your natural selves. Just as you used to offer the parts of your body in slavery to impurity and to ever-increasing wickedness, so now offer them in slavery to righteousness leading to holiness. When you were slaves to sin, you were free from the control of righteousness. What benefit did you reap at that time from the things you are now ashamed of? Those things result in death! But now that you have been set free from sin and have become slaves to God, the benefit you reap leads to holiness, and the result is eternal life. For the wages of sin is death, but the gift of God is eternal life in Christ Jesus our Lord. (Rom 6:11–23)

39. See Holland, "Paschal," chapter 5.

6:11 In the same way, count yourselves dead to sin but alive to God in Christ Jesus. In making this statement, Paul is not inviting his readers to dream about an impossible situation. He adopts a term used in accounting,[40] so that the phrase "count yourselves dead to sin" actually means "credit to yourselves that you are dead" because Christ has died in the Roman believers' place. Because of this death, the old relationship with Sin has been brought to an end and the church has been brought out of the domain of Sin (the kingdom of darkness) and into the kingdom of light. The requirements have not been violated but fulfilled. There is no possibility of evidence being found that will show the new relationship is over and fellowship must terminate. No, theirs is an absolute right. The people of God are not in God's presence because of their achievements but because of what God has accomplished through the death of his Son.

Paul introduces us to the expression "in Christ." This expression is at the heart of his soteriology and, because of it, some have suggested that Paul's emphasis is not on atonement but rather on the representative nature of Christ's death in which his people shared. This is known as Participation Theology. There is no doubt that this is an aspect of Paul's thinking. However, the Paschal background to his argument about the significance of Christ's death demands that propitiation is at its heart.[41]

6:12 Therefore do not let sin reign in your mortal body so that you obey its evil desires. Paul appeals to the Roman church to exercise covenant loyalty. It would be easy to abuse the grace of God and use this freedom as an excuse for sin, as Israel had done. As the same appeal is given to the Corinthian church in 1 Cor 10:1ff., it would be foolish not to see if the first Corinthian letter could help us understand the argument in Romans. The context of both passages is baptism (Rom 6:1–4; 1 Cor 10:1–4). In the original OT type, Israel, after her baptism unto Moses, abused the covenant relationship and sinned against God. Paul appeals for loyalty–a loyalty that only a few of the Mosaic covenant community displayed.

In making this appeal, it is easy to think that Paul is calling each believer to live a holy life. He does this elsewhere (1 Thess 4:3–8), but it is not the thrust of the argument here. His appeal is not to the believer to control his body, but to the church to maintain her purity. The term "body" is corporate: ὑμῶν (hymōn) "your" (pl.) σῶμα (sōma) "body" (sing.). The phrase τῷ θνητῷ ὑμῶν σώματι (tō thnētō hymōn sōmati) "your mortal body" is not a reference to the physical body of the believer but to the physical existence of the church in Rome. This verse is an appeal to the church to discipline its members who refuse to live the new life in Christ. Paul reflects on the failure of the Jews to deal with sin, for he is keenly aware of how it had spread through the community and damaged the whole nation.

1 Cor 5:6–8 is a passage that is not only Paschal/new exodus as in Rom 6, but is part of a passage calling for the church to hand over to Satan the one guilty of incest (1 Cor 5:5). While the exhortation applies to each individual, its language is corporate

---

40. Käsemann, *Romans*, claims that the real issue Paul is dealing with is not freedom from guilt but from the power of sin.

41. For extensive discussion, see Holland, *Contours*, 157–286.

and makes better sense when seen as an appeal to maintain purity in the church by the in a believing community. Paul's concern is that Satan seeks every opportunity to re-establish himself so as to regain control. A community that tolerates sin will soon find that it is living under the control of Sin and living off the evil desires it feeds into its heart. Many Christian communities have been sucked into the abyss of moral and spiritual decline because they have refused to deal with the sin that has become established in their members.

6:13 Do not offer the parts of your body to sin, as instruments of wickedness, but rather offer yourselves to God, as those who have been brought from death to life; and offer the parts of your body to him as instruments of righteousness. This exhortation could well have been given to the Jewish nation after being delivered from its captivity in Egypt. To Moses' horror, the Israelites turned away from the responsibilities of the covenant and sought the favor of the gods of the surrounding nations (Exod 32:1).

Again, this passage in Romans parallels a passage in Paul's first letter to the Corinthians (1 Cor 10:1–14). It is not an appeal to individuals to control their bodies[42] (an appeal which is normally taken to highlight sensual sins), but an appeal for purity in the life of the believing community in Rome. This broader corporate appeal identi-fies a wider range of sin that Paul was concerned with. For example, in the Corinthian situation, he was concerned with schism (1 Cor 1:11–17, 3:1–9), fornication (1 Cor 5–6), occult issues (1 Cor 8:1–13, 10:14–33), and doctrinal unfaithfulness (1 Cor 15:12–34). He urges the church not to tolerate or promote wrongdoing in believers who sin after the nature of the issues he raises in the letter.[43] He expressed this same concern in 1 Cor 5:6–8: "Your boasting is not good. Don't you know that a little yeast works through the whole batch of dough? Get rid of the old yeast that you may be a new batch without yeast—as you really are. For Christ, our Passover lamb, has been sacrificed. Therefore let us keep the Festival, not with the old yeast, the yeast of malice and wickedness, but with bread without yeast, the bread of sincerity and truth."

The ground for the appeal in Romans and in 1 Corinthians is the same. Christ, the Passover sacrifice, has died, and with him have died the people of God. Just as Israel died to the rule of Pharaoh when she left Egypt, so the Christian community has died

---

42. Horst, *TDNT*, 4:562 note 64, points out that the relationship between σαρχ *sarx* (flesh) and μελη *melē* (members) is different in Rom 7:25. There, it is *sarx* which is ruled by sin instead of *melē* ruled by sin. Horst suggests that Paul is speaking of corporeal human existence rather than individual experience. He says that, while it is clear that parts of the body could be at the disposal of sin (see Matt 5:29–30; Jas 3:5–6), the Pauline use has to be weighed carefully. He can refer to parts of the body as its members, but he never speaks of the parts of the human body being members of Christ. It is only the *sōma* that is given this des-ignation, 564. Horst uses 1 Cor 6:15 to expound the meaning of *melē*, but keeps to a highly individualistic interpretation of the text; see Holland, *Contours*, chapter 5. Wright, *Messiah*, 149, says that Rom 6:21 refers to Gen 1:28, showing that Paul saw the church to be the new humanity. This lends weight to the corporate setting of the passage. The constant concern of the NT is the purity of the church, even though it means the "destruction" of some of its members (see 1 Cor 11:29–32; 1 Tim 1:20; Rev 2:16, 21–23; 3:19).

43. The exhortation for believers to examine themselves when they come to the Lord's Table (1 Cor 11:28) is in this context. Pressing people in a highly introspective and individualistic way to search their consciences about an undefined list of possible offences has serious pastoral implications. The practice normally burdens those with sensitive consciences, but passes over those who are more robust.

to the rule of Sin. The church's responsibility is not to live as she had previously lived by fulfilling the whims of the old master or husband. She is to live a new life that pleases and honors the one who died for her and who is now her new betrothed and Lord.

This corporate perspective is not limited to Paul. For example, Jesus' teaching in the Sermon on the Mount makes better sense when seen to be directed to the repentant elect from the nation. (His teaching must be interpreted in the context of his association with John the Baptist who, like himself, calls Israel to repentance.) The exhortation to pluck out the eye is not as grotesque as is normally interpreted. It uses the imagery of the body to describe the people of God—the exhortation by Jesus being: "Have no dealings with those who compromise the calling of the community. Even though they might be valued as much as the eye—get rid of them if they keep on sinning." The discipline of removal from the community is to be exercised, regardless of status and importance. In the OT, ungodly kings, priests and prophets should have been treated in this way, but they continued in their roles without receiving discipline[44] and, for the most part, brought ruin to the nation. Such parallels, sadly, exist in the Christian church today, where people are excused sinful behavior because of the role they play in the church community. Tolerating such behavior will eventually bring greater harm to the individual and to the church.

So, in this verse Paul addresses the church. This is not to deny that individuals must put the apostle's teaching into practice (Rom 12:1—15:33), but an exclusively individualistic focus misses the corporate context of his reasoning. If the individual Christian does not wholeheartedly obey (v. 17), profound repercussions may be felt throughout the congregation of believers. Paul is saying to the congregation in Rome that although they tolerated godless living when they were part of the kingdom of darkness, their toleration must cease now that they are part of the body of Christ. The members of the church are members of one another, and Paul is appealing for corporate holiness. Not only is it the duty of the church to restrain evil, it is the duty of the church to promote righteousness among the believers. While the last thing Paul wants to encourage is a secret police mentality, he urges the church to face up to the reality of evil and recognize how a little leaven leavens the whole lump (1 Cor 5:7–8).

6:14 For sin shall not be your master, because you are not under law, but under grace. Once again, we must understand that when Paul speaks of sin, he is speaking of Sin (Satan).

Satan's exploitation of the law has been answered fully in the death of Jesus. By his death, Christ Jesus satisfied the law's demands, for its penalty has been paid. By his death, the covenant—by which Sin demanded obedience and control—has been brought to an end for those who are now in Christ. Under the new head (Christ), the law of Sin and Death (the reign of Satan) is terminated, and Sin's control of redeemed humanity has been brought to an end.

In saying that believers are "not under law," Paul opens up an issue that has occupied the attention of scholars for centuries. What does he actually mean? Does the law have

---

44. The case of David's adultery was one of the few occasions when a king was disciplined with beneficial effects.

no relevance for the believer? Paul will discuss this in chapter 7. What we can say here is that the context is the fulfillment of God's promises, that is, the covenants he made with Abraham and David. If Paul's understanding of law is removed from this covenantal context, there is no possibility of understanding his rationale.

This corporate interpretation has massive pastoral implications. It shows that Paul is not urging some form of sinless perfection. Such teaching has crushed millions of Christians who have been tormented by their failures when urged to attain perfection. The passage makes no such demand. It tells the Roman believers that they are to live in the light of the greatest reality of history: Christ has rescued them from the kingdom of darkness and made them his people, his own special possession, his bride. It urges them to live out this glorious status and calling in the Empire's capital city.

6:15 What then? Shall we sin because we are not under law but under grace? By no means! Once again, Paul challenges the suggestion that being under grace rather than law means that one can continue sinning without fear of consequence. Only after one sees the hatred that God has toward sin will the distress of such a suggestion be felt. Grace and sin cannot be mixed. To think that they can harmoniously coexist is to think that light can coexist with darkness, or that life can coexist with death. Paul responds much more strongly than the NIV suggests. His retort to the proposal is "God forbid!" Paul is not responding to the question he posed in the opening of the chapter, when he wrote "shall we sin that grace might abound?" In this verse the argument is: "Since we have been removed from the realm of sin, what we do now has no spiritual consequence."

It is clear that Paul holds a sharp distinction between the realms of sin and grace. We shall soon see that these terms are not abstractions of some kind but are shorthand pointers to relationships that exist between humanity and Satan, and humankind and God. In all relationships, there are frameworks that are essential and common, regardless of how good or bad the relationships are. Long ago, the Puritans saw that there was grace in law and law in grace.[45] God only abandons people at the last day when all of his pleas have been rejected. Despite this, we must not forget that Paul sees further than these distinctions of law and grace. He sees the great realities of enslavement and liberation, to which these concepts point. A mark of maturity in any person is that they see the bigger picture and, for the believer, that bigger picture is God's purposes being worked out in Christ.

6:16 Don't you know that when you offer yourselves to someone to obey him as slaves, you are slaves to the one whom you obey—whether you are slaves to sin, which leads to death, or to obedience, which leads to righteousness? At this point, we encounter a difficulty with the word *doulos*, which is normally translated "slave." This is an understandable translation, as the word meant "slave" in classical Greek. It was a word used to describe slaves who had no rights. Their masters owned them, and their only justification for being allowed to live was that they fulfilled the wishes of their owners. Often, such wretched people were the victims of war and subsequent deportation. It is

---

45. Kevin, *Law*.

thought by some that Paul calls himself "a slave" of Christ, and that in this verse he is saying that the Roman believers, having once been slaves of Sin, are also Christ's "slaves."

Many sermons have been structured on this understanding. The thrust of such teaching is that the Christian has no rights. He is owned by Christ who has absolute claim upon him. Such a picture is powerful, inspiring many into sacrificial service. But is that what Paul is saying?

We have seen in Rom 1:1 that *doulos* has at least two meanings in the OT. This fact needs to be remembered as we seek to understand what Paul is saying about being "slaves" to righteousness. We found earlier that *doulos* can only be understood by giving attention to the context in which it is used. The context of the word has to be examined to see if it befits the appellation "slave" or "servant." The latter will be expected to have terms associated with it that echo the OT. In the OT, the servant's role and his relationship with God are spoken alongside terms such as "calling" and "election." This is exactly what we find in Paul's writings. Repeatedly, he uses *doulos* in contexts in which the Servant Songs of Isaiah are echoed or quoted (Acts 26:15–18; 2 Cor 6:1–10).

What difference does this make to our understanding of the passage in chapter 6? First, it helps us see that the OT is still the background for Paul's message. We have already seen that he described Jesus as the "Son of David" through whom the prophets promised deliverance from exile. Paul says that these promises are now being fulfilled.[46] He has used sacrificial language with clear Passover echoes (Rom 3:21–26), and has used imagery that speaks of the Christian community on pilgrimage (Rom 5:3–4). In addition, he has spoken of being baptized into Christ (Rom 6:1–4), echoing the exodus when the Jews were baptized into Moses (1 Cor 10:2). If this strong new exodus theme runs through the letter—and it was Paul's intention to show how the Scriptures have been fulfilled in the Son of David, the final Passover bringing about the liberation of the people of God from bondage to Sin and Death—then the correct understanding of *doulos* in Rom 6:16 becomes clear. The church is the servant of the Lord. Her members are the people called by God to do his will, serving him by taking the Gospel to the nations as the Jews should have done. The status of "servant" confers on the church and her members the highest honor as she and they are called to serve the living, saving God.

Paul's appeal to the Romans to turn from sin parallels Moses' appeal to the Jews to stay faithful to their God. Again, a parallel passage is found in 1 Cor 10:1–14, where Paul warns the Corinthians that sin leads to death. Earlier, he showed that a congregation which tolerates sin in the lives of its members comes under the sentence of judgment. Ultimately, that will mean temporary separation from the wider redeemed community and its God-given blessings. It also means being handed over to Satan (1 Cor 5:3–5; Rev 2:20–23), whose rage will be used by God to correct the wayward church or believer.[47]

6:17 But thanks be to God that, though you used to be slaves to sin, you wholeheartedly obeyed the form of teaching to which you were entrusted. What had kept the Roman believers from falling into the same condemnation as the Jews under Moses? Paul

---

46. He is saying nothing that Jesus himself has not already said, see Luke 4:16–21.

47. For a fuller treatment of this subject, see Holland, *Contours*, chapter 5.

writes: ὑπηκούσατε δὲ ἐκ καρδίας εἰς ὃν παρεδόθητε τύπον διδαχῆς (*hypēkousate de ek kardias eis hon paredothēte typon didachēs*) "you wholeheartedly obeyed the form of teaching to which you were entrusted." The Jews of the exodus had refused to do this, and had not submitted themselves to its authority. They rejected the message that Moses proclaimed to them, even though they had experienced such a marvellous act of deliverance. Before Moses came down from his meeting with God on Mount Sinai where he was given the law, the people were worshipping a golden calf that Aaron, the priest, had made for them (Exod 32:8). Despite all that the Lord had done for them, the people broke faith with God, turning to idols to lead them and worshipping them for the deliverance they had supposedly wrought (Exod 32:1,8b). For believers, the importance of the biblical message cannot be overstated. Their correct understanding of it and their obedience to it keep them from being seduced back into the life they once lived before they were brought out of the kingdom of darkness.

As we have seen, the term *doulos* in Rom 6:16 should be translated "servant" rather than "slave." "Servant" keeps the argument in the flow of redemption history. Nevertheless, in Egypt the Israelites were slaves. In this verse there is a subtle switch: once, slaves (*doulos*) to Sin (or Pharoah); now, servants (*doulos*) to Yahweh. What a contrast!

The phrase "obeyed the *form of teaching* to which you were entrusted," may have pastoral implications. The expression is not so much about delivering formal teaching but living out the teaching as a visual aid.[48] The preacher who is anxious to proclaim God's word verbally must be as anxious to live it out before his people as Paul was careful to do in the churches for which he was responsible.

6:18 You have been set free from sin and have become slaves to righteousness. Paul is confident that what he has heard of the Roman believers is genuine, so he encourages them that they have a true knowledge of God. They have changed their allegiance and are no longer part of the kingdom of darkness. When Paul says that they have been set free from "sin," we should again read it as "Sin." The reality is that all the Roman believers will continue to be prone to sin and will fail to be the people they ought to be, but that is not the same as living under the rule of Sin (Satan). Someone who takes out citizenship in a country other than his country of birth illustrates the point. Legally, he has a totally new identity and set of obligations. The old allegiance is over. Nevertheless, he is still the product of the first nation's culture and history. He must go through the long process of leaving that identity behind in his lifestyle, worldview, expectations and commitments, and become what his new citizenship signifies.

Again, we should translate "slaves to righteousness" as "servants to righteousness." Paul sees Christians as servants of Christ, with all the privileges and dignity that this status bestows.[49] Following the exodus type, Israel was Pharaoh's slave, but through her redemption she became Yahweh's servant. The relationships were totally different. The term "righteousness" is a synonym for God (and has been used as such throughout the

---

48. Stowers, *Rereading*.

49. For a fuller discussion, see Holland, *Contours*, chapter 4.

chapter), just as Sin is a synonym for Satan. The Roman believers had been slaves of Satan, but now they are servants of God!

6:19 I put this in human terms because you are weak in your natural selves. Just as you used to offer the parts of your body in slavery to impurity and to ever-increasing wickedness, so now offer them in slavery to righteousness leading to holiness. In what way does Paul want the Romans to understand him when he says they are "weak" in their "natural selves"? It can hardly refer to physical weakness—even though this is a consequence of the fall and something from which the church waits to be delivered at the *parousia*, the Second Coming. It cannot mean intellectual weakness, for there would be no point in Paul writing such a detailed letter which clearly presupposes intellectual capacity. The weakness must be spiritual. While Paul has asserted his confidence that they have obeyed from the heart the teaching delivered to them, they need to continually have the Word of God carefully explained and applied so that they can profit from it.

The goal of this exhortation is that the church will live in holiness, reflecting the exhortation of Yahweh to Israel to be holy, as he is Holy.[50]

6:20 When you were slaves to sin, you were free from the control of righteousness. Paul is not saying that the Roman believers were free from responsibilities of personal righteousness before their conversion. Everyone is aware of the struggle between good and evil, whether a believer or not. There are many non-Christians who live noble lives—striving to promote justice and righteousness in their communities—while there are those who call themselves Christians who have little concern for social issues. Paul would have been as aware of this fact in his day as we are in ours.

However, he is not talking at the level of personal morality or social justice. As has been argued throughout this exposition, Paul is evaluating the condition of the human race rather than individual people. He has divided humanity into two groups—those in Adam and those in Christ. Here, he speaks of the Roman church's deliverance from the kingdom of darkness, the realm where Sin rules. Before their deliverance, God (righteousness) had no control over the Roman believers as they were covenanted to Sin and were its willing servants. Paul says that before God saved them and brought them under his control, the Roman believers were under the control of Sin (Satan).

6:21 What benefit did you reap at that time from the things you are now ashamed of? Those things result in death! Paul reminds the believers of the futility and shame of their former lives.[51] They had given themselves to the service of Sin; but such service was rewarded with death. Satan was a ruthless master, with no care for those who served

---

50. Cranfield, *Shorter*, 145, disagrees with the translation of holiness, saying the term is not about a state but a process. He favors instead "sanctification." It is difficult to follow Cranfield's argument, as sanctification can also mean a state. However, in the context of the new exodus, it fits Cranfield's understanding, for they are to strive to be holy in an ongoing process—as with Israel's neglected calling.

51. The punctuation of v.21 poses difficulties. Does the phrase "from the things you are now ashamed of," link with "what benefit did you reap," or with "those things result in death"? The NRSV & NIV follow the former, while the NEB & REB follow the latter, so following the Nestle-Aland Greek text. This is possibly the better choice because of the presence of the Greek word *gar* which the NIV fails to translate.

him–no matter how willingly. The only end that such service was going to bring was death. This would be physical (as Paul has argued in chapter 5) and spiritual (exile from the presence of God). The glory of the proclamation in this letter is that this exile is over for the people of God and that Death, the last enemy, has been conquered. This is the heart of the Gospel (see 1 Cor 15:37–58).

6:22 But now that you have been set free from sin and have become slaves to God, the benefit you reap leads to holiness, and the result is eternal life. The Jews were set free from Pharaoh's enslavement and became the servants of God. This was not merely a transfer of allegiance but a change of lifestyle. The nation's calling was to live out the will of God. She was his servant, and her call was not only to be holy (Lev 20:7) but also to bring the knowledge of the God of Abraham to the Gentiles (Gen 12:2–3), so that the other nations might worship him also.

This, Israel singularly failed to do. She became obsessed with her own concerns, which distracted her from doing the will of God. The reality was, without the fulfillment of her missionary task, the most careful observance of the law was bound to degenerate into hollow religious activity that was nothing more than self-justification. At that stage, Israel not only failed to give the message of God's love to the nations but she began to misrepresent him.

This is a salutary warning to the Christian church. Her calling is not to be comfortable and self-satisfied but to be a servant who takes the message of the living God to those in darkness. Her calling is to be the servant of the Lord, whose ministry brings light and life to the nations. For Paul, faith results in risk. It was this unwillingness to take risks that caused Jesus to warn Israel that what she had been given was about to be taken from her and given to another (Luke 19:11–27).

6:23 For the wages of sin is death, but the gift of God is eternal life in Jesus Christ our Lord. Moses and Joshua warned the Jews after they had come out of bondage that there were two ways ahead of them (Deut 30:15–16; Josh 23:1–16). One way rejected the law and led to death; the other way obeyed the will of Yahweh from the heart and led to life. Paul seems to be reflecting that same exhortation. This time, however, the appeal is directed to the church in Rome, urging her to be fully committed to loving and serving God. Again, we notice the personification of Sin, this time as a master who pays a wage. The echoes of the appeal made by Moses further confirm the new exodus context of Paul's mindset.

CONCLUSION TO ROMANS 6

Paul has modeled the experience of the Christian community on that of Israel, and her exodus from Egypt in particular. At that time, the Hebrews died to the power of Pharaoh. Now, the church has died to the power of Satan who has held her in his kingdom of darkness. The key to her deliverance was not the slain lamb as of old but the death of Jesus, God's beloved (firstborn) Son.

The solidarity of the nation of Israel was the consequence of her baptism into Moses, who then functioned as her representative before Yahweh. The solidarity of the new covenant community (the church) was the consequence of her baptism (by the Spirit) into Christ, who functioned as her representative before God. Because of this baptism, the church (comprising all believers) shares all that Jesus experienced and all that God bestows upon him. She has died to her enslavement to Sin and has been raised to newness of life. Having been freed from Satan's control through the death of her representative Redeemer, she is to live a holy life, reflecting the character of the God to whom she now belongs and serves. She has been redeemed, and is on pilgrimage to her inheritance which her Savior has secured.

ROMANS 7

EXCURSUS F: SIN IN THE THEOLOGY OF PAUL

Paul has much to say about humankind's sinful condition. His understanding has huge implications for the Bible's teaching on the state of man, i.e., how he stands before God and how he relates to the rest of creation. The following discussion is an attempt to highlight the danger of absorbing ideas from the culture which Paul would have never owned, particularly about sin, and reading them back into Scripture. These non-Hebraic thought-streams have become so embedded in Western Christian thinking that we unintentionally misrepresent what Paul and the other Scripture writers actually teach.[1]

OT Background of NT "sarx" (NIV Translation: "sinful nature")

The Greek word σὰρξ (sarx) is used in the LXX to translate the Hebrew בָּשָׂר (bāsār), the accepted English translation of both sarx and bāsār being "flesh." It requires a close study of each OT passage in which the term is found to understand how it should be interpreted because it has a number of meanings. This brief OT survey will attempt to show the various ways in which the term was used by the OT writers.

The Use of "flesh" to Describe a Covenant Relationship

An important use of "flesh," is found in the latter part of Gen 2:23–24, where we find Adam saying of Eve: "This is now bone of my bones and flesh of my flesh; she shall be called 'woman,' for she was taken out of man." The writer of Genesis continues: "For this reason a man will leave his father and mother and be united to his wife, and they will become one flesh." Here, "flesh," implies the covenant relationship a man has with his wife. She was "one flesh" with him. The provision of this relationship was Yahweh's response to Adam's loneliness and frailty. Despite it being a holy relationship (it was approved by God before the fall), it did not change the creaturely vulnerability of man.

The Use of "flesh" to Describe Human Frailty

The condition of human frailty is also called "flesh" in the OT. It is found in the writings of prophets such as Isaiah and Ezekiel. Isaiah, with his lofty view of Yahweh, emphasized

---

1. One of the most thorough studies of Paul's use of anthropological terms in the last fifty years has been that of Jewett, *Terms*. His conclusion have been summed up by Aune, "Nature," 298 who says: "Jewett's own thesis is that conflict situations are the primary reason for inconsistencies in Paul's anthropology." This inconsistency is the inevitable outcome of reading Paul as a Jew who has embraced Hellenism.

that flesh was weak compared to the might of God. He paints a powerful picture of man's frailty: "all men (flesh) are like grass . . . the grass withers and the flowers fall" (Isa 40:6). The prophet Ezekiel promised that the great gift of the new covenant would be a "heart of flesh" which would replace a "heart of stone" (Ezek 36:26–27). Clearly, Ezekiel does not liken "flesh" to sin but to a heart dependent on God.

The Use of "flesh" as a Term for Mankind

Isaiah indicates that "flesh," can have another meaning, which the NIV translates "mankind": "all mankind ('flesh') will come and bow down before me" (Isa 66:23). He says that, in the day of Yahweh: "all mankind ('flesh') will know that I, the LORD, am your Savior, your Redeemer, the Mighty One of Jacob" (Isa 49:26). Furthermore, the prophet Joel promised that Yahweh would pour out his Spirit on all people (flesh) (Joel 2:28).

The Use of "flesh" as a Term for the Physical Body

In Gen 17, the term "flesh," was used for man's flesh, that is, his body. So, Abraham and the males in his household were to be "circumcised in the flesh" (Gen 17:14). In the OT, "flesh," is also used for animals. When the Flood was predicted, "all flesh" was to be destroyed. This judgment was particularized when God said he would destroy "every creature ('flesh') that has the breath of life in it" (Gen 6:17). After the Flood, it was recorded that "every living thing ('flesh') that moved on the earth perished – birds, livestock, wild animals, all the creatures ('flesh') that swarm over the earth, and all mankind" (Gen 7:21). Here, we see man grouped under the comprehensive description of "all flesh" which ranges from insects to man. Further, "everything on dry land that had the breath of life in its nostrils died" (v.22). We can see from this the narrower use of "flesh," restricting it to creatures that were air-breathing, that is, sustained by the breath of life. (cf. Gen 9:16; Job 34:15; Ps 136:25).

In conclusion, "flesh" can be interpreted in a number of ways in the OT, depending on context. It is very important to note there is no suggestion in the OT that "flesh" is in any way sinful or unclean. This is the very opposite to Greek understanding, which holds to a dualistic existence: spirit is pure and matter is evil. It would be easy to be influenced by Greek ideas and begin to think that flesh/body is evil, but this is something a Jew would never do. This assertion is supported by the fact that the blessing of the new covenant was the giving of a "heart of flesh" to his people by God (Ezek 36:26–27), and it was this that brought them near to him. On occasions, priests or people had to wash their bodies because of uncleanness. However, this was ceremonial uncleanness and not moral impurity (Lev 15:10). There is no more guilt in a dirty man than there is in an unclean garment that needs to be washed to fulfill ceremonial requirements. Dirtiness would only become the occasion of sin if the person refused to undergo the prescribed cleansing, for then he would be rejecting the command of Yahweh.

A Special Case?

There is an OT text which, while it does not contain the word *bāsār*, is deeply significant for OT support of the traditional Christian doctrine of sin. This text comes from David's writings. In Ps 51:5, he writes: "Behold, I was shapen in iniquity, and in sin did my mother conceive me" (KJV). This well-known rendering of David's statement has since been modified by translators. As a result, it fails to convey the proper meaning of the text. The NIV translates it as: "Surely I was sinful at birth, sinful from the time my mother conceived me." The NAS has: "Behold, I was brought forth in iniquity, and in sin my mother conceive me." The NET version has: "Look, I was guilty of sin from birth, a sinner the moment my mother conceived me." Clearly, such a text has to be evaluated and the translators' preferences considered. If it is speaking of being conceived in sin, then it is suggesting that David could not help his actions because of the sinful nature with which he was born. This is a major departure from what the rest of the OT teaches and what we know Jews throughout history have held to. The statement is intended to contrast the truthfulness of God with the deceitfulness of David. In fact, "the Psalms and the OT in general speak less in terms of 'being' (ontology) than in terms of experience and history (existence)."[2] David is not speaking about his nature but the social/spiritual environment into which he was born. This condition, which we shall see ties into what Paul has to say about being "in Adam," does not deny David's sinfulness but understands it in the framework of OT thinking.

So, what does David mean when he says he was "conceived in sin"? Scholars have noted the term יחם (*yḥm*) "to be hot, rut, conceive"[3] describes raw sexual passion or sexual intercourse. It must be noted that David is not speaking of his own behavior but his mother's, for she conceived him "in sin" (KJV). In an attempt to resolve the use of this term (a term not normally used for conception), some have gone so far as to say the statement relates to adultery on the part of David's mother. This leaves us with a quandary, because there is no suggestion David describes his Jewish home-life as being anything other than normal and stable, albeit with typical sibling tensions.

Can there be another explanation for this offensive language? The fact is that David speaks of having two mothers, and it is important that we recognize the one to whom he is referring in this psalm. The idea of Zion being a mother is found throughout the OT (Isa 3:16; 37:22; 62:11; Jer 4:31; Lam 1:6; Mic 1:13; 4:10), and the idea of Zion "bearing"

2. Broyles, *Psalms*, 228. However Kraus, *Psalms*, 1–59, 503, says: "the total depravity that is determinative for humans from the beginning is here acknowledged." Kraus appeals to Gen 8:21; Job 14:4; 15:14ff.; 25:4; Ps 143. However, none of these texts assert the innate sinfulness of man's being, rather the impossibility of his being able to come up to God's standards. This is not the same as asserting "original sin." Mays, *Psalms*, 200, notes that the idea of being conceived in sin has led to a very negative attitude to human procreation, and claims that the statement is not about David's conception in sin but the rebellious, spiritual, and social environment that characterized Israel. Thus, he was conceived and born into a state of sin. Born into such a community, he cannot but sin. Goldingay, *Psalms*, vol. 2:128, says: "One can see how this declaration would apply to Israel as a whole, whose sinfulness goes back to the moment when its relationship with Yahweh was sealed at Sinai." I consider that such an understanding reflects what the whole of Scripture is saying.

3. Tate, *Psalms*, 18, who cites supporting evidence. The Oxford English Dictionary defines rut as: "the periodic sexual excitement of a male deer, goat, sheep etc." The Hebrew clearly suggests aggressive sexual animal activity.

children is also found (Ps 87:5). Admittedly, Ps 87 is not David's composition–but psalm 9 is attributed to him, and in that psalm he writes: "that I may declare your praises in the gates of the Daughter of Zion and there rejoice in your salvation" (Ps 9:14).

So could David be saying that, because he was born into a community which constantly broke Yahweh's commandments, he was set on the path of disobedience and sin? Is this why his conception is described as being "in sin"? It would certainly make sense of his use of חם "to be hot, rut, conceive" because Zion/Israel is repeatedly called a "harlot," going after other gods and leaving her husband (Isa 1:21; Jer 5:7; Ezek 16:28). In addition, there were many children of Zion who were described as being illegitimate (Hos 1:2; 2:4).

This line of reasoning is supported by the text of Ps 51:18, where David pleads: "In your good pleasure make Zion prosper; build up the walls of Jerusalem." The psalm recognizes Israel's sin, and, in a typically Semitic way, David confesses the sin of his people of which his own is a part. Forgiveness is not solely for himself but also for his wayward people, and it results in the rebuilding of the walls of Zion—the protection of Yahweh's inheritance. In other words, being born "in sin" is a reference to the type of community into which David was born, and he is conscious that his behavior has followed the national characteristic of unfaithfulness to Yahweh. Such an understanding is in complete harmony with the rest of the OT Scriptures and has stayed totally within a Jewish framework.

To summarize the OT's teaching on "flesh," we can note that the term is morally neutral, speaking of man's creaturely existence and frailty. There is no lexicographical evidence to suggest that the term carried any negative moral connotation.

A Major Conundrum

That "flesh," is a morally neutral term is a vitally important point. In Christian thinking, "flesh," normally implies a condition of sinfulness in an individual. If the OT does not use it in this way, and it is widely accepted that Jews do not see their physical existence as in any way impure, then we have to ask if Jesus, a Jew, ever used "flesh" in our Hellenized Christian way. The answer has to be negative. The founder of Christianity, who lived and ministered entirely within the Jewish nation, shared that same understanding of "flesh"— an understanding based on the Jewish Scriptures.

If this assertion is true, and few would doubt it, then the question has to be asked: "where did the idea that "flesh" is sinful come from?" Did Paul introduce this concept into the church's understanding and teaching? If he has done this, he has added something very un-Jewish and, therefore, very different from what Jesus himself taught. If the understanding did not come from Paul, where did it originate?

The OT use of "flesh" outlined above is the complex background to Paul's Jewish thinking. If, after his conversion, he stayed within its framework, this semantic domain has to be consulted when interpreting his writings. However, if Paul moved into Hellenism—where "flesh" is intrinsically evil—we must interpret his letters accordingly. We have to make a decision as to whether Paul and the NT writers continued in the restricted stream of OT thought or whether they "advanced out," absorbing Greek ideas. Certainly, these Greek ideas would have been familiar to the growing number of Gentile converts in the early church.

If we find that the OT understanding continues, it would have been necessary for the early church to have devised a program of careful instruction for the Gentile converts in order to bring their understanding in line with Jewish thought. This would not have been as formidable a task as might at first appear, for, in the early years of the church, almost all of the teachers were Jews. Indeed, we must remember that Gentile converts were being filtered into congregations which were mostly Jewish. They would have been taught from the LXX, and, finding that their understanding of the term *sarx* clashed with that of the Jewish community, would have been taught its "true" meaning by their Jewish brethren. If this did not happen, a Gentile takeover would have occurred causing serious problems for the Jewish majority and the church's apostolic theology in its formative days.

The Use of "flesh" in the NT: A Caution

The translators of most English versions try to help their readers understand the term "flesh" by rendering it in ways they think appropriate. This seems reasonable, but, unfortunately, the translations often contradict the contexts in which the term is found. To translate "flesh" as "sinful nature" (as in the Romans passage under consideration) does not normally convey what Paul was writing but, instead, misrepresents him on a vitally important issue.[4]

The Use of "flesh" in the Gospels

Of all the references to "flesh" in the Synoptics, only one statement (recorded by Matthew and Mark [Matt 26:41; Mark 14:38]) appears to be a possible reference to the human body. However, this is debatable as the phrase: "the spirit is willing but the flesh is weak" could imply the frailty of the human condition, where man without God is limited to his creaturely resources. Certainly, this interpretation is in agreement with one of the Jewish meanings of "flesh" and reflects the "heart of flesh" in Ezekiel. This meaning conveys an awareness of creaturely weakness and dependency upon God.

Another possible reference to "flesh" as "body" is in John 6:51–56. Since it is a controversial passage which is difficult to expound (it is the key text in support of the doctrine of transubstantiation, i.e., the changing of the Eucharistic elements into the body and blood of Christ), it would be easy to ignore. To do so would leave a weakness in the argument being presented. I will, therefore, suggest another possible interpretation.

In his Gospel, John repeatedly shows that Jesus was misunderstood. In chapter 1, the Jews failed to perceive the identity of the Son of God (John 1:10–11). In chapter 2, they thought he was referring to the temple of Herod when he said the temple would be destroyed and raised in three days (John 2:19–22). In chapter 3, Nicodemus misunder-

---

4. Sadly, the NIV—upon which this commentary is based— is one of the worst examples of this misrepresentation as we soon shall see.

stood the nature of the second birth (John 3:3–9). In chapter 4, the Samaritan woman failed to understand the nature of living water (John 4:15) and in chapter 5, the Jews misunderstood the message of the Scriptures (John 5:39–40). When we come to chapter 6, the Jews were offended when Jesus said that unless they ate his flesh, there would be no life in them (John 6:53). Their thinking would have been consistent with OT ideas of "flesh" so they assumed that Jesus was referring to his body, a meaning that is in the OT semantic domain for *bāsār*. They misunderstood his words because they took them literally! Jesus was not speaking of his body any more than the "temple" of chapter 2 was a reference to the building in Jerusalem. So, how can we understand Jesus' use of "flesh"?

The time of the statement was Passover (John 6:4), and Jesus was reminding the Jews that the manna sent down from heaven sustained their ancestors as they journeyed to the promised land. Now, God has sent living bread for people to eat, to sustain them until the last day when they will be raised up (John 6:40). Jesus is saying that believers must partake of him by faith, in order to be sustained on life's journey. In the context of a relationship between himself and his needy people, his use of "flesh" reflects the way its used in Gen 2:24—it refers to the inaugural statement of marriage. This original marriage in Genesis foreshadowed the divine marriage of Yahweh and his people at Sinai, which, as we have seen earlier, was the purpose of the Passover and is the theme being traced in this commentary.[5] The concept of the divine marriage had already been introduced by John. He recorded that Jesus attended the wedding feast in Cana of Galilee in order to typify the forthcoming new relationship between Yahweh and his people.[6] John the Baptist bore witness that he was the friend of the bridegroom, and that, having heard his voice, he rejoiced (John 3:29).[7] It was no coincidence Jesus' statement was made near the time of the celebration of the Jewish Passover—a motif which is ongoing in John's Gospel.[8] If this understanding of "flesh" is correct, i.e., it is covenantal and speaks of the marriage relationship between Christ and his people, then the statement is only sacramental in that it is speaks of the "mystic" union between Christ and his bride. In other words, it carries the same significance as Paul's understanding of what it means to be "in Christ" and nothing more.

Paul's Use of "flesh"

As I have already stated, we have to decide if the teaching on "flesh" in the NT reflects the OT understanding or whether it widens to embrace Greek language and culture. Many

---

5. For the influence of the exodus/Paschal model on Paul, see Holland, *Contours*, 207–86.

6. If the early church read the texts in this OT manner, i.e., as the fulfillment of the promises of the new exodus and divine marriage, they would identify the point of the statement. Their sustenance comes from the relationship they have with Christ.

7. The theme of the divine marriage in John's Gospel has been established by McWhirter, *The Bridegroom*. This study, establishing the presence of the divine marriage imagery in John, supports evidence that the early church knew of the presence and importance of this OT motif and that she understood references to it in the writings of the apostles. It, therefore, supports the reading that I am suggesting for Romans, where the divine marriage is a key component of the apostle's thinking.

8. John 2:13, 23; 6:4; 11:55; 12:1; 13:1; 18:28; 19:14.

scholars believe Paul was influenced by Greek thought, and that this was reflected in his teaching.[9] Certainly, as noted, a growing number of converts to the Gospel were Greek-speaking Gentiles, and it would seem reasonable for Paul to adapt his message to make it more "Gentile-friendly."

However, we have seen in the Greek understanding of "flesh" that it was sinful because all material things were considered evil. If the assumption is correct that Paul adapted his message, we should find evidence that Paul uses "flesh" in this Greek way. However, when we look closely at his letters, we find that he does not introduce this meaning but continues to make use of its multi-faceted, OT perspective.

Paul's Use of "flesh" to Describe a Covenant Relationship

We have seen that the term "flesh" in the OT can refer to a covenant relationship, e.g., in the creation account. Paul uses this meaning when writing of the Jews, the covenant people of God. He makes it clear that he puts no confidence in this covenant relationship ("flesh"), despite his own pedigree and achievements as a Jew: "For it is we who are the circumcision, we who worship by the Spirit of God, who glory in Christ Jesus, and who put no confidence in the 'flesh'—though I myself have reasons for such confidence. If anyone else thinks he has reasons to put confidence in the flesh, I have more: circumcised on the eighth day, of the people of Israel, of the tribe of Benjamin, a Hebrew of Hebrews; in regard to the law, a Pharisee; as for zeal, persecuting the church; as for legalistic righteousness, faultless. But whatever was to my profit I now consider loss for the sake of Christ" (Phil 3:3–7).

Paul is not saying that his background and ambition to be a faultless Jew were sinful in themselves. Rather he is saying now that he is in Christ, he recognizes that before his conversion, he had been in Adam and living outside of God's kingdom and covenant relationship. Everything he did, including the meticulous practice of his religion, was an expression of his separation from God. When he says "the acts of the sinful nature (flesh) are obvious: sexual immorality, impurity and debauchery; idolatry and witchcraft; hatred, discord, jealousy, fits of rage, selfish ambition, dissensions, factions and envy; drunkenness, orgies, and the like" (Gal 5:19–21a), he includes his own failings. His "noble achievements" in trying to destroy the church before his conversion, dragging men and women off to prison and breathing out murderous threats against the Lord's disciples (Acts 8:3; 9:1), would surely have qualified for acts of "hatred," "jealousy," "selfish ambition," and "fits of rage." These and other acts of the "flesh," were evidence that Paul was in the wrong kingdom or the wrong covenant, i.e., that he was "in the flesh."

Again, Paul makes use of the covenantal OT perspective of "flesh" when he states that being "in the flesh" is the same as being "in Adam." Both terms describe the condition of being unregenerate and disobedient to God's word (cf. Rom 5:12ff.; Gal 3:10ff.). Paul says: "those controlled by the sinful nature ('flesh') cannot please God" (Rom 8:8). He is not writing with an individualistic Greek understanding of the spirit of a man being polluted by his sinful body ("flesh") but of the solidarity of mankind with Adam. In other

---

9. See Casey, *Jewish Prophets*; Barth, *Colossians*, 248; Wright, *Colossians*, 68.

words, unredeemed mankind is "in Adam," and controlled by Satan. These unredeemed members of the human race form the "body of Sin."[10] The picture is of a covenant community, which is outside of the kingdom of God.

This is made plain in Rom 8:9, where Paul tells the Romans that they are not controlled by the sinful nature ("flesh") but by the Spirit, "if the Spirit of God dwells in you." Paul appears to be saying that those who are in Christ are not controlled by Satan but by the Holy Spirit. To be "in the Spirit" is to be "in Christ" where no confidence is placed in human ability or attainment, but all confidence is placed in Christ (cf. Rom 6:5–11; 8:4–8).

In Rom 7:5, Paul speaks of being "in the flesh" as a past experience: "For when we were controlled by the sinful nature (flesh), the sinful passions aroused by the law were at work in our bodies, so that we bore fruit for death." Since nothing acted to control them, the "sinful passions" had free reign to steer them into even greater rebellion against God, producing the works of the flesh (Gal 5:19–21), leading to "fruit for death."

All this is made clear when Paul's statements concerning "flesh" and "Spirit," when "lust" and "sin" are considered.[11] The Mosaic law was powerless in that it was "weakened by the flesh" because man, in Adam, was under the law of Sin (or Satan). Therefore, while man was in this covenant relationship with Satan, he could not respond to God's demands or claims. However, God rescued him from this relationship by "sending his own Son in the flesh ('likeness of sinful man' [NIV]) to be a sin offering" (Rom 8:3). "And so he condemned sin in the flesh ('sinful man' [NIV]) in order that the righteous requirements of the law might be fully met in us, who do not live according to the flesh ('sinful nature' [NIV]), but according to the Spirit. Those who live according to the flesh ('sinful nature' [NIV]) have their minds set on the things of the flesh ('what that nature desires' [NIV]); but those who live in accordance with the Spirit have their minds set on what the Spirit desires" (8:3b–5).[12]

In the Corinthian letter, Paul implies that Sin[13] is related to man's weakness. He draws on the OT covenantal meaning of "flesh," insinuating that believers, because of being in the "flesh" can be enticed back into darkness and bound by the power of Satan. He actively encourages the Corinthian believers not to trust in their own abilities, gifts, wisdom and influence (1 Cor 1:18–25). In their folly, they concede to temptation and begin to boast of their prowess. They are in danger of turning from Christ and substituting other gods in place of him. Paul develops this line of thinking later, especially in Rom 8:1–13; 10:1–22; 11:17–34. The implication is that there is an attempt by Satan to re-establish the relationship he had with them when they were part of the kingdom of darkness (that is, part of "fallen flesh") and Sin (Satan) was their "husband." Acting "in the flesh" causes man to trust in his own abilities and to secure his salvation without taking God's claims to heart. In this sense, Sin and flesh are related. This OT concept is

---

10. For details of this term, see notes on Rom 6:6.

11. For the covenantal-exodus background of this language in Gal 5:18, see Wilder, *Echoes*.

12. There is more said in this passage that needs clarification. It will be dealt with as the commentary proceeds.

13. The upper case is used to emphasize that Sin is personal. It refers to Satan.

not compatible with Hellenistic ideas. For Paul, a Jew, the issue is essentially relational: living in the flesh was living as though he was still in Adam and serving the purposes of the kingdom to which he has succumbed.[14]

Paul's Use of "flesh" to Describe Human Frailty

On occasions, Paul uses the term "flesh" to speak of man's creaturely limitations, reflecting another OT usage: "No one ('flesh') will be declared righteous in his sight by observing the law" (Rom 3:20), and Christ came "in the likeness of sinful man ('flesh') to be a sin offering" (Rom 8:3). Clearly, Paul is not saying that Christ shared our sin but that he shared our creaturely limitations.

In Gal 2:20, Paul says: "I have been crucified with Christ and I no longer live, but Christ lives in me. The life I live in the body (flesh), I live by faith in the Son of God, who loved me and gave himself for me." Here, Paul acknowledges that he continues to live in a state of weakness. In his earthly body, he is in the "flesh."

When writing to the Corinthians, Paul was aware there were some who no longer realized their limitations! They prided themselves in their intellectual gifts and oratorical powers. They no longer felt a need to depend on God. So, Paul tells them: "Brothers, think of what you were when you were called. Not many of you were wise by human standards (flesh); not many were influential; not many were of noble birth. But God chose the foolish things of the world to shame the wise; God chose the weak things of the world to shame the strong. He chose the lowly things of this world and the despised things—and the things that are not—to nullify the things that are, so that no one may boast before him" (1 Cor 1:26–29).

Paul's Use of "flesh" as a Term for Humankind

Surprisingly, when Paul uses "flesh" to speak of man, at first glance, it seems that he never uses the term to speak of humankind as a corporate entity but to refer to the individual person. This emphasizes his argument that each individual, Jew or Gentile, will be treated in the same way by God: "Therefore no one ('flesh') will be declared righteous in his sight by observing the law; rather, through the law we become conscious of sin" (Rom 3:20), and "no one ('flesh') may boast before him" (1 Cor 1:29). However, it could be argued that "no flesh" is distinguishing between Jew and Gentile rather than individuals, in which case the argument continues to be corporate and the texts are not exceptions to what has been said above.

Paul's Use of "flesh" as a Term for the Physical Body

Paul was aware that the OT concept of "flesh" could refer to the bodies of men and beasts, and we find him employing this in 1 Cor 15, where he differentiates between man's flesh

---

14. This understanding is supported by what Paul says in 1 Cor 5–6. In 1 Cor 6:16 he warns the Corinthians of the danger of being delivered over to Satan—a condition which he calls "one flesh" (their pre-converted state). For details of this argument, see Holland, *Contours*, 85–139. See also remarks made on Rom 7:1–6 in this commentary.

and that of animals: "All flesh is not the same: Men have one kind of flesh, animals have another, birds another and fish another" (1 Cor 15:39). Apart from this one mention of animal "flesh," Paul reserves the term for man and his experience, and follows the LXX in using κρέας (kreas) for animal meat (Rom 14:21; 1 Cor 8:13).

In Rom 12, Paul urges the believers in Rome to: "offer your bodies as living sacrifices, holy and pleasing to God" (v. 1). He is not suggesting their sinful bodies[15] can be changed, but he is calling the believers to respond to the claims of God by changing their attitudes as they submit to the word of God. The result will be that the church becomes "a living sacrifice," offered to God in the city of Rome. In the statement: παραστῆσαι τὰ σώματα ὑμῶν θυσίαν ζῶσαν ἀγίαν εὐάρεστον τῷ θεῷ "offer your bodies as living sacrifices, holy and pleasing to God," it is only "your bodies" (ta sōmata hymōn) which is plural. In other words, the NIV's "living sacrifices" should be translated "a living sacrifice," making it a corporate offering. This is made explicit when Paul goes on to tell the church: "Do not conform (μὴ συσχηματίζεσθε [mē syschēmatizesthe], pl.) any longer to the pattern of this world, but be transformed (μεταμορφοῦσθε [metamorphousthe], pl.) by the renewing of your mind (τοῦ νοός [tou noos], sing., literally 'of the mind'). Then you (ὑμᾶς [hymas], pl.) will be able to test and approve what God's will is—his good, pleasing and perfect will" (Rom 12:2). Paul's argument is typically Semitic. Conceptually, he thinks in corporate terms, and these ideas are very much part of the OT understanding of "flesh." The key point to note is that if Paul had adopted a Hellenistic understanding of man (i.e., his body is sinful), he could not have appealed to the believers in Rome to offer their bodies as a living sacrifice to God. A sacrifice has to be clean and holy—an impossible requirement within Hellenistic dualism.

There are other examples of Paul using the term "flesh" to describe man's physical make-up. In speaking of Christ, he says: "who as to his flesh ('human nature,' [NIV]) was a descendant of David" (Rom 1:3). When speaking of circumcision, he speaks about it being "in the flesh" (Rom 2:28; Eph 2:11 ["body," NIV]). He speaks of the necessity of remaining "in the flesh" (Phil 1:24 ["body," NIV]) and of his sufferings "in the flesh" (2 Cor 12:7; Gal 4:13, 14 ["illness," NIV]; Col 1:24). Finally, Christ suffered "in the flesh" (Eph 2:15; Col 1:22 ["physical body," NIV]).

Paul—a Jew

The difference between a Hebraic reading of Paul and a Hellenistic reading ought to be clear. The latter assumes that "flesh" is sinful, physical, and rebellious. However, the OT uses "flesh" in a way that is diametrically opposed to such a reading. The term is morally neutral and its meaning has to be decided from its context.

In conclusion, our study has shown that Paul followed the OT understanding when using the term "flesh."[16] He made use of its wide variety of meanings and applied the term in differing contexts to support what he was teaching. He made particular use of

15. Paul's use of "body" (σῶμα) is typically Hebraic and his appeal is holistic. Thus, Paul is saying that corporately, they should yield their entire being as "a living sacrifice." See Holland, *Contours*, 85–110, 179.

16. "Paul was not a dualist. He proposed that it was God himself who subjected creation to 'futility' and that he had done so 'in hope' planning for its redemption." See Sanders, *Paul*, 39.

the term when writing of the frailty of man as well as of his solidarity to his representative head, Adam. What Paul did not do was use "flesh" in the Greek way and so teach the Roman church it was intrinsically sinful.

We can draw two conclusions from this study. First—and more importantly—Paul did not embrace Greek thinking on "flesh," but stayed within the OT framework. Second, a well-developed program for educating Gentile believers, who were steeped in Greek ideas, would have been a necessity in the early church.

Hellenism and Christian Thought

In the light of all this, we must recognize that the Hellenistic meaning of "flesh" has dominated Christian thinking.[17] If we claim this was the way that Paul thought and taught,[18] then we have to acknowledge that he introduced ideas and teachings into Christian thinking which are at variance with those of the Lord Jesus, who, as a Jew, was reared on the OT. If this is the position we come to accept, then we have to designate Christianity as the religion of the Apostle Paul, who has hijacked Jesus and repackaged him for the Gentile world.

If, however, we accept that the multitude of OT quotations and allusions in Paul's letters, along with his dependence on OT theological structures, demonstrate that he was as much a Jew as was Jesus, then we have to do everything in our power to avoid translating "flesh" in a way that suggests our physical condition is "sinful," i.e., believers have sinful "natures" which have permanently tainted their physical, fleshly bodies. This leads us to reflect on the biblical doctrines of sin and the fall to rediscover the distinctive roots of Jewish-Christian understanding.

Sin

If I am correct in claiming that the NT meaning of "flesh" has Jewish roots and that there is a need to be alert to Hellenistic influences in Western Christian understanding of the doctrine, then we need to ask if the doctrine of sin has been influenced by Hellenism in any significant way. The normal Western Christian understanding of sin is something like this: "acts which break the laws of the OT." This is an understandable definition, but it is not entirely in tune with Scripture.

To construct a doctrine of sin which emphasizes wrong actions rather than wrong relationships is akin to a builder failing to examine the foundation before building a superstructure. For most people, the belief is that wrong actions (sins) come from indwell-

---

17. See, for example, Jewett, *Terms*, 154, who, commenting on Paul's use of the term, says: "For the sake of communication he took over the usage which had become current in Corinth and possibly elsewhere in the Hellenistic church."

18. As claimed by Blocher, *Original*, 27, who says: "Paul's extraordinary development of the idea, whereby the flesh becomes the seat and power of indwelling sin, even the hypostasis of sin's tyranny, maintains continuity with previous usage; (*kata anthrōpon*) and 'being human beings' (1 Cor 3:3ff.). This language describes the fact that human nature *concretely* is at enmity with God; hence the meaning attached to 'flesh.'" (Original emphasis.)

ing sin or man's sinful nature. Such an understanding of sin allows Hellenistic dualism to filter unchallenged into our understanding, leading us away from biblical thinking.

A typical dualistic approach sees that for everything good there is a corresponding evil. In terms of anthropology, man is seen as having two natures: one that is good and the other that is evil. If such an understanding of man takes control of our theology, we will find great difficulty in reconciling it with what the Bible says about the believer and humankind in general. We will have departed from the holistic, OT understanding of man which holds that his being is indivisible. The Hebraic view of man has no place for the dualism of the Greeks who see man as being tripartite: body, soul, and spirit.[19]

What, then, is sin? The OT sets out its stall very clearly. Hosea, commenting on Adam's disobedience, says: "Like Adam, they have broken the covenant . . . they were unfaithful to me there" (Hos 6:7). Hosea lays the charge at Israel's door that she is being unfaithful to Yahweh, who is likened to her husband. She is playing the prostitute, taking other lovers (gods) and breaking her covenant relationship with God. This, says Hosea, is what happened in Eden.[20] Adam rejected God's good and pure love for him and, in its

19. The nearest that the NT apparently gets to such a view is found in 1 Thess 5:23, but most commentators are very clear that the description is not tripartite but reflecting different aspects of the one being a person. For standard expositions see p. 64 n. 17. However, it is clear from how Paul constructs the prayer that he does not pray primarily for the individual believer in Thessalonica but for the community as a whole. Paul writes: "May God himself, the God of peace, sanctify you through and through. May your whole spirit, soul and body be kept blameless at the coming of our Lord Jesus Christ" (1 Thess 5:23 NIV).

The Greek reads: Αὐτὸς δὲ ὁ θεὸς τῆς εἰρήνης ἁγιάσαι ὑμᾶς ὁλοτελεῖς, καὶ ὁλόκληρον ὑμῶν τὸ πνεῦμα καὶ ἡ ψυχὴ καὶ τὸ σῶμα ἀμέμπτως ἐν τῇ παρουσίᾳ τοῦ κυρίου ἡμῶν Ἰησοῦ Χριστοῦ τηρηθείη (1 Thess 5:23 BGT).

Paul prays that God would sanctify them ("you" ὑμᾶς—pl.), by keeping their (ὑμῶν "your"—pl.) πνεῦμα (spirit—sing), ψυχὴ (soul—sing), and σῶμα (body—sing) blameless. In other words, Paul's prayer is not for the sanctification of the individual believers' spirits, souls and bodies, but for the sanctification of the spirit, soul and physical wellbeing of the community, the church. This is in keeping with OT thought where, for example, in Isa 57:15 Yahweh says "I live in a high and holy place, but also with him who is contrite and lowly in spirit, to revive the spirit of the lowly and to revive the heart of the contrite." Here the element "spirit" רוּחַ (ruach) is seen in the form ὀλιγοψύχας in the LXX. So the same idea is present where Yahweh cares for the spirit of the community, the servant he encourages. While the individual is clearly included, it is the nation that has acted unrighteously (see v 9–10) and is called to humble herself. Furthermore, in Isa 58:11 the prophet says: The LORD will guide you always; he will satisfy your needs נַפְשֶׁךָ (nephesh soul) [desire so RSV, ESV and NAS; needs so NJB and NIV; soul KJV] in a sun-scorched land and will strengthen your frame. Again it is the nation that is addressed (v. 2) but the call expects individual Jews to respond. In the LXX נַפְשֶׁךָ is translated ψυχή (For similar uses in which the spirit and the soul of the church is referred to see 1 Cor 6:20 and 1 Pet 2:11). These same Hebrew and Greek terms רוּחַ (ruach)/ πνεῦμα (spirit) are used Deut 6.5: "You shall love . . . with all your soul." We have seen elsewhere (see comments on 6:6) that σῶμα (body) is normally used with a corporate meaning (For the same use in the LXX see Zeisler, "Soma,"133–45). Clearly the same terms found in 1 Thess 5:23 are present in the OT with application to the community. Thus Paul is not praying for the believers as tripartite beings, but for the community which experiences a range of realities and through which Paul longs they will be preserved and blessed. Thus, as individuals (sanctify you pl.) they will know the blessing of sanctification as the community experiences God's blessings. The point of this observation is that Paul by his use of the singular along with the plural is shown to be referring to the constituent parts of the believing community and not the tripartite nature of man.

20. A reference to Adam's disobedience in Eden is disputed by most OT scholars on the grounds that Genesis makes no mention of Adam being in covenant with God. See Macintosh, *Hosea*, 236–39, who says: "It is doubtful, however, whether Adam could be said to have transgressed a covenant or whether his

place; he embraced the lies of the serpent. He went after another god, putting him before the God who made him.

In other words, sin is essentially relational.[21] Breaking God's law is the symptom of the problem. Man has declared himself to be a lover (a covenant partner) of the one who is at war with Yahweh. This imagery continually appears throughout the OT, sin is betrayal. It is rejecting Yahweh and the espousal of other gods. Thus, Adam was not merely disobeying Yahweh but forming a new relationship with God's adversary. In NT terms, at the time of the fall, Adam entered into a relationship with Satan himself.[22]

This relational definition of sin is found throughout the OT. In Deut 5:9, God said to Israel: "You shall not bow down to them or worship them; for I, the LORD your God, am a jealous God, punishing the children for the sin of the fathers to the third and fourth generation of those who hate me."

In Deut 6:14–15, Israel is again warned: "Do not follow other gods, the gods of the peoples around you; for the LORD your God, who is among you, is a jealous God and his anger will burn against you, and he will destroy you from the face of the land."

Again, the definition of sin is made clear in Deut 32:15–19, where it is written: "Jeshurun grew fat and kicked; filled with food, he became heavy and sleek. He abandoned the God who made him and rejected the Rock his Savior. They made him jealous with their foreign gods and angered him with their detestable idols. They sacrificed to demons, which are not God–gods they had not known, gods that recently appeared, gods your fathers did not fear. You deserted the Rock, who fathered you; you forgot the God who gave you birth. The LORD saw this and rejected them because he was angered by his sons and daughters."

It is true, of course, that Israel broke the commandments of God, and because she did not repent, this brought punishment. These disciplinary episodes took place when the nation turned away from the God who had done everything for her and embraced

---

transgression of the divine command is here referred to since that is not the case anywhere else in the OT," 236. Stuart, *Hosea*, 111; Anderson & Freedman, *Hosea*, 438; although Landy, *Hosea*, 84–85, offers reasons why Hosea does refer to the Genesis story. Most scholars claim that Hosea refers to an East Jordan city called Adam, where something terrible was done that violated Israel's covenant with Yahweh. This suggestion is weak because all attempts to find evidence of such covenant-breaking behavior in the city of Adam has failed. In support of Hos 6:7 being a reference to Eden, we find in Hosea a reference to Yahweh leading Israel out of Egypt, as a bridegroom woos a bride, to marry her in the wilderness (Hos 2:14–16). Such an understanding of the exodus was not found in Israel's literature prior to Hosea's writings. So if he was able to create, or preserve, this previously unknown tradition concerning the significance of the exodus event, was he not able to create or preserve a previously unwritten tradition about Eden? If Hosea did create a new understanding of what happened in Eden, i.e., that it was about Adam breaking the covenant relationship with Yahweh, then he has provided new insight into the significance and nature of Adam's disobedience. Thus, the objection raised by Macintosh that the concept occurs nowhere in the OT is answered in the divine marriage imagery, which many of the writing prophets utilized. Indeed, once it is recognized that the divine marriage metaphor has been created by Hosea, it is only a small step for him to read it back into the Eden story and thereby expand its meaning and significance.

21. "sin as covenant disloyalty permeates most of the Hebrew Bible," Sanders, "Sin," VI.36.

22. This is far from being a novel concept. Israel exchanged her relationship with Yahweh—her husband—for a relationship with other gods. The OT is full of this imagery. For a fuller discussion, see Holland, *Contours*, 85–139.

other gods instead. In other words, sin is not essentially legalistic—it is covenantal and relational.

In most countries today, when a man is unfaithful to his wife and commits adultery, no legal infringement has occurred, even though court proceedings may follow. Adultery is relational. It is the betrayal of the covenantal promises which were entered into when marriage vows were made. The husband's or wife's unfaithfulness brings their covenantal relationship to an end. No husband should ever say: "My nature merely got the better of me and nothing has changed in our marriage." He should say: "I chose to do this because it appealed to my desires and instincts. I preferred to break my marriage vows rather than be faithful to my wife. I chose infidelity." This is what sin is. It is man's betrayal of God's covenant love so that he can embrace another. The created one is unfaithful to his Creator. In terms of identifying sin "in" man, it is found in his stubborn refusal to obey God and keep his covenant. The seat of sin is the will of man.

This covenantal understanding of sin is found in texts whose significance and meaning scholarship has failed to appreciate. Many recognize that in Rom 5–7, Paul speaks of sin in the singular. Indeed, there are many who recognize that this singular use of sin is intended to portray sin as a force or as a person (Sin).[23] Sin is repeatedly contrasted with God or righteousness, and most scholars understand that righteousness is an example of a metonymy (a substitute name) for God. In other words, in this scheme, sin is Satan.

This use of "Sin" (which I have suggested should be identified as personal [Satan] by the use of the upper case) alerts us to Paul's much larger view of the doctrine than many understand. It is Sin which has taken humankind captive, and it is the law of Sin (the authority that Sin has over people, similar to the authority that a husband has over his wife) that controls mankind in Adam. As we have seen, Sin is Satan, and the adulterous relationship—the idolatry—has been formed with him. All who are in Adam, i.e., "in the flesh," are in this relationship.

Western Christianity has mostly lost this OT understanding. The subject has been wrenched from its covenantal context and interpreted in a legal setting. Sin is seen as breaking God's law, a crime that requires punishment. In contrast to this forensic understanding, the OT sees sin to be essentially the betrayal of Yahweh's love and the sacrifices which are provided to restore the relationship. The OT concept of sacrifice is, therefore, covenantal rather than judicial. It is not so much the punishment of man's sin but the removal of the fundamental problem that had violated the covenant. In the OT the problem of sin is much more serious than breaking any of the laws, it is about the betrayal of Yahweh's covenantal love. Turning OT sacrifice into an essentially legalistic issue loses a vitally important dimension of its significance; it is about the restoration of the covenant relationship by dealing with the issues that have caused the "divorce." This does not deny the need for a legal element, that is, a need for propitiation, etc. Nevertheless, this legal issue is subordinate to the much greater theme of covenant restoration which requires the termination of the relationship with Sin which in the OT is the ending of the relationship with foreign gods.

23. See Dunn, *Romans*, 1:360; Wright, *Romans*; Sanders, *Paul*, 43. Kennedy, *Conception*, 102 n. 2; Sandy and Headlam, *Romans*, 169; Wedderburn, *Structure*, 342.

By interpreting "sin" mainly in legal terms, we miss a more important framework, which places its emphasis on a God who is the lover of mankind rather than its judge. We have noted in our comments on chapter 4 that justification is rooted in covenantal ideas. These observations lend support to the need to define "sin" in the same terms.

Is Rabbinic Judaism the Source of Paul's Doctrine of sin/Sin?

Some scholars argue that the Christian doctrine of "sin" bears a resemblance to the rabbinic doctrine of *yesher hara*, which is about the human tendency towards evil.[24] At first glance, such a case seems attractive, for Jesus was familiar with rabbinic teaching. Moreover, before his conversion, Paul trained as a rabbi under Gamaliel. One problem with Rabbinic Judaism being the source of Christian understanding is that Jesus clashed with the teaching of the rabbis on various doctrines and refused to be entangled in their web of traditions.[25] Because he challenged his hearers with the direct meaning of the OT text, the people were amazed: "he taught as one who had authority and not as their teachers of the law" (Matt 7:29). The rabbinic perspective is far from what the NT teaches, and it is abundantly clear that Paul had rejected such understanding.[26] Just how much Rabbinic Judaism was influenced by Hellenistic Judaism to become a law bound religion is a point of disagreement amongst scholars.[27] However, far more important is the observation that the meaning of the concept of *yesher hara* was not uniform throughout Judaism. In the midrashim of Rabbi Akiba, the concept implies a natural tendency which is not inherently evil. It functions quite differently from the concept found in the teaching of the school of Rabbi Ishmael.[28] If this is right, Paul could not have been influenced by the later "negative" concept of the *yesher hara*, because Ishmael ben Elisha, known as Rabbi Ishmael (90–135 CE), was yet to be born!

Is Hellenistic Judaism the Source of Paul's Doctrine of Sin?

However, the above Jewish evidence does not affect the argument of some scholars. They see Hellenistic Judaism to have influenced NT understanding concerning the doctrine of "sin." The argument of those who hold this position is that, because Judaism had interacted with Hellenism, the texts of Hellenistic Judaism provide us with the evidence for unraveling Paul's thinking. Some of these texts, which reflect the interface between Judaism and the Hellenistic world, are found in the literature of intertestamental Judaism.

But is this a valid position? It is a huge assumption that Paul ever quoted from these texts. Despite the lack of evidence, scholars assume that Paul derived his dualistic

---

24. Davies, *Rabbinic*, 25.

25. Matt 5:21–22, 27–28, 31–32, 33–34, 38–39, 43–44.

26. The only explicit evidence of Paul's rabbinic background is found in Gal 4:21–31 where he gives a typical Midrashic exegesis of the story of Sarah and Hagar. For a view that sees more extensive influence see Davies, *Paul*, and Hanson, *Methods*.

27. See Davies, *Rabbinic*, who argues for significant influence, as does Powys, *Hard Question*. Ridderbos, *Outline*, 101, rejects any rabbinic influences in Paul's doctrine of "sin."

28. Rosen-Zvi, "The Origins." I owe this information to Seung-Ho Kang.

teaching on "flesh" from these texts.[29] We have already explored the supposed influence of Hellenistic Judaism, and found that its teachings have repeatedly masked what the Scriptures actually teach. So, for example, we have found that *doulos* is not a "slave" but a "servant,"[30] and that the "body of sin" is not the human body but the corporate body of man in his allegiance to Satan.[31] We have also found that "righteousness" in Paul's writings is not a law-court image (a fundamental Greco-Roman concept of legal perfection) but has roots in Isaiah and the psalms, where the "righteousness of God" is his covenant-faithfulness and saving activity.[32]

Elsewhere it has been shown that the teaching of Wisdom Christology; which depends heavily on Jewish Hellenistic texts, has misrepresented Paul's thinking. The key term in Wisdom Christology is *prōtotokos*, which has not been derived from Hellenistic literature as is widely held. It is rooted in the OT account of the Passover where the first-born was the designated object of judgment.[33] In each of these cases, using the literature of Hellenistic Judaism has been disastrous. Rather than opening up the teaching of Paul, it has imposed a mindset on his teaching which has distorted many of his key concepts. This fact alone ought to dissuade us from embracing this literature in order to discern Paul's understanding of "sin."

Sinful Nature

Another expression which influences our understanding of "sin" needs to be considered. Peter appears to write indirectly about man's "sinful nature." When speaking of the promises of God, he says: "through them you may participate in the divine nature and escape the corruption in the world caused by evil desires" (2 Pet 1:4). The reference to being partakers of the "divine nature" is read by some[34] as the counterpart of the condition of unbelievers, i.e., of not having the "divine nature" but having a "sinful nature."

---

29. See Dunn, *Theology*, 84–90. Dunn's evidence that Paul used this literature is his claim that Paul draws on intertestamental wisdom sources in his discussion on "sin" in Rom 1:18–32. Dunn says: "Of greater importance is the Wisdom of Solomon. Its particular relevance for us lies in the fact that Paul certainly knew and seems deliberately to echo this in his opening indictment (Rom 1:19—2:6)." See also Lincoln, *Wrath*, 137. However, despite Dunn's confidence in this matter, his claim is challenged by the exposition of Jewett, *Romans*, 191, who shows the OT (LXX) source of many of Paul's ideas that make up the argument of the passage. Indeed, Jewett gives specific examples of how Paul's argument clashes with Hellenistic understanding: "The content of Hellenistic Judaism was the exact opposite of what we encounter in Romans," (154). To see how this literature has obscured what the NT writers are saying, see, Holland, *Contours*, 339–51.

30. See Holland, *Contours*, 69–82.

31. Ibid., 85–11.

32. Zeisler, *Righteousness*; Hill, *Greek Words*.

33. For further information, see Holland, *Contours*, 237–86; 339–51.

34. The Platonic influences on the understanding of "divine nature" are widely recognized without acknowledging that the term has a natural Hebraic content of "divine kingdom." See Sherlock, *Humanity*, 77; Owen, *Temptation*, 13–14. Green, *Peter*, 184 recognizes the significance of the promises and their place in redemption history but does not appreciate how they link with the believers being partakers of the divine nature (kingdom), so argues for a moral significance for "nature." Kelly, *Peter*, 301–4, also acknowledges links with OT vocabulary but drifts into what he acknowledges is a Hellenistic interpretation of "the divine nature" which he says the first century church received from Plato and Aristotle.

Against this traditional understanding of "nature" is that the Greek term φύσις (*physis*) has two possible meanings. It not only refers to "nature" in terms of an ontological state, but also to a system or order. For most people 'human nature' is in contrast to the divine nature that Peter speaks of, and it is this sinful nature that is thought to be replaced or held in check when the divine nature is given. It is this close relationship between the two natures that allows the term "divine nature" in Peter to support the idea of the existence of a human or sinful nature. This understanding is resting on a fundamental misunderstanding, for neither meaning of φύσις (*physis*) necessarily carries a negative connotation.[35]

Clearly, the believers Peter writes to have escaped the corruption that is in the world. When he speaks of θείας κοινωνοὶ φύσεως (*theias koinōnoi physeōs*) "partakers of the divine nature,"[36] he could mean sharing in the divine order, i.e., the kingdom of God. This way of thinking is supported elsewhere in the NT[37] and by Peter himself: "you will receive a rich welcome into the eternal kingdom of our Lord and Savior Jesus Christ" (2 Pet 1:11).

I am suggesting, therefore, that the term "nature" refers to the *order* to which a person belongs–the kingdom of darkness into which he was born in Adam or the kingdom of God. The natural order of the kingdom of darkness is rebellion against God and the natural order of the kingdom of God (into which a person comes through faith in Christ) is obedience to the will of God. The term does not define the intrinsic being of man but the ontological and moral reality of the realm to which he belongs.[38]

It is important to clarify what is going on in this passage in Peter. Clarity over the way use of the way φύσις is used will guide us to appreciate the OT roots of the term.

When Israel was redeemed from Babylon, she was brought out of the pollution of a pagan society (Isa 52:11; Jer 13:27). The dry bones in Ezek 37 exposed the nation itself as dead and polluted (evidenced by the need for cleansing after a corpse has been touched [Lev 22:4; Num 5:2; 6:7; 9:6.]) This situation was dramatically changed when Israel was brought back to her own land where she could be in fellowship with God. If this is how

---

35. φύσις,εως ἡ "nature," "natural endowment," or "condition." See, Rom 2:27; 11:21, 24; Gal 2:15; Eph 2:3. Also, φύσις means "natural characteristics" or "disposition," (Gal 4:8; 2 Pet 1:4). Furthermore, it may be used with the sense of "nature," carrying the meaning of the regular natural order. See Rom 1:26; 2:14; 1 Cor 11:14. Finally, it can be used with the sense of (natural) "being," "creature," "species," "kind." See Jas 3:7a and, probably, 3:7b (BDAG).

36. The subject becomes more difficult because the NIV (though not limited to it) keeps translating σάρξ as "sinful nature," when there is nothing in the language or text to support this choice. See, Rom 7:5, 18, 25; 8:3–5, 8–9, 12–13; 13:14; 1 Cor 5:5; 11:14; Gal 5:13, 16–17, 19, 24; 6:8; Eph 2:3; Col 2:11, 13; 3:5. Also σάρξ is found in 2 Pet 2:10, 18, where the NIV again translates as "sinful nature." Translating the term as "sinful nature," (as is done throughout the NIV), seriously misrepresents what Paul and Peter are saying.

37. Acts 14:22; 1 Cor 6:10; Eph 5:8–20; Col 1:13–20; 2 Pet 2:19.

38. John Murray describes the pollution of sin in this way: "This refers to the depravity of disposition and character. Man is totally unholy. All of his functions and exercises are unholy because they lack conformity to the will of God; they come short of the perfection which his holiness demands. Man's understanding is darkened, his will enslaved, his conscience perverted, his affections depraved, his heart corrupted, his mind at enmity against God." Murray, *Writings*, 80. Such understanding fits the covenantal model of being "in sin" that I am suggesting, and does not imply anything of a "sinful nature."

Peter's comments should be read—and in its favor, it is not dualistic and contrary to Jewish thinking—then the text does not support the admittedly convoluted suggestion that man has a "sinful nature." The recipients of Peter's letter had been in a state of sin not because they had a sinful nature that needed to be replaced by a new nature, but because they had belonged to the kingdom over which Satan ruled—a kingdom that had polluted them but from which they had been delivered.

This logic fits Paul's statement in Eph 2:3: "All of us also lived among them at one time, gratifying the cravings of our sinful nature ('our flesh') and following its desires and thoughts. Like the rest, we were by nature objects of wrath." In the first chapter of the letter to the Ephesians, Paul lists the blessings that the church experienced as a result of being under the headship of Christ (Eph 1:18–23). These blessings are the result of God's saving mercy when she was rescued from Satan's control: "In him (Christ) we have our redemption through his blood, the forgiveness of sins, in accordance with the riches of God's grace" (Eph 1:7). Like the Israelites, the church has been brought into another kingdom where she is to serve God. This is the context in which the statement "objects of wrath" must be interpreted. Before their conversion, the Ephesian believers had been, like the Jews in Egypt, living under a system that was in rebellion against God and was part of the order that was under God's wrath. Here, "nature" refers not to the ontological condition of man but to his relational condition, as in 2 Pet 1:3. As members of the community that is in Adam, the Ephesians were under God's wrath. They were, by "nature," rebellious children of wrath, but because of God's grace towards them, all of this had changed!

The Heart

There is one final term that we need to consider—the use of "heart" in both the OT and NT. One obvious reference seems to suggest the heart of man is corrupt. Jesus states: "But the things that come out of the mouth come from the heart, and these make a man 'unclean.' For out of the heart come evil thoughts, murder, adultery, sexual immorality, theft, false testimony, slander. These are what make a man 'unclean'; but eating with unwashed hands does not make him 'unclean'" (Matt 15:18–20).

The problem with presenting this as firm evidence that the very being of man is sinful is that the term "heart" is used positively elsewhere in scripture without any suggestion of innate sinfulness. If the "heart" is sinful in the way normally understood, then all references to it would support this view. The fact is that this is not the case, in either the OT or the NT. This ought to cause us to reconsider the traditional understanding of Matt 15:18–20.

The following is a selection of references which speak of the heart of man in a positive way. Of course, there are others that speak of the heart as being evil, hardened, polluted, etc. It is undeniable that different people at different times have hearts in these conditions—but this is not always the case. To have the heart spoken of in the following positive ways can only mean that the heart of man, i.e., his nature (however that is defined), is not permanently wicked or corrupt:

everyone who was willing and whose heart moved him came and brought an offering to the LORD for the work on the Tent of Meeting, for all its service, and for the sacred garments. (Exod 35:21)

Only be careful, and watch yourselves closely so that you do not forget the things your eyes have seen or let them slip from your heart as long as you live. Teach them to your children and to their children after them. (Deut 4:9)

But if from there you seek the LORD your God, you will find him if you look for him with all your heart and with all your soul. (Deut 4:29)

Love the LORD your God with all your heart and with all your soul and with all your strength. (Deut 6:5)

So if you faithfully obey the commands I am giving you today—to love the LORD your God and to serve him with all your heart and with all your soul. (Deut 11:13)

The LORD your God will circumcise your hearts and the hearts of your descendants, so that you may love him with all your heart and with all your soul, and live. (Deut 30:6)

"Do not be afraid," Samuel replied. "You have done all this evil; yet do not turn away from the LORD, but serve the LORD with all your heart." (1 Sam 12:20)

But the LORD said to my father David, "Because it was in your heart to build a temple for my Name, you did well to have this in your heart." (1 Kgs 8:18)

Because your heart was responsive and you humbled yourself before the LORD when you heard what I have spoken against this place and its people, that they would become accursed and laid waste, and because you tore your robes and wept in my presence, I have heard you, declares the LORD. (2 Kgs 22:19)

You found his heart faithful to you, and you made a covenant with him to give to his descendants the land of the Canaanites, Hittites, Amorites, Perizzites, Jebusites and Girgashites. You have kept your promise because you are righteous. (Neh 9:8)

Delight yourself in the LORD and he will give you the desires of your heart. (Ps 37:4)

My heart is steadfast, O God, my heart is steadfast; I will sing and make music. (Ps 57:7)

I will be careful to lead a blameless life—when will you come to me? I will walk in my house with blameless heart. (Ps 101:2)

May my heart be blameless toward your decrees, that I may not be put to shame. (Ps 119:80)

Love the Lord your God with all your heart and with all your soul and with all your mind and with all your strength. (Mark 12:30)

The good man brings good things out of the good stored up in his heart, and the evil man brings evil things out of the evil stored up in his heart. For out of the overflow of his heart his mouth speaks. (Luke 6:45)

> But what does it say? "The word is near you; it is in your mouth and in your heart," that is, the word of faith we are proclaiming. (Rom 10:8)

> For it is with your heart that you believe and are justified, and it is with your mouth that you confess and are saved. (Rom 10:10)

> Obey them not only to win their favor when their eye is on you, but like slaves of Christ, doing the will of God from your heart. (Eph 6:6)

> The goal of this command is love, which comes from a pure heart and a good conscience and a sincere faith. (1 Tim 1:5)

There is one OT text that speaks about the human heart being sinful which appears to contradict what has been argued above. It is Jer 17:9, which says: "The heart is deceitful above all things and beyond cure. Who can understand it"? However, when the text is read in its context it takes on a different meaning from that normally understood.

> He will be like a bush in the wastelands; he will not see prosperity when it comes. He will dwell in the parched places of the desert, in a salt land where no one lives. "But blessed is the man who trusts in the LORD, whose confidence is in him. He will be like a tree planted by the water that sends out its roots by the stream. It does not fear when heat comes; its leaves are always green. It has no worries in a year of drought and never fails to bear fruit." The heart is deceitful above all things and beyond cure. Who can understand it? "I the LORD search the heart and examine the mind, to reward a man according to his conduct, according to what his deeds deserve." Like a partridge that hatches eggs it did not lay is the man who gains riches by unjust means. When his life is half gone, they will desert him, and in the end he will prove to be a fool. A glorious throne, exalted from the beginning, is the place of our sanctuary. O LORD, the hope of Israel, all who forsake you will be put to shame. Those who turn away from you will be written in the dust because they have forsaken the LORD, the spring of living water. Heal me, O LORD, and I will be healed; save me and I will be saved, for you are the one I praise. They keep saying to me, "Where is the word of the LORD? Let it now be fulfilled!" I have not run away from being your shepherd; you know I have not desired the day of despair. What passes my lips is open before you. Do not be a terror to me; you are my refuge in the day of disaster. Let my persecutors be put to shame, but keep me from shame; let them be terrified, but keep me from terror. Bring on them the day of disaster; destroy them with double destruction. (Jer 17:6–18)

In its context it is clear that the statement about the heart of man being deceitful above all things is not intended to categorize the whole of humanity, for the heart that has confidence in God cannot be desperately wicked. While Jeremiah speaks of a forthcoming new covenant in which the covenant community will receive a new heart, the statements he makes about himself in this passage refer to the present, and cannot be read as though he only speaks of the time in the future when the new covenant is established. The statement concerning the wickedness of the human heart refers to those who keep saying: "Where is the word of the LORD? Let it now be fulfilled!" It is clear that Jeremiah sees himself as having been faithful to Yahweh, he has been a faithful shepherd

(17:16) and one who has been planted by the water (17:8). It is those who have turned away from God who are described as being desperately wicked and they are contrasted with those who seek to walk in the ways of the Lord and who will be rewarded with blessing (17:7, 14). The passage is an expansion of Ps 1 which uses the same imagery of the tree planted by the water, and in that psalm is also found the contrast between the righteous and the ungodly that we find here.

The reason for citing these passages is to show that the blanket statement which says the human heart is continually and permanently wicked is not tenable. There are times when it is wicked, and there are times when it is not. Just as in our earlier study on the use of "flesh," we have to listen to the context of each use of the term "heart" and interpret it appropriately. The reasoning given to support the doctrine of the total depravity of man does not always discern the range of uses for the term. Indeed, the doctrine falls apart if this is its only foundation.

While there are individual texts that when collected together form the basis of the traditional doctrine of sin, it is not an adequate biblical theology that depends on ignoring texts which speak to the contrary. If we are to achieve a truly biblical doctrine of sin then we are obliged to search for an explanation that holds all the evidence together in one cohesive understanding.

The NT and the Doctrine of Sin

However we define "sin," we must not be influenced by the dualism of Greek understanding. If we are, our understanding will differ from the OT writers and Jesus himself. As a Jew, he was saturated in the OT Scriptures, and his understanding was essentially covenantal and relational. If we argue that Paul's understanding of "sin" was different from Jesus', we claim that Paul turned from the understanding into which he was born. This understanding of Paul's development has been widespread as a result of the twentieth century German Religio-Historical School's assumption that Hellenism was his natural home. This has now been rejected by much of recent scholarship. Because Paul's commitment to the OT Scriptures has been recognized, fewer scholars now want to defend direct Greek influences on his thinking. This gives good grounds for questioning the assumed meaning of "sin" in Paul's writings. For Paul, being "in sin" is the consequence of being Adam's offspring. It is relational. We were born outside of the covenant with God which man was created to enjoy, and into a covenant with the very enemy of God. The consequence of Adam's disobedience was universal, as all his descendents were driven out of God's presence with him. For Paul, this is what it means to be a sinner. Committing wrong actions is a consequence of being born into a kingdom that is at war with God. Wrong actions are a consequence of sin, not the root of it. To "walk in the flesh" is to "live in Adam," preferring to live by the values of the "kingdom of darkness." It is to deny God his right in our lives, and the awful consequence of this choice is death. If believers continue to flirt with the realm that is opposed to the rule of the God of heaven, they will suffer discipline as happened in the OT (Deut 28:15–68; Neh 1:2–3; Ezek 21:1–32) and in the NT (Matt 18:18; 1 Cor 5:1–11; 10:1–22; Rev 2:4–5, 14–16, 19–23).

The reason for much of the confusion about the nature of "sin" is because Bible translators have been unclear about its biblical, covenantal dimension. They have been guided by syncretistic (especially legal) ideas, which have prevailed in Western Christianity. These views have produced deep pastoral problems, with many people in distress because they fear that they continually sin against God. Most translators—especially those who have produced the NIV—have done a huge disservice to the Christian public by constantly translating *sarx* as "sinful nature."[39] Such a translation has enforced a dualistic understanding of man, locking many believers into a state of ignorance and despair.

It is clear that the NT has a doctrine of "sin." The sins that Paul refers to have to do with the failure of Christians to live within the new covenant's ethos. Instead of living or walking in the Spirit (that is, living under the Lordship of Christ), the Roman believers are being enticed back into the lifestyle of the kingdom of darkness from which they have been rescued. Such behavior—such sins—will bring God's judgment on them, and Paul warns them of this very forcefully.

Thus, Paul's teaching on "sin" is essentially the same as that found in the OT. All unbelievers are in Adam and, because of this, they share his fate. Their union with him means that they are bound up in the covenant relationship into which he entered.[40] Through Adam, man is bound in a covenant relationship with Satan. This is the reason for God's judgment, and the sins that spring from this condition are the result of freely made choices to live independently of God. This independence may express itself in gross immorality or in devoted religious pursuits. Whatever its expression, all that is done within this relationship (a relationship that excludes the living God) is of the "flesh."

There is, therefore, no "sinful human nature." Such an understanding leads right into the jaws of Hellenism where Christian truth is devoured. Rather than speaking of the NIV's "sinful nature," we must learn to speak of the "fallen condition" of man. He is born in Adam, and in that state he can neither please God nor know him. He is cut off from God, and in this condition of death he will eternally remain. This can only change if God comes to his aid, and does something so God-like that it secures the overthrow of Satan and releases him from the master who has ruled over him. God secured this salvation when he came into the world in the person of his Son and died on a cross at the hands of Roman soldiers.

Sin is not found, therefore, within a distorted human nature. It is the result of Satan enslaving the will of man. This bondage is nothing less than Luther's *Bondage of the Will.* As a fallen human, man is not intrinsically evil in his physical make-up. He is a part of Evil, a part not only of Adam but of Satan.[41] In this condition, he cannot love God; for Satan, who holds the heart and will of man in Adam, is the very opposite of God. In such a condition, man is not "less sinful" but "more sinful" than the prevailing Hellenistic view understands. He is not physically, intrinsically evil. His sinfulness is in a different dimen-

---

39. Rom 7:5; 8:4–5, 8–9, 12–13; 13:14; 1 Cor 5:5; Gal 5:13, 16–17, 19; Eph 2:3; Col 2:11, 13; 3:5; 2 Pet 2:10, 18.

40. See comments on pages 159–60.

41. "Paul regards sin not merely or in the first place from the individual and personal, but from the collective and supra-individual point of view." Ridderbos, *Outline,* 125.

sion. He is in covenant with Satan–held captive by him and unable to deliver himself from his clutches (Rom 7:21–25).

It is because this is the NT's understanding of the sinfulness of man that we can recognize that the image of God continues to be reflected in our fellow men (Luke 18:21; Acts 10:1–2).[42] We do not have to search for flaws in their characters to prove they are sinners. We can acknowledge the reality of God's common grace, and be delighted at their achievements and moral virtues. However, no matter how fine they may be, un-redeemed men and women are still in Adam, cut off from their Creator and under the sentence of eternal separation from him. This separation is finally sealed as irrevocable in death, when the awful condition of being "in Adam" will be fully realized by those who have rejected the "last Adam" in life (Rom 5:15–19; 1 Cor 15:45–49).

In this excursus, and earlier in the commentary, we have examined a range of terms which have traditionally been thought to speak about "sin" in man. Such terms as the "body of sin," the "old man," "flesh" and "sinful nature" have all been explored and found to be Hebraic terms describing corporate states. We have also examined chapter 7 of Romans, finding that its argument has a corporate dimension and that its language should be read in terms of man's condition in Adam rather than seeing sin as dwelling inside of each person. These key terms, interpreted individualistically, have been used to build the church's doctrine of "sin." As a consequence, she has embraced an understand-ing which has taken her from her Jewish foundations and which has replaced it with a Hellenized view of the being of humanity. What has been constructed is at serious odds with the intended teaching of the NT.[43]

In concluding this excursus, I want to affirm the Scriptures teach that when it comes to sinfulness, humanity is totally depraved because Adam's sin has alienated all his off-spring from God, leaving them enemies of their maker. Furthermore, because of human-ity's solidarity with Adam, his sin and guilt have been imputed (credited) to everyone of his descendents.[44] Because of this, subsequent generations are left with no hope of ever being accepted by a God who is holy. We must understand that this relational model of sin speaks of man being in a far worse condition than does the Hellenistic model. Man "in Adam" is helpless and sentenced to an ongoing separation unless his Creator can, or will, bring about a salvation that is "godlike and divine."

---

42. Of course, no matter how attractive and decent a person is, being "in Adam" means that the disposi-tion is of no consequence. In the Second World War, there were many, very decent German people who did not want war but were under Hitler's "headship." That determined their state as enemies of the allies.

43. The claim that the terminology under consideration has been interpreted through inappropriate categories has also been noted by Jewett, *Term*, 248, in relation to the widespread understanding of the term "body of Christ."

44. The term—despite objections from Wright, *Really Said*—is used deliberately, as it is the language used by Paul himself in Rom 5:18.

D O YOU NOT know, brothers—for I am speaking to men who know the law—that the law has authority over a man only as long as he lives? For example, by law a married woman is bound to her husband as long as he is alive, but if her husband dies, she is released from the law of marriage. So then, if she marries another man while her husband is still alive, she is called an adulteress. But if her husband dies, she is released from that law and is not an adulteress, even though she marries another man. So, my brothers, you also died to the law through the body of Christ that you might belong to another, to him who was raised from the dead, in order that we might bear fruit to God. For when we were controlled by the sinful nature, the sinful passions aroused by the law were at work in our bodies, so that we bore fruit for death. But now, by dying to what once bound us, we have been released from the law so that we serve in the new way of the Spirit, and not in the old way of the written code. (Rom 7:1–6)

Introduction

The seventh chapter of the letter to the Romans has a long history of conflicting interpretation. For the most part, the debate has been about whether Paul is describing his pre-conversion experience or his post-conversion experience. In recent years, there has been a move away from seeing the passage as Paul recording his own experience to one where Paul acts out the historical experience of a community of which he is a representative member. As to the identity of the community, there is lively debate. Some scholars say that Paul is playing out the experience of the whole human race—locked into its bondage to Sin—while others see the community to be Israel. This latter view focuses on her relationship with Sin from which she thought she had been redeemed through the experience of the exodus from Egypt.

There are some good reasons for accepting a corporate perspective for the passage. First, it begins with an illustration based on marriage. The significance of this is that the marriage analogy is never used in the OT or NT to speak of an individual's relationship with God. This sort of language is used for describing the relationship of Israel with Yahweh in the OT and the relationship of the church with Christ in the NT. To impose an individualistic interpretation[45] on this illustration would be contrary to the way such language is used in Scripture.

The passage that opens chapter 7 may be introducing Rom 7:7ff. or concluding chapter 6.[46] Identifying the passage as a conclusion rather than an introduction makes good sense. Paul's argument from chapter 5 has been that man is naturally in Adam and under the curse. He has shown in Rom 6:1–4 that the new solidarity, which the church enjoys, results from the Spirit's baptism of members who have been called from the body of Sin into union with Christ. These members do not include all who are in the of the body of Sin, but only those who God knew in his foreknowledge would call on the name

---

45. As does Wright, *Romans*, 558, when he says: "the Christian is now, in some sense, the 'bride' of Jesus the Messiah."

46. Hellholm, "Funktion," correctly, in my view, argues that Rom 1:1–6 serves as a thematic introduction to what follows, taking up the theme of Rom 5:20a and 6:14.

of his Son for salvation. The Spirit's baptism formed "one new body," and its members are those who have been brought out of darkness into light. The members of this new body have shared in the death of Christ (their new federal head),so the relationship to Sin has ended. The community has been freed from its covenant bondage to Sin, and Christ is able to take it as his bride. Because the death of Christ is a reality, the former covenant with Sin (Satan) has been cancelled and Paul can say that those who have died are justified from sin (Sin) (Rom 6:7). In other words, Satan cannot lay at the door of either the church or Christ the accusation of adultery.

Paul then urges the local Roman church to live as the servant of God, just as Israel was urged to after her redemption from Egypt. This redemption/marriage analogy is the very heart of Israel's own experience, for she had been redeemed from bondage in order to be the bride of Yahweh (Ezek 16:8; Hos 2:2). Thus, the passage is a perfect conclusion to the argument that Paul has been developing in the two preceding chapters. Indeed, it can be argued that it goes back to Rom 3:21–25, where the background was the event which inaugurated the exodus, i.e., the Passover.

But Rom 7:1–6a is also an introduction to Rom 7:6b,[47] and this is the setting for the rest of the chapter. Paul is not writing an apology for the law, nor is he digressing. He comments on the nature of the old relationship and contrasts it with the new. He has to explain how the old has passed away and how the new has come into being. To do this, he must show how the law had functioned and how it now functions. Thus, Rom 7:1–6a is the conclusion of chapters 5–6 and the introduction to Rom 7:7—8:34.

As a result of the argument given above, the chapter would have been better started at Rom 7:7. This is evident from the start of the verse, where Paul says: "What shall we say, then?" This is Paul's typical way of introducing a new section in which he develops insights out of the teaching expounded in the preceding passage.

Having explained his argument, he asks his hearers for their response to what he has written. The statement marks the beginning of Paul's application of all that he has written in Rom 5:12—7:6.

7:1 Do you not know, brothers for I am speaking to men who know the law—that the law has authority over a man only as long as he lives? Paul uses an illustration that spans all cultures—marriage (Rom 7:1–2). The relationship of marriage is permanent, and, in biblical thinking, can only end through the death of one of the parties as death terminates a covenantal relationship. This termination is absolute. No charge of unfaithfulness can be brought against a survivor who remarries. In the case of remarriage, the surviving spouse does not have two marriage partners, one dead and one living. He or she has only one marriage partner, and that is the one who is living. The authority of the dead husband ceased when his life ceased because the marriage covenant ended. Thus, a remarried woman does not have to try to meet the wishes of two men. In fact, the authority (law) of the former husband ended before her new marriage.[48] Even if she chose never

---

47. See Käsemann, *Romans*, 210, who also sees that Rom 7–8 form a unity.

48 The perspective that Sin (Satan) is the former husband, as argued in Rom 6:7, is supported by Giblin, "Monotheistic," 544, who says that the law of the husband "is the husband himself as the living, determin-

to remarry, he no longer had authority over her because death had terminated their legal bond.

⟶7:2 For example, by law a married woman is bound to her husband as long as he is alive, but if her husband dies, she is released from the law of marriage. Paul amplifies his introductory statement. He introduces the universally familiar example of a woman whose husband's death leaves her a widow. Even without a new husband, she is released from the law of her former husband because the old relationship came to an end with his death. This is a vital point for Paul. Christ's death, on behalf of his people, ended the former relationship they had with Sin (Satan). Through his representative death (in which his people have shared [6:1–8]), those who were once prisoners of the body of Sin have been freed. They have a new status; having died with Christ, they are no longer bound to the law of the old husband—the law of Sin and Death.[49]

At a corporate level, this illustration echoes the experience of Israel. In Egypt, she was bound up with the relationship that the Egyptians had with their gods. When she came out of Egypt at the exodus, she died not only to the reign of Pharaoh, but also to her involvement, through him, with his gods. Following this release, or redemption, she became the bride of Yahweh at Sinai.

The trouble was that Israel betrayed the covenant love that Yahweh lavished upon her, and, in her heart, returned to her former lovers (Exod 32:1, 4, 8) at the beginning of her marriage. For this reason, Israel was repeatedly accused of playing the harlot (Ezek 16:26–58; Hos 4:15—5:7).

⟶7:3 So then, if she marries another man while her husband is still alive, she is called an adulteress. But if her husband dies, she is released from that law and is not an adulteress, even though she marries another man. For many scholars, it has been difficult to know what law the believer has died to. If the exegesis given is correct, it will be clear the argument is about the church and not the believer. Certainly, the individual believer in some way shares in the consequences of this death to law, but it ought to be

---

ing factor of the bond under consideration . . . law is somebody's law." Thus, he can speak of the law of the husband (Rom 7:2). Kuss, *Römer*, 1:119, points out that Yahweh was betrothed to Israel in righteousness (cf. Isa 46:13; 51:6, 9). As we have seen, righteousness is a major theme of Romans. It is clearly part of the eschatological perspective of Paul, which culminates in the eschatological marriage, thus linking back with Isaiah's new exodus theme. Derrett, *Law*, 461ff. says that Israel thought law bound her to God in marriage covenant. Wright, "Messiah," 148, argues that the former husband is Adam. However, he is right when he says: "We believe that the majority have taken the whole argument out of specific covenantal context in which alone it could be understood." Wright, "Narrative Structure," 39 says: "In Paul's usage, 'sin' refers not just to individual human acts of 'sin,' of missing the mark (the basic meaning of the word) as regards the divine intention for full human flourishing and fulfillment. 'Sin' takes on a malevolent life of its own, exercising power over persons and communities. It is almost as though by 'sin' Paul is referring to what some other parts of the Bible meant by 'Satan.'" Thus Wright would have been more consistent if he had seen that the marriage is not to the law, but to the one behind the abuse of the law, Satan. 2 Cor 11:2; Eph 5:25–33; Rev 19:7.

49. Thus Earnshaw, "Analogy," 68–88, is right to see that the passage is about the believers' union with Christ and the freedom that follows, but he is wrong to see it about individual Christian experience and the first husband being the law.

obvious what law the church has died to.[50] Paul states: ἐλευθέρα ἐστὶν ἀπὸ τοῦ νόμου (*eleuthera estin apo tou nomou*) "she is released from that law," i.e., the law of the former husband. To use another description that Paul has already employed, it is the law of Sin and Death.[51] As we have noted previously, these terms are used as descriptions of Satan. He is the former husband. While it is true that Satan himself has not died, that is not a problem for death has taken place through Christ. By Christ's representative death—into which his people were baptized—the church has been set free. Her former husband has no legal power over her. She has died to his authority—his law—and is legally betrothed to another. Because she has died with Christ, she is justified from the law of her former husband. No legal charge can be upheld against her.

7:4 So, my brothers, you also died to the law through the body of Christ, that you might belong to another, to him who was raised from the dead, in order that we might bear fruit to God. Paul brings his argument to its conclusion. The purpose of Christ's death was to free his people from Sin so that he could take them as his bride.[52] This is possible because Christ not only died but was raised from the dead. His death is a historical fact, but its significance is a present reality. Through his death, the covenant his people once had with Sin (the old husband) has ended and the risen Christ has taken the "raised widow" unto himself.[53] Christ thus fulfills the role of the OT redeemer, who married the childless widow of his near kinsman. We have seen that Christ is not called the Redeemer in the NT, but his work is certainly described in terms which are modeled on the OT redeemer figure. Yahweh promised to fulfill this role for the Jews in exile. He planned to redeem the nation so that she could become his bride (Isa 49:20–21; 50:1–8; 62:4–5). Paul uses the same imagery of bride-purchase elsewhere (Acts 20:28; 1 Cor 6:20; 2 Cor 11:2; Eph 5:25). These texts are evidence that the NT writers saw marital imagery as describing the church's relationship to God (Matt 22:1–4; 25:1–13; Luke 14:15–24; John 3:27–30; Rev 19:9).

The reference to bearing "fruit to God" is a clear echo of the command to Adam to be fruitful and replenish the earth. Here, the statement is not about replenishing the natural order but is about the new creation. The church is called to enlarge the family of God, not through natural procreation but through the proclamation of the life-giving Gospel. The original context of the quotation from Genesis was marital. As the church lives under the law (or covenant authority) of her new husband she fulfills the command to be fruitful and replenish the earth. This fruitfulness is the natural consequence of the outflow of her love for her Redeemer husband.

50. The argument that I am making is supported by Winger, "Law," 537–46, when he claims that the Law of Christ in Gal 6:2 is not about a specific legal instruction, but rather the way in which Christ exercises his lordship over those called by him.

51. For supporting evidence that Death is another pseudonym for Satan, see p. 235 n. 70.

52. Käsemann, *Romans*, 188, notes that v.4 draws the conclusion. The aorist tense and the context unmistakably look again to baptism. What is said in Rom 6:4ff. in relation to the power of sin is self-evidently transferred to the law.

53. Not as Wright, *Romans*, 559, who comments on Rom 7:7: "'You' in the first half of 7:4 is the 'former husband'; 'you' in the second half is the wife."

We now come to a passage that has not only had a profound influence on the doctrine of sin, but has also been at the center of much theological debate in recent years. Some have claimed that in this passage Paul describes his own Christian experience. Those who hold this view argue that the next chapter is about the victory of the Christian over sin and death. Amongst its advocates are those who teach some form of "higher spiritual life," which emphasizes a post-conversion experience of the Holy Spirit, bringing the believer from defeat into victorious Christian living. Those who have supported this understanding include Wesley; the holiness movements of the past two hundred years; and, especially, the original Keswick movement, which popularized this view to hundreds of thousands of believers. (The present Keswick message has changed from its original position on this teaching.) The other traditional view of this passage argues that Paul is not speaking of his past but his present experience as a believer. This position, which is held by most Reformed teachers, holds that sin is not eradicated until the believer is completely transformed at the coming of Christ.

Both of these positions have been challenged in recent years.[54] As we have already noted, the passage has not been seen to be specifically about Paul's own experience but either about the history of Israel or the history of humanity in Adam. The reason for this conclusion is that the passage is at odds with other statements Paul has made about his attitude to the law before he became a follower of Christ. In Phil 3:6, he describes his pre-Christian legal status as faultless, and in Gal 1:14, he writes that he advanced in Judaism beyond many contemporaries, being zealous for the traditions of his fathers. Both statements suggest Paul was a man who had a very positive attitude towards the law and what it demanded. Indeed, recent intertestamental and rabbinical studies have shown that Paul was not alone in this position. It is now appreciated that many in first century Judaism saw the law as the most precious gift God had given them, safeguarding their relationship with him. Rabbinical studies have shown that NT Judaism was far from being a community crippled with guilt and self-despair (experiences familiar to some parts of the Christian church).[55] Rather, for many Jews, their attitude to the law was one of tremendous appreciation and gratitude. However, caution does need to be exercised over this rabbinical evidence. First, some rabbinic texts (albeit few) do not convey this positive attitude.[56] Second, the rabbinical writings were not recorded until the end of the second century—much later than the NT period. Although it is generally believed the writings have accurately preserved the oral tradition they transcribe, nevertheless, some scholars challenge their use because there is no external testimony to corroborate their faithfulness to the tradition they were supposed to preserve. Indeed, some scholars see a possibility that particular traditions were invented.[57]

Returning to Romans chapter 7, the question must be asked: "About what or about whom is Paul writing?" In answering this question, scholars have pointed out Paul makes

---

54. See Dunn, *Romans*; Wright, *Romans*.

55. See Sanders, *Palestinian*.

56. Bockmuehl writes, "Scholars in the past tended to take their pick from this complex evidence, alternatively stressing either the elements of grace or those suggesting a strict legalism" ("Salvation," 411).

57. Chilton & Davies, "Aqedah," 534–36.

a statement that cannot be part of his experience. He says: "Once I was alive apart from law; but when the commandment came, sin sprang to life and I died" (v. 9). The fact is there was never a time when Paul lived apart from the Mosaic law. Born into a devout Jewish home, he would have known something of the law from his childhood, and it would have been the greatest influence on his life as he grew into adulthood. Consequently, the statement does not reflect any part of his experience. If it is argued Paul meant that, although the law existed objectively in his life, he had not experienced a personal sense of guilt that comes when the Spirit works through the law to produce repentance, then we have a position with a little more substance. But the problem with this interpretation is the notion that sin is dead without the law, which suggests there was no guilt until the law condemned. This is not a position that echoes the rest of scripture. Sin exists, even when there is no law. If sin does not exist without the law, it is better for people to be left in ignorance. Sin is not brought to life by the law; it is increased by it (Rom 5:20).[58]

But doubt should be raised over the highly individualistic interpretation outlined above, i.e., that of Paul battling with his own sins. This is because the passage is introduced using a corporate illustration (Rom 7:1–6). Paul uses the example of marriage and remarriage to show how a new relationship can come into existence. As noted earlier, the analogy of marriage is regularly used throughout the whole of Scripture to depict the relationship of God with his people. This analogy is never used for the relationship of an individual with God. It is always corporate, describing the experience of the covenant community.

So, what is Paul talking about if it is not about his own experience? Two suggestions have been put forward. First, he is acting out the role of humanity. He enacts the drama in the Garden of Eden. There, Adam was alive without the law. Then God gave the command not to eat of the tree of the knowledge of good and evil (Gen 2:15–17) and the command provoked the desire to have knowledge that was denied to him as a creature. Adam disobeyed, ate, and sinned. It was through this act of disobedience that Sin established its bridgehead and man died to his relationship with God. He was driven from the Garden and from the tree of life (Gen 3:23–24).

In its favor, the corporate interpretation has an individual representing a community.[59] This is not only a biblical way of expressing something corporate, it is used in many other cultures—even twenty-first century Western ones. The one representing the many is seen in international sporting events, and sometimes, within these events, conflicts of history are focused in an individual as he does battle with the nation's enemy!

Second, while agreeing that Paul acts out the experience of a group, another interpretation says it is not mankind he is representing but the Jewish people. It is pointed out that the commandment: "you shall not covet," was not established until the Ten Commandments were given to the nation of Israel (Exod 20:17). This interpretation sees

---

58. It will be noted that I have spelled "sin" using the lower case. The reader will recall the difficulty in chapter 5 about deciding whether Paul is speaking of sin as guilty actions or sin as Sin (or Satan). Here, I judge, he is dealing with the guilt of not keeping the Mosaic law.

59. For an overview of the debate regarding theories of solidarities in the Bible, see Rogerson, "Corporate," especially 14–16. See also, Rogerson, "Responsibility," 1156–57.

the entrance of sin as referring to the giving of the covenant law at Sinai, when Israel's covenant with God was to be ratified. What should have been the climax of the salvation event—Israel being brought as a bride to be united to her husband at Sinai—was disastrous. Instead of entering the fullness of life, she came under the sentence of death. The law that should have sealed her relationship with God did the very opposite—it condemned her and excluded her from her great calling.

This interpretation is not appealing for two reasons. First, the claim that the command: "You shall not covet," came with the establishment of the law cannot be maintained. It was the very essence of the command to Adam: "You must not eat from the tree of the knowledge of good and evil." This command was to tell Adam that he must not covet God's omniscience. Second, the idea that the law could sentence Israel in this way was not part of Jewish understanding. As we have seen earlier, Jews generally had a positive view of the law. New Perspective theologians claim the law was not the source of guilt and death but of privilege and life.

The suggestion that Paul is taking the part of Adam is supported by the unfolding argument of the letter. Chapter 5 described the fall and chapter 6 showed how the fall could only be reversed when the solidarity with Adam was cancelled. The chapter also showed how this was done through the creation of a new humanity, which was brought into existence through the death of Christ when the Spirit baptized its members into union with their Savior. The remainder of chapter 6 was an appeal to the redeemed community to live as servants of God. The opening of chapter 7 reviewed how the authority of Sin was brought to an end for the new covenant community through the representative death of its head, Christ, the last Adam. In the flow of this argument, the section we are currently dealing with (Rom 7:7ff.) is best understood as a review of the condition of man following the fall. Paul wants to emphasize that, outside of Christ, there can be no salvation. Christ alone is the true Passover/sin offering that brings the old relationship with Sin to an end. Thus, Paul is not recounting personal biographical details but is giving a historical biography of which he is part.[60]

Can it be shown elsewhere that Paul uses this literary technique of entering into the experience of others in order to act out the corporate/individual relationship? If this can be demonstrated, it would be useful in supporting the argument given. We do, in fact, find an example of this in Paul's letter to the Philippians. In Phil 1:18b–19, Paul seems to echo the experience of Job as found in Job 13.[61] He expresses, in his isolation, the same confidence that God would eventually vindicate him. If taking an OT story and moulding the experience of the apostle or church around it can be established as a literary technique, it would support the suggestion that chapter 7 is an example of intertextuality.

This technique, in fact, is not limited to Paul but has been recognized by scholars to be a literary device used within the NT. We find the phenomenon of one person representing the many in the Servant Songs. These Isaianic texts have long fascinated scholars, and most now agree the Songs reflect a corporate relationship between an individual and

---

60. "We should not attempt to decide between these two (Sinai and Eden): Paul's point is precisely that what happened on Sinai recapitulated what had happened in Eden." Wright, *Romans*, 563.

61. See Hays, *Echoes*.

the community of which he is the head or part. In the Songs, it is extremely difficult to answer the following: "Who is speaking, what is his status, and what is he saying?"[62]

The same phenomenon is found in Ps 69. The psalm is a confession of David, but as it progresses, it is difficult to know whether he is speaking of his experience or the nation's. As the psalm ends in vv.34–36, they seem to merge with the focus being on the experience of the nation returning to Zion. Other OT texts that use the personal pronoun to denote the nation of Israel include: Ps 44:4–8; Mic 7:7–10; Jer10:19–22; Lam 1:9–22; 2:20–22. It is worth noting the confessions in Ezra 9:7 and Neh 9:2, 34, where the two reformers prayed and confessed as representatives of the nation. The features noted in Ps 69 are present in these texts.

The difficulties associated with the traditional reading of chapter 7 have been caused by the failure to recognize the Jewish character of the text and to appreciate that it does not speak of one person's experience alone. It speaks of the experience of one and of many, all of whom have a range of social and religious positions within history and within the text.

I believe, therefore, that Paul is acting out the experience of humanity in Adam. Because he has come to see that Israel is still in Adam (in Sin), he knows she does not have the covenant relationship with God of which she boasts. She is, therefore, included in the story, her experience occasionally breaking through into the narrative. In the illustration that Paul has just used, he makes it clear the law could do nothing to change the relationship that humankind has with Sin. Indeed, the law's effect is to ratify the relationship. This same impotence is seen in civil law. It creates a marriage in legal terms but is utterly helpless to change a bad marriage and make it good. Indeed, even though the marriage might not be good, the law has to uphold the rights of both partners. In this way, the law of God had become the servant of Sin. Satan could appeal to the law for his exclusive rights to the obedience of man, and the law could do nothing but recognise them. Those rights, as we have seen, were ended by the death of Christ for his people.

But some would argue that if the law had been used by Sin, it was sinful itself! Part of Paul's following argument is to reject such a claim—a claim that would have been abhorrent to any Jew. His concern is not only to pacify the Jews, however, but also to make sure that Gentile believers do not become caught up in an anti-law movement. This would throw out the moral teachings of the law, leaving the believers in Rome exposed to the very corruption from which they had been redeemed.

62. Note Rowley's comment, *Faith*, 118: "This narrowing down of the community is found in the Old Testament in other forms. Attention is frequently called to the Hebrew conception of corporate personality. The term occurs nowhere in the Bible, but is a modern creation to express a view that is common in the Old Testament. It is a particular form of the concentration of the life of the community for the moment, often in a single individual, and much wider in its reference than the thought of the Remnant. For any purpose the Hebrew could think of an individual who was the representative of the community, or whose experience was typical of that of the community, as identified with the community. *For the time being he was the community, and he could use the first person singular when he was speaking in the name of the community. He could equally speak of the community in the third person. For there was in his thought a fundamental fluidity, whereby he could pass back and forth from the thought of himself to the thought of the community, and from the thought of the community to himself, in whom for the moment its experience or its life is concentrated or represented.*" (emphasis added)

7:5 For when we were controlled by the sinful nature, the sinful passions aroused by the law were at work in our bodies, so that we bore fruit for death. The interpretation of this text was inevitably driven by presuppositions made by the translators as they grappled with the meaning of the passage. To translate *sarx* as "sinful nature" assumes that the argument is about individual human experience. If it is translated as "human weakness," it leaves the door open for other possibilities. Before any decision is made as to how to translate the text, its context has to be considered, along with the theological tradition of which Paul was part.

The foundation of the ongoing argument was laid in chapter 5, a chapter which reviewed historical, corporate realities. Without those realities as the foundation, the teaching of chapter 6 cannot be unlocked. I suggest this understanding continues into chapter 7, and that the term *flesh* (*sarx*) should be rendered "human weakness" and not "sinful nature." The argument is that humanity is not in the covenant relationship for which it had been created, but is under the control of Sin, exposing its individual members to all the guiles of the tempter. Humans sin because they are in solidarity with the community of Sin which is alienated from God. What Paul is *not* saying is that the individual human body is sinful; it is not driving and controlling wicked passions.

If this corporate interpretation is accepted, then Paul, representing either Adam[63] or the Jewish nation,[64] speaks about the frailty of his "members" (not "bodies," as the NIV translates[65]). His members are individual people who have difficulty resisting the temptations that Satan lays before them, as did Adam in the garden.

Although the term "members" is often seen as representing particular body parts, i.e. the eye, a hand, a foot, etc., the legitimacy of understanding "members" as individual people is supported by the use of μέλος (*melos*) which has strong corporate associations in Paul's theology.[66] This statement, therefore, summarizes the description of the human condition that Paul has given in Rom 1:18–32.

7:6 But now, by dying to what once bound us, we have been released from the law so that we serve in the new way of the Spirit, and not in the old way of the written code. The corporate dimension of the argument continues. Paul cannot say "what bound you," as it was never an act of delivering an individual but that of the community of which he was a part. Of course, individuals made up the community and shared in the saving event, but Paul's argument is not about the solitary believer—his argument is about the people of God.

He is not appealing to the Roman believers to die. He is saying they, with all believers, have already died. He is focusing on the event that Rom 6:1–6 and 7:1–6 have spoken about, i.e., their death with Christ as a result of the union created with him by the Spirit.

---

63. Emphasized amongst others by Dunn, *Romans*, 1:378, and Käsemann, *Romans*, 196–97.

64. Emphasized amongst others by Wright, "Messiah," 93–96; Whiteley, *Theology*, 51–53, and Karlberg, "Personified," 68–69.

65. Such liberty in translating reflects the translators' failure to follow the narrative and the theology it creates.

66. For a discussion of this, see Holland, *Contours*, 124–28.

This is the historic, spiritual reality of which Paul says the church is part. The wedding gift brought to this marriage is the Spirit who will help the church live in newness of life. Here, Paul begins the argument that he will develop more fully in the following chapter. Before that, however, Paul explores the relationship of the new covenant community to the Mosaic law, and how the Spirit has changed that relationship.

THE MESSIAH KING AND THE DISTRESS OF HIS BRIDE

WHAT SHALL WE say, then? Is the law sin? Certainly not! Indeed I would not have known what sin was except through the law. For I would not have known what coveting really was if the law had not said, "Do not covet." But sin, seizing the opportunity afforded by the commandment, produced in me every kind of covetous desire. For apart from law, sin is dead. Once I was alive apart from law; but when the commandment came, sin sprang to life and I died. I found that the very commandment that was intended to bring life actually brought death. For sin, seizing the opportunity afforded by the commandment, deceived me, and through the commandment put me to death. So then, the law is holy, and the commandment is holy, righteous and good. Did that which is good, then, become death to me? By no means! But in order that sin might be recognised as sin, it produced death in me through what was good, so that through the commandment sin might become utterly sinful. We know that the law is spiritual; but I am unspiritual, sold as a slave to sin. I do not understand what I do. For what I want to do I do not do, but what I hate I do. And if I do what I do not want to do, I agree that the law is good. As it is, it is no longer I myself who do it, but it is sin living in me. I know that nothing good lives in me, that is, in my sinful nature. For I have the desire to do what is good, but I cannot carry it out. For what I do is not the good I want to do; no, the evil I do not want to do—this I keep on doing. Now if I do what I do not want to do, it is no longer I who do it, but it is sin living in me that does it. So I find this law at work: When I want to do good, evil is right there with me. For in my inner being I delight in God's law; but I see another law at work in the members of my body, waging war against the law of my mind and making me a prisoner of the law of sin at work within my members.

What a wretched man I am! Who will rescue me from this body of death? Thanks be to God– through Jesus Christ our Lord! So then, I myself in my mind am a slave to God's law, but in the sinful nature a slave to the law of sin. (Rom 7:7–25)

7:7 What shall we say, then? Is the law sin? Certainly not! Indeed I would not have known what sin was except through the law. For I would not have known what coveting really was if the law had not said, "Do not covet." Paul introduces the problem he knows must be tackled: the relationship of the law to Sin.[67] Does the fact that the law brings knowledge of sin make it sinful? Paul could not tolerate such a thought, but knows that he must defend his position lest weaker brethren accept it. The length that he goes to in order to remove misunderstanding is a model for all Christian preachers and teachers. Not all are privileged to have the heritage that gives a relatively comprehensive worldview. New converts come into their faith in Christ with philosophical and cultural baggage that is often the opposite of Christian truth. It is not sufficient to instill Christian

---

67 The higher case has been deliberately used in order to identify Satan.

dogma, although there is a place for this. The individual needs time and help to bring his understanding in line with God's word. Without this care, the convert is likely to get into all sorts of dangerous positions as a result of incorporating pre-Christian thinking into their newfound faith. He or she can easily believe this hybrid thought system is biblical Christianity. The fact is, this unconscious syncretism is more dangerous than teachings that are overtly anti-Christian. The false beliefs which were carried over from the convert's pre-conversion days have been hidden within a genuine Christian profession and treated as biblical truth. In this chapter, Paul shows his sensitivity. He is aware the Jews will be offended by the claim that the law is sin, but is also concerned about the damage that could be done in the minds of the Gentile Christians if false teaching goes unchallenged.

Paul's first argument is that the law has made him (that is, humankind) know what Sin is.[68] There are two points that support this interpretation. First, he shows that the intention of the law is to prevent sin. The law says "you shall not covet," rather than "you can covet." For Paul (humankind) the law unlocked an understanding of sin. There is no suggestion the law itself stirs up desires for sin, that it serves Sin by giving man a liking for it which turns into an appetite. No, it is the very opposite. The law is in direct conflict with Sin. It presents the very standard that Sin opposes, i.e., God's standard. It is like light, and its introduction into darkness shows what was hidden. The problem is not the law; the problem is the "heart" or condition of man.

Second, when Paul says: "I would not have known what sin was except through the law," he uses γινώσκω (ginōskō) "known." This is normally reserved for experiential knowledge rather than academic, intellectual knowledge.[69] The law did not merely give a correct "academic" understanding of sin; it made man aware of its power and authority. The light of the law exposed the full horror of Sin's (Satan's) true nature.

7:8 But sin, seizing the opportunity afforded by the commandment, produced in me every kind of covetous desire. For apart from the law, sin is dead. Here we can see a shift from the concept of sin as breaking the law to Sin as being a person who entices or seduces. The one who entices or tempts is Satan.[70] So, we have the same pattern as we observed in chapter 6—Satan is spoken of as Sin. It is possible that in v. 7, where Paul says he would not have known Sin but for the commandment, he is not referring to sin as acts of violation of the law but to Sin as a person. Indeed, in biblical terminology, to "know" someone is a reference to the relationship of marriage. It is intensely personal and not limited to intellectual or experiential knowledge. "Knowing" in this sense is essentially covenantal (Amos 2:3 "known," as AV) and is the knowledge two people have of each

---

68. Schreiner, *Romans*, 371, notes that: "Paul's personal history is paradigmatic because it is the story of all people who live under the law."

69. γινώσκω "to come to an understanding as the result of ability to experience and learn, to come to understand, to perceive, to comprehend." Louw-Nida. (Gen 22:12; Ps 134:5; Matt 25:24; Luke 8:46)

70. For synonyms of Satan, see Martin, *Colossians*, 51; Dunn, *Romans*, 1:360; MacGregor "Principalities," 342; Sanday and Headlam, *Romans*. Ford, "Euphemism," 189ff., shows how euphemizims were used to avoid the use of an offensive or sacred original. Sin is personified in the OT and Paul's writings; see Wedderburn, "Structure," 342.

other as a result of having entered into an exclusive and permanent relationship.[71] While there could be some debate as to the meaning of "sin" in v. 7, there can be little doubt in v.8. Here Paul brings Sin into the open and speaks of it as the enemy that has gained a foothold in man's experience.

Paul states that Sin produced covetous desires. We can only speculate on the problem of evil. While the Bible gives us certain parameters for our thinking, it does not try to give us a neat philosophy which meets the probing demands of the philosopher. Not all truth is reduced to a rational formula. How can humanity, created in God's image, be capable of sin? This seems an impossible quandary to solve. All we do know is that man had to be capable of choosing sin if he was to have free will and be responsible before God. Indeed, this freedom to choose is part of man being made in God's image.

Paul says that apart from the law, Sin is dead. He has already said that the Christian community has died to Sin (Rom 6:6). In that passage, death terminated the covenant relationship that man had with Sin (Satan). If the same imagery is applied in v. 8—and we recognize that when Paul says "Sin is dead" he is speaking of Satan (as in chapter 6)—then he is saying that when Adam was in the garden, Sin had no power over him. This changed when he violated the command not to eat from the tree of the knowledge of good and evil, for through disobedience the covenant with God was terminated. At this point, man entered into a relationship with Sin (Satan), and the law was powerless to change it. Thus, in this covenantal/marriage paradigm, Sin had no power before man disobeyed, for God was humankind's husband and the law was his will. Once Adam disobeyed, however, and acted like an adulterer by rejecting God's love and embracing Satan (Sin), the law became powerless when it came to backing up Yahweh's covenantal claims. Through Adam's representative action, the covenant with God was severed and humankind became legally bound to another husband.

In writing: "apart from the law, sin is dead," the absence of the law needs to be emphasized. Before God gave the command in Eden, Satan had no opportunity to seduce Adam. But the giving of the command changed that, and Satan seized his opportunity to challenge man's love for, and obedience to, his Creator.

7:9 Once I was alive apart from law; but when the commandment came, sin sprang to life and I died. Paul, as Adam, remembers the start of the story, before the tree of the knowledge of good and evil had been mentioned. As soon as the command was given, temptation presented itself and lured him to disobey the command of God. When Paul says: "sin sprang to life," he is referring to Satan, who took the opportunity to seduce Adam with false promises. This brought an end to fellowship with God and established

71. Espy, "Robust," 161–88, suggests that "knowing" in Rom 7:7 has a possible hint of knowledge within a marriage relationship. Moo, "Law," 78, says that the law of sin is better understood as the authority or power exercised by sin. Allison, "Jesus," 57, acknowledges there are elements of covenantal nomism in Paul's theology (denied by Sanders, *Palestinian*, but supported by Hooker, "Nomism"). However, he says that it is not the key to his thought. This commentary assumes the opposite, but does not accept that covenantal nomism characterized the whole of Judaism (it was far too diverse to be put under any one description). See Holland, *Contours*, chapters 9–10. Eskola, "Predestination," 390–412, argues that the covenantal nomism defined by Sanders is the opposite of Paul's soteriology.

humanity's bondage to Sin. Satan assumed the place of the Creator and became man's master, and Adam died (i.e., "I died") to all that God had created him for.

7.10 I found that the very commandment that was intended to bring life actually brought death. At no point does Paul blame the law or God for sin, or for man's condition of being under condemnation. He knew the command was given for positive reasons, to bless and protect man. Adam's perversity in believing Satan's lie and in accusing God of malice was the problem. Because Paul is steeped in the OT Scriptures, he has a mindset that acts as a hedge, preventing him from questioning certain assumptions. Some of the truths that were foundational to the Jewish nation, and therefore to Paul, had to do with monotheism: God is the Creator, he is holy and just. For this reason, the Scriptures are not concerned with raising questions that twenty-first century debaters would rush to ask. The wisdom material of the Bible (Job, Proverbs, Psalms and Ecclesiastes) bears no relation to the notions taught in modern schools of philosophy. This is not an attempt to run away from "the truth," it simply reflects human existence as it is today. In loving, stable marriages, certain questions about a spouse's character or intent would never be asked. In a divorce court, by contrast, these questions are at the heart of accusations made by estranged partners. Because believers do not challenge God with the sort of questions non-believers pose does not make them foolish. It shows that they have a relationship with God from which unbelievers are excluded.

7:11 For sin, seizing the opportunity afforded by the commandment, deceived me, and through the commandment put me to death. Paul sees Sin as a predator, waiting to attack and kill. Satan saw his opportunity in Eden when the command was given, and realized that the law of God—given for man's blessing—could be used against Adam. By enticing him to disobey, he secured the decisive victory that he wanted. He turned man against God and put him into a position of guilt before the one who loved him. Adam fled from the pure love of God into the deceit and destruction of Satan. Satan had now, in effect, taken God's place, but without the truth, purity, holiness, and love that characterized the relationship he had destroyed. Adam's disobedience meant that Sin would reign over man "to death" (Rom 5:17; cf. Rom 7:2). Thus humankind, through its disobedience, died to the relationship with God for which it had been created. In so doing, it had come under the authority of Satan, who would remain in control unless an adequate Redeemer could come to humanity's rescue.

Sin (Satan) achieved the death (or termination) of the covenant, which man was created to enjoy, and put Adam to death in terms of his relationship with God.

7:12 So then, the law is holy, and the commandment is holy, righteous and good. This statement is at the heart of a crucial debate. Some think that Paul was speaking here of himself, either before or after his conversion. Those who think it could not be Paul's pre-conversion experience argue that the unregenerate man has no pleasure in the word of God. They believe the verse to speak of Paul's post-conversion experience, where he had been brought to love God and his word. The rest of the passage—the struggle with sin—is seen as Paul's Christian experience. The doctrine of sanctification then, is not about a naïve triumphalism but about continual conflict with the consequences of humanity's fallen condition. This view prevails amongst most Reformed scholars, and certainly matches the experience of countless believers.

The problem with this understanding is that, as we have previously noted, Judaism did not have this continual conflict with the law. The average Jew rejoiced in it as the gift of God and, far from seeing it as accusing him, he saw it as protecting him and maintaining the covenant Yahweh had so graciously established between himself and his people (e.g., Ps 19:7–14, 119:129–36). Paul testifies that he had this type of confidence in the law in his pre-Christian days (Phil 3:4–6). So the premise for such an interpretation is unreliable. Of course, this understanding envisages sin as indwelling but, as we have seen in chapter 6, Paul has a much bigger perspective of Sin. Also, the traditional Reformed understanding, like most others, begins from an individualistic interpretation of the passage. I have suggested the evidence is not compatible with this. Rather, it points to the passage being corporate. Scholars from a wide range of theological traditions are sharing this conclusion.

In making these comments about the passage, I am not denying that Paul struggled with sin or that individual believers continue to do so. I am saying that this existential reality should be interpreted from texts which deal with the issues of individual responsibility and conflict. The bigger picture that our text presents may not match the individual's experience in every detail, but you can be certain the individual's experience will fit into the properly understood corporate picture of Sin and salvation.

Even though many in Judaism had positive thoughts towards the law like the psalmist, clear evidence shows that not all Jews shared this understanding. Others saw the law as making demands that they could not meet (Acts 13:39). In other words, there was not just one Jewish viewpoint regarding the law. This warns us of the danger of pigeonholing Paul and then assuming we understand his writings. We must make every effort to listen to him carefully and reflect on the totality of the argument he is making.[72]

It is likely that, for most of his life, Paul rejoiced in being a son of the law. His letters do not reveal the point in his life when he became alert to the condemning role of the law.

7:13 Did that which is good, then, become death to me? By no means! But in order that sin might be recognised as sin, it produced death in me through what was good, so that through the commandment sin might become utterly sinful. Paul reflects on the law and how it cornered him with guilt. He sees Adam questioning the purpose of the commandment that had been given and which he had broken. He hears Adam reasoning that it was because the commandment had been given that the fruit of the tree of the knowledge of good and evil was so appealing! "It wasn't my fault," he argued. "It was the commandments. It had a negative effect by presenting me with temptation." In other words, Adam was innocent; the commandment was to blame.

---

72. For further discussion, see Holland, *Contours* chapters 9–10. See also Holland, *Paul, Israel's Law and God's Spirit*, (forthcoming).

Such reasoning might be possible for a twenty-first century secularist, but it would be blasphemy for any first century Jew who gloried in the covenant God had made with his people. While the text suggests that Adam is the one who is making the case, Paul identifies with his argument. The apostle and his ancestor struggle with the effect of the law in exciting sin. They realize the law's negative effect is in stark contrast with its intrinsic goodness which reflects the character of God. The law has to be good because it is God's law. Paul reasons that it does what it does precisely because it is holy and true. The law, therefore, excites sin because it confronts it and accuses it (Jas 1:23–25). It does not make man sinful; it exposes him to be so.

7:14 We know that the law is spiritual; but I am unspiritual, sold as a slave to sin. Israel's calling was to be the bride of Yahweh. He redeemed her from bondage (Isa 43:1; 44:22) and bought her to be his bride (Isa 54:5; 62:5). This went disastrously wrong when his bride became the possession of other gods. She repeated Adam's error and sold herself to Sin (Satan).

Paul employs the same imagery he used earlier in chapter 6 and the beginning of chapter 7. The language is not about slavery but about covenant and the dignity of obedience to the divine call. He says that humanity is found in a relationship for which they were not created. This is the consequence of rejecting the covenant and embracing the promise of Satan, who was a liar from the beginning. The adulterous relationship humanity has been seduced into is not the law's doing, but neither is it one the law can undo. In the case of civil law, the law is intended to uphold and protect the sanctity of marriage. However, when the law is rejected, it is powerless to change the consequences. Law can only identify guilt and demand appropriate action. So it is with the God's law. Israel understood the law to be the greatest gift given to humanity and evidence of God's commitment to his creation. But when a marriage fails, the law can do nothing to change the heart of fallen humankind. In the bigger picture, it cannot save. Instead, it condemns and leaves people unchanged, in bondage to Sin.

The language of being bought/sold, which is often found in Paul's writings, is normally seen to reflect his use of slave imagery. It is a natural extension of the analogy of being a *doulos,* a "slave" of Christ. I have questioned this understanding of *doulos,*[73] pointing out that the context, not the etymology, must decide the meaning Paul intended. I have argued that its proper setting is the "servant of the Lord" imagery of the OT. In the OT context, Israel was called to be the servant of the Lord, and her ultimate goal was to be Yahweh's bride. This bride-purchase context—so common in the ancient Near East—is the setting for Paul's statement about being "bought with a price" (1 Cor 6:20). Confusion with the imagery of Hellenistic slavery has masked the much richer OT perspective which depicts God redeeming his people so they could become his bride.[74]

---

73. See Holland, *Contours,* 69–82.

74. For bride-purchase in the ancient world, see Balsdon, *Women,* 179–80. Kosmala, "Husband," 16, points out the close connection between circumcision and marriage, based on Exod 4:22 and ancient marriage rites. We have already had Paul arguing the only circumcision that matters is that of the heart (Rom 2). In Col 2:10, there is reference to the circumcision of Christ, which took place in his death, while Eph 5:24ff. associates marital imagery with the death (that is, the circumcision [Col 2:10]) of Christ. This

(If there is any doubt this is the setting in the passage we are considering, readers are encouraged to consult the opening verse of the chapter once again.) So, when Paul says: "but I am unspiritual, sold as a slave to sin," he is speaking of the condition of humankind which is in bondage to Sin through Adam. Instead of humanity being the bride of Yahweh, it is the bride of Sin (Satan).

It is natural to think that the slave setting is upheld by the phrase: "sold as a slave to sin." However, as just explained, the passage is not drawing on the slave-market analogy but bride-purchase imagery, the wife in Ancient Near-East culture relating to her husband as her lord.[75]

7:15 I do not understand what I do. For what I want to do I do not do, but what I hate I do. People are no longer in control of their lives. It is not that they sin within the limits of comfort—they are dragged down into shame and disgrace, identifying themselves as fallen creatures. They struggle to live according to their conscience, but find that their conscience accuses them. This was not only the experience of Adam, but of Paul; and it is the experience of all who have begun to realize that they are not citizens of the kingdom of God. The promises that once gave an assurance of freedom, meaning and fulfillment are discovered to be empty lies. The one who offered deity delivers nothing other than despair and hopelessness. The realization that we are powerless to change our condition is the first step towards receiving the grace of God.

7:16 And if I do what I do not want to do, I agree that the law is good. This statement is the pivotal point of the chapter. Some scholars say Romans 7 is Paul's defense of the law. In this statement, he has come to the point in his argument where he says the law is not at fault. This is demonstrated in his attempts to keep the law because he knows it to be right. Again, the drama can be observed at several levels, one being Adam's discovery that the law he had rejected was not meant to limit him, as Satan had claimed, but to protect his liberty. Having rejected the law and tasted Satan's false brand of "freedom," Adam/Paul longs to keep the law in the way God intended. The experience is true for Adam, Israel, Paul and all human beings.[76]

7:17 As it is, it is no longer I myself who do it, but it is sin living in me. Whether Adam, Israel or Paul, this is the reality of every man's experience. There is something that overpowers humanity in its corporate, as well as individual, existence. It is the reality of Sin. We have already seen that Paul's understanding of "the body of Sin" is mainly

---

is a powerful image, and was employed by the OT writers in connection with the exodus. See Holland, *Contours*, chap. 8. The same imagery is found in the NT to describe the purpose of Christ's death, i.e., the purchasing of a people to be his bride and the preparation for the union (so, Eph 5:25ff.; Rev 19:7–9). See Holland, *Contours*, chapter 5.

75. "like Sarah, who obeyed Abraham and called him her master. You are her daughters if you do what is right and do not give way to fear" (1 Pet 3:6).

76. In this sense, Aletti, "Rom 7.7–25," 358–76, when after noting that all the rhetorical techniques support the non-Christian identity of the ἐγώ "I" in Rom 7:7–25 is correct. Aletti claims that the background of the ἐγώ must be Jewish and Greek, and stresses the relevance of such a double background to the understanding of the anthropology of the pericope.

corporate. As a part of the body of Sin, every person in Adam is under Sin's control. No matter how strenuous and urgent the struggle to be free, humankind is under the power of Satan and helpless to change its condition.

Questions are often raised about the expression: "sin living in me." In what way does sin live in Paul if the text is corporate? This text is the basis for the doctrine of sin which holds that it is "biologically inherited." I have argued this is a Hellenistic intrusion into Paul's Hebraic mindset and ought to have no place in biblical thinking. The reason for so strongly denying this view is that it is essentially dualistic and, therefore, pagan. The NT reflects the OT in asserting the goodness of God's creation, even though it is seriously weakened and marred by the coming of Sin into the world. The entrance of Sin has bound man into a fallen, federal (corporate) existence. This is the perspective of the NT doctrine of sin—not some dualistic intrusion from the patristic period.

The expression: "sin living in me," does not have the Hellenistic, dualistic connotations once the argument is read at the corporate level. The statement is about Adam seeing his offspring controlled by Sin (Satan) in the most terrible way. In other words, the text should be read with the OT Hebraic mindset. In those writings, the one and the many merge into an almost indistinguishable relationship with the head or king figure. Again, this is seen especially in the Servant Songs and some of the psalms (Isa 42:1–9; 50:4–10; 52:13—53:12; Ps 69; 89; 108. Also, see how the Son of Man is both Israel and Israel's king in Dan 7:22).

7:18 I know that nothing good lives in me, that is, in my sinful nature. For I have the desire to do what is good, but I cannot carry it out. The statement speaks of the utter despair when realizing that all of the greatest achievements of people have been contaminated by the corruption of Sin. There is no part of their experience—culture, education, music, art, politics, commerce, religion, psychology, ethics, etc.—that has not been defiled, corrupted, and flawed. This condition in Adam debases him, making him want what will never truly satisfy. He longs for the restoration of paradise but rejects the affiliation that made it possible—the relationship of the creature and his Creator whom he loves and obeys.

Translating σάρξ (sarx) "flesh" as "sinful nature" leads the reader in the direction of an inherited human nature rather than to a federal understanding. Of course, the term can equally be translated "fallen condition," referring to the frailty of humankind in Adam and without God. This legitimate translation avoids the Greek dualism suggested by "sinful nature."[77]

7:19 For what I do is not the good I want to do; no, the evil I do not want to do—this I keep on doing. Satan's promise was that Adam would be as God, but it has become clear he became a stooge of the one who fooled him. He is now a slave of Sin, with no claims to the blessings of his Creator, whom he abandoned.

7:20 Now if I do what I do not want to do, it is no longer I who do it, but it is sin living in me that does it. Paul has already reasoned that, because he does not agree with

---

77. See the discussion on the meaning of this term on pages 202–11.

what he himself does, he agrees with the law instead, acknowledging that it is good (Rom 7:16). Now he argues about mankind's condition. He establishes there is something more evil than people—something that controls them that they cannot master. This does not take away his responsibility, but it does acknowledge an evil force that is greater than himself. Whereas Paul's struggle to keep the law acknowledged its intrinsic goodness, his struggle with Sin demonstrates Sin's intrinsic evil. Paul is arguing for more than the weakness of humankind; he argues for the reality of evil, which is personified in Satan. It has deceived humanity, bringing it into a condition from which it cannot escape.[78]

7:21 So I find this law at work: When I want to do good, evil is right there with me. In referring to the law, Paul is not concerned with a particular commandment but with a principle or authority. He has already spoken of the woman who was under the law of her husband. This is the law of Satan, i.e., of Sin and Death, from which man cannot escape. Because it is legally binding, it effectively renders God helpless when it comes to rescuing humankind—their condition is the consequence of the relationship Adam willingly accepted. In this way, the offspring of Adam is like the helpless woman who is married to an abusive husband. There is no one to call upon who can legally interfere because her relationship with her husband is protected by the law! Of course, the laws of many nations now give women rights with which they can appeal, but such provisions are very late in terms of human history and do not invalidate the argument Paul is making.

The only legitimate termination of marriage is death. This is not saying Paul was immune to the realities of marriage (as the discussion in 1 Cor 7:12ff. shows all too clearly). However, in absolute terms, there is no divorce procedure to which man can appeal in order to gain freedom from the law of Satan. Although there were grounds for divorce in the OT, it was only the husband (Satan!) who could free the wife by issuing the divorce certificate (Deut 24). The only sure way out of marriage for the wife was death—a situation that pertains to the Jewish community to this day.

7:22 For in my inner being I delight in God's law. Despite the sinfulness of the descendents, the honor and perfection of God's law is still recognized. Paul has a tortuous fascination with that which condemns. It ought to comfort him, but it terrifies him. Within his heart, there is a cry for the security the law once gave in protecting the relationship with God for which he had been created. But now, while Paul delights in acknowledging its perfection, at the same time, he experiences dread in anticipating its condemnation.

The transition from chapter 7 to chapter 8 is unnatural if read on an individualistic level. Some claim the closing verses in this chapter and the opening of chapter 8 have been dislocated. This suggestion is attractive when it is realized that removing 7:23—8:1 (while keeping Rom 7:25a in place) leaves a text that reads naturally. Some commentators seek to resolve the difficulty by proposing that the section just mentioned was originally

---

78. Wright, *Romans*, 720, says: "Why does he emphasise this point so strongly? Have traditional readings missed something within the dense jungle of chapter 7?" In this statement, the failure of the individualistic reading of the text is illustrated.

in a different order. It is suggested the statement: "I myself in my mind am a slave to God's law, but in the sinful nature a slave to the law of sin" should follow v. 23 and lead into v. 24. The thanksgiving of v. 25a is placed after these verses, followed by Rom 8:2 and then Rom 8:1. Using this suggested order, the passage would read:

> v. 23 but I see another law at work in the members of my body, waging war against the law of my mind and making me a prisoner of the law of sin at work within my members.

> v.25b So then, I myself in my mind am a slave to God's law, but in the sinful nature a slave to the law of sin.

> v. 24 What a wretched man I am! Who will rescue me from this body of death?

> v. 25a Thanks be to God—through Jesus Christ our Lord!

> 8:2 For through Christ Jesus the law of the Spirit of life set me free from the law of sin and death.

> 8:1 Therefore, there is now no condemnation for those who are in Christ Jesus.

While this may appear to be an attractive explanation to the problem, relocating texts creates another obstacle that must be overcome. There is no textual evidence to support this suggested order; it is entirely based on speculation. A lack of textual support from the oldest manuscripts also applies to another suggestion that scholars have made. They say that Rom 7:25b and Rom 8:1 are insertions by copyists.

Others have argued that the problem is not as difficult as it first appears and that the structure of the text should be retained. In psalms, we find similar abrupt transitions. For example, in Ps 22:22–23 and Ps 69:30–31, members of the congregation interrupt the laments by declaring their testimonies to God's saving grace. It is argued that the passage in chapter 7 could have been modeled on this structure. The lament in Rom 7:7–24, with its sudden expression of gratitude in v. 25a, conforms to the pattern seen in these psalms and, like them, the letter was heard by an assembled congregation. In other words, both the format and the liturgical setting of the chapter match these representative psalms exactly.

Another reason for accepting the given structure of the text is that, in Jewish and Hellenistic teaching, it was common to begin, or summarise, lectures with maxims that could easily be remembered. Such a practice had the benefit of emphasizing the point of the teaching. Two such maxims exist in Rom 7:25b and Rom 8:1. If this observation is correct, Paul summarizes what he has expounded and what he intends to expound, and he does it in a way that parallels his thought in Rom 7:5–6.

But the above suggestions fail to notice one critical fact. They all embrace the passage as Paul's personal testimony, whereas many scholars have been persuaded that the perspective is corporate. This is an extremely important argument to consider. In my opinion, the corporate view makes better sense of the earlier part of the passage and treats the text of the conclusion of the chapter with respect. The individual perspective has had to ignore and rewrite the translated text in order to make some sense of the passage.

7:23 But I see another law at work in the members of my body, waging war against the law of my mind and making me a prisoner of the law of sin—at work within my members. The other law Paul writes about functions in a different way. It is also the Law of Moses that was given to rule the life of Israel. It was taught to every generation of Jews from infancy and it was intended to be a law that protected from the people of God from Satan, but it became a law that bound man to him. The essence of this law had been planted in the heart of the human family and so operated as a safeguard to protect man from the father of lies. This law is holy and good, but now, because of the fall, it condemns! Its function in condemning makes it into "another law" that wars against the fallen will of man. In a similar way, the civil law protects but also condemns.

It is easy to read the statement: "the members of my body," as a reference to Paul's physical body if an individualistic perspective for interpreting the passage is adopted and, therefore, to see his problem as sensual. Apart from the fact that the letter is addressed to a church and heard in a corporate setting, there is another difficulty with reading this verse individualistically—the illustration of marriage that began the chapter. We have noted this marriage imagery is not used in Scripture to speak of the individual's relationship with God but the corporate relationship of the covenant community with him. I have sought to demonstrate there are statements in the letter which only make sense in a corporate context (e.g., Rom 2:17–24; 6:1–7; 7:1–5) and we shall see that this corporate perspective functions well in the remainder of the letter.[79]

So, what does Paul mean by: "the members of my body"? If I am right to interpret the "body of [S]sin" (Rom 6:6) as corporate and the exhortation not to yield members to unrighteousness as an appeal to the church to exercise discipline, then the expression "members of my body" focuses on the experience of Adam and his offspring. Adam, represented by Paul, sees his progeny being taken over by Sin, with murder, deceit, sexual impurity, etc. (Rom 1:16–31) coming to fruition among them. Some see this passage in chapter 1 to be describing the human disintegration following the fall of Man in Adam. The statement in chapter 7 is about human irrationality—excusing the inexcusable and defending the indefensible in the face of his Creator's charge.

7:24 What a wretched man I am! Who will rescue me from this body of death? Paul cries out the lament of death. He sees the condition of humanity as hopeless and bound up with that condition is its own eternal fate. However, the cry is not for deliverance from his earthly body. It is much more than this. The argument continues to address the corporate aspects of Sin. "This body of death" is nothing less than the body of Sin—the bride of Satan. So Paul's cry is: "who will deliver me from the kingdom of darkness?"

79. Garlington, "Creation," 197–235, places this closing passage into the framework of chapters 5–8. It deals with the believer as an inhabitant of the new creation, i.e., the realm of Christ and the church, not in Israel and the Torah. Paul's hatred of sin brings forth the cry: "Wretched man that I am!" This is not an admission of defeat but of frustration in falling short of new-creation ideals.

The rule of Satan has determined the developing argument since Rom 5:12 when the description of the human race in Adam was introduced. This is what Paul discovered through his encounter with Christ. His privileges as a Jew had counted for nothing, for he, like his fellow Jews, had been as much part of the kingdom of darkness as the Gentiles had been.

7:25 Thanks be to God through Jesus Christ our Lord! So then, I myself in my mind am a slave to God's law, but in the sinful nature a slave to the law of sin. Deliverance can come through none other than God. He has done something God-like to achieve the redemption of his creation by making a way "through Jesus Christ." We shall soon see that this way has been made by God sending his Son as a sin offering. This is critical as the power of Sin and the guilt of sins needs to be dealt with before there can be peace with God. Here, in his triumphant proclamation, Paul anticipates the next stage of his argument when he will continue to explain the process and significance of release from Satan's power and the provision that God has made for his people's subsequent pilgrimage.[80]

CONCLUSION OF ROMANS 7

The theme of redemption and pilgrimage dealt with in chapter six proceeds to the glorious event that awaited Israel—her marriage. At Sinai, she was to become the bride of Yahweh.[81] This is the theme that Paul develops in this section of his letter. He opens the chapter with an illustration of how a woman is bound by the law of her husband. This law cannot recognize any relationship that overrides the existing one. The only way this can happen is when the husband dies, releasing the woman from his authority and the law of God that bestowed it on him.

---

80. Stendahl, "Introspective," 205, has shown the text has not been treated with the respect that it deserves. The description is not about Paul's personal experience of salvation–and not even man's–but the salvation of the whole cosmos. Stendahl makes the following comment on the trend of Western commentators to individualise the teaching of Paul: "This Western interpretation reaches its climax when it appears that even, or especially, the will of man is the centre of depravation. And yet, in Rom 7, Paul had said of that will: 'This will (to do what is good) is there' (v. 18). What we have called the Western interpretation has left its mark even in the field of textual reconstruction of this chapter in Romans. In Moffat's translation of the NT, the climax of the whole argument about the Law (v. 25b, see above) is placed before the words 'wretched man that I am . . .' Such a rearrangement—without textual basis—wants to make this exclamation the dramatic climax of the whole chapter, clarifying for the reader that Paul answers the problem of human existence. But, by such arrangements, the structure of Paul's argument has been destroyed." Stendahl went on to say that if Paul had meant the individual perspective of Western exegesis, he would have spoken of the "body of sin" rather than "body of this death." This statement exposes the limited progress of Stendhal's understanding, for the term "the body of sin" is corporate, in keeping with the corporate focus of the letter. For a critical assessment of Stendahl's position, see Espy, "Robust," 161–88. Donaldson, "Curse," 104, says: "For Paul, all human existence apart from Christ, Jewish or Gentile is characterised by bondage to the elemental spirits of the universe." For a discussion on the corporate meaning of the "body of sin," see Holland, *Contours*, chapter 5.

81. In rabbinical understanding, the Passover was the marriage of Yahweh to Israel, as was the covenant-making ceremony at Sinai.

The illustration indicates the problem of bringing the redeemed community into this marriage relationship with her Redeemer. She had been the "property," i.e., the bride of Sin (Satan). Only death can end this relationship so that a new one with God can be established.

Following the principle of chapter 5, where the sin of Adam—humanity's representative head—brought death to his offspring through his disobedience, Paul now says that the sinless Christ—his people's representative head—has brought life to his people through his obedience. His death has released them from the law of Sin and Death. The divine marriage can, at last, take place because the church has become the bride of Christ. Just as in the book of Ruth, the redeemer has become the bridegroom. However, this argument is not guided by that story but the one proclaimed by Isaiah—Israel's Redeemer becomes her husband.

Paul then explores the role of the law in salvation history. He shows that the law, which was given at Sinai and was to be recognized to be Yahweh's marriage gift, is not sinful but is spiritual, true and good. As the antitype the church has now reached the parallel Sinai event. Here, Israel was made Yahweh's bride and was given the law. In the Christian counterpart, Paul must explain how the church can become the bride of a holy Savior and how the law will function in this new divine relationship. The argument is based on the parallel experiences of the church and Israel, Israel being the type and the church's experience being the anti-type.

EXCURSUS G: ISAIAH AND THE NEW EXODUS

The perspective that has been advanced in these pages echoes the prophet Isaiah's account of Israel's experience.[82] He says:

> LORD, our God, other lords besides you have ruled over us, but your name alone do we honor. They are now dead, they live no more; those departed spirits do not rise. You punished them and brought them to ruin; you wiped out all memory of them. You have enlarged the nation, O LORD; you have enlarged the nation. You have gained glory for yourself; you have extended all the borders of the land. LORD, they came to you in their distress; when you disciplined them, they could barely whisper a prayer. As a woman with child and about to give birth writhes and cries out in her pain, so were we in your presence, O LORD. We were with child, we writhed in pain, but we gave birth to wind. We have not brought salvation to the earth; we have not given birth to people of the world. But your dead will live; their bodies will rise. You who dwell in the dust, wake up and shout for joy. Your dew is like the dew of the morning; the earth will give birth to her dead. (Isa 26:13–19)

Reflecting on how other lords had ruled over them, Isaiah goes on to say:

82. Note Hays, "Believed," 47, "The explicit citations are merely the tip of the iceberg; they point to a larger mass just under the surface, Paul's comprehensive construal of Isaiah as a coherent witness to the gospel. I believe that Paul had read and pondered the scrolls of Isaiah as a whole, over the years of his apostolic ministry, and developed a sustained reading of it as God's revelation of the 'mystery that was kept secret for long ages but is now disclosed, and through the prophetic writings is made known to all the Gentiles, according to the command of the eternal God, to bring about the obedience of faith' (Romans 16:25–26)."

> So this is what the Sovereign LORD says: "See, I lay a stone in Zion, a tested stone, a precious cornerstone for a sure foundation; the one who trusts will never be dismayed. I will make justice the measuring line and righteousness the plumb-line; hail will sweep away your refuge, the lie, and water will overflow your hiding-place. Your covenant with death will be annulled; your agreement with the grave will not stand. When the overwhelming scourge sweeps by, you will be beaten down by it. (Isa 28:16–18)

The reference to the covenant with death is probably a reference to their alliance with the Egyptians in which they would have been required to accept the lordship of Môt, the god of death. They would have entered into a relationship with Môt rather than pursuing the God of their fathers and Môt would have become their new master and husband.

Israel was to be delivered from this relationship by the direct intervention of Yahweh himself. The salvation or deliverance from this unholy alliance with Egypt would repeat the process and pattern of the original exodus under Moses:

> Awake, awake, O Zion, clothe yourself with strength. Put on your garments of splendor, O Jerusalem, the holy city. The uncircumcised and defiled will not enter you again. Shake off your dust; rise up, sit enthroned, O Jerusalem. Free yourself from the chains on your neck, O captive Daughter of Zion. For this is what the LORD says: "You were sold for nothing, and without money you will be redeemed." For this is what the Sovereign LORD says: "At first my people went down to Egypt to live; lately, Assyria has oppressed them. "And now what do I have here?" declares the LORD. "For my people have been taken away for nothing, and those who rule them mock," declares the LORD. "And all day long my name is constantly blasphemed. Therefore my people will know my name; therefore in that day they will know that it is I who foretold it. Yes, it is I." How beautiful on the mountains are the feet of those who bring good news, who proclaim peace, who bring good tidings, who proclaim salvation, who say to Zion, "Your God reigns!" Listen! Your watchmen lift up their voices; together they shout for joy. When the LORD returns to Zion, they will see it with their own eyes. Burst into songs of joy together, you ruins of Jerusalem, for the LORD has comforted his people, he has redeemed Jerusalem. The LORD will lay bare his holy arm in the sight of all the nations, and all the ends of the earth will see the salvation of our God. Depart, depart, go out from there! Touch no unclean thing! Come out from it and be pure, you who carry the vessels of the LORD. But you will not leave in haste or go in flight; for the LORD will go before you, the God of Israel will be your rear guard. (Isa 52:1–13)

The deliverance would be through the sufferings of the Servant of the Lord:

> Yet it was the LORD's will to crush him and cause him to suffer, and though the LORD makes his life a guilt offering, he will see his offspring and prolong his days, and the will of the LORD will prosper in his hand. After the suffering of his soul, he will see the light of life and be satisfied; by his knowledge my righteous servant will justify many, and he will bear their iniquities. Therefore I will give him a portion among the great, and he will divide the spoils with the strong, because he poured out his life unto death, and was numbered with the transgressors. For he bore the sin of many, and made intercession for the transgressors. (Isa 53:10–12)

It would be the Spirit of the Lord who would bring the salvation of the Servant to fruition:

> "The Redeemer will come to Zion, to those in Jacob who repent of their sins," declares the LORD. "As for me, this is my covenant with them," says the LORD. "My Spirit, who is on you, and my words that I have put in your mouth will not depart from your mouth, or from the mouths of your children, or from the mouths of their descendants from this time on and forever," says the LORD. (Isa 59:20–21)

The outcome of this salvation would be the restoration of Israel to her previous calling to be the bride of Yahweh:

> I delight greatly in the LORD; my soul rejoices in my God. For he has clothed me with garments of salvation and arrayed me in a robe of righteousness, as a bridegroom adorns his head like a priest, and as a bride adorns herself with her jewels. For as the soil makes the young plant come up and a garden causes seeds to grow, so the Sovereign LORD will make righteousness and praise spring up before all nations. (Isa 61:10–11)

There are other literary/theological parallels between the first seven chapters of Romans and OT themes which are embedded in Paul's argument. In both the Egyptian exodus and the Babylonian exodus, the Jews were exhorted to repent and put their faith in the provision that Yahweh was about to make. In the Passover account, the people were urged to kill the Passover sacrifice and apply the blood of the lambs to their doorposts and lintels. They were instructed to remain indoors throughout the night (Exod 12:19–22). The Jews had to accept that they were in the same danger as the Egyptians, and that the Lord would slay their firstborn if they did not obey. A similar exhortation to repent sounded from the prophets when they urged the nation to turn from her sins and seek the Lord, who would save her from the coming judgment (Hos 7:1–2; 14.1–3; Isa 1:18–20).

With these warnings came statements concerning the sacrifice for dealing with the peoples' sin. In the first Passover, there was a propitiatory element, i.e., a turning of God's wrath away from the Jewish homes. In the Babylonian exodus, atonement would be made by the Servant, who would die for the sins of the people (Isaiah 53).

Following the act of atonement is the pilgrimage out of bondage. In the case of the Egyptian exodus, it was accomplished by the mighty act of God at the Red Sea, where Israel was delivered from Pharaoh's control when his armies were wiped out.

Having been delivered from Egypt, the Jews were led by Moses to Mount Sinai where the law was given. The eighth century prophets developed this picture in more detail by arguing the event was, in fact, the marriage of Israel to Yahweh (Ezek 16:1–14; Hos 2:14–20). The same picture is used for the deliverance from Babylon. Israel is to return to Zion, where there will be the remarriage of Yahweh to his people.

Within these promises of a new exodus from Babylon is the declaration that Yahweh would create a new covenant. This new covenant will not be like the Sinai covenant for it would be about circumcising the hearts of the people, not their bodies. This is a theme that Paul stresses in the opening chapters of Romans. Moreover, the new covenant is unlike the Sinai covenant in another remarkable way. In this covenant, the Jews will have no priority over the nations. The Gentiles will be accepted without embracing Judaism. This is the theme that Paul emphasizes, and is a truth he will not compromise. The heart of the Gospel is that nothing can be added to what Christ has done—no matter the pedigree or religious initiation ceremony.

This is the pattern we find in the early chapters of Romans. In Rom 1:18ff. Paul describes the condition of humankind as a result of Adam's sin. He warns the Jews they are not exempt because they are also under the law's condemnation. He directs them to the Paschal provision that God has made for his people (Rom 3:21–27), and he emphasizes that all have sinned (Rom 3:23); Jew and Gentile alike are under this same condemnation.

In Rom 5:1–8, Paul uses pilgrimage imagery to explain the consequence of the Son's death (Rom 5:8). In the Egyptian exodus, the pilgrimage was part of the deliverance at the Red Sea. This is where the Hebrews were baptized into Moses and died to Pharaoh (Sin). So, in his letter to the church in Rome, Paul tells the believers about the occasion when they died to Sin (Satan) (Rom 6:1)—it was when they were included in Christ's death by the Spirit's baptism. It was then, in Christ's exodus (Luke 9:31 τὴν ἔξοδον αὐτοῦ (tēn exodon autou) "his exodus"), that they died to Sin (Satan).

Through this series of events—repentance, Passover, pilgrimage, and deliverance—the nation is brought to the climax of the salvation event which is its marriage to Yahweh.

And *this* is the culmination of the opening chapters of Romans. The church becomes Christ's bride (actually, his betrothed; for the marriage will only be consummated at the coming of her Savior) and the possession of the one who died to release her from the covenant she had been in through Adam. She has died to Sin (Satan) and has been taken by Christ who acts as her Redeemer. This parallels what Yahweh did in the Egyptian and Babylonian exoduses when he acted as Israel's Redeemer. Just as Israel was to continue her journey from Sinai as Yahweh's bride (which, of course, did not happen because of her unfaithfulness), so the Christian community continues on her pilgrimage (Rom 8:31ff.) as Christ's betrothed. The marriage is not yet consummated, but this will happen at her Savior's glorious appearing.

The literary/theological parallels are too exact to be coincidental, especially when seen in the light of the way the exodus events shape the thinking of the Apostle. Paul follows the pattern of salvation history as found in the pages of the OT scriptures which, as he has said earlier, are the basis of the gospel of Christ (Rom 1:2).

THE MESSIAH KING AND HIS BRIDAL GIFT

THEREFORE, THERE IS now no condemnation for those who are in Christ Jesus, because through Christ Jesus the law of the Spirit of life set me free from the law of sin and death. For what the law was powerless to do in that it was weakened by the sinful nature, God did by sending his own Son in the likeness of sinful man to be a sin offering. And so he condemned sin in sinful man, in order that the righteous requirements of the law might be fully met in us, who do not live according to the sinful nature but according to the Spirit.

Those who live according to the sinful nature have their minds set on what that nature desires; but those who live in accordance with the Spirit have their minds set on what the Spirit desires.

The mind of sinful man is death, but the mind controlled by the Spirit is life and peace; the sinful mind is hostile to God. It does not submit to God's law, nor can it do so. Those controlled by the sinful nature cannot please God.

You, however, are controlled not by the sinful nature but by the Spirit, if the Spirit of God lives in you. And if anyone does not have the Spirit of Christ, he does not belong to Christ. But if Christ is in you, your body is dead because of sin, yet your spirit is alive because of righteousness. And if the Spirit of him who raised Jesus from the dead is living in you, he who raised Christ from the dead will also give life to your mortal bodies through his Spirit, who lives in you.

Therefore, brothers, we have an obligation—but it is not to the sinful nature, to live according to it. For if you live according to the sinful nature, you will die; but if by the Spirit you put to death the misdeeds of the body, you will live, because those who are led by the Spirit of God are sons of God. For you did not receive a spirit that makes you a slave again to fear, but you received the Spirit of sonship. And by him we cry, "*Abba,* Father." The Spirit himself testifies with our spirit that we are God's children. Now if we are children, then we are heirs—heirs of God and co-heirs with Christ, if indeed we share in his sufferings in order that we may also share in his glory.

I consider that our present sufferings are not worth comparing with the glory that will be revealed in us. The creation waits in eager expectation for the sons of God to be revealed. For the creation was subjected to frustration, not by its own choice, but by the will of the one who subjected it, in hope that the creation itself will be liberated from its bondage to decay and brought into the glorious freedom of the children of God. We know that the whole creation has been groaning as in the pains of childbirth right up to the present time.

Not only so, but we ourselves, who have the firstfruits of the Spirit, groan inwardly as we wait eagerly for our adoption as sons, the redemption of our bodies. For in this hope we were saved. But hope that is seen is no hope at all. Who hopes for what he already has? But if we hope for what we do not yet have, we wait for it patiently. In the same way, the Spirit helps us in our weakness. We do not know what we ought to pray for, but the

Spirit himself intercedes for us with groans that words cannot express. And he who searches our hearts knows the mind of the Spirit, because the Spirit intercedes for the saints in accordance with God's will.

And we know that in all things God works for the good of those who love him, who have been called according to his purpose. For those God foreknew he also predestined to be conformed to the likeness of his Son, that he might be the firstborn among many brothers. And those he predestined, he also called; those he called, he also justified; those he justified, he also glorified. What, then, shall we say in response to this? If God is for us, who can be against us? He who did not spare his own Son, but gave him up for us all—how will he not also, along with him, graciously give us all things?

Who will bring any charge against those whom God has chosen? It is God who justifies. Who is he that condemns? Christ Jesus, who died—more than that, who was raised to life—is at the right hand of God and is also interceding for us. Who shall separate us from the love of Christ? Shall trouble or hardship or persecution or famine or nakedness or danger or sword? As it is written: "For your sake we face death all day long; we are considered as sheep to be slaughtered."

No, in all these things we are more than conquerors through him who loved us.

For I am convinced that neither death nor life, neither angels nor demons, neither the present nor the future, nor any powers, neither height nor depth, nor anything else in all creation, will be able to separate us from the love of God that is in Christ Jesus our Lord. (Rom 8:1–16)

INTRODUCTION

The relief of acquittal marks the opening of the eighth chapter. Paul states that the longed-for salvation has been realized, not on the grounds of man's actions but God's. This acquittal is not according to the flesh, but according to the Spirit (Rom 8:5–7). It is not through keeping the law but because of a perfect sacrifice for sin (Rom 8:3). This statement picks up all the cultic statements made earlier in the letter (see commentary on Rom 1:4; 3:25ff.; 4:25; 5:5–11; 6:1–4), and emphasizes that the sacrifice was the Son of God, freely given by the Father. It is Christ's death that liberates and brings the children of God out of bondage. By entering the realm of Sin's domain, the Son challenged Sin at the point where Satan's power was strongest. Subjecting himself to the full force of Sin's attack, Jesus (in the realm of human likeness and weakness, but without sin) entered into conflict to deliver his own (Rom 8:3).[1] This fulfilled the righteous requirements of the law. Indeed, it was to this event that the law and the prophets had pointed (Rom 1:2; 3:21). Although the exodus under Moses was a national, geographical, and political deliverance, it failed to remove Israel from her spiritual bondage because she was still in Adam and under the same condemnation as the Gentiles. However, as a type (1 Cor 10:1–6), the exodus under Moses pointed to the greater exodus, which Christ would bring about. When Paul speaks of living "according the flesh" (Rom 8:5 [sinful nature NIV]), it could mean living in flagrant opposition to the law or in such a way as to meet the law's demands in an attempt to achieve righteousness. Such righteousness rejects the divinely appointed way (Rom 10:1–4).

---

1. As argued in Heb 2:5–18.

The unbelieving Jew put his confidence in Moses and the sacrifices of the temple, not in God (who had set the temple sacrifices aside) or in the sacrifice of his Son. He was the Christ, the Passover sacrifice, who had wrought salvation from Sin and Death. Paul insists there can be no neutral zone in man's relationship with God (Rom 8:6), for to reject his purposes is to be at enmity with him. This does not necessarily mean a deliberate rejection of the law's requirements but of failing to grasp, and then live up to, its intent. This is where Paul and his fellow countrymen had stumbled so often. Rather than being guided by the law, they had made adhering to it their goal. It had become the barrier to doing the will of God, for they made its keeping—which they gloried in—he grounds for hope that they would participate in the eschatological salvation. The law had become an idol—their object of worship.

The difference between a man under law and one under grace was the possession of the Spirit. It was this gift that formed part of the promises to the community in exile (Isa 44:3; 59:21; 61:1–3; Ezek 36:24–28). The Jews were assured that because they could not achieve what Yahweh had purposed for them in their own strength, they would be empowered by the Spirit. He would not only guide, but sustain and comfort them in their pilgrimage, finally establishing them in their inheritance. To walk in the Spirit was to walk by faith and to receive the righteousness to which the law pointed. As with Abraham, it meant being a son of God through faith, leaving the natural dwelling place, and making a journey by faith to the promised land. It meant keeping the Passover as Moses had done, but acknowledging that Christ, the true Passover, was slain (Rom 3:21–26; 1 Cor 5:7). It meant abandoning all privilege and respectability as David had, and receiving the promise of mercy and forgiveness (Heb 11:24–29).

To enter this righteousness was to enter into the eschatological community. While the church continues to live under the physical sentence of death, awaiting its final redemption, the gift of the Spirit (Rom 8:11) guarantees what was to come. His presence not only transforms the believers' lifestyles in the present (Rom 8:13), but will bring about a metamorphosis of the church's physical existence in the resurrection (Rom 8:16–17).

Paul's theme of sonship has long been regarded as being modelled on Roman adoption law. However, this has been questioned because his reference to the gift of the Spirit, with Messianic associations of sonship, suggests that he continues to draw from the concepts of OT redemptive history. The Messiah was the figure that Yahweh would raise up to accomplish his redemptive purposes for his people, and the giving of the Spirit was one of the essential provisions for accomplishing this task. The king, who was endowed with the Spirit, was the supreme model of the long-awaited Messiah, the Son of God. It is this Messianic imagery that Paul draws upon when he describes believers as "children of God," who are destined to rule the world on his behalf.

Jesus is described as the "firstborn among many brothers" (Rom 8:29), a description that has major redemptive significance. Certainly, the term "firstborn" has Messianic significance (Ps 89:27), but its emphasis is on the Son of God—the firstborn—who died for his people in the Passover setting (see comments on Rom 3:21ff.). Ideally, the eldest brother (the firstborn) was the redeemer of the family, responsible for the well-being of his brothers and sisters. Jesus is described as the one who was made a sacrifice for sin

(Rom 8:3) and who redeemed our bodies (Rom 8:16–17). He is the one who redeemed creation, restoring it back into the possession of the new man (the eschatological family of God), which he was responsible for creating (Rom 8:19–22). Because Jesus is the Redeemer, the Christ, the Son of David, the Son of God, and the beloved firstborn Son, he is able to lead his people safely through their earthly pilgrimage, no matter what they face from the enemy of their souls (Rom 8:30–39).

8:1 Therefore, there is now no condemnation for those who are in Christ Jesus. Paul discussed the theme of condemnation in Rom 5:16 when he wrote: "the judgment followed one sin and brought condemnation, but the gift followed many trespasses and brought justification." In chapters 6–7, Paul explained the solidarity that man has with Sin and Death. The only way out of this condemnation was through the sacrifice of Christ. He was the last Adam, who acted for his people.

The opening of chapter 8 is a cry of glorious assurance. In Adam, there was nothing but condemnation and hopelessness; but in Christ, there is redemption, for he has brought his people out from under the rule and authority of Sin. The end of this rule was not merely that their sins had been forgiven but that the covenant relationship, which had bound them into an existence with Sin and Death, had been terminated.[2] The consequences of that relationship have been ended through the annulling of the covenant (Rom 7:1–4).

There are distinct echoes of the original exodus in this verse. The Hebrews in Egypt were under condemnation for worshipping Egypt's gods. Pharaoh determined to crush them out of existence (Exod 1:16). If God was to intervene, he had to deal with them in righteousness, dealing with their sin before he could deal with their need of salvation. This is why the Passover had to take place. When the LORD passed through the land, he came in judgment–visiting the sins of the Egyptian people. The Jews were spared his visit upon their firstborn because each family obeyed the command to slay a lamb and smear its blood on the doorpost and lintel (Exod 12:23–24). The evidence that vicarious sacrifices had been made meant that judgment did not come upon the Hebrew families. Thus, in two very distinct ways, the Jews at the Passover could assert that they were no longer living under condemnation. The power of Pharaoh to harm, or even destroy, was removed, and the fear of Yahweh's judgment was ended. He spared them because of the death of the lambs, and so they were safe.

Through the death of Christ, our Passover sacrifice (1 Cor 5:7), God has provided the only adequate sin offering. He had to surrender his only Son to rescue His people from destruction. Like the deliverance of the Jews from Egypt, this deliverance was double edged. First, there was deliverance from Satan who determined to heap destruction on the people of God, seeking to control and silence the church's testimony. Second, there was deliverance from the judgment that God, the holy and righteous one, must pass on all who break his holy law. Thus, the deliverance of the Jews at the exodus was truly a type of that which Christ would secure for his people.

---

2. For a fuller discussion, see Holland, *Contours*, chapter 10.

This deliverance does not benefit everyone. It is only for those who are "in Christ Jesus." Those who choose to remain members of the body of Sin stay in the kingdom of darkness, remaining under condemnation and judgment put on Adam.

As we have seen, *sarx* has many meanings.[3] In an attempt to help their readers, it is interpreted by most modern translators as "sinful nature." This translation hides the multifaceted nature of *sarx*, robbing the reader of better alternative interpretations of the passages in which the term occurs.[4]

One meaning of *sarx* describes the sinful state of man (Rom 8:5), while another simply refers to his weakness without God. Paul said in the letter to the Romans that Jesus, "as to his human nature (*sarx* 'flesh') was a descendant of David" (Rom 1:3). *Sarx* is a morally neutral word, only its context telling us what sense it is meant to convey. This is rather like the word "sleep," which can mean, among other things, a state of rest and a state of death. Only the context can tell how the word should be interpreted. Here in Rom 8:1, *sarx* is better interpreted as the condition of weakness that man is in because he is a creature and not the Creator. It was into this condition of weakness and vulnerability that the Creator came (2 Cor 8:9; Phil 2:7; John 1:3). Paul is not saying that Jesus was "contaminated by sin," but that his birth brought him solidarity with man—sharing with him his frailty and vulnerability, but not his sinfulness. Christ has no covenantal relationship with Satan as fallen man has. Paul makes this clear in 2 Cor 5:21 and Phil 2:5–11, while Peter and John make it clear in 1 Pet 2:21–22 and John 1:1–14.

Paul says that those who are in Christ Jesus do not live according to the flesh but according to the Spirit. Again, there is an allusion to the Jewish experience in the exodus. In Egypt, the life of Israel was dictated by the will of Pharaoh, but, as a result of the exodus, she came under the rule of God. Throughout the exodus events, the life of the nation was, or was intended to be, under the control, guidance and authority of the Holy Spirit–the pillars of cloud and fire marking his presence with them (Isa 63:11,14). The turning point for Israel was its baptism into Moses (1 Cor 10:2), when the nation came under his representative headship.

The removal of condemnation is "for those who are in Christ Jesus." The acclamation refers only to those who have accepted Christ's lordship and who are no longer in (or under) Adam's representative authority. They are now in (or under) Christ's representative authority, and in that relationship they share all of the blessings of salvation.

As always, Paul is careful how he expresses himself. Not only is he saying that condemnation is over for those who are in Christ Jesus, but he qualifies their condition. This is inevitable, because no man can demonstrate his position in Christ other than by a transformed life. Israel had professed to be under the authority of (or in) Moses, but the lives of her people did not demonstrate this to be true. Those delivered by Christ are not to live according to the flesh, their fallen condition in Adam, but according to the Spirit. In other words, those who are truly under the headship and lordship of Christ will live in

---

3. See Excursus F: Sin in the Theology of Paul, pages 203–25.

4. Russell, "Argumentation," 333–57, claims that Paul's use of the terms "flesh," and "spirit" in Gal 5:13–26 should be interpreted in a redemptive-historical sense. They represent modes or eras of existence, not parts or entities within the Christian. The same term is used in the argument of Rom 8:1ff.

a way that pleases him. This is possible because they are not living in their own strength but in the strength of the Spirit, who dwells among them and in them.

8:2 Because through Christ Jesus the law of the Spirit of life set me free from the law of sin and death. By using the phrase "set me free," Paul continues to act out the experience of man outlined in chapter 7. The opening verses of chapter 8 are the conclusion to chapter 7 and not the start of a new section. They describe the new man's liberation from bondage to Sin and Death. The section they introduce still deals with the process of redemption and describes the Spirit's involvement. The corporate reading of the text must continue.

The new section describes life in the Spirit. It does not start until v.5, where Paul says that the new life is determined by a totally different principle from the law of Sin and Death. We have seen in Rom 7:1–6 that this law refers to the authority Satan has over all those who are in Adam. It is the covenant authority of Satan which has now been cancelled through the representative, covenant-annulling death of the last Adam. Those who have called on Christ are part of the church. This is his body, the eschatological bride who is under the law of her new husband.

In this state of transition—when the church waits for the completion of her redemption and the consummation of her wedding to the lamb—the groom is represented by the Spirit who acts as the bride's custodian. (Note the same idea in John's Gospel. He makes the same use of the Passover/new exodus model. In John 3:27–30, the Baptist acted as the best man while in John 14:25–27, the Spirit fulfills this role as the church waits for the return of her groom who has been snatched away before her marriage has been consummated [Matt 9:15]). It is the Spirit who is charged with leading the people of God to glory for the final revelation of Christ's love toward his people. Thus, the law of the Spirit is the law of Christ. It is the authority that the Spirit has as he guides, protects, teaches, and prepares the bride for her presentation before her groom, the Son of God.

The paradigm is clearly that of the exodus—whether Egyptian or Babylonian—for the Spirit was active in both with the same goal of bringing the people of God to their inheritance and their final experience of God's love in the eschatological marriage (Matt 22:1–14; 2 Cor 11:2; Eph 5:25–27; Rev 19:7).[5]

The Spirit's work is not independent—it is through Christ Jesus. In other words, it is only because Christ has died for his people that the Spirit can lead them as the son(s) of God. As the Spirit is obeyed, the old life is forsaken and his ministry completes the deliverance that was the purpose of the Son's death (Rom 7:4–6). The Spirit applies to the church what the Son achieved through his death. In this way, his ministry sets the church free from the law of Sin and Death. It is a constant reminder to the church of what Christ has done for his people, so the threatening accusations of Satan ("Sin and Death") can be seen for what they are. This assurance gives the church the freedom to enter the life into which Christ has called her.

---

5. The same marriage imagery—with its new exodus background—is found in Rom 7:1–4 and 1 Cor 6:14–20. See Holland, *Contours*, 111–39.

8:3 **For what the law was powerless to do in that it was weakened by the sinful nature, God did by sending his own Son in the likeness of sinful man to be a sin
offering. And so he condemned sin in sinful man.** Once again, the translators have
opted for "sinful nature" to translate *sarx*. This translation dominates the passage we are
considering. Unfortunately, it is not the best rendering for this verse. It is clear that the
argument is about the condition of man rather than the sins he has committed. This misunderstanding has been a problem with most translations and interpretations of Paul's
letters. While most scholars acknowledge that, for Paul, *sarx* describes man in Adam (or
in the kingdom of darkness), many commentators prefer an understanding of personal
guilt. While Paul clearly had a doctrine of personal sin, most Western commentators
read Paul's letters (and the NT in general) from an Augustinian perspective. Augustine's
understanding of the biblical teaching on sin was tainted by his background in Greek
philosophical schools, which he explored before his conversion. The consequence of this
mindset was that Paul's corporate view of sin was minimized and the power of his argument lost. What I am saying is that we must not allow this individualization of the argument to control the passage. In the context of Rom 8:3, Paul is not writing about man's
"sinful nature" but his fallen condition in Adam. This, as has been shown,[6] is a natural
and legitimate understanding of *sarx*.

So, Paul is not describing the individual believer's conquest of sin but man's condition in Adam (continuing the argument begun in Rom 5). The law was helpless to change
this situation in the same way that the law is helpless to change a marriage if it goes
wrong. The law was never intended to change the hearts of people but to protect the
relationships that it recognized. The law was given as the covenant gift to protect Israel's
relationship with God. Tragically, God's law was unable to do this. Through his law, God
was bound to condemn Israel who violated the relationship and to acknowledge that a
new lover had taken the heart of his divine bride. This protective and then condemning
role is true of both human law and God's law. God's law acknowledges the claim that
Satan, the husband of the body of Sin, makes on those who have chosen to be in covenant
union with him. God's law can do nothing but recognize the existence of the relationship.
For this reason, Paul says that the law was powerless to do anything. If that relationship
came to an end through death, and the surviving partner entered into another relationship, the law of God would recognize that union. However, to begin a new relationship
while the former husband lives would be adulterous, and this the law condemns.

However, what the law could not do, Christ has done. Through his death, he condemned Sin (Satan) in the flesh and brought to an end its (his) dominance and authority.
Christ's death (as the last Adam) terminated the previous marriage. The law was not
"weakened by the sinful nature" but by man's relationship with Sin (Satan], and this
the law recognized. It was into this fallen condition that Christ came, experiencing the
weakness and utter vulnerability of man. This was more than the weakness of being a
creature–it was the weakness of being stripped of glory (Heb 2:5–18). Christ's experience
was not identical with man's because he did not share man's guilt, having never sinned

6. See Excursus F: Sin in the Theology of Paul, pages 203–25.

(2 Cor 5:21). For this reason, Paul qualifies his description of Christ's coming by saying that he came in the "likeness of sinful man." Such a statement is not suggesting that Christ was less than truly human. The statement is not docetic; it is incarnational.

Paul says that Christ's death was a sin offering.[7] We have seen that he views it as a Paschal offering, as do the other NT writers. Most scholars deny any atoning significance in the Passover but I have shown earlier (see comments on Rom 3:21–26) this misses vitally important OT evidence. Ezekiel describes the Son of David offering the sacrifices of the Day of Atonement at the eschatological Passover, in order to deal with the covenant community's sin (Ezek 45:18–25). I have also shown that the original Passover took place so that Yahweh could take Israel as his bride. It is out of this type of the Paschal new exodus that Paul continues to argue. Christ's death is a sin offering; it is the Paschal offering that brings deliverance. It is the Messiah's death alone that is the foundation of the new age, for he established a new relationship with God for his people. In this new age, the Spirit is given and the promises of Yahweh made to the prophets are brought to their completion: "For no matter how many promises God has made, they are 'Yes' in Christ. And so through him the 'Amen' is spoken by us to the glory of God" (2 Cor 1:20).

8:4 In order that the righteous requirements of the law might be fully met in us, who do not live according to the sinful nature but according to the Spirit. Again, I would question the prevailing understanding of this verse. It has Paul saying that the penal demands of the law have been met. While this is part of the picture, it is probably the secondary meaning. Paul, I would claim, is saying that the death of Christ has brought to an end all former relationships for his people, and the law's demand regarding the establishment of a new relationship has been met. Paul is repeating what he has said in Rom 6:7, that those who have died with Christ are justified from Sin. There is no charge that can be made against the new relationship. It is not an adulterous one as the law's righteous requirements have been met in the representative, covenant-annulling death of Christ. The argument continues to be a corporate one, describing the conditions of two communities.

---

7. Dunn, *Romans*, 1:413. Citing support from Wilckens, Denny, and Michel, he says that the translation should be "sin offering," so following the LXX of Lev 5:6–7,11; 16:3, 5, 9; Num 6:16; 7:16; 2 Chron 29:23–24; Neh 10:33; 2 Esd 20:34; Ezek 42:13; 43:19. See also Moule, *Romans*, 139; Wright, "Messiah," 155, and Gager, "Functional," 327. All see Rom 8:3 to be a covenant sacrifice looking back to Rom 5:12–21, which Whiteley, "Atonement," 250, has identified as Paschal. Stuhlmacher, *Reconciliation*, 175, also sees Rom 8:3 and 2 Cor 5:21 as referring to the sin offering on the Day of Atonement. However, Hooker, "Interchange," 350, says that becoming sin is not cultic, but refers to the incarnation and obedience which Christ rendered to the will of God, which included obedience unto death. She also sees the chapter reflecting a second Adam theme, 355, 358. Whiteley, "Atonement," 244, says that Rom 8:3–4; 2 Cor 5:21 and Gal 3:13 are foundational to the substitutionary theory, but that none of these verses either necessitates or excludes a substitutionary explanation. This is not so if the new exodus is the model being followed by Paul. The event concentrates on the principle of substitution. By the substitution of the lamb for the firstborn and then the replacement of the Levites for the firstborn, the wrath of God is averted from the people (see comments on Rom 3:21–25), and the merger that Ezekiel has made between Passover and Day of Atonement in 45:18–25 powerfully endorses such a propitiatory view. See Holland, *Contours*, chapter 9. Thus, the texts cannot be removed from the realm of substitutionary theology.

Again, as argued above, it is misleading to translate *sarx* as "sinful nature" as it does not stay within the bounds of Paul's corporate argument. He is saying that the requirements of the law have been met for those who live under the authority of the Spirit, the one who is the custodian of the bride. However, these requirements are not met for those who continue to be part of the body of Sin. As fallen humanity, they reject the application of the covenant-annulling death of Jesus. Thus, living "according to sinful nature" is not primarily about gross sins (the acts of the "sinful nature" as given in Gal 5:19–21 are much broader than what most would consider as sins) but about continuing to live in Adam.[8] This is the inevitable consequence of rejecting the lordship of Jesus, the last Adam.

8:5 Those who live according to the sinful nature have their minds set on what that nature desires; but those who live in accordance with the Spirit have their minds set on what the Spirit desires. Once again, it would be wise to replace "sinful nature" with "flesh." Paul is saying that those who are members of Adam (the body of Sin) live[9] governed by the headship of Satan (or Sin). Those who have received the Spirit—who are part of the eschatological community—live under the authority of the Spirit. They desire to do what is asked of them because they are being prepared for their entrance into the presence of their Redeemer God. The motivation for those who live according to the Spirit is God's love because this has been poured out, by his Spirit, into the hearts of his redeemed people (Rom 5:5).

8:6 The mind of sinful man is death, but the mind controlled by the Spirit is life and peace. In its translation, the NIV tries to maintain continuity with the earlier verses. These passages are understood by the NIV translators to be describing an individual perspective rather than a corporate one. Because of this, they translate *sarx* as "sinful man," rather than "the flesh." In this verse, the "mind of sinful man" ("flesh,") means the value system of man in Adam, i.e., the carnal (or old) man.[10] Living in this condition means eternal separation from God. Paul's statement to the believers in Rome (v.6a) reflects the warning given to Adam in the Garden before the fall: "when you eat of it you will surely die" (Gen 2:15–17) and the exhortation given to the Israelites before they crossed the Jordan into the promised land: "I (Moses) set before you today life and prosperity, death and destruction . . . I have set before you life and death, blessings and curses. Now choose life" (Deut 30:15, 19). Thus, Paul is writing about the realm of human experience without God–the condition Adam chose in preference to loving obedience to his Creator. Paul is saying that all who choose this way will know death or eternal separation from the lover of their souls.

In contrast, the pilgrim people of God, led by the Spirit, are being taken to their inheritance. This will include the experience of dwelling forever with God, which is life

---

8. See Wilder, *Echoes*.

9. In fact, the term "live" is an added term that does not exist in the Greek text. Paul actually says "those who are according to the flesh," οἱ κατὰ σάρκα ὄντες (*hoi kata sarka ontes*).

10. "Old man" is a corporate term. See Holland, *Contours*, 95ff.

and peace. The statement in Rom 8:6b is not about the believer experiencing peace at all times in this life, nor does it imply that when a believer is robbed of peace, his salvation should be doubted. (Paul himself knew times of acute anxiety as 2 Cor 2:4, 13; 11:28–29 make clear.) The statement is about the end of the pilgrimage, when the new covenant community—led by the Spirit—is brought safely into her inheritance, experiencing life and peace. Indeed, a characteristic of the new covenant was that it established peace (Isa 52:7; 54:13; Ezek 34:25; 37:26).

So, in conclusion, Paul, like Moses[11] (Deut 30:15–16), is telling the people there are two ways set before man: the way of life and the way of death. Just as Moses urged the Israelites to choose the way of life, Paul urges the Roman church to do the same and accept that believers have no abiding place on earth. They are part of the pilgrim community whose home is in heaven (Phil 3:20). Pilgrimage language has been used in Rom 5:1–4 and we see it again in Rom 8:35–39. The parallel between Israel's pilgrimage and that of the church continues.

8:7 The sinful mind is hostile to God. It does not submit to God's law, nor can it do so.12 For "sinful mind," read ungodly or carnal mind, as this allows the concept of Sin to be seen in terms of man's condition in Adam rather than his "degree of sinfulness." This does not deny the fundamental reality of the sinfulness of each individual but does more justice to Paul's corporate perspective of man's state in Sin through Adam.

The ungodly or carnal mind leaves the true and only God out of consideration and is concerned with man's immediate existence. Paul is saying that its refusal to accept the commands of God is hostility towards the one who has absolute sovereign right over the whole of his creation. In denying him his right, man affirms his allegiance to Satan–the one who led a rebellion in heaven in an attempt to dethrone God.[13]

Sin is more than choosing something that does not have God's approval; it is no less than declaring a spiritual war of independence. This condition of rebellion is a result of man's complicity in the sin of Adam and is what Paul calls the "carnal mind." It seeks independence from God at every turn, often presenting itself as righteous. In doing this, it makes God out to be the offender and guilty of sin. In this, the perversity of Sin is

---

11. See Holland, *Contours*, 339–51, where it is argued—contrary to Davies, *Rabbinic*—that the contrast in 2 Cor 3:5–18 is not between the ministry of Moses and Jesus but between the ministry of Moses and Paul, so also Hanson, *Techniques*, 152. If this argument is correct, it supports the claim made here that Paul sees himself as acting out Moses' prophetic ministry to Israel. This does not deny that Jesus is the prophet like unto Moses, but it does identify that Paul, as a servant of the Lord who continues that same ministry of witnessing to the covenant people of God. Hays, *Echoes*, 14, says: "To read Paul against this background of inner-biblical exegesis is to understand his place in the stream of tradition in a new way. He saw himself as a prophetic figure, carrying forward the proclamation of God's word as Israel's prophets and sages had always done, in a way that reactivated past revelation under new conditions." See also Byrne, "Boldly," 83–96; Mallard, "Communion," 242–48; Lane, "Conflict," 3–30.

12. The Greek has the conjunction γάρ (*gar*) "for," (thus: "for the sinful mind," or better, "for the carnal mind"), which, for some reason, the NIV translators have thought to be redundant. Its presence naturally suggests that the statement builds on earlier arguments made, the core of which is death to Sin (Rom 5:12–21 and Rom 7:1–14).

13. Luke 10:18.

shown: light is called darkness and darkness is called light. It ignores, or excuses the evil of Satan but accuses God, who is loving and good, of wrongdoing.

8:8 Those controlled by the sinful nature cannot please God. Yet again, the rendering ought to be: "those who are in the flesh (*sarx*) cannot please God."

Paul sums up his preceding argument. He is concerned for the believers in Rome to appreciate that being in Adam (in the flesh) is to be incapable of pleasing God. It is for this reason that he is convinced of the necessity for all men to believe in Christ. From his experience, and from his knowledge of the Scriptures, Paul had come to understand that his sincerity in keeping the highest religious ideals and practices had not changed his state of "being in Adam." He had been at enmity towards God, and his religion had been an excuse for dismissing the claims of his Creator—the God of Abraham, David, and Jesus.

8:9 You, however, are controlled not by the sinful nature but by the Spirit, if the Spirit of God lives in you. And if anyone does not have the Spirit of Christ, he does not belong to Christ. Because of Paul's use of the pronoun ὑμεῖς (*humeis*) "you" (pl.), we know that he is addressing the church community in Rome. Having explained the condition of man in Adam (or in the flesh), he wants to assure the believers there they have nothing to fear. He is persuaded they are not in Adam but in Christ, i.e., they have the "Spirit of Christ." In this realm, the church has the "firstfruits" of all future blessings that will be enjoyed in heaven. In other words, on the basis of the work of Christ in his death, the Spirit is present with the believing community in Rome, leading her to the New Jerusalem.[14]

When the Roman church was established, the community was given the Spirit (Rom 5:5; see Acts 2:1–5; 8:14–17; 10:44–48; 19:2 for the giving of the Spirit when churches were founded, and Eph 1:13–14; 2 Cor 1:22; Gal 3:5; 1 Thess 1:5; 1 Pet 1:2 for references to these events). This giving of the Spirit fulfilled the promise to the new covenant community (Ezek 36:26–27). (This is not the same event as the baptism of the community by the Spirit into the dying Christ.[15] In this baptism—which is the anti-type of the baptism of the Jews into Moses in the exodus—the Roman Christians [along with all other believers] were united with Christ by the Spirit [Rom 6:1–4; 1 Cor 10:1–4; 12:13; Gal 3:25–27; Eph 4:5][16]). Here, in Rom 8:9, Paul is writing about the Spirit who has been given to the Roman community to guide and protect her as she makes her eschatological pilgrimage to her inheritance. Along with all other believing communities she is making her pilgrimage to her heavenly home.

---

14 Wright, *Romans*, 551, says: "God has dealt with sin once and for all on the cross, and now the life of the Spirit is given to bring the new-exodus people home to their promised inheritance (5:1–5, 6–10; 8:12–30)."

15. See Excursus E: "Baptism into Christ," pages 168–77. This event is not the same as the one Paul speaks about here. The former was hidden and historically completed, only God knowing what was done; the gift or outpouring of the Spirit was public and witnessed by many (Acts 2:1–12; 8:1–8; 10:44–48; 19:1–7).

16. See Holland, *Contours*, chapters 6–7.

Proof that a community is part of the eschatological people of God is the Spirit's presence. This was the reason behind the question Paul asked the Ephesians when he first met them: "Did you receive the Holy Spirit when you believed?" (Acts 19:2). This was not a personal interrogation of the believers but the natural enquiry of an apostle to a believing community (see Acts 8:14–17), for the Spirit was, and still is, the birthright of every church. Of course, the Ephesian disciples of John were not believers in Christ, but their outward appearance misled Paul into treating them as such until they confessed what they had not experienced.

The problem is that most expositors apply statements concerning the Spirit directly to the experience of the individual believer. This is an unfortunate mistake, as it takes the reader away from the NT dimension of the Spirit and the church. I have already tried to show that letters to churches would not have been read privately but communicated publicly. It is a false methodology to individualize the pneumatology of a letter before it has been appreciated and interpreted as a statement of the Spirit's work in the community. Only then can its significance and meaning be extrapolated for the individual. This must be done with great care, however, as what is true for the church is not always true for the believer.

One such example concerns the indwelling Holy Spirit. While the Scriptures call the church "the temple of the Holy Spirit," it is not true of the individual believer.[17] It is true that the Spirit dwells in the individual (2 Tim 1:14), but to say that a person is a temple is to say that God dwells in his fullness in each believer. Such a claim is not scriptural. The NT is not different from the OT. The fact that God's Spirit will be poured out on all flesh in the last days (Joel 2:28), does not justify individualizing the promise. Paul is saying to the church in Rome that she is not under the dominance of Sin (Satan) and living in the flesh, but is in Christ and living in fellowship with the Spirit who leads her.[18] The church has already been described as the community on pilgrimage (Rom 5:1–4), and Paul will soon echo those same themes of perseverance and triumph (Rom 8:35–39). He has not lost sight of the fact that he is dealing with the experience of the eschatological community on its earthly, heaven-bound pilgrimage. This parallels how the Spirit was the key to the Jews' survival and ultimate arrival in the promised land.

So, Paul is saying that the key to triumph for the Roman church is twofold: "recognize the provision that has been made to bring you safely to your destination, and live in obedience to God." When Peter reported to the council of leaders in Jerusalem what God had done in accepting the Gentiles, his argument could not have been clearer (Acts 15:7–9). Evidence of their divine acceptance was that they had received the Spirit of God as had the Jerusalem church at Pentecost. Throughout the Acts of the Apostles, the Spirit never came upon an individual. He was poured out only on communities (Acts 2:15–17; 4:31; 8:17; 10:44–45; 19:6). This is especially significant when we examine the account of the conversion of Paul. Even though his conversion is held up to the church as a model of the work of God, there is no mention of the Spirit coming upon him. He was filled with

17. See Holland, *Contours*, chapter 10, for further discussion.

18. Ayodej, "Spirit," 71–84, reminds us there is a strong connection between the Holy Spirit and Paul's ethics–a connection that has often been overlooked.

the Holy Spirit (Acts 9:17), but most would agree this is quite a different experience from the outpouring of the Spirit. When Paul speaks of a community having received the Holy Spirit, he is thinking of the local church at its historic inception. He does not think of the individual's experience of conversion and gift of the Spirit, confirming his place in the believing community. (In reality, a believer becomes part of the church at the moment of Christ's death. See comments on Rom 6:1–5).

The switch from the Spirit of God to the Spirit of Christ—made so naturally without need for explanation—is evidence of the early church's "Trinitarianism."[19] This is not at the ontological level, which would be developed later, but is more of a "functional Trinitarianism."[20]

8:10 But if Christ is in you, your body is dead because of sin, yet your spirit is alive because of righteousness. Literally, the text reads: "But if Christ is in you (pl.), the body (sing.) is dead because of sin, yet the spirit (sing.) is alive because of righteousness." If Paul is writing about the experience of the individual believer, as many think, he would be saying that his physical body was still under the sentence of death, eventually yielding to the reality of its mortality. However, this is not the destiny of his spirit, which will not suffer death because of the righteousness he has entered into through Christ. This is in line with the OT, which focuses on separation and not extinction (see Gen 3:3–4). The problem with this interpretation is that it has departed from the corporate perspective of the letter. Evidence of the corporate context continuing is that the phrase: "If Christ is in you," is not the type of language that is used of the individual.[21] Indeed, "you" is plural. It is similar to the phrase in Col 1:27: "Christ in you (pl.) the hope of glory." Here, as in other passages, the emphasis is not on Christ in the individual but in the church. The argument is similar to that found in 2 Cor 5:1–21 where Paul speaks of the nature of the earthly dwelling place. Again, the evidence is that it is corporate:[22] "*we* have" (2 Cor 5:1), "*our* heavenly dwelling" (2 Cor 5:2), and "while *we* are in this tent (sing.)" (2 Cor 5:4).

---

19. For a discussion on Paul's contribution to the doctrine of the Trinity see, Young, "Meaning," 255-60.

20. Fee, "Christology," 327, sees "soteriological trinitarianism" in Rom 1–8; 2 Cor 3:1–4, 6; Gal 4:4–6; Eph 1:3–14; Tit 3:5–7. He does not find it in Rom 8:9.

21. Zeisler, *Romans*, 211, recognizes the unusual term, and notes that Paul normally speaks of the Spirit being "in us." He explains this by saying that Paul switches from Spirit-indwelling language to Christ-indwelling language. Paul sees the Spirit of God to be the Spirit of Christ, and, therefore, to be interchangeable.

22. This corporate suggestion is supported by Dunn, *Romans*, 1:431, who says: "As usual, σῶμα does not mean physical body but humanity embodied in a particular environment (see 6:6). As most modern commentators recognize, it should not be individualised ('your bodies', as RSV); rather, the singular denotes the embodiment which characterizes all human existence in this age. That is to say, it is τὸ σῶμα τῆς ἁμαρτίας (*to sōma tēs hamartias*), 'the body of sin' (6:6), τὸ σῶμα τοῦ θανάτου τούτου (*to sōma tou thanatou toutou*), 'this body of death' (7:24), because this age as such is still under the rule of sin and death, and precisely as σῶμα all humanity is part of this age. This truth of fallen humanity is individualized in v.1." This understanding is supported by Turner, *Spirit*, 119, who, without indicating that he appreciates the wider corporate implication, says the following when commenting on 2 Cor 3:3: "As the context of 2 Corinthians 5:17 is a continuation and development of the theme handled in 2 Corinthians 3, it might seem inviting to explain Paul's language of 'new creation' and of regeneration of God's people promised by

In Rom 8:10, Paul does not say: "your bodies are dead," but, "your body (sing.) is dead," ("your" being better translated "the," making the phrase read as, "the body is dead"). While the reference in the NIV to "your spirit" naturally suggests the spirit of the individual believer, the original Greek implies a reference to the Holy Spirit who dwells among the believers.[23] This reading of Spirit is supported by Paul's following statement, which speaks about the Holy Spirit of God without introduction (Rom 8:11).

There are other reasons to suspect a corporate dimension in this passage.[24] The mention of the Resurrection suggests that Paul is dealing with the same theme he dealt with in 1 Cor 15. There is evidence[25] that the Corinthian chapter had been influenced by the prophecy of Ezekiel, who saw a valley of dry bones representing the Jewish nation (Ezek 37). He was told to prophesy to the bones and, as a result, the Spirit turned them into a resurrected and powerful army. It was a vision of the resurrection of the nation, and it was this army that was led by God's Spirit on pilgrimage to its inheritance.

This imagery is part of the new exodus motif which is the theme of chapter 8.[26] The corporate exegesis of the letter is supported by the pilgrimage motif. It was never used

---

Ezekiel, as little more than powerful metaphors for the individual inward renewal of heart and spirit by the indwelling Spirit of God. But this proves unsatisfactory for two reasons. First, it ignores the predominately corporate focus of the new covenant promises in the Old Testament. Ezekiel 36–37, for all the prophet's individualism, concerns the re-creation of the nation and the righteous people, and a similar corporate dimension to new creation language is well brought by e.g., Isa 65–66." Turner goes on to say: "Paul himself echoes the corporate (ecclesial) dimension of this new covenant/new creation work of the Spirit in God's people in the anti-Judaizing polemic of Philippians 3:2–3 (and co-texts), and in the more pastoral contexts of e.g., 1 Corinthians 12–14 (esp. 12:12–28; 14:12, 26); 2 Corinthians 13:13, Romans 12:4–8, etc." He further goes on to note that, in the apocalyptic eschatology of the rabbinic writings and early Christianity, "new creation" referred either to this national restoration in history or to the state of affairs Christians associated with the Parousia. Following on from Turner's observation, we also note that Isa 65:17–18 used language about the creation of a new heaven and new earth as a way of speaking of the anticipated transformation of Jerusalem, i.e., it was essentially corporate language. Ellis, "11 Corinthians," when examining the eschatology of 2 Cor 5 notes this corporate dimension to Paul's reasoning. He comments: "Paul's primary thought is not of individual bodies at all, but of corporate solidarities which inhere in Adam and in Christ, the old aeon and the new aeon" (222).

23. Note the comment of Schreiner, *Romans*, 415: "The decisive argument against a reference to the human spirit is the word ζωή, for that word never means 'alive' but always means 'life'. It is difficult to imagine what Paul could possibly mean in saying that the human spirit is life. By contrast, the connection between the Holy Spirit and life permeates this section."

24. This corporate understanding of the resurrection is no new development but reflects Hebraic expectation. Wright, *Romans*, 584, says: "It should be noted most emphatically, that, although 'resurrection' is naturally something that individuals can hope for, for themselves or for those they love, the belief we have studied is always focused on a general resurrection at the end of the present age and the start of the age to come. This will be a raising to life in which all Israel (with suitable exceptions, depending on one's point of view) will haste. Seen from this angle, it will constitute Israel's salvation: after long years of oppression and desolation, she will be rescued at last." Despite this helpful statement, Wright interprets this passage individualistically.

25. Schreiner, "Corporate," 144–61.

26. See Keesmat, *Traditions*. Fee, "Christology," 323–24, says: "the linguistic ties to 6:4–14 are so unmistakable that it is hard to escape the conclusion that Paul is here intentionally tying together what was said there about Christ with what is said here about the Spirit." We noted in the exposition of chapter 6 that it is both corporate and framed in the exodus event. See, Holland *Contours* chapter 7, for fuller discussion.

of an individual but of the church.[27] Being part of second exodus imagery, it was natural for Ezek 37 to become the model of the final resurrection, when God would raise his people from the dead in order to bring them into their inheritance. The point to note is that the resurrection of Ezek 37 is corporate—it is the nation that was raised. The Jew had no notion of an individual resurrection because he saw the nation's resurrection as the fulfillment of covenantal promises. These promises are not the property of the individual Jew but of Israel. The slide into individualism takes us out of the biblical mindset—including Paul's—for, while resurrection embraces individuals, it is an experience of the community.

This corporate dimension is found elsewhere in Paul's letters. For example, in Col 3:1–13, Paul[28] writes:

> Since, then, you have been raised with Christ, set your hearts on things above, where Christ is seated at the right hand of God. Set your minds on things above, not on earthly things. For you died, and your life is now hidden with Christ in God. When Christ, who is your life, appears, then you also will appear with him in glory. Put to death, therefore, whatever belongs to your earthly nature: sexual immorality, impurity, lust, evil desires and greed, which is idolatry. Because of these, the wrath of God is coming. You used to walk in these ways, in the life you once lived. But now you must rid yourselves of all such things as these: anger, rage, malice, slander, and filthy language from your lips. Do not lie to each other, since you have taken off your old self with its practices and have put on the new self, which is being renewed in knowledge in the image of its Creator. Here there is no Greek or Jew, circumcised or uncircumcised, barbarian, Scythian, slave or free, but Christ is all, and is in all. Therefore, as God's chosen people, holy and dearly loved, clothe yourselves with compassion, kindness, humility, gentleness and patience. Bear with each other and forgive whatever grievances you may have against one another. Forgive as the Lord forgave you.

Clearly, this exhortation, which reflects Rom 8, is corporate. This is evidenced by the statement: "put on the new self, which is being renewed in knowledge in the image of its Creator. Here there is no Greek or Jew, circumcised or uncircumcised, barbarian, Scythian, slave or free, but Christ is all, and is in all" (Col 3:10–11). In saying: "Here there is no Greek or Jew, etc.," the reference is to a community that Paul calls the "new self" ("new man"). Once this is appreciated, the flow of the argument parallels that found in Rom 8.

Thus, τὸ σῶμα (*to sōma*)[29] "your body" in Rom 8:10 is corporate, and speaks of the solidarity the Roman believers have in Christ. However, the church's physical condition

27. Shogren, "Entering," 180. Of course, though corporate the community is made up of individual people and how this text downloads to individual participation is an important part of the theologian's enquiry, but that is not the issue here for we are, as a biblical theological commentary, seeking to follow and keep to the argument that Paul is making.

28. For discussion on Pauline authorship of Colossians, see Wright, *Colossians*; Holland, *Contours,* ch. 12.

29. So overcoming the problem posed by Sanders, *Palestinian*, 42, who claims that "Paul's rhetoric has led him into obscurity, and that, in order to provide a neat contrast to the second half of the statement about 'your spirits', he comes out with something well-nigh unintelligible." Cited by Zeisler, *Romans*, 221.

is still in the realm of fallen humanity and under the sentence of death. The argument focuses on the physical dimension of its existence. The church's earthly physical existence, which was once part of the body of Sin[30] but is now the body of Christ, is sentenced to death. This is because her members are still descendants of Adam and have yet to experience the completion of salvation. They are still "in the flesh," which does not mean they are corrupt but that their earthly condition is yet to experience release from the flawed, weakened, fallen condition. They are legally in Adam as far as their earthly existence is concerned until the redemption of their bodies (vv. 11, 21). But their condition of weakness, with its inevitable death, is not irreversible. The same Spirit who dwells among them (NIV: "in") is the one who raised Jesus from the dead. They will be raised also, and be transformed by the same Spirit to become the vehicle through whom the glory of God is, and will, be displayed to the whole of creation.

"Your body is dead because of sin (Sin)," is better translated: "The body being dead with respect to Satan."[31] The statement refers to the death to Sin that Paul has explained in Rom 7:1–6. It is through the death of Christ that the termination of the covenant with death (Death/Sin/Satan) has been accomplished. Satan's authority, by virtue of being the husband (the law of Sin and Death), is over. The people of God in Rome, with all other believers, are free to live in the Spirit and serve their new master. The church is, therefore, no longer under the power of Death/Sin/Satan. Paul will expound this tension of being in Christ yet still bound to the fallen earthly existence later in the chapter (8:21) where he says that: "that the creation itself will be liberated from its bondage to decay and brought into the glorious freedom of the children of God."

8:11 And if the Spirit of him who raised Jesus from the dead is living in you, he who raised Christ from the dead will also give life to your mortal bodies through the Spirit, who lives in you. Elsewhere, Paul calls Jesus the "firstfruits of those who have fallen asleep" (1 Cor 15:20). In the OT, the priest brought the first gathering of the wheat harvest, the firstfruits, into the tabernacle or temple to dedicate the coming harvest to the Lord (Lev 23:9–11). The fact that Paul has called Jesus the "firstfruits" is most interesting. The firstfruit offering was made three days after Passover.[32] This explains the early church's insistence that Jesus rose on the third day (1 Cor 15:3). His resurrection was seen as the fulfillment of the type found in the book of Leviticus. In other words, the Easter events were interpreted as being the fulfillment of the Passover. This same type is being explained here. Paul encourages the believers that, because Jesus has been raised from the dead by the Spirit, they will be raised in the same way.[33]

---

30. Käsemann, *Romans*, 225, acknowledges the corporate nature of the argument when he says: "But here the Spirit is obviously regarded as the true resurrecting force, as is evident in Eph 1:19ff. For us, he is the pledge that we shall be made like the resurrected Christ (Asmussen)–and in this new corporeality as the sign of a creation which is no longer subject to assault."

31. Käsemann, *Romans*, 224.

32. See Bruce, *1 Corinthians*, 140.

33. Fee, *Empowering*, 543, has argued for the well-attested variant reading that God will give life to your mortal bodies "because of," rather than "through," the indwelling Spirit (cf. NRSV margin).

The framework of the argument is the community, not the individual. This is made explicit by the Greek which the NIV translators mask. Paul speaks of the Spirit "living in you (pl.)"(ἐν ὑμῖν [*en hymin*]). However, the focus is about to change, as Paul writes that the Spirit will give life to "your mortal bodies," σώματα being the plural of σῶμα (*soma*) "body." In other words, the focus is no longer the corporate experience of resurrection but that of each believer.[34] Paul speaks of their common experience as members one of another and as members of Christ.

The concluding statement ἐν ὑμῖν (*en hymin*) "through the Spirit, who lives in you," can refer to the Spirit in them individually or collectively. If we accept that the arguments of letters written to churches are about God's saving action toward his people, i.e., the church, then the latter reading is natural. The former is not found in any of Paul's other letters to the churches, but it is found in the personally addressed letter 2 Tim 1:14. Thus, because the Spirit dwells in them collectively, as God's temple, he will care for them and raise every individual member of that community on the last day.[35]

8:12 Therefore, my brothers, we have an obligation—but it is not to the sinful nature, to live according to it. Once again, the NIV translators opt for "sinful nature" when translating *sarx*. Once more, we are led away from Paul's thinking. It is better to translate *sarx* as "flesh," as discussed earlier.

Paul is arguing that, because the church is the redeemed community and her ultimate deliverance is certain, she has no reason to live as though she is a part of the body of Sin, the kingdom of darkness. Her destiny is to be revealed as the spotless bride of the Messiah (Eph 5:25–27). Her obligation, therefore, is to prepare for that momentous day and not live her life as though destined for judgment. Her destiny is glorious and secure because her Redeemer, the *gōēl*, the firstborn, has died.

Christ not only redeemed her through his death but will fulfill his redeemer role by marrying her (Rom 7:1–4. See Deut 25:5–10 and Ruth 3:12; 4:1–8 for the laws of levirate marriage). This marriage imagery is part of the second exodus motif (Isa 49:20–21; 50:1–2; 54:1–8; 62:4–5). We have seen this imagery in Rom 7:1–6 and shall see it in themes developed later in the chapter, reinforcing the new exodus paradigm that is guid-

---

34. Contra, Wright, *Romans*, 598, who, in commenting on Rom 8:23, says: "Paul uses the singular 'body' rather than the expected plural, as in 8:11, but there seems no particular significance to this change . . . The Christian in the present time is but a pale shadow of his or her future self."

35. Rom 8:10–11 is difficult to follow because Westerners naturally read the passage individualistically. The following paraphrase may help guide you through the corporate/individualistic nuances of the passage: "Even though Christ dwells among you because you are his people, it must be recognized that you have not yet attained the fullness of his salvation. Your earthly existence is still linked to the penalty that Adam has caused to come on his descendants—your physical state will still suffer death. But this is not the end. You see, the Spirit who dwells among you is the same one who raised Jesus from the dead. Just as he transformed Jesus' earthly condition of death, he will transform yours. Your bodies, as members of his church, are going to be raised and transformed when Christ returns for his people. Then you will not merely be in a right relationship with God, but you will be as you were intended to be when God created man for himself. And it is the Spirit who will achieve this." For further information on Paul's use of body language, see Holland, *Contours*, chapter 5, and Holland, "Mistaken."

ing our exegesis. Because the church is betrothed to Christ, she is obliged to live a life that pleases him.

8:13 For if you live according to the sinful nature, you will die; but if by the Spirit you put to death the misdeeds of the body, you will live. The statement echoes again Moses' warnings to the Jews in Deut 30:15–16 (cf. Jer 21:8). He set before the Israelites two ways: the way of life and the way of death. Moses urges them to choose life. The law was thought to have brought life; to reject it was to embrace death and judgment.

Yet again, the NIV's "sinful nature" is not the best rendering in this context. Paul is saying that, if the lives of the Roman believers are characterized by independence from God, they will die. This reference to death can be seen at several levels. It can refer to death as separation from God, but the problem with this reading would be the denial of eternal safety for the believers in Rome. However, if the corporate setting is taken seriously, the problem is removed. In this setting, the statement means that the church in Rome would die. She would come under judgment, and her "candlestick," or witness, would be removed (Rev 2:5). This is an experience that has fallen on some Christian communities. Indeed, some backslidden members of congregations might die, as happened in Corinth (1 Cor 11:29–32). The importance of guarding a congregation from entering this realm cannot be over-emphasized. This is the reason for the appeal and warnings in the first letter to the Corinthians (1 Cor 5–6; 10:1–22).[36]

Paul has said that the Spirit will give life (Rom 8:11); now he says that the same Spirit will help the believers die to their old existence in Adam. The "misdeeds of the body" are not necessarily to do with physical sin, such as sexual immorality, but have more to do with the lifestyle of the body of Sin, i.e., the life that characterizes those who are in Adam. This is the OT pattern of the exodus. It was the Spirit who was instrumental in the deliverance of the Jews from the domain of Pharaoh (Exod 14:21; 15:10–13, Yahweh's *rûah* "wind" is his Spirit),[37] but it was also the Spirit who chastised them for willful disobedience, struggling with them to bring them back to repentance (Isa 63:10). This same struggle is re-enacted in the new covenant community as she journeys on her pilgrimage to her inheritance. The same argument is found with more immediate application in 1 Cor 10:1–11. Here, in his attempts to warn the Corinthians of the dangers of deliberately sinning against God, Paul reminds them of the particular sins that caused the Israelites to come under the judgment of Yahweh.

8:14 Because those who are led by the Spirit of God are sons of God.[38] This statement has been characteristic of the people of God throughout the ages. It was true of

---

36. The same argument is found in great detail in Heb 4 and 6, where the exhortation is clearly to the believing Jewish community. The comparison is between the unbelieving generation of the exodus (who fell in the wilderness) and the recipients of the letter who are tempted to turn back in unbelief.

37. Cf. also Ezek 37, for the Spirit's work in the second exodus.

38. The view that Sonship was modelled on Roman law of adoption has given way to the realization that the imagery is thoroughly Semitic. It is drawn from OT concepts of Israel being adopted as Yahweh's son and the king being made the Son of God and Yahweh Israel's "Father." See Stott, *Ephesians*; Lyall, "Writings," 458–66; Hester, "Concept," 12; Dunn, *Baptism*, 113; Bryne, *Seed*, 1ff.; Scott, "Adoption," 13–18; Schreiner, *Romans*, 425. Ridderbos, *Outline*, 201, points out that Sonship is corporate.

Abraham as he obeyed the command to leave his father's family and country. It was true of Israel when she was led by the Spirit (seen in rabbinical writings to be symbolized by the pillar of cloud by day and the pillar of fire by night), and it was true of Israel when she returned from exile in Babylon (Isa 44:3; 59:21; 61:1–3; Ezek 36:24–28; 37:1–4).

In this verse, the new exodus theme is again the backdrop of Paul's thinking.[39] He is saying that there can be no individualism, with believers separating themselves from the body of Christ's people. The leading of the Spirit is essentially a corporate experience, when the covenant community is guided on its pilgrimage to the New Jerusalem (Acts 15:28; 16:7–10).

(In arguing for a corporate setting for the passage, I am not denying that the Spirit can give specific individual guidance at crucial times in the life of a believer [Acts 8:26; 13:1–3; 18:9]. However, even in these texts, the guidance is about major steps that need to be taken to further the Gospel's proclamation rather than about individual preoccupations.)

8:15 For you did not receive a spirit that makes you a slave again to fear, but you received the Spirit of sonship. And by him we cry, "Abba, Father." We can hear Moses saying the same thing to the Jews as they panicked in the wilderness, wanting to return to the "comfort" and "security" of Egypt. The Spirit had been overtly present with them, guiding and protecting. To have gone back to Egypt would have exposed the nation to far greater dangers, for she would have forsaken the presence and promise of Yahweh.

Now Paul applies the same sort of exhortation to the believers in Rome. He urges them to continue living as the redeemed people of God. Such commitment brings difficulties—even hostility and persecution. He urges the church not to be afraid but to recognize these have been the experience of the people of God throughout the centuries. Indeed, persecution is evidence of her calling. Without it there would be grounds for questioning her testimony (Acts 14:22; 2 Tim 2:11–13).

The presence of the Spirit changes the circumstances of the people of God. It is not that they have learned to grin and bear their sufferings, but rather that their sufferings have been transformed and they can rejoice in them (Rom 5:3; Jas 1:2). Paul speaks regularly about how the world is challenged by the way Christians suffer for their Lord (2 Cor 12:7–10; Phil 1:12–30; 1 Thess 1:6–8). The Spirit, as the Spirit of adoption, gives them joy. He reminds them their suffering is vital evidence that they are part of the eschatological community, and that they have left the acceptance and security of the world as they journey towards their inheritance (Rom 5:1ff.).

There is an alternative reading of the text, depending on how a problem of punctuation is resolved. The end of Rom 8:15 is ἐν ᾧ κράζομεν· αββα ὁ πατήρ (*en hō krazomen abba ho patēr*) "And by him we cry, "Abba, Father." This phrase continues the sense of the previous one in the NIV, while in the KJV it is a phrase which concludes the

---

39. Note Wright's, *Romans*, 581, comment: "it becomes clear that the Spirit 'indwells' God's people in Christ, as the Shekinah 'indwelt' the tabernacle in the wilderness or the temple in Jerusalem; so we should not be surprised to discover in the following paragraphs that the Spirit takes on the role, within the wilderness wanderings of the liberated people of God, that in the exodus story was taken by the pillar of cloud and fire."

sentence. The NRSV uses the phrase to introduce the next verse and the NEB combines the two verses: "a Spirit that makes us sons, enables us to cry 'Abba! Father!'. In that the spirit of God joins with our spirit in testifying . . ."

The Aramaic term "Abba" was deeply personal and carried huge respect. It is the type of greeting that a child might give to his father as he cries out: "Daddy, Daddy." It speaks of belonging and confidence in a father's care. Using the term "Abba" in a letter to people unfamiliar with Aramaic seems remarkable.[40] Of course, it is not so surprising if the passage preserves a liturgical formula that was used by the church's evangelists and teachers. If this is the case, its meaning would have been explained to the Gentile converts and retained in its original form as an expression of the church's heritage. Alternatively, the church may have taught its converts the Lord's corporate prayer in Aramaic as this was also part of its heritage. In comments on chapter 12, it is noted that Rom 12:9–21 and Matthew's account of the Sermon on the Mount (Matt 6:9–13) in which Jesus taught his disciples how to pray are similar. The idea has been propounded that the early churches possessed copies of Matthew's Gospel.[41] If that was so, the term "Abba" at the opening of the prayer would be familiar to believers such as those in Rome.

We cannot tell if it was Paul or an earlier teacher who promoted the use of "Abba" among believers, but we do know that Paul has used the term in Gal 4:6. Before Jesus taught his disciples how to use this term, "Abba" was used to speak of Israel's relationship with God.[42] However it was never used by individual Jews to address Yahweh.[43] This corporate use may be key to how Paul intends to use the term, for although it is normal to read the passage as a commentary on individual Christian experience, its corporate dimension should not be overlooked.

So, the Spirit prompts the believing community to affirm God's Fatherhood. Israel was called God's son when she was brought out of Egypt (Exod 4:22) and, at that time, she was given the gift of the Spirit as a down payment of the bridal gifts that were to be given at Sinai and on entering Canaan. Here, the same pattern is followed; for the church is not only redeemed and forgiven, but given the Spirit to create the covenant/marriage relationship with Christ, her Redeemer.

In recent years, a different emphasis has been placed on the significance of the use of "Abba." It has been argued that Sonship is not so much a title of privilege but of responsibility. The king, as the son of God, was responsible for doing God's will and ordering the kingdom in accordance with his wishes. While intimacy remains, the emphasis is one of obedience, the cry of "Abba" denoting surrender and obedience.[44]

---

40. See Zeisler, *Romans*, 214.

41. Lauer, "Rediscovery."

42. God's relationship with Israel is often spoken as being that of a father and child, so Ps 103:13; Isa 22:21; 63:16.

43. Jeremias, *Prayers*, 57 comments: "In the literature of Palestinian Judaism *no evidence has yet been found* of "my Father" being used by an individual as an address to God . . . It is quite unusual that Jesus should have addressed God as "my Father"; it is even more so that he should have used the Aramaic *Abba* . . . We do not have a single example of God being addressed as *abba* in Judaism, but Jesus always addressed God in this way in his prayer" (emphasis original). See also Jeremias, *Theology*, 65–66.

44. See McKnight, *Vision*, 58–59; Caird, *Theology*, 401–4; Charlesworth, "Caveat"; Dunn, *Study*, 39.

8.16 The Spirit himself testifies with our spirit that we are God's children. The Spirit has always been the undisputed evidence that God has accepted a people for himself. Peter was confident that the household of Cornelius had been accepted by God (Acts 15:6–9) when he saw how the Spirit came upon them. Because of that, he dared not refuse them baptism—even though they were not circumcised. This acceptance was a massive shift of position for such a rigid Jew, and shows how important the testimony of the Spirit was for the early church.

But the Spirit's work is not only historical. Paul uses the present tense when he says that the Spirit testifies with our spirit that we are God's children. His work is an ongoing work, in which he brings assurance and guidance to each generation of believers. The construction τῷ πνεύματι ἡμῶν (*tō pneumati hēmōn*) "with our spirit," suggests it is the church that is witnessed to, but it is individuals who are confirmed to be God's children. Just because Yahweh's dealings with Israel were at the corporate, covenantal, and historical level, they did not override the individual Jew's response to God or his calling by him. The covenant community was the context in which the individual experienced all that God was to him. This same corporate experience of the people of God is found in this letter to the Romans. For Paul and the Roman believers, it would have been the most natural way of reading and understanding the letter.

THE MESSIAH KING AND HIS BRIDE'S SUFFERING

Now if we are children, then we are heirs—heirs of God and co-heirs with Christ, if indeed we share in his sufferings in order that we may also share in his glory. I consider that our present sufferings are not worth comparing with the glory that will be revealed in us. The creation waits in eager expectation for the sons of God to be revealed. For the creation was subjected to frustration, not by its own choice, but by the will of the one who subjected it, in hope that the creation itself will be liberated from its bondage to decay and brought into the glorious freedom of the children of God. We know that the whole of creation has been groaning as in the pains of childbirth right up to the present time. Not only so, but we ourselves, who have the firstfruits of the Spirit, groan inwardly as we wait eagerly for our adoption as sons, the redemption of our bodies. For in this hope we were saved. But hope that is seen is no hope at all. Who hopes for what he already has? But if we hope for what we do not yet have, we wait for it patiently. In the same way, the Spirit helps us in our weakness. We do not know what we ought to pray for, but the Spirit himself intercedes for us with groans that words cannot express. And he who searches our hearts knows the mind of the Spirit, because the Spirit intercedes for the saints in accordance with God's will. And we know that in all things God works for the good of those who love him, who have been called according to his purpose. For those God foreknew he also predestined to be conformed to the likeness of his Son, that he might be the firstborn among many brothers. And those he predestined, he also called; those he called, he also justified; those he justified, he also glorified. What, then, shall we say in response to this? If God is for us, who can be against us? He who did not spare his own Son, but gave him up for us all—how will he not also, along with him, graciously give us all things? Who will bring any charge against those whom God has chosen? It is God who justifies. Who is he that condemns? Christ Jesus, who died—

more than that, who was raised to life—is at the right hand of God and is also interceding for us. Who shall separate us from the love of Christ? Shall trouble or hardship or persecution or famine or nakedness or danger or sword? As it is written: "For your sake we face death all day long; we are considered as sheep to be slaughtered." No, in all of these things we are more than conquerors through him who loved us. For I am convinced that neither death nor life, neither angels nor demons, neither the present nor the future, nor any powers, neither height nor depth, nor anything else in all creation, will be able to separate us from the love of God that is in Christ Jesus our Lord (Rom 8:17–39).

8:17 Now if we are children, then we are heirs—heirs of God and co-heirs with Christ, if indeed we share in his sufferings in order that we may also share in his glory. Here we begin to see more clearly the model Paul has used for sonship. There are scholars[45] who would argue that he used the pattern of Roman adoption procedures to illustrate adoption and sonship. They point out that a Roman could adopt his slave into his family, and the law would give the adopted slave the same status and rights of inheritance as the natural-born children. They argue that Paul is saying that, although the Gentiles were once slaves, God has chosen them. Now they have a status equal to those who are naturally of the family, i.e., the Jews. They are co-heirs with Christ.

While this is an attractive picture of adoption, some things Paul says do not fit the scheme. First, in the Roman legal procedure there is nothing that can be compared to a Spirit of adoption. The gift of the Spirit has no part in this model, yet it is at the heart of Paul's description of sonship. Also, the reference in this verse to the necessity of suffering as part of sonship is absent from the Roman model. To make this position even less reliable, recent research has shown that this adoption procedure only happened in a very remote province of the Empire. It is most unlikely that Paul ever knew of this practice, or that the Roman Christians would have had sufficient familiarity with this adoption procedure to understand an argument based upon it.

But these factors are not a problem for the OT pattern of adoption. Indeed, they are essential parts of the picture. Israel was called God's son when she obeyed and followed Moses out of slavery: "Out of Egypt I called my son" (Hos 11:1). She was given the Spirit to guide and protect her, and her obedience brought conflict with the enemies of Yahweh so that her pilgrimage was characterized by suffering. This OT background for understanding Paul's doctrine of adoption is being increasingly appreciated and accepted by scholars.[46]

The picture of Israel being the son of God is supported by chapter 9. Paul writes that it is not the physical descendants of Abraham who are the sons of God but his spiritual descendants (Rom 9:8). It is clear that being a son of Abraham is the same as being a son of God (Gal 3:25–29, where the sons of God are Abraham's seed).

There is also another model of sonship in the OT—the king was called "God's Son." Ps 2 is a coronation psalm in which the following is declared of the newly crowned king.

45. See Bruce, *Romans*; Burke, *Adopted*.

46. See Scott, "Adoption," 15–18.

Verse 7 says: "You are my Son; today I have become your Father." The king, like Israel, was called into a covenant relationship with God, and his task was to represent God to the nation. He was given the Spirit to equip him for his calling, and he knew continual conflict as he upheld the word of God by applying it to the nation's life.[47] Thus, sonship in the NT could include this OT picture of kingship. It is this idea of ruling that is probably reflected in the statement of the verse we are considering (Rom 8:17), "that we may also share in his glory." This same theme of believers ruling with Christ is found in Rev 5:10: "You have made them to be a kingdom and priests to serve our God, and they will reign on the earth."

It is clear that the NT writers saw believers to be kings, and that their destiny was to rule with Christ (1 Cor 6:1–2). They share in his Messianic Kingship and, because they share in this, they are sons of God. (It is clear from this that being sons of God has nothing to do with being deified—only Christ is the God-Man.) So, again, we meet an example of the Messianic use of the term where believers are joint heirs with Christ.

The Lord Jesus Christ, of course, claimed something for himself that no other son can share. It was because of his claim of equality with God that the Jewish leaders turned on him and sought to stone him (John 10:33). For further discussion on this theme, see comments on Rom 1:4.

The picture Paul seems to have in mind is that of a people who are accompanying the Messiah, Jesus, on his pilgrimage. Because they share with him in his suffering, they will also share with him in his glory. This is another way of saying they are co-heirs with him (Eph 3:6). In the OT, God promised to give the land to Israel (God's son) as an inheritance. As we move from the OT into the NT, the promise no longer focuses on the physical land of Israel but on the kingdom of God (Col 1:13–14). This is in keeping with the fact that sonship has transferred from the physical descendants of Abraham to his spiritual descendants (Rom 4:12).

8:18 I consider that our present sufferings are not worth comparing with the glory that will be revealed in us. This is the same theme Paul takes up in 1 Cor 2:9, where he quotes Isa 64:4: "No eye has seen, no ear has heard, no mind has conceived what God has prepared for those who love him." In its original context, Isaiah's message was given to encourage the pilgrim community that the sufferings they experienced were of little consequence when compared to their future blessing. Paul is clearly using the same exhortation language to encourage the Roman church to persevere on its pilgrimage. While the believers must have often been tempted to be afraid of the authorities, Paul refuses to dwell on their earthly sufferings. He is not a pessimist. He says that, no matter what sufferings he and the Roman believers endure, they are not worthy of comparison with the glory that is to be revealed in them.

"The glory that will be revealed εἰς ἡμᾶς (eis hēmas) in us" implies that believers are not merely to have a vision of God's glory (as implied by the NRSV), or to have glory appear within them. Glory will be bestowed upon them from above as a gift to the believ-

47. O'Brien, *Ephesians*, 102; Byrne, *Seed*; Trumper, "Son," 17–19.

ing community. The bestowal of this glory will transform the church and bring her to the perfection that Christ's redemption has secured (Eph 5:25–26).

8:19 The creation waits in eager expectation for the sons of God to be revealed. One of the promises of the Babylonian (second) exodus was that, when the people of God returned to their inheritance, a new creation would come into existence (Isa 65:17; 66:22). The valleys would be raised up and the mountains made low (Isa 40:3–5), the desert would spring forth and blossom, and the wolf would lie down with the lamb (Isa 65:25). This was to be the response of creation[48] to the saving activity of Yahweh.

Paul is saying that the final pilgrimage is now under way. It is the event that brings with it the completion of the eschatological hope—the renewal of creation. This renewal of creation—when God makes all things new (2 Cor 5:17; Rev 21:5)—will take place when the people of God enter into their inheritance. When the promised new creation is handed over to them, the people of God will be finally justified.[49]

8:20 For the creation was subjected to frustration not by its own choice, but the will of the one who subjected it in hope. Once again, we find the theme of the fall and the representative role of Adam embedded in the text.[50] Indeed, it has never left the thinking of Paul—although it can slip from our own as we read the letter. All that Paul is saying about the liberation of man is against the backdrop of the Genesis story. He is clear that, although creation is a pointer to God's creative activity, it no longer reveals the perfection of its original order. It has suffered under the curse as well as from man's abuse and misuse. Yet, despite the spoiling of creation, it has been subjected in hope. It has not been cast off. God still values it and his plan is for its final transformation. Jesus is the one whose death has redeemed creation and who is, therefore, its firstborn (Col 1:15). He is the firstborn of all creation—its Redeemer.

The verse does, however, pose this question: "who has subjected the world to bondage?" The background of Gen 3:1–3 is important for resolving this puzzle. From the Genesis text, it could be argued that it was Adam who subjected the world as a result of his disobedience.[51] However, there is no direct statement to this end in the account. Because of the lack of an explicit statement, most commentators see that it was God who subjected creation to bondage.[52] Support for this comes from the fact that only God could subject "in hope," which Paul explicitly states is the destiny of the cursed creation. Also, in the Genesis story it is God who curses and, therefore, who does the subjecting.

---

48. Wilckens, *Römer*, II.152ff. and Cranfield, *Romans*, 41, contend that the term does not include Christians.

49. See Nwachukwu, *Justification*.

50. The idea of the restoration of creation causes difficulties for many scholars. Gager, "Diversity," 329, considers that it refers to the non-believing human world, and Käsemann, *Romans*, 233, says: "There can be no doubt that non-Christians are included. Difficult though it is to the modern mind, there can be little alternative to facing the fact that Paul intends the physical creation to be meant."

51. See O'Neill, *Romans*, 141; Robinson, *Wrestling*, 102.

52. See Cranfield, *Epistle*, I.414; Leenhardt, *Romans*, 220; Sanday and Headlam, *Romans*, 208; Bruce, *Romans*, 172; Käsemann, *Romans*, 235 and Murray, *Romans*, 303.

A difficulty in accepting that God was the one who subjected creation to bondage is the absence of an explicit mention of such. However, the difficulty is not insurmountable, for it is in keeping with Paul's Hebraic divine passive thinking to have God as the implicit agent, thereby avoiding anthropomorphism.

8:21 That the creation itself will be liberated from its bondage to decay and brought into the glorious freedom of the children of God. Redemption is not just about the liberation of people from the body of Sin; it is the release of the whole created order that has languished in decay, pain, and chaos. Creation is seen as suffering and in need of redemption. This is not some Gnostic development of the sinfulness of the physical world but is taken directly from the story of the fall in Genesis. As a result of Adam's disobedience, not only his descendents, but also the whole of creation, were plunged into turmoil as it came under the curse (Gen 3:17–19). For this reason, the Redeemer must restore creation, and, to undo Adam's "mess," he will need to be its firstborn—the "firstborn of all creation" (Col 1:13–20).

Isaiah had predicted the second exodus would be accompanied by the removal of the curse (Isa 65:23)—clear evidence that the reign of God had at last become a reality (Isa 66:1–22). This theme is found throughout the Scriptures—the closing message of the last book of the NT trumpets the promise that God will be "making everything new!" (Rev 21:5). In this new creation, the righteousness of God will not only be seen but it will permeate the whole created order. It will be heaven on earth! It will not be like the old creation which Adam, as its master, brought into a state of curse. It will be ruled by the redeemed people of God, who will be the opposite of the fallen Adamic community. The redeemed of the Lord will share in the glory of God. Through them, as a result of their Savior's death, the created order will enjoy the status it had at the beginning of time.

8:22 We know that the whole of creation has been groaning as in the pains of childbirth right up to the present time. The picture of childbirth was used by the prophets to speak of the sufferings that creation must go through before the coming of the Messiah.[53] The imagery became known as the "Messianic birth pangs" and pictured creation being brought forth into a new existence.[54] This process of birth would be finalized with the coming of the Messiah (Isa 26:16–18; Mic 4:9–10). Paul envisages the whole of creation being in travail, waiting for the pain of the final contraction. Then, the cursed creation would emerge from its old order into a new life through the redemption secured by Christ. This redemption is of a cosmic dimension. Jesus is the Paschal sacrifice, the firstborn of all creation (Col 1:15), who reconciles all things in heaven and earth to himself through his blood shed on the cross (Col 1:20).[55]

---

53. Amos 5:16–20; Isa 28:17–23; Dan 12:1; Joel 2:1–11, 28–32; Zeph 1:14–18. The theme is found in developed forms throughout Jewish apocalyptic literature. See, *4 Ezra* 7:37f; *Jub* 23:11; 24:3; *2 Bar* 55:6; *1 Enoch* 80:40,45.

54. Morris, *Romans*, 323, thinks that the idea of Messianic birth pangs is too specific for what Paul is saying here.

55. See also Heb 1:1–6, for the same Paschal exodus theme. Note the presence of similar motifs found here in Romans as well as in Colossians.

Even though Jesus' death has taken place (witnessed by Paul's repeated reference to it), it has not brought an end to the suffering of the people of God. Like the Jews who had been delivered from Egypt, their sufferings will continue until they arrive at their inheritance. This suffering precedes the birth of the Messianic kingdom, the comfort for the believer being that it indicates the consummation of all things is at hand. Paul's argument implies that creation is not to be destroyed but it is to undergo a new birth. What will emerge will not be something totally different but something that is transformed through the redemption that is in Christ Jesus. This renewal of creation is important, for as Abraham was promised the land as an inheritance, the true children of Abraham are promised a redeemed earth. Thus the redemption of creation is implicit in the Abrahamic covenant.

8:23 Not only so, but we ourselves who have the firstfruits of the Spirit, groan inwardly as we wait eagerly for our adoption as sons, the redemption of our bodies. Paul recognizes the tension for believers as they wait for the release from Sin that has been promised. The anticipation of the completed work of redemption is highlighted by the presence of the Spirit. He not only gives the community a taste of what is to come, but encourages her that her sufferings are part of God's purposes.[56]

The unity of man with creation has been increasingly recognized as the ecology movement has made its message known. The Jewish-Christian scriptures have been speaking of this for thousands of years.[57] Paul is not unifying man and nature in some cosmic, mystical union. He sees, as does the rest of scripture, that man is the crown of God's creation; yet, while sharing in its weakness and vulnerability, he is still distinct from it. He is its master and not its slave. It is true, of course, that he has abused his authority. However, a theology of creation that does not understand God as creator, man as his vice-regent, the fall as a reality, and the death of all creation's firstborn as essential elements in achieving cosmic redemption, is an inadequate Christian theology.

Paul envisages that the redemption process will be complete when the people of God are transformed, becoming the people that God intended. The redemption of the "body of Christ" is the final act of salvation. Paul, being a Jew, could not conceive of man's salvation without it also including his physical existence. This is what marked out the Christian gospel from all competing ideologies of the first century. It must have been a large hurdle to overcome, because the Greeks would have strongly opposed it. For them, salvation was not the restoration of the body but its destruction. It is here that we can see how faithful the early church was to the Jewish tradition of Jesus. She did not reinterpret

---

56. Tsumura, "Background," 620–21, suggests the background to Rom 8:23 is not only the widely recognized text of Gen 3:17 but also Gen 3:16a, which refers to the "trembling pain" that Eve was to go through in childbirth. Here, the pain is connected to the birth of many firstborn sons.

57. The sabbatical requirements of the OT all structured the cycle of Jewish life so as to respect nature (Lev 25:10–54). These encompassed the weekly Sabbaths that allowed man to rest as well as nature not be overworked (Exod 12:23), the rotation of crops and land (Lev 25:3–4) or the year of Jubilees with its insistence on the resting and returning of land and other properties to the families who had been the original owners.

its message for the sake of acceptability as many have argued,[58] but stayed faithful to the OT Scriptures, proclaiming the resurrection of Jesus as the event that defined the Christian Gospel.

The OT has several descriptions or titles for Israel. Two of the most important are that she was God's son and his bride. The OT sees that, while Israel was Yahweh's bride on earth, the consummation of the marriage would happen in the future. In contrast, sonship is fully established on earth, with no future development or fulfillment of the imagery.

Despite the NIV translation, the church has the firstfruits of the Spirit and not the individual believer, for Paul actually writes: "we wait for the redemption of *our* body (sing.)."[59]

The "firstfruits of the Spirit" probably refers to the beginning of the Spirit's work. What the church has already experienced is but a token of what she will experience on the day of Christ's coming. The lives of her members have been transformed by the presence of the Spirit but, when Christ returns, "their body" (the church) will be transformed. It will be the Spirit who will change her—raising her to immortality, just as he did when he raised the Lord Jesus (Rom 8:11).

There have been times, such as revivals and other outpourings, when the Spirit's presence has been beyond the expected, and miraculous happenings have become the norm rather than the exception. Such events anticipate the eschatological goal when God will dwell among his people in all of his fullness. When outpourings occur, his presence affects not only the church's spiritual life but her physical well-being also.

8:24 For in this hope we were saved. But hope that is seen is no hope at all. Who hopes for what he already has? All that Paul has been describing lies in the future. He has already said that believers are groaning for the completion of their redemption. This is a future hope, but it is a hope that is grounded in the historical happening of the death and resurrection of Jesus. It is, therefore, not a vain hope. The hope of the Christian is not something akin to whistling in the wind; it is singing the songs of heaven, strengthened by the promises of the God who will never fail.

Paul acknowledges that this hope is not verifiable. It is the same as when Israel was in Babylon, waiting for her release. She knew the prophets had set a limit on her captivity and waited for that time to pass (Jer 25:11). The Babylonians would have mocked any suggestion that her God was in control, demanding that she must face the facts of the

---

58. See, e.g., Chadwick, "All Things," 273, says: "The eschatological and apocalyptic character of the primitive Palestinian Gospel was a grave liability in preaching the Gospel of Christ to an audience of Hellenistic intellectuals. He boldly reinterpreted the Gospel so as to put into the background the concept of the end of the world, and interpreted the supremacy of Jesus Christ in terms of Cosmic Wisdom, the agent of God in creation."

59. Contra, Wright, *Romans*, 598, who notes: "Paul uses the singular 'body' rather than the expected plural, as in v. 11, but there seems no particular significance to this change." Such a conclusion is the result of a faulty reading methodology, for while Wright regularly stresses the importance of the corporate, he often fails to apply the principle to the texts he is interpreting.

situation. However, it was her Babylonian masters who were not facing the facts, for they did not acknowledge that Israel was the covenant community of God.

This is the present condition of the church. Many despise the faith of the people of God; others, at least, acknowledge that "simple faith" comforts Christians in their sorrows and supports them in their need. But the fact is that such reasoning refuses to investigate the evidence. Jesus has been raised, and he is the firstfruits of those who sleep. All those who are dead in Christ are destined to share in his victory over death and to be transformed into the likeness of the Son of God.

8:25 But if we hope for what we do not yet have, we wait for it patiently. Anxious to clarify what Christian hope is, Paul stresses that at the present time, it is not the fulfillment that he and the Roman believers enjoy but the promise. He argues in the following way: "We will continue to suffer and be frustrated. But this certain hope, founded on the promises of God and the work of Christ, will one day be completed, and the fullness of our redemption will no longer be a hope, but a reality!"

8:26 In the same way, the Spirit helps us in our weakness. We do not know what we ought to pray for, but the Spirit himself intercedes for us with groans that words cannot express. Paul has been referring to the work of the Holy Spirit throughout his letter.[60] In Rom 1:3, he spoke of the resurrection as being the work of the Spirit, and in this chapter he says that the Spirit will raise the church (Rom 8:11). The Spirit is bound up with the believers' adoption as sons, and in this verse Paul tells us that the Spirit is the one who aids believers in their weakness by interceding for them.

These three ministries of the Spirit echo the experience of the Jewish people in their return from exile. It was the Spirit who raised them from the dead (Ezek 37), it was he who conferred on them sonship (Isa 51:1–3), and it was he who strengthened and supported them on their pilgrimage back to the promised land (Isa 42:13–16; 48:16–18). This is the theme that Paul is developing here. Israel was the type; the church is the antitype. Recognizing the importance of typology for Paul's theology makes understanding his teaching that much easier.

The people of God, once bound to Satan as members of the body of Sin, have been released through the covenant-annulling death of Jesus, the last Adam. The Christian community has experienced the eschatological (end of time) new exodus the prophets had spoken about. This deliverance, as they had predicted, has been accomplished through the Son of David. It is the Spirit who has raised this community from spiritual death and given her life, and it is he who made her into the army of the living God. Having been freed from her bondage, the church is now led by the Spirit. He makes her believers into sons of God who, through him, cry: "Abba! Father!" It is he who assures, comforts, and strengthens them as they face all the opposition arrayed against them. It is he who triumphs over the forces of darkness which seek to stop the believers (the sons of God) from arriving at their promised inheritance. This will become clearer towards

---

60. Smith, "Function," 29–38, claims that Paul uses ὡσαύτως (*hōsautōs*) "likewise" to link, by way of comparison, the active ministries of the indwelling Spirit described by Paul in Rom 8:16, 26.

the end of the chapter, where Paul writes about the impossibility of being separated from God's love (Rom 8:31–39).

It is clear from this that the work of the Holy Spirit is vital for the life of the church (local or world-wide). He is responsible for her beginning, her continuation, her preservation, and her eventual triumph. It ought to be clear that any Christian who does not understand the essential biblical teaching concerning the Holy Spirit is going to be confused and badly equipped for the Christian life.

Although there are several dimensions of the Spirit's work and power, in this particular context, the Spirit is spoken of as the one who sustains the people of God when they are overwhelmed in desperation. Paul says that the Spirit helps us in our weakness. It is often thought that endowing with some sort of exhilarating power is the defining characteristic of the Spirit's work in toward God's people. While there is certainly truth in such understanding this limited perspective can easily become a distorted understanding. Paul is saying something that is recognized in both the OT and NT. Before the Spirit's power can be displayed, the recipient must be brought to experience and acknowledge his total weakness (Zech 4:6).[61] At times the Spirit's ministry is like that of a lifesaver, who responds when the one in need comes to the end of his resources. The Spirit does not come to the church's aid to boost her strength; he comes to her aid when strength is completely gone. At that point, believers must say: "salvation is of the Lord." He helps them in their weakness–at the point of their despair and anguish (cf. Rom 5:6–8). He is the God who calls those things that are not as though they were; and it is into utterly hopeless situations that he comes in graciousness, power, and might. Israel was "dead" in Babylon, and, step by step, the Spirit worked to achieve her deliverance and return. Whenever the exiles took the matter into their own hands, they hindered the work of the Spirit but, at every point when they felt their weakness and cried to God for help, he responded by coming to them in the person of his Spirit. While Paul's perspective is the church's experience, this experience is mirrored in the lives of millions of individual believers. Of course the Spirit's work is not just about giving power, he give gifts and empowers for witness etc.

Paul says that the Spirit intercedes with groanings that words cannot express. Some commentators see this to be a reference to the ecstatic utterances that the church knew and experienced. These utterances (known as the gift of tongues) are not mentioned in the letter to the Romans. Indeed, they are only recorded in the Acts of the Apostles (Acts 2:4–8; 10:45–46; 19:6) and in Corinthians (1 Cor 12:10, 30; 14:4–28). It is difficult to say exactly what these tongues were intended to achieve. In some places, they were the instrument of praise (Acts 2:11), in others they were the means of private edification (1 Cor 14:4), and of delivering exhortations (1 Cor 14:26–28).

The context in Rom 8:26 does not suggest that Paul has this gift of the Spirit in mind. The experience he describes seems to go beyond the exercising of a spiritual gift.

---

61. Wo, "Intercession," 13, suggests that the reference to the universal sufferings and groans in Rom 8:17–25 draws a parallel between Jesus' prayers in Gethsemane and the believers' attitude as children of God.

It denotes despair, which is only reversed because the Spirit comes to the church's aid.[62] In the midst of such an experience, there is only place for gratitude that the God who came to the aid of the Jews in their desperate plight in Egypt has come to the aid of his people in Rome. He not only gave the church his indwelling Spirit to intercede on her behalf, but also his Son, who intercedes for her at the right hand of God as the perfect high priest (Rom 8:34).

8:27 And he who searches our hearts knows the mind of the Spirit, because the Spirit intercedes for the saints in accordance with God's will. Understanding this verse is problematical. It is difficult to know who it is that searches the hearts. Is it the Father or the Spirit? If it is the Father, then Paul is saying that the Father knows the mind of the Spirit and understands his groans. If it is the Spirit, then he is saying that the Spirit knows the mind, or desires, of the spirit of man and, as a result, reliably represents those longings to the Father with groans that he can understand. Because of the previous verse where Paul wrote that the Spirit "helps us in our weakness," it would be natural to expect that he continues to write about the Spirit's work. If this is the case, then Paul is saying that the Father knows the mind of the Spirit who intercedes for the believers as they attempt to pray. Because the Spirit is one with the Father, he prays for the believers according to the will of God.

We can understand this in one of two ways. First, Paul could be saying that the saints are the object of the Spirit's prayers. This is not suggested anywhere else in Scripture. What is taught is that Christ, as his people's high priest, prays for his people (1 Tim 2:5; Heb 4:14–16). The second possibility, and probably the correct one, is that the Spirit helps the believers pray and sustains them, so that, in their weakness, their prayers become effectual. Their prayers are not merely the prayers of men but they were empowered by God, through the groans of the Spirit.

In the phrase: "in accordance with the will of God," it is clear that prayer is not about changing the mind of God or about man achieving God's goals through his help. It could be about the will of man conforming to the will and desires of God so that, when he prays in the way that Paul speaks about, he prays according to God's will. Alternatively, it could be that God transforms believers' prayers so that they accord with his will, as there is no reference to man's will being conformed to God's will in the text.

8:28 And we know that in all things God works for the good of those who love him, who have been called according to his purpose. As we shall see, this concluding section gathers together the themes of the earlier part of the letter and brings them to a glorious ending. Paul's purpose is to encourage the Roman church about the certainty of her future and destiny. This would prove essential as, in the days to come, the might, pride, and ruthlessness of the Roman Empire were unleashed against her with the intention of wiping the Christians from the face of the earth. The recollection of Paul's words from this part of his letter must have brought unspeakable comfort to many of the be-

---

62. See also Käsemann, *Romans*, 239–42; Cranfield, *Romans*, 420–24. For an argument that defends the position that this passage is about speaking in tongues, see Fee, *Empowering*, 577–86.

lievers when they were crushed and killed by the empire's barbaric and cruel onslaught. Amazingly, despite the awful persecution, the Roman church grew while the decadent state went through its death throes.

The historical realities of suffering and the seemingly meaningless triumph of evil over good must make us wary of interpreting Paul's statements in too idealistic a way. It is easy for those who have had few knocks in life to recall this verse, but Paul did not write these words to assure comfortable believers that God would look after their every interest. He wrote them to those who were about to be deprived of the most basic of human rights and who knew that they could lose everything they owned, including life itself. For these people—whose testimony in the face of the most appalling suffering won the admiration of the most skeptical of historians—Paul's words would have provided comfort, enabling them to see a far greater treasure and a more glorious citizenship.[63]

The knowledge that Paul writes about in Rom 8:28 is the product of relationships.[64] Paul and the Roman believers knew how things would eventually turn out because they knew the one in charge had ultimate authority to achieve his will. Paul is not saying that God intervenes at every point of threat. History and our own human experience challenge such a claim as being totally unrealistic. Importantly, the Scriptures do too. We only have to read the Acts of the Apostles to see how Christians suffered poverty, famine, injustice, and untimely death. The early church would hardly interpret Paul's statement as being some sort of heavenly insurance from the ills of this life. Her experience could not allow such an interpretation, and it certainly did not fit Paul's own experience either (2 Cor 11:23–29).[65]

The loaded phrase, "all things" is a reference to the list of saving decisions and actions found in Rom 8:29–30, i.e., God's foreknowledge, and our predestination, calling, conformation, justification, and glorification. These are all the glorious things that work together for good in the lives of all believers, regardless of their circumstances. They call from Paul the magnificent statement "if God is for us, who can be against us?" (Rom 8:31).

So, Paul emphasizes that in all these things God is working "for the good of those who love Him." This is quite different from certain translations, which say that all things work together for good (so, GNV, NIB, NJB). They promise the innocent reader that everything will turn out well in this life—each incident serving his eventual, greater good. These translations fall woefully short of the mark and, as has been indicated earlier, history and experience—as well as the scriptures—do not support such naive optimism. Of course, the trials of life can work for the maturing and character-building of people, but this applies to believers and unbelievers, and is not Paul's point here.

63. Olyott, *Romans*, 79–80, notes the sobering corollary: "in the final analysis we shall see that nothing has worked for the good of the wicked."

64. Dunn, *Romans*, 2.480, sees this knowledge as coming from Israel's experience; while Moo, *Romans*, 527, sees it to be based on Christian experience.

65. The phrase "his will" has textual difficulties, for the word "his" does not appear in any MSS. This leaves the sense of the statement less secure than what most think (even translators). The majority suggest "his" to help the English reader. For a discussion on the possible meanings which take into account the nature of the Greek text, see Witherington, *Romans*, 227.

We must ask if Paul is making this statement about the individual or the Christian community. If we accept the proposed understanding, which is set in an eschatological context—that the ultimate goal of God is to work for the good of those who love him—then there is little difference between the two. The vindication of both community and member, and their ultimate blessedness, are not for this life but for the time when the believers enter into their inheritance. However the corporate concepts of the OT persist in the thinking of Paul, for Israel had been called to fulfill the purposes of Yahweh (Gen 12:3b). Tragically, she failed because she did not love the Lord her God and the covenantal purposes of her calling were transferred to the church (Eph 1:3–14; Heb 7:22). The church now has the high calling to represent Yahweh to the nations (Matt 28:18). As she fulfills this calling, the believers are strengthened in the knowledge that God, who foreknew their commitment to him, will justify, conform, and ultimately glorify them. Events in Rome may crush the Christians, but Paul has already comforted them by saying that their sufferings are not worth comparing to the glory that will be revealed in them (Rom 8:18).

The focus of "God's purposes" is described as "those who love him." In a passage such as this, which is reminiscent of the exodus event, it is difficult not to detect an echo of the Shema: "Hear, O Israel: The LORD our God, the LORD is one. Love the LORD your God with all your heart and with all your soul and with all your strength" (Deut 6:4). The motivation to fulfill the Shema comes from recalling God's mercy in the exodus (Deut 6:20–25). This act of salvation should have motivated love for God and also compassion for others (Deut 24:10ff.), but it was only the remnant who sought to fulfill this mandate. Paul describes "those who love him" as being the true sons of Abraham (Rom 4:17).

There is debate over the subject of the verb συνεργεῖ (*synergei*) "work together." Some propose it is the Spirit,[66] an understanding conveyed by the NEB. It is argued that the work of the Spirit has been the main topic ever since Rom 8:1. The difficulty with this view is that the subject has changed—it is God, not the Spirit, who is the subject of Rom 8:27. Because of this, several versions, including the NRSV and the KJV, accept the variant reading of a number of manuscripts and opt for the subject being God. Thus, it is God who is the one who works for the good of his people. This interpretation is supported by Rom 8:29, where God is the subject of the continuing theme.

8:29 For those God foreknew he also predestined to be conformed to the likeness of his Son, that he might be the firstborn among many brothers. The foreknowledge of God is not only about his omniscience. It is gloriously true that the God of creation, who knows all, saw from eternity those who would love him as they responded to the Gospel. However, in saying that God "foreknew"[67] those who would be saved, Paul is not necessarily saying that they had been elected as individuals. "Foreknowledge" has to do

---

66. Advocated by Fee, *Empowering*, 587–90.

67. "Those God foreknew," refers to the community. It is corporate. See, Zeisler, *Romans*, 226; Fitzmyer, *Romans*, 524. Dunn, *Romans*, 1.482, suggests that "foreknew" has in view the more Hebraic understanding of "knowing" as a relationship. This is unnecessarily rejected by Witherington, *Romans*, 228, as he fails to appreciate the marital language/imagery that is present in the text of Romans—a marriage rooted in the exodus event—when Christ died for his people (Eph 5:25ff.).

with God's covenantal relationship, and, once the term has been put into its OT setting, it naturally conveys the idea of election—but it is an election of the nation. Yahweh said to Israel: "I have loved you with an everlasting love; I have drawn you with loving-kindness" (Jer 31:3). This same love is what Paul focuses on here as he tells the Romans of the certainty that God's purposes will be fulfilled.

Within the theological context of the OT, the term "foreknowledge" has a distinctive Calvinistic dimension. What, however, needs to be remembered is that, if the proposed corporate reading of the letter is correct, this election is of a community like that in the OT. Those who are in Christ are God's elect. As I have pointed out earlier, this does not deny that there is a doctrine of personal election in the NT. However, it does not have the prominence of corporate election, as texts cited in support of individual election are more often about the community. Thus, individual election is subservient to the doctrine of corporate election.[68]

There are two dimensions to the concept of "being conformed to the likeness of his Son"—individual sanctification and, together with other believers, corporate transformation. First, the individual believer is sanctified or transformed by the work of the Spirit (1 Thess 4:3–8). This change is a microcosm of a second, greater transformation which involves the church. It is this community, having been rescued from the kingdom of darkness (the body of Sin), which is transformed into the likeness of Christ (Rom 8:9; 2 Cor 3:18; Phil 2:5–11). It is the covenant community (not the individual) that is created in the image of the heavenly man.[69] Being transformed is not essentially about physical appearance (although this will be part of the ultimate transformation) but about readiness to do the will of God (Rom 12:1–2; cf. Heb 1:8–9).

This was the supreme quality which characterized the life of Jesus. As the church delights to do God's will, she is being conformed to the image of his Son. The nation of Israel had been called to do God's will by taking the message of salvation to the nations (Isa 49:3, 6; 52:7), but she failed in her task, as Jesus made clear (Luke 11:1–14). So, the church was given the mantle of faithful servanthood, and her task remains to take the "word of life" to the ends of the earth (Matt 28:18–20; Rom 10:14–15).

To be conformed is not some eschatological goal but the present reality of what God expects of his people. In his letter to the Philippians, Paul encourages the believers to have the same attitude as Christ, so that they would "become blameless and pure, children of God without fault in a crooked and depraved generation . . . hold(ing) out the word of life" (Phil 2:15–16). Transformation is costly. It will involve representing God in an evil, hostile, and indifferent world. The church should not take the option of keeping her head below the parapet with her mouth sealed in the hope of dwelling in peace. If

---

68. Klien, *Chosen*, cover summary, says that "in scripture you do see individuals chosen/elected to tasks, service, and functions, as well as corporate bodies of people elected/chosen to tasks and services, but nowhere in scripture do you see individuals elected/chosen for salvation. Wherever you do see an election in the context of salvation, the focus is always on the people (pl.) as a corporate body, not on an individual. Principally, Christ is seen as the elect one, and if you are found in him, by virtue of that you are elect."

69. See Holland, *Contours*, 95ff., for discussion on the corporate nature of the new man imagery.

she does, God may confer on her the name *Lo-Ammi,* "not my people," as he did with Israel (Hosea 2:23).

This interpretation is supported by the context because the passage in Romans is about the community on pilgrimage.[70] Further evidence for this interpretation comes from the description of the church's future in Rome when it will experience many trials (Rom 8:31–39). Such tribulation marked the pilgrimage of the nation of Israel as she journeyed to the promised land.

The culmination of the church's transformation into the image of Jesus is when she completes her faithful witness to the nations and brings about the triumph of the kingdom of God. Only then will creation be transformed, for the redemption of all things, through the death of Jesus, will be completed. It is for this reason that Jesus is called "the firstborn of many brothers." The firstborn was the redeemer in the Jewish economy. If one of its family members was forced to sell its inheritance through hardship, it was his responsibility to redeem what was lost to the family and resort it as part of their inheritance.[71] In this way, Jesus is the firstborn, or Redeemer, of many brethren. Through his death, redemption has been secured. He has not only attained the salvation of his brethren but has recovered what they had lost as a result of man's sin. Through his death as the firstborn of all creation, he has redeemed the whole created order (Col 1:13–21) which had come under the curse as a result of the sin of Adam. Now, through the last Adam, it is restored to its perfection and returned to the new man (the church), who will once again rule over it as God's vice-regent (1 Cor 6:2; Gal 3:25–29; Heb 2:5–9; Rev 1:5–6).

Thus, the term "firstborn of many brethren" has a distinctively redemptive content. It speaks of Christ as the Redeemer of his people and the restorer of all that had been lost through the disobedience of Adam.[72] This fits perfectly with the theology of the Christ hymn in Col 1:15–20, where the focus is on the redemption that has been achieved through the death of the firstborn (Col 1:15, 20). The hymn says Christ's death has achieved not merely the redemption of man but the redemption of the whole of creation (hence, he is its firstborn).

8:30 And those he predestined, he also called; those he called, he also justified; those he justified, he also glorified. The language Paul uses is taken directly from the OT Scriptures. He is saying that the privileges of Israel are now the possession of the church. The OT speaks of the experience of Abraham, who was called to leave his homeland

---

70. See also Rom 10:14–21, which is part of a new exodus discussion. The members of the new covenant community are the ones with the "beautiful feet." They are the fulfillment of the type of the returning remnant from the Babylonian exile who were the original pilgrim community.

71. See Lev 25:25–26, 48–49.

72. Dodd, *Romans,* 156; Sanday and Headlam, *Romans,* 218; Buchsel, *TDNT,* 4:353–54. The reference to Christ being the firstborn of many brethren is a further expression of Adamic theology. See, Black, "Adam," 175; Dunn, *Making,* 108; Zeisler, *Romans,* 227. Keesmaat, "Intertextual," 37ff. and Thielman, "Story," 182–83, who suggest an exodus background to the term. Thus, Paul continues to use the backdrop of the universal effects of the fall of Man, and shows that the extent of the salvation Christ achieves before his brethren is the reconciling of all things to himself. His brethren share in that renewed creation. Robichaux, "Christ," 30–38, correctly notes that the term "firstborn"—when used by Paul of Christ—refers to his humanity. However, he fails, like most others, to connect with the Paschal significance.

(Gen 12:1–4), and of the nation of Israel, which was called out of Egypt (Exod 3:10) and Babylon (Isa 62:11–12). The language is essentially corporate, conveying how God fulfilled his promises in bringing people out of slavery to Sin into the freedom of the saints in the kingdom of light. We have already noticed how Paul was able to apply this transition language of the OT to the experience of the church. For further discussion on the use of OT justification language, see comments on Rom 3:21ff. and Rom 4:2.[73]

The OT repeatedly speaks of the pilgrim community journeying to Jerusalem to appear in the presence of God, so seeing his glory. In this way, the pilgrims were "glorified." This is the meaning of the word here, for it is also part of pilgrim imagery.[74] Being "glorified" is essentially being delivered from the damage inflicted by Sin as well as its power, and being restored to the perfection of Adam's pre-fallen condition in the presence of God. The OT presents the completion of the second exodus as a return to Eden (Isa 51:3; Ezek 36:35).

8:31 What, then, shall we say in response to this? If God is for us, who can be against us? Some scholars think this statement preserves part of a primitive hymn.[75] Israel's call to return home meant danger as she journeyed from the land of exile through the wilderness to the promised land. It was a journey beset with crises: wild beasts and bandits, internal strife within the oft-divided community, threats from surrounding nations, and physical discomfort. But God's presence was with her, and, with hindsight, the Israelites could respond to the fears that welled up in their hearts and cry: "If God be for us, who can be against us?"

Paul encourages the Roman believers that no opposition arrayed against them could overcome the purposes God has for them. No doubt, in future days, these words would be repeated time after time as believers watched the gates being opened in the Coliseum, crowds pouring their vile scorn upon them. As lions ran to tear their bodies apart, these words would be a triumphant testimony to the faithfulness of God and their future glory.

8:32 He who did not spare his own Son, but gave him up for us all—how will he not also, along with him, graciously give us all things? Again the theme of pilgrimage is the background to this verse. As the Roman believers journeyed in their weakness, Paul reminds them that, if God went to the lengths of giving up his Son, he will not rescind the purposes he has for them in Rome, or for himself as he pursues his missionary calling. God has given them his Spirit and now gives them "all things."

---

73. See Holland, *Contours*, chapters 8–9, for a discussion on justification and chapter 4 in this commentary.

74. Rom 8:31-39 bristles with traditional Jewish concepts of the suffering of the righteous or elect. In vv. 33–34, the formulations θεὸς ὁ δικαιῶν (*theos ho dikaiōn*) and τίς ὁ κατακρινῶν (*tis ho katakrinōn*) echo Isa 50:8 LXX, the servant's triumphant cry before his coming vindication: ἐγγίζει ὁ δικαιώσας με, τίς ὁ κρινόμενός μοι (*engizei ho dikaiōsas me, tis ho krinomenos moi*).

75. See Krimmer, *Römer*, 226; Kramer, *Son*, 116; Zeller, *Römer*, 166; Best, *Romans*, 103; Taylor, Romans, 57; Wilckens, *Römer*, 1980. However, others see Isa 53 to be the source, see Hahn, *Titles*, 60. For a more recent and novel approach, see Hamerton-Kelly, "Violence," 116.

The pilgrimage in the OT was no different in that God provided for his people in order to bring about his purposes for the nation(s). The uncertainty of undertaking the journey without basic necessities must have created tremendous pressure on the Israelites. But the OT records how God provided for those who responded in faith. The manna in the wilderness (Exod 16:13–16) was evidence of his care. The same imagery is found in John 6, suggesting its familiarity to the early church. Paul takes up the pilgrimage theme, assuring the pilgrim community in Rome that it can be confident that basic needs will be met.

The reason why he can be so positive is because of the logic of God's grace. Having given up his only Son to death to bring his people out of their captivity, he is not going to fail to bring them safely through their pilgrimage to the promised land. Many scholars see the phrase "giving up his own Son" to be an echo of the sacrifice that Abraham was willing to make of Isaac, an event that is known in Jewish writings as the *Aqedah* (the binding), because Isaac was bound on the altar in preparation for his death.[76] The Jewish rabbinical writers argued that the willingness of Abraham to make this sacrifice was so pleasing to God that he treated Abraham and his family as though the sacrifice had actually been made, even though it had not. The Rabbis argued this meant that Isaac had "died" for the sins of his people and that his death had atoned for their sins. The argument of the Jews that they had their own firstborn, whose death had freed them, was used to counter the preaching of the early church.

While there may be an echo of the *Aqedah* in this verse, the reference is better seen as a reference to the death of Jesus as the Passover victim. On the night of the Passover that the life of every beloved firstborn son was taken from the Egyptian families. For the Jews, there was a way of salvation. This was by shedding the blood of lambs in place of the lives of their firstborn. In the Christian Passover, the firstborn Son is not spared but is given up by the father. So, in the OT, the death of the lambs that were substituted for the firstborn began the process of redemption. In the NT, it is the death of Jesus—the beloved firstborn Son of the Father—that has redeemed his brethren and brought them out of bondage to Satan (Col 1:13–22). Having redeemed believers by the blood of his Son, God is not going to turn against them when, in weakness, they strive to obey him.

"How will he not also, along with him, graciously give us all things?" Paul told the believers in Corinth that they had become rich because Christ, who was rich, had become poor (2 Cor 8:9). This is an amazing insight. God did not achieve salvation for his people, and then expect them to battle through in their own strength and ingenuity. No! In Christ he provided all the resources his people would need. Success is assured. Indeed, the church/Christian is called a co-heir with Christ (Rom 8:17), sharing the same resources the Father provided for his Son so that he could fulfill his mission. Paul will develop the theme of the church's pilgrimage and her mission in Rom 10:14–15.

The term χαρίσεται (*charisetai*) "graciously" is a cognate of the Greek word χάρις (*charis*) "grace." Everything that God gives us—even the ongoing provision to his people

---

76. See Wright, *Romans*, 610; Cranfield, *Shorter*, 208. Contra, Chilton and Davies, "Aqedah," 546. Käsemann, *Romans*, 247, considers that the phrase, "gave him up for us all," had been preserved in either a baptismal or Eucharistic confession.

following their salvation—is from his grace. God's grace in giving believers "all things" is never earned or limited: τὰ πάντα ἡμῖν χαρίσεται (*ta panta hēmin charisetai*) "graciously give us all things." It is probable that Paul uses the expression "all things" in the light of its earlier use in Rom 8:28ff.

8:33 Who will bring any charge against those whom God has chosen? It is God who justifies. Paul has already dealt with the possibility of an accusation of guilt being brought against the church for entering into another marriage relationship (Rom 6:7; 7:1–4). Satan will accuse Christ and the church that their union is not lawful. Should the call go out: "if anyone can show any just cause why they may not lawfully be joined together in matrimony, let him now declare it, or else hereafter for ever hold his peace" he is ready to cry out: "She is mine. She is already married." It is into this awful scene that Paul confidently declares: "It is God who justifies!" The judge of the whole earth will not accept there is a charge to answer, and Paul states why this is so in the next verse. Of course, if Satan cannot persuade believers that it was unlawful for Christ to take his people as his bride then he will find other means to charge them. The answer to all charges, whatever they may be, is: "Christ has died and is risen! Hallelujah!"

This marital context for the charge against God's people is supported by those who identify vv. 33b, 34 as an echo of Isa 50:8. In this prophecy, the Servant asks: "He who vindicates me is near. Who then will bring charges against me?" If we examine this Isaianic text in its wider context, we find that the prophet has been explaining the marital status of Israel after God sent her into exile. Isa 50:1 asks: "Where is your mother's certificate of divorce with which I sent her away? Or to which of my creditors did I sell you?"

The prophet is soon to say: "I delight greatly in the LORD; my soul rejoices in my God. For he has clothed me with garments of salvation and arrayed me in a robe of righteousness, as a bridegroom adorns his head like a priest, and as a bride adorns herself with her jewels." (Isa 61:10). In Isa 62:5, he will say: "As a young man marries a maiden, so will your sons marry you; as a bridegroom rejoices over his bride, so will your God rejoice over you."

If Paul is consciously intertextualizing his sources (as he clearly does elsewhere) then he is deliberately feeding off the divine marriage theme, and it is in this context that the significance of the charge should be read. There is no charge that can be brought that would nullify the relationship God is bringing his church into, i.e., the consummation of the divine marriage.

8:34 Who is he that condemns? Christ Jesus, who died—more than that, who was raised to life—is at the right hand of God and is also interceding for us. The accusation cannot stand. There is no illegal relationship. The death of the second Adam has brought to an end the reign of Sin and Death; the people of God have been released; and the pilgrimage, which will culminate in their marriage to the Lamb, has begun!

While on pilgrimage, the Jews had a high priest who constantly represented them before God (Heb 5:1–4; 9:7–10). Throughout their journey, they faced spiritual and moral temptations as well as dangers from enemies who sought to prevent them from reaching their inheritance. Because of this, the ministry of the high priest was crucial. He offered sacrifices for the sins of his people and interceded for them. Yet this very high priest was under the same ultimate sentence of judgment and death as the ones he represented.

However, this is not so for the high priest of the Christian church. He has a ministry which is based on the power of an endless life (Heb 7:16), for he was raised to life. He does not have to sacrifice animals, for he has put away sin by offering himself (Rom 3:21ff.; Heb 9:11–15; Rev 1:4–6). His priestly ministry is complete, for he has brought all his people out of the kingdom of darkness and made them fit for the kingdom of light. Jesus is able to do this because he is the Melchizedek priest who is the Son of David (Ps 110:1–4; cf. Matt 22:41–45; Heb 5:1–10; Rev 1:12–18). As the promised descendant of David (Rom 1:3), he is the fulfillment of the Melchizedek priesthood in being both king and priest. It was Jesus who was raised up to bring salvation to his people, as the prophets had foretold (Luke 1:46–55, 67–79; 2:8–38).

The theme of Christ's intercession is throughout the NT. His priesthood is not only in this passage but lies beneath the surface of much of the Gospel material. It is found throughout the Pauline letters, in Peter, Revelation, and, particularly, the Epistle to the Hebrews.[77] Clearly, it was a theme from which the early Christians would have drawn comfort and assurance during the sufferings that engulfed them.

We have seen that the previous verse echoes Isa 50:8. In Paul's statement concerning Christ's intercession, it is possible there is an echo of the intercessory work of the Servant, who is spoken of in Isa 53:12.

8:35 Who shall separate us from the from the love of Christ? Shall trouble or hardship or persecution or famine or nakedness or danger or sword? Paul continues to paint the picture of the church's security in her Savior. It began in v. 33 with: "Who will bring any charge against those whom God has chosen?" and continues in v. 34 with: "Who is he that condemns?" Now, in v. 35, Paul asks: "Who shall separate us from the love of Christ?" Of course, the answer is "No one!" The Roman Christians are absolutely safe. God's good purposes for them stand secure, and nothing—not even the extreme experiences of life in Rome—can affect their relationship with Christ, who intercedes for them at the Father's right hand.

While the list of hardships in v. 35 can find a natural home in Paul's life and ministry (2 Cor 4:4–10; 6:4–10; 11:23b–28), they also reflect the extremes the OT pilgrim community experienced as they travelled through the wilderness following their deliverances from Egypt and Babylon.[78] We shall see, in chapter 10, that Paul deliberately adopts the pilgrimage language of Isaiah and applies it to the church, the NT pilgrim community.

The description in this verse is not limited to physical hardships either. Many believers have suffered psychological persecution for being Christians: famine in their

---

77. See Holland, "Motif," chapter 5.

78. Belli, "Is 50:8–9," 153–84, analyses Rom 8:31–39, with particular attention to its structure and rhetorical composition. He concludes that its allusion to Isa 50:8–9 is identifiable at literary, stylistic and thematic levels. He also notes that Paul's use of Isa 50:8–9 in Rom 8:31–39 displays the particular role assumed by the Isaianic Servant of Yahweh for understanding God's fidelity toward his elect, and the paradoxical character of justification through suffering and death. This is similar to the view of Maartens, "Inference," 1046–87.

souls, nakedness in their spirits, and dangers at every level (2 Cor 1:8–9a; 4:8; 6:8–10; 11:28–33). While the term "danger" might refer to the normal mishaps that befall all people, it is more likely that Paul had in mind the sort of experiences he had throughout his life as a Christian (2 Cor 11:26). The reference to the sword, however, possibly refers to the persecution of believers. This would be particularly pertinent to the church in Rome as, in coming days, the sword would strike her as she sought to bear witness in a city where lives hung on the word of a despot. However, this fragile Christian community was going to experience the power of God in her suffering, and triumph over all that the forces of darkness would bring against her.

8:36 As it is written: "For your sake we face death all day long; we are considered as sheep to be slaughtered." The quotation used by Paul is from Ps 44:22. Its context is the Babylonian exile, and the psalm speaks of how the covenant community was treated by its conquerors.[79] They have no regard for the welfare of the people they have conquered– their lives are of little importance and they are seen as having no value (Ps 44:13–16; cf. 2 Cor 6:8–9). The exiles will be put to death at the first sign of dissent (Ps 44:10–11, 22), yet the psalmist writes that their deaths will be "for your (God's) sake."

The fall of Jerusalem was only part of the conquering ambition of the Babylonians and the deportation of most survivors into exile would ensure subordination. Among those deported were Jews who stayed true to Yahweh, despite the waywardness of the rest of Israel (Ps 44:8–12). The psalmist focused on the Lord's chastening of this remnant for, despite being faithful, these innocent Jews suffered with the guilty during their time in exile (Ps 44:17–19).

The remnant recalled the victories God secured for his people in the past, and they cried to him for help, asking that he would redeem them again (Ps 44:23–24, 26). The outcome of such redemption would be the extolling of Yahweh's glorious name among the nations as they witnessed his righteous dealings with Israel (Ps 44:24–25). Such a clear display of his holiness would send out a warning to the nations that they must seek him while he could be found. Paul quotes from this psalm because it reflects the experience of the new covenant pilgrim community, the OT remnant, and NT church suffering in spite of their integrity and faithfulness to God.

There is another way in which the phrase: "for your sake" might be understood. It could refer to the fact that, once in exile, the covenant community was faced with the startling choice of conforming or suffering. The clearest example of dedication to faithfulness is found in the book of Daniel, which records the story of a group of Jews who were ready to die rather than deny the God whom they served. They were the Hebrew equivalent of the Holiness Club that developed in Oxford University. Here, some of its brightest men vowed that they would spend their lives serving God and extending his kingdom. From this group emerged such men as Wesley and Whitfield, whose preaching changed the destiny of nations.

79. Morris, *Romans*, 339, points out that the NIV has weakened the force of Paul's statement, for he follows Ps 44:22 and says: "We are being killed all day long." Barrett comments, "Suffering and persecution are not mere evils which Christians must expect and endure as best they can; they are the scene of the overwhelming victory which Christians are winning through Christ" (*Romans*, 137).

Any commitment is costly, and there will always be enemies. The tragedy is that persecution can come from within the church itself. It often springs from self-interest when established power structures are threatened. Jesus had to face this reality, and his disciples were not protected from it either (John 15:18–27; Acts 4:1–22; 6:8–15; 7:54–60). Paul is expounding on the earlier theme of being "conformed to the likeness of his Son" (v. 29). "Being conformed," means sharing in his sufferings and becoming like him in his death (Phil 3:10). To say that we want to be like Jesus is to say that we want the very foundations of our existence challenged, shaken, and possibly replaced. Such talk is dangerous indeed! Yet this is what God's people are called to.

8:37 No, in all of these things we are more than conquerors through him who loved us. The anticipation of suffering and death should not deter the members of the pilgrim community. If the phrase: "all of these things" refers to the list of tribulations in vv. 35–36, Paul is saying that, in all these experiences, he and the Roman Christians are more than conquerors because of Christ's love for them.

The alternate interpretation of the phrase: "all these things" is that it is a recurrence of "all things" in vv. 28, 32. In light of this reading, Paul is saying: "No one can bring a charge against us! We have been called by God and our relationship with Christ is settled. No one can condemn us, as Christ has died to redeem us, and, what is more—having been raised—he now intercedes for us. He will never stop loving us. We are his bride whom he will never abandon. Even though the whole world is arrayed against us, we will remain conquerors because our election still stands, our calling still stands, our justification still stands, and our future glorification still stands. And how can we be so certain? Because Christ; the lover of our souls and our betrothed, is forever faithful."[80]

Paul knows that believers have not been redeemed to be eventually forsaken. The history of the covenant people of the OT demonstrates the faithfulness of God and his commitment to his people. Not even judgment and exile could bring God's love for his people to an end. His covenant to Abraham was not abandoned, but moved towards its fulfillment in the new covenant promised to those in exile. These new covenant promises (Jer 31:31–34; 33:4–26; Ezek 36:22–32) focused on blessing the Gentiles through raising up the descendant of David who fulfilled the promise of the covenant made with Abraham (Isa 11:1–10; 19:16–25; 42:1–9; 60:1–3). Thus, the new covenant brings to completion the promises God made to Abram (Gen 12:1–3), and to David (2 Sam 7:4–17).

---

80. Even though he does not recognize the power of the divine marriage motif in Romans, Wright, "Theology," 55, says: "Rom 8:31–39, like a musical coda, picks up the theme of the entire letter thus far and celebrates them in good rhetorical style. The divine love, which has been under the argument since 5:6–10, re-emerges as the real major theme of the entire gospel message. This is covenant love, promised to Abraham and his family, a family now seen to be the worldwide people who benefit from Jesus' death. Since this love is precisely the Creator's love, it remains sovereign even though the powers of earth and heaven may seem to be ranged against it. Since it is the love of the covenant god, it rests on his unbreakable promise. The language of the law court and the language of the marriage contract thus merge (8:33–34; 35–39), with both of them now revealed as vital metaphorical aspects of the one more fundamental truth, which can be expressed both as δικαιοσύνη γὰρ θεοῦ ('righteousness of god') and as ἀγάπη θεοῦ ('love of God'): the covenant faithfulness of the Creator god, revealed in the death and resurrection of Jesus the Messiah and the gift of the Spirit."

The two possible interpretations of "all these things" imply that believers were (or would be) victims of awful circumstances. But, there is an alternative reading that could suggest otherwise.

The early church was clear there would be a reward for suffering (Matt 19:27–30; 1 Cor 2:6–16; Phil 1:19–30; Heb 12:28). However, Paul does not focus on reward in this verse but goes to the very heart of the Gospel. It is the love of Christ that has set believers free, and through him they conquer. This all-conquering love has driven thousands, including Paul, to take calculated risks for the sake of the Gospel, putting themselves in the way of trouble, hardship, persecution, famine etc., and death. Compared to the magnitude of God's self-giving in the person of Jesus, the magnitude of their self-giving is reckoned as very small indeed. Many, like Paul, count it joy to suffer in "the going and making disciples of all nations," because Christ is with them "to the very end of the age" (Matt 28:19–20). Thus, in this context—which can be supported by what Paul will go on to say about the church's mandate to be the suffering servant who declares Yahweh's salvation (Rom 10:5–15)—Paul refers to the sufferings of the church as the "all things" that she conquers. Thus, the focus is much more honed—suffering is not about the consequences of being the people of God but are about the consequences of *living* as the people of God, fulfilling the master's mandate to make disciples of all nations. Sadly, there are many Christians who never experience suffering because they never bear witness when the going gets tough.

8:38 For I am convinced that neither death nor life, neither angels nor demons, neither the present nor the future, nor any powers, The strength of Paul's confidence in the faithfulness of God to keep his covenant promises enables him to make use the strongest language to encourage the church as she faces the conflicts that will arise during her pilgrimage and service. This is no whistling in the dark with the hope that dangers may never materialize, for Paul has already faced most, if not all, of them. He was crushed and almost destroyed when fulfilling his calling (2 Cor 11:16–33). He knew this suffering had not been an unfortunate accident but had been an inevitable part of the commission to preach the Gospel to the nations (Acts 9:16; 2 Tim 1:8–14; 2:8–13).

For the Jew—without the certainty of resurrection—there was the ever-threatening presence of death. Paul would remember the days when he feared that death would cause his separation from the covenant people and fellowship with God. This fear is evidenced throughout the OT, especially in psalms (Ps 30:8–12; 88:4–5, 10–12; 102:23–24; 116:3–4). Believers in the early church, however, knew that, as a result of the resurrection of Jesus Christ, life and immortality had been brought to light (2 Tim1:10). It is difficult for those who have known the Christian message from childhood to appreciate the darkness that many people live under as they face death. No unconverted person can have the confidence Paul speaks of in this verse, but, in contrast, the believer knows that his relationship with God will never be severed—not even by death. This is the wonder of the Gospel!

However, it is not only death that threatens fellowship with God—it is life itself. Certain experiences can overwhelm people. They can find themselves swamped by dangers that threaten not only their lives but their confidence in God's love for them. Such experiences are well recorded in the psalms, where we find psalmists crying to God for help. Heman's psalm (Ps 88) is one such psalm. Grandson of Samuel and a Levite in charge of music before the tabernacle (1 Chron 6:31–34, 39), Heman rose to become David's seer (1 Chron 25:5). He knew God's blessing on his life (1 Chron 25:4–5) but drew near to death alone and in deep distress. He expresses the feelings of many a broken Christian when he writes: "darkness is my closest friend" (Ps 88:18b).

However, the psalms which express anguish repeatedly show that, even though their composers may be distressed and feel abandoned; God had not left them or turned his face from them. A Psalm of David (Ps 22) speaks of this misconception. David graphically describes his brokenness of spirit, and, as he starts writing, his immediate complaint to God is: "Why have you forsaken me?" As he continues composing, his faith in the ever-present God is rekindled, and a wonderful cry of faith is given in v. 24: "he has not despised or disdained the suffering of the afflicted one; he has not hidden his face from him but has listened to his cry for help." This psalm, thought to be the one Jesus quoted from the cross (Matt 27:46), is said to provide evidence that God turned away from his beloved Son in his passion. The justification for his action is said to be that God could not look on sin. This apparent severing of the relationship between the Father and his Son, it is argued, was the greatest pain that Jesus bore at Calvary—greater, indeed, than his physical sufferings. However, if Jesus was identifying with this psalm, we have, in his passion, a magnificent demonstration of faith. Despite his brokenness and *feeling* of abandonment, God had not turned away from him and hidden his face, but inclined his ear toward him and listened to his cry for help. The very request of the psalm that God would come to David's aid quickly (v. 19) was met in the manner of Christ's death (Mark 15:44–45). The persecuted people of God, such as the Roman believers, are united with their Savior in his experience, and, throughout their innocent sufferings and feelings of abandonment, they prove the everlasting love and faithfulness of God, and receive his vindication.

Paul writes to the believers about his conviction that neither angels nor demons could separate Paul and the church in Rome from the love of God in Christ Jesus. The forces of darkness were no match for the power of God that was promised to his people as they made their journey back from exile in Babylon to their inheritance in the promised land. Travelling at night across the desert (a place where the forces of evil were understood to dwell) would have been a terrifying experience for the Jewish community. Even the heavenly bodies seemed to have deadly and lethal powers that could strike at night (Ps 121:6).

As for the church in Rome, she is making her pilgrimage through a hostile world. Some of the hostility that greets her is nothing more than normal human conflict, which is an expression of a fallen world. However, some is of a different order, threatening her very existence and testimony. Such hostility comes from beyond those instruments of opposition—it comes from the forces of darkness, which Paul says believers must stand against (Eph 6:10–18).

In saying the present and the future are not being able to separate Paul and the believers in Rome from God's love, it is notable that he does not mention the past. For him the believers have nothing to fear from what has gone before. The death of Christ has dealt completely and finally with the guilt that lurks in their consciences—their pasts will never catch them up, at least, not in terms of it being brought before God for judgment.

However, what could there be about the present or the future that would threaten the Roman believers as they seek to follow Christ? Perhaps they are afraid their faith might fail, their status might be lost, or reputation discredited. They may fear the consequences of ill health, unemployment, bereavement, and any one of a host of social, spiritual, physical, and economic dangers. Paul knew these fears as well; he was no different from them. At one time he despaired of life itself (2 Cor 4:7–18), but his testimony to them is that none of these things "will be able to separate us from the love of God that is in Christ Jesus our Lord" (v. 39). The security of the Roman believers lies not in their ability to negotiate the perils of life but in the certainty that God has promised to care, protect, and bring them safely home.

Paul leaves nothing outside of this tremendous declaration of confidence. Through these and the following phrases he gathers together everything that can possibly harm the believers in Rome, concluding with the affirmation that there is no power that can separate them from God's love in Christ Jesus.

8:39 Neither height nor depth, nor anything else in all creation, will be able to separate us from the love of God that is in Christ Jesus our Lord. Paul concludes his declaration of confidence by exposing every possible opposition.[81] He goes to those regions that are outside of the experience of man and says that there is no dimension that has the power to sever him and the believing community in Rome from the love of God.

Paul uses the same word for "height" when speaking about the nature of his ministry and the warfare in which he is engaged (2 Cor 10:5). In that passage, he speaks about demolishing the "arguments and every pretension that sets itself up against the knowledge of God."

The term "depth" has roots in OT thinking. In Ezek 32:24, the prophet spoke about Israel's enemies being consigned to the pit. We have seen how Ezekiel influenced Paul's theological understanding and this suggests that he might well be reflecting Ezekiel's meaning of the term. If true, it suggests Paul is saying that all the enemies that Christ has conquered—including death itself—can do no harm to his church.

In conclusion, absolutely nothing–not even events or powers that come from those areas that terrify man—can separate the people of God from the one who loves them. Hallelujah!

CONCLUSION OF ROMANS 8

Paul's teaching reflects the setting of Sinai where Israel received the law and became the bride of Yahweh. Here she sinned, becoming the unfaithful wife on the first night of her

---

81. Morris, *Romans*, 340, points out that the terms are often used in astronomy. If this is Paul's reference point here, then he is saying that neither the height (when a star is at its zenith) nor the depth (with its entire unknown potential) is strong enough to separate believers from God's love.

marriage. Paul assures the church that her experience of redemption has not brought her into condemnation. There is now no condemnation to those who are in Christ Jesus. This is a work of God that the law—holy and good though it was—could not achieve. The decisive factor is the presence and work of the Spirit in the life of the community.

Chapter 8 uses pilgrimage imagery. The church is called to walk in the Spirit and not to live after the flesh—leaving God out of her world view as Israel had done. She is journeying to the inheritance that her Redeemer has secured. No matter how the forces of darkness attempt to discourage her, she can have absolute confidence that God will bring her safely through all the perils of the journey and the sufferings her mission brings her into. Nothing can separate her from the love of God.

Again the argument has been driven by the new exodus theme. However, the inheritance of the church is not just to live in Zion; it is to be with Yahweh. This encounter will lead to the celebration of God's love for his people. It will result in the wedding feast of all wedding feasts and the marriage of all marriages, for the bridegroom is none other than Jesus! While the church—and indeed, all of creation—awaits this great celebration, nothing can separate the people of God in Rome from the love Jesus has for his betrothed.

ROMANS 9

THE MESSIAH KING AND ISRAEL'S HARDENING

I SPEAK THE truth in Christ—I am not lying, my conscience confirms it in the Holy Spirit—I have great sorrow and unceasing anguish in my heart. For I could wish that I myself were cursed and cut off from Christ for the sake of my brothers, those of my own race, the people of Israel. Theirs is the adoption as sons; theirs the divine glory, the covenants, the receiving of the law, the temple worship and the promises. Theirs are the patriarchs, and from them is traced the human ancestry of Christ, who is God over all, forever praised! Amen. It is not as though God's word had failed. For not all who are descended from Israel are Israel. Nor because they are his descendants are they all Abraham's children. On the contrary, "It is through Isaac that your offspring will be reckoned." In other words, it is not the natural children who are God's children, but it is the children of the promise who are regarded as Abraham's offspring. For this was how the promise was stated: "At the appointed time I will return, and Sarah will have a son." Not only that, but Rebekah's children had one and the same father, our father Isaac. Yet, before the twins were born or had done anything good or bad—in order that God's purpose in election might stand: not by works but by him who calls—she was told, "The older will serve the younger." Just as it is written: "Jacob I loved, but Esau I hated."

What then shall we say? Is God unjust? Not at all! For he says to Moses,

"I will have mercy on whom I have mercy, and I will have compassion on whom I have compassion."

It does not, therefore, depend on man's desire or effort, but on God's mercy. For the Scripture says to Pharaoh: "I raised you up for this very purpose, that I might display my power in you and that my name might be proclaimed in all the earth." Therefore God has mercy on whom he wants to have mercy, and he hardens whom he wants to harden.

One of you will say to me: "Then why does God still blame us? For who resists his will?" But who are you, O man, to talk back to God? Shall what is formed say to him who formed it, "Why did you make me like this?" Does not the potter have the right to make out of the same lump of clay some pottery for noble purposes and some for common use? What if God, choosing to show his wrath and make his power known, bore with great patience the objects of his wrath—prepared for destruction? What if he did this to make the riches of his glory known to the objects of his mercy, whom he prepared in advance for glory—even us, whom he also called, not only from the Jews but also from the Gentiles? As he says in Hosea:

"I will call them 'my people' who are not my people; and I will call her 'my loved one' who is not my loved one,"

and,

"It will happen that in the very place where it was said to them, 'You are not my people,' they will be called 'sons of the living God.'"

Isaiah cries out concerning Israel:

"Though the number of the Israelites be like the sand by the sea, only the remnant will be saved. For the Lord will carry out his sentence on earth with speed and finality."

It is just as Isaiah said previously:

"Unless the Lord Almighty had left us descendants, we would have become like Sodom, we would have been like Gomorrah."

What then shall we say? That the Gentiles, who did not pursue righteousness, have obtained it, a righteousness that is by faith; but Israel, who pursued a law of righteousness, has not attained it. Why not? Because they pursued it not by faith but as if it were by works. They stumbled over the "stumbling-stone." As it is written:

"See, I lay in Zion a stone that causes men to stumble and a rock that makes them fall, and the one who trusts in him will never be put to shame." (Rom 9:1–33)

INTRODUCTION

Chapters 9–11 have been at the heart of attempts to understanding Paul's understanding of election. Many scholars have seen the section as an intrusion into the letter, disrupting the argument that was being made; but, in recent decades, it has been appreciated that these chapters are the purpose for Paul writing the letter.[1] In fact, the continuity of the argument is evident in that Rom 9:4–23 has a number of close parallels with Rom 3:1-7.[2]

Some Jewish believers were insisting that in order to be true members of the covenant people, Gentile believers had to keep the law and submit to circumcision. While such demands may have come from sincere attempts to apply the law, it is likely they were motivated by unspoken political concerns. The believing Jews must have been intimidated by the ever-increasing number of Gentiles who were professing faith in Jesus as Messiah and God's Son. At Paul's insistence, which was strengthened by the agreement he had won from the Jerusalem Council (Acts 15:12–35), the Gentiles were being admitted into the community of the Messiah on the same terms as the Jews. They were of little threat while their numbers remained relatively low. However, the blessing that accompanied their evangelization and the increasing resistance of the Jewish people to the message of the crucified Messiah meant that the Gentiles were speedily taking the reins of power in local believing communities by virtue of their numbers.

The problems produced by this growth were tearing the early church apart. A number of Jewish disciples came to believe that the only way to rein in the growing influence and power of the Gentile converts was to demand that they be circumcised. By controlling who was accorded full covenant membership, they could keep the upper hand. It was a simple, effective move, but one that Paul could not tolerate.

The danger with a divided community was that each faction would see the other as renegade. This was Paul's deepest fear as it would damage the gospel message incalculably. On the other hand, believing Jews and Gentiles living in harmony with each

---

1. Wright, *Messiah*, 166, says the theology in chapters 1–11 remains the same. Stendahl, "Introspective," 205, claims that chapters 9–11 are not an appendix but the climax of the letter. Räisänen, "Conversion," 410, says chapters 9–11 are about rejecting covenantal privilege. Gaston, "Enemies," 415, points out that the phrase "instruments of wrath" is based on Isa 53. This, once again, links the argument with the exile and new exodus promises.

2. See Williams, "Righteousness," 281.

other would be a great demonstration of the power of God to restore relationships and overcome the evil of hatred and alienation.

Paul devotes the next section of his letter (chapters 9–11) to show that believing Jews and believing Gentiles are part of God's salvation purposes and how the rejection of one by the other is a denial of the Gospel. He shows that it is God's intention, as expressed in the Law and the Prophets, for Gentiles to be converted and for their successful evangelization to provoke unbelieving Jews to turn to the Messiah. Paul also wants the believing Gentiles to realize that they cannot exist, as far as God is concerned, without believing Jewish people—the remnant in Israel cannot be treated as having been cast off by God and, therefore, irrelevant.

However, Paul has to address another sensitive matter—the status of unbelieving Israel. In keeping with the corporate, covenantal framework he has been using throughout the letter, the text will be interpreted as a development of the new exodus theme. Paul is concerned to show that Israel is in danger of being left outside of the covenant, which has been brought to fulfillment in Christ. Ironically, this is the very covenant made with Abraham, the father of the Jewish nation. We have seen the developing new exodus theme in chapters 1–8, Rom 8:29–36 uses pilgrimage language to speak of opposition to the pilgrim community as it journeys to its inheritance. We also saw that Rom 7:1–4 summed up the argument of Rom 5:12—6:23. The issue at stake was how a people could be brought out of a relationship with Satan and into a new relationship with God. This relationship, in keeping with OT imagery and the expectation of a second exodus, was described using marital language. Israel was called to be Yahweh's bride, and she gloried in this privilege and status.

The question Paul must now answer is: "where do the Jewish people fit into the new exodus?" Are they automatically included on the basis of having been the people of the Egyptian exodus? Do they bypass the conditions that are imposed on Gentiles who wish to be part of this community? Do they have a privileged status within it? Can they cast a deciding vote over who is included?

Paul fears that this new community–this new man–is in danger of self-destruction as Jews and Gentiles argue over their status before God. The Jews can, of course, appeal to their history and the promises given to their ancestor, Abraham. The Gentiles, however, can claim that the experience of the Jewish people *is* history, and that God has cast them aside in favor of blessing Gentiles. Their growing numbers and increasing dominance in the church must have seemed like undeniable evidence that this was so.

In chapter 9,[3] Paul begins his defense of Israel's status. Conscious of how crucial this issue is, he is concerned that the Gentile converts understand God's purpose for his ancient people so that they can relate appropriately to them. However, behind Paul's argument is a further concern: "if God can cast off his ancient people who were bound to him by covenant, what security can there be for the new covenant community? Can God's promises be taken seriously if he was able to abandon his people when they failed him? Is God's commitment to the New Israel as frail as his commitment to her predeces-

---

3. Martin, "Kerygma," 308, considers that chapters 9–11 recapitulate the argument of chapters 1–8.

sor? If he chooses to disengage himself from his covenant promises to her, will not his reputation and the confidence of his people be at stake?" Paul reminds the Romans that the Jews have the birthright. They had received blessings from which the Gentiles were excluded. They had been privileged beyond any other nation on earth (Rom 9:1–5).

Paul goes on to show the principles of foreknowledge and election operating throughout salvation history. They were active when he called Jacob instead of Esau (Rom 9:6–17) and when he dealt with Pharaoh. God is at liberty to show mercy or to judge as he wills–and none can argue.[4] As the potter has freedom to mold clay however he wishes, so God has the right to express his will by exercising justice in the form of judgment (which all deserve) or mercy and forgiveness (which none deserve) (Rom 9:14–24).

It would be wrong to use these texts to support individual election.[5] In line with the argument of the whole Epistle, they are dealing with representative heads of communities. The freedom that a person has to enter or reject membership is a different matter. As this material applies primarily to states of solidarity, there are hermeneutical issues that need to be faced before truths are removed from their intended context and applied to the salvation of the individual. There are important overlapping concepts and principles in corporate and individual models, and these must be worked through and clarified before using them without reference to their original context and purpose.[6] In general, out of its great traditional concern for the salvation of the individual, Reformed theology has given insufficient emphasis to the corporate dimension of the argument being presented by Paul in this passage. However, while the corporate perspective must be kept to the fore, the argument in this section is presented in terms of individuals as Paul deals with heads of communities. This indicates that there must be individual significance in what is being said even though personal salvation is not the primary thrust of the passage.[7]

What is most significant is that Paul uses OT material that prophesies the Babylonian exile, bringing it into the developing new exodus theme. He says that the final manifestation of Yahweh's righteousness is displayed in the fulfillment of the promise he made long ago to include the Gentile nations in the experience of the new exodus salvation. This new exodus is about bringing out the new covenant people of God from the domain of Sin. It does not deny the earlier covenants made with Israel–faith has always been the principle of initiation for sharing in the righteousness of God. Israel "after the flesh" was not being rejected, but invited into the new covenant. Many would refuse, preferring to misuse the law in a hopeless attempt to secure righteousness. Nevertheless, a remnant in

---

4. Later, I will suggest that the argument is not principally about showing mercy in salvation (as is often understood) but more about grace in granting unmerited privilege, see Excursus H: Election to Privilege and Service, page 310.

5. For discussion on Rom 9 and individual election, see Schreiner, "Election," 25–40.

6. See, for example, the discussion on justification in Excursus D: Justification in the Theology of Paul, pages 107–30.

7. The case parallels what we find in Rom 5:12ff. Adam, as the representative of his descendents, responds to God in such a way that they will know alienation and personal judgement. While the focus is Adam's sin, they are all involved because, collectively, they are "in Adam." Here, Pharaoh represents his people, who will come under judgment as a result of his decisions. If the corporate focus is taken away from either passage, a very different and inadequate reading will be produced.

Israel would be saved. This was a constant principle in the old covenant. A remnant had always stood against the Jewish community's popular mindset (2 Chr 34:21; Isa 10:20; 11:16; 37:32; Zeph 3:13). They would share in the faith of the Messiah as true people of God. This is in complete accord with the principle of election and is fundamental to all that the prophets had taught (Rom 9:25–33).

The new exodus motif is further underlined as Paul considers Pharaoh. The hardening of his heart was prior to the exodus (Rom 9:17–18) and, amazingly, Paul applies the same principle to his own kinsmen, unbelieving Israel (Rom 11:25)! By refusing to become part of the remnant, they have become the victims of the divine hardening and, as a result, have been excluded from the experience of the new exodus. In this attitude of disobedience, they have done everything they could to deter their fellow countrymen from joining the people of the Way. In other words, unbelieving Israel in the new exodus reflects Pharaoh in the Egyptian exodus. They both resist God and both have hardened hearts.

We have already noted the extensive use that Paul makes of Isaiah. Here, in chapter 9, there are quotations from Isaiah in vv. 15, 27, 29, and 33. Each of these has been carefully chosen by Paul to support his ongoing argument, without doing injustice to their original contexts.[8]

9:1 I speak the truth in Christ—I am not lying, my conscience confirms it in the Holy Spirit. Paul is concerned that he is not seen as rejecting his kinsfolk. He swears an oath, affirming that what he is about to say is a true reflection of his feelings for his kinsmen. Paul expresses grief over the state of unbelieving Israel. It was vital for the Roman Jewish believers to know that his grief was genuine as fabricated distress was a feature of their culture. The presence of professional mourners at the deathbed of Jairus's daughter in Capernaum is an example of such disingenuous sorrow, which turned so quickly to mocking laughter (Luke 8:51–53).

In the past, Paul's word had been doubted. Three years after his conversion, believing Jews in Jerusalem did not accept his story as true (Gal 1:18–20) and Barnabas had to speak, on his behalf, to the apostles (Acts 9:26–27). It was fourteen years later that Paul's testimony was believed in Jerusalem when he was accepted by the "pillars" of the church as an apostle to the Gentiles and given the right hand of fellowship (Gal 2:1–10).

No wonder Paul had such strong feelings about telling the truth and defending his trustworthiness—a matter he touched on in a number of his letters. He warned of untruthfulness in his letter to the Colossians (Col 3:9–10), where, interestingly, he raised the issue in the context of church unity. When defending his ministry to the Corinthians, Paul wrote: "The God and Father of the Lord Jesus, who is to be praised forever, knows that I am not lying" (2 Cor 11:31).

---

8. Aletti, "L'argumentation," 41–56, claims that Paul's argument in Rom 9 is concentric: A (vv. 6–9) and B (vv. 10–13): the divine choice, C (vv. 14–18) and C' (vv. 19–24): questions and answers concerning God and his justice, B' (vv. 25–26) and A' (vv. 27–29): the divine choice. Such an analysis reveals that Paul's emphasis in this chapter concerns the contrast between the elect and the non-elect. This observation suggests that chapter 9 is closely connected to chapter 8.

Paul stressed that he is speaking the truth "in Christ." This is a solemn claim for him to make as he has written in chapter 8 about the one who "searches our hearts" (v. 27). In order to fully appreciate the corporate nature of his arguments, it is important to keep in mind that Paul normally applies the term "in Christ" to communities of believers rather than individuals. Some of the believing communities that he describes in this way are the Ephesian (Eph 2:13), Corinthian (1 Cor 15:18; 16:24), Philippians (Phil 1:1; 4:21), and Colossians (Col 1:2).

Paul writes that his conscience supports his claim of truthfulness and adds the phrase "in the Holy Spirit." This could be a reference to Rom 8:26, where he acknowledged the help given by the Holy Spirit to all believers, aiding them in areas of weakness.

9:2 I have great sorrow and unceasing anguish in my heart. Paul's experience can only be understood by those who have been rejected by the people they love. He was not alone in having such an experience. David is considered by some to have composed Psalm 22 after fleeing from Jerusalem to escape the tyranny of his son, Absalom. He described the emotion of such rejection in this way: "I am poured out like water, all my bones are out of joint. My heart has turned to wax; it has melted away within me" (Ps 22:14).[9]

From his letters and the Acts of the Apostles, we learn of Paul's intense sufferings, including those he experienced at the hands of his fellow Jews. He was stoned in Lystra and left for dead (Acts 14:19), publicly misrepresented in Ephesus (Acts 19:9), beaten in Jerusalem (Acts 21:27–32), and lashed on five occasions (2 Cor 11:24). In addition to physical sufferings, Paul writes these telling words in his letter to the Corinthians: "Besides everything else, I face daily the pressure of my concern for all the churches. Who is weak, and I do not feel weak? Who is led into sin, and I do not inwardly burn?" (2 Cor 11:28–29).

Such openness helps us to appreciate the man behind this statement in Rom 9:2; for, in addition to his immense concern for his kinsmen, he carried the memory of all that he had suffered at their hands as well as his daily concern for the churches. In spite of the ever repeating cycle in his heart of sorrow and anguish, Paul could not help but love his unbelieving brethren.[10] He felt this way because he knew the privileges that his kinsmen were rejecting, and of the judgment that faced them (Rom 9:25–29) if they lived and died rejecting the Savior whom God had sent (Rom 11:26).

9:3 For I could wish that I myself were cursed and cut off from Christ for the sake of my brothers, those of my own race, the people of Israel. The intensity of Paul's

---

9. The psalm is, of course, applied to Jesus, the Messiah, in the NT. As a Psalm of David, it best fits the circumstances of his flight from Jerusalem (2 Sam 15:13–31; 16:5–14), when his enemies divided his garments and he felt all strength drain from him as a result of the horror of his son's betrayal. Even the reference to the piercing of hands is poetic language, describing his utter helplessness. Of course, the psalm has a far more glorious fulfillment in the suffering of his descendant (Rom 1:3), whose hands were literally nailed and whose garments were divided.

10. Contra Davies, *Jewish*, 137, and Campbell, "Freedom," 28, who suggest the emphasis is to answer those who have accused Paul of denying his heritage and national identity.

love and concern is such that he would be willing to exchange his own position of blessing for the awful state of condemnation[11] if that would secure the salvation of his "brothers and fathers" in Israel. Scholars have noted the similarity between Paul's willingness to take the place of his people and the willingness of Moses to be cut off for the sake of the rebellious Israelites (Exod 32:32). Some have argued that Paul saw himself to be a new Moses.[12] This may be so, as in 2 Cor 3:7–18 Paul seems to compare his ministry with that of Moses. However, this latter point is disputed by some scholars.[13]

9:4 Theirs is the adoption as sons; theirs the divine glory, the covenants, the receiving of the law, the temple worship and the promises. This verse lists the remarkable privileges the Jews[14] had as the covenant people of God.

They had been adopted as God's son(s) (Exod 4:22–23), had the Lord dwelling among them in his divine glory (Exod 40:34), and had been the only nation with whom God had entered into covenants. (Paul is probably referring to covenants with Abraham [Gen 15:1–21], Moses [though, in reality, he was the mediator of the covenant between God and Israel], and David [2 Sam 7:12–16].) Furthermore they had received the law of God, which Paul sees as a privilege, even though he speaks elsewhere of it bringing condemnation.[15] They also had the temple in which the Creator God dwelt and his promise of blessing when he sent his Messiah into the world.

The significance of these privileges is difficult for Gentiles to appreciate; they define the Jewish people and their relationship with God. How could a nation be more blessed? However, despite all of these privileges, Paul describes unbelieving Jews as fallen olive branches (Rom 11:17–21), in desperate need of being grafted back into the tree. (This description of unbelieving Jews bears similarity to Jesus' words in John 15:1–11, a passage often used to challenge the fruitfulness and assurance of Christians. Such a reading fails to recognize that Jesus was speaking to the apostles who, as Jews, were still under the old covenant. He was warning them of apostasy within the nation, describing unredeemed Israel as unfruitful branches on the vine, which God, the divine gardener, cuts off. They wither and are cast into the fire. The fruit they failed to produce included truth, justice, righteousness, and purity. To preach the danger of Christians losing their salvation from John 15 misses the crucial meaning of the original context and wrongly identifies the subjects of the warning.)

So, Rom 9:4 is a reminder of the immense privileges afforded to Israel. It contains important information that will help us confirm the earlier claim that the letter should be read from an OT perspective, carefully considering the legitimacy of importing into it Greco-Roman cultural thought.

11. The term is "anathema," which originally meant "devoted to destruction." In Paul's day, it had become a formula for excommunication.

12. See Munck, *Israel*, 12ff., 29ff., who argues that Paul saw himself as a significant eschatological figure, parallel to Moses. Contra Siegert, *Argumentation*, 12.

13. For further discussion, see Holland, *Paul, Israel's Law and God's Spirit*, forthcoming.

14. Moo, *Application*, 292, notes that, when Jews speak about themselves and their special place in salvation history, they call themselves "Israelites."

15. See Holland, *Paul, Israel's Law and God's Spirit*, forthcoming.

The first of the privileges was that the Jews had been adopted as sons. We have seen in Rom 8:17 that many scholars believe Paul's teaching on sonship to be modeled on the Roman practice of slave adoption, giving the slave the same legal status as natural siblings. Here, the word υἱοθεσία (*huiothesia*) "adoption" is used again, but it is clear that this has nothing to do with Roman adoption patterns.[16] The background is Israel's adoption as Yahweh's son, the nation coming under God's covenantal care (e.g., Exod 4:22; Deut 14:1; 32:6; Jer 31:9; Hos 1:10; 11:1). This model pre-dates adoption in the Roman legal system. Indeed, those who cite the Greco-Roman model often fail to note that the practice was restricted to a very remote province. It is unlikely that the general public in Rome would have known of its existence.

However, Paul and the Roman believers did have a shared narrative context—the OT, This is attested to by the many OT quotations in the letter. Indeed, Paul builds his theology on the basis of these citations. It would seem reasonable to begin with these sacred texts to see if his doctrine of adoption reflects them.

The significance of this particular text (Rom 8:17) for Paul's doctrine of adoption is important. If he is following the OT understanding of sonship, it would confirm that, when he calls the believers *douloi* (which can be translated "slaves" or "servants"), he has "servants" in mind.[17] Israel was God's servant to the nations as well as being his son, and was commissioned to take the message of the knowledge of Yahweh to those in darkness. This is a task the nation was to perform as a son and not as a slave, serving the father willingly within the covenant. In this context, individual Jews were servants of Yahweh.

However, if we follow Paul's argument in the unfolding chapters, we will find him explaining how unredeemed Israel failed to fulfill this role. This is why the nation eventually lost the unmerited privileges that God graciously bestowed upon her when he elected Israel to be his servant.

Paul describes how the Gentiles are being grafted into the original stock as they take up the mantle of service. They draw nourishment from its root, as do the branches of the redeemed remnant of Israel. One assumes that, in Paul's mind, the stock is Abraham and the believers have become his true seed. Together, redeemed Gentiles and redeemed Jews fulfill the purposes of the covenant to the end that all the nations of the earth will be blessed.

The second privilege was that the Jewish people knew the presence of God in a way that no other nation did. The divine glory was exhibited at the exodus when they were brought out of Egypt (Exod 15:11) and in the second exodus when they were brought out from exile in Babylon (Isa 40:5). The divine glory is the manifestation of God's presence and person. This is what Moses longed to see and of which he was granted a glimpse (Exod 33:18). The prophets looked forward to the day when, along with the nations, they would see the glory of God (Isa 66:18).

---

16. See Scott, *Sons of God*, 174. Wilder, *Echoes*, 77, (Contra, Burke, *Adopted*) says that Scott's insights need to be pressed further, so that they might yield their full measure of corresponding reality and open up Paul's teaching regarding the law.

17. See Holland, *Contours*, chapter 4; Thielman, *Story*, 185–89.

The third privilege was that, throughout OT history, God made a series of covenants with the Jewish people. He promised Adam that he would protect him and send a Redeemer from his family, Noah that he would not flood the world again, Abraham that he would establish him as the head of a nation that would represent him, and David, that one of his sons would always rule over the house of Judah. While these are the key covenants of the OT, God made many less significant covenants with individuals for various reasons. In all of these covenants, Yahweh was committing himself to his people. These unique, privileged agreements were focused on the people of Israel and were for their blessing.

The fourth privilege was that the Jewish people were blessed by the giving of the law. They esteemed it so highly that their teachers taught creation happened so that God could give his law to his people. The psalms express the delight that devout Jews had in the law, for it instructed them in Yahweh's ways and guided them in the paths of truth and righteousness. The commandments were not arid regulations that had to be observed but expressions of Yahweh's love for his people and, because of this, they were joyfully observed (Ps 1:2; 94:12; 119:29, 55–92; Isa 51:7). Of course, something went seriously wrong, for this same law became the means of Israel's condemnation.

Israel's sixth privilege concerned the Temple, the importance of which cannot be exaggerated. It was where Yahweh met with his people and where he dwelt. (Before King Solomon built the temple, God tabernacled with his people by dwelling in a temporary "tent.") However, Solomon's temple was razed to the ground when Nebuchadnezzar invaded Judah and destroyed Jerusalem. Removing this privilege from Israel symbolized the end of her covenantal relationship with God, and she was taken into exile in Babylon.

Seventy years later, a remnant returned to Jerusalem to rebuild the city, and its first priority was to rebuild the temple. According to promise, this would be achieved by a descendant of David. However, no such leader emerged, and the community decided to restore the building itself.

This building was eventually replaced by the temple that King Herod built. By means of this gesture, the Gentile king hoped to endear himself to the Jewish people; but his hope was in vain. It was in this edifice that Jesus declared: "destroy this temple and I will raise it again in three days" (John 2:19), confusing the Jews who did not realize that he was talking about his own body. As a result, the early church regarded Herod's temple as redundant because the living temple (the church), in which God dwelt by his Spirit, was raised to life in the death and resurrection of Jesus. The Jews, however, continued to see themselves as custodians of temple worship. They believed that they alone had access to the living God and that he was delighted to receive their praise and worship, which could only be offered in the appointed place. Of course, such confidence was severely shaken as a result of the war in 70 AD, when the Romans destroyed the temple.

Finally, the promises had been the unique property of the Jews. Eventually, however, they were given to bless the Gentiles. Different promises had been given at various points in Israel's history, all encouraging and looking forward to the nation's blessing and usefulness. The key promises have been considered in the introduction of this chapter.

9:5 Theirs are the patriarchs, and from them is traced the human ancestry of Christ, who is God over all, forever praised! Amen. Paul has a theological understanding of history: "but when the time had fully come, God sent his Son, born of a woman, born under law, that we might receive the full rights of sons" (Gal 4:4). His understanding is like Matthew's (Matt 1:1–17) and Luke's (Luke 3:23–38)—both gospel writers being anxious to show the lineage of Jesus, the promised seed. Paul asserts that there was nothing haphazard about Jesus' line, for it came about through the purposes of God. He was the one whom Joseph predicted would be raised up to secure his brothers' welfare (Gen 49:10), the one about whom Nathan spoke (2 Sam 7:11–16), and the one anticipated by the prophets (Isa 9:2–7; Jer 23:5; 30:9; 33:17; Ezek 34:23; Rom1:3).

The statement "who is God over all," is evidence that the early Christian community acknowledged the divinity of Jesus. The early church came to this conviction through her understanding of the OT Scriptures as well as from her experience and growing understanding of the salvation Jesus had secured. The NIV translates ὁ ὤν ἐπὶ πάντων θεὸς εὐλογητὸς εἰς τοὺς αἰῶνας (*ho ōn epi pantōn theos eulogētos eis tous aiōnas*) "who is God over all, forever praised." While such a reading is supported by the word order of the original Greek text, word order alone does not decide meaning. Punctuation must also be considered. Unfortunately, the punctuation of this text is not clear, for there is little or no punctuation in the earliest manuscripts.[18] The following are the possibilities that the Greek will bear:[19]

1. From them comes the Messiah according to the flesh, who is over all, God blessed for ever, Amen. (Comma after "who is over all")

2. From them comes the Messiah according to the flesh, who is over all. God be blessed for ever, Amen. (Full stop after "who is over all")

3. From them comes the Messiah according to the flesh. God who is over all be blessed forever, Amen.

The following considerations favor the meaning of the first possibility, with the consequence that Paul ascribes divinity to Christ. First, the grammatical argument heavily supports this interpretation. For such an expression of praise as "Amen" not to be linked to a word in the preceding sentence is exceptional in Paul's writings. Second, the confession in Rom 1:3–4 is widely considered to be programmatic for the letter. In that passage, Paul described Jesus as the "Son of God." In the light of this, a statement about Christ's deity in the body of the Epistle would be expected. (While the term "Son of God" in Rom 1:4 can be interpreted as a Messianic description and not a proof of divinity, Christ's status as being "over all" is repeatedly asserted in Paul's writings [Eph 1:22; 4:6; Col 2:10],[20]

---

18. See Metzger, "Punctuation," 95–112; Harris, *Jesus*, 144–72; Turner, *Grammatical*, 13–17; Cullmann, *Christology*, 312–13; Moule, *Origin*, 137.

19. As listed by Wright, "Romans."

20. Of course, many scholars would not accept the Pauline authorship of these letters. I have argued that the evidence for rejecting Paul's authorship of the letter to the Colossians is methodologically flawed. See Holland, *Contours*, ch. 12, etc. The arguments given are also applicable to the letter to the Ephesians.

and these texts have high Christologies.) Third, the whole argument of Rom 9–11 moves towards the final affirmation of the universal sovereignty of Jesus as Messiah and Lord.

A key piece of evidence is found in Rom 10:4–13, where Paul calls Jesus Κύριος (*Kurios*) "Lord." This title is used in a section in which he quotes from the book of Joel 2:32 (3:5 [LXX]). There is no doubt that in the LXX, the title *kurios* stood for the Tetragrammaton—YHWH—the sacred name of Israel's God. Paul says: "For there is no difference between Jew and Gentile—the same Lord is Lord of all and richly blesses all who call on him, for, 'Everyone who calls on the name of the Lord will be saved'" (Rom 10:12–13). The inclusion of this passage from Joel 2:32 is telling. It determines the way Paul uses the term *kurios* in the earlier part of the passage. He (the Lord) is the same LORD (Yahweh) who is spoken about by the prophet, and Paul says that he is Jesus.

Some scholars are understandably hesitant to embrace the statement as an expression of high Christology, believing this came much later in the understanding of the church. Also, they reason that trinitarianism was framed when the church confronted several challenges stemming from Greek philosophy in the second and third centuries. But the statement should not be seen as a flight into ontological theology. Its setting is that of salvation history. It asserts that Christ is the Redeemer of his people and, indeed, of creation itself. As the OT made abundantly clear, only Yahweh can redeem creation.[21] Therefore, it must follow, that if Jesus is the Redeemer, he must be Yahweh (God). Such a pathway to a high Christology is driven by the very doctrines of God, creation, and salvation, and is not dependent on any form of philosophical speculation or argument.[22]

9:6 It is not as though God's word had failed. For not all who are descended from Israel are Israel. In human terms it appeared that the word of God had failed. When, from his "Christian" perspective, Paul considered the condition of Israel's unredeemed majority, it looked as though the promises given to his people had failed—indeed, that the word of God had failed. But, as the opening sentence in the verse states, his word had not failed! As the chapter unfolds, Paul quotes the prophet Isaiah, who stated that only a remnant of Israel would be saved while the majority would be condemned (Isa 10:27–28). He also quotes from the book of Hosea, in which God said of the Gentiles: "I will call them my people who are not my people" (Hos 2:23).

So Paul is saying that, despite the pain Israel's condemnation brings him, God's word is true, and he plays on the name "Israel" to explain how this is so. There are a number of ways of interpreting this verse. Paul could be saying that not all of the descendants of the nation of Israel are members of the true Israel. While he does not state the fate of Israelites who do not belong to the true Israel, we know from previous verses that he mourns their rejection and the fact they will be condemned should they fail to acknowledge Jesus as the Messiah. On the other hand, Paul could be saying that all who are descended from the patriarch Israel–Yahweh's name for Jacob (Gen 32:26–28) —are not members of the true Israel, i.e., the church (the body of redeemed people from all nations, including Israel). The implication of this is that the promises were not given to

21. Isa 41:18–20; 42:5–17; 44:24–26; Jer 36:8–12.

22. See Holland, *Contours*, chapter 12.

Abraham's natural descendants but to his sons of promise, such as Jacob. It is interesting that when Isaac blessed Jacob (Gen 28:3–4), he said: "May God . . . increase your numbers until you become a community of peoples" (Gen 28:3), the blessing being confirmed to Jacob by God in a dream (Gen 28:13–14).

At Pentecost, there was a tremendous wave of Jewish conversions (Acts 2:41; 4:4). To the disciples, it must have looked like God was bringing the nation to her Messiah. Sadly, this promising start did not continue, for many of those who came into the church in those early heady days[23] misunderstood the makeup of the new community. Their confusion is seen in the letter to the Hebrews and in the closing chapters of the Acts of the Apostles, where divisions between the Jewish believers became obvious as some sought to impose the law on Gentile converts.

This major disagreement about the Gentiles and the law almost ripped the church apart. Many of the Jewish converts found it impossible to move on from the security that the law had given them into total confidence in the completed work of redemption accomplished by Christ. They tried to straddle both camps, creating an ongoing problem for those who sought to welcome the uncircumcised Gentiles on an equal footing with the circumcised Jews.

So, in conclusion, it seemed that the promises of God to the patriarchs (including Abraham) had failed as the number of Jewish converts was declining rather than increasing. However, Paul refused to accept this as the true picture. The physical descendants of Abraham (and, therefore, of Jacob [or Israel]) are not his true children. His true descendants are those who share the same faith as Abraham. It was not correct to count the number of Jews coming into the church as a measure of the fulfillment of scripture. The Gentile converts were just as much the children of promise, and, in Paul's view, they must be taken into account when deciding whether the promises to the patriarch were being fulfilled.

9:7 Nor because they are his descendants are they all Abraham's children. On the contrary, "It is through Isaac that your offspring will be reckoned." Paul presses home the truth that being a physical descendant of Abraham does not mean automatic membership of the new covenant community. To show this, he points to the fact that the original promise was not given to all the physical descendants of Abraham such as Hagar's son, Ishmael, or the sons of his wife, Keturah (Gen 25:1–4), or of his concubines (Gen 25:6).

At the time when Abraham was promised he would father a son (Gen 15:2–6), he was not told the identity of the mother. So, many years later, when his old and barren wife, Sarah, insisted that he should father a family for her through her handmaid, he agreed.

---

23 Even after a period of intense intimidation (Acts 5), Luke says: "So the word of God spread. The number of disciples in Jerusalem increased rapidly, and a large number of priests became obedient to the faith" (Acts 6:7). It is understandable why, at this time, the church would have thought that Israel was embracing her message and her Savior.

His first child was born to Sarah's Egyptian handmaid, who came to be known as Hagar. When Hagar became pregnant, she was told by the angel of the LORD that her son, to be named Ishmael, would father numerous offspring (Gen 16:9–11). If Abraham had listened carefully to Hagar's account of the meeting, he would have realized that Ishmael was not to be the "son of promise" because the LORD had warned Hagar that Ishmael would live in hostility towards all his brothers. In contrast, Abraham's descendants, through his "son of promise," would be a blessing to the nations. Despite Ishmael being his firstborn son (and being circumcised with the patriarch), Abraham's "son of promise" had yet to be born.

When Ishmael was fourteen years old, Sarah gave birth to Isaac. Paul confirms that he was the child of promise through whom Abraham's offspring would be reckoned.

In Galatians, Paul goes even further, pointing out that the Scriptures say the nations would be blessed through Abraham's "seed"—not "his seeds" (Gal 3:16). He argues that the promise is directed to a specific descendant, i.e., Jesus, the Christ. The NIV has obscured this particular point that Jesus is the true seed of Abraham in Paul's letter to the Romans. It has translated σπέρμα (*sperma*) "seed" in Rom 9:7 as "offspring," hiding Paul's technical use of the term. Paul uses "seed" in this verse in the same way as he has used it in Galatians. The point he is making is that the promised seed is a particular descendant of Abraham's line. The term is not to be understood as encompassing all of Abraham's spiritual descendants.

In a parallel argument in Galatians, Paul appeals to the church to stay committed to the person of Christ. His argument presents him as the one true seed of Abraham and rejects all possible contenders for Jewish allegiance—even such luminaries as Isaac, Jacob, Moses, Elijah, and David. Jesus alone is the true seed of Abraham, and it is through him that the covenant promises are fulfilled.

9:8 In other words, it is not the natural children who are God's children, but it is the children of the promise who are regarded as Abraham's offspring. What Paul is arguing would have been bewildering for Jews in Rome. They regarded the fact that they were the physical descendants of Abraham and of Jacob ("Israel") as synonymous with being the children of the promise. Paul cuts right across this thinking—the same thinking he had once upheld. His claim that the Gentiles are equally, without reservation, children of Abraham through faith in Christ Jesus is the basis of his following argument. Indeed, their union with Christ, who is the true seed of Abraham, makes them not only the true seed, but also the remnant spoken so much about by the prophet Isaiah (Isa 10:20–22; 11:11–16; 28:5; 37:4, 31–32. See also, Jer 23:3; 31:7; 42:2; 43:5; 44:7; 50:20).

9:9 For this was how the promise was stated: "At the appointed time I will return, and Sarah will have a son." Paul quotes from Gen 18, where the visit of the three men to Abraham is recorded: "Then the LORD said, 'I will surely return to you about this time next year, and Sarah your wife will have a son'" (Gen 18:10). It is of interest how, in Gal 4, Paul saw God's involvement in the birth of Isaac. When considering Ishmael and Isaac, he writes: "At that time the son born in the ordinary way persecuted the son born by the power of the Spirit" (Gal 4:29). The statement suggests that Sarah was enabled to conceive by the "power of the Spirit." This is a misleading translation of ἀλλ᾽ ὥσπερ τότε ὁ κατὰ σάρκα γεννηθεὶς ἐδίωκεν τὸν κατὰ πνεῦμα, οὕτως καὶ νῦν. The NAS gives a better translation: "But as at that time he who was born according to the flesh persecuted him who was born according to the Spirit, so it is now also" (Gal 4:29 NAS). In other words, the birth of Isaac was the result of the divine promise and not the result of extraordinary faith as discussed earlier (see pages 140–49).

So, Paul's argument hangs on a correct understanding of the promise. The fact that Abraham and Sarah had to wait for the LORD's return in order for the promise to be fulfilled emphasizes that this birth was dependent on divine intervention. In human terms, God's appointed time for the couple was hardly their best time. They were both advanced in years (Abraham was one hundred and Sarah was ninety when Isaac was born) and the birth of a child, while joyous beyond measure, would usher in years of anxiety.

9:10–11 Not only that, but Rebekah's children had one and the same father, our father Isaac. Yet, before the twins were born or had done anything good or bad—in order that God's purpose in election might stand. Again, Paul focuses on the descendants of the promised seed. Isaac's wife, Rebekah, experienced years of barrenness until God answered his prayer. His wife conceived and she bore non-identical twin boys. Paul makes the point that one was chosen and the other was not. This choice was not made after they were reared, when their developing personalities and characters could be assessed, but in the womb and before they were known to their parents.

How could there be anything to distinguish between the babies while they were still in the womb? From a human perspective, priority would be decided at the point of birth. The son who was born first—Isaac's firstborn—would be given the birthright and claim to the promised inheritance conferred on Abraham and his seed.

The point Paul is emphasizing is that human choice is not necessarily God's choice. He is not swayed by personality, talent, and achievement; or bound by "rights" and privileges of any kind. God alone makes his choices. These cannot be predicted because they are of a different order from those made by humans. Again, the emphasis is on the two boys having done nothing to determine the election of Yahweh. While they were still in the womb, God decreed that the firstborn would serve his younger brother. Paul is demonstrating that nothing can control the choices that God makes.[24] The one chosen will not be able to claim that this privilege was his right by birth or because of his works.

9:12 Not by works but by him who calls—she was told, "The older will serve the younger." The phrase "not by works" recalls similar words in Eph 2:9: "not of works, so that no one can boast." This is the essence of the Gospel Paul proclaimed—absolutely no one can boast in his or her status before God (1 Cor 1:26–31). Nothing can be brought to God to convince him of human worth. Indeed, any such attempt to do so is grounds for rejection, as God will not share his glory with another (Eph 2:9b). While it is valid to

---

24. Cranfield, *Romans*, 11, 480, says that if there is a hint of predestination here, it is strictly focused on the progress of God's saving activity within the process of history and not on individuals. Cf. Wilckens, *Römer*, 11, 196–97, and Käsemann, *Romans*, 265. That accepted, it still does not deflect from the sovereignty of God in making choices over individuals to achieve his purposes.

recall Eph 2:9, it must be realized that, in Rom 9:12, Paul is not dealing with how God chooses people for salvation but how people are chosen for privilege and responsibility. (We shall see that this perspective continues into chapter ten.) Indeed, when Eph 2:9 is examined, it is found to be saying a similar thing. Paul tells the Gentiles that they had been included into the covenant community solely because of God's grace and kindness. Therefore it is not in its intent a proof text for evangelism but a declaration of God's kindness to them. It is a corporate statement of the change of status afforded to all believing Gentiles—they have been included in the covenants of promise by God's grace and not by law observance. In that covenant, they share God's saving grace. Since they are saved from the judgment that will come upon the godless, the covenant speaks ultimately of salvation. Indeed, even though Paul's argument is about being elected for service, it moves on to salvation from judgment (v. 27), i.e., the salvation of the believing community from the wrath it deserves. We shall see that Paul is insistent that this community is not exclusively Jewish or Gentile but made up of those who have faith in the redemptive purposes of God.

The detailed argument Paul has made prepares the believers in Rome for his claim that God has brought the Gentiles into the new community ahead of the Jews. He will go on to declare that God has set aside privilege, exalting those with none.

The term "works" in the phrase "not by works" has been interpreted by those favoring the "New Perspective" on Paul as referring to the law's requirements of rituals and practices. It is claimed that the term is not about keeping the moral or religious requirements of the law but about issues such as circumcision, diet, and Sabbath-keeping. While Paul does make use of this meaning for "works" in Rom 3:27 and Rom 9:4, there are other times when its meaning is much more than this. This meaning encompasses the keeping of the law's commands as a set of moral precepts as understood by the Reformers (Acts 13:38–39; Rom 3:19–20; 5:13, 20). What Paul is saying is that Jacob, the heir, was not chosen because he had attained a greater righteousness than Esau through his devoted obedience to the law.

9:13 Just as it is written. "Jacob I loved, but Esau I hated." In saying that God hated Esau–the firstborn and natural inheritor of the promise—there is no intention to suggest there was malicious ill will towards him. The expression is a familiar Hebraism speaking of "loving less."[25] It does not necessarily imply that Esau had been rejected by God in terms of his love; it simply means that he was not chosen to be the bearer of the promise made to Abraham.[26] The same idiom is found in one of the sayings of Jesus.

25. Hodge, *Romans*, commenting on 2 Sam 12:11; 16:10 and Ps 105:25 says, "from these similar passages it is evident that it is a familiar scripture usage to ascribe to God effects which he allows in his wisdom to come to pass" (316).

26. Heb 12:15–17 says: "See to it that no one comes short of the grace of God; that no root of bitterness springing up causes trouble, and by it many be defiled; that there be no immoral or godless person like Esau, who sold his own birthright for a single meal. For you know that even afterwards, when he desired to inherit the blessing, he was rejected, for he found no place for repentance, thought he sought for it with tears." This text does not challenge the reading offered above, for it speaks of a different event. The event in Rom 9:13 is about Esau being denied the role of Redeemer as a result of Yahweh's sovereign choice, whereas the Hebrews text is about the bitterness that set into his heart as a result of losing his inheritance

He said that unless a man hates his father, mother, and wife, he could not be his disciple (Luke 14:26). Jesus was not calling for his followers to hate their families but to love him more than them. In a similar way, the choice of Jacob did not mean God did not love Esau; it simply meant that he had chosen Jacob to continue the line through which his covenantal purposes would be fulfilled.

EXCURSUS H: ELECTION TO PRIVILEGE AND SERVICE

Contrary to the claims of some scholars, there are a number of significant factors in Romans 9 Paul speaks about election for honor (privilege) and service rather than salvation.

First. As we have been discovering, the letter to the Romans makes better sense when interpreted as a document with the church's experience of God's saving work as its focus rather than that of the individual Christian. This corporate reading has resolved many of the difficulties presented by traditional individualistic readings.[27]

Second. In reference to Paul's statement that he is willing to be cut off from Christ for the sake of his brethren, some claim that he would not show this extreme distress over the loss of national privilege but only for the eternal salvation of individual Israelites.[28] This position, however, is not tenable. Most scholars acknowledge that, in his distress, Paul is identifying himself with Moses, who anguished over the judgment that was about to come upon Israel. Few, if any, would argue that Moses had an understanding of individual salvation. This was a doctrine that developed through succeeding generations, finally coming to its climax in the death and resurrection of Christ (2 Tim 1:10). If Paul keeps faithful to the original theological context and content (as many now recognize him to do), imposing a notion of individual salvation that was not in the original text needs to be justified. Furthermore, to see the loss of privilege and status as of little consequence is to fail to see the statement in its historical setting. The covenantal curses were spelt out in Deut 29–32, and among these curses, which were to fall on Judah in 586 BC, were conquest and deportation. It is significant that Moses prayed because he feared that as a result of the covenant being broken by the people's idolatry that Yahweh's wrath would come upon Israel, despite the judgment that the Levites had exercised (Exod 32:27–35).

---

to his younger brother through selling his birthright. The point of the Hebrews text (written, of course, to Jews), is that they must strive not to lose their inheritance of the blessings that believers are entitled to. The discussion of both texts is about covenant privilege and responsibility, not salvation.

27. For support of this corporate reading, see Thiselton, *Doctrine*, 187, 480.

28. Schreiner, "Teach," 27; Moo, *Romans*, 559. This is also the argument of Piper, *Justification*, 156, who sees only an individualistic meaning in Rom 9:1–3. He acknowledges that this individualistic reading of Rom 9:1–4 is the key to his interpretation of Rom 9:18. Without it, his "election to judgment" reading of Rom 9:18 falls. However, he does not consider Israel's immediate 70 AD danger (see following). If the impending siege is the context of Paul's statement, his focus is not the individual Jew, and Piper's interpretation of Rom 9:18 collapses. He acknowledges this himself when he says: "Therefore the solution which Rom 9:6–13 develops in response to this problem *must* address the issue of individual eternal salvation," Piper, *Justification*, 64–65 (emphasis Piper's).

In Paul's day, many were growing concerned about the the increasing danger Israel was putting herself into as she provoked Rome by pressing her national aspirations.[29] The church must have been alarmed as she knew of Jesus' prediction that Jerusalem would be razed to the ground within the generation of those who heard him (Matt 24:1–2). To say that Paul would not know about this too is to be theologically and historically naive.[30] In this context it is more than understandable why he identifies with Moses. In both cases, the nation is at risk of coming under the covenantal curse. Paul is sharing in exact detail the concern of Moses and makes the same plea. It is natural that he would wish to be cut off for Israel's sake–he would not be a true son of Abraham if he did not. (Sadly, as feared, judgment was poured out in all of its destructive brutality when the Roman army laid siege to the city in 70 AD). In recognizing this to be the setting of Paul's anguish, what he says matches the theology of Moses' prayer perfectly.

Third. While Paul expresses deep grief for his brethren, who now stand under the curses of the covenant, the opening section of the chapter cannot be used to justify individualizing the verses that follow. In this introductory passage, Paul is saying that it is *as a nation* that the Jews have received the adoption, have known the divine glory, have partaken in the covenants, have received the law, have known temple worship and have received the promises. He writes: "*Theirs* are the patriarchs" (ὧν οἱ πατέρες Rom 9:5) and "out of *them* is the Christ" (ἐξ ὧν ὁ Χριστὸς Rom 9:5). Clearly, none of these blessings belong to an individual Jew—it is the community that received them. What Paul is preparing to deal with is not individual salvation but how a people, who had been blessed above all others, could lose the privileges they once had. If this setting is not appreciated, alien issues will

---

29. See, for example, Wright, *Victory*.

30. Wright, *Perspectives*, 142, sees 2 Thess 1:6–9 to refer to the fall of Jerusalem. The argument that Paul is not interested in the fate of his brethren other than their eschatological judgment asks us to accept that a deep concern held by Jesus and his disciples (Matt 24:1–2) had evaporated from the thinking of the early church. The possibility of the fall of Jerusalem is evident in texts throughout the NT. Heb 10:30–32 and Luke 12:58–9 have these sorts of ideas behind them. The cry of Jesus over unrepentant Jerusalem (Luke 13:34–35) is a lament that pervades much of the NT. Following his reference to her as a city set on a hill, giving light to the world (Matt 5:14), Jesus warns of Jerusalem's future judgment if she does not build on the rock of his words (Matt 7:26–27). See also Matt 21:18—22:14; 24–25 and parallels, especially Jesus' teaching on the significance of the curse of the fig tree. The same theme of Jerusalem's judgment is found in Revelation. Bauckham, *Climax*, xv, xvii., says: "The world created by the text is intended as an interpretation of the real world in which John and his readers live . . . In his symbolic vision of the past, present and future of the Roman empire, he brings together accurate references to the apparent contemporary realities of Roman power and prophetic perception of the hidden reality of divine power." See also, Hendriksen, *Conquerors*; Smolarz, *Marriage*. Regardless of the legitimacy of interpreting Revelation in the context of the church's future experience, the exegete's first task is to interpret it as it would have been understood by the intended readers. If this is valid, then it is clear that the fall of Jerusalem continued to be a vitally important topic for the church. Indeed, not to consider this context is a strange way of exegeting the teaching of the apostles, for if they had forgotten, or overlooked, Jesus' prophesy, how could they be trusted to communicate the rest of his teaching? Consequently, while Paul's main concern regarding salvation is eschatological, he is also deeply distressed over the impending judgment of his people. This said, as pointed out by Beale, *Revelation*, 45, the problem of limiting the judgment of Rev 13:7–8 to AD 70 is the need to: "provide an exegetical rationale both for exchanging a pagan nation with Israel as the primary object of Daniel's final judgment and for limiting the last judgment mainly to Israel and not applying it universally."

be imported into the case that Paul is making. As noted in our comments on v.4, while the benefits of the blessings are individually appropriated, they are corporately received.

Fourth. We have found throughout our exposition of Romans that Paul argues from OT models and texts. For this reason, it is important to guard against inadvertently introducing ways of thinking into Paul's perspective that are not supported by his firm grasp of OT theology. The fact is that there is no theology of individual election to salvation or damnation in the OT. The OT understanding of salvation is about God saving people from physical and moral danger. For example, Abraham and Lot were called to leave places saturated with ungodly practices, and when Yahweh rescued Israel from Egypt, her salvation was delivery from captivity and restoration to the role she was elected to fulfill. This is not to deny that a development of the doctrine of personal election took place in the NT. However, while I want to stand by the teaching that holds to God's electing grace toward the individual, I also want to assert that basing arguments for individual election on this particular passage confuses the discussion and misses some important issues that Paul is expounding.

Fifth. Immediately before the passage that speaks of God's judgment on Pharaoh, Paul recounts the principles of covenant theology, the essence of which is rooted in corporate representation (Rom 9:6–12). In v. 7, he says: "It is the children of the promise who are regarded as Abraham's offspring." Because they are Abraham's seed, they have the blessings of the covenant that Yahweh made with Abraham. This is followed by a discussion concerning Esau. He was Isaac's firstborn, who forfeited his inheritance by giving it to Jacob in exchange for a pottage of meat. Although Jacob was an unworthy inheritor, through this transfer of privileges, the rights of the firstborn were bestowed upon him. In receiving this blessing, Jacob became the head of Abraham's family and, as a result, all his children became the inheritors of the promises that Yahweh had sworn to the patriarch.

Paul continues to explore the crucial issue of how Israel could lose her inheritance. This is the great theme that is thrashed out throughout the chapter, continuing on into chapters 10 and 11. It is clear that the metanarrative of these chapters is that Israel has lost all that she has been blessed with and that the believing Gentiles have been brought into the blessing promised to Abraham (Gen 12:3). Thus, the examples that Paul draws upon to introduce his argument concerning Pharaoh's judgment are essentially about Jewish and Gentile election to privilege and service rather than to salvation. At no point in this prologue is there any suggestion that the discussion is about individual salvation.[31]

---

31. Contra, Schreiner, *Romans*, 519, who says: "The strongest evidence that salvation is in view is the contextual flow of thought that informs Rom 9–11." As demonstrated above, the overall Paschal/New Exodus corporate argument of the letter along with the flow of the introduction to chapters 9–11 support a corporate argument. To shore up his argument concerning election to judgment, a topic that he can find no evidence for in any other text of scripture, Schreiner, op cit 521, has had to appeal to extra-biblical literature, saying: "Double predestination is also evident in Jewish sources, particularly Qumran." He also cites in support 1QS 3:15–16; 4:24–26; 1QH 7(15) 16–26, and then refers to Sir. 33:7–13, Apoc. and Abr. 22.1–5 (op cit 522 n. 23). Schreiner dismisses the reading of Caird on the basis that: "he asserts mistakenly that the term 'vessels of destruction' does not relate to God's decree concerning the eternal destiny of individuals" (op cit 522 n. 24). Schreiner's dismissal of Caird rests on what I seek to show is a misplaced confidence in his own exegesis. Basically, the essence of his argument is "because Caird does not agree with me, he is wrong."

Sixth. Paul follows the discussion of Pharaoh's judgment with a citation from the book of Isaiah. There is some debate as to which passage he cites. The majority of scholars[32] identify Isa 29:16 as the source:

> You turn things upside down, as if the potter were thought to be like the clay! Shall what is formed say to him who formed it, "He did not make me"? Can the pot say of the potter, "He knows nothing"? (Isa 29:16)

However, while Isa 29:16 is found word for word in Rom 9:20, it lacks the question τί "why." The element τι is, however, found in another passage, which has a potter making a pot (Isa 45:9). In this passage, the clay challenges the potter as to why he has made it into the vessel it does not want to be. It is because of the presence of τί in Isa 45:9 that some believe Paul to have conflated the two texts, Isa 29:16 being augmented by the question of Isa 45:9.[33]

While scholars have highlighted their preference for the origin of the quote in Rom 9:20, those who recognize that Paul has introduced τί from Isa 45:9 fail to ask the fundamental question, "Why has Paul done this?" Surely the answer is that Paul wants both passages to contribute and, in order to find out why, we need to consider their contexts. Isa 29:13–16 says:

> The Lord says: "These people come near to me with their mouth and honor me with their lips, but their hearts are far from me. Their worship of me is made up only of rules taught by men. Therefore once more I will astound these people with wonder upon wonder; the wisdom of the wise will perish, the intelligence of the intelligent will vanish." Woe to those who go to great depths to hide their plans from the LORD, who do their work in darkness and think, "Who sees us? Who will know?" You turn things upside down, as if the potter were thought to be like the clay! Shall what is formed say to him who formed it, "He did not make me"? Can the pot say of the potter, "He knows nothing"? (Isa 29:13–16)

What is interesting is that the illustration of the potter has Israel asserting that she has achieved her status by her self effort. She thinks that her own wisdom has guided her through the dangers she has faced and that her own effort has elevated her.

But Yahweh warned, "the wisdom of the wise will perish, the intelligence of the intelligent will vanish" (Isa 29:14). Her leaders are told that they are foolish if they think they can do anything in secret, hiding their plans and guilt from God (Isa 29:15). They do not realize that Yahweh is totally different from them (Isa 29:16). They are arrogant, thinking that they are the designers and craftsmen of their own status and achievements. Indeed, they actually ask if Yahweh really is responsible for their achievements (Isa 29:16).

The picture is of Israel, boasting of her independence from Yahweh and refusing to credit anything to him. Her perception is that he had no hand in her development, it being the result of her own wisdom. Yahweh's accusation against Israel is upheld by his distress in Isa 28:18 that she had entered into a covenant with death (believed by many to refer to the Egyptian god of death, Môt).

---

32. Os, "Isaiah," 75–78; Barrett, *Romans*, 188; Cranfield, *Romans*, 2:491; Piper, *Justification*, 195.

33. Morris, *Romans*, 365; Dunn, *Romans*, 2:356; Fitzmyer, *Romans*, 369.

The above picture of Israel and how Isaiah uses the potter illustration in Isa 29:16 is very different from the way it is used in Isa 45:9. This text, which was about the clay's complaint against the potter, is not coming from one who boasts of her achievements but from the nation, who complains to Yahweh for preferring Cyrus above herself and appointing him to be Yahweh's anointed. This is the very status that Israel forfeited through her disobedience. This Isaianic text is crucial for grasping the argument that Paul is making because, as previously noted, scholars are increasingly agreeing that he uses the OT with great respect, transferring texts along with their theological contexts. This key fact precludes us from using the quote to support an individualistic reading as it is *Israel* who is objecting to her God.[34] It is also crucial as Paul has taken the trouble to conflate the two texts, so that they make their own contributions to his case against Israel. Bringing the question from Isa 45:9 into such a brief extract from Isa 29:16 suggests that it is a vital part of his argument in the compiled citation. We would, therefore, be wise to pay close attention to what the question is focusing upon. Isaiah says:

> "This is what the LORD says to his anointed, to Cyrus, whose right hand I take hold of to subdue nations before him and to strip kings of their armor, to open doors before him so that gates will not be shut: I will go before you and will level the mountains; I will break down gates of bronze and cut through bars of iron. I will give you the treasures of darkness, riches stored in secret places, so that you may know that I am the LORD, the God of Israel, who summons you by name. For the sake of Jacob my servant, of Israel my chosen, I summon you by name and bestow on you a title of honor, though you do not acknowledge me. I am the LORD, and there is no other; apart from me there is no God. I will strengthen you, though you have not acknowledged me, so that from the rising of the sun to the place of its setting men may know there is none besides me. I am the LORD, and there is no other. I form the light and create darkness, I bring prosperity and create disaster; I, the LORD, do all these things.
>
> "You heavens above rain down righteousness; let the clouds shower it down. Let the earth open wide, let salvation spring up, let righteousness grow with it; I, the LORD, have created it.
>
> "Woe to him who quarrels with his Maker, to him who is but a potsherd among the potsherds on the ground. Does the clay say to the potter, 'What are you making?' Does your work say, 'He has no hands'? Woe to him who says to his father, 'What have you begotten?' or to his mother, 'What have you brought to birth?'" (Isa 45:1–10)

The context of the potter illustration in Isa 45:9 is very different from that of Isa 29:16. Here, the focus is not the arrogance of Israel but her confusion and frustration that another has been given the privilege of being the anointed (servant) of the Lord. Cyrus is not only given this most prestigious position, but all that had been said of Israel is now promised to him as he fulfills the ministry entrusted to him by Yahweh:

The Lord takes Cyrus's right hand (Isa 45:1). Nations are subdued before him and their might removed (Isa 45:1). All obstacles are removed that would hinder his progress (Isa 45:1–2). He is given an intimate knowledge of God and an assurance as to his calling

---

34. Implied by the designation "anointed."

(Isa 45:3). The purpose and goal of his mission is made clear, it is to serve the people of God and act as their deliverer (Isa 45:4). His calling is totally of grace (Isa 45:5). The purpose of his calling is that Yahweh will be exalted among the nations (Isa 45:6). The LORD who has called Cyrus is sovereign (Isa 45:7–8).

All of these statements had been said of Israel, her mission, and her God. Now, they are addressed to Cyrus.

Unlike the potter's illustration in Isa 29:16 (which highlighted Israel's arrogance), this illustration highlights her confusion over her loss of privilege. She has learned that Yahweh has chosen Cyrus to be his servant (Isa 45:1). She cannot cope with this news, and asks him why she has been given a lower status, for she will be dependent upon Cyrus. This is at the heart of what Paul is about to argue. Believing Israel has to come to terms with the fact that the Lord has called the Gentile church to be his servant. Israel—even believing Israel—has no precedence over the new servant of the Lord.

Indeed, this is the very theme that Paul has raised in the opening of the chapter, where he laments the imminent judgment on Israel. Like her ancestors in Isaiah's time, she has abused her privilege and status, and is to be judged. If Paul was talking about individual salvation when considering God's dealings with Pharaoh, he has now introduced a theme that is completely against the flow of his earlier argument. The link between the judgments on Israel and Pharaoh is underlined by his statement that Israel has been hardened (Rom 11:7). If this is not the focus of his theme, it would mean that, as soon as Paul completes his discussion on Pharaoh's hardening (a hardening to eternal damnation, as is argued by those who support the double jeopardy reading), he jumps back to the theme of Israel's displacement in his citation of Isa 45:9, and then on into a further expansion of corporate election to honor and service (Rom 9:22–10:4). This construction has Paul wandering from subject to subject, without giving any clear pointers to the changing context of his ongoing argument and exposing him to the charge of inconsistency.

This proposed "election to honor" reading does not deny that the theme of individual salvation is raised in chapter 10 (Rom 10:9–11). However, introducing it into chapter 9 is contrary to the literary and theological controls of the passage, and cannot be justified. The proposed reading does not deny the doctrine of election to salvation; but it is on the evidence of other texts that it must be established.

Seventh. Most tellingly, as noted earlier, the proposed election to damnation reading of Rom 9:18 has support from no other biblical texts. Its proponents fail to present one piece of textual evidence to show that the doctrine is present in the wider cannon.[35] The

---

35. Piper cannot give one example of Isa 45:9 or Isa 29:15–26 being adapted in biblical literature to speak of individual judgment. Because of this (as Schreiner [*Romans*, 517]), Piper, *Justification*, 196, resorts to citing support from a text outside of the authoritative sources of the early church, i.e., the book of Wisdom. Indeed, Piper says of Wisdom 15:7—a text that is the bedrock of his case— "What is frustrating is that the meaning of Wis 15:7 has almost nothing in common with Paul's meaning." This hardly instils confidence for building an argument on this literature! Indeed, this is not an isolated case of such dependence. Piper cites five pages of NT texts in the index of his book *Justification*, half of which comes from Romans and approximately one third from the other NT letters. Surprisingly, approximately one quarter of the index comes from intertestamental literature. Such influences from sources that often taught the op-

absence of this evidence causes them to go outside of the Christian Scriptures to draw support from the writings of other Jewish groups. This methodological issue has been discussed elsewhere,[36] but what is surprising is how scholars with a very high view of scripture are prepared to borrow from non-apostolic sources in order to create and support their case.

In addition to this lack of biblical support is the fact that when the potter imagery is used elsewhere in scripture, Isa 29:17; 45:7; 64:8; Jer 18:19; 19:11, the pottery is never an individual Israelite but always the nation of Israel. There have to be very good reasons for shifting from a corporate perspective to an individual one in the application of these passages, and none are given.

Eighth. The individual election argument assumes that Paul picks up the Exodus narrative where Moses addresses Pharaoh with the subsequent hardening of his heart and applies it to individual election.[37] Such a reading is common, because it has long been assumed that the hardening of Pharaoh happened after Moses delivered his declarations from Yahweh. It is therefore argued that the hardening followed the pronouncement and had nothing to do with anything that Pharaoh had previously done. The election to judgment was therefore not based on works but Yahweh's sovereign decision.

We need to be careful that we don't allow often-valued traditions of interpretation to control the message of this passage. Allowing the text to have its own voice is an essential part of the Reformed tradition. We have seen in chapter 4 how traditional readings have missed important pointers regarding the significance of Paul's argument about justification, because details that were not present in his exposition have been unintentionally imported into the narrative. We found that the justification of Abraham did not take place at Isaac's birth but in his willingness to sacrifice his son as an act of obedience to Yahweh (Gen 22:10). I want to suggest that the same mistake is being made here.

Paul was of course fully aware of the narrative of Israel's deliverance from Egypt. We cannot follow his logic about Pharaoh unless we expose this shorter account (i.e., Rom 9:14–24) to the wider version of the Exodus narrative, allowing the latter to control how we interpret Paul's reasoning. The text of Exodus makes it clear that Yahweh told Moses that Pharaoh's heart would be hardened after Moses made his declaration to the Egyptian ruler (Exod 4:21–23).

However, the message that Moses was instructed to deliver to Pharaoh suggests that this was not the first time Pharaoh had heard the demand to let the Israelites go into the desert to worship their God. This text is crucial, for it suggests that Pharaoh's hardening

---

posite of apostolic teaching is very concerning. It is only fair to say that not all of Piper's arguments rely on these quotations as crucial evidence, but a methodology that uses non-Christian texts as crucial evidence to defend arguments that lack supporting biblical evidence can hardly serve as a reliable foundation for a good Reformed biblical theology. As noted above (fn 33), the same reliance on this literature applies to Schreiner, *Romans*, 522.

36. See pages 23–25. Also, Holland, *Contours*, 51–68.

37. See Moo, *Romans*, 599: "Here, however, Paul is speaking about the work of God in individuals. And v. 22–23, where Paul expands on the idea of both God's mercy and his hardening, suggests that the division between those individuals who receive mercy and those who are hardened is basic and final."

had begun *prior* to the time Moses delivered his message.[38] Indeed, this is clearly the case, for the Hebrew of Exod 4:22, 23 is about God having spoken in the past to Pharaoh regarding the release of Israel. Thus Yahweh warned Pharaoh before Moses delivered his message to Pharaoh and the final judgment was not made in a moral vacuum.

וְאָמַרְתָּ אֶל־פַּרְעֹה כֹּה אָמַר יְהֹוָה בְּנִי בְכֹרִי יִשְׂרָאֵל: 23 וָאֹמַר אֵלֶיךָ שַׁלַּח אֶת־בְּנִי

וְיַעַבְדֵנִי וַתְּמָאֵן לְשַׁלְּחוֹ הִנֵּה אָנֹכִי הֹרֵג אֶת־בִּנְךָ בְּכֹרֶךָ:

(Exod 4:22–23 WTT)

This reading has been followed by several translations:

> And thou shalt say unto Pharaoh, Thus saith Jehovah, Israel is my son, my first-born: and I have said unto thee, Let my son go, that he may serve me; and thou hast refused to let him go: behold, I will slay thy son, thy first-born. (Exod 4:22–23 ASV)

> And thou shalt say unto Pharaoh, Thus saith the LORD, Israel is my son, my firstborn: and I have said unto thee, Let my son go, that he may serve me; and thou hast refused to let him go: behold, I will slay thy son, thy firstborn. (Exod 4:22–23 ERV)

> Then say to Pharaoh, 'This is what the LORD says: Israel is my firstborn son, and I told you, "Let my son go, so he may worship me." But you refused to let him go; so I will kill your firstborn son.'" (Exod 4:22–23 NIV)

Each of these translations observes the fact that the Hebrew speaks about a past event(s), when Yahweh demanded that Pharaoh let his people go to worship him. Even in the later stages of hardening, Yahweh offers mercy to Pharaoh.

If this is correct, then the hardening that followed Moses' message was an extension, possibly at a more significant pace, of what had already been going on. In the light of this, it is incorrect to argue that Yahweh's judgment was without reference to the works of Pharaoh.[39] We must also remind ourselves that this was not an eschatological judgment concerning Pharaoh's eternal salvation; rather, it was God's judgment upon a ruler and his people for challenging his will and purposes. Thus, the order of how the hardening progressed is, in reality, very different from the case made by those who see the passage dealing with election to individual hardening and damnation. The hardening had already begun when Yahweh offered a stay of execution to the increasingly reprobate ruler. Mercy had been shown long before Moses came on the scene; however, this "passing over" was coming to an end with the threatened slaying of the firstborn.

---

38. This earlier ongoing hardening of Pharaoh's heart is overlooked by Piper, *Justification*, 174: "not once in Exod 4–14 is the assertion of God's hardening of Pharaoh *grounded* in any attitude or act of Pharaoh. Instead, again and again the reason given for the hardening is God's purpose to demonstrate his power and magnify his name. Paul picks up precisely this theme in Rom 9:17. With this selection and adaptation of Exod 9:16 Paul indicates his understanding of the Exodus context: the action of God in Pharaoh's life is determined ultimately by the *purposes* of God, not Pharaoh's willing or running." (Emphasis Piper's.)

39. Because I am not claiming that election in Rom 9:18 is to eternal salvation, the claim has no bearing on Paul's doctrine of salvation.

Ninth. God's willingness to stay judgment on a Gentile king/nation is found elsewhere in the OT. There is no difference between God's intention to judge Pharaoh and his intention to judge Nineveh. "When God saw what they did and how they turned from their evil ways, he had compassion and did not bring upon them the destruction he had threatened" (Jonah 3:10). This is in line with other NT texts, such as: "This is good, and pleases God our Savior who wants all men to be saved and to come to knowledge of the truth" (1 Tim 2:3–4). It is extremely serious to use a badly founded argument (such as election to damnation) to overturn such an important and unambiguous statement concerning the character of God. While there is general agreement over what 1 Tim 2:3–4 means, there is very real doubt over the syntax and, therefore, the meaning of Rom 9:17.[40] Furthermore, there are numerous verses that support 1 Tim 2:3–4,[41] while there are no biblical statements to support the reading of individual election to damnation. In dealing with other doctrines, strenuous efforts are made to harmonize the statements made with the rest of scripture and to ensure that the interpretation of a passage with justifiable concerns over its exegesis does not dominate others. The proposed reading of election to honor and service is supported by the whole of OT theology, whereas as we have seen earlier, nothing supports election to damnation.[42]

To demand the passage teaches that God elects individuals to damnation rather than to salvation from the judgment that reprobate humankind deserves, goes beyond biblical evidence. Those who propose this argument appeal to texts such as Rom 8:32–34, Eph 1:4 and 1 Thess 1:4.[43] However, they fail to note that these texts say nothing about election to damnation but are about a corporate calling to be God's people.[44] Not to notice these things is a serious failure. It can only suggest that such exegetes are so determined to uphold their understanding that they fail to notice the inappropriateness of their evidence is. Furthermore, the emphasis of scripture is that God is gracious and longsuffering; delighting in mercy and wanting all to come to the truth. While this may be difficult to reconcile with the doctrine that God elects some and not others, we still have to recognize the overwhelming emphasis of scripture is that God is merciful and does not delight in the destruction of the wicked.

Tenth. The double jeopardy reading has failed to appreciate the servant theology that is operating in Rom 9–11. By citing a conflation of Isa 29:16 and Isa 45:7 (as discussed ear-

---

40. See Schreiner, *Romans*, 519, who acknowledges the complexity of the syntax and accepts that nothing can be based upon it.

41. Matt 28:19; John 3:16; 5:34; 1 Thess 2:16. Of course, the matter of the election of individuals to salvation is a different issue altogether.

42 As noted earlier (page 312 n. 33), neither Schreiner, *Romans*, 522, nor Piper, *Justification*, 196, can offer one biblical text to support their arguments; both have had to seek support from intertestamental literature.

43. See Piper, *Justification*, 58.

44. Interestingly Schreiner, "Election," 39, acknowledges that these texts could be interpreted corporately and appeals to John 6:37, 44–45, 64–65; 10:26; Acts 13:48; 16:14. I have no hesitation in endorsing them as the correct source for a doctrine of election to salvation; however, they say nothing about an election to damnation.

lier), Paul is introducing, albeit indirectly, the figure of Cyrus. He was another pagan king appointed by Yahweh to achieve his purpose. In Isa 45:9, Israel complained that Cyrus had been appointed to be Yahweh's anointed (Isa 45:1). This interplay with another pagan king's calling to serve Yahweh's purposes supports the claim that Pharaoh's calling was to serve the historical, saving purposes of the living God. Pharaoh, like Cyrus, was appointed to be a savior-redeemer figure to Israel, as were all the examples given in Rom 9:6–13. Here, Isaac–though not Abraham's firstborn—is given the status of head of the people of promise and is, therefore, their redeemer figure. As such, he was chosen to care and provide for the promised seed. Similarly, Jacob—though not Isaac's firstborn—emerged as the appointed head. This servant theme is, therefore, at the heart of the argument that is being advanced. Consequently, this must be brought to the table when considering God's choice of his servant, Pharaoh. Central to this discussion is God's right to appoint people who have no natural claim to service—a role that bestows not only responsibility but gave honor. Within the story of Esau and Jacob, God takes the birthright from the one who, by order of descent, has a right to it and gives this blessing to another. This is the theme that drives Paul's discussion on the hardening of Pharaoh and Israel and the supplement of the calling of Cyrus in Rom 9:20.

The Pharaoh, who had been chosen as Yahweh's servant at the time of Joseph, had been a true shepherd of Israel. Exalting Joseph to a role that allowed him to welcome and provide for his family was clearly vital to the survival of the promised seed. However, when a later Pharaoh emerged who had not known Joseph, he abused his calling and sought to slaughter Israel's sons. Clearly, he was setting himself up to become a vessel of wrath. Later again, when Cyrus became Israel's shepherd, he provided the best resources for rebuilding the temple. Indeed, even King Nebuchadnezzar acted as a shepherd of Israel, exalting Daniel to a privileged position, which enabled him to care for the nation.

If the backgrounds regarding the role that the Pharaohs played in relation to the preservation of the seed of Abraham is not allowed to determine the interpretation of the hardening passage, then we will have failed to hear what Paul is arguing. This is given considerable support, as noted earlier, by the fact that Paul brings Cyrus into his argument by citing Israel's objection to his appointment.

Furthermore, this reading is demanded not only by the verses that immediately precede this passage but also by the ongoing argument, which runs into chapters 10 and 11. The whole thrust of the discussion is how Israel could lose her special status of being Yahweh's chosen servant. Because she failed to fulfill her divine appointment to be a light to the nations, she has been hardened and is under judgment. As a result, God has called the Gentiles to fulfill the role she has chosen to vacate. This concluding argument cannot be separated from what has gone on in the earlier chapter.

Significantly, the appointment of unworthy pagans to serve Yahweh by protecting his people is not limited to the above examples. Paul expands the theme in chapter 13 vv. 1–7, when he argues that the ruling authorities have been established by God to do the Roman believers good, and that its servants are to be honored and obeyed.

Eleventh. The OT examples that Paul uses can only point in one direction—Paul is discussing the election of people to be Yahweh's servants.[45] Indeed, the same language is used in 2 Tim 2:20–21, where we read: "In a large house there are articles not only of gold and silver, but also of wood and clay; some are for noble purposes and some for ignoble. If a man cleanses himself from the latter, he will be an instrument for noble purposes, made holy, useful to the Master and prepared to do any good work." The passage is clearly urging Timothy to ensure that he does not do anything that would damage his usefulness as a servant of the Lord, the very theme that I am arguing Rom 9:19–24 addresses. Pharaoh was disqualified from further use as a vessel of honor because of his disobedience. That led to the hardening of his heart. He was given over to the same hardening and ultimate destruction that Paul outlined in Rom 1:18–32.

THE MESSIAH AND HIS SERVANT'S HARDENING

9:14 What then shall we say? Is God unjust? Not at all! Paul responds to a possible charge that, by reversing the natural order of priority, God is being unjust. His point is this: because neither Jacob nor Esau deserved this honor, neither could claim merit. If they were to receive anything, it must be given by God out of his grace.

God has determined that those who are given this honor will not be able to claim it was their's by right This is demonstrated by the twists and turns seen in the progressive succession of those who were selected to carry forth the covenantal promises given to Abraham. Scripture shows that God has regularly taken a surprising course, choosing the unexpected to be the bearer of the promises.[46] Yet, in doing this, he is always faithful to the covenant he swore with Abraham.

---

45. This is a view that is supported by Herman Ridderbos, *Outline*, 345–46, who says: "The purport of Paul's argument is not to show that all that God does in history has been foreordained from eternity and therefore, so far as his mercy as well as his hardening is concerned, has an irresistible and inevitable issue. Rather, it is his intention to point out in the omnipotence of God's activity the real intention of his purpose. Everything is made subservient to the electing character of God's grace, not based on human merit or strength, and of the calling and formation of his people. So did God originally display it in Israel and to Israel, contrary to all human calculations, and contrary to all human resistance. And so does God maintain this sovereign electing character of his work of redemption over against Israel, when Israel misjudges this nature of its election as the people of God and has come to trust in its own righteousness, instead of in the righteousness of God (9:30ff.). Thus it can happen that Israel because of this misjudgement of its calling and election is placed next to Pharaoh as the exemplification of God's reprobation and hardening, and that what applied to Pharaoh holds for Israel as well, namely, that God by Israel's hardening and fall has chosen to make known the riches of his mercy (to the Gentiles) (Rom 11:7–10, 12, 15). At the same time, however, it is evident that one may not identify the omnipotence and sovereignty of God's grace thus upheld on the one hand and of his reprobation and hardening on the other with irrevocable 'eternal' decrees, in which God would once and forever have predestined the salvation or ruin of man: for God has not only reprobated and hardened Israel in order to display his mercy to the Gentiles, but no less to provoke Israel itself to repentance and 'jealousy' (Rom 11:11ff.). This concept of election denotes the omnipotence, not the deterministic character of God's work of grace and of the formation of his church. Election is an election of grace (*ekloge charitos*), that is to say: it does not take place on the ground of works (Rom. 11:5, 6). This contrast between grace and works dominates the whole argument of Romans 9–11 with respect to the calling and election of the people of God."

46. See, Levinson, *Death*.

9:15 For he says to Moses, "I will have mercy on whom I have mercy, and I will have compassion on whom I have compassion." To drive home his claim that election to honor and service is not based on merit or status, Paul again appeals to the Scriptures. The use of Exod 33:19 has particular relevance because of its context. Moses had asked Yahweh if he might see his glory, and, in reply, he was told: "I will cause all my goodness to pass in front of you, and I will proclaim my name, the LORD, in your presence." Yahweh then made the statement: "I will have mercy on whom I will have mercy, and I will have compassion on whom I will have compassion." The point is clear. God reveals himself to those who seek him, but not on the grounds of merit—his revelation is based solely on mercy. In this statement to Moses is echoed the divine name, which he revealed to him in Exod 3:14: "I AM WHO I AM" (or I WILL BE WHAT I WILL BE)—a name that speaks of God's refusal to be contained by a definition or expectation.

That God takes the initiative in salvation history has been demonstrated in the call of Abraham. The ancestor of the Jewish people was not chosen to be the conduit of God's blessings to all the families of the earth on the grounds of his merit but on the grounds of God's free electing grace. The same applies to the true descendants of Abraham—the sovereign God elects those who are allowed to see his glory. Our election to service and the privileges this brings is all of God's grace, prerogative, and initiative.

However, the case being argued is not for individual election but for that of peoples. God elected the Jewish people in their ancestor, Abraham. Now the Gentiles are part of his elect people and included in the covenant. As such, they are chosen by God to serve his purposes in redemptive history, i.e., they are included in the servant community that is appointed to take the good news of God's grace to the nations.

9:16 It does not, therefore, depend on man's desire or effort, but on God's mercy. This is the only conclusion that can be reached from the texts considered. The Scriptures Paul selects are not taken out of context but faithfully portray the nature of God's sovereign choice. Being chosen to serve God's purposes springs from his mercy and has nothing to do with man's achievements or rights by birth (John 1:12).

9:17 For the Scripture says to Pharaoh: "I raised you up for this very purpose, that I might display my power in you and that my name might be proclaimed in all the earth." We can easily miss the argument that Paul is making. We need to remind ourselves that Paul is discussing the judgment that has come on Israel. To illustrate this judgment, he considers God's dealings with Pharaoh. Many see this verse to be saying that God created Pharaoh in order to destroy him, so showing himself to be greater than the Egyptian ruler. But was Paul saying this? All that God would have achieved by such destruction would be a reputation that no person could get the better of him. However, the emphasis of this verse (and that of the exodus narrative) is God's mercy. This message of how God's mercy triumphs over man's sinfulness will characterize Paul's conclusion to this entire section (Rom 11:33–36).

The text that Paul quotes must be considered in its original setting. Failure to contextualize the quotation and so grasp its intended meaning has frequently caused Paul's argument to be misunderstood. God was not going to destroy Pharaoh in order to display his power; he was, in fact, doing the very opposite. The power of God was demonstrated through his patience and kindness to a disobedient Pharaoh:

‏16: כִּי עַתָּה שָׁלַחְתִּי אֶת־יָדִי וָאַךְ אוֹתְךָ וְאֶת־עַמְּךָ בַּדָּבֶר וַתִּכָּחֵד מִן־הָאָרֶץ‎

‏וְאוּלָם בַּעֲבוּר זֹאת הֶעֱמַדְתִּיךָ בַּעֲבוּר הַרְאֹתְךָ אֶת־כֹּחִי וּלְמַעַן סַפֵּר שְׁמִי בְּכָל־‎

‏הָאָרֶץ:‎

(Exo 9:15–16 WTT)

> For by now I could have stretched out my hand and struck you and your people with a plague that would have wiped you off the earth. But I have raised you up for this very purpose, that I might show you my power and that my name might be proclaimed in all the earth. (Exod 9:15–16 NIV)

> For by now I could have put forth my hand and struck you and your people with pestilence, and you would have been cut off from the earth; but for this purpose have I let you live, to show you my power, so that my name may be declared throughout all the earth. (Exod 9:15–16 RSV)

Examining the Exodus passage in its context[47] makes it clear that Yahweh's intention was not to glorify himself through the destruction of Pharaoh but through his

---

47. Piper, *Justification*, 64, considers that he has observed this method, i.e., of the context controlling his exegesis. He says: ". . . to understand Paul's intention in Rom 9:6–13 we must keep in view that these verses are an attempt to solve the problem raised in 9:1–5, namely that many within the elect nation of Israel are accursed and cut off from Christ. Many individual Israelites within the chosen people are not saved (cf. Rom 11:14). Paul is not moved to constant grief (9:2) because Israel has forfeited her non-salvific 'theocratic privileges' while another people (the church or the remnant) has taken over this 'historical role.' He is grieved because all the privileges of Israel listed in Rom 9:4, 5 imply the eschatological, eternal salvation of his people . . . but many individual Israelites—his kinsmen according to the flesh—are damned in their unbelief . . . Therefore the solution which Rom 9:6–13 develops in response to this problem must address the issue of the individual, eternal salvation." But Piper's argument has several inherent weaknesses. First is that the blessings listed were not individual blessings, they were the blessings given to the community. Apart from community membership, these blessings could not be experienced. Also, Paul is clearly recalling Moses' request that Yahweh blot him out of the book of life if, by being judged, the people would be spared (Exod 32:32). It is widely recognized that the theology of the original OT passages cited in the NT are transferred with the citation (so, Dodd, *According*; Hays, *Echoes*; Beale, "Wrong Text") The concern of Paul, therefore, echoes the concern of Moses, and Moses was not concerned about individual Israelites but about the nation, and the fact that she was Yahweh's representative. If she is cast off, the nations would say that Yahweh was not a covenant-keeping God and his name would be dishonoured. This is Moses' concern, and I would assert it is the nature of Paul's concern. Indeed, Rom 9–11 demonstrates this to be so. Piper refutes this, *Justification*, 155–6 and further justifies his individual reading (even though he acknowledges the corporate thrust of the overall text) by appealing to Rom 8:32, Eph 1:4, and 1 Thess 1:4. These texts, however, are of no value to his case. Eph 1:13 shows that the "you" in Eph 1:4 refers to "you Gentiles." This is supported by the overall corporateness of the letter. (See Holland, *Contours*; Crozart, "Ephesians") Again, the Thessselonian reference does not prove that Paul refers to the individual election of the believers for, as in Ephesians, it is a statement about the elect community–the church. I have shown how the letter to the Romans concerns the life and experience of the Roman church and not individuals. Rom 8:32 is about God's election of the church to be his people and of his faithfulness to the promises he had made to them. In the light of these facts, Piper has no grounds to impose an individualistic reading on Rom 9:17. This is not to deny that election of the individual to salvation is taught in the NT, but this teaching must be based

patient call to repentance. Indeed, although there is the warning of a future harden-ing, Pharaoh's heart had been hardened long before Moses addressed him.[48] He had sought to kill the newborn sons of the Hebrew families, and it is impossible to ar-gue that he could do that without hardening himself towards Yahweh's word. When Moses stood before him, Pharaoh was already a hardened man to whom Yahweh, in his mercy, continued to give the opportunity to repent and thereby save his people from impending judgment. Even the consequence of Pharaoh's rejection of god's word did not impact only on him, every Egyptian family was judged! Thus, the order of progres-sion of hardening is in reality very different from that which supporters of the election to divine hardening and damnation rely on. The hardening had already begun when Moses offered a stay of execution to the increasingly reprobate ruler. Mercy had been shown long before Moses came on the scene, but this was coming to an end with the threatened slaying of the firstborn. Inserting a discussion on election to damnation is not appropriate; indeed, it abuses the text.

Although God's show of power was demonstrated initially through his patience to Pharaoh, it became the grounds for God's judgment. In response to Pharaoh's willful-ness, Yahweh began the process of divine hardening as distinct from the hardening that Pharaoh's guilt had produced. The Lord had had every reason to judge him, but he de-sisted in order that his power should be shown through his mercy. But because Pharaoh rejected his mercy and continued to harden his heart, Yahweh sealed his fate with his divine hardening. Yahweh had no other option but to bring judgment upon him.

However, this was not the reason for raising Pharaoh up. The statement made to Pharaoh (quoted by Paul) has nothing to do with God choosing him in order to harden his heart so that God could display his power in judgment. Granted, the judgment did display his power—but that is not the context of the quoted verse. God wanted to change the heart of Pharaoh through patience and kindness. He was urging Pharaoh to receive mercy through repentance and obedience.[49]

Pharaoh had been chosen by God to rule, as had the Pharaoh who was ruling at the time of Joseph. In the closing chapters of Genesis, Joseph invites his father and his family to dwell in Egypt to escape famine. He could only do this with the consent of the Pharaoh ruling at that time, and, by granting Joseph's request, the Pharaoh acted as the Hebrews' benefactor, protecting them from danger. In the course of time, this benevolent relationship between Jacob's descendants and the Pharaoh changed. Rather than seeking to protect the Hebrews, a later Pharaoh sought to destroy them. He who had been ap-

---

on better exegesis than has been presented thus far. Indeed, Piper's own disciple Schreiner, "Exegetical," 38, notes the corporate setting of these texts. His argument is that, if the texts are corporate (dealing specifi-cally with Eph 1:4), it still does not deny individual election. He says: "In fact individual election cannot be dismissed, since it is taught in too many texts (e.g., John 6:37, 44–45, 64–65; 10:26; Acts 13:48; 16:14)." I want to affirm Schreiner's correct identification of texts that support individual election, but to claim that they can be imported into Rom 9 to support an individualistic interpretation of the hardening of Pharaoh, and through this a doctrine of election to damnation, is not admissible.

48. For textual evidence of this progression, see pages 316–17.

49. For a study on how God chooses the outsider and not the one designated by the law, see Levinson, *Death*.

pointed as a vessel of honor became a vessel fitted for destruction! This was a distressing development since he who had been given the privilege of acting as a redeemer figure to Jacob's descendants—a role that Cyrus would assume in the future—had not been elevated to be judged but to serve. We will find that Paul echoes the role of Cyrus as he deals with the protest of the vessel which the potter has made. This juxtaposition of pagans in the text is crucial. While no one would doubt the role that Cyrus was called to, most fail to see that it was also the role that the Pharaoh at the time of Moses was called to, and so filter out his calling from their discussion on the divine hardening.

The statement: "I could have stretched out my hand and struck you and your people with a plague that would have wiped you off the earth. But I have raised you up for this very purpose, that I might show you my power and that my name might be proclaimed in all the earth" (Exod 9:15–16) expresses God's focus was not one of salvation but of serving and honor. This is the central subject Paul continues to deal with when he turns to the story of Pharaoh. He is addressing the fact that Pharaoh's position had been given to him by God, but that he had abused it. He was created for honor but, by steadfastly rejecting God's word and purpose, his heart was hardened and, after exercising much patience, God judged him. Thus Pharaoh, who was chosen for honor, became a vessel prepared for destruction (v. 22). References to God telling Moses that he would harden Pharaoh's heart (Exod 4:21–23; 7:2–4; 14:4ff.) clearly speak of what will happen when Pharaoh rejects Moses' message. Taking our hermeneutic from Paul's ongoing argument concerning men whom God raised up to bless and protect his people, Pharaoh is judged, i.e., hardened, because he refuses to be the servant he has been appointed to be. He failed to protect the promised seed.

We need to remind ourselves that Scripture has no difficulty in seeing pagan kings and leaders as "servants of God." God referred to Cyrus as his "anointed . . . whose right hand I take hold of" (Isa 45:1).[50] Cyrus was a pagan king who served his own deities; nevertheless, God said of him: "He is my shepherd and will accomplish all that I please" (Isa 44:28). Cyrus did what Pharaoh refused to do—he served as a shepherd for the promised seed. Of course, Paul will refer to this shortly (vv. 19–20). The example is part of the argument that he is making about God's sovereignty and, as we will see, vv. 19–20 is corporate and not about election to salvation.

Thus, if a pagan leader can be God's servant, chosen for noble purposes (i.e., a vessel of honor), then Pharaoh had the potential to be a vessel of honor too. Looking again at the context of Paul's quotation in Rom 9:17, Yahweh says to Pharaoh: "For by now I could have stretched out my hand and struck you and your people with a plague that would have wiped you off the earth" (Exod 9:15). By delaying the judgment of the Passover night, God exercised mercy by calling the ruler to humble himself in his presence (Exod 10:3). With this invitation, God was not playing a game of cat and mouse with Pharaoh; he was appealing to him from the same heart that, in future years, would ache and call to Israel, his firstborn servant, to turn from her sins and receive mercy.

---

50. KJV has servant.

Not all of Pharaoh's court agreed with the position their master took. As the plagues fell, some of the Egyptians responded in fear to God's display of power (Exod 8:19; 9:20). Many in the country thought highly of Moses and the Israelites (Exod 11:3), and, by implication, respected their God. Were these the first Gentile converts—the firstfruit from among the Gentiles? As many were familiar with the Hebrew people, did they hear about the coming plague on the firstborn? Did they avail themselves of the power of the blood of the Passover lamb?

The narrative of the pre-exodus events suggests an apparently repentant Pharaoh to whom God extends mercy and answers requests (Exod 8:8, 12–13, 28, 30–31; 9:27–28, 33; Exod 10:16–17 in particular). Yet, the moment he had relief from the plagues, Pharoah's feelings of remorse were forgotten. He hardened his heart further (Exod 8:15, 19, 32; 9:12, 34; 10:20, 27–28) and any fear of the Lord was snatched away. Tragically, the seed of God's word had fallen on "thorny ground."

Pharaoh's rejection of God's mercy meant that "he sinned" (Exod 9:34). He and his officials hardened their hearts. This was expressed in Pharaoh's final venomous address to Moses: "Get out of my sight! Make sure you do not appear before me again! The day you see my face you will die!" (Exod 10:28). This hardening was the result of rejecting Yahweh's word. It was, therefore, the word of God that ultimately hardened Pharaoh.

Tragically and inevitably (Gen 15:13–14, where the covenant with Abraham promised blessing on those who dealt well with his descendents and wrath on those who sought their harm), Pharaoh's hardening was now to reap its just reward, and he was to become a vessel of wrath. Judgment, so long held back, was to visit him and all of the Egyptian people who disregarded God's word. Aaron and Moses did see Pharaoh again as, during the night of the Passover (after the death of the firstborn), they were summoned to the palace and granted freedom for themselves and their people. The one who had been chosen for noble purposes (v. 21) had hardened his heart to the responsibilities his privileges demanded. He became, instead, a vessel of wrath. This new role manifested other aspects of God's character as his righteousness and judgment were revealed.

The principle that noble "vessels of honor" can become "vessels of wrath" not only applies to Gentile rulers and the people they represent, but it also applies to Israel herself.

> "O house of Israel, can I not do with you as this potter does?" declares the LORD. "Like clay in the hand of the potter, so are you in my hand, O house of Israel. If at any time I announce that a nation or kingdom is to be uprooted, torn down and destroyed, and if that nation I warned repents of its evil, then I will relent and not inflict on it the disaster I had planned. And if at another time I announce that a nation or kingdom is to be built up and planted, and if it does evil in my sight and does not obey me, then I will reconsider the good I had intended to do for it.
>
> "Now therefore say to the people of Judah and those living in Jerusalem, 'This is what the LORD says: Look! I am preparing a disaster for you and devising a plan against you. So turn from your evil ways, each one of you, and reform your ways and your actions.' But they will reply, 'It's no use. We will continue with our own plans; each of us will follow the stubbornness of his evil heart.' Therefore this is what the LORD says: 'Inquire among the nations: Who has ever heard anything like this? A most horrible thing has been done by Virgin Israel.'" (Jer 18:6–13)

Clearly, individual leaders and the nations they represent are not necessarily vessels of honor forever. God responds and acts in mercy when a people repent and turn to him. In addition we can note that the warning of Israel's destruction if she refuses to repent is clearly not at the level of annihilation, for Israel survived the exile. It thus speaks of God's judgment, whatever the form, as essentially removing privilege from those who had enjoyed it previously and exercising appropriate judgment. This observation supports the case being made that becoming a vessel of wrath, as a term used in Rom 9:22, is not about eternal damnation.

While we have noted that Paul is making a corporate argument, it is more significant to note that this was not a battle of wills with Yahweh triumphing over Pharaoh. Rather, the exodus was a battle between Yahweh and Ra,[51] the Egyptian god. This god was seen to control the Egyptians and aliens (like the Hebrews) who lived within their borders. However, Yahweh had made a covenant with the Hebrews through their ancestors. If Ra triumphed over Yahweh, salvation history would be scuttled, Yahweh would be disgraced, his rule of creation and faithfulness to his covenant ended, and his reputation and character irreparably damaged.

In this drama, we see the outworking of the same principles that determined the destiny of the first man. Designed for honor and fellowship with God, and made to rule over God's creation as his vice-regent, Adam turned from his Creator and became a vessel of wrath. In the Garden, in one act of disobedience, man lost his honorable status and was prepared to be a vessel for destruction (Rom 1:18–32).

All of this supports the case that Paul's purpose in chapter nine is to demonstrate how God elects the people who are to serve him and to show that God can and does overturn privileges that he has given. "Now," says Paul, "Yahweh rejects the claims of the very people to whom he had previously committed himself—the Jews.[52] The firstborn nation (Exod 4:22), the nation with the divine calling and privilege, is to be replaced by a people who had no prior claims to his favor. The people who were 'no people' (Hos 2:23) are to be called 'the people of God' (Rom 9:25), just as Hosea had predicted." Further support for this position will unfold as we look further at specific verses. Thus, God is able to overturn the privilege of representation of those appointed through birth or even election, be it Esau, Pharaoh, Cyrus or Israel, and it is this theme that ties the section together. To depart, without any justification, into a discussion on people's eternal destinies and to use this passage as the key text is to miss what the passage is saying. There is a biblical doctrine, in my understanding, of individual election to salvation, but it should not in any way draw from this passage which is about something quite separate.

---

51 Dozeman, *War*, 3, says: "The destruction of the Egyptians is a story of holy war." For further details of God as a warrior, see Longman, *Warrior*, 31ff.

52. Getty, "Salvation," 456–69, holds that several ideas in Rom 9–11 were probably written to check a trend of anti-Jewish sentiment within the church. She claims that this is evident in Paul's rebuke of the Gentiles for their anti-Jewish sentiment, their pride (Rom 11:20), their relative newness in the kingdom (Rom 11:24), and their status as grafted branches (Rom 11:17–18). For God's overturning of privilege, see Levinson, *Death*.

9:18 Therefore God has mercy on whom he wants to have mercy, and he hardens whom he wants to harden. If the argument outlined above is correct and Pharaoh was a vessel of honor until he rejected Yahweh's word, then it changes the reading of the text significantly.[53] The emphasis is not that God has created people to be damned but that he created *all people* for dignity and service, i.e., to be vessels of honor.[54] In writing about salvation history and men who represent their respective nations, Paul focuses on communities, not individuals.[55] By addressing God's dealings with Moses and Pharaoh as representative heads, he shows how God chooses people groups to fulfill his purposes.[56] As Israel discovered, the fact that a people has been chosen does not mean that she is exempt from God's judgment. Indeed, it was because she had abused her privileged calling that God said to Israel: "You only have I chosen of all the families of the earth; therefore I will punish you for all your sins" (Amos 3:2). The promise of punishment was fulfilled in her conquest and exile. Thus, the proposed interpretation of this notoriously difficult section[57] is supported by the way Yahweh elected and then held Israel to account. She had been a vessel of honor, chosen to be the people through whom Yahweh would bless the nations (Gen 12:2; 17:16; 18:18; 26:4) but who, because of disobedience and the hardening of her heart, (Ps 95:8–11; Isa 63:17) was replaced by a people who "were no people" (Hos 1:10). This is the OT theme that is being thrashed out in Rom 9–11, and so the proposed reading stays firmly within the tradition of OT theology.

This divine principle of showing mercy to people groups can be seen throughout history. Nations and communities have experienced the mercy of God, with large numbers of their people turning to him in repentance. In Isa 34–35, the Gentile nations were warned of judgment but promised restoration and redemption if they sought the Lord. Yahweh even says to *Gentiles* who have come under judgment (Isa 34:1–17) but who call on him for mercy: "Be strong, do not fear; for your God will come with vengeance; with divine retribution he will come to save you" (Isa 35:4).[58]

Thus, blessing and salvation is never an end in itself, nor is judgment.[59] Any claim to having received God's blessing and mercy must be supported by evidence of service,

53. Schreiner, *Romans*, 518, changes the meaning of the text by asserting: "the choice of one for eschatological honour and the other for judgement from the same lump indicates that those chosen had no special merits or distinctiveness that accounted for their being chosen." Thus, Schreiner has introduced the dimension of eschatological judgment when there is no mention of this in the text. Admittedly, once this has been introduced the case for election to judgment is stronger but the grounds for introducing the concept are not present.

54. Clearly, at the socio-historic level there have always been leaders, (vessels of honor) but, in absolute terms, everyone is called to the service of God and have been created for honor and glory (Rom 3:23).

55. See Wilckens, *Römer*, 2:196–97; Käsemann, *Romans*, 265; Hays, *Echoes*, 66.

56. See Munck, *Israel*, 38, 42; Leenhardt, *Romans*, 249; Campbell, "Freedom," 29.

57. Murray, *Romans*, 2:29, softens the example by saying that the hardening is the consequence of Yahweh not intervening to soften Pharaoh's heart. Hodge, *Romans*, 316, makes the case that: "Pharaoh was no worse than many other men who have obtained mercy, yet God, for his wise and benevolent reasons, withheld from him the saving influence of his grace." Both explanations are clearly pulling away from where their exegesis has led, i.e., Yahweh elected Pharaoh to be damned.

58. For another example of God's mercy to the Gentiles, see Isa 19:19–25.

59. Note Ridderbos, *Outline*, 112: "God's wrath places itself in the service of his love."

exhibiting concern for others that they will become recipients of the same grace. For the Christian, the reality of blessing ultimately turns on a concern for people as they seek to reach them with the message of the Gospel of peace (Isa 42:1).

This principle also applies to local churches. All too often, when a time of revival recedes, the responsibility to witness to others wanes and energies become focused on divisive, peripheral issues. Believers within a church that has known blessing often become confused as non-essential features of its theology or cultural identity are seen as responsible for spawning the work of God. The congregation reasons that, in order to experience another visitation, its culture and values must be maintained.

When this stance is taken, the church unwittingly puts controls on God and exalts her own understanding. But God is never limited in this way. This was Israel's sin when she tried to impose non-essential practices on the Gentiles, idolizing her own status. When a church does this, her witness is often lost; her light goes out and her candlestick is removed (Rev 2:15). Even a church that has been richly blessed and used powerfully to advance the Gospel can become arrogant, proud, and hardened. If she falls into this state and rejects the call of her Lord (as did Pharaoh and Israel), she will become a vessel of dishonor and destruction (1 Cor 5:1–8; 10:1–13; Rev 2:4–6, 14–16, 21–23; 3:1–3).

9:19–20 One of you will say to me: "Then why does God still blame us? For who resists his will?" But who are you, O man, to talk back to God? Shall what is formed say to him who formed it, "Why did you make me like this?" Paul again anticipates an objection: "If we are what we are because God has determined what we shall be, how can he judge us?" There is apparent substance to the complaint, but not when it is put into the context of God's sovereignty. Paul answers the anticipated objection by quoting what God said in response to a similar complaint made by Israel in Isaiah's prophecy.

The allegation of God's injustice is only possible because of the freedom he has given to the people he has made. The very fact that the creature can call the Creator to account is evidence that man has attempted to usurp God's authority. As the author of Lamentations wrote: "It is because of the LORD's unfailing mercies that we are not consumed" (Lam 3:22). Those who are embittered and who make a charge of injustice against God have been spared by his unfailing mercy, as God's justice without mercy requires that sentence be served forthwith. But they have been shown mercy, and the Day of Judgment is postponed.

To rain accusations upon the God who has shown such mercy, allowing opportunity for repentance, demonstrates man's sinful rebellion to overthrow his rule. However, if it had been God's will to withhold mercy so that swift judgment was meted out, what right did man have to challenge him?

We have seen that the letters to the churches had to be read corporately as they were not written to individuals but to congregations. Their arguments are concerned with God's ways throughout salvation history. As we have seen, rather than creating Pharaoh for destruction, he was created for honor. It was his refusal to hear and obey God's word that brought the hardening of heart and consequent judgment.

The narrative about people appointed to be vessels of honor continues in this passage. This time, however, Paul alludes to a passage that has in its background another world leader whom God raised up. Paul quotes from Isa 45:9: "Woe to him who quarrels with his Maker, to him who is but a potsherd among the potsherds on the ground. Does the clay say to the potter, 'What are you making?' Does your work say, 'He has no hands?'"

The passage is Israel's response on hearing that Cyrus had been raised up to serve Yahweh's purposes. Earlier, Isaiah recorded:

> "This is what the LORD says to his anointed, to Cyrus, whose right hand I take hold of to subdue nations before him and to strip kings of their armor, to open doors before him so that gates will not be shut" (Isa 45:1). After Israel complained about not having the status granted to Cyrus, God responds: "*I will* raise up Cyrus in my righteousness: *I will* make all his ways straight. He will rebuild my city and set my exiles free, but not for a price or reward, says the LORD Almighty." (Isa 45:13)[60]

We cannot separate the quoted text in Romans from its original OT context of Israel's complaint to God about decisions he had made. The theme of this passage in Rom 9 continues the argument about Pharaoh being raised up to display God's power. This is also the theme of Isa 45, from which Paul quotes the complaints that God anticipates Israel will make (Isa 45:9b). Rom 9–11 is about God's sovereignty in choosing people to fulfill his purposes, and Paul gives biblical evidence that he reserves the right to include Gentiles among those whom he uses. In the past, his choices included Pharaoh and Cyrus; now they include Gentile believers and the Jewish remnant. God has now chosen these to serve him and, as in the past, the physical descendants of Abraham complain.[61]

9:21 Does not the potter have the right to make out of the same lump of clay some pottery for noble purposes and some for common use? The imagery of the potter was well known to the Jews (Isa 29:16; 30:14; 45:9; 64:8; Jer 18:4–6). Here in v. 21, the potter takes clay and, pulling from it smaller pieces, he begins to work each piece. He forms different types of pots: some beautiful—skillfully turned for eating and drinking—and some roughly made for common use. The potter made different pots in different ways and for different purposes. The clay had no choice as to how it would be worked, and it

---

60. Emphasis added to show that Yahweh refuses to be controlled by the petty complaint of Israel.

61. Yahweh's desire and determination to bless all the peoples of the earth –even in the face of Israel's complaint—is echoed in many parts of the scripture. The book of Jonah typifies this as do many other texts, such as: "In that day there will be an altar to the LORD in the heart of Egypt, and a monument to the LORD at its border. It will be a sign and witness to the LORD Almighty in the land of Egypt. When they cry out to the LORD because of their oppressors, he will send them a savior and defender, and he will rescue them. So the LORD will make himself known to the Egyptians, and in that day they will acknowledge the LORD. They will worship with sacrifices and grain offerings; they will make vows to the LORD and keep them. The LORD will strike Egypt with a plague; he will strike them and heal them. They will turn to the LORD, and he will respond to their pleas and heal them. In that day there will be a highway from Egypt to Assyria. The Assyrians will go to Egypt and the Egyptians to Assyria. The Egyptians and Assyrians will worship together. In that day Israel will be the third, along with Egypt and Assyria, a blessing on the earth. The LORD Almighty will bless them, saying, 'Blessed be Egypt my people, Assyria my handiwork, and Israel my inheritance'" (Isa 19:19–25).

was the choice of the potter as to what it would become. There had to be vessels made for noble purposes and there had to be vessels made for lesser purposes.

This was also the case with the families of man. Some nations were elected for what appeared to be noble tasks, while others, in comparison, had less significant functions. Paul's argument is that just as clay has no right to argue with the decisions of the potter, so man has no right to argue with the decisions of God. It is not that such decisions are fixed—if a beautiful drinking vessel leaks and no longer serves its purpose, it is destroyed. As we have seen, vessels of honor can (and do) come under judgment for turning away from God, and those that did not have honor can be promoted instead. As indicated in the earlier argument, this is how God has always dealt with men (Rom 9:6–13 [see also Hos 1:10]; 9:25–26).

In writing Rom 9:21, Paul may have had the Genesis creation story in mind. This narrative describes how man was made from the dust (or clay) of the earth. What God, the potter, decides regarding his creation is his own prerogative. In this argument, Paul is not saying that God is capricious, but that he does everything, at all times, according to truth and justice. He takes the fallen children of man (who, because of the hardening of their hearts through unbelief [Rom 1:18–32] were under judgment) and bestows honor and blessing upon them. Who can complain about God's dealings?

9:22 What if God, choosing to show his wrath and make his power known, bore with great patience the objects of his wrath—prepared for destruction? Paul is writing to the believers in Rome to say that they must understand they cannot question God's actions and decisions. He asks the question: "What right do you have to challenge God if he chooses to show his wrath and display his power to rebellious people?" Paul reasons from what, at first, appears to be a hypothetical case. He focuses on the great patience of God, who keeps back his wrath from those who deserve judgment.[62]

Paul's argument emphasizes that the only thing that is not fair or just is that God has acted in mercy. Man's attempt to usurp the position and authority of his Creator (an attempt that eventually resulted in the death of God's Son) should have left him under the sentence of separation from God and eternal judgment. When Paul writes: "prepared for destruction," he does not necessarily mean that man was created for destruction but that, as a consequence of disobedience, he is prepared for destruction. Even though the line of demarcation has been crossed and man's heart has become hardened, Yahweh still pleads with the ones who disobey him to repent and avoid judgment. This is nothing new; it replicates his pleadings with Israel before they were cut off, in accordance with the covenantal curses. The ones who are put aside in terms of being instruments for achieving God's purposes continue to experience his patience and mercy until the very last moment. Of course, for those who fail to fulfill their assigned task and reject God, the consequence is not merely a loss of status; they also come under judgment for

---

62. Schreiner, *Romans*, 519, acknowledges the complexity of syntax of vv. 22–23 and accepts that argument cannot be settled on this evidence. He concedes that it is the flow of the argument that is important for interpreting these verses.

misrepresenting him and for the unrighteousness in which they took part. This is true for the Gentiles as much as it was for Israel.

9:23 What if he did this to make the riches of his glory known to the objects of his mercy, whom he prepared in advance for glory. Another question is raised: "How are people prepared for glory?" Earlier, Paul discussed the redemption that is in Christ Jesus (Rom 3:21ff.) and his role in undoing the work of Adam (Rom 5:12ff.). The letter pivots around the exodus of the people of God from Egypt and then from Babylon. Both OT redemptive events show how God, having committed himself to his people in covenant, prepared for their deliverance. He made plans to bring them out of bondage, misery, and shame, in order that he might bring them into his glory (Isa 41:8–16).[63]

Using these powerful OT models, Paul is saying that God will be as glorified by his new covenant people's eschatological exile as he was when he made the ancient people a vessel of honor, delivering them first from captivity in Egypt and then from Babylon. The mercy that was extended to Israel has now been extended to nations that she considered to be "vessels of destruction." It is believing people from these Gentile people groups who, along with believing Jews, have been rescued from exile and brought into the kingdom of God (Col 1:13–14). Those who thought that they had divine rights to inclusion have been excluded.

9:24 Even us, whom he also called, not only from the Jews but also from the Gentiles? God extended his mercy in order to bring about a single covenant community made up of believing Jews and believing Gentiles. The original argument against God having the right to reject or elect as he wished (v. 19) has not been fully developed. Now, Paul returns to his premise, spelling out the background to the calling of the Jews and their salvation history. Yahweh's purpose in choosing them was to bring to himself a people of Jews and Gentiles who would love him and display his grace and mercy to the whole of creation (Eph 2:8–18).

9:25 As he says in Hosea. "I will call them 'my people' who are not my people; and I will call her 'my loved one' who is not my loved one," Paul adapts the text of Hos 2:23. The original passage was from Hosea's life when, tragically, the prophet realized that the child his wife had borne was not his but her lover's. Yahweh uses the pain of Hosea to speak of his own anguish. He calls the northern kingdom of Israel "not my people." She had broken away from Judah and Benjamin (who stayed loyal to the line of David) and had played the harlot, setting up her own shrines to worship false gods (Hos 3:1; Ezek 16:23–34).Yahweh said that the children of Israel were not his, and separated himself from them by exiling them at the hand of the Assyrians (2 Kgs 18:11).

---

63. Despite not interpreting the text corporately, Seifrid, "Romans," 647, notes: "Paul does not identify God with a hidden election of some to destruction and some to glory. Paul affirms that the Creator acts in sovereign freedom, but his response to the impertinent question of the human being does not rest with abstract assertion of the Creator's right; rather, he bears witness to the promise of the gospel, that the Creator's purpose is the restoration of his glory to those whom he is now preparing."

Paul now adapts the original passage to speak of the Gentiles, whom God has brought to himself. God honors them with the title "my people." The text was originally applied to a people who had forfeited their privilege by joining themselves to other gods—the very condition of man in Adam. God is going to accept the repentant children of Adam (believing Gentiles) back into his presence. The use of the quotation does not violate the original message given by the prophet but expands it.

9:26 And, "It will happen that in the very place where it was said to them, 'You are not my people,' they will be called 'sons of the living God.'" Paul again quotes from Hosea 1:10. If he is deliberately emphasizing the place where the Gentiles will become part of the covenant community (Eph 2:11–15), he might have had in mind the prediction of the Gentiles going up to Jerusalem. The prophets saw Jerusalem as the place where the Gentiles would assemble when they sought Yahweh (Isa 2:1–4; 19:24–25). Some think this was the prophecy that motivated Paul to lead a deputation of Gentiles into Jerusalem with an offering for the believers who were suffering through extreme poverty (Rom 15:25; 1 Cor 16:1–3). Scholars reason this visit was a symbolic act on Paul's part, fulfilling the predictions of the prophets that the Gentile nations would come up to Jerusalem to worship the Lord.[64]

What is significant is the unquoted opening sentence of Hos 1:10: "Yet the Israelites will be like the sand on the seashore, which cannot be measured or counted." This is nothing less than a renewal of the Abrahamic covenant. It is a quote from Gen 22:17 and is not included in the earlier promises concerning the covenant (Gen 12:1–3; 15:5) or in the later promises given to Isaac and then Jacob. Just as Yahweh had given Isaac back to Abraham from the "dead" (Heb 11:19—later rabbinical writers interpreting the sacrifice of Isaac as atonement for Israel's sins), so now many sons (including Gentiles) are being brought from the "dead."

9:27 Isaiah cries out concerning Israel. "Though the number of the Israelites be like the sand by the sea, only the remnant will be saved. Here we see a transition in Paul's argument. We have noted earlier in the chapter that the argument was not about election to salvation but to service. However, salvation terminology is introduced here, and Paul begins his discourse as to the condition of Israel in relation to God's saving activity. While the argument moves on to Israel's salvation rather than her call to service, the argument does, of course, continue to be corporate rather than individualistic. It is about Israel's salvation; not about individual salvation.[65]

We noted in the comment on the previous verse that the unquoted introductory sentence of Gen 22:17 in Hos 1:10 promised that Israel would be as "the sand on the seashore." Instead, Paul draws on the fuller statement from Isa 10:22: "Though your people, O Israel, be like the sand by the sea, only a remnant will return." The promise that Abraham would have a multitude of descendants was clearly important to the eighth

---

64. See Munck, *Israel*.

65. While that is the argument here, the preaching of the apostles stressed the importance of individual response in becoming members of the covenant community, so Acts 2:40; 3:19; 8:31–35; 10:32–34; 13:32–34; 13:47–48; 16:31–34; 17:16–17; 18:5–11; 19:8; 20:25–26; 28:20.

century prophets. It must have sustained them, assuring them that Yahweh was bound by his own oath to save, at the very least, a remnant. If Yahweh allowed the extinction of Israel, his promise to Abraham could never be fulfilled.

Paul, of course, has demonstrated that the true children of Abraham—the children of the covenant—are those who share Abraham's faith in the God who keeps his promises to all who call upon him. In the original passage of Isaiah, there is an intended note of distress that only a remnant would be saved; but here, Paul writes out of hope. Despite the sinfulness of Israel, a remnant would still be saved. The emphasis is on the fact that even Israel's rebelliousness could not frustrate the sovereignty of God. This is the first direct mention that a remnant of Israel will be saved, although Paul has been implying it throughout the section since v.6.

By incorporating Isa 10:22 into his evidence, Paul is able to show that Gentiles are included in the pilgrim community that returns from exile in Adam.

9:28 For the Lord will carry out his sentence on earth with speed and finality." The final part of the Isa 10:22–23 passage makes it clear that God's judgments are final and that it is he who determines the time of their fulfillment. Throughout history, some have seen the longsuffering of God as a sign of weakness or non-existence. Both conclusions are foolish and dangerous. If his judgment could come on his covenant people with such devastation and ferocity that surrounding nations were aghast (Jer 22:8; 46:12–13; Ezek 5:15; 28:19), how foolish it would be to suggest that God would not bring judgment on all who rebel against him (1 Cor 10:1–11).

9:29 It is just as Isaiah said previously: "Unless the Lord Almighty had left us descendants, we would have become like Sodom, we would have been like Gomorrah." The fall of Jerusalem at the hands of the Babylonians was so complete that it appeared to be the end of the covenant. It is true that Israel would survive in exile, but what sort of survival would it be? Without the temple and land, her people were disinherited. In ancient understanding, it was unthinkable for a people to be without their land and their god. Even in modern thinking, nationhood is often thought to be inseparable from homeland. This, sadly, is the reality for many millions of refugees at the beginning of the twenty-first century.

Those who survived the dreadful slaughter following the fall of Jerusalem were exiled to Babylon. Eventually, they came to terms with their new circumstances and started to make a life for their families. Many had worked successfully during the seventy years since their deportation and had been absorbed into Babylonian society. When Yahweh called them to return to their homeland, most chose to forsake their inheritance; they stayed in their new home, despite the promise that God would restore the nation after seventy years of exile (Jer 29:10–14). The return to the promised land was going to cost the Jews; they would have to endure great hardships, and, in so doing, deprive their families of the benefits they had as a community living in an advanced society. As a result, most rejected God's call to go back. The descendants referred to in Rom 9:29 must be the remnant who continued to believe Yahweh's promises given through the prophets. These people recognized that Yahweh would fulfill his word. He was a God who kept covenant with his people and who freely gave mercy. They knew that if this had not been so, Israel—like Sodom and Gomorrah—would have ceased to exist.

In mentioning these two notorious cities, Isaiah was acknowledging not merely the necessity for Jerusalem's judgment but her undoubted oblivion if God had not intervened. Jerusalem not only deserved a similar judgment to Sodom and Gomorrah but doubly deserved it (Gen 19:24–25, 28). These two cities had sinned in ignorance, but the people of Jerusalem had sinned in the face of all the warnings of the prophets and their appeals for them to turn from their sin. Israel's willful disobedience brought direct shame on Yahweh, whose servant she was supposed to be and whose honor she should have upheld. She was the one who had been called into covenant with Yahweh, and it was her rebellion, rather than the holiness of Yahweh (Lev 19:2), that the nations of the world had witnessed.

Paul skillfully uses the comparison with these two ancient cities to emphasize that no one can accuse God of being unjust for acting in judgment. Indeed, if God is to be accused of anything, it is that he has not given man the judgment he deserves. This has been delayed; and for those who believe, it has been averted at great cost—the cost of his own Son's death (Rom 8:32).

9:30 What then shall we say? That the Gentiles, who did not pursue righteousness, have obtained it, a righteousness that is by faith; The irony is obvious. How could it be that those who sought to live according to the law have been rejected, while those who had such little concern have been accepted? To be told that neither good deeds nor religious activities earn God's salvation is still an unspeakable offense for many today. Such a claim, when referring to individual election, seems to make a monster out of God, as though he had lost his senses and ceased to uphold the moral law! From a strictly human perspective that would be right, for it is saying that man's efforts are worthless. But the argument that Paul is making is not about morality (how some define the "righteousness of God") but about how God does not choose a people to represent him, i.e., to be his servant, on the basis of works.[66] To read "righteousness" as another term for morality is to impose Hellenistic understanding on Paul's use of "righteousness," when what he is writing about is God's saving activity. The God of Scripture has revealed himself as the one who deals with all men on the same basis, that of his grace. Only in this way can they be released from their bondage to Sin and be brought into the covenant community.

For Paul, there is only one saving righteousness—one divine saving act—and that is what Christ's redeeming death is all about.[67] Thus, the term "righteous" is not limited to moral uprightness or vindication before the law. Paul uses the term with the meaning given by Isaiah within the context of redemptive history—it is God's saving activity (Isa 56:1 cf. Rom 1:17). God has visited the Gentiles who had not sought him, and has brought representatives of all the nations into a covenant that binds them into the promises made to Abraham (Rom 2:25–29; 4:16–17). They have been redeemed from sin and condemnation, and brought into the kingdom of the Son he loves (Col 1:13–14).

---

66. But of course election of people to salvation is a part of the gospel and it does offend many.

67. For further discussion on righteousness, see comments on Rom 4:3.

⟐ **9:31 But Israel, who pursued a law of righteousness, has not attained it.** The NIV rendering has been chosen out of a range of possibilities in an attempt to explain a difficult expression. Paul writes literally: "But Israel, did not catch up with the law." One suggestion is that Paul means Israel was pursuing uprightness through the law, but fell short.[68] Paul is not criticizing the Jews for pursuing the law; he simply laments that they have missed its purpose. The law was intended to be the nation's "schoolmaster/supervisor"[69] in order to bring the Jews to Christ (Gal 3:24), and not to be an end in itself.

⟐ **9:32 Why not? Because they pursued it not by faith but as if it were by works. They stumbled over the "stumbling stone."** Paul's question: "Why not?" anticipates an objection to the above statement. Paul's answer is that man's way of righteousness is not the same as God's. It never has been and never will be. It has been argued by New Perspective theologians that Paul misrepresents the Jews[70] as they never were (certainly not in Paul's time, according to the rabbinical evidence) a people who thought that keeping the law earned them salvation. The New Perspective argument proposes that the Jews understood the law to be a gift from God and that this gift was bestowed upon them *after* he had accepted them as his covenant people. Their argument concludes with the question: "If this was their mindset, how is it that Paul could be interpreted as accusing the Jews of seeking righteousness by the law?" Of course, the question assumes this is how they did understand the law.

But for Paul, the issue was not how the Jews thought they were made right with God but how the Gentiles were to be made right with him. Their insistence that the Gentiles had to be circumcised was the acid test. If they really believed their relationship with Yahweh was without the law and that the law "merely" spelled out the covenantal obligations, what right did they have to require circumcision of the Gentiles? Their confidence and their understanding were flawed. Like Jonah, who feared that Yahweh would be merciful to Nineveh, they were demonstrating how far they were from the true meaning of the covenant. They wanted this grace solely for themselves and sought to protect their unique status by demanding that the Gentiles be circumcised. In other words, they taught that salvation could only be obtained within Judaism. They had turned the grace of God into a set of legal requirements. Their understanding of what would save the Gentiles defined how they saw their own salvation; in other words, it was achieved by keeping the works of the law.[71]

---

68. See Fitzmyer, *Romans*, 578.

69. These are the most widely accepted meanings of *paidagogos*. For an understanding that sees the law functioning as a "best man" preparing for a wedding, see Holland, *Contours*, 212 and *Paul, Law and Spirit*, forthcoming.

70. See Sanders, *Palestinian*.

71. However, we must not forget that Judaism was not a homogeneous set of beliefs. A critique of a particular part of Judaism must not assume that the problem or misunderstanding being addressed was throughout the nation. See Holland, *Contours*, 202–3.

9:33 As it is written: "See, I lay in Zion a stone that causes men to stumble and a rock that makes them fall, and the one who trusts in him will never be put to shame." Paul cites the text that predicted the Jews would stumble. The NT understanding of Isa 28:16 speaks of those who reject the Messiah king. However, in its historical setting, Isa 28:16 spoke of the coming judgment on Judah and her subsequent exile. The whole section (Isa 28:11–16) is a key passage for NT theology. Isa 28:11 is quoted by Paul in 1 Cor 14:21 and Isa 28:16 (the stone text) is the most quoted OT verse in the entire NT. I will argue that Isa 28:15 is part of the background that informs Paul's understanding of what it means to be in Adam (see comments on Rom 10:11). Isaiah is saying that, rather than trusting in alliances with other nations for security—alliances made by the king that would cause the fall of Jerusalem—Yahweh would raise up a true Son of David. Those who put their trust in him would be brought out of the exile that had resulted from their forefather's sin. Again, we see Paul staying true to the original meaning of the Scriptures. The argument is that God has raised up the righteous Branch, who brings the sons of Adam out of the exile into which they had been sentenced as a result of the fall.

CONCLUSION OF ROMANS 9

Paul shares the distress he experiences over the unbelief of his own people, the Jews. They had been privileged above all other nations, but they misunderstood their situation. In their minds, they would always be first in line for the blessings of God. To dispel this illusion, Paul highlights examples in Scripture. These show that God will not be bound to Israel's belief that Yahweh owes the nation privilege and protection. Even Pharaoh, Israel's great enemy, had been raised up by God (as had Cyrus) so that he could use him to achieve his sovereign purposes.

Paul answers the arrogance of his unbelieving kinsmen. Foolishly, Israel thinks she has a unique relationship with God that guarantees her privileged role. Paul answers from the Jewish Scriptures, and shows that what he says is no different from what the law has always said. He demonstrates that the promotion of the Gentiles above Israel for given periods of time had always been part of redemptive history.

The citations all come from texts that warn Israel of judgment and the calling of the Gentiles—themes that are part of the second exodus preaching of the prophets. The new exodus was brought about so that Yahweh would have his bride, and Paul has made it clear that his bride would include Gentile believers.

Although this chapter is often used to support doctrines relating to individual election, that was never its purpose. It is about how God has, throughout history, chosen people and nations to be his servants. In being chosen, they are appointed to positions of honor. If they abuse their privilege, they are warned of the danger of judgment. If they continually resist God's appeals to repent, they are removed from their calling, become vessels of wrath, and are judged for resisting and seeking to overthrow God's purposes. This was, of course, the pattern of the fall of Adam—Yahweh's first servant.

ROMANS 10

THE MESSIAH KING AND HIS COVENANTAL PURPOSES

Brothers, my heart's desire and prayer to God for the Israelites is that they may be saved. For I can testify about them that they are zealous for God, but their zeal is not based on knowledge. Since they did not know the righteousness that comes from God and sought to establish their own, they did not submit to God's righteousness. Christ is the end of the law so that there may be righteousness for everyone who believes. Moses describes in this way the righteousness that is by the law: "The man who does these things will live by them." But the righteousness that is by faith says: "Do not say in your heart, 'Who will ascend into heaven?'" (that is, to bring Christ down) "or 'Who will descend into the deep?'" (that is, to bring Christ up from the dead). But what does it say? "The word is near you; it is in your mouth and in your heart," that is, the word of faith we are proclaiming: That if you confess with your mouth, "Jesus is Lord," and believe in your heart that God raised him from the dead, you will be saved. For it is with your heart that you believe and are justified, and it is with your mouth that you confess and are saved. As the Scripture says, "Anyone who trusts in him will never be put to shame." For there is no difference between Jew and Gentile—the same Lord is Lord of all and richly blesses all who call on him, for, "Everyone who calls on the name of the Lord will be saved." How, then, can they call on the one they have not believed in? And how can they believe in the one of whom they have not heard? And how can they hear without someone preaching to them? And how can they preach unless they are sent? As it is written, "How beautiful are the feet of those who bring good news!" But not all the Israelites accepted the good news. For Isaiah says, "Lord, who has believed our message?" Consequently, faith comes from hearing the message, and the message is heard through the word of Christ. But I ask: Did they not hear? Of course they did: "Their voice has gone out into all the earth, their words to the ends of the world." Again I ask: Did Israel not understand? First, Moses says, "I will make you envious by those who are not a nation; I will make you angry by a nation that has no understanding." And Isaiah boldly says, "I was found by those who did not seek me; I revealed myself to those who did not ask for me." But concerning Israel he says, "All day long I have held out my hands to a disobedient and obstinate people." (Rom 10:1–21)

INTRODUCTION

In chapter 10, Paul continues to express his deep longing for the salvation of his kinsmen (v. 1). He argues that, while the Jews think that they have been zealous for God, in reality they have been obstinate and disobedient, refusing to submit to the only righteousness that God can accept, i.e., the righteousness that is by faith in Jesus Christ (Rom 10:2–4).

Their pride in being "people of the book" actually hindered them from discovering what the message of the book (the Torah) is all about. By quoting Deut 30:12–13 in Rom 10:6, Paul demonstrates that the law intended righteousness to be a gift given by faith.

Within this OT text, there are references to "ascending into heaven" and "descending into the deep." These phrases—familiar to Paul's Jewish readers—refer to the finding of the law. Paul applies them now to the finding of Christ. He can do this with great confidence because the law and the writings of the prophets point to Jesus, their decrees all being fulfilled in him who is the end, or goal, of the OT revelation.

Thus, Christ is to be found. He is not far off but is near to all who call upon him. Paul drives this lesson home by explaining how salvation is to be received: "If you confess with your mouth, 'Jesus is Lord,' and believe in your heart that God raised him from the dead, you will be saved" (Rom 10:9).

Paul highlights the vital importance of this message of faith by explaining that throughout history people have heard it. He stresses the necessity of it being told. He likens the witnessing NT believers to the exiles leaving Babylon. Using second exodus material (Isa 52:7), he writes that, just as the former exiles returned home announcing their message of salvation to all who would listen, so the NT believers, on their pilgrimage, announce that the second exodus of God's people has been accomplished. They declare that all those who hear and believe can share in the salvation and come out of their bondage to Sin. The summons to declare that Jesus Christ is Lord echoes Rom 1:4, where Jesus the Son of David, through the Spirit of holiness, was proclaimed to be the Son of God by his resurrection from the dead.

Paul uses the words of Isaiah to describe those who preach the Gospel (v. 15): "How beautiful are the feet of those who bring good news!" As already noted, the prophet was speaking about the Jews who, on returning to Jerusalem from Babylon, rejoiced that God had delivered them from their exile. As they journeyed towards Zion, they brought good news for the Jews who still lived there, that God would comfort, restore and exalt the ruined city. He would deliver her inhabitants from their shame—even raising up the promised Davidic prince who would bring the remnant into a glorious salvation. The NT constantly asserts that Jesus is this promised Davidic king. However, before sharing in His glory, the believing community must share in his sufferings (Rom 8:18).

The few who returned from the Babylonian exile joined the small number of Jews still living in the city. Together, they were the remnant through whom Yahweh would continue his purposes. Paul writes there is still a remnant of Jews who have heard God's call and obeyed, but the majority reject the call to join the redeemed community. He is distressed that his unbelieving kinsmen refuse to take their place in the eschatological community and to experience the salvation to which the exodus had pointed (Rom 10:16–21).

10:1 Brothers, my heart's desire and prayer to God for the Israelites is that they may be saved. The Jews considered themselves to be saved and in a right relationship with God because, in the time of Moses, Pharaoh had been overthrown and their ancestors had experienced the exodus. Paul has made it clear in chapter 9 that in clinging to their history and privileges, the Jews are rejecting the eschatological reality to which their historical experiences point. Just as a wedding ceremony is prepared for by means of a rehearsal so that all in the bridal party can know their parts in the event, so the exodus was a rehearsal for what Yahweh was to do for his people in the death of his Son. In ultimate terms, it was not intended to establish the relationship that was going to happen in the eschatological exodus, but the tragedy was that the Jews confused the rehearsal with the real event. They concentrated on the fact that they were redeemed from Egypt when they had not been redeemed from Sin. This redemption was to what the rehearsal had pointed.

Paul has written in chapter 9 of God's mercy in bringing the Gentiles into the covenant community. However, it must be remembered that in the Acts of the Apostles, Paul went to the Jews first with the good news. He visited their synagogues, proclaiming to worshippers that Jesus was the Messiah for whom they had been waiting. Indeed, earlier in the letter, he wrote that the Gospel is to the Jew first and also to the Greek (Rom 1:16).

In this verse, Paul pauses to share his constant burden. He knew the Jews had been blessed with many privileges and that nothing more could be done for them. Yet, despite their unique privileges, they, like the unbelieving Gentiles, were children of the kingdom of darkness. The realization of their condition caused Paul to cry to God.

Paul distinguishes between longing ("my heart's desire") and prayer. It is a fact that sometimes we pray because we know that we should rather than because we are driven by a burning desire. Paul probably knew the sort of praying that responded to duty rather than compassion. Here, however, he writes that whenever he thinks of his countrymen, he cannot but pray—his heart going out to God for them. The dynamism that drives such prayer is love, and Paul's affection and concern for his people result in deep distress over the dangerous condition they are in.

How easy it would have been for Paul to wash his hands of any responsibility for his fellow countrymen. They had done everything to silence him: they had planned his death (Acts 9:24), slandered him (Phil 1:17), and sought to ruin the work he had sacrificed everything to do (Gal 1:6–9). Yet, their eternal welfare was his primary concern. God blesses such a man who gives himself—regardless of the cost—to those who need to hear the good news of Jesus Christ.

10:2 For I can testify about them that they are zealous for God, but their zeal is not based on knowledge. Paul is able to acknowledge the zeal that drives the Jews to silence him. It is the same zeal that had controlled him before his conversion (Acts 8:3). It now led them to go to incredible lengths in their attempts to assassinate him (Acts 23:12–15; 2 Cor 11:25). They belonged to the chosen nation, with privileges and blessings above all other nations.[1] How could they accept that a Galilean, crucified by the Romans,

---

1. Smiles, "Concept," 282–99, notes that "zeal" in Second Temple Judaism had to do with an impassioned defence of the covenant by observance of the law. Covenant and law were so bound together that they were essentially synonymous terms. Prior to becoming an apostle, Paul would have defended such a view. In this context, Gentiles were only important insofar as they affected Israel's capacity to be faithful to the covenant. Separatism was for the sake of obedience; the reverse was never true. Smiles argues that what Paul found

could possibly be the Messiah of God? It was this utter revulsion that drove them—as it had driven Paul—to persecute the Jewish followers of Jesus (Acts 22:3–5). While their rejection of Jesus seemed logical, their presuppositions were wrong. They interpreted the promises of God in terms of privilege and innocence, and not in terms of responsibility and guilt.

10:3 Since they did not know the righteousness that comes from God and sought to establish their own, they did not submit to God's righteousness. In saying that they did not know the righteousness of God, Paul is not saying that the Jews were ignorant of God's requirements but that they had refused to accept what God had provided. This is what alarmed him for he had been like them at one time. He thought that he was pleasing God by his commitment to destroy the church, but, instead of pleasing God, he was actually fighting against him.

Before his conversion, Paul could not have accepted that God's righteousness had been made known and made available through the crucifixion of one at the hands of the Gentiles. To accept that the death of Jesus, sentenced as a common criminal, was part of the purposes of God was something Jews could not accept. They reasoned that nothing could transcend the events of their history. What could be greater than the revelation of God in saving his people from bondage in Egypt and in bringing them to Sinai, where he revealed himself in glory and majesty? What could be greater than the messages of the prophets and the deliverance from exile in Babylon? The answer to these questions was the resurrection of Jesus Christ from the dead. This alone was able to change Paul from persecutor to disciple and from destroyer to proclaimer. Until they faced this historic reality, which overshadowed all other demonstrations of God's power and presence, the Jews would continue to reject the message of the cross, preferring to embrace their own righteousness (that is, the experience of salvation through Moses) which actually held them captive to darkness.

10:4 Christ is the end of the law so that there may be righteousness for everyone who believes. This has been a much discussed verse for obvious reasons.[2] Is Paul actually saying the law has no relevance because its life span is over? Such a suggestion would do nothing but terrify a devout Jew, for the law is an essential part of the covenant. In Jewish thinking, "no law" meant "no covenant." The end of the law would mean the end of the unique relationship between the Jewish people and Yahweh. This is a point that Paul is well aware of, and it is going to be the thrust of his argument in the next chapter. Here, he

---

wrong with the zeal of his opponents was the faulty understanding of their covenant which, in his judgment, made "works" its bedrock. For Paul, it was essential to understand that the covenant was wholly a matter of grace (Rom 4:4, 16; 11:5–6).

2. For a summary of different understandings of Paul's attitude to the law, see Westerholm, *Law*, who argues that the law has no validity for the Christian. This was challenged by Cranfield, "Place," 50–64, saying that Paul continued to find the will of God in the law but in a new and distinctively Christian way. Schreiner, "View," 113–35, argues that the "end of the law" refers solely to the law as a means of salvation having come to an end. Further discussion on the various views on the law can be found in Stickland, *Law*.

is specifically focusing on the law's role in achieving righteousness.[3] Paul is not rescinding the need for righteousness; he is redefining the scope of those who are its recipients, making it clear it is no longer limited to the Jews who alone had the law.

We need to remember that when Paul speaks of "righteousness," he uses it in the way that the OT prophets, especially Isaiah, used the term. In their writings, "righteousness" referred to the saving activity of God in delivering his people from exile in Babylon, so that they could return to their inheritance and appear in his presence. This is the argument Paul is making here. It is not only the Jews who are able to come into the presence of God as rescued and forgiven sinners; the Gentiles also are included in this act of salvation. It is not an act of redemption based on the OT acts of God and into which the Gentiles are invited to share (provided they convert to Judaism and come under the law). It is a salvation, or a righteousness, that has come through Christ's death and is available to all who believe. The old law is no longer applicable. There is a new covenant and, therefore, a new law—the law of Jesus, the new husband (Rom 7:1–6).

Paul is not saying the ethics of the law have no relevance to Christian living. His concern has to do with the law's role in establishing righteousness. Later in the letter, he says that love is the fulfillment of the law (Rom 13:8). For many Jews delivered from Egypt, it was the keeping of the law that demonstrated their gratitude to Yahweh. But the law, with its high principles, could only regulate outward behavior. Love regulates the whole life, the heart of man especially. For the new covenant, the law is inadequate and has to be replaced by the command: "Love." It is love for Christ that causes the believer to accept gladly the authoritative law of the new husband, the law of Christ.[4]

However, it is possible that Paul means that Christ is the end of the law in another way as well. We have noted the ongoing priestly theme of the letter. In Rom 8:34, Paul has written: "who is he that condemns? Jesus Christ who died—more than that, who was raised to life—is at the right hand of God and is also interceding for us." Such a strong statement concerning Christ's priesthood should not be overlooked. We have already noted that there are strong thematic links between the letter to the Romans and the letter to the Hebrews.[5] In the latter letter, the writer explained that the change of administration (i.e., the establishment of a new covenant), meant a change of priesthood and, with it, a change of law. If this is the background to the statement in Rom 10:4, then Christ is the end of the law because he is the end of the old administration. He is the High Priest of

3. Hills, "Goal," 585–92, says Paul's meaning is that Christ was the goal of the law from the very beginning. He based this claim on the absence of a copula (i.e. a linking verb) between his use of τελος (*Telos*) and Χριστος (*Chrsitos*). Thus Christ was, from the very beginning, the goal of the law. This is a similar understanding to that of Bechtler, "Telos," 288–308, who argues that the key to the meaning of Rom 10:4 is to be found in the relationship between Rom 9:30–33 and Rom 10:1–4, two paragraphs whose parallelism renders them mutually interpretative. The logic of the passage in chapter 9 demonstrates that Paul identified Christ not as the termination of the law but as the goal toward which God intended the law to lead Israel. In the logic of this argument, Jews who reject Christ reject the purpose and goal of the law.

4. See comments on Rom 7:1–4.

5. See excuses B (pages 84–91) for the influence of Ezekiel on Pauline theology. See also Moo, *Romans*, 246, who lists parallels between Ezekiel and Romans. However, Moo did not notice the absorption of the Day of Atonement sacrifices into the Passover as described in Ezek 45:25 and how this matches the merging of the Day of Atonement and Passover found in the letter to the Hebrews.

the new one and, in this new administration of grace, the law of Christ replaces the law of Moses and the priesthood he established. This suggestion makes good sense in the light of the argument that Paul is about to make for, as we shall see, the question: "'Who will ascend into heaven?' (that is, to bring Christ down)" (Rom 10:6), is better understood as a reference to Christ's ascension rather than to his incarnation. If the ascension reading is correct, then it links into the start of Christ's priestly which resulted from his ascension where he now intercedes for his people. Thus the law has come to an end because a better law has been established based on a new High Priest and a new covenant.

10:5 Moses describes in this way the righteousness that is by the law: "The man who does these things will live by them." At first reading, this verse suggests that Paul is speaking about attaining righteousness by observing the law. This is an understandable interpretation, but it tends to exclude the OT's covenantal dimension of the term: "the righteousness of God." I have sought to show[6] that there are passages in his letters where Paul can be read against the background of covenantal nomism. This is the understanding that the law did not terrify the Jews but was seen as their greatest blessing and gift from a loving God to his covenant people. If this is so, then the "righteousness that is by the law" (v. 5), does not refer to salvation that is secured by its keeping for it had not been given for that purpose. Indeed, when we recall that righteousness in the OT is not essentially about character but about God's saving activity, we find that Paul is saying that the law does not secure this salvation. Indeed, in the Leviticus passage that Paul quotes (Lev 18:5), the thrust is not "keep the law and you will gain salvation" for the passage implies that the Israelites had already been saved: "You must not do as they do in Egypt, where you used to live" (Lev 18:3a). The passage continues: "and you must not do as they do in the land of Canaan, where I am bringing you" (Lev 18:3b). In other words, to know the fullness of the blessing of salvation, the Israelites now had to live according to the law of God.[7]

Thus, Paul's statement should be read in the same context as Moses' address to Israel: the saving activity of God is brought to completion by his people's response to the teaching of the law. The righteousness of God is initially established in the church (or the lives of believers) by the deliverance that comes through Christ's death. It is completed and finalized when those who have been redeemed are transformed at the appearing of Christ (Phil 3:21). It must be emphasized that this reading of righteousness, i.e., in a covenantal context rather than in a legal/forensic setting, still requires the free gift of God's forgiveness. This is because the covenant could not exist unless God was prepared to deal with man on the basis of grace rather than on his ability to fulfill the law. The passage is saying nothing different from Eph 2:4–10.

The Greek text of Rom 10:5 begins with the word γαρ (*gar*) "for," which is omitted in the NIV. This word links vv.5–9 with the four opening verses of the chapter, where Israel's condition under the law and her attempt to use it to attain righteousness (salva-

---

6. See Holland, *Contours*, 183–236.

7. For further discussion, see comments on Rom 4:2, and Holland, *Contours*, chapter 9.

tion) have been discussed. Paul is explaining, therefore, how the law is fulfilled in a totally unexpected but, nevertheless, predicted way in Christ.

10:6 But the righteousness that is by faith says: "Do not say in your heart, 'Who will ascend into heaven?'" (that is, to bring Christ down) Before attempting to unravel the meaning of the passage in its wider OT context (the source to which Paul and the Roman church unquestionably had access), we need to note that, once again, Paul demonstrates a high regard for the context of his OT quotations. The chapters preceding Deut 30 warned Israel of the danger of not keeping the covenant. If she lived according to its precepts, she would be richly blessed, but if she went after other gods, she would be uprooted from the land and given over to her enemies. While Deut 28–29 anticipated Israel's unfaithfulness and judgment resulting in her exile, the nation was also given a promise that she would be restored to her inheritance when she returned to Yahweh. As outlined in Deut 30, the process of turning back would be a national undertaking which required Israel's heartfelt repentance and call to God for mercy and deliverance.

Aware of the value his countrymen placed on the law, Paul sought to show them its limitations. To do this, he turned to another key statement of Moses in Deut 30:11–14. Paul used the Greek conjunction δε (*de*) "but" at the beginning of Rom 10:6 to turn the tide of Moses' statement to favor his own argument. While Moses taught the people to keep the law, Paul reasoned that Moses knew this could not be achieved and, because of this, told the people of another righteousness. Paul unpacks Moses' statement to show that this speaks of Christ.

Moses' question can be expressed as: "Who will ascend into heaven to get it (i.e., the book of the law) and proclaim it to us so we may obey it?" (Deut 30:12b). It was addressed to the Israelites before they entered the promised land and the question probably echoed their experience at Sinai when Moses, their leader, ascended the Mount for the final time. He carried in his hands the two stone replacement tablets upon which the Lord would inscribe the Ten Commandments—the words of the covenant. When Moses descended, he gave the Israelites all the commands the Lord had given him (Exod 34:1–32).

In Deut 30:11–12, 14, Moses told the Israelites not to look for anyone to ascend a mount again in order to receive a new revelation. They were to recognize that Yahweh had provided for them through the giving of the book of the law on Sinai. This would stand during their time in the promised land and after the return of their descendants from exile. That same word would always be near them—it was in their hearts and would be in the hearts of their descendants because it had been taught since the nation's inception. Moses pronounced that no new teaching or revelation would be needed for Israel—just willingness to obey what had already been given (Deut 30:10).

Paul chose to use Deut 30:11–14 as its second exodus context fitted his argument perfectly. He could bring the text over into his letter because it fitted its theological framework about God's salvation being accomplished through the new exodus. This suggested use of typological correspondence is also seen when Paul quotes Isa 52:7 later in the chapter (Rom 10:14–17). This Isaianic passage recounts how the returning exiles entreated those residing along their route to join their pilgrimage to Jerusalem. They urged the people to become part of the returning community that was obeying the call to worship Yahweh in Zion.[8] It is clear that Paul transfers the Isaianic text to the church, for, in her pilgrimage to the heavenly Zion, she is also called to welcome all who will join her in seeking the Lord. Paul makes this link between the pilgrim communities without any explanation to the Roman believers—typological exegesis, evidently, did not need to be defended.[9]

Before attempting to unravel the meaning of Rom 10:6, attention must be paid to the widespread understanding among scholars that Paul has constructed a wisdom Christology and that Rom 10:6 speaks of Christ's incarnation.

Moses' original statement urged the Israelites to stay faithful to the law. Scholars[10] have noted how Deut 30:12 was used by the writers of the Jewish pseudepigraphal works *4QMMT* and *Baruch 3*. In these texts, the theme of wisdom is linked with the quotation. This has lead many scholars to hold that the intertestamental wisdom theme was the source of Paul's teaching about Jesus being the wisdom of God. They reason that, by using this material from the pseudepigraphal writings,[11] Paul has built a Christian doctrine which speaks of the incarnation of wisdom. However, while this suggestion has gained widespread acceptance, it poses insurmountable problems.

First, it relies on texts from Second Temple Judaism that do not have a homogeneous message. The construction of a doctrine from a set of texts requires that they all testify to the same thing—and this is something that the texts from Second Temple Judaism do not do. The fact is that the texts expressed many Jewish positions (often radically different) on any one theme, often using the same vocabulary to convey different meanings. As a result, constructing a reliable teaching of Second Temple Judaism becomes an unrealizable aspiration. Scholars who use these texts to explore Second Temple theology cannot possibly establish that it presented a unified perspective because there was not one but there were many theologies. In spite of this, having supposedly discovered the original fertile thought world of the NT, scholars often go on to impose their new found

---

8. The setting of Deut 30:12 was the bringing down of a new law from Sinai (or heaven). When Moses originally went to receive the law, the Jews thought he had deserted them because of his delayed return. It may have struck the Roman believers that, while Moses was away forty days in the Mount, Jesus had been away from his people for many years. It would have been natural for them to have asked, "What must we do to bring him back among us?" This makes sense of Paul's answer: "He is already intimately with you. Faith will recognize that fact and rejoice in all of the blessing that the ascended Christ has poured upon you." Such a question certainly became part of a later period of Judaism for it was not uncommon for rabbis to argue that the Messianic kingdom would not come until the law had been kept perfectly, cf. Jewett, *Romans*, 626–27. Indeed, the letters to the Hebrews and the Colossians indicate that believers were tempted to return to the law—probably claiming that they would embrace it in a new way as a result of the coming of Christ. Regardless of this aspiration, they were subjecting themselves to the law and this was something that Paul could not tolerate.

See Lincoln, *Ephesians*, 243. Kaus, *Psalms 60–150*, 53, links the ascension with the exodus.

9. See Goppelt, *Typos*; Friedbert, *Indicators*.

10. Bekken, *Near You*; Wright, "Romans," 662. See Jewett, *Romans*, 626, for an explanation of how Paul has altered the text so as not to follow the pseudepigraphal wisdom reading of Deut 30:12. Moo, *Romans*, 652–53, acknowledges the wisdom tradition but thinks it is not as widespread or important for Paul's Christology as some make it.

11. Also found in other texts, such as *Sir* 24:8–12; *Wis* 9:9–10.

understanding on the NT texts they are attempting to exegete. However, their findings do not recover first century understanding but display twenty-first century methodological incompetence. It is akin to a scholar of contemporary Christian theology daring to use the teachings of Presbyterianism to understand the doctrines of Methodism. Such practice would never be countenanced, for the mixing of texts from different traditions does not lead to a greater understanding but an increased confusion.[12]

Second, reliance on Second Temple texts assumes that Paul knew them well enough to construct arguments from them and that his readers were sufficiently familiar with them to follow his reasoning. However, the likelihood that these texts were known and deliberately used by him to construct, in this case, a wisdom Christology and known well enough by the Roman believers to identify and decipher the relevance of allusions in his arguments is too remote for serious consideration. Alarmingly, this assumption is made by many respected scholars in their interpretation of numerous NT texts.

Third, the personification of wisdom in intertestamental literature has no links with a dying Messiah—yet this is clearly implied in Paul's statement: "God raised him from the dead" (Rom 10:9).[13] Moreover, this confession, which is at the end of the passage giving it the status of the purpose of its argument, focuses on the resurrection/ascension of Christ while saying nothing about his incarnation. This confession is the key to the use of Deut 30:12, for the argument that Paul has developed out of Moses' statement is part of the pathway to the confession of Christ's Lordship. The conclusion must control the reading of the preamble.

Fourth, there is no anticipation of an incarnate Messiah in the OT in any theology in Judaism or even in the pseudepigraphal writings. None of these sources saw someone ascending to heaven in order to escort the Messiah down to earth. Moreover, there is no suggestion of such an understanding in the NT. Nevertheless, despite an absence of evidence to support the interpretation, the incarnational meaning that relies on the Wisdom teaching of intertestamental literature is the one followed by most scholars.[14]

So, if evidence supporting the claim that Rom 10:6 speaks of Christ's incarnation is unreliable, is there an alternative reading worthy of serious consideration? I believe there is. It speaks of Christ's ascension into the Father's presence. I shall attempt to show that Deut 30:12 has become part of an extensive ascension tradition in the OT[15] and that it is one of a number of passages taken over into the NT and used by Paul as a type of Christ's ascension.[16]

---

12. Holland, *Contours*, 51–68, and page 23–25 in this commentary.

13. Davies, *Rabbinic*, 155.

14. The intertestamental Wisdom theme is not the same as that taught by John (John 1:1–3) nor should it be confused with the Wisdom theme that is rooted in the OT. For further discussion see Holland, *Contours*, 339–51.

15. Present in the coronation psalms (Ps 24; 47; 68; 110; 118). In the LXX, ascent language is used in Ps 24(25LXX):3; 47(48LXX):5; 68(69LXX):18.

16. Nearly all NT writers testify to the ascension, although the Epistles (Rom 8:32; Eph 1:20–21; 4:8–11; Heb 6:20) assume rather than describe it. The Gospels focus on the physical aspects, whereas Paul, the theologian, emphasizes Christ's spiritual body. The Johannine pericopes do not mention the ascension but imply it on several occasions (John 8:14, 21; 13:3, 33; 14:4–5, 28; 16:5, 10, 17, 28). See Gulley, *Ascension*.

In Rom 10:6, Paul has brought Deut 30:12 into an argument saturated with quotations from the OT with second exodus themes pulsating within them. In this new setting, i.e., of the new exodus that Paul is developing, the true Son of David has ascended into heaven from where he sends down the gift of himself to his people in the person of the Holy Spirit. Because of the descent of the Spirit of Christ, no one needs to go up into heaven in order to bring Christ down. He is already with his people by his Spirit.

The key for understanding Paul's fuller meaning of Deut 30:12 is the ongoing story of the new exodus. While the prediction of a second exodus is the original setting of Moses' words, the new exodus context of the letter is much more developed than the original promise of a return from exile. It is this new exodus "flavor" that Paul's use of Deut 30:12 absorbs. Without appreciating this wider theological context, much is lost and logical consistency is impossible. Since Deut 30:12 is used by Paul to support an argument that brings his readers to the resurrection and ascension of Christ, I am persuaded that he has made the text refer to Christ's ascension and glorification.[17]

The difficulty with interpreting the statement: "Do not say in your heart, 'Who will ascend into heaven?' (that is, to bring Christ down)" (Rom 10:6) as a reference to the ascension of Christ is that the passage goes on to ask: "or 'Who will descend into the deep?' (that is, to bring Christ up from the dead)" (Rom 10:7). The difficulty with interpreting the statement in Romans 10:6 "Do not say in your heart, 'Who will ascend into heaven?' (that is, to bring Christ down)" as referring to the ascension of Christ is that the passage goes on to ask in verse seven, "or 'Who will descend into the deep?' (that is, to bring Christ up from the dead)." It is argued that the bringing of Christ up from the dead is a reference to his resurrection—the event preceding the ascension. The statement "who will ascend" cannot, therefore, refer to Christ's ascension. As a result, it is linked to his incarnation as an event that proceeds being brought up from the grave.

Evidence for this ascension tradition is found in Eph 4:8, where the writer cites Ps 68:18:

> This is why it says: "When he ascended on high, he led captives in his train and gave gifts to men." (What does "he ascended" mean except that he also descended to the lower, earthly regions? He who descended is the very one who ascended higher than all the heavens, in order to fill the whole universe.)

The ascension theme is implied in that Christ first descended to the lower earthly regions, a clear reference to his burial, and this defined the one who had ascended on high. With the passage of time, the original text in the Psalms has been loaded with an expanded meaning. The psalm originally spoke of Yahweh ascending Sinai after his conquest of the Egyptians. It was later interpreted as a reference to his ascent of Zion to rule Israel and then to the ascent of David to occupy the throne of Zion after the conquest

---

17. Strictly speaking, the "going up" is not about the ascension of Christ but the challenge of someone ascending to bring Christ down. The point is that no one needs to ascend because Christ has already descended and is now amongst his people. This justifies focusing on an ascension reading of the passage. The ascension was the climax of Christ's saving work, and only because he was exalted to the Father's side was he able to fulfill the promise and send the Spirit. For the importance of the ascension in the NT, see Maile, "Ascension"; Donne, *Ascended*. Dunn, *Making*, 184–86 also sees the focus being the ascension and thinks that the event order is controlled by the original wording of Deut 30:12.

of his enemies. This association of key OT texts had been made by the rabbinic writers who saw Ps 68:8 as speaking not only of the ascension of Yahweh and David but also of Moses.[18] In later history it was claimed by the church as evidence of the ascension of Christ to his heavenly throne from where he distributed the gifts "of war" to his people. With this Christian reinterpretation, a full circle has been turned. It now speaks of King David's greater Son (who is none other than Yahweh) taking his throne. In addition, significant textual editing has taken place so that the version used in the letter to the Ephesians, the psalm has "you received gifts from men" to "and gave gifts to me."[19]

What this reading of Eph 4:8 shows us is that there was a richly developed ascension tradition in the early church.[20] An examination of other NT texts suggests this tradition was extensive and formed a major part of the church's teaching.[21] If this is so, grounds are given to return to Rom 10:6 to see if, despite the apparent inappropriate word order, it reflects the same ascension tradition as found in Ephesians.

As has been stated, the only problem for an ascension reading of Rom 10:6 is its word order as following an ascension reading it puts ascension before resurrection. But if the word order can be resolved satisfactorily, a typological exegesis would be the most natural reading of Paul's use of Deut 30:12. The question has to be asked whether the word order is as crucial as is commonly understood or, indeed, has it been correctly interpreted?

What is clear from other Pauline passages is the way he utilizes OT texts. Paul is flexible, appearing comfortable with the way he adapts and applies the OT Scriptures in support of the cases he is making. So, for example, in Rom 11:26, he quotes from Isa 59:20–21 but does not quote the Hebrew or LXX text. Instead, Paul alters the text so that it serves his theological purpose. He identifies its original second exodus context

18. The Targum on the psalm has "You have ascended to heaven, that is Moses the prophet; you have taken captivity captive, you have learnt the words of the Torah; you have given it as a gift to men," cited by Lincoln, *Ephesians*, 242–43. Lincoln, op cit, 243, goes on to say: "The 'Moses mysticism' with which this interpretation of the psalm is to be associated was widespread. It can be found elsewhere in the rabbinic writings (e.g., *Midr. Tĕhillim* on Ps 24:1 and Ps 106:2; *b. Sabb.* 88b) and in Philo (e.g., *Quaest*, Ex. 2.40, 43; *Mos*, 1.158; *Poster*, 14; *Somn*. 1.186–88: cf. also, W. Meeks, *The Prophet-King* [Leiden: E.J. Brill, 1967], 122–25, 205–9)." According to the Targum, the gifts given in Ps 68 were the Torah and the heavenly secrets.

19. There is a major change from the original LXX text of psalm 68 from "you receive" to "you give." This change is found in the Targum on the Psalms, and although the Targum is a late work, it is held that it has made use of an ancient rabbinical tradition. See Lincoln, *Ephesians*, 243. This suggests that the Christians have not had to create this tradition for themselves but may have received it from an established Jewish tradition.

20. The descent theme in Eph 4:9–10 has three possible interpretations. First, it speaks of the descent of the pre-existent Christ in his incarnation. This reading is supported by Ernst, 352; Mitton, 147–48; Schnackenburg, 18–81; Barth, 433–34 (listed by Lincoln) and Moo, *Romans*, 656. In its favor is the descent—exaltation Christology found elsewhere in the NT, especially in the Fourth Gospel (cf. John 3:13; 6:62) and in Paul (Phil 2:6–11). Second, it speaks of Christ's descent to the underworld following his death. This was popular among the patristics and has support from Robinson, 180; Dunn, 186f.; Arnold, 57 and Kreitzer, 127 (listed by Muddiman, *Ephesians*, 192–93). Third, some see it as referring to the descent of the exalted Christ in the Spirit (Supported by Caird, "Descent," 73–75; Kirby, *Ephesians*, 187 n. 51; Harris, "Descent" 235–65 [listed by Lincoln, *Ephesians*]).

21. See Maile, *Ascension*; Zwiep, *Ascension*.

and this gives him the freedom to make it serve the new exodus model he is developing.[22] So, it is possible that Psalm 68 had undergone a refocusing on who ascended and gave gifts. Indeed, it is quite possible that the editing of Isa 59 in Rom 11:26 is evidence of the reshaping of a text to make it clear that no one had to ascend up to Jerusalem to meet with the Redeemer.[23]

But such textual adaptation was not even necessary in the case of Deut 30:12. It was abundantly clear that *Moses was a type of Christ* and that his ascent of the Mount represented the ascension of the leader of the eschatological new exodus. As a result—if our reasoning is correct—Deut 30:12, as part of the ascension tradition found in the OT, did not require adaptation to make it fit the church's message.[24] All that was required for referencing Deut 30:12 in Rom 10:6–7 was a straightforward typological application and reading—a process that has been established as widely practiced by the early church.

Indeed, the difficult matter of the order of the terms "ascend" and "descend" may not be the problem that it first appears. Paul may be more careful in his use of the Deut 30:12 text than has been recognized. It is possible that he is reading back through redemption history and, as he looks back, the most recent event was the ascension and gift (or outpouring) of the Spirit (Rom 10:6), preceded by the death and resurrection of Christ (Rom 10:7). Viewed in this way, the statement is effectively saying that the Easter/Ascension and Pentecost events (death and resurrection/ascension and outpouring of the Spirit) have been accomplished, and it was these events that brought an end to the old covenant and the law that expressed it.[25] In comparison to other examples of textual adjustment, the practice of reading historical events retrospectively is easy to establish. It is something that Paul does on several occasions. Indeed, immediately following this instance he uses the same method of citation again: "How, then, can they call on the one they have not believed in? And how can they believe in the one of whom they have not heard? And how can they hear without someone preaching to them? How will they preach unless commissioned? Just as it has been written: How lovely to see the feet of those announcing good news!" (Rom 10:14–15).

If Paul is looking back through the events of salvation history, the apparent "awkwardness" of his ascension reading of Deut 30:12 is resolved. He has no need to change the position of the events in the Deuteronomy text. He can leave them as they are for their existing order serves his purpose perfectly. He can begin with the climax of the covenant promise—the giving of the Spirit, which was secured by Christ's ascension. In reality it is more than this, for the ascension not only secured the outpouring of his Spirit on his people but also his exaltation as Lord, in whose presence every knee will eventu-

---

22. While the model was given by the prophets, then fulfilled and given new meaning by Christ, and was also used as the framework of his teaching ministry (see Wright, *Victory*), the apostles clearly developed themes within the context of the paradigm to make particular points.

23. See comments on Rom 11:26.

24. For a summary of this teaching, see Gulley, *Ascension*. For the ascension in Luke, see Zwiep, *Ascension*. The ascension has been described as the most neglected doctrine of the church. See Jansen, *Ascension*, 17.

25. See comments on Rom 10:4.

ally bow in submission. Indeed, it is by professing Jesus' Lordship that salvation is given before the Day of Judgment. The importance of this event is laid down in the confession of faith required in Rom 10:9 and this should control the earlier reading of Deut 30:12.

This proposed reading of Rom 10:6, i.e., the ascension of Christ and the giving of the Spirit (the descent of Christ to his people), parallels the reading of Eph 4:8 where the gift was the promised presence of Christ himself to the believing community (John 14:15–21; 15:26–27. Paul had written of this as the right of the church in Rom 8:10–17). This ascension and outpouring happened because God raised Jesus from the dead. As a result, there was no need for anyone to descend into the deep to bring Christ up, for it had been done and settled for all time.

Reading Rom 10:6 as referring to the ascension rather than the incarnation is supported by the fact that, throughout the letter to the Romans, Paul makes considerable use of Isaiah's writings—particularly his second exodus perspective. He uses these ancient texts to direct his readers to the Redeemer—the Son of David, on whom the prophets focused—as the bringer of deliverance.[26] As a result, Christ the Redeemer and Son of David, whose triumph was his ascension to his throne along with his delivered people (Rom 8:34), significantly it informs Rom 9–11; and this section is, of course, the new context for Deut 30:12.[27] Thus, the teachings of other OT texts that form this ascension tradition are echoed in the citation of Deut 30:12. These echoes support the exegesis that has been offered that the text is about the ascension of Christ (the son of David) and his giving of the Spirit, no one needing to go up "to bring Christ down."

Thus the typological argument guiding the reading of Deut 30:12 and the introduction of Moses into Psalm 68 found in the rabbinic traditions suggests there existed a willingness to replace Moses by David and vice versa. Thus the replacement of Moses by David in the NT (which had been in reverse in parts of second temple Judaism, Moses substituted for David) justifies the retrospective introduction of David into the Deuteronomy text. This was especially made possible because of its typological reading in which Moses anticipates Christ who was identified as the son of David. Thus for the early church, Deut 30:12 naturally referred to the ascension of Moses and to his new exodus successor, David. Thus, the great son of David, who came down in the incarnation, has come down again in the person of the Spirit and now resides with his people as he had promised.

This reading is supported by the conclusion of the section. As noted earlier, this is what Paul's argument is working towards, which is why the quote from Deut 30:12 is at the heart of his preamble. Rom 10:6–7 leads to the declaration about how to become a member of the new covenant community in v.9: "if you confess with your mouth, 'Jesus is Lord,' and believe in your heart that God raised him from the dead, you will be saved." The resurrection of Christ is central to this confession; any reading of Rom 10:6–7 that fails to take this into account is more than likely to miss the point of Paul's discourse.

---

26. Something of this is reflected in Acts 15:15–19; Gal 4:21–27; Heb 12:18–28. In each case, the progression of Moses to David and then to Jesus is evident.

27. For a detailed examination of the influence of the exodus theme in chapters 9–11, see excursus J: The new exodus framework of Romans 9–11 and pages 6–15.

The relation of Deut 30:12 to the confession is best appreciated when we read the text as a whole:

> But the righteousness that is by faith says: "Do not say in your heart, 'Who will ascend into heaven?'" (that is, to bring Christ down) "or 'Who will descend into the deep?'" (that is, to bring Christ up from the dead). But what does it say? "The word is near you; it is in your mouth and in your heart," that is, the word of faith we are proclaiming: That if you confess with your mouth, "Jesus is Lord," and believe in your heart that God raised him from the dead, you will be saved. For it is with your heart that you believe and are justified, and it is with your mouth that you confess and are saved. (Rom 10:6–10)

The relation between the statement of Moses and the confession that a seeker must make becomes evident and so the ascension reading of Rom 10:6 becomes much more secure.

In addition, Paul has prepared the Roman church for a Christological/ascension reading of Deut 30:12 by emphasizing at the opening of his letter that the resurrection of the Son of David declared him to be the Son of God (Rom 1:4). This resurrection/ascension emphasis is consistent with the importance Paul has given the resurrection throughout the letter (Rom 4:25; 6:1–4; 8:34). This emphasis on the death and exaltation of the Son of David, which leads to the outpouring of the Spirit, is found throughout the preaching of Acts (Acts 2:24–36; 3:21; 4:24–31; 5:29–34; 10:39–44; 13:22–52; 24:21; 26:23).

In conclusion, this reading of Deut 30:12 in Rom 10:6 directs the Roman church to the one who has replaced David and Moses in the new exodus (Rom 6:4; 7:4–6; 8:31–39; 1 Cor 10:6–13; Col 1:13–14). His conquests have brought about the eschatological new exodus event and with it the creation of a new covenant. With this new covenant, a new law (that is, the gift of the Spirit) has been given. Indeed, we saw in the introduction[28] the massive transition in the Jewish prophetic tradition of the eighth century BC in which the future hope of Israel was no longer bound up with Moses but rather with the victory and, therefore, ascent of David's descendant (that is, Jesus Christ).[29]

Thus, the question, "Who shall ascend into heaven?" is understood to be about receiving the benefits of the work that the glorified Redeemer has achieved. It is not about receiving the law (as with Moses) but what the law pointed to, i.e., the fulfillment of the covenant and all of its blessings—not least, the gift of the Spirit. It is because of this that Christ is the end of the law for all who believe (Rom 10:4; cf. Gal 3:25; 5:18).

The argument that has been made for the meaning of Rom 10:6 has assumed a new exodus setting of the text. That this is the correct setting can be further demonstrated when the wider context of the text is considered.[30]

10:7 "or 'Who will descend into the deep?'" (that is, to bring Christ up from the dead). Paul considers the second obstacle that Moses said did not need to be overcome

---

28. See pages 6–12.

29. See Strauss, *Davidic*.

30. See Excursus J: The New Exodus Framework of Rom 9–11 and Other NT Passages, [x-ref].

by the Israelite people. However, Paul changes the obstacle from the sea to the grave of the Messiah.

Paul does not strictly follow Deut 30:13, which says: "who will cross the sea to get it [the book of the law] and proclaim it to us so that we may obey it?" Rather, he has:

"'Who will descend into the deep?' (that is, to bring Christ up from the dead)." We will consider this change in a moment.

In human terms, descending into the deep—the grave—is an impossible and hopeless situation. The most that could be hoped for would be that, in some way, the death of Jesus might inspire others to keep faith with what they believe, even to the point of death. But that was not God's intention. Jesus had not been abandoned in the grave by God, so man does not have to go searching for him in the terrifying arena of death. God has acted decisively by raising Jesus from the dead. Jesus is neither limited to heaven nor is he a prisoner of death. He is near to all who would call on him.[31]

The statement about going into the grave echoes Deut 30:13 (LXX). However, it is held by some scholars that Paul has used a translation of the text which is found in the Targums.[32] This echoes the wording of Ps 106:26 (LXX) (Ps 107:26, in most English translations). They consider that this source is preferred because the original text in Deut 30:13 has: "Nor is it beyond the sea, so that you do not have to ask, 'Who will cross the sea to get it and proclaim it to us so we may obey it?'" Those scholars who favor the Targum as Paul's source think it explains his revised text: "Who will descend into the deep?" The difficulty with this suggestion is this: how are the readers and hearers of the letter (particularly Gentiles) expected to know the Targum so as to understand the change that has been made to Deut 30:13? (As with other intertestamental literature, great care has to be exercised. Few seem to appreciate this need for care as the appropriate controls for the interpretation of texts are not being exercised.[33] Indeed, at this point in Israel's history, the Targums were still in oral form and only rabbinical scholars had access to them).

A more simple suggestion is that Paul made this connection between Deut 30:12 and Ps 107:26 and, as a result, produced the new reading. This hypothesis does not require the Roman believers to have had prior knowledge of rabbinic sources as they had the same ability as Paul to reflect on internal echoes of Biblical texts.[34] This suggestion is reasonable because Ps 106 (LXX) (Ps 107 in the English Bible) recalls the experience of Israel in times of crisis and the subsequent mercy of Yahweh. There is widespread agreement that the psalm is a second exodus psalm about Jews returning from exile.[35] Indeed,

---

31. For a fuller discussion, see Humphrey, "Demonstration," 129–48, who argues that Paul is denying any need for visionary experience in order to hear and respond to the word of Christ. Paul's argument is that what is needed has been revealed in the Scriptures.

32. See Jewett, *Romans*, 627.

33. Controls such as those outlined by Hays, *Echoes*, 29–33.

34. Again, so following the argument given by Hays, op cit.

35. Allan, *Psalms, 101–150*, 88–89; Harman, *Psalms*, 354; Mays, *Psalms*, 346; Kraus, *Psalms*, 60–150, 330. Goulder, *Psalms*, 118ff., gives a detailed analysis of the psalm, showing how the imagery fits Israel's experiences in exile and during her journey from it.

the Jews used it in the Temple to celebrate Yahweh's faithfulness in rescuing the nation from Babylon. Through this liturgical use, it became well known and easy to recall.

So, the believing congregation in Rome could immediately see that Paul had legitimately embraced a typological application and that this had also been done with Deut 30:13, Paul inserting the Christological interpretation of Ps 68.[36] With David's approval (in that it could be argued David had written this paraphrase of Deut 30:13 in Ps 106 [LXX]), Paul had no need to defend his rendering!

The psalm lists four examples of Yahweh's saving activity toward Israel. What is especially interesting is that Ps 106:26 (LXX) has the phrase καταβαίνουσιν ἕως τῶν ἀβύσσων while Paul has Τίς καταβήσεται εἰς τὴν ἄβυσσον "Who will descend into the deep?" The passage in the psalm tells of how Jews on a journey out of exile faced death (v.26). They were caught in a terrifying storm at sea where waves lifted their boat up before throwing it down into a watery abyss. The craft was totally at the mercy of the wind, causing the waves to buffet the vessel. The similarity between the two texts (Rom 10:6 and Ps 106:26 [LXX]) persuades many to believe that Ps 106 reshapes the Deuteronomy text quoted in this verse (Rom 10:7), for Paul neither quotes the Masoretic text nor the LXX of Deut 30:13.

The interesting feature about Ps 106:26 (LXX) is that its theme of danger faced by the pilgrim community is echoed in Rom 10. Chapter 10 parallels Israel's pilgrimage as evidenced by the way that Isa 28:16 is quoted in v.11 and Isa 52:7 in v.15. The citation of Isa 53:1 in v. 15 ("Who has believed our message and to whom has the arm of the LORD been revealed?") brings to mind those in Babylon who refused to hear the message of the prophets concerning Yahweh's promise to save Israel from her captivity. As a result of their refusal to heed the prophets, they did not join the remnant community that returned to Jerusalem. The way Paul links Deut 32:21 and Isa 65:1 in vv. 20–21 serves to drive forward the theme of Israel's disobedience and the refusal of most of the exiles to hear the call to return to the promised land. The latter of the two citations warns unbelieving Israel that she will be replaced by the Gentiles. Ps 106 (LXX) describes four groups of people who were in danger, the psalmist telling how God delivered them. The important thing to note is that each of these groups cried to the Lord (vv. 6, 13, 19, 28) and he heard their cries and rescued them.[37] This fits Rom 10:13 where there is a quotation from Joel 2:32: "for everyone who calls on the name of the Lord will be saved."

There is a further reason for believing that Paul brought Ps 106 (LXX) into Deut 30:13. Ps.106:26 (LXX) says: "They mounted up to the heavens and went down to the depths; in their peril their courage melted away." The mention of "going up to the heavens and going down into the depths" is an ideal paraphrase of Deut 30:13 and offers the opportunity to make it clear that Christ will not be brought from across the seas but from

---

36. The psalm is, of course, post-exilic; but all of the psalms carry David's authority, for they are treated by the Jewish community as the "Psalms of David."

37. The psalm is possibly the theological structure used by Luke in Luke 8. Here, the narrative records a series of saving events that Jesus performed. Each of the sub-narratives appears to correspond to one of the four saving activities found in Ps 106 (LXX). If this is true, it suggests the passage was read in the way that is proposed in the argument given above.

the depths of the abyss (the grave).[38] By this creative merger, Paul has given the words of Moses far greater significance. The one like unto Moses has not been brought from across the sea but up from the grave to speak Yahweh's decisive last word (Heb 1:1–4). Indeed, the one who has done this is none other than the Son of David (Rom 1:3), so it is appropriate that the words that bear his name (Ps 106 LXX) are used to instruct the church in Rome.

There could also be a subtle apologetic message in the transformation of the text so that it speaks of not having to cross the sea to meet with Christ. When we examine Rom 11:26, we shall see that Paul is not averse to making a fine adjustment to a text if it ensures that his readers understand its proper meaning in the light of the Christ event. This is especially important in situations like this where the unaltered text could lead to a false understanding of the role of Judaism and God's dealings with men. Could it be that, in his transformed text, Paul is directing the believers in Rome away from any thought that they needed to travel across the seas to meet with the Messiah? There was no need for them to make a pilgrimage to Jerusalem, and the following verse gives the reason why.

10:8 But what does it say? "The word is near you; it is in your mouth and in your heart," that is, the word of faith we are proclaiming: Moses pronounced that the requirements of the law were clear to any who were truly seeking to know God's ways. When Moses said these words to the Israelites, he was about to leave them. They were soon to cross the Jordan under a new leader, Joshua. Moses assures them that, although he will not be with them to teach them, they know the message of truth for it is in their hearts. If they seek God with all of their hearts they will find him, for they have been taught his word.

Paul's reference to the word being in their mouths and in their hearts probably recalls Jer 31:33–34, where God declares that he will put his law into the minds and hearts of members of the new covenant community.

10:9 That if you confess with your mouth, "Jesus is Lord," and believe in your heart that God raised him from the dead, you will be saved. Contrasting with the uncertainties of the legalistic use of the law and the inaccessibility of God is the ringing certainty, "you will be saved." But what is required of man to secure his release from Sin and bring him into the certainty and assurance for which his heart longs? It is the simplest thing that can be asked of any man: "confess . . . and believe."

However, confessing Jesus as Lord is no small thing. The Roman Christians knew it meant saying that the will of Jesus came before any claims that Caesar or any other being could make upon them. Life in Rome meant daily confrontations with claims for allegiance, and faith required that, into these situations, confessions of Christ's Lordship were spoken immediately. There was to be no hiding behind some indecisive gesture or

---

38. The "abyss" is used elsewhere in the OT to speak of realms beneath the earth, so making it an ideal picture of the grave. See Deut 8:7; 33:13; Ps 71:20–21; 107:26. To change "sea" for "abyss" is not difficult for the Hebrew mind. Both are linked with the picture of the separation, both had the same connotation in spiritual terms.

turn of phrase that left onlookers uncertain as to what was being proclaimed. The confession had to be clear, unequivocal and absolute. It was not sufficient to say that Jesus was a lord or a great figure. To confess him as Lord was to say that there was no rival.

The Lord's will was for the early disciples to be committed to him, even if it cost them their lives. For many Roman Christians, this was exactly the price they paid. Just as a bridegroom and bride confess their acceptance of each other, regardless of the circumstances that will face them, so commitment to Jesus as Lord begins at the point of confession. Living with him and for him has to be worked out daily in every detail of life.

Surprisingly, the exhortation is not "believe and confess," but "confess . . . and believe." This was possibly the order required by the apostles as it followed the sequence given by Jesus to those who claimed allegiance: "Whoever acknowledges me before men, I will also acknowledge him before my Father in heaven" (Matt 10:32). This cuts through the danger of mere intellectual assent. Indeed, faith is born in the act of confession. In the indifferent West, the implications of this order can easily be missed. This is not so for those who live in hostile parts of the world, where to confess can be the most costly thing a person can do.

10:10 For it is with your heart that you believe and are justified, and it is with your mouth that you confess and are saved. Paul spells out the way God saves people. It is with a simplicity that offends many because he demands no great feat from them. They presume the almighty sovereign Lord ought to be demanding great demonstrations of sacrifice and loyalty to his laws. Instead, Paul writes to the Romans that all he demands is confession of Jesus as Lord and obedience to him.

Paul is not bypassing the seriousness of sin. He has already spelled out the devastating consequences of it in the early chapters of the letter. He has shown how extremely serious sin is, and how dreadful it will be for any person to give an account before God. However, he has also explained that God has made a way of escape through the death of his Son.

In the first part of the verse, the NIV translators have interpreted the Greek noun δικαιοσύνην (*dikaiosunēn*) as "justified." The passage literally reads: "for with the heart one believes into righteousness." The use of ἐις (*eis*) before the verb and noun gives: "you believed into righteousness" or "you believe, resulting in righteousness." Thus, they will be made right with God, their Creator, and restored to the relationship they were created for. The important difference between justified and righteousness is that the former is an event whereas the later is a status. Righteousness leads to justification; they are not the same. In the justification and righteousness language of the prophets when used in relation to Israel, Yahweh acted in righteousness toward her—saving her from her oppressors. As a result, she was justified, i.e., brought back into the relationship she had lost with her God.

The statement reflects the confession that each of the converts were required to make. While I have argued for a corporate baptismal significance of Rom 6:1–4 and other Pauline baptismal texts[39] I do not deny the practice of the early church in baptizing

---

39. See Excursus E: Baptism into Christ, pages 168–77.

those who came to faith (1 Cor 1:14,17), as evidenced throughout the book of Acts (Acts 2:38, 41, 47–48; 13:24; 19:5). The NT writers saw baptism as the natural way of confessing faith, i.e., acceptance of the Lordship of the Savior, Christ Jesus. Indeed, it was not only the natural way, it was what Jesus commanded (Matt 28:19).

10:11 As the Scripture says, "Anyone who trusts in him will never be put to shame." Paul demonstrates that the principle of faith is not his invention. In quoting the prophecy of Isaiah (Isa 28:16), he is not making use of a text that is unrelated to his theme. The original context of the quotation is about Israel turning from God and entering into a covenant with Môt, the Egyptian god of death (Isa 28:15, 18). By means of this covenant, Israel sought protection from Yahweh's anger. Isaiah promised the people that Yahweh would protect those who returned to him; moreover, he would not put them to shame. If Môt, the god of death,[40] could be thought to offer protection to his subjects, how much more could Yahweh, the living God, secure his own from the onslaught of Satan?

This picture of Israel entering into a covenant with the enemy of Yahweh is the same picture that is used in the NT. Unredeemed humankind—including the Jews—is related to Satan in a similar way. Jesus told the Jews: "You are of your father, the devil" (John 8:44). While the Jews could accept this as a description of the Gentiles, this allegation of a relationship with Satan would have infuriated them. It was tantamount to saying they had no covenantal relationship with Yahweh and were children of darkness. Indeed, it was saying they were in the same desperate plight as the Gentiles—people they despised and regarded as unclean.[41]

Paul seeks to make it clear that, while Jews and Gentiles are equally blessed in being offered salvation, they are also equally in danger if they reject God's offer of mercy. All unbelieving Jews and Gentiles are in covenant with Satan. This concern has been at the heart of Paul's Gospel exposition in chapters 5–7. While the Jews had been delivered from the dominance of the Egyptian gods (the covenant with Môt was abolished through the representative death of the lambs in place of the Hebrew firstborn), most in Israel had yet to be rescued from the reality that the exodus pointed to, i.e., the cosmic bondage to Sin and Death. This is the condition of unredeemed humankind for all are caught up in this reality of bondage and exile and need deliverance.

The NIV translates καταισχυνθήσεται (*kataischunthēsetai*) as "put to shame." This rendering is too weak a translation. The meaning is "ashamed," and the opposite of "being ashamed" is "being saved." There are echoes of its use in Rom 1:16; 5:5; 9:33.

10:12–13 For there is no difference between Jew and Gentile—the same Lord is Lord of all and richly blesses all who call on him, for, "Everyone who calls on the name of the Lord will be saved." Paul again turns to an OT prophet to support his argument. Joel 2:28 was directed to those who were in exile. The prophet predicted the coming of

40. "Death" was a term the NT writers used as a pseudonym for "Satan" (1 Cor 15:26, 55; Rev 20:13). See also, Ps 49:14; *4 Ezra* 8:53; *Apoc Bar* 21:23; *Test. of Levi*, 18, for evidence that the imagery was used elsewhere in Judaism.

41. See Holland, *Contours*, chapter 10, for fuller discussion.

the Day of the Lord, when the Spirit would be poured out. His prophecy was fulfilled on the Day of Pentecost, when Peter, in his sermon, referred to the same text (Acts 2:21). The Day of the Lord was the Day when Yahweh raised up his servant, the descendant of David, to bring the captives out of exile (Isa 52:3–10). Paul, along with all of the NT writers, is saying that the Day of the Lord has come. Jesus, the Son of David, has delivered his people from exile.

Joel also declares that any who call on the name of the Lord will become part of the covenant community and experience deliverance. Again, the invitation is to all unredeemed Jews and Gentiles. The quotation naturally picks up on the use of Ps 106 (LXX) where those in exile and tribulation called upon the Lord and he answered them (see comments on v. 7). Paul stresses the universality of the Gospel; the Jews, as far as salvation is concerned, have no favored status. Their entrance into salvation is the same as that of Gentiles. They must call on the name of the Lord who is rich in mercy.

10:14–15 How, then, can they call on the one they have not believed in? And how can they believe in the one of whom they have not heard? And how can they hear without someone preaching to them? And how can they preach unless they are sent? As it is written, "How beautiful are the feet of those who bring good news!" Paul asks a series of questions, drawing the Roman believers along his line of reasoning to the point where they recognize how important it is that the message of salvation is proclaimed. Paul's intention is not only to emphasize the need for the Gospel to be preached, but also to stress that it is part of the OT picture—it is the fulfillment of God's purposes. God's intention has always been to save through preaching the message of salvation.

The quotation is from Isa 52:7. It refers to the Jews returning from exile. As they journeyed through the wilderness, they announced to all they met that they were returning home because Yahweh had redeemed them. Isaiah described these returning exiles as having "beautiful feet." They announced that their exile was over, and invited all the Gentiles that they met to journey with them to Jerusalem where they could worship God together.[42] The returning remnant gave this invitation because the prophets had said that, once the exile had ended, the nations would come to Jerusalem to worship the Lord (Isa 56:6–8; 60:8–16).

This is how Paul envisages the ministry of the church in Rome. Having been delivered from the kingdom of darkness, she journeys towards her heavenly home. As she journeys, she tells everyone she meets—in and beyond the city—that her God has redeemed her. Everyone is invited to join her in her pilgrimage and become part of one of the witnessing redeemed communities at the heart of the Roman Empire.

10:16 But not all the Israelites accepted the good news. For Isaiah says, "Lord, who has believed our message?" Isaiah was distressed because, as Jews in Babylon began their journey home, many refused to join the redeemed band (Isa 53:1). Their refusal was partly due to disbelief that deliverance really was at hand, but also to their unwillingness to identify with the ministry of the Suffering Servant. Many declined to leave the

---

42. Bornkamm, *Paul*, 165.

security they had acquired in Babylon. They preferred to stay under the headship of the Babylonian king rather than return to a disgraced and troubled Jerusalem and to the service of Yahweh who had been the nation's judge. It was more comfortable to stay in Babylon than to undertake a demanding pilgrimage and the enormous task of rebuilding Jerusalem with all its attendant problems and deprivations.

This is obviously how Paul is using the text, for the first part of the verse is clearly linked with the ministry of the returning exiles in the previous verse. Paul removes Isa 53:1 from its OT context (i.e., the ministry of the Suffering Servant and the people's refusal to believe the prophets' message that Yahweh had redeemed them. The apostle then applies the passage to unbelieving Israel of his own day whose preference for the security of the old covenant over the suffering that the new covenant would bring gives a stark parallel.

In the original context, the description of the Suffering Servant applied to one who the kings of the earth could not speak about (Isa 52:15). This is an important clue for identifying the Servant. Aristocrats are rarely moved by the suffering of ordinary people, however, they are alarmed when one of their own suffers. We saw something of this when members of the Russian royal family were assassinated during the Bolshevik revolution. It sent shivers of fear throughout the royal families of Europe. They realized the same fate could be theirs, and mere mention of the tragedy distressed them.

This is what is happening in Isa 53. The Servant is Israel's king, and he is the one the nation had hoped would come in glory to deliver her from Babylon. Instead, she is told that he will be treated like a common criminal. Isaiah sees the Servant's death (that is, the king's death) as a sin offering for rebellious Israel. He goes on to say (Isa 55:3) that the suffering of the Servant brings the sure mercies of David to those who believe, confirming the royal significance of the Servant figure. While it is important to understand Isa 53 in its original context, it has become a key passage by which Christians interpret the death of Jesus—and rightly so. It is their king—the Jewish Messiah—who has died for their salvation.[43]

This ties in with the early proclamations made in Acts. Here, the Christological statements are almost entirely about Jesus being the promised Davidic King (Acts 2:25–36; 5:29–32; 13:32–39). The Christology of Acts and the Gospels is not at variance with Pauline Christology, despite what many scholars claim. Their Christologies are at one and stay firmly within the orbits of the OT and the testimony of Jesus. In his letter to the Roman believers, Paul says that the same rejection the Messiah suffered at the hands of his chosen people continues. They cannot accept that they are saved only through the death of God's representative, Yahweh's Messiah King.

10:17 Consequently, faith comes from hearing the message, and the message is heard through the word of Christ. Paul takes the principles of the returning exiles' ministry and uses them to describe the ministry of the Christian community such as the one in Rome. However, the message the NT pilgrims carry is far more exalted because

---

43. See Holland, *Contours*, 81–82, for a discussion on the use of this passage in the NT and why its atoning significance is not stressed in the way we might expect.

they are proclaiming Christ. He is not only the Son of David, leading his people to their inheritance, but he is the one who gave his life as the sacrifice which broke the power of Satan, delivering his people from bondage. Again, Paul emphasizes the importance of the Christian community emulating the example of the OT covenant people and fulfilling her role in a way that Israel had failed to do (Jer 5:11; 31:22; Ezek 39:23; Hos 4:12).

Since the message creates faith, Paul sees its telling to be crucial, even though its proclamation has put his life in danger. He was not so much threatened by the unbelieving pagan world but by the Jews, who were aghast at his betrayal of their heritage and the denial of their unique status as a result of election. Religious hatred like this can often spawn violence and injustice as communities defend their perceived purity and privileges. Paul will have none of this. All of these privileges are meaningless outside of Christ.

10:18 But I ask. Did they not hear? Of course they did. "Their voice has gone out into all the earth, their words to the ends of the world." Paul anticipates that one of the Roman believers, listening to his letter being read, will suggest that perhaps the Jews had never heard the good news. He discounts this doubt by citing Ps 19:4, where the psalmist reasons how creation itself disperses the knowledge of God throughout the universe: "The heavens declare . . . the skies proclaim . . . Their voice goes out, etc." Paul argues that the creation displays the glory and knowledge of the Creator God. The psalm continues by extolling the Scriptures—the Jews will have known them from childhood and could be lead by them in the way everlasting. According to the psalm, they are perfect, revitalizing, trustworthy, wise, right, joy-giving, radiant, enlightening, sure, righteous, precious, and sweet . . . and what is more, they are accessible to every Jew. So, because he had the witness of creation and the Scriptures, no Jew could excuse himself from seeking a right relationship with God.

However, despite the witness of creation, few responded to God. They silenced their consciences and persuaded themselves of their innocence before him (Rom 1:18–32). If men turn from the revelation of God in nature, how will they react when confronted with the actual preaching of the Gospel? The revelation contained in nature was, as it were, "testing the waters" for the reception of the declared word.[44] Paul's argument concerning the witness of nature applies especially to the Gentiles. It cannot apply in the same way to the Jews for they have the oracles of God (Rom 9:4) and are without excuse. The details of the immediate argument suggest that Paul's focus has moved away from unbelieving Israel to the unbelieving world. He will return to the specifics of unbelieving Israel in Rom 10:19.

While Paul argues that all have heard,[45] the dilemma remains that his fellow countrymen are outside of the true covenant that God has established through Christ. All

44. Contra Moo, *Application*, 344, who thinks the use of the psalm demonstrates the looseness with which Paul is able to use the OT—applying it in ways that were never intended. We have seen, however, that Paul always respects the context and meaning of the original quote and does not take liberties in using the quoted texts as dysfunctional proof texts (see Holland, *Contours*, chapter 2).

45. Munck, *Christ*, 95–99, argues that "all" refers to representatives of all nations, so focusing on the concept of corporate solidarity.

other covenants have either been ended or have found their fulfillment in him, and there is no automatic transference from the old into the new. What is required is for unredeemed Israel to see that, by entering the kingdom of God, she would experience the vitally needed rebirth. Jesus expressed this to Nicodemus—a member of the Jewish ruling council—when he said to him: "you must be born again" (John 3:7).[46] In this phrase, the Greek for "you" is plural because Jesus was speaking about the nation that Nicodemus represented. Her rebirth would be as a result of the Spirit's activity. In the absence of national repentance, the individual must make his stand in the midst of unbelief and hostility.

10:19 Again I ask. Did Israel not understand? First, Moses says, "I will make you envious by those who are not a nation; I will make you angry by a nation that has no understanding." What Paul is arguing for is not something new—certainly not something that should take his fellow countrymen by surprise. The apostle appeals to Moses, who was cherished by his countrymen above all other OT figures. Moses warned the Jews that Yahweh would make his people envious by giving his attention to the Gentiles (Deut 32:21). The blessings that God would pour upon them would provoke the Jews to envy.

Deut 32:21 is one of three citations from Deut 32 (the Song of Moses) in the letter. In Rom 12:19 Paul cites Deut 32:35, and in Rom 15:10 he cites Deut 32:43. It is clear that the Song of Moses was well known to Paul and to the believers in Rome. He expects them to identify with the original passages and their context. In the Song of Moses, Israel was warned about her rebelliousness (Deut 32:15–18) and threatened that God's judgments would come upon her (Deut 32:19–25). The warning is given in Deut 32:21. Because Israel had provoked God to anger by worshipping false gods, Yahweh would provoke Israel to jealousy by taking a people that were not his people in the place of those who had been his people.[47] Paul clearly sees this text as a prophecy of the calling of the Gentiles and continues this theme of jealousy into chapter 11.

10:20 And Isaiah boldly says, "I was found by those who did not seek me; I revealed myself to those who did not ask for me." Paul demonstrates that the Jews ought to have realized that the nations would come into a special relationship with Yahweh. He quotes from Isa 65:2 in which the prophet warned the people that God would be found by those who had not sought him. The Gentiles would not have sought the Lord but for the fact that he revealed himself to them. This was tantamount to saying that Israel, who had been the recipient of this same divine self-disclosure, was no longer the sole benefactor of Yahweh's electing grace. Others whom the Jewish people despised were to come into the same privileges. No doubt this would cause violent protest from Paul's Jewish kinsmen, but he could respond by asking the question: "Don't you remember; this is the

---

46. The words of Jesus spoken to Nicodemus are essentially about Israel's condition and need. While it is legitimate to apply them to individuals when urging the exercise of faith and repentance, it must not be forgotten that the thrust of the original conversation was not about the salvation of an individual.

47. See Ryan, "Fidelity," 89–93, for a discussion on Yahweh's faithfulness to Israel in electing gentiles.

very same state that we were in when Yahweh elected us?" The Jews were also chosen when they were not a people and had no prior claims on Yahweh.

10:21 But concerning Israel he says, "All day long I have held out my hands to a disobedient and obstinate people." The same Scriptures are now used to warn Israel. Despite having the blessings of the covenants, she did not want the intrusion of Yahweh into her national life and would not respond when he made his rightful claims upon her. To emphasize his point, Paul cites Isa 65:2. Like Hosea, Isaiah depicted Yahweh as the husband and Israel as his bride. Yahweh had rescued Israel when no one else wanted her, and he secured her life. He nurtured her until she became strong and beautiful, and then took her as his wife. She committed adultery, however, turned to the gods of the surrounding nations, rejected Yahweh's love, and spurned his pleas (Ezek 16:15–29). This is a picture of Israel that all Jews are familiar with from the writings of the prophets.

The Jews of Paul's day could not see that they were doing exactly the same as their forefathers. Indeed, they were doing worse. For the love of God had been revealed in a way that was beyond anything the Jews of the OT period could have envisaged. Yahweh had sent his beloved Son to die as the Passover victim, to bring them out of their bondage to Sin, and to make them the new covenant community—the bride of Christ. The marriage theme is such a part of Jewish understanding that, at every Passover meal, the Song of Songs is read. It speaks of the love between a man and a woman, which points to a far greater love—the love of Yahweh for his people. The Passover celebrates the divine marriage, when Yahweh took Israel as his bride on the first Passover night.

Thus, Romans 10 pulls together the theme of the exhortation of Moses in Deut 30:12–13 with the instruction that, when the Israelites return from exile, they are not to search for someone who will represent them before God in the mountain as Moses had done. They are not to send emissaries overseas either to find someone of the caliber of Moses who was brought to the nation by Yahweh from beyond the Red Sea. There would be no "new revelation" from God. He would give his people all that they needed in the person of the prophet who would be raised up from among them. This prophet would be like Moses, and his words were to be obeyed. This is the exhortation which is accompanied with the powerful themes of pilgrimage and deliverance from exile—themes that resonate throughout Paul's letter to the Romans.

CONCLUSION OF ROMANS 10

Paul continues his exposition of the condition of Israel. She has pursued God but not according to knowledge. Instead of focusing on faith, she has focused on works—seeing the law as a means of retaining a status that had, in fact, been lost at Sinai. Her unique status did not exist, and she had no grounds for boasting.

Paul takes his readers back to the Sinai event, and forcefully argues that the principle of faith was embedded in the giving of the law. Again, it is exodus-type material that floods into his mind as he makes his case against Israel's unbelief.

He stresses again that the Scriptures are full of warnings to Israel that her unbelief will exclude her from God's blessings—blessings that the Gentiles will be brought into ahead of her. The proof texts are all from passages that have to do with the original exodus or the promises that accompanied the second exodus preaching of the prophets. Paul quotes from Ps 19, which speaks of the word of God being like the sun. According to the psalm, the sun is like a bridegroom who runs a race (Prov 19:5; cf., Isa 61:10). In missing the true meaning of the Scripture, Israel has missed her encounter with the bridegroom! She is missing the immense purpose and privilege of the new exodus and, because of this, the Gentiles have responded ahead of her.

EXCURSUS J: THE NEW EXODUS STRUCTURE OF ROMANS 9–11 AND OTHER NT PASSAGES

The following overview of the OT texts Paul used in Rom 9–11 supports the argument that Rom 10:6–7 refers to the victorious ascent of the Son of David. The OT citations all have second exodus roots and David is the center of the event. They act, therefore, as a catalyst for this new reading of Deut 30:12:[48]

> As the Scripture says, "Anyone who trusts in him will never be put to shame." (Rom 10:11, citing Isa 29:16)

> for, "Everyone who calls on the name of the Lord will be saved." (Rom 10:13, citing Joel 2:32)

> And how can they preach unless they are sent? As it is written, "How beautiful are the feet of those who bring good news!" (Rom 10:15, citing Isa 52:7)

> But I ask: Did they not hear? Of course they did: "Their voice has gone out into all the earth, their words to the ends of the world."[49] (Rom 10:18, citing Ps 19:4)

> Again I ask: Did Israel not understand? First, Moses says, "I will make you envious by those who are not a nation; I will make you angry by a nation that has no understanding." (Rom 10:19, citing Deut 32:21)

> And Isaiah boldly says, "I was found by those who did not seek me; I revealed myself to those who did not ask for me." (Rom 10:20, citing Isa 65:1)

> But concerning Israel he says, "All day long I have held out my hands to a disobedient and obstinate people." (Rom 10:21, citing Isa 65:2)

These eight OT texts in Rom 10 cannot but influence the way Deut 30:12 is read. Paul's use of it is controlled by the new exodus context in which it is placed. This is not an abuse of the text, for Moses was saying that the Jews, who returned from exile following punishment for breaking the terms of the covenant, were not to abandon the revelation

---

48. We need to remind ourselves that such "new readings" were given by the prophets. For example, Hosea's new reading concerning what happened at Sinai transformed the significance of the exodus event from that given in the original exodus narrative. We shall find that Paul does this again in Rom 11:26.

49. This unexpected text in a such a list of new exodus allusions might be explained by the fact that the following verse says that the law of the Lord "is like a bridegroom coming forth from his pavilion, like a champion rejoicing to run his course" (Ps 19:5). It might be this bridegroom theme that Paul uses in support of his new exodus understanding of Deut 30:12. In other words, the law—which represents Christ— is the Bridegroom who seeks his bride.

given to them at Sinai as "the word is in your mouth" (Deut 30:14). (In a short time the people would, indeed, have God's words in their mouths. Israel was to learn a hymn that God would recite to Moses and Joshua in order to stand as a witness to him against his people. The hymn would remind them of God's dealings in their past and warn them of such in the future, and Moses insisted that it must be passed down through the generations [Deut 31:19—32:47]).

This new exodus framework is not a sudden introduction, for chapter 9 made similar use of these themes, supporting them with an array of OT texts. Paul lists the blessings his people have been given to prepare them for the coming of Christ, and writes:

> Theirs are the patriarchs, and from them is traced the human ancestry of Christ, who is God over all, forever praised! Amen. (Rom 9:5)

This designation of Christ as being "God over all" is a key to understanding the meaning of the phrase, "to bring Christ down."[50] The description clearly sees the Messiah to be exalted because he has fulfilled his Father's will. It is because salvation is through such a rejected servant that such offense is caused (Rom 9:33).

> Nor because they are his descendants are they all Abraham's children. On the contrary, "It is through Isaac that your offspring will be reckoned." (Rom 9:7, citing Gen 21:6)

> For this was how the promise was stated: "At the appointed time I will return, and Sarah will have a son." (Rom 9:9, citing Gen 18:10, 14)

> Just as it is written: "Jacob I loved, but Esau I hated." (Rom 9:13, citing Mal 1:23)

> What then shall we say? Is God unjust? Not at all! (Rom 9:14, citing Exod 33:19)

> For the Scripture says to Pharaoh: "I raised you up for this very purpose, that I might display my power in you and that my name might be proclaimed in all the earth." (Rom 9:17, citing Exod 9:16)

> But who are you, O man, to talk back to God? Shall what is formed say to him who formed it, "Why did you make me like this?" (Rom 9:20, citing Isa 29:16 or Isa 45:9)

> As he says in Hosea: "I will call them 'my people' who are not my people; and I will call her 'my loved one' who is not my loved one." (Rom 9:25, citing Hos 2:23)

> It will happen that in the very place where it was said to them, "You are not my people," they will be called "sons of the living God." (Rom 9:26, citing Hos 1:10)

> Isaiah cries out concerning Israel: "Though the number of the Israelites be like the sand by the sea, only the remnant will be saved." (Rom 9:27, citing Isa 10:22–23)

> For the Lord will carry out his sentence on earth with speed and finality. (Rom 9:28, citing Isa 10:22–23)

---

50. See notes in the main body of the commentary on the possible meanings of Rom 9:5.

It is just as Isaiah said previously: "Unless the Lord Almighty had left us descendants, we would have become like Sodom, we would have been like Gomorrah." (Rom 9:29, citing Isa 1:9)

As it is written: "See, I lay in Zion a stone that causes men to stumble and a rock that makes them fall, and the one who trusts in him will never be put to shame." (Rom 9:33, citing Isa 28:16)

The linking of the original promise to Abraham with the promises of the new exodus emphasizes that the latter have not superseded the former. Instead, the new exodus is its rightful fulfillment. What is more, this concentration of interlinking thematic texts is not limited to chapters 9–10, for the same theme is continued in chapter 11:

And David says: "May their table become a snare and a trap, a stumbling block and a retribution for them." (Rom 11:9, citing Ps 69:22)

May their eyes be darkened so they cannot see, and their backs be bent forever. (Rom 11:10, citing Ps 69:23)

And so all Israel will be saved, as it is written: "The deliverer will come from Zion; he will turn godlessness away from Jacob." (Rom 11:26, citing Isa 59:20)

And this is my covenant with them when I take away their sins. (Rom 11:27, citing Jer 31:33–34)

Who has known the mind of the Lord? Or who has been his counsellor? (Rom 11:34, citing Isa 40:13)

Who has ever given to God, that God should repay him?" (Rom 11:35, citing Job 41:11)

This mass of OT second exodus material controls the theology of the section. It supports the claim that we should neither focus on the achievements of Moses nor on the parallels that are supposed to be in the NT, for, as we have seen, he is superseded by the Davidic king. This fulfillment becomes the springboard for examining the way Paul uses his OT texts. The predictions of Moses must be understood through the lens of David who is the type of his greater son, Jesus. We also need to remember the pervasive control that Isaiah's vision of a second exodus, under the leadership of the Son of David, the Servant of the Lord, has on the theology of the letter as a whole. This was identified by the way the quotes from Isaiah were carefully placed throughout Romans (see pages 13–15).

When this prophetic control of Deut 30:12 is appreciated, it becomes clear that the order within it is of little significance for Paul. He is happy to follow Deuteronomy's order. However, he does not commit himself to forcing the events of Jesus' incarnation into Moses' statement for they cannot fit—even with manipulation. There is no suggestion in Scripture that anyone brought Christ down for his incarnation; indeed, the statement of Moses in Deut 30:12 is never found to have a Messianic fulfillment in the literature of Judaism.

In addition to these considerations, we have noted the presence of the priestly theme in Romans (Rom 1:1, 3; 5:2–3, 9; 6:10; 8:34; see also 12:1; 15:16) and how this matches the teaching found in the letter to the Hebrews. Here, the change of priest brings a change of law—the former law passing away with the displaced priesthood.[51]

> If perfection could have been attained through the Levitical priesthood (for on the basis of it the law was given to the people), why was there still need for another priest to come—one in the order of Melchizedek, not in the order of Aaron? For when there is a change of the priesthood, there must also be a change of the law. (Heb 7:11–12)

It is the priestly theme that prepares for the exposition of the new covenant in Heb 8. Again, the change of law is implied when the writer quotes from Jeremiah, saying:

> For if there had been nothing wrong with that first covenant, no place would have been sought for another. But God found fault with the people and said: "The time is coming," declares the Lord, "when I will make a new covenant with the house of Israel and with the house of Judah. It will not be like the covenant I made with their forefathers when I took them by the hand to lead them out of Egypt, because they did not remain faithful to my covenant, and I turned away from them," declares the Lord. "This is the covenant I will make with the house of Israel after that time," declares the Lord. "I will put my laws in their minds and write them on their hearts. I will be their God, and they will be my people. No longer will a man teach his neighbor, or a man his brother, saying, 'Know the Lord,' because they will all know me, from the least of them to the greatest. For I will forgive their wickedness and will remember their sins no more." By calling this covenant "New," he has made the first one obsolete; and what is obsolete and aging will soon disappear. (Heb 8:7–13)

Here we see the same themes as in Rom 10. With the inauguration of a new covenant, the Mosaic law is terminated (Rom 10:4; Heb 7:12).[52] The new law is established as the result of a priest-king ascending on high. In both letters, Jer 31:31–34 is quoted (Rom 11:27; Heb 8:8–12) and emphasis made that Christ, the priest-king, has ascended to heaven and will not appear again until he comes to complete his saving work (Rom 1:4; Heb 9:24–28). In addition, both letters say the law has been brought to an end because the promised new covenant, with its new priesthood, has been inaugurated. Thus, the proposed reading of Rom 10:4–10 as a reflection on the benefits of the resurrection has the support of the letter to the Hebrews, suggesting widespread familiarity with the themes identified. No extra-biblical documents have to be appealed to—only the OT Scriptures and those which formed part of the identifiable emerging cannon of the early church. The OT texts were not only available to the community but known by its members in considerable detail, evidenced by the way they were repeatedly used by Paul to sustain detailed and, at times, complex arguments.

---

51. See Rom 10:4.

52. The new exodus theme which lies behind Romans has been shown to lie behind the letter to the Hebrews also. See Shin, *Hebrews*.

Further support for this ascension reading of Ps 68 is a text that is used in Eph 4:7–13, where Paul[53] writes about the ascension: "This is why it says: 'When he ascended on high, he led captives in his train and gave gifts to men.'" The distribution of gifts by the ascended victorious Christ is a development of the original psalm in which Yahweh receives gifts from the spoil. In the Ephesian text, it is clear that the ascended Christ does not give a new law but spiritual gifts. The Spirit takes the place of the law, the Spirit of Christ being given as the new law (Rom 8:3–4). Christ, in the person of his Spirit, has come down, and no one else was needed to bring this about. He (the Spirit) came down because a fitting person ascended the hill of the Lord; the Lord God was pleased with his intercessions for his people and delighted to send his Spirit. His final self-disclosure was complete. It is of no small significance that Pentecost—celebrated by the early church as the sending of the Spirit—was the occasion of the giving of the law in the Jewish calendar.[54]

This reference to the exalted Christ in Eph 4:8 does not stand on its own. Earlier in the letter, Paul expanded on the same theme. In chapter 1, he wrote:

> He raised him from the dead and seated him at his right hand in the heavenly realms, far above all rule and authority, power and dominion, and every title that can be given, not only in the present age but also in the one to come. And God placed all things under his feet and appointed him to be head over everything for the church, which is his body, the fullness of him who fills everything in every way. (Eph 1:20–23)

Many scholars see this passage about Christ's exaltation to be a direct echo of Ps 110, which concerns the Davidic king's enthronement. In the second chapter of Ephesians, Paul describes the church's union with Christ in his death and resurrection, and goes on to say:

> By abolishing in his flesh the law with its commandments and regulations. His purpose was to create in himself one new man out of the two, thus making peace. (Eph 2:15)

He then writes:

> In him the whole building is joined together and rises to become a holy temple in the Lord. (Eph 2:21. See also, Eph 1:13; 4:4)

So, again, we find that "the new law" which was promised to Israel in the OT has been given from heaven by the man Christ Jesus (i.e., through the death and resurrection of God's own Son). He continues to be present among his people by his Spirit. Such a natural interchange between God, the Spirit, and Christ has clear Trinitarian implications.

Thus, in Ephesians, we have what we found in Rom 10:6. As a result of the ascension, Christ has brought an end to the law and the division that existed between Jews and

---

53. I hold that, when Ephesians and Colossians are read corporately and through the lens of the Paschal new exodus paradigm, there are no conflicts between these writings and the "officially recognized" letters of Paul. The supposed conflict is not in the documents but in the manner of their reading.

54. See Kirby, *Ephesians*; Lincoln, *Ephesians*, 243.

Gentiles. The new community that has been created from the two warring communities is the dwelling place of God's Spirit—it is the living temple made without hands.

The same themes of death, resurrection, ascension, and termination of the law are found in Colossians:

> giving thanks to the Father, who has qualified you to share in the inheritance of the saints in the kingdom of light. For he has rescued us from the dominion of darkness and brought us into the kingdom of the Son he loves, in whom we have redemption, the forgiveness of sins.
>
> He is the image of the invisible God, the firstborn over ("of " RSV) all creation. For by him all things were created: things in heaven and on earth, visible and invisible, whether thrones or powers or rulers or authorities; all things were created by him and for him.
>
> He is before all things, and in him all things hold together.
>
> And he is the head of the body, the church; he is the beginning and the firstborn from among the dead, so that in everything he might have the supremacy. For God was pleased to have all his fullness dwell in him, and through him to reconcile to himself all things, whether things on earth or things in heaven, by making peace through his blood, shed on the cross. Once you were alienated from God and were enemies in your minds because of your evil behavior. But now he has reconciled you by Christ's physical body through death to present you holy in his sight, without blemish and free from accusation. (Col 1:12–22)

The hymn has all the essential features we identified in our reading of Romans. The Davidic king (the firstborn from the dead), having died to secure his people's redemption as well as that of the rest of creation (he is the firstborn over all creation), has presented his people perfect before his father. Christ is not merely the Jewish Messiah but is the Creator of all things. It is because of this cosmic redemption and reconciliation that the church has been released from the law and brought into a totally new relationship with God. This relationship is not achieved through law-righteousness but through the redeeming work of Christ.

This salvation has changed the very nature of the Jewish law. What it required has been fulfilled in a completely different way from what its adherents expected, but in a way that is in complete harmony with its original intentions.

> In him you were also circumcised, in the putting off of the sinful nature (Gr *sarx*, flesh), not with a circumcision done by the hands of men but with the circumcision done by Christ. (Col 2:11)

As we have seen elsewhere—but especially in Rom 10:4—the law has been brought to an end through the death of Christ:

> having cancelled the written code, with its regulations, that was against us and that stood opposed to us; he took it away, nailing it to the cross. (Col 2:14)

The Colossian community, having died with Christ, has received the gift of the Spirit from the ascended Lord. We know this because Paul commends her members for their love in the Spirit (Col 1:8). Thus, as in Hebrews and Ephesians, Jesus—having died for his people and having brought the law to an end through the establishment of a new

Melchizedek priesthood and a new covenant—has given his people his Spirit. This teaching is also the basis of Paul's argument:

> You, however, are controlled not by the sinful nature but by the Spirit, if the Spirit of God lives in you. And if anyone does not have the Spirit of Christ, he does not belong to Christ. (Rom 8:9)

The whole idea that Christ is among the believers (i.e., the Spirit of Christ, who is the Spirit of God) confirms that the paradigm fits the evidence and the argument. Furthermore, the death and resurrection of the Davidic king is at the heart of Paul's message to the Roman church (Rom 1:3–4; 3:21–27; 5:8).

So, through the gift of the Spirit, the promised eternal presence of God among his people has become a reality. God is no longer far off but near to all who call on him. Paul has called the Spirit, "the Spirit of God" and "the Spirit of Christ" (Rom 8:9). He is the Spirit of truth and he leads his people. There is no further revelation to be given. All has been given in the gift of the Spirit. He is the gift of the ascended Son to his bride.

From this exploration of Rom 10:6, we see that it is all too easy to lose the flow of the argument and finish up with a different story from what Paul and the other NT writers were telling. This is more likely to happen when we appeal to extra-biblical texts to construct the argument—a practice that has determined the meaning of this text for many modern scholars. It is not because these sources are not "Scripture," but because they are not the story of the Christian community—a story that is fundamentally different from those of other Jewish communities. Because the pseudepigraphal texts are narratives of different communities within Judaism, they should not be merged with the Christian story in an attempt to give a common account.[55] Such a method leaves the reader with elements of narrative reconstruction that do not belong to each other and do not match the Christian story. The proposed readings of these non-canonical texts introduce understanding into apostolic teaching that seriously disfigures the message it proclaims.

So, to be faithful to the narrative, someone must go up to heaven. Like Moses who ascended Sinai, Christ ascended into heaven following his resurrection. Because of his ascent, a new high priest has been inaugurated and the church given a new law—the law of the Spirit. This resulted in the outpouring of the Spirit who is the gift of Christ to his people. Thus, Paul writes: "Christ is the end of the law so that there may be righteousness for everyone who believes" (Rom 10:4). While no new law came down from heaven, the Holy Spirit did! It is the law of the Spirit that is life in Christ Jesus. Paul writes: "through Christ Jesus the law of the Spirit of life set me free from the law of sin and death" (Rom 8:2). The gift of the Spirit has been given, and his coming is the direct consequence of Christ's ascension. Thus, someone has ascended to heaven and, as a result, the new revelation—the law of the Spirit—has been given to the church.

---

55. It is obvious that the Pharisees and Sadducees read the history of redemption differently than the disciples of Jesus and from those residing at Qumran. Each community's story must be kept separate as an amalgamation is not the story of any community.

ROMANS 11

THE MESSIAH KING AND HIS NEW COVENANT PEOPLE

I ASK THEN: Did God reject his people? By no means! I am an Israelite myself, a descendant of Abraham, from the tribe of Benjamin. God did not reject his people, whom he foreknew. Don't you know what the Scripture says in the passage about Elijah—how he appealed to God against Israel: "Lord, they have killed your prophets and torn down your altars; I am the only one left, and they are trying to kill me"? And what was God's answer to him? "I have reserved for myself seven thousand who have not bowed the knee to Baal." So too, at the present time there is a remnant chosen by grace. And if by grace, then it is no longer by works; if it were, grace would no longer be grace. What then? What Israel sought so earnestly it did not obtain, but the elect did. The others were hardened, as it is written: "God gave them a spirit of stupor, eyes so that they could not see and ears so that they could not hear, to this very day." And David says: "May their table become a snare and a trap, a stumbling-block and a retribution for them. May their eyes be darkened so they cannot see, and their backs be bent forever." Again I ask: Did they stumble so as to fall beyond recovery? Not at all! Rather, because of their transgression, salvation has come to the Gentiles to make Israel envious. But if their transgression means riches for the world, and their loss means riches for the Gentiles, how much greater riches will their fullness bring! I am talking to you Gentiles. Inasmuch as I am the apostle to the Gentiles, I make much of my ministry in the hope that I may somehow arouse my own people to envy and save some of them. For if their rejection is the reconciliation of the world, what will their acceptance be but life from the dead? If the part of the dough offered as firstfruits is holy, then the whole batch is holy; if the root is holy, so are the branches. If some of the branches have been broken off, and you, though a wild olive shoot, have been grafted in among the others and now share in the nourishing sap from the olive root, do not boast over those branches. If you do, consider this: You do not support the root, but the root supports you. You will say then, "Branches were broken off so that I could be grafted in." Granted. But they were broken off because of unbelief, and you stand by faith. Do not be arrogant, but be afraid. For if God did not spare the natural branches, he will not spare you either. Consider therefore the kindness and sternness of God: sternness to those who fell, but kindness to you, provided that you continue in his kindness. Otherwise, you also will be cut off. And if they do not persist in unbelief, they will be grafted in, for God is able to graft them in again. After all, if you were cut out of an olive tree that is wild by nature, and contrary to nature were grafted into a cultivated olive tree, how much more readily will these, the natural branches, be grafted into their own olive tree! I do not want you to be ignorant of this mystery, brothers, so that you may not be conceited: Israel has experienced a hardening in part until the full number of the Gentiles has come in. And so all Israel will be saved, as it is written: "The deliverer will come from Zion; he will turn godlessness away from Jacob. And this is my covenant with them when I take away their sins." As far as the gospel is concerned, they are enemies on your account; but as far as election is concerned, they are loved on account of the patriarchs, for God's gifts and his call are irrevocable. Just as you who were at one time disobedient to God have now received mercy as a result of their disobedience, so they too have now become disobedient in order that they too may now receive mercy as a result of God's mercy to you. For God has bound all men over to disobedience so that he may have mercy on them all. Oh, the depth of the riches of the wisdom and knowledge of God! How unsearchable his judgments, and his paths beyond tracing out! "Who has known the mind of the Lord? Or who has been his counselor?" "Who has ever given to God, that God should repay him?" For from him and through him and to him are all things. To him be the glory forever! Amen. (Rom 11:1–36)

INTRODUCTION

In the eleventh chapter,[1] Paul continues to express his concern about the present state of Israel. He shows that the principle of the "remnant" is not new but has been part of God's purpose and Israel's history throughout the ages (Rom 11:1–6), as demonstrated by the Scriptures (Rom 11:7–10). Paul explains that the rejection of Israel is not final, but temporary and partial (Rom 11:11–12), and he makes reference to the firstfruits offering (Rom 11:16) and the grafting of olive branches (Rom 11:17–21) to illustrate his argument.

These two illustrations are significant as they are both images from exodus material. Instructions for the firstfruit offering of bread were given at Sinai in Lev 23:17, when the children of Israel were at the beginning of their journey to the promised land. Reference to the olive tree was made in Jer 11:16–17 and in Hosea 14:4–6 where a promise of blessing was given for those who would be brought out of the predicted exile in Babylon.

Thus, the new exodus motif emerges once again in Paul's argument. His reasoning is at two levels. First, he wishes to show that a new exodus has taken place of which the church is the firstfruit, creation itself sharing in this eschatological event. Second, he wants to demonstrate continuity. There has not been a total break with the purposes of God as revealed in the OT. The original, cultivated olive tree, which was not yielding the fruit it should have done,[2] has now been pruned of most of its branches and has new branches (albeit from wild stock) grafted in amongst the remaining old ones. This second picture was given to illustrate that Gentiles from many nations have been brought into the community of faith to receive the blessings promised to Abraham alongside the believing Jewish remnant. These Gentiles are also now Abraham's children by virtue of sharing his faith (Gal 3:6–9, 26–29). Paul writes to the Jewish and Gentile believers in Rome that originality (the creation of a new covenant people) and continuity (the fulfillment of the OT promises) are distinguishing features of the purposes of God (Rom 11:22–24).

1. See Johnson, "Structure," 91–103, for discussion on the structure of Rom 11.

2. Isa 5:1–7 makes the same point about Israel's unfruitfulness but Isaiah bases his illustration on the vineyard.

In the conclusion of the section, Paul insists that unbelieving Jews could still have a place in these purposes. However, they will be accepted on the same terms as all other people. Israel's salvation is conditional (as is that of the Gentiles) on recognition of need and reception of saving mercy (Rom 11:25–32). This will happen when the deliverer comes from Zion.

The reference to the "deliverer" coming "from Zion" (Rom 11:26) is a distinctively Pauline adaptation. The prediction is based on Isa 59:20: "The Redeemer will come to Zion, to those in Jacob who repent of their sins." Paul's use of the quotation involves significant alterations. He does not appear to think that the term "Redeemer" is appropriate when writing about Christ's future saving of Israel. He chooses to use the title "deliverer."

The conclusion of this theological section of the letter is a doxology in which the wisdom of God in his saving purposes is proclaimed, reinforcing the claim made earlier that wisdom is not ontological for Paul but rather the origin of salvation.[3]

11:1 I ask then. Did God reject his people? By no means! I am an Israelite myself, a descendant of Abraham, from the tribe of Benjamin. Because he had quoted from the prophets who speak about Yahweh bringing Gentiles into a special covenant relationship (e.g., Isa 10:20), Paul feared that some of the Gentile believers in Rome might think they had replaced the Jews as the covenant community. He is careful to show this is not the case.[4] If Yahweh could abandon his covenant with the Jewish people, he could not be trusted–and Christian confidence in him would be undermined. After all, if Yahweh had given up the Jews, could he not also abandon the Gentile believers in Rome?

Paul begins his response to the claim that God had abandoned the Jewish people by outlining his own Jewish pedigree. Paul always held that he had not compromised his Jewish heritage even though he now valued it differently. Before he met the risen Lord when he was on the way to Damascus to arrest followers of Jesus, he hated everything about what he knew concerning the new sect known as the Way (Acts 19:23). His encounter with the Living Lord changed everything. Paul came to see that Jesus did not destroy his Jewish faith, he fulfilled it. Elsewhere Paul used his personal testimony as a corrective to possible error, so for example, when writing to the Philippian church to warn the believers about the teaching of Judaizers who were pressing for Gentiles to be circumcision (Phil 3:2–14).

11:2–3 God did not reject his people, whom he foreknew. Don't you know what the Scripture says in the passage about Elijah—how he appealed to God against Israel: "Lord, they have killed your prophets and torn down your altars; I am the only one left, and they are trying to kill me"? By asking if God has rejected "his people," Paul uses the Greek word σπερμα (*sperma*) "seed." He has used this term in Rom 8:7–9, and the expression clearly has important theological significance. It refers to the promised

---

3. See Holland, *Contours*, 339–51, for further discussion.

4. See Given, "Restoring," 89–96, who makes a case for restoring "the inheritance" to the text of Rom 11:1. Given seeks to demonstrate the superiority of the marginal reading through a combination of text-critical and intertextual arguments.

descendants of Abraham.[5] The point that Paul repeatedly makes is that descent from Abraham is no guarantee of covenant membership—at least, not of the covenant that ultimately matters.

Paul continues his argument by appealing to the Scriptures. This time he considers the era of Elijah (1 Kgs 19:10, 14), reminding his readers that the prophet thought all had forsaken Yahweh. Evidence supporting Elijah's despair was all around him: the Israelite people, now following Baal, had torn down the altars where Yahweh was worshipped and were seeking the prophet's life. It was no idle threat. They had already killed many of Yaweh's prophets. It seemed to Elijah that the covenant had been rescinded—Israel's sin finally brought her relationship with God to an end.

11:4 And what was God's answer to him? "I have reserved for myself seven thousand who have not bowed the knee to Baal." Yahweh told Elijah that even though he could see no obvious evidence to support the LORD's answer, the situation was not hopeless (1 Kgs 19:18). He was not alone as other prophets had also stayed true to Yahweh and been preserved. They were the remnant and the object of Yahweh's concern. Who could harm them when under the protection of the living God?

The point Paul is making is that even during one of the worst periods of apostasy in Israel's history, Yahweh had still preserved a remnant for himself who remained faithful to Him and His covenant. It was a time of famine, so the pressure for the Israelites to worship Baal—the god of fertility—must have been immense. Yet despite that it had not rained for three and a half years, seven thousand refused to bow the knee to Baal. The drought was Yahweh's judgment on the sinfulness of Israel, and only when she responded in repentance was the judgment lifted (1 Kgs 18:39, 45).

11:5 So too, at the present time there is a remnant chosen by grace. Although it appeared that God's purpose for Israel was thwarted, there was no possibility of this happening as, through his saving grace, Yahweh had preserved a remnant for Himself. Paul writes that the same thing is true in his day.

That Paul reasoned in this way is evidence of a massive change in expectation from the immediate post-Pentecost days when Jews, in their thousands, were entering the kingdom of Christ (Acts 2:36–41; 6:1–7). In those heady days, it must have seemed as though Israel's acceptance of Jesus as her Messiah was imminent.[6] How quickly this optimism changed, and how difficult it was for Jewish believers to accept that Gentiles were coming into the kingdom ahead of their kinsmen. These types of misplaced expectations, leading to disappointment, have characterized the church over the centuries. As a result of misinterpreting certain texts, God's people have often been mistaken when it comes to the timing and the way that Scriptures will be fulfilled. Such exegesis has resulted in

5. See Gal 3:16–29, where Paul applies *sperma* to Christ (the true descendent of Abraham according to the seed of promise) and to believers (the community that are the offspring of Abraham according to faith).

6. Despite these comments, it must be noted that Paul's argument is one of optimism. God has not abandoned his promises to Abraham. There will be a future ingathering of the Jewish remnant and it will acknowledge Jesus as the true Messiah King.

optimism and expectation that have conflicted with fundamental biblical truths, causing confusion and harm to the people of God.

In seeing the Jews who believed in Jesus as a remnant, Paul makes a comparison with the remnant that refused to worship Baal. The logical conclusion of Paul's argument is that he considers Judaism to be a pagan religion akin to Baal worship—a concept that would have horrified the orthodox Jews. It was pagan because it sought to demand allegiance from the Jewish people in the face of the claims of their Messiah. It has been suggested that Paul uses this ploy in his letter to the Colossians.[7] In that letter his argument follows the same line of thought—Judaism is a religious system that has rejected the Messiah. In so doing she has become nothing less than pagan.

11:6 And if by grace, then it is no longer by works; if it were, grace would no longer be grace. The believers were not in relationship with God as a result of their own work. Paul introduces the word "grace" into the argument despite the fact there is no mention of it in the original OT incident involving Elijah. Paul legitimately embellishes the story by the addition of the word "grace" because the remnant has received far more than those of Elijah's day for they have now been brought into the Messiah's kingdom! Yahweh's incredible mercy could only be summed up by the term "grace"–total and absolute unmerited favor. The contrast is clear. While it was God who kept the remnant in Elijah's day safe, because they had remained faithful, so it could be claimed they were rewarded for faithfulness or works. In the new exodus however, the Jews were not present because of their commitment to Yahweh, but because of His commitment to them as fallen and defiled sinners. This is why Paul wrote to the Ephesians: "For it is by grace you have been saved, through faith—and this not from yourselves, it is the gift of God—not by works, so that no one can boast" (Eph 2:8–9).

11:7 What then? What Israel sought so earnestly it did not obtain, but the elect did. The others were hardened. What is tragic in this analysis of Israel's history is that although driven in her pursuit to please God, she fell far short of the target. This is a shocking claim for any Jew to consider. Paul argues that those whom the Jews despise— who have not followed their path of works—have received that which they had never sought: a right relationship with God.

The tragedy of unbelieving Israel is that she has been hardened. This was the description of the condition of Pharaoh's heart (Exod 8:32; 9:12) as he sought to stop the Jews from leaving Egypt for the promised land. Paul is in effect saying that in the early years of the Christian church's pilgrimage, the one who now plays the role of Pharaoh is unredeemed Israel. She is seeking to prevent the people of God from leaving the kingdom of darkness to follow the Davidic Messiah on his triumphant march to the promised land. To suggest such a startling reversal of roles would have left any orthodox Jew appalled.

11:8 As it is written: "God gave them a spirit of stupor, eyes so that they could not see and ears so that they could not hear, to this very day." Paul appeals to the writings of Isaiah (Isa 29:9–10), in which he warned Jerusalem of her forthcoming judgment. He

7. Wright, *Colossians.*

also appeals to Moses (Deut 29), who summoned the Israelites to renew their covenant with God.

Isaiah warned Jerusalem not to be complacent because her situation was immensely dangerous. The reason for the Jews' ill-judged perception of security was because Yahweh had given them a spirit of stupor. It was as if they were dazed and unable to reason. God had turned against his own people because they continually rejected his word.

In Deut 29, Moses said a similar thing to the Israelites. Despite all that he had done in delivering them from Egypt and in keeping them during forty years of wanderings in the desert, they still had a warped understanding of God. Moses said the Lord had blinded their eyes and stopped up their ears (v. 4), effectively causing them to stumble as if their senses were withdrawn.

Paul is making the point that the present hardening of heart his kinsmen were experiencing was not a unique event—God had acted in judgment against his own covenant people throughout the OT. While the Jews thought the covenant protected them from Yahweh's chastening, the Scriptures made it clear that, because they were the covenant people of Yahweh, they would be chastised ahead of the Gentiles (Amos 3:2).

11:9–10 And David says: "May their table become a snare and a trap, a stumbling block and a retribution for them. May their eyes be darkened so they cannot see, and their backs be bent forever." Now, to add insult to injury, Paul brings the words of their own Messianic king to witness against his unbelieving subjects (Ps 69:22–23). David's prayer was for Yahweh to exact vengeance on his enemies, but Paul applies it to the Jews. Paul does not misuse the passage as those who sought to overthrow David were members of his own family.

There is another reason why Paul uses David's psalm. Paul has been describing how the Gospel is the fulfillment of the promises made to David and Abraham. To reject Jesus, therefore, is to reject David and the covenant made with him (2 Sam 7:5–16). It is entirely appropriate to apply David's cry in Ps 69:22–28 to the Jews of Paul's day, for they persecuted their own countrymen who had turned to the Son of David for salvation.

The mention of the "table" in David's psalm may have a significance that is not immediately obvious. The term was used by Paul in 1 Cor 10:21: "You cannot drink the cup of the Lord and the cup of demons too; you cannot have a part in both the Lord's Table and the table of demons." This possible link suggests that the term has a cultic significance for Paul. He may be suggesting through the use of "their table" that the Jewish sacrificial system has become a snare and a trap, preventing the Jews from seeing their need for Christ's death.[8] This is also the thrust of the argument in the letter to the Hebrews. If this suggestion is correct, Paul is saying that David's psalm predicted the obsolescence of the sacrificial system as a means of getting right with God.

11:11 Again I ask. Did they stumble so as to fall beyond recovery? Not at all! Rather, because of their transgression, salvation has come to the Gentiles to make Israel envious. In responding to his own question concerning the permanence of Israel's

---

8. See Käsemann, *Romans*, 302.

fall, Paul answers an emphatic: "Not at all!" He explains that the very purpose of the Gentiles being brought into the covenant was to provoke Israel to envy. It is doubtful if Paul intended the Roman believers to think this was the only reason for the salvation of the Gentiles because the rest of Scripture presents a much higher motive—the glory of God himself (Eph 2:10; 3:10–11). The provocation of Israel to envy is with the intention that Jews will seek Yahweh and so bring him more glory.[9]

11:12 But if their transgression means riches for the world, and their loss means riches for the Gentiles, how much greater riches will their fullness bring! The method of argument in this verse was well known in Judaism. If negative events bring positive results, then positive events would bring positive results of a greater magnitude. A modern equivalent would be the question: "If a sick child can make so many people happy, how much more joy will he bring when made well?"

Paul asks the church in Rome a similar question about his kinsmen: "if their sin, with its consequential loss of blessing, is the cause of the Gentiles coming into blessing, how much more blessing will overflow to the Gentiles ("salvation has come to the Gentiles" [Rom 11:11]) when God graciously, out of his mercy, restores the Jews to their forfeited place in the covenant?"[10]

In writing about Israel's "transgression" παράπτωμα (*paraptōma*), Paul uses the same term he used in Rom 5:15: "But the gift is not like the trespass. For if the many died by the trespass of the one man, how much more did God's grace and the gift that came by the grace of the one man, Jesus Christ, overflow to the many!" Again, in Rom 5:20 we read: "The law was added so that the trespass might increase. But where sin increased, grace increased all the more." This suggests that not only Israel's historic national failure (the focus of the discussion), but also her inclusion in Adam's sin is the transgression which brought the Gentiles blessing. In chapter 5, Paul made it clear that all humanity is in Adam, and in Adam all have sinned and come short of the glory of God (Rom 3:23).

Of course, the greatest sin Paul's people have been guilty of is rejecting their Messiah and their part in his death (Acts 7:51–53). This is certainly the transgression that has brought riches to the world. It reflects man's rejection of Yahweh in the garden and its tragic consequences. The parallel between the two events has been drawn by Paul in Rom 5:15–21, and is likely therefore to be behind the repetition of the term here in chapter 11.

What exactly is Paul referring to when he writes about "their gain"? The immediate reference to "their loss" must refer to expulsion from the Garden or from the land. Both themes are fundamental for the understanding of what the death of Christ achieves. He undid what Adam had done and liberated his people from the enslavement Adam produced. In light of this comparison, "their fullness" must be their restoration to covenantal relationship and blessing—becoming part of the new covenant people of God.

---

9. Paul has already introduced the Gentiles' provocation of the Jews in Rom 10:19–20.

10. See Donaldson, "Riches," 81–98, who argues that the logic in Paul's statement is not the spatial logic of displacement but the temporal logic of delay. Donaldson says that Israel's failure to respond to the gospel makes possible the "riches for the Gentiles" by opening up time, not space.

Paul seems to anticipate future blessing for his kinsmen: "how much greater riches will their fullness bring!" Such blessing will lead to even greater blessing for the Gentiles, not the sidelining of them because of the blessing of the Jews.

11:13 I am talking to you Gentiles. Inasmuch as I am the apostle to the Gentiles, I make much of my ministry. Paul addresses the Gentiles in the congregation and reminds them of his status. He is the apostle who has been called specifically to minister to them (Acts 9:15–16; Rom 1:5). His calling gives him the right to speak with authority. Paul's instruction is not from an academic, detached position; it is the exhortation of a man who is investing his life in bringing the good news to those who were estranged from the covenants of God (Eph 2:11–13).

While it would be understandable for the Gentiles in Rome to resent intrusion from an outsider, Paul states his credentials ("*the* apostle to the Gentiles" [emphasis added]) and his life's commitment to reaching them with the Gospel. With these come his right to correct any behavior that is unbecoming of those who have been "brought near."

11:14 In the hope that I may somehow arouse my own people to envy and save some of them. Paul says that part of his ministry to the Gentiles is directed towards his own countrymen.[11] This is a fascinating insight into his mind, and an example of how it has been shaped by the Scriptures. This same desire to jolt Israel out of her sinfulness by showing that the Gentiles are preferred before her is also in the heart of God (Isa 19:23–25).

The use of the term τινας (*tinas*) "some" is telling. Paul is not expecting that the entire nation of Israel will be saved through his ministry. He understands the promise to Abraham was there will always be a true and saved seed, and his argument flows from this expectation that a remnant—bearing witness to Yahweh's faithfulness—will be preserved. These are the Jews that Paul is longing to reach!

11:15 For if their rejection is the reconciliation of the world, what will their acceptance be but life from the dead? Paul reasons in the manner of many rabbis, i.e., from the lesser case to the greater. He tells the Roman Gentiles they must not cast the Jewish people off as though they had no further purpose in the plans of God.[12] Indeed, he reasons that the real blessing of mankind through the Jewish people is yet to happen. If her casting off brought salvation to the Gentiles, what will her return bring? Paul says it would be wrong and foolish to discount the Jewish people with the assumption that they no longer had any place in the purposes of God.

The expression of "life from the dead" echoes Ezek 37, the vision of the valley of dry bones where Israel was resurrected. It spoke, of course, of her return from exile. Its significance for our discussion on Israel's future is that only the remnant came back from

---

11. The Greek term that the NIV translates as "countrymen" is σαρξ, "flesh." This picks up other uses of *flesh* in relation to Israel's status; see also chapters 7–8; 9:3. The implication is that Paul is deliberately placing Israel in the same sphere as Adam.

12. Chilton, "Dialogue," 27–37, says that although Paul's argument demands reinterpretation of Judaism and its Scriptures, it prohibits a supersessionist view of Israel.

the dead. The majority of the nation remained in exile and continued to suffer the consequences of the covenantal curses—they remained cut off from fellowship with God, for sadly, they chose to remain in a foreign land rather than to be faithful to their calling and the claims of Yahweh.

In saying that believing "Israel" would be part of redemptive history (not lording it over Gentile believers but sharing with them as co-heirs of the covenants of promise [Isa 19:19–25; Eph 2:19]), Paul is not saying that her acceptance is a future event which will happen before the resurrection of the dead. He is saying the resurrection of the Jewish people has taken place, or is taking place (1 Cor 15:52; cf. Hos 13:14). The imagery of resurrection was used to describe Israel's return from exile (Hos 13:14 [cited in 1 Cor 15:55]; Ezek 37:1–14; Dan 12:2).[13] If this is the imagery Paul is alluding to, he writes that in turning to the Messiah, Israel is being resurrected from from spiritual death. She comes from exile, returning to God to worship him.[14] The fact that his is a present reality is evidenced by the growing community of Jews who, as a result of Yahweh's faithfulness to the covenant he made with Abraham, are now coming to Christ.

What a glorious finale to human history! The promises of God are completely fulfilled so the whole of creation can be in no doubt that he is to be worshipped as the covenant-keeping God.

11:16 If the part of the dough offered as firstfruits is holy, then the whole batch is holy; if the root is holy, so are the branches. The previous suggestion of the eschatological ingathering of Israel just prior to the resurrection is born out in the reference to the "firstfruits." Paul used the term in 1 Cor 15:20 with distinct reference to the resurrection: "But Christ has indeed been raised from the dead, the firstfruits of those who have fallen asleep."

In Lev 23:9–15 (v.11 especially), we find that the firstfruits were offered three days after the offering of the Passover sacrifice.[15] In 1 Cor 15:3, Paul writes that Jesus rose from the dead on "the third day according to the scriptures," and then adds that he is the "firstfruit of those who sleep" (v. 20).[16] It is clear Paul places the death of Jesus in the context of the Passover (1 Cor 5:7), as did the Gospel writers, and he interprets its significance from that setting.

In the Jewish practice of offering firstfruits at the harvest, the first of the gathered fruit (or grain) was offered to God to indicate that the rest of the harvest belonged to him. Paul applies this concept to the Jews. He writes in effect, that because Abraham was the firstfruit, the rest of the nation is not only offered to God but is also holy. This

---

13. While normally seen as referring to the resurrection at the end of the ages, Daniel shares the same hope as Hosea and Ezekiel of a return from exile that is likened to the resurrection of the nation. The text, like the prophecies of Ezekiel and Hosea, has a more immediate application as well as eschatological hope. I owe this insight to Dr. Piotr Lorek.

14. By this observation, I do not deny the general resurrection as a future hope.

15. See Bruce, *Corinthians*, 140.

16. It must be noted that, while the ideas of firstborn and firstfruits are related (being Paschal themes), the firstborn has a particular redemptive/propitiatory role that the firstfruits do not have. See comments on Rom 3:21–26; Holland, *Contours*, 237–73.

has nothing to do with her achievements, any more than the Gentiles could claim it was their achievements that saved them. God accepted them out of his grace in order to stay faithful to the covenant he had made with Abraham.

Paul now brings to the Gentile believers' attention the image of the olive tree, a long established symbol of Israel (Jer 11:16–17; Hos 14:6; Zec 4:3, 12–14). He has already written about Abraham being the father of all who believe within Judaism and within the nations of the world (Rom 4:16–17). In making use of the picture of the olive tree, it seems probable that Paul saw its root to represent the promises made to Abraham and its branches to represent his spiritual offspring—believing Jews and Gentiles who are justified and made holy by the same faith as their "father."

> So then, he (Abraham) is the father of all who believe but have not been circumcised, in order that righteousness might be credited to them. And he is also the father of the circumcised who not only are circumcised but who also walk in the footsteps of the faith that our father had before he was circumcised. (Rom 4:11b–12)

By arguing in this way, Paul begins to prepare his hearers to view soberly their inclusion in the new covenant community.

11:17 If some of the branches have been broken off, and you, though a wild olive shoot, have been grafted in among the others and now share in the nourishing sap from the olive root. Paul now asks the Christians in Rome to imagine a situation where some of the branches of the olive tree have been broken off. It seems likely that Paul had Jeremiah's description in mind by which he warned the houses of Israel and Judah: "The Lord called you a thriving olive tree with fruit beautiful in form. But with the roar of a mighty storm he will set it on fire, and its branches will be broken. The Lord Almighty, who planted you, has decreed disaster for you, because the house of Israel and the house of Judah have done evil and provoked me to anger by burning incense to Baal" (Jer 11:16–17).

Paul will go on to say that the branches were broken off because of unbelief, but at this point in his argument he is more concerned to illustrate the picture of the Gentiles' inclusion in the covenant community, and he uses his readers' knowledge of grafting to achieve this.

Paul asks the Roman Gentiles to imagine the situation where an olive grower would break off the many unproductive branches from a cultivated olive tree and, having cut a branch from a wild olive tree, graft it into the cultivated stock among the few remaining productive branches. This picture alone will have made an uncomfortable point for many of his hearers. How foolish for an olive grower to invest time and effort in grafting a wild branch into a cultivated stock. How limited his harvest will be!

Nevertheless, this is what the grower has decided to do, and the success of his grafting (however limited) will depend upon an ongoing supply of water and minerals being drawn up from the ground by the cultivated root. Paul's point is clear: the very inclusion of the Gentiles in the covenant community is by grace. They are dependent upon the continuance of God's purposes for his ancient people because the root, which transports the nourishing sap, is their "father" Abraham. They must remember that the covenant made with Abraham, as well as the promises given to the patriarchs and reiterated by the prophets, allow the Gentiles into the grace they now enjoy. Any temptation to reject their believing Jewish brothers and sisters would be a rejection of Abraham himself–the root upon which they depend.

While the salvation of the Gentiles has not replaced the salvation of the Jews[17] (the grafted shoot is sharing the same rising sap as the remaining, original branches), the prophets promised their conversion as the consequence of Israel coming into her own inheritance (Isa 42:1–7). It is interesting that the order expected by the reforming prophets was not fulfilled, because the Gentiles came into the new covenant ahead of the majority of Jewish people.[18] However, their inclusion is still dependent upon the promises Yahweh made to Abraham and his descendants.

This rearrangement of key redemptive, historical events takes place elsewhere in the NT. For example, the Gentiles were brought into the covenant without circumcision (Acts 10:44–48; 15:14–21). Also, the Spirit, who was expected to be poured out when Israel was restored to her promised glory, is poured out on the church who has shared in the death of her Savior. Yahweh had returned to his temple as promised, but it was no longer a building made with hands, it was, as it had always been intended, his people (Ps 114:2; John 2:18–21; 1 Cor 6:19–20; Eph 2:18–20; 1 Pet 2:4–6; Rev 21:22–26).

Here in Romans, the prophetic predictions about the Gentiles' acceptance have been rearranged so that it happened *during* redemptive history rather than at its end. In Jewish expectation, this event was to be the climax of history. Isa 19:19–25, which looks forward to this occasion, is one of the most remarkable passages in the OT relating to the in-gathering of the Gentiles. There we read they will be accepted as nations in their own right, with no suggestion that they will be required to convert to Judaism.

Paul has not only rearranged the order of key OT redemptive expectations, he has also, as has been hinted, changed the order of the illustration. Normally, branches grafted into a stock have superior, desirable features. The old stock, while hardy, is merely used to support and nourish each scion. Paul reverses this situation in his illustration as the root is superior to the grafted branch. It is quite possible that Paul has done this deliberately in order to emphasize, as he has stated earlier, that the Gentiles are dependent on the promises made by Yahweh to the Jews. It never is, or was, the other way around.[19]

11:18 Do not boast over those branches. If you do, consider this: You do not support the root, but the root supports you. Paul's concern is to stress to the Gentiles that they must not become arrogant towards the believing Jews in the congregation. At the

---

17. Of course, it was Jews who first entered the new covenant community (Acts 2).

18. Note Paul's statement to the Ephesians. Speaking to the Gentiles he says, "In him we were also chosen, having been predestined according to the plan of him who works out everything in conformity with the purpose of his will, in order that we, who were the first to hope in Christ, might be for the praise of his glory. And you also were included in Christ when you heard the word of truth, the gospel of your salvation" (Eph 1:11–13). The "we" is likely to refer to the Jewish believers and the "you" to the Gentile believers. If so, Paul's order implies that the conversion of Jews by their acceptance of Christ leads to the blessing of Gentiles.

19. See Esler, "Differentiation," 103–24, for a fuller discussion.

heart of his concern is that the Gentile believers were beginning to look at their Jewish brothers and sisters with disdain, and their arrogance offended him deeply.

He had to warn them their conceit was dangerous. Indeed, esteeming themselves over the Jews in the church would reverberate back down through the generations to Abraham, the Jews' natural ancestor. Paul is concerned for the Gentiles respect the patriarch. He was the one with whom God made His covenant to the eternal benefit of the Gentile nations.

Paul has already written about the patriarch in his letter (Rom 4:1–3, 12, 13, 16, 18; see also Gal 3:6, 8, 9, 14, 16; 4:22), and now reminds the Gentiles that as a branch of the olive tree, they do not support Abraham, the root. On the contrary, the Gentiles are totally dependent on the covenant which God entered into with Abraham and the promises made to him, because "Abraham believed the Lord, and he credited it to him as righteousness" (Gen 15:6). The Lord said to him, "I will make you into a great nation . . . and all peoples on earth will be blessed through you" (Gen 12:2–3) and, "As for me, this is my covenant with you: You will be the father of many nations . . . I will establish my covenant as an everlasting covenant between me and you and your descendants after you for the generations to come, to be your God and the God of your descendants after you" (Gen 17:4, 7). Paul's words to the Jews in Rom 3 seem just as appropriate for the Gentiles: "Where, then, is boasting? It is excluded" (Rom 3:27).

Paul continues to use this fitting illustration of the olive tree, developing and applying it as the passage unfolds (see v. 24).[20]

11:19 You will say then, "Branches were broken off so that I could be grafted in." Paul moves away from the main thrust of his argument so that he can deal with the response he anticipates his Gentile readers will make. He expects them to say something like: "God has put almost all of the Jews out of the covenant community and we have replaced them. We were chosen, and grafted into the tree in their place. We are the privileged people and they, the removed branches, have been abandoned." This was the very attitude of pride which took over the hearts of the Jews in the OT and led to their ultimate downfall (Isa 25:11).

It is vital for Paul to warn the Gentiles about their attitude as they must not be under any illusion regarding their spiritual security now that they are covenant people. God can treat them in exactly the same way as he treated the Jews–chastening them for their pride and arrogance. The same hand of correction that had fallen on the covenant people of the OT could just as easily fall on them (Ex 32:1–35; Jer 11:1–17; 1 Cor 10:1–22).

11:20 Granted. But they were broken off because of unbelief, and you stand by faith. Do not be arrogant, but be afraid. Paul grants the claim of the Gentile believers concerning their status and also that of the unbelieving Jewish community as far as the new covenant blessings are concerned. However, he warns them of the danger of ar-

---

20. Baxter & Zeisler, "Arboriculture," 25–32, note that Paul's use of the grafting picture produces problems for various commentators but they argue the point of the grafting in Rom 11 was the rejuvenation of the tree and that the illustration was used primarily to stress God's intention to save Israel.

rogance and of not being fearful of the living God, lest they become like the unbelieving Jews and fall under judgment.

The reason Israel was brought under judgment was more than the term "unbelief" implies–a term which can suggest a period of grave doubt. The term Paul uses is ἀπιστία (*apistia*). Surprisingly, it is not found in any of the OT writings and is used only five times in the NT (Mark 9:24; Rom 3:3; 4:20; 11:20, 23; 1 Tim 1:13). The term can mean "unfaithfulness," making Israel's removal from the covenant community understandable. She did not merely have a lapse of confidence in God but displayed a rebellious and determined turning-away.

The same imagery of branches being lost is used by Jesus in John 15:1–4, where the Lord refers to vine branches being cut off. However, in Romans 11 the branches were "broken off" from the olive tree–not a technique used in tree management. Perhaps Paul envisaged them as being diseased and blown off in a storm: "The Lord called you a thriving olive tree with fruit beautiful in form. But with the roar of a mighty storm he will set it on fire, and its branches will be broken. The Lord Almighty, who planted you, has decreed disaster for you, because the house of Israel and the house of Judah have done evil and provoked me to anger by burning incense to Baal" (Jer 11:16–17).

In Jesus' analogy, the divine gardener cut the branches that did not bear fruit, but in Paul's illustration the gardener only came into view when he chose to graft in the wild branch. Why was this? Perhaps the answer lies in the term ἀπιστία (*apistia*) which as has been noted can be translated "unfaithfulness." In the quotation from the book of Jeremiah, Jews had been unfaithful to Yahweh, the nation's "husband," and had "turned to the right and to the left" in their worship of false gods. As a result, they had died to Him. They had broken covenant with him and could no longer be part of his covenant community. This awful "break" of the covenant led to an appalling consequence—the branches fell. The Jews who were removed from the covenant had, in essence, removed themselves.

It should be noted that when Jesus spoke of branches being removed (John 15:1–8), he used the imagery of the vine. This plant was another well known description of Israel (Ps 80:8–18). By means of this imagery, Jesus was effectively saying: "I am the true son of God. Unlike most of Abraham's descendants, I am the one whose disciples will bear fruit pleasing to the Divine Gardener." It was a powerful image but not appropriate for Paul's argument as Jesus was speaking to, and about, Jews. Paul needed a horticultural example where grafting was a common practice because he wanted to illustrate how God was bringing in the Gentiles and joining them to the covenant community. Grafting into a vine, though possible, was infrequently done. The image of Israel as an olive tree (a tree with which the technique of grafting into old stock was practiced) was well known in the ancient world, and it provided Paul with the picture he needed. Thus, the unfruitful branches were broken off and the Gentiles grafted in.

(As a side note, the illustration of the vine and branches used by Jesus in John 15, and which, at first glance seems to be related to Paul's example in this passage, is often misunderstood, The imagery used by Jesus in John 15 has been seen by many to challenge the doctrine of eternal security. This is not the case. In this passage, Jesus was speaking to the Jewish people and not to the church, which his death and resurrection had yet to bring to birth. He speaks at two levels: to the nation of Israel and to the individual Jew. The cutting off and burning of the branches specifically applies to the nation[21] albeit that individuals make up its identity.

In the first exodus, such "breaking off and burning" took place when the wilderness generation came under judgment and could not enter the land of promise. It also happened in the second exodus when the nation was delivered up to the Babylonians and the Jews were deported–cut off from the blessings of the covenant [Ezek 19:10–14]. In John 15, Jesus warned his disciples they were members of another generation that was in danger of such judgment. It soon happened, for Rome destroyed Jerusalem and drove the nation from the land.

Thus, we must not read Jesus' words as a direct warning to the individual Christian about his fruitfulness. They are about Jewish apostasy and its consequences.)

Paul has already told the Gentiles in Rome not to boast to their Jewish brethren. Now he tells them, "Do not be arrogant," because he fears this attitude may lead to their own judgment. Paul and the Gentiles would have been familiar with many examples of such arrogance in the OT and of the Lord God's attitude towards it: "'Surely the day is coming; it will burn like a furnace. All the arrogant and every evil doer will be stubble, and that day that is coming will set them on fire,' says the Lord Almighty. 'Not a root or a branch will be left to them'" (Mal 4:1). When writing to the church in Corinth, Paul was concerned about the attitudes of the believers there also. He warned them in 1 Cor 10:12: "So, if you think you are standing firm, be careful that you don't fall!"

However, Paul's warning to the Gentiles in Rome was not that they would lose their salvation but that they would experience the Lord's discipline. This would be exercised with the intention of bringing them back to him in repentance and renewal.[22] Paul has already implied that not all of the broken branches (the Jews) were discarded or consumed. The gardener (God) clearly preserved them so that he could, if he wished (i.e., when the Jews did "not persist in unbelief" but turned back to God in repentance) graft them in again to the olive tree (the covenant community), so re-establishing his covenant with them.

Finally, in this verse Paul instructs the Gentiles to "be afraid." He fears that unless they revere the Lord, their attitude may bring the Lord's chastisement: "'Should you not fear me?' declares the Lord. 'Should you not tremble in my presence?'" (Jer 5:22–25). "I tell you my friends, do not be afraid of those who kill the body and after that can do no more . . . Fear him who, after the killing of the body has power to throw you into hell. Yes, I tell you, fear him" (Luke 12: 4–5). "Now all has been heard; here is the conclusion of the matter. Fear God and keep his commandments, for this is the whole duty of man. For God will bring every deed into judgment, including every hidden thing, whether it is good or evil" (Eccl 12:13–14).

---

21. Ps 80:16: "Your vine is cut down, it is burned with fire; at your rebuke your people perish." See also Ps 80:8–18.

22. Paul deals with this theme in 1 Cor 5–6. See Holland, *Contours*, chap 6.

11:21 For if God did not spare the natural branches, he will not spare you either. Paul presents the inevitable logic of his reasoning with clarity and force. What right has the Gentile believing community to think that it will survive if the natural branches suffered chastisement for the same sin of arrogance? It is too easy for the Gentiles to think they are a special, privileged case whom God will excuse. Once they begin to think in such a way, they are in grave danger of being cast out of the covenant community as a consequence of the Lord's discipline.

11:22 Consider therefore the kindness and sternness of God. Sternness to those who fell, but kindness to you, provided that you continue in his kindness. Otherwise, you also will be cut off. It is disturbingly easy to take the grace of God for granted; but Paul reminds his Gentile readers that the character of God has not changed. He is both stern (the term can mean "severe" and is never applied to God or any person elsewhere in the Scriptures) and kind. He is kind to those who feel their need and turn to him in humble repentance. On such he pours his love and forgiveness without measure (Rom 2:4). But to those who are proud or arrogant, he sets himself against them in judgment. He has always been such a God. Paul urges the Gentiles to remember this and not presume they have a relationship with a God who changes his character.

Paul's warning still applies today. When Christians become inflated with pride and self-satisfaction, they are in danger of losing the sense of God's graciousness and of falling into a deepening abyss of conceit and obstinacy. The judgment of God on his people is a theme all too rarely heard from the pulpits of twenty-first century Christendom. The modern message focuses on the certainty of forgiveness. In some respects, this is right, but if salvation loses its transforming effect as a result of indifference to what God has done in giving up his own Son to death, there is real danger of his new covenant people coming under a discipline no less severe than the Jewish people experienced and of which the Gentile Christians in Rome were warned. Hence, the awfulness of the warning: "you also will be cut off."

This warning is not addressed to individuals regarding the loss of their salvation but to Christian communities, whose behavior may cause them to come under discipline with the subsequent removal of their witness (Rev 2:5). Similar language was addressed to Israel when she was warned of being cut off by being sent into exile (Deut 29:18–29). There, she was chastened until she repented and accepted the call from God to return to her inheritance.

11:23 And if they do not persist in unbelief, they will be grafted in, for God is able to graft them in again. Far from God having closed the door to the Jews, Paul asserts they also can come into the blessings of the new covenant—not on the basis of merit or ancestry but on the same basis as Abraham, i.e., by faith. It is unbelief (unfaithfulness) which has caused the Jews to be cut off from their glorious destiny; but this destiny will be restored to them as soon as they exercise the same faith as their illustrious ancestor.

11:24 After all, if you were cut out of an olive tree that is wild by nature, and contrary to nature were grafted into a cultivated olive tree, how much more readily

will these, the natural branches, be grafted into their own olive tree! Paul now brings his illustration of the olive tree to an end. His closing point is a further warning to the Gentile believers. It is as easy for God to reverse the position they are boasting about as it is for him to restore believing Jews to their former place within the covenant community. This would not be difficult for God to do. Even in horticulture, it would be more fruitful, reliable and easy to graft a previously cultivated branch back into its old cultivated tree than to graft in a branch from a wild tree. The latter process is notoriously unfruitful. Yet, this is what God did when he introduced the Gentiles into the new covenant community of faith. Paul must have left his Gentile hearers in no doubt that their inclusion in the community was purely of grace. He had, indeed, chosen a very effective and telling illustration!

11:25 I do not want you to be ignorant of this mystery, brothers, so that you may not be conceited: Israel has experienced a hardening in part until the full number of the Gentiles has come in. Paul calls the inclusion of the Jews back into the covenant community a "mystery."[23] This term is used elsewhere to describe the inclusion of the Gentiles (Eph 3:4–6). A "mystery" in biblical terms is not a puzzle. It is used to speak of something that could never be known unless God revealed it.[24] As an expression of his grace and according to his own wishes, he reveals his mystery and purposes to all sorts of people, regardless of their intelligence or station in life.

Too often, wrong attitudes emerge in the lives of Christian people because they fail to see God's greater plan. When the picture of God's saving purposes is out of focus, spiritual life can be damaged. Theological distortions are of grave concern as, instead of believers developing attributes that reflect the character of God, they are spiritually "defaced" and exhibit characteristics that are more like their former father, the devil (John 8:39–44). The tragedy of this truth litters the pages of history. For this reason, Paul does not want his hearers to be ignorant of this mystery.

In speaking of Israel's salvation as being dependent on the in-gathering of the Gentiles, Paul has reversed Jewish expectation. The OT clearly shows (Isa 42:1; 49:6; 49:22; 56:7; 62:2; 66:12; Ezek 38:23; Mic 4:2; Mal 1:11) that the blessings of the new covenant will come to the Gentiles following the in-gathering of the Jewish people. Paul says they have come in ahead of the Jews because Israel has rejected the Messiah. Consequently, the Jews must now wait for the blessing of the Gentiles to be completed before the nation can enter into the promises made to Abraham.

---

23. Kim, "Mystery," 412–29, claims the concept of mystery came from a very early interpretation of Paul's Damascus revelation in which he reflected on the significance of Isa 6:49 for his apostolic ministry.

24. Glancy, "Israel," 191–203, claims that Paul's situation overcame him, causing his logic to fail. She understands Paul to be arguing that Israel suffers in her loss of identity. This means that Israel, by this suffering, is symmorphic with Christ. This vicarious suffering offers Gentiles an opportunity to also become symmorphic with Christ. Israel will be resurrected in her eschatological encounter with the Redeemer from Zion. While Glancy's position probably reflects the tension that is in Paul regarding his kinsmen, to say his logic has failed places the blame for inconsistency on the apostle's mindset rather than on the reader's. Accusations such as Glancy's litter Pauline commentaries.

No wonder the Jewish community had great difficulty in coping with Paul. Not only did he insist that the Gentiles should not be made to undergo circumcision, he also taught they were now the conduit for Israel's blessing!

▬▬▬11:26 And so all Israel will be saved, as it is written: "The deliverer will come from Zion; he will turn godlessness away from Jacob. The first question the text raises is whether "and so" is a correct translation of οὕτως (*houtōs*). It has been suggested it should be translated "only then" or "in this way."[25] The second question is: "who is Israel in this passage?" Is Paul still thinking of spiritual Israel as discussed in Rom 2:28–29 and in Rom 4:11–12, i.e., Jews and Gentiles who share the same faith as Abraham? If so, then he refers only to those who believe and are the true sons of Abraham.[26] Or is Paul using the term with its national historical meaning, i.e., the nation of Israel?[27]

It is difficult to avoid the conclusion that Paul meant the latter because of what he goes on to write in Rom 11:28—how can the members of spiritual Israel, the true sons of Abraham, be described as "enemies" in relation to the Gospel?

However, if this is accepted as the meaning another question is raised: "Is Paul saying that *all* of the nation of Israel will be saved?" This question is difficult to answer, but it could be resolved if the term "all" is intended to convey all believers in Christ in the nation. However, in accepting this meaning, we still have to resolve the problem that all believing Jews are described as "enemies."[28]

In seeking to understand the scope of "all Israel," it is helpful to recognize that the term in the OT does not include every Jew but a large number of representative Jews (1 Sam 18:16; 28:4; 2 Sam 3:21).

This section concerning Israel's calling is notoriously difficult to unravel, so, it will be helpful to give careful attention to Paul's use of Isaiah 59. Resolving Paul's meaning here might assist in unravelling the meaning of the rest of the passage. Unfortunately, Paul's use of the quotation is complicated by the fact that he follows neither the Hebrew nor the Greek text of the LXX. Clearly, Paul's alteration of the Isaianic text requires attention.

First, we should note that the Hebrew text speaks of the "Redeemer coming to Zion."[29] "'The Redeemer will come to Zion, to those in Jacob who repent of their sins,'

---

25. Van der Horst, "Meaning," 521–25, argues that while most translators and commentators take *outws* in Rom 11:26 in a moda—("and so [or 'thus'] all Israel will be saved")—he presents evidence from Greek authors as well as Jewish and Christian writings to show that a temporal sense of *outws*—("and then [or 'only then' or 'thereafter'] all Israel will be saved")—is more widespread than is commonly assumed.

26. See Calvin, *Romans*, 440; Wright, "Romans," 691, and *Climax*, 246–51.

27. See Käsemann, *Romans*, 307; Zeisler, *Romans*, 285; Carbone, "Israele," 139–70; Cranfield, *Shorter*, 282; Moo, *Romans*, 722; Wright, "Romans," 689.

28. Interestingly, Calvin, *Romans*, 440, who favours reading "Israel" as the church, has nothing to say about Paul describing her as an enemy. Neither does Wright, op cit. The normal argument is the preceding discussion determines that Israel refers to the church. Murray, *Romans*, 96, says: "It is exegetically impossible to give 'Israel' in this verse any other denotation than that which belongs to the term throughout this chapter."

29. Johnson, "Tongues," 102, points out that the reference to the Redeemer coming out of Zion in Rom 11:26b is based on an amended text of the LXX of Isa 59:20. This has ἕνεκεν Σιων. Johnson says there is no sure way of knowing whether ὁ ῥ′υομενος 'the Redeemer' refers to Jesus Christ or to God. See also

declares the Lord" (Isa 59:20). However, Paul alters the text, writing: "The *deliverer* will come *from* Zion; he will turn godlessness away from Jacob" (emphasis added). Paul alters the text in two significant ways: he calls Isaiah's Redeemer "the deliverer" and writes that he comes "from Zion" rather than "to Zion." Why has he made these changes?

It may be he wants to emphasize that the salvation which the deliverer will bring is not a salvation for the Jews alone. Paul may be writing, in effect, that the deliverer is more than a national figure. He is the Savior of all men; so he does not come "to Zion" but "from Zion," i.e., he is the Jewish Messiah coming to the remnant to save his people including those in the Gentile world. This fits in perfectly with what we have noted and with contemporary scholarship. Paul did not abandon his Jewish heritage but stayed within its boundaries as he expounded the Gospel for the Gentile world.[30]

But there is another possibility. In writing that the deliverer will come "from Zion," it could be Paul is implying that he is coming to those who do not make Zion their hope, leaving behind those who stress that Zion is the place of salvation. In other words, Paul writes that salvation is not found "in Zion" but comes "from Zion" to those who know that there is no salvation in the institutions of Judah.[31]

The image of the Messiah coming to the Israelite people of faith who are nonetheless outside of Zion (that is, not depending on its institutions), fits the picture drawn in the letter. These people are the believing Jews who wait for the return from exile, i.e., the eschatological exodus of the people of God. They recognize there is another Jerusalem (see Gal 4:24–27; Heb 12:22; Rev 21:1–2) to which they must come and have no confidence in national achievement or historical privilege. Indeed, they recognize they are outside of Zion (their heavenly home) as they make their pilgrimage, and it is from there (the heavenly Zion) that the deliverer comes.[32] The argument is about the salvation of the Jews. It suggests they share the same faith as the Gentile believers among whom they dwell, for they also await the coming of the deliverer. If this is the perspective of Paul's argument, he is saying that "all Israel" is "believing Israel" who, with all believing Gentiles, comprise the true seed of Abraham, i.e., the ones who will be saved.[33] Although the argument Paul makes in this passage has nothing to do with Gentiles believers, we know that he sees them to be part of spiritual Israel by what he has already written in the letter (Rom 2; 4; 9:6).

This line of exegesis is supported by Paul's use of Isa 52:7 in Rom 10:15. The original setting of the Isaianic passage was the return of the exiles when they proclaimed to all who wanted to hear that Yahweh had redeemed them from bondage. The task of the remnant was to encourage the Gentiles to join them on their pilgrimage. This task has

---

Davies, "People," 25, who further says it is most natural to assume it refers to Yahweh. See also, Stuhlmacher, *Reconciliation*, 178.

30. See Dunn, *Theology*; Hays, *Echoes*; Wright, *Climax*.

31. Contra Seifrid, "Romans," 674–75, who see the reference to coming from Zion be intended to say that the Redeemer comes to confront the threatening nations; i.e., to defend Israel.

32. The reference can, of course, be to the Redeemer's first coming or to his second coming. As Paul's discussion is about Israel's future salvation, it suggests that he is focusing on the Redeemer's second coming.

33. See Calvin, *Romans*, 437.

been transferred to the church, which is made up of the remnant of Jews and Gentiles. It is her task, while on her eschatological pilgrimage, to encourage others to join her and experience the grace of God's redeeming love. If this is a correct understanding of the way that Paul has adapted the OT scripture, it suggests that the true people of God are still to enter Zion and that Paul's alteration of the OT is intended to point to this fact. Moreover, Paul goes on to quote from Jer 31:33 (Rom 11:27). This is, of course, a promise regarding the new covenant, suggesting that his argument is not about the *parousia* but the coming of the Gospel.

Whoever is the intended focus of the adjusted prophecy's fulfillment, it is clear that the deliverer will transform the lives of those he has come to—"he will turn godlessness away from Jacob" (see conclusion of Rom 11). From the quote borrowed from Isaiah, the Roman Gentiles would have known that "godlessness" (a term only used by Paul) would have been "turned away from Jacob" when those in Jacob repented of their sins (Isa 59:20).

Before moving on to Rom 11:27, we need to note that Paul—in keeping with the rest of the NT—has avoided calling Jesus "the Redeemer." This is especially significant here for it would have been natural to follow the Hebrew text. Instead, Paul chooses the term "deliverer." This is in keeping with his paschal theology where the term "Redeemer" has been dropped in preference for the more definitive title: "Firstborn."[34] Paul, as do the other NT writers, keeps in step with this paschal theology.

From this discussion, it appears that Paul cannot bring himself to say national Israel has been abandoned but that the conditions of her acceptance are the same as the Gentiles. She will only be restored through the salvation that Christ has made possible through his death and resurrection. "All Israel," therefore has two meanings. First, it refers to all believing Jews; second, to all the sons of Abraham, i.e., Jewish and Gentile believers. Paul, it would seem, is quite fluid in the way he uses the term. What it does not refer to is the nation of Israel.

11:27 "And this is my covenant with them when I take away their sins." Paul continues to make use of the Isaianic quote by combining the first phrase of Isa 59:21 with the sense of Isa 59:20b.

The above suggestion that the "Israel" who will be saved refers to those in spiritual exile from Zion,[35] fits the theme of the new exodus around which, some suggest, the letter to the Romans was constructed. We have repeatedly heard echoes of the fulfillment of prophecy in connection with the homecoming of Israel from exile under the leadership of a Messiah of Davidic descent. For the eighth century prophets, the "return from exile" was the forgiveness of sins.[36] We have seen that many of the Scriptures Paul uses are from this period in Israel's history when the prophets were comforting the nation that it had

---

34. See Holland, *Contours,* chapter 10.

35. Contra Sanders. He says Jews will be saved by covenant and sinners by Christ. This is rejected by Allison, "Jesus," 66; Davies, "People," 39, says: "to argue that God saves Israel apart from Christ rests on silence and some improbable interpretations of Rom 11:25–27."

36. See Wright, *Victory.*

not been cast off forever. Paul supplements this eighth century material by drawing upon aspects of the Passover, the central event of the first exodus.[37] This indicates forgiveness is not without the shedding of blood but is based on the fact that "Christ our Passover has been sacrificed for us" (1 Cor 5:7).

It is clear that Paul instinctively looks to the prophecy (Jer 31:33–34) of a new covenant, which promised that Israel's sins would be forgiven. This is significant, for this promise was made to the Jews in exile. If Paul is exercising his usual respect for the original context of the passage he quotes, the application has to be to those who are exiled from Zion. Indeed, the promise originally made by Jeremiah was not to all the Jews. Most stayed in Babylon, refusing to respond to the call to return to Zion. Such people excluded themselves from this new covenant. The promise was not for those who refused the hardships of the return but for those who responded in faith and went back to their homeland—despite those hardships—in order to serve and worship their God.

It does not take much imagination to see the NT parallel. The "exile" is not separation from the earthly Zion but from the heavenly one. Those living in the earthly Zion are the ones who refuse the call to faith and the challenge to leave behind all that is precious to them. Those to whom the deliverer comes are the ones who find no comfort in Zion with its nationalism and hardness of heart. They wait for their deliverer to appear and lead them to the heavenly Zion for which their hearts long.

The above exegesis suggests that the reference to "all Israel" in v. 26 includes the physical descendants of Abraham who share his faith and look for a country that has not yet been given to them.[38] It would be unwise to go beyond this by saying that "all" refers to all of Abraham's physical offspring. This glorious conclusion is available to all Israel, but it will only be a reality for an individual Jew if he rejects what once he had gloried in and embraces what once he had despised. The statement: "I will forgive their sins" was equivalent to: "I will bring them out of exile," for it was because of their sins that they had been cut off from their inheritance.

11:28 As far as the gospel is concerned, they are enemies on your account; but as far as election is concerned, they are loved on account of the patriarchs. Paul has already used the term "enemies" ἐχθροὶ (*echthroi*) in his letter. Indeed, he included himself in the term when describing God's saving activity on behalf of his people in Rom 5:10. He wrote: "For if, when we were God's enemies, we were reconciled to him through the death of his Son, how much more, having been reconciled, shall we be saved through his life!" In Rom 5, Paul writes that God's enemies are people who have not been reconciled to him, and this seems to be the sense of the term in Rom 11. He uses the term "enemies" in a number of his letters.[39] In Phil 3:18–19, Paul elaborates, with tears, on the lifestyle

---

37. See comments on Rom 3:21–25.

38. See Calvin, *Romans*, 441, who says: "Paul maintains that the purposes of God stand firm and immovable, by which he had once deigned to choose them for himself as a peculiar nation. Since then, it cannot possibly be that the Lord will depart from that covenant which he made with Abraham, 'I will be the God of thy seed' (Gen XV11.7). It is evident that he has not wholly turned away his kindness from the Jewish nation."

39. Rom 12:20; 1 Cor 15:26; Gal 4:16; Phil 3:18; 2 Thess 3:15.

and destiny of people who live in enmity to the Gospel: "I have often told you before and now say it again even with tears, many live as enemies of the cross of Christ. Their destiny is destruction, their god is their stomach, and their glory is in their shame. Their mind is on earthly things."

Paul is not intending to convey the sense that the Jews are hated as far as the Gospel is concerned but, at this point in their history, they are loved less (or, to use a better term, "behind")[40] the believing Gentiles, who have been reconciled to God and brought into the kingdom ahead of them.

Yet, even though this is so, it is only temporary. The Jews are loved on account of the patriarchs and their election has not been put aside. Paul has been at pains to stress how the new covenant has redefined Israel, and this redefinition has not reneged on the promises made to the ones with whom God had made the preparatory covenant. It is the fulfillment of these ancient covenants (those made with Abraham [Rom 4:1–25] and David [Rom 1:3]) that brings blessing to the Gentiles and for which they should be eternally grateful.

11:29 For God's gifts and his call are irrevocable. Regardless of what the Roman Gentile believers think about his explanation of the Jews' standing, Paul reminds them that ultimately their status is not dependent on the consent of men. It is settled by a sovereign God whose decisions cannot be challenged. This is true of God's right to bestow gifts to men and his right to exercise his prerogative in choosing who he will save and in what order.

We need to keep in focus the fact that Paul is not discussing individual election but that of people groups, namely Jews and Gentiles. This does not alter the fact that, elsewhere, the same principle is applied to individuals (Acts 13:48).

11:30 Just as you who were at one time disobedient to God have now received mercy as a result of their disobedience. Upon hearing Paul's letter read to the gathered church, the Gentile believers in Rome were reminded there was a time when they also were disobedient to God and enemies of the cross of Christ. Indeed, at the opening of his letter, Paul exposed the fact that he knew of the depraved behavior and ongoing disobedience among some of the believers. Rom 2:1–16 must have made very uncomfortable listening for some.

But, despite their disobedience, the Gentiles had received mercy when they responded in repentance to the Gospel which was extended to them as a result of God's grace. Paul writes: "Through him and for his name's sake, we received grace and apostleship to call people from among all the Gentiles to the obedience that comes from faith. And you also are among those who are called to belong to Jesus Christ" (Rom 1:5–6).

Had the Gentiles in the congregation been listening carefully to the letter as it was being read to them, they would have known their call came about because of the disobedience of the Jews. Paul had already reminded them of the words of the prophet Hosea

---

40. See the meaning of "hated" in Luke 14:26.

(Hos 2:23) in Rom 9:24–26 that God would call them "my people" who were not his people and "my loved one" who was not his loved one.

11:31 So they too have now become disobedient in order that they too may now receive mercy as a result of God's mercy to you. Paul clearly sees that responsibility accompanies the mercy which has been extended to the Gentiles. They are obliged by divine grace to bear witness to the unbelieving Jews so that they too may hear the good news of God's saving activity in Christ, repent, and be reconciled to the God of their fathers.

It might seem strange that Paul says the Jews will receive mercy because of the mercy that the Gentiles have received, but this is not so strange when it is appreciated that, once again, his frame of reference is the prophetic word of the OT. The prophets had said the Gentiles would be brought into the covenant community, and that God would provoke the Jews to jealousy by calling a people he had not formerly known to be his people (Rom 9:25). The Gentiles were actually being used to provoke the Jews—to make them realize that their unbelief was denying them the blessing of fellowship with God.

Of course, arguments alone from the believing Gentiles would not win the Jews to Jesus the Messiah—they would do that through their lives. They had to demonstrate to the Jews that they had turned from their sin and disobedience to serve the living God in the very way that the Jews had been called, but had failed, to do. Rather than being the cause of boasting, the calling of the Gentiles gave them a great and awesome responsibility to live as the servants of God.

11:32 For God has bound all men over to disobedience so that he may have mercy on them all. There is no limit to the "all" in this statement. All the children of Adam—whether descendants of Abraham or not—who actively disobey the command of Yahweh (i.e., those who are outside of Christ) are under judgment (Rom 3:22–24). It can no longer be said that Yahweh gives Israel privileges over the Gentiles. Indeed, all her privileges have come to an end in terms of her special relationship with him. She is now in the same position of danger as the Gentiles. She must turn to her God in repentance and, like them, seek the same kindness and mercy.

11:33 Oh, the depth of the riches of the wisdom and knowledge of God! How unsearchable his judgments, and his paths beyond tracing out! Paul has come to the end of his presentation on the equality of Jews and Gentiles before God. The first eleven chapters of his letter have argued for this equality on theological grounds—the next section will argue for it in practice.

At this point of transition, Paul pauses. He is not able to conclude his argument without reflecting on the wonder of what he has been presenting. His heart rings with praise and thanksgiving to God, and he writes the longest doxology that appears in any of his extant writings.[41] This brief, concluding section is possibly a key passage in an unexpected way. It shows us that the man God used not only knew his theology but was overwhelmed by its message and the God about whom it spoke. Paul is a powerful

---

41. Or hymn. See Jewett, *Romans*, 716.

example to those of us who love theology that a passion for academics can never be a substitute for loving God himself. May we not be like some of the Pharisees and Scribes who pursued theology as an intellectual exercise but, rather, like the Apostle Paul who was moved by its truths.

He begins his eulogy by dwelling on the "depth of the riches of the wisdom of God." Both Jews and Gentiles have challenged God's decisions and callings throughout history, seeing them—at times—as arbitrary, ruthless and cruel. When tempted by adverse crushing circumstances to doubt God in such a way, we need to ask if such judgments reflect the character of the God who gave his own Son up to death for the salvation of those who hated and abused him. How can such evil be charged to such a God? We can only conclude that any evidence which suggests that God is ruthless and merciless is unreliable and untrue. This does not deny that he will judge—sometimes in this life—but it does warn us of the danger of attributing characteristics to him that befit the prince of lies.

Paul declares the depth of the richness of God's knowledge. The term "depth" is used throughout the Scriptures to denote those areas that are beyond the inspection of man (e.g., Prov 18:4; 1 Cor 2:10; Phil 1:9). In his letter, Paul has argued for God's right to make decisions that man may not approve. He would not be God if he had to seek the endorsement of man for his decisions and actions. Because he is uniquely omniscient no one should challenge his wisdom. How dare we, in our foolishness, question the judgments and decisions of the Lord God! "How unsearchable his judgments, and his paths beyond tracing out!" God's judgments are at a depth that man cannot fathom, and his actions, therefore, are always going to be beyond what man can comprehend.

11:34 "Who has known the mind of the Lord? Or who has been his counsellor?" While there is an echo of Job 15:8 in this verse, Paul clearly relies on Isa 40:13, which he also uses in 1 Cor 2:16: "Who has understood the mind of the Lord, or instructed him as his counselor?"[42] The questions are rhetorical, and asked not because Paul was expecting an answer (for he and his hearers knew that the answer was "No one") but because he intended that their very asking would remove any complacency.

The original text in Isa 40 celebrated the wonder of Yahweh who announced that he would deliver his people from exile in Babylon. The declaration by Isaiah was to answer those who challenged the prophet's message by claiming there was no possibility that God would bring Israel back home to Zion. No one would have advised God to act in this way as it was contrary to all that the nation deserved. However, instead of casting her off forever, God was working to redeem her and re-establish the relationship she had rejected. Of course, what Isaiah declared about God redeeming his people from bondage in Babylon pales into insignificance when we recall the length to which God went to redeem his people from bondage to Satan. He did this so that he could bring his people home to the heavenly Jerusalem.

I have argued the letter is set within a new exodus framework, and here, in the closing section of the theological discussion, Paul again uses the words of Isaiah. The

---

42. See Holland, *Paul, Israel's Law and God's Spirit,* forthcoming.

390

presence of Isaiah's oracles is a clear reminder of the importance of this eighth century prophet's perspective and the many predictions and comforts he brought to Israel in that crucial period of her history. Paul's use of the prophet of the second exodus, underlines the continuity of these great themes and promises that have, and are, being fulfilled in Christ.

Paul asserts the impossibility of any man being able to instruct God: "who has been his counselor?" To think that we can manage, understand, and advise God in a way that satisfies our puny, fallen, darkened minds is ridiculous. Such arrogance is ludicrous, and beyond comprehension. God is not beholden to man. He does not have to seek man's approval for his decisions and goals. He is the Creator who answers to no man, thing, or being. He is not a capricious God. He is the God who redeems and saves those who call on him. The sufferings of creation are not the result of his affliction but the consequence of humankind's fall. Into this sin-cursed existence, God has come in the person of Jesus, to bring life and immortality by means of the Gospel (2 Tim 1:10). His judgments are unsearchable and his paths beyond finding out.

This has been the thrust of Paul's argument throughout his letter to the Romans. Man has given himself over to Sin (Satan). As a result of this covenant relationship with Satan, man is in exile; there is nothing he is can do to annul this relationship and reverse its consequences. The quotation from Isaiah is a comment on the theology of the letter over which the previous verse has burst into gratitude and praise. The attention of such a God to the wellbeing and deliverance of his people is a source of unspeakable comfort (Isa 40:1).

11:35 "Who has ever given to God, that God should repay him?" The quote is difficult to identify with any certainty, but it is possibly based on Job 41:11.[43] This section of Job concludes a long, searching debate between Job and his "comforters," finally ending with God's challenge to Job as to his authority to question his Creator. Job responds with a hymn of intense praise, which glorifies Yahweh for his wisdom, power, and might.

The point Paul is making is that no man can understand God's ways; it is only as Yahweh reveals himself that man can possibly begin to understand his own insignificance and frailty. There is nothing man can give to God; he needs to receive everything from him. The relationship is not one of equals, and yet, incredibly, God desires to treat man as though he was an equal. In the light of God's perfection, majesty, and power, the redemption of man is beyond anything that could have been contemplated. "Where," asks Paul, "has this salvation come from?" He answers: "From the heart of God himself."

11:36 For from him and through him and to him are all things. To him be the glory forever! Amen. There is no praise for man. He deserves nothing but judgment and condemnation, as he is guilty and totally helpless.

All of God's gracious dealings with redeemed men and women, Jew or Gentile, are because God has purposed to do "all things" for them: "And we know that in *all things*

---

43. Jewett, *Romans*, 718, thinks that Paul has carefully selected Job 41:3, along with the earlier use of Isa 40:3, so as to construct a chiastic development of the riches, wisdom, and knowledge of God referred to in Rom 11:33.

God works for the good of those who love him, who have been *called* according to his purpose. For those God *foreknew* he also *predestined* to be *conformed* to the likeness of his Son, that he might be the firstborn among many brothers. And those he predestined, he also called; those he called, he also *justified*; those he justified, he also *glorified*" (Rom 8:28–30, emphasis added). Thus the "all things" are those things that pertain to salvation.[44] Paul can only respond: "To him be the glory forever! Amen."

CONCLUSION OF ROMANS 11

Paul puts Israel's unbelief in context. He shows that it has been the pattern of her history throughout the OT. How different her story would have been if she had truly believed and repented!

Yet, in spite of this unbelief, Paul insists the purposes of God still stand—he is living evidence that a believing remnant still exists, just as it has existed throughout Israel's history.

He fears that some Gentile believers in Rome are in danger of falling into Israel's sin of pride and unbelief (disobedience). He urges them not to boast that they have replaced Israel, showing them that the Jews are the "natural, cultivated, fallen branches of the olive tree," and that it would not be difficult for God to bring them back into the blessings promised to Abraham. After all, God had grafted the Gentiles into the tree as wild branches, so why could he not restore the natural branches to the site where they once grew?

He concludes with an affirmation that all of believing Israel will be grafted back into the tree. The spiritual Israel will be saved in the fullness of time when the Gentiles have been brought in as predicted by the prophets. This argument is brought to its climax with the declaration from the prophet Isaiah that the deliverer (Hebrew גּוֹאֵל "redeemer") would come from Zion. The culmination of his coming is found in Isa 61:10, where Isaiah testifies: "he has clothed me with garments of salvation and arrayed me with a robe of righteousness, as a bridegroom adorns his head like a priest, and as a bride adorns herself with jewels." Believing Israel will, at last, be joined with the Gentiles to form the bride in the divine marriage.

---

44. See also Peter's argument in 2 Pet 1:3.

ROMANS 12

THE MESSIAH KING AND HIS PRIESTLY PEOPLE

THEREFORE, I URGE you, brothers, in view of God's mercy, to offer your bodies as living sacrifices, holy and pleasing to God—this is your spiritual act of worship. Do not conform any longer to the pattern of this world, but be transformed by the renewing of your mind. Then you will be able to test and approve what God's will is—his good, pleasing and perfect will. For by the grace given me I say to every one of you: Do not think of yourself more highly than you ought, but rather think of yourself with sober judgment, in accordance with the measure of faith God has given you. Just as each of us has one body with many members, and these members do not all have the same function, so in Christ we who are many form one body, and each member belongs to all the others. We have different gifts, according to the grace given us. If a man's gift is prophesying, let him use it in proportion to his faith. If it is serving, let him serve; if it is teaching, let him teach; if it is encouraging, let him encourage; if it is contributing to the needs of others, let him give generously; if it is leadership, let him govern diligently; if it is showing mercy, let him do it cheerfully. (Rom 12:1–8)

INTRODUCTION

PAUL HAS NOW CONCLUDED the theological section of his letter in which hugely important issues have been patiently yet decisively presented. However, Christian living is not only about understanding theology but also about living it out, and it is to this that Paul now turns.

God saved his people to serve him in truth and holiness, qualities which Israel tragically failed to display. Living as faithful servants is obligatory, for we have been saved from the awful judgment that awaits those who are not in Christ. Like the Jews in the Exodus who benefitted from the death of the lamb, the church is saved as a result of the death of its paschal sacrifice, Jesus the Firstborn and Redeemer. Because of this, "there is now no condemnation for those who are in Christ Jesus" (Rom 8:1).

As a result of Israel's exodus from Egypt she was called to be a priestly people, and this, Paul says, is now the calling on the church.

12:1 Therefore, I urge you, brothers, in view of God's mercy, to offer your bodies as living sacrifices, holy and pleasing to God—this is your spiritual act of worship. In using the adverb "therefore," Paul is effectively saying: "In light of what I've written, this is how you should respond." It does not refer to the material of chapter 11 alone (where

Paul explained the role of the Jews in the purposes of God) but to the argument that has gone on from the beginning of the letter.

Throughout the letter, Paul has focused on the history of God's saving activity, showing the believers that Jesus, the Son of David, has fulfilled all the predictions of the OT prophets, bringing salvation to those who looked to the living God. Despite Israel's rebellious history, God's many promises and the examples of how he acted in history show that he would continue to have compassion on them and be merciful to them (Isa 63:9; Neh 9:31). It is into this mercy that the Gentiles have now been brought, sharing with those in Israel who have true faith.[1]

By appreciating that the first eleven chapters of the letter provide the backcloth of the exhortation of chapter 12, we can understand more clearly what motivated Paul's appeal. The prophets had, albeit implicitly, anticipated the death of Jesus.[2] His death was nothing other than the great eschatological Passover. Paul discussed this is Rom 3:21–26, and the ramifications of this awful event overshadow the rest of the letter.

In the original Passover, the Jewish firstborn sons were spared death because lambs were slain on their behalf. These firstborn sons were then claimed by God as priests, and were set apart to represent the nation in worship (Exod 13:2; 22:29b). God then provided an alternative arrangement, allowing the Jewish families to keep their firstborn sons by substituting the tribe of Levi for them (Num 3:12–13). The Levites acted in their place as the priesthood of the nation. Regardless of this arrangement, God named those who had been spared (indeed the whole nation) his "firstborn," calling them all to a ministry of priestly service (Exod 4:22–23; 19:6).[3]

This is Paul's argument. He has explained how through the death of Jesus—God's beloved son and firstborn of all creation—believers have been spared. No spotless lamb was killed in their place but, as with the Egyptian families, the victim of judgment was their elder brother (Rom 8:3–4, 29). Note the theme of redemption throughout chapter 8 in which the life of the firstborn was surrendered as God, through Christ, became his people's Redeemer.[4]

The death of Jesus means that believers have been set free—released from bondage and impending judgment. Just as those Jews who were spared the judgment of the first Passover were claimed by God as priests, so, in the great Passover when Christ died, God claimed those he had spared as his priestly people. All the redeemed of the Lord were henceforth called to be a holy nation and a royal priesthood (1 Pet 2:5, 9).[5]

---

1. Campbell, "Rule," 278, stresses that Paul seeks to create a community ethos in Rome so that there can be unity within diversity: one church made up of Jews and Gentiles.

2. See comments on Rom 3:21–26.

3. According to rabbinic tradition, the firstborn had been the servants of the sanctuary but lost the office owing to the worship of the golden calf. The honor went to the Levites (Ginzberg, Legends, 3:211). The Levites were substituted for the firstborn, the tribe having the responsibility of atoning for the sin of the firstborn among the children of Israel (Legends, 3:226). This connection of the priesthood of believers with the Paschal theme is supported by other parts of the NT, suggesting that the Paschal paradigm was the origin of the believers' priestly ministry. See Holland, Contours, chapter 10.

4. See Holland, Contours, 237–73, for discussion on the firstborn in redemptive history.

5. Commenting on Rom 12:1, Campbell, Deliverance, 651, notes the cultic setting and comments on the presence of cultic imagery throughout Romans saying: "All this material is just too pronounced to ignore.

The priestly theme is part of the exodus, second exodus and the new exodus. Not only was Israel redeemed to be Yahweh's bride but also his priestly people. Isa 61:10 describes the condition of restored Israel not only in terms of being the bride of Yahweh but also his priesthood: "I delight greatly in the Lord; my soul rejoices in my God. For he has clothed me with garments of salvation and arrayed me in a robe of righteousness, as a bridegroom adorns his head like a priest, and as a bride adorns herself with her jewels."

This is the background of Paul's appeal to the believers of the Roman church that they offer themselves as a living sacrifice. That was precisely what the priesthood was meant to be in the OT—the people were to be a living sacrifice. This is the basis of Christian living for all believing people. It is not a calling for special classes of Christians such as "full-time" and "cross-cultural workers." Such distinctions were never suggested in the NT. All Christians are "full-time" because they have been fully redeemed, and the implications of this are far reaching for the way they live their lives. What we expect from certain "categories" of Christians is no different from what God expects of all his people. As priests of the living God, believers are called to minister in intercession as well as instruction, for the priests of the OT formed a teaching community (2 Kgs 17:27; 2 Chr 15:3; 17:7; Ezek 44:21–23). The NT knows nothing of a division between laity and ordained as all believers are "priests unto God" (Rom 15:16; 1 Pet 2:5; Rev 1:6). All are called to serve by making Christ known, being totally committed to this task because they have been redeemed and are not their own.[6]

When Paul urges the Roman believers to yield their bodies, he is not limiting his appeal to the dedication of their physical bodies. His appeal includes the whole of their persons, and could legitimately be translated as "yield yourselves" (Rom 6:13–14). This is not playing with words, for scholars who have studied the way the ancient Jews used the term "body" (soma), have shown that it was used differently by the Greeks for whom it mostly meant "physical body."[7] However, for the Jews it was a term that embraced the whole of the person—it encompassed mind, emotions, will, and physical being.

Thus, Paul's appeal is for the Roman believers to be totally and completely dedicated to God, recognizing that they belong to the one who has given his Son for their forgiveness and salvation. If, when listening to the letter being read to them, they grasped the enormity of what God had done for them in Christ, Paul's appeal for dedication would have been met with ready assent from the assembled congregation.

The NIV translation of this verse reads: "Therefore, I urge you, brothers, in view of God's mercy, to offer your bodies as living sacrifices, holy and pleasing to God—this is your spiritual act of worship." It is understandable for this exhortation to be seen as an individualistic, introspective appeal to all the believers in Rome to live holy lives which

---

Christ, the Spirit, Paul himself, and the Christian community all receive overtly cultic coding at certain points in Romans."

6. Stuhlmacher, "Theme," 341, comments that "Rom 12–16 belongs inextricably to the letter . . . because the apostle nowhere (and certainly not in Romans) expounds abstract theology, but always only concrete exhortation. Whether the Romans really believe in Christ as their redeemer and Lord will be evident, according to Paul, by how they (as Gentile and Jewish Christians) deal with one another and how they resolve the tensions among one another in Rome."

7. Holland, *Contours*, chapter 6.

can be offered to God as individual living sacrifices. The picture this conjures up is of Roman believers striving to live holy lives in the context of their families and social responsibilities within the city. They come together to be strengthened and helped through the teaching of the Scriptures and the celebration of the Lord's Supper so that they are prepared for the more important task of living their independent, sacrificial lives in the days ahead.

However, Paul is saying more than this. The fuller picture is hidden by the translators' lack of respect for the use Paul makes of individual and corporate vocabulary. As the believers listened to the letter being read, they would have heard the appeal more like this: τὰ σώματα ὑμῶν θυσίαν ζῶσαν (ta sōmata humōn thusian zōsan) "offer yourselves (pl.) as a living sacrifice (sing.), holy and pleasing to God—this is your (pl.) reasonable service." Paul had already addressed them corporately in Rom 6:12: Μὴ οὖν βασιλευέτω ἡ ἁμαρτία ἐν τῷ θνητῷ ὑμῶν σώμαται (mē oun basileuetō hē amartia en tō thnētō humōn sōmati) "do not let sin reign in your (pl.) mortal body (sing.)."

I think what Paul is saying to the believers in Rome is something like this: "Remember how I told you earlier in the letter that God rescued you from bondage to Sin through the death of his Son and gave you life through his Spirit? In response to his mercy and grace that has given you these things, I urge you to offer yourselves to him as a corporate sacrifice. You are all equally part of Christ's church. You are all children of Abraham, and despite the differences that have divided you in the past and made you suspicious of each other (I hope you now know that these must stop), you are to recognize that God has accepted you all. So, you are all called to priestly service, Jew and Gentile alike, and you are all to offer yourselves in order to make the church in Rome a living sacrifice. And I want this offering to be a sacrifice that God can accept. In other words, the church must be spotless and without blemish. This means that you all must be holy—conformed to the image of his Son—and you must be united. If, as a church, you make an offering to God of this quality (and, after all the things that he has done for you, this is surely not too much to ask), you will bring him great pleasure and be effective in his service."

Since sacrifices were offered in the temple by priests, Rom 12:1 suggests that Paul saw priestly ministry as continuing in the NT church. This is indeed how the early church saw her service, for when they chose seven of their number to serve as "deacons," the apostles prayed and laid hands on them (Acts 6:6). When Barnabas and Saul were set apart to do their missionary work among the Gentiles (Acts 13), the elders also laid hands on them in the manner of setting priests apart.[8] Later in this letter (Rom 15:15–16), Paul writes: ". . . because of the grace God gave me to be a minister of Christ Jesus to the Gentiles with the priestly duty of proclaiming the Gospel of God, so that the Gentiles might become an offering acceptable to God, sanctified by the Holy Spirit." Paul is clearly saying that as a NT priest his responsibility is to make the Gospel known to the Gentiles. It is through his proclamation that Gentiles will believe and become proclaiming priests in turn, so becoming part of the "offering acceptable to God." Of course, while the priesthood of the NT draws from imagery from the OT institution, it is unlike that order, for it is not

---

8. Kidner, "Metaphors," 119ff., points out that in Num 8:10ff., the Levites had hands laid on them and were offered as living sacrifices to the Lord.

about offering physical sacrifices but rather spiritual ones. Also, unlike the OT priesthood which was exclusive, the NT priesthood is all inclusive. Every believer, regardless of ethnicity and no matter position in society or gifting in the church, is a priest.

As I have noted, Paul did not use the term πνευματικος pneumatikos "spiritual" but λογικος logikos "logical" or "reasonable," and so he writes: "This is your reasonable (or logical) service."[9] So Paul writes that in light of God's faithfulness, the gift of the Spirit, and the taking of the church as his bride "your (pl.) reasonable (sing.) service (sing.)" is to be a living sacrifice. Again, there is a corporate dimension to this phrase—all the believers contributing to the single, united, acceptable, holy offering to God that is the redeemed community, i.e., the church in Rome. All the believers are to see that, as a church, their priestly act of service was the reasonable response to God's undeserved mercy and that all are responsible for maintaining the church's integrity as a holy and pleasing sacrifice. This interpretation is supported by what Paul says in Rom 15:16 where he speaks of his own calling: "to be a minister of Christ Jesus to the Gentiles with the priestly duty of proclaiming the gospel of God, so that the Gentiles might become an offering acceptable to God, sanctified by the Holy Spirit."

12:2 Do not conform any longer to the pattern of this world, but be transformed by the renewing of your mind. Then you will be able to test and approve what God's will is—his good, pleasing and perfect will. Another way of saying "do not conform to the pattern of the world," is to say "do not let the world mold you." The Roman church had two options. It could either allow God to mold it (by submitting to the Spirit, to God's word as revealed in the OT, and to its leaders [including Paul] as they interpreted and taught the Scriptures) or the church could allow Roman society to shape it as it had the believers before they were converted.

The tragedy is that this molding of lives often takes place unnoticed. Values are disseminated throughout popular culture, being expressed through media, science, and non-Christian families, friends and work colleagues. They change people imperceptibly. Regardless of how noble our societies may appear, Paul would urge: "Brothers and sisters, do not conform any longer." The values believers embrace are to be based on those of another kingdom—the one that Christ rules.

In saying this, Paul is not urging believers to be less than human. Culture is an expression of man's creativity. It is a gift from God and part of the enriching experience of life. His concern for the Roman Christians is that the city's prevailing culture can be anti-God and an instrument by which he can be deposed from the throne of the church's heart and mind. He wants the believers to control its influence. In Phil 4:16, he writes "Whatever is true, whatever is noble, whatever is pure, whatever is lovely, whatever is admirable—if anything is excellent or praiseworthy—think about such things." We are to reject what is base, crude, false, and unkind as part of our refusal to be molded by the world (Rom 6:13–14).

---

9. Bruce holds that there is a contrast here between "the externalities of Israel's temple cult." Cited by Morris, *Romans*, 434.

When Paul uses the term "world" in the phrase "Do not conform any longer to the pattern of this world," it has a particular meaning. It speaks of the activities of people from which God is excluded. (This is the way that the Apostle John used the term when he wrote "Do not love the world or anything in the world. If anyone loves the world, the love of the father is not in him" [1 John 2:15]. The usual meaning of the term "world" in his gospel is "humankind," e.g., John 3:16.)[10] Paul's use of ἀίων (*aiōn*) "age," links into one of the meanings of a common term encountered throughout the letter: σαρχ (*sarx*) "flesh." To be conformed to (or molded by) the world is to live "in the flesh" (Rom 8:13).[11]

The condition of unredeemed humanity, i.e., "being in the flesh," is a result of Adam's disobedience to God's commands. The scriptures say that there is a spiritual war raging between God and Satan (Dan 10:12–14; Mark 3:23–29, 4:15; 2 Cor 10:1; Eph 6:10–18; Rev 12–17) into which man, through Adam, has been drawn. His decision to reject God's offer of mercy leaves him bound in covenant to Satan and the life he lives "in the flesh" reflects the character of the federal head he has chosen.

For those who embrace God's mercy, the death of Christ—their "firstborn"—breaks this covenantal binding, setting them free to enter into covenant with Christ (Rom 7:1–4). However, Christ's redeemed people on earth are still living in the world, interacting with many who are "in the flesh" and feeling the pull of their old allegiance to it. Their minds need to be constantly renewed, and this can only be achieved when they take the message of Scripture seriously and evaluate everything in its light. Only when they do this will they see the significance of issues that face them. Paul urges the church in Rome to seek such a Christ-centered worldview.

Paul urges the church to be "transformed by the renewing of your (pl.) mind (sing)." He continues to be concerned for its corporate identity and witness (see also Eph 2:16; 4:17–32; Col 3:5–17), urging a renewal that comes from submission to the word of God. A renewed mind will enable the church to test and evaluate the issues it faces in Roman society as well as discern God's will. No promises are made that the church would be given direct revelation of God's will in the way Paul had experienced. The believers would discover the sort of life that God wanted them to live as they listened to the Scriptures being explained when they met together under the ministry of gifts given to the church.

It is likely that Paul speaks of the renewing of the church's mind in contrast to what he has said in Rom 1:28 about those living "in the flesh": "since they did not think it worthwhile to retain the knowledge of God, he gave them over to a depraved mind, to do what ought not to be done."[12] The renewing of the church's mind, therefore, is a rediscovering of God's perspective by a community of people who value the retention of his word and values. The effectiveness of a church that is renewed in this way is described by Paul in his letter to the Philippian church: "Do everything without complaining and arguing, so that you may become blameless and pure, children of God without fault in

---

10. There could also be a literal element to "the world," creation being redeemed through the death of Christ by the God who loves it. See Rom 8:18–25.

11. For Paul's use of "flesh," see Excursus F: Sin in the Theology of Paul, page 203–25.

12. See Peterson, "Worship," 271–88.

a crooked and depraved generation, in which you shine like stars in the universe as you hold out the word of life" (Phil 2:14–16a).

Paul describes God's will as "good, pleasing and perfect." Some see this statement to speak of Paul's conviction that there is a perfect, unique plan for the life of every Christian. If Paul believed this, supporting texts would be needed to confirm this view. However in this statement he is addressing the church. This is clearly indicated by his urging of the Roman believers to σώματα ὑμῶν (somata humōn) "offer themselves" ("your bodies"). By doing this, the church will come to know God's perfect will.

I would question whether there is an individual plan for a believer's life. Verses that are usually appealed to in support of such a conviction are not normally about the experience of the individual but of the church. The "plan" is for the people of God collectively, and it is the responsibility of each Christian to strive to fulfill his part in it. God's will is that the community will fulfill its role as a servant of the Lord, bringing knowledge of him to those who are in darkness.[13]

Statements which indicate that the will of God may be known are found elsewhere in Paul's writings (1 Thess 5:18; Eph 5:17; Col 3:15). When it is remembered that these letters are addressed to churches and not individuals, "his will" is found to have a corporate perspective. The letters speak of the churches' corporate experience of the peace of God as evidence of his will being revealed. (We have already noted that this corporate experience is reflected in λατρείαν ὑμῶν [latreian humōn] "your reasonable [or logical] service," where "your" is plural and "reasonable service" is singular). In other words, it is a corporate act of worship.[14]

The plan is for the people of God as a whole, and it is the responsibility of each Christian to seek to fulfill his part in the corporate plan so that the community will be a faithful servant of the Lord, bringing the knowledge of God to those who are in darkness, under the control of Satan, and living in the flesh. Just as God spoke to Moses "Speak to the entire assembly of Israel and say unto them: 'Be holy because I, the LORD your God, am holy'" (Lev 19:2), so Paul speaks to the Roman church. Just as all the children of Israel were asked to be holy, so every member of the Roman congregation had to put the teaching into action and live out the challenge before the pagan world.

The question must be asked: "How does the church know God's will?" First, his will can be known from the Scriptures (Ps 119:7–112; Prov 3:5; Rom 15:4). The Scriptures make clear what God's plan is for his people and it is in them that we find how the church was led in its mission in the early years. Although Paul says that Christ is the end of the law for those who believe (Rom 10:4), it is clear that he constantly referred to the OT and used it as an inspired tool as he taught the early church. Second, his will can be known through the Holy Spirit who guides and prompts the church to fulfill her mission (Acts 13:2; 16:7). In addition to these foundational means of knowing God's will, there is the counsel of mature believers who are able to give advice in the light of Scripture and their knowledge of the leadings of the Holy Spirit in similar circumstances. However, these

13. See Friesen and Maxson, *Decision*, for an excellent discussion.

14. The corporate dimension of the argument is noted by Witherington, *Romans*, 297–98. He rightly says that the ethics that follow are about the community's behavior.

"secondary means" are subjective in nature and can easily be misinterpreted. Because of this, secondary means must never be contrary to the clear message of Scripture.

12:3 For by the grace given me I say to every one of you: Do not think of yourself more highly than you ought, but rather think of yourself with sober judgment, in accordance with the measure of faith God has given you. The direction of the appeal changes in this verse, for Paul now addresses the individual believers using his apostolic status: "For by the grace given me I say . . ."

In his appeal to the believers, Paul is effectively saying: "If apostles are called not to become conceited, then so are you." Elsewhere, Paul highlights the danger of people having over-inflated opinions of themselves. Such people are:"arrogant and boastful . . . they know God's righteous decree that those who do such things deserve death" (Rom 1:30, 32) and he also says that an overseer: "must not be a recent convert, or he may become conceited and fall under the same judgment as the devil" (1 Tim 3:6). Conceit is a serious sin. It was the root of Satan's rebellion, for in aspiring to be like God, pride entered his heart.

Exercising an over-inflated self-opinion is a sin that is all too easy to commit and Paul felt obligated to write to the congregation about this sensitive matter. Seducing Christians to seek their own advancement at the expense of others is one of Satan's most effective ploys. When writing to the church in Philippi, Paul urged the believers: "Do nothing out of selfish ambition or vain conceit, but in humility consider others better than yourselves. . . . Your attitude should be the same as that of Christ Jesus" (Phil 2:3, 5).

God is not as concerned about our gifts as about his grace being manifest in our lives. Conceited Christians can so easily become Absaloms in their local churches (2 Sam 15:1–4), despising and passing judgment on church leaders. Often this sort of criticism comes from hearts that have failed to think of themselves with sober judgment and where the interests of others are subjugated to their own. Perhaps Paul had heard reports about such believers in the church in Rome and was concerned about the damage that they could do to its witness (Rom 14:10). Perhaps he had in mind the bringing together of the Jews and Gentiles in the birth of the Roman church and was appealing to the two communities not to think more highly of themselves than they should. He goes on in the letter to say: "Live in harmony with one another. Do not be proud, but be willing to associate with people of low position. Do not be conceited" (Rom 12:16). Certainly, this understanding maintains the corporate dimension of the letter.

The reference to "the measure of faith" could be understood in one of three possible ways. First, the measure of faith could refer to the amount of faith or trust that a person has. If this is what Paul meant, he is in danger of driving vulnerable believers to continual self-analysis and deprecation, particularly in the presence of those with faith to "move mountains."

Second, the measure of faith could refer to the degree of faithfulness that the believers have, for that is how faith is evident. If this is correct, then Paul is writing that the believers ought to assess themselves in light of their commitment to Jesus Christ.

Without such commitment, their gifts might prove to be a liability leading to boast-fulness and conceit. This sort of meaning is behind Paul's warning to Timothy not to appoint a young, unproved convert—no matter how talented—to the role of overseer or elder as he may become conceited and fall under judgment (1 Tim 3:6). Sadly, history is strewn with examples of those who once ran well as young Christians but who were "promoted" within their churches too early. This was something that Paul feared could even happen to himself (1 Cor 9:27).

Third, the measure of faith could refer to zeal for the Gospel. Paul uses it in this way in his second letter to the Corinthians, where he says:

> We do not dare to classify or compare ourselves with some who commend them-selves. When they measure themselves by themselves and compare themselves with themselves, they are not wise. We, however, will not boast beyond proper limits, but will confine our boasting to the field God has assigned to us, a field that reaches even to you. We are not going too far in our boasting, as would be the case if we had not come to you, for we did get as far as you with the gospel of Christ. Neither do we go beyond our limits by boasting of work done by others. Our hope is that, as your faith continues to grow, our area of activity among you will greatly expand, so that we can preach the gospel in the regions beyond you. For we do not want to boast about work already done in another man's territory. But, "Let him who boasts boast in the Lord." For it is not the one who commends himself who is approved, but the one whom the Lord commends. (2 Cor 10:12–18)

If this is the correct meaning, Paul is encouraging the believers to measure them-selves in the light of the sacrifice they have made for the sake of the Gospel. Such people know, of course, that the sacrifice is never adequate when compared to the one made to save them from sin. But lest there be any who might boast about his opportunities for service, Paul goes on to expand his teaching on the body, its gifts, and the honor given to its members. He does this to put every form of Christian service into its right perspective.

12:4 Just as each of us has one body with many members, and these members do not all have the same function. Paul now prepares to tell the Roman believers how they can make sober judgments of themselves. He is going to remind them of the gifts God has given them. It will be through their ministry that the church will know how to renew her mind. Once again, he draws their attention to the corporate reality of their situation. No gift is given for the recipient's sake but for the benefit of the believing community.

Paul has used the imagery of the body to describe the church in his first letter to the Corinthians (1 Cor 12, 14). "Body of Christ" imagery comes naturally from the concept of the divine marriage, which—as we have seen—is threaded throughout the argument of the letter to the Romans. The church is the "bride of Christ." Just as the body of a bride belongs to her husband, the church (the new covenant community) becomes the body of Christ. Note that the same language is used in Eph 5:25–26, the background of which is clearly marital and new exodus.

Paul not only applies this imagery to the worldwide church but also to the local church. He sees each believing community to be the witnessing "body of Christ" in its particular locality (1 Cor 1:2; 1 Thess 1:1). In preparation for using "body of Christ" imagery, Paul reminds the believers of the makeup of the human body. He will soon use this analogy to illustrate the corporate body, the church—to which they belong.

Paul's initial point is that there is diversity among the members of the human body, each member having a particular role in its healthy functioning. It is obvious to all that the body will be impeded in health and vitality if certain of the observable members fail—eyes no longer seeing, ears no longer hearing, tongue no longer speaking, etc.

12:5 So in Christ we who are many form one body, and each member belongs to all the others. Paul then applies this simple illustration to the church, which is comprised of many believers to form one body, and just as in the human body, there is diversity among its members. This diversity is fundamental to the understanding of the status and dignity of individual believers. In 1 Cor 12 and 14. Paul argues this principle more fully, his main thrust being that hidden parts of the body are often the most important while obvious parts, despite attracting the greatest attention, are of less consequence for its ongoing maintenance. It is more disastrous if the brain malfunctions than if an eye is lost.

Paul stresses the unity of the local body of Christ. He does not write that each member belongs to Christ, which they obviously do by virtue of being "in Christ," but that "each member belongs to all the others." This is a beautiful way of expressing a church's interdependence and unity. Gifts are given for the building up of the local body of Christ. Although given to individuals, they are not for their blessing but for the benefit of the whole body.

Many believers think that they have been denied gifts; but this is not so. All gifts given to the church are for the sake of all. They are given in order that everyone can be built up so that, corporately, believers can progress in an understanding of God's purposes and love to the end that he will be glorified in the church.

A believer's transformation—making him more like Christ—is not an individualistic matter any more than it was an individualistic concern for the Jew to make the pilgrimage from exile back to the promised land. His return was only achievable when he was part of the pilgrim community. Individually, it was highly unlikely that his return from Babylon could be achieved, but corporately it was possible.

So this transformation is experienced in the individual believer as he recognizes that he goes on a pilgrimage to the heavenly home with other believers in the church. Together they encourage each other as they benefit from the gifts God has given them. In Paul's thinking, being renewed in the image of Christ is a corporate concept of the church becoming like its savior (Eph 4:20–24; Col 3:10).

12:6 We have different gifts, according to the grace given us. If a man's gift is prophesying, let him use it in proportion to his faith. In v. 3, Paul spoke of the grace that had been given to him. Now he applies the giving of grace to the Roman church. He is clearly concerned that the believers grasp the truth that there are different gifts bestowed on believers in the church through God's grace. A failure to appreciate this can lead to divisions as a result of petty jealousies and rivalries.

Many Christian fellowships have been divided over gifts because of pride, jealousy, and hurt. The danger of division is avoided when it is understood that God has given gifts according to his will. They are not inherited talents whose distribution among men is governed by genetic makeup. However, despite these gifts having a divine origin, churches often select leaders on the basis of talent, personality, status, and family, seeing these as indicative of divine gifting. Such appointments may place churches in danger of damage from pride and ambition.

Paul begins to specify gifts that are given by the Spirit. He does not mention that these gifts are the gifts of the Spirit as he does in his first letter to the Corinthians (1 Cor 12:8–11). Here, the gifts are simply the gifts that God has bestowed. This is an indication of Paul's "Trinitarian" understanding—a term that he, of course, does not use. He often attributes OT descriptions of God to either Christ or the Spirit (e.g., 1 Cor 8:6; 2 Cor 13:14. See also Phil 2:10–12, where the quotation from Isa 45:23b originally applied to Yahweh).

When Paul encourages the gift of prophecy, he qualifies its use by saying "let him use it in proportion to his faith." This exhortation is unlikely to refer to the confidence the recipient has in his powers of oratory as that would promote self-confidence, leading to arrogance. The term "faith" is likely to mean "faithfulness," as discussed earlier. A church should only encourage the gifts of it members when it sees them living in faithfulness to Christ. The exercising of gifts without the appropriate grace leads a church into a spiritual minefield.

Prophesying was clearly a common ministry in the early church. The NT prophets' responsibility was to apply the word of God. This had been the function of the prophets in the OT. They did not bring a new revelation to Israel but constantly reminded them of the covenant of which they were part. That is not to deny that they occasionally predicted the future or that they developed themes that had previously been known only in part. However, their main task was to remind the people that because of the covenant, Yahweh made claims upon them. Their preaching was essentially a reiteration of the promises and warnings of the covenant in which Israel was urged to walk obediently (Isa 40:1–5; Jer 34:1–10; Hos 14:1–3; Amos 5:4–5).

This was no less the function of the NT prophets. Their gift was to direct the church to the OT Scriptures, which spoke prophetically about the coming age. They were able to draw from those Scriptures the obligations of the new covenant and to urge the church to fulfill them. In this, God would be glorified; and, in turn, he would respond in blessing. Although the church was given teachers (v. 7), the prophets' ministry also included teaching. It is possible that the prophet spoke with more authority—the Spirit of God empowering his message. Because of this, the word of God came to the people with a sense of "the Holy Spirit says" (Acts 13:2; 21:11).

It is clear from the first Corinthian letter that Paul thought highly of the gift of prophecy—a gift which he said was for believers (1 Cor 14:22): "But everyone who prophesies speaks to men for their strengthening, encouragement and comfort . . . he who prophesies edifies the church" (1 Cor 14:4).

12:7 If it is serving, let him serve; if it is teaching, let him teach. The gift of serving is the next gift listed by Paul. While it is difficult to know exactly what he had in mind regarding this gift (and in 1 Cor 12:5 he states that there are different kinds of service), it is of interest that Paul placed serving between prophesying and teaching, suggesting that its place in church life was of great importance.

It has often been thought that "serving" refers to the meeting of practical needs within the local church and amongst needy believers in other churches. When he wrote the letter, Paul was on his way to Jerusalem with a gift for those who were suffering from poverty and he describes his anticipated visit as being "in the service of the saints" (Rom 15:25). In his first letter to the Corinthians, Paul commended to them the household of Stephanas because of their "service to the saints" (1 Cor 16:15–17).

The role of deacons in the early church has often been linked with the gift of "serving" (1 Tim 3:10, 13) as has the general expression of concern that believers show for one another within a fellowship (Rom 12:9–11; Gal 5:13). In his letter to the Ephesians, Paul says that apostles, prophets, evangelists, pastors, and teachers have been given to the church "to prepare God's people for works of service, so that the body of Christ may be built up" (Eph 4:12). While we shall consider the outworking of "works of service" later in the chapter, an alternative understanding of the gift of "serving" may be of interest.

At the opening of his letter, Paul assured the believers of his prayers by writing these words: "God, whom I serve with my whole heart in preaching the gospel of his Son, is my witness how constantly I remember you in my prayers" (Rom 1:9–10). Moreover, in Rom 15 he wrote: "I am a minister of Christ Jesus to the Gentiles with the priestly duty of proclaiming the gospel of God . . . Therefore I glory in Christ Jesus in my service to God" (Rom 15:16–17). It is, therefore, possible that Paul saw the gift of serving—the second gift in his Romans list—to be the proclamation of the gospel, i.e., the gift of evangelism (Eph 4:11–12).

Support for this view is found in the letter to the Corinthians. Paul—who sees his work as priestly ("serving at the altar" rather than at tables)—wrote that those who preach the Gospel should receive their living by it (1 Cor 9:13–14). In his second letter to the church, he reminded the Corinthians that he had served them by "preaching the gospel of God" (2 Cor 11:7–8). Finally, the letter to Timothy states: The glorious gospel of the blessed God was entrusted to me. I thank Christ Jesus our Lord, who has given me strength, that he considered me faithful, appointing me to his service" (1 Tim 1:11–12).

It is clear that those who did the work of evangelism exercised other gifts in the church. Philip—one of the seven deacons in Acts 6:1–6—became known as "Philip the evangelist" in his town of Caesarea (Acts 21:8–9) and Timothy—who was urged to devote himself to preaching and teaching in Ephesus (1 Tim 4:13–14)—was encouraged to "do the work of an evangelist" (2 Tim 4:5). Thus, if the gift of service is evangelism, Paul sees the proclamation of the gospel to be one of the foundational gifts to the church because of its prominent position in his list—a position not so suitable for its traditional meaning.

Teaching is the next gift to be mentioned. It may refer to the catechizing of new converts, enabling their understanding of basic Christian truths, or to its more public ministry to the gathered church. Whatever the form of teaching received by the Roman church, Paul commends the believers' whole-hearted obedience to it. As a result of teaching, they had been set free from sin and had become servants to righteousness (Rom 6:17–18). Paul appreciated how vital teaching was for the health of the church. It would prepare the congregation for service, building its members up in the knowledge of God and bringing them to maturity (Eph 4:11–14).

Teaching was a gift that the apostles exercised when they taught the young church in the days following Pentecost (Acts 2:42). Indeed, they recognized the danger of neglecting the gift when the practical needs of the infant church pressed in upon them. So, after the church had chosen seven wise, spirit-filled men from the congregation and the apostles had set them apart to ensure that the social needs of the believers were not overlooked, they gave themselves to prayer and teaching. The results were remarkable! (Acts 6:1–7).

Like the apostles, many Christian leaders feel the pressure of being expected to do a wide range of tasks in their congregations to the neglect of their teaching ministries. The consequence of yielding to such pressure is that believers are not well taught and are left exposed to false teachings. As a consequence, the word does not spread in the locality and the leaders are left exhausted. Even the Roman congregation, with its obedient assent to the teaching it received, had to be warned against its exposure to false teaching (Rom 16:17–19).

Those who have responsibility for teaching in a church need mentors like Jethro, who, on drawing alongside Moses, saw the pressure he was under and suggested the appointment of officials to lighten his load. Moses was then free to teach decrees and laws to the people as well as to settle major disputes (Exod 18:17–26). The NT shows that church leaders need to be part of a leadership team, which provides a forum for mutual support and understanding within the church. So we find Paul urging Titus to appoint elders in every town (Titus 1:5). Such men, like the apostles, corporately bore the load, each contributing his particular gift(s) to the building up of the church for which they were responsible. The support, understanding, and mutual encouragement necessary in church leadership cannot be provided by inter-church fraternals alone, however valuable they may be. The NT does not recognize the "one-man ministry" that characterizes many churches. The "minister" is the church—the people of God—and it is their collective gifts that make Christian service possible. The church, of course, requires leadership to oversee the ministry in which the believing community is engaged, but this leadership is the community's servant rather that its dictator.

Timothy was told not to neglect his gifts of preaching and teaching but to be diligent in their use. He was also told to watch his life and doctrine closely. It is clear that "the knife can be blunted" through sin and laziness, to the detriment of the preacher/teacher and the congregation he serves.

12:8 If it is encouraging, let him encourage; if it is contributing to the needs of others, let him give generously; if it is leadership, let him govern diligently; if it is showing mercy, let him do it cheerfully. Paul now urges those in the congregation with a gift of encouragement to exercise their gift. The Greek noun παρακλησις (*paraklēsis*) allows for this to mean "bringing comfort," and this was how the term was used in some NT passages (Acts 15:22–31; Eph 6:21–22). It is the same term that Jesus used when he described the ministry of the Holy Spirit: ἄλλον παράκλητον δώσει ὑμῖν (*allon paraklēton dōsei humin*) "He will give you another Counselor" (John 14:16).

Paul himself benefited from encouragement. Barnabas whose name means "the son of encouragement," befriended Paul as a new convert, introducing him to the leadership of the church in Jerusalem (Acts 9:27). Moreover, he was Paul's co-worker on his first missionary journey during their time in Antioch (Acts 11:26). In his second letter to the Corinthian church, Paul told the believers that he and Timothy had been "comforted" by Titus and the church in Corinth at a very difficult time in their ministry (2 Cor 7:5–7), and, in a sensitive letter to Philemon, he expressed his gratitude for the encouragement he had received from Philemon's love for the saints (Phlm 4–7).

But is this encouragement and comfort what Paul had in mind when writing about the gift of encouragement? It is possible that the gift of encouragement was more a gift of exhortation: "he who exhorts, in exhortation" (Rom 12:8 NKJ), the Greek allowing for this meaning of the term. This would fit neatly into Paul's list as it is the gift that follows prophesying, serving (evangelizing), and teaching—all gifts concerned with the ministry of the word.

Encouraging by means of exhortation can be done by members of the congregation. For example, the believers in Thessalonika were urged to "encourage each other" about the coming of the Lord (1 Thess 4:13–18; 5:11). However, it is probable that the gift refers to a more public ministry of encouragement (Acts 13:14–52; 14:21–22; 1 Cor 14:3; 1 Thess 2:1–3, where "appeal" [NIV] is "encouragement" or "exhortation;" 2 Tim 4:2; Titus 1:7–9). The following is written to Timothy: "Until I come, devote yourself to the public reading of Scripture, to preaching and to teaching" (1 Tim 4:13). In this NIV translation, "preaching" (παρακλήσει *paraklēsei* "comfort") would be better translated "encouraging" or "exhorting." To conclude, if the gift of encouragement is a public ministry, its exercising in a congregation would reflect the ministry of the Godhead to his people—God encouraging them through the Scriptures he has given for their edification (Rom 15:4–5).

The next gift in the list—"contributing to the poor"—is usually seen to refer to the support of needy believers. Paul's desire is that this gift be exercised "generously." The Greek carrying the idea of giving without reservation. The idea is of a bountiful generosity that springs from a desire to help those in need. Paul uses the verb μεταδιδωμι (*metadidōmi*)—which can be translated "impart," "share," or "give"—on three other occasions in his letters. On one occasion, he uses the sense as translated by the NIV: "He who has been stealing must steal no longer, but must work, doing something useful with his own hands, that he may have something to share with those in need" (Eph 4:28).

However, in 1 Thessalonians and Romans, the term is used differently: "We loved you so much that we were delighted to share with you not only the gospel of God but our lives as well, because you had become so dear to us . . . For you know that we dealt with each of you as a father deals with his children, encouraging, comforting and urging you to live lives worthy of God" (1 Thess 2:8, 11–12). Here, Paul uses the term "share" to describe the proclamation of Christ as well as the giving of himself and his co-workers.

He uses the term at the beginning of his letter to the Romans where the NIV translates it as "impart": "I long to see you so that I may impart to you some spiritual gift to make you strong—that is, that you and I may be mutually encouraged by each other's faith . . . That is why I am so eager to μεταδιδωμι (metadidōmi) "share/preach the Gospel . . ." also to you who are at Rome" (Rom 1:11–12, 15). Paul seems to be using the term to speak of his personal imparting of the good news, to the end that he and the believers would be encouraged in their faith.

The term translated "to make strong" in Rom 1:11 στηριδω (stērizō) can be translated "to establish" and it is used by Paul at the close of his letter: "Now to him who is able to establish you by my Gospel and the proclamation of Jesus Christ " (Rom 16:25a). This verse together with Rom 1:11 suggests that it was Paul's desire that the Roman believers would be encouraged and established by God in their faith when they received Paul's spiritual gift, that is, his ministry of the word, which he would impart to them or share with them when he came to visit them personally.

So, the phrase under consideration in Rom 12:8 would perhaps be better understood as "he who imparts or shares the things of God and himself, with the result that believers are encouraged and established in their faith." This understanding reflects the ministry of Jesus to his disciples. He shared with them the good news and gave himself for their blessing and establishment.

Paul says in Rom 12:8 that this gift of "imparting," "sharing" or "contributing to the needs of others" must be done "generously." This term ἁπλότητι (aplotēti) also means (with) singleness, simplicity, sincerity, and frankness. It richly describes aspects of effective ministry to believers and personal work among them. In conclusion, it seems possible that the gift of "contributing to the needs of others" is pastoral ministry (Eph 4:12), and a believer gifted with this spiritual gift to the church is a pastor. Elsewhere Paul has written:

> It was he who gave some to be apostles, some to be prophets, some to be pastors and teachers, to prepare God's people for works of service, so that the body of Christ may be built up until we all reach unity in the faith and in the knowledge of the Son of God and become mature, attaining to the whole measure of the fullness of Christ. (Eph 4:11–13)

Next Paul addresses himself to the leaders of the congregation, writing to them that, if leadership is their gift, they must "govern diligently." It is no surprise that leadership is listed with gifts that benefit the work of the Gospel in the local church. Its diligent exercise is crucial, as ineffective leadership results in an undisciplined church where lives are damaged. Extreme outcomes of bad leadership were on display in Corinth where there was toleration of incest (1 Cor 5:1–2),[15] an involvement in occult practices (1 Cor 10:21–22), a lack of propriety in worship (1 Cor 11:2–16; 14:33b–35), unresolved divisions

---

15. Taking a stepmother (as the verse implies) is a prohibited relationship but is not strictly incest. Incest legally applies to one's own birth mother.

(1 Cor 11:18), disrespect for the Lord's Supper (1 Cor 11:17–34), and disorderly worship. Crucially, there was a denial of the resurrection (1 Cor 15:12–18). Understandably, these issues necessitated Paul's detailed instructions to correct (1 Cor 14:26–33).

The leadership of a local church was the province of elders who were set apart for the task (Titus 1:5). Their appointment was not to be made in haste as the scrutiny of their lives was essential (1 Tim 3:1–7; 5:22; Titus 1:6–9). Their work was extremely demanding. In writing to the Thessalonian believers, Paul urged them to "respect those who work hard among you . . . Hold them in the highest regard in love because of their work" (1 Thess 5:12–13). It was demanding because their ministry involved preaching and teaching—with all of the resulting pastoral needs of people seeking to apply what they had heard—as well as the oversight of the church's affairs (1 Tim 5:17; Titus 1:9). In addition to these demands, all their dealings had to be conducted with a godly attitude (1 Pet 5:1–3).

The comments I cited from Paul's Corinthian letter give some insight into a church's oversight. When the congregation gathered for worship its meetings had to be ordered and organized, the practicing of spiritual gifts had to be controlled—and the presence of gossiping women had to be managed. The Lord's Supper had to be celebrated in a worthy fashion and ungodly believers had to be warned and disciplined. In addition to all this, elders had to vigorously refute those who opposed sound doctrine (Titus 1:9, 11, 13) while carrying, at the same time, the worry of potential accusation (1 Tim 5:19).

The term that Paul uses for "leader" (Rom 12:8), προϊστάμενος (proistamenos), can also be translated "being over," "superintending," and "presiding"—and it was God's household over which the elders had to exercise leadership (1 Tim 3:15). The same term that is applied to an overseer's and deacon's management of their homes and families in 1 Tim 3:4,12.

As Paul appreciated from the situation in the Corinthian church, leadership could be of poor quality. So he urges the leaders in the church in Rome to exercise their gift "diligently" (NIV). The term translated "diligently" can be translated "eagerly," "enthusiastically," and "zealously." It can also be translated "speedily" and "hastily." Perhaps in choosing this term, Paul had in mind the re-building of the temple in Jerusalem during Ezra's time: "The work is being carried on with diligence and is making rapid progress" (Ezra 5:8). Paul would have loved to have heard a similar report from the leaders of all the churches because he would then know that the lives of believers and the churches to which they belonged were being built up.

Finally, in the Romans verse under consideration Paul writes to the believers "if it is showing mercy, let him do it cheerfully." It is difficult to be certain who Paul is referring to as recipients of mercy, what the gift entailed, and who exercised it.

The term translated "showing mercy" can also mean "has or shows mercy or pity." Paul used this term when speaking of the Lord's mercy in 1 Cor 7:25, and in Phil 2:27 when speaking of God's mercy to the sick Epaphroditus. The Romans text is Paul's only reference to mercy being extended by and to a believer.

The same term is used in Matt 5:7 when Jesus promises that God will show mercy to the merciful, and in Matt 18:33 when the wicked servant in the parable was rebuked for not showing mercy, Jesus equating mercy with "forgiving your brother from the heart." In addition, Jesus spoke of the rich man, in torment in hell, asking Abraham to show mercy to him (v. 24).

The Phil 2 text cited above, however, informs us that mercy was shown by God to Epaphroditus and to Paul without the context of forgiveness. God took pity on Paul's very sick companion who had travelled on behalf of the Philippian church to meet the apostle's needs. In doing this God had also shown mercy to Paul, who would have been heartbroken, had Epaphroditus died. Clearly in this case the showing of mercy was not about God forgiving the two men but caring for them in their frailty.

So, while the term can be used to speak of forgiveness, it is also used to speak of compassion to the needy and it is likely that this meaning is the context for "showing mercy" in Rom 12:8. This gift would have been exercised, at the very least, by deacons in the church—men who were set apart for the task of dealing with pressing social concerns in the fellowship so that the prophets, evangelists, teachers, pastors, and elders could give full attention to exercising their gifts (Acts 6:1–6; 1 Tim 3:8–13). Perhaps Paul had the deacons in mind when he wrote this to the church in Rome.

He urged that the gift of showing mercy be carried out with "cheerfulness." This reflects the wisdom of the book of Proverbs, which says: "a cheerful heart is good medicine, but a crushed spirit dries up the bones" (Prov 17:22). The term "cheerfully" ἱλαρότητι (hilaroteti) means "with gladness," "with graciousness," "without reluctance," and even "with hilarity"—qualities and attitudes that would be invaluable to deacons carrying out their role of "showing mercy" to the needy!

In conclusion, it is possible that in Rom 12:6–8 Paul encourages the prophets, evangelists, teachers, preachers, pastors, elders, and deacons to exercise their gifts in the church in Rome. Like Timothy, they would probably exercise more than one gift, fulfilling their calling so that together they would "prepare God's people for works of service, so that the body of Christ may be built up until all reach unity in the faith and in the knowledge of the Son of God" (Eph 4:12–13) What a powerful, public display of a living sacrifice to God in Rome that would be!

THE MESSIAH KING AND HIS PEOPLE'S CHARACTER

LOVE MUST BE sincere. Hate what is evil; cling to what is good. Be devoted to one another in brotherly love. Honor one another above yourselves. Never be lacking in zeal, but keep your spiritual fervor, serving the Lord. Be joyful in hope, patient in affliction, faithful in prayer. Share with God's people who are in need. Practice hospitality. Bless those who persecute you; bless and do not curse. Rejoice with those who rejoice; mourn with those who mourn. Live in harmony with one another. Do not be proud, but be willing to associate with people of low position. Do not be conceited. Do not repay anyone evil for evil. Be careful to do what is right in the eyes of everybody. If it is possible, as far as it depends on you, live at peace with everyone. Do not take revenge, my friends, but leave room for God's wrath, for it is written: "It is mine to avenge; I will repay," says the Lord. On the contrary: "If your enemy is hungry, feed him; if he is thirsty, give him something to drink. In doing this, you will heap burning coals on his head." Do not be overcome by evil, but overcome evil with good. (Romans 12:9–21)

In Rom 12:9–21, Paul returns to his concern that the believers in Rome live holy lives as priests of the living God (v.1), so that they can offer to him a church that is "a living sacrifice, holy and pleasing." He has urged all of the believers to evaluate their lives seriously and honestly (Rom 12:3; Matt 7:1–5), reminding them of the gifts that God has given the church (Rom 12:6–8). As they benefit from these, Paul hopes that the corporate body of believers will rise to the challenge to renew its mind.

In the passage we are now considering, Paul begins to tell the church how it can stop conforming to the world and become a transformed, renewed, believing community. His appeal echoes the teaching of Jesus in his Sermon on the Mount (Matt 5–7).[16] Indeed, it seems possible that Paul applied the teaching of Jesus to his disciples to the context of the local church (Matt 7:24–27; Eph 2:22).

The following table compares the parallel themes found in the Gospel and the letter.

---

16. See, Fitzmyer, *Romans*, 652. Barrett, *Romans*, 240, considers Paul to be using a Semitic source. This probably originated in the very early church because of the presence of participles instead of imperatives. Further support for dependence on Matthew has been provided by Stuart Laurer, "Written." His case is that the Gospel of Matthew was a standard text in the early church. It was used by the apostles and left with the churches they established as an authoritative reference source. Laurer's work focuses on the saying in 1 Cor 4:6: "Do not go beyond what is written." His conclusions suggest that Matthew's Gospel was distributed widely throughout the apostolic ministry, a conclusion that fits uncomfortably with the prevailing documentary hypothesis.

Romans 12:9–21	Matthew 5–7
Theme: "Love must be sincere" or "Sincere Love."	Theme: "Love you neighbor as yourself"
v. 10 Hate what is evil; cling to what is good.	If your right hand causes you to sin. Blessed are the pure in heart 5:8; 5:29–30; 6:19–21, 24.
v. 10 Be devoted to one another in brotherly love.	You are the salt of the earth (salt being a symbol of lasting concord) (5:13; 7:12)
v. 11 Honour ("honor") one another above yourselves.	Blessed are the poor in spirit (5:3)
v. 12 Never be lacking in zeal, but keep your spiritual fervour ("fervor"), serving the Lord.	Blessed are those who hunger and thirst after righteousness (5:6; 6:33)
v. 12 Be joyful in hope,	Rejoice and be glad because great is your reward in heaven (5:12)
v. 12 patient in affliction,	Blessed are you when people insult you (5:10–12, 38–42)
v. 12 faithful in prayer.	And when you pray, do not be like the hypocrites (6:5–15)
v. 13 Share with God's people who are in need. Practice hospitality.	Blessed are the merciful (5:7; 6:1–4)
v. 14 Bless those who persecute you; bless and do not curse.	Pray for those who persecute you (5:44)
v. 16 Rejoice with those who rejoice; mourn (weep) with those who mourn (weep).	Blessed are those who mourn (5:4)
v. 16 Live in harmony with one another.	Anyone who is angry with his brother will be subject to judgment (5:21–26)
v. 16 Do not be proud, but be willing to associate with people of low position. Do not be conceited	Blessed are the meek (5:5, 22b)
v. 17 Do not repay anyone evil for evil	Do not resist (5:39)
v. 17 Be careful to do what is right in the eyes of everybody	You are the light of the world (5:14–16)
v. 18–19 If it is possible, as far as it depends on you, live at peace with everyone. Do not take revenge, my friends, but leave room for God's wrath, for it is written: "It is mine to avenge; I will repay," says the Lord.	Blessed are the peacemakers (or peace-lovers 5:7, 23–24) Every tree that does not bear good fruit is cut down and thrown into the fire (7:17)
v. 20 On the contrary: "If your enemy is hungry, feed him; if he is thirsty, give him something to drink. In doing this, you will heap burning coals on his head."	Love your enemies and pray for those who persecute you (5:44, 40–42)
v. 21 Do not be overcome by evil, but overcome evil with good.	If you forgive men when they sin against you (6:14)

Paul begins his exhortation by introducing its theme—"Sincere Love." His desire is that the greatest fruit of the Spirit will be demonstrated in the believers' lives. This will transform the church in Rome, affecting those within the fellowship and those outside in the wider community.

When the believers heard this passage read, they would have taken from it a challenging pattern for individual living. While Paul's exhortation in chapter 12 is to individuals in the congregation, it must be remembered that his emphasis throughout the letter has been the church—the body of believers. Although his desire was that the lives of the individual believers would be built up (Rom 15:2; 1 Thess 5:11), his greatest desire was that the local church would be built up to become a "dwelling in which God lives by his Spirit" (Eph 2:22).

12:9 Love what is sincere. Hate what is evil; cling to what is good. As previously mentioned, Paul begins his exhortation with what seems to be its theme: "Sincere Love." The adjective "sincere" ἀνυπόκριτος (*anupokritos*) "without hypocrisy," is related to the verb ὑποκρινεσθαι (*hypokrinesthai*) "to answer." It was used to speak of the reply an actor gave on stage and was associated with the pretence of the performer in his role. Affection that is a pretense of friendship is odious (1 John 4:20–21). It is the very opposite of Christian love, which must be the expression of genuine concern.

In his letter to the Galatians, Paul wrote that love ἀγάπη (*agapē*) was one of the fruits of the Spirit (Gal 5:22), and in his first letter to the Corinthians, he described the transformed attitudes of people who display this love (1 Cor 13:4–8a). In 1 Cor 13:13, he says that it is the greatest spiritual fruit that we can exhibit, reflecting the love that God has for his people (Rom 5:8). Indeed, it is the essence of God himself, for he is its source (Rom 5:8; 1 John 4:7–19). So, how do the believers in Rome love in sincerity? Paul cuts straight to the chase by telling them to engage their wills. They are to "hate what is evil."

God's standard is clear—he hates evil (Amos 5:14–15; Ps 97:10). Those who would have fellowship with him must share his concern and values. Despite the values of those around, the Roman believers must be concerned about pleasing God alone (Rom 12:21). This is the only time that Paul—or any NT writer—tells believers to "hate" evil, ἀποô τυγοῦντες (*apostugountes*) being better translated "abhor." As mentioned, it is a position that God himself takes and which he wants to see his people follow. After bringing the children of Israel out of Egypt, God comforted them with these words: "I will not abhor you … you will be my people" (Lev 26:11–12). However, they broke covenant with him and his abhorrence of them returned (Lev 26:14–17, 30; Amos 6:8). It is also an attitude that King David displayed. In the psalms, he wrote that he "hated and abhorred falsehood" and he expressed his abhorrence for men who actively rebelled against God (Ps 119:163; Ps 139:19–22).

The believers in Rome were told to abhor evil—the objects of David's abhorrence being examples of the evils they should abhor. Jesus said that men are "unclean" because of the evils that come from within, such as "evil thoughts, sexual immorality, theft, murder, adultery, greed, malice, deceit, lewdness, envy, slander, arrogance and folly" (Mark 7:20–23; Luke 6:45). He also said that his disciples would be the recipients of evil because of their allegiance to him (Matt 5:11).

The Christians in Rome were to abhor evil within their hearts and any expression of it in society. If the church had access to the Gospel of Matthew (as has been suggested), the believers would know from Jesus' Sermon on the Mount that in being recipients of evil as a result of their allegiance to Christ, they must not hate the evil-doers but take encouragement from the fact that persecution will bring blessing.

While hating what is evil, the believers were told to "cling to what is good." The phrase suggests a desperate situation, like a drowning man in a storm clinging to a beam of wood, and feeling so weak that he does not know how he can survive. All he must do is keep on clinging! The problem is that this understanding places all the responsibility on the believer to keep hold of what is good, despite all the pressures that buffet him.

The word translated "cling" can be translated "join oneself to," "join closely together," or "unite." It is the same term used by Paul in 1 Corinthians, where he writes: "Do you not know that he who unites himself with a prostitute is one with her in body? For it is said, 'The two will become one flesh.' But he who unites himself with the Lord is one with him in Spirit" (1 Cor 6:16–17). In light of this usage, perhaps Paul is writing that the Roman believers must abhor evil by changing their allegiance and uniting to what is good. The union is an act of their wills, reflecting the covenant of marriage. The believers are to commit themselves to the Lord and his people.

12:10 Be devoted to one another in brotherly love. Honour one another above yourselves. The exhortation to be devoted to one another in brotherly love is an out-working of sincere love (v. 9). Paul uses φιλαδελφία (*philadelphia*) "brotherly love" in one other letter: "Now about brotherly love we do not need to write to you, for you yourselves have been taught by God to love each other. And in fact you do love all the brothers throughout Macedonia. Yet we urge you, brothers, to do so more and more" (1 Thess 4:9–10).

In his letter to the Romans, Paul's instruction is clearer than the "more and more" of 1 Thess 4:10. He tells the believers to be "devoted" in brotherly love—taking this love to a deeper, more personal, and committed level. The term translated "devoted" is used nowhere else in the Scriptures.

Peter, when writing to the scattered believers, also urged a deepening of love for each other. He recognized the sincerity of their brotherly love but urged them to love "fervently" or "intently" (1 Pet 1:22). His appeal is consistent with Paul's that the believers in Rome, benefiting from the ministry of the Scriptures, make devoted brotherly love a hallmark of the church.

Being devoted to one another is not a directive to accept everything that a fellow Christian does. Such mindless acceptance will not bring glory to God but will be an opportunity for Satan to exploit. God was devoted to the Jewish people throughout the long history of the OT—but that commitment resulted in tough action. He not only spoke against them when they were breaking his commandments but also warned them that he would use the armies of mighty Babylon to wield the sword when they repeat-edly refused to hear and obey his word. So, being devoted to one another may mean the leaders of the church exercising "tough love" in situations where the word of God is being rejected or ignored. Such "tough love" was prescribed by Paul for the church in Corinth when it refused to deal with the case of incest (1 Cor 5–6), and is seen in the warnings that Jesus gave the churches in the book of Revelation (Rev 2:1—3:22).

Paul now tells the believers to "honor one another above yourselves." Honoring one another would have been hard enough for the Jewish and uncircumcised Gentile believers in Rome, but honoring each other above themselves would have seemed well-nigh impossible. Another challenge for the believers would have been the honoring of disadvantaged brethren in the congregation. This would have been particularly challenging for those in leadership positions. However, in his letter to the Corinthians, Paul leaves us in no doubt as to God's wishes in this matter (1 Cor 12:22–26).

It would have been a crushing command for the believers but for the fact that God had sent his Spirit into their hearts (Rom 8:15), bringing with him a different set of values from the ones they had lived by (Rom 8:9, 12–13; Gal 5:16–26). Later, when writing to the church at Philippi, Paul referred to a very early Christian hymn. It shows how the infant church dwelt on the example of Christ's death and how believers drew inspiration to consider others better than themselves.

The hymn has an introduction:

> Do nothing out of selfish ambition or vain conceit, but in humility consider others better than yourselves. Each of you should look not only to your own interests, but also to the interests of others. Your attitude should be the same as that of Christ Jesus.

The hymn follows, focusing on the example of Christ:

> Who, being in the very nature God, did not consider equality with God something to be grasped, but made himself nothing, taking the very nature of a servant, being made in human likeness, And being found in appearance as a man, he humbled himself and became obedient to death—even death on a cross! Therefore God exalted him to the highest place and gave him the name that is above every name, that at the name of Jesus every knee should bow, in heaven and on earth and under the earth, and every tongue confess that Jesus Christ is Lord, to the glory of God the Father. (Phil 2:6–11)

12:11 Never be lacking in zeal, but keep your spiritual fervor, serving the Lord. Paul has just exhorted the believers to be devoted to each other in brotherly love and to honor each other above themselves. He now exhorts them to maintain their zeal.

A believer's first rush of excitement on discovering the glorious reality of God's love can easily become fossilized. An improvement in living standards (resulting from a more disciplined lifestyle) can become the purpose of life and an intellectualization of newfound faith can replace the warmth of first love. The zeal of loving and serving Christ can disappear like the morning dew—it happened to Israel's love for Yahweh (Hos 13:3) and sadly it happens to Christians' love for Christ (Gal 1:6; 2 Tim 4:10; Rev 2:4).

The NIV translation of this verse gives the impression that Paul is exhorting the church to be "zealous."[17] Certainly, being zealous was a characteristic of his people, the Jews. In Rom 10, Paul testifies that the Jews display ζῆλος (zēlos) "zeal" in the defence of their faith (v.2), and in his letter to the Philippians he writes retrospectively of himself, "as for zeal ζῆλος (zēlos) persecuting the church" (Phil 3:6). However, he uses a term here which means "diligence" or "earnestness," ζέοντες (zeontes) translating literally as "boiling in spirit." So, the opening phrase of v.11 would be better translated "never be lacking in diligence or earnestness." Paul uses this term again when writing his second letter to the Corinthians (2 Cor 7:11; 8:7–8) and in all cases it is translated "earnestness" by the NIV translators.

Perhaps Paul is referring to what he has just written—urging the believers to be diligent, with no hint of laziness, in their devoted love and preference for each other. The writer to the Hebrews exhorted the Christians to "keep on loving each other as brothers" (Heb 13:1), having previously written: "God is not unjust; he will not forget your work and the love you have shown him as you have helped his people and continue to help them. We want each of you to show this same diligence to the very end, in order to make your hope sure. We do not want you to become lazy, but to imitate those who through faith and patience inherit what has been promised" (Heb 6:10–12).

As the believers in Rome heard the letter read to them, they heard an exhortation to be "fervent in spirit, serving the Lord" (NKJ—a better translation than NIV). The term fervor ζέοντες (zeontes) can be translated "hot." It is a term that implies passion. The RSV translates it "aglow" in an attempt to portray the passion of the term.

But how can the believers maintain fervor? Paul has given the answer in the earlier part of his letter. By reflecting on who Christ is and what God has done for them through his death their hearts will be moved (Rom 8:1–3). This means that the believers must put themselves under the authority of the Scriptures, for these were written for their instruction (Rom 10:14b;17;15:4).

The call to serve the Lord has a textual variant. Some MSS[18] have δουλευοντες τυ καίρω (douleuontes tu kairō) "serve the hour" instead of κυρίῳ (kyriō) "Lord." The latter is possibly the result of a copyist's confusion of an abbreviation where Kō has been read as Krō.[19]

---

17. The Zealot movement, which emerged out of the Maccabean revolt (167–160 BC), takes its name from this term. Its adherents drew their inspiration from the story of Phinehas, the priest. Burdened with the dishonor brought to God by Israel's idolatry, he slew an Israelite man and a Midianite woman in their blatant act of immorality, thereby staying the wrath of God from destroying Israel: "The LORD said to Moses, 'Phinehas son of Eleazar, the son of Aaron, the priest, has turned my anger away from the Israelites; for he was as zealous as I am for my honour among them, so that in my zeal I did not put an end to them'" (Num 25:10–11). As this story was well-known in Judaism and in the early church, Paul's appeal to be zealous would be heard by many in light of it. Of course, the believers were not to execute judgment in their zeal but to direct people to the one who turned God's wrath away from sinners by his propitiatory death (Rom 3:25–26).

18. D and G.

19. See, Metzger, Text, 187.

12:12 Be joyful in hope, patient in affliction, faithful in prayer. Paul writes to the believers in Rome telling them that they should be "joyful in hope." He has already written sublimely about this theme in the opening verses of chapter 5. Having described the extraordinary access that the believers have to God through Christ (vv. 1–2a), he then explains the hope that galvanizes Christians. He does not exhort the believers to hope, but tells them of the sure and certain hope they have of sharing in the glory of God (Rom 5:2b).

Having explained the sufferings that the church is called to endure as she bears witness to the one who has called her, Paul writes "and hope does not disappoint us because God has poured out his love into our hearts by the Holy Spirit, whom he has given us" (Rom 5:5). Clearly, this hope sustains and empowers the church—it is a hope that is founded in God's love for his people.

Paul will reaffirm the importance of the Scriptures in chapter 15, when he will writes "For everything that was written in the past was written to teach us, so that through endurance and the encouragement of the Scriptures we might have hope" (Rom 15:4). At the close of the chapter, Paul will describe God as being the God of hope who fills the believers with all joy and peace so that they will overflow with hope by the power of the Holy Spirit (Rom 15:13).

In other words, the future for the Roman Christians is so glorious that joy ought to characterize their lives. No matter what happens—and appalling persecution was soon to come—their hope remains a sure certainty. Loss of status, health, wealth, friends, etc. could not affect their certainty, for their inheritance is laid up in heaven (1 Cor 2:9; 1 Pet 1:4–5). Only the Christians in Rome could rejoice in what lay ahead. For everyone else, death would be the entrance into God's presence where they will be judged. For the Christians, it will be altogether different. Instead of this frightening scenario, death will be their glorious entrance into the Lord's presence and into joy unspeakable. The Christians' hope should permeate their lives so that they are characterized by joy (Ps 16:11; John 16:20; Rom 14:17; 15:13; 1 John 1:4).

Paul writes that they should be "patient in affliction." The term "affliction" θλίψις (*thlipsis*) should be translated "tribulation," which has a more serious tone. He had written to them in chapter 5: ". . . we also rejoice in our sufferings (tribulations), because we know that suffering (tribulation) produces perseverance; perseverance, character; and character, hope" (Rom 5:3–4).

Should any of the believers be experiencing tribulation, much of Paul's letter would prove to be an enormous comfort and encouragement. As Paul says earlier in the letter:

> "I consider that our present sufferings (tribulations) are not worth comparing with the glory that will be revealed in us. . . . We ourselves, who have the firstfruits of the Spirit, groan inwardly as we wait eagerly for our adoption as sons, the redemption of our bodies. . . . If we hope for what we do not have, we wait for it patiently. . . . Who shall separate us from the love of Christ? Shall trouble or hardship or persecution or famine or nakedness or danger or sword? . . . No, in all these things we are more than conquerors through him who loved us . . ." (Rom 8:18–39)

The patience in tribulation that Paul desired the church to have is rooted in her hope in the Lord Jesus Christ. This hope marked out the believers in Thessalonika. Paul wrote to the church there, commending the believers for their patience in tribulation (1 Thess 1:3b; 2 Thess 1:4).

Being faithful in prayer was essential if the believers were to be patient in tribulation and joyful in hope. Prayer is about committing ourselves and the things that concern us into the hands of God. When we are confident that our lives are in his hands we can know the sort of confidence that these verses speak about. When we are confident in the unchanging dependability of God's covenant love, we are empowered to face the problems of life (Rom 5:1ff; Jas 1:2–8; 1 Pet 4:12–16). It is then that we can share in the psalmist's experience that we shall not fear what men will do to us (Ps 27:1–3).

Prayer is the natural expression of spiritual life. When Paul was conquered by the realization that Jesus was the Christ and had been raised from the dead, spiritual life flowed through his soul. When Ananias was told by the angel to go to Paul and pray for the restoration of Paul's sight, Ananias was told "he is praying" (Acts 9:11). Spiritual life begins with prayer, and prayer upholds it. The Acts of the Apostles demonstrates that just as prayer was vital to Jesus (cf. Matt 14:23; 14:23; 26:36; Luke 3:21; 5:16; 6:12; 9:28), so it was to the church he left behind (Acts 1:14; 2:42; 3:1; 6:4; 12:5; 16:13–16).

If the believers in Rome are not faithful in prayer, there will be no possibility of them living lives that will corporately make their church a living sacrifice, and no possibility that they will patiently bear the awful tribulations yet to come.

12:13 Share with God's people who are in need. Practise hospitality. One of the characteristics of the early church that made an impact on the unconverted was their care for one another (Acts 2:44–45; 4:32–35; 6:1–4). This sprang from their brotherly love and was expressed in many ways. Here, Paul identifies a specific aspect of care—that of sharing with those in need. This was a ministry that he benefited from himself when the church at Philippi met his needs while in chains (Phil 4:10, 14–16, 18). How staggering it must have been for the people of Rome to see wealthy Christians being concerned for those Christians who had very little—if anything—of this world's goods.

The Gospel abolishes all sorts of barriers. The removal of social distinctions is because believers are loved and valued by the God who has made them in his own image. They know that only the death of Jesus was sufficient to redeem them from the kingdom of darkness and the guilt of sin, and that the cost of this redemption underscored the value God placed on them all.

This injunction to care for one another regularly appears in the NT (Acts 24:23; Gal 6:10; Eph 4:28; Phil 2:25; 1 Tim 6:18; Heb 13:16). The apostle clearly could not conceive of a believing community not giving care towards those who were in need as his letters to the Corinthians make abundantly clear (1 Cor 16:1–4; 2 Cor 8–9). It is thought by some that there is the possibility of a veiled hint that the Roman church was providing for the destitute members of the impoverished Jerusalem church.[20]

---

20. So Fitzmyer, *Romans*, 655.

Paul's comments to Timothy are interesting in this regard. Paul is quite specific on who qualifies for help in the church in Ephesus: "Give proper recognition to those widows who are really in need" (1 Tim 5:3). "No widow may be put on the list of widows unless she is over sixty, has been faithful to her husband, and is well known for her good deeds . . ." (1 Tim 5:9–10). However, "If any woman who is a believer has widows in her family, she should help them and not let the church be burdened with them, so that the church can help those who are really in need" (1 Tim 5:16; 5:4,8). There are few things more disgraceful than Christians who neglect the needs of elderly parents, preferring to invest their time and gifts into the life of their local church while leaving others to make up for their lack of care. Jesus spoke against those Jews who avoided family obligations. By saying that all they had was "Corban," devoted to God (Mark 7:11) they were able to claim that their money was not theirs to use—it was God's! Such a "tax haven" was abhorrent to Jesus. Christian duty is to provide for our families (1 Tim 5:8), especially needy parents!

Hospitality was an important demonstration of the Gospel in the days of the early church (3 John 3–8). As Christian workers moved around the empire, there were few places where they could stay safely. The inns were not the most desirable of places and would expose itinerant preachers (such as Tychicus, Eph 6:21–22) to physical and moral danger. The *Didache*—a second century document of basic Christian teaching—instructed the believers to extend hospitality for no more than three nights. If the one being entertained was a true servant of Christ, he would not want to stay longer, being anxious to move on in order to fulfill his ministry. The implication is that the early church discovered how easy it was for some unscrupulous people to present themselves as dedicated servants of Christ in order to take advantage of hospitality in the homes of caring Christians.

When writing his letter, Paul tells the believers about the hospitality that he had received in the home of Gaius (Rom 16:23) and commends Phoebe to them for their help and hospitality when she arrives (Rom 16:1–2). When writing to Timothy about the eligibility of widows for church help, the author says that one of the conditions was their giving of hospitality (1 Tim 5:10, and John commends Gaius for his hospitality to fellow workers in the Gospel (3 John 5–8).

From the above citations it is possible to get the impression that hospitality was merely given to itinerant preachers and visitors from afar, but Peter encourages the practice of willing hospitality within the local church (1 Pet 4:9).

12:14 Bless those who persecute you; bless and do not curse. Paul extends the principles of Christian living to the area of personal persecution.[21]

At first sight, it seems that v.14 should be relocated before v. 17, a verse which introduces a section concerning the pressure from hostile relationships. Sadly, it appears that

---

21. Braaten, "Romans," 12:14–21, 291–29, considers the genre of the passage to be a moral discourse with a wisdom flavor that has parallels in other religions. However, Paul's ethic is rooted in the love of God, which is displayed in the giving up his Son to death (Rom 5:8). In that sense, there is no comparison between this and the texts of other faiths.

Paul sees the need to advise faithful believers in Rome on their response to persecution within the church (Rom 2:1; 14:10–13).

Paul was writing out of experience as he had enemies within the wider church. Some of his greatest opponents were "believing" Jews who saw him as a betrayer of all that was eternally true, i.e., a betrayer of what God had given to Moses. These "believing" Jews—including circumcised Gentiles—would have applauded Paul if he had led the Gentiles into the fold of Judaism through their submission to circumcision. The hatred that his non-compliance generated is difficult to appreciate but is evident throughout his letters and the Acts of the Apostles (Gal 6:12; 1 Thess 2:13–16; Acts 21:20–22; 23:12–22).

In urging the believers to bless those who persecute them, Paul was not asking them to abandon principles of justice. In Rom 13:1ff., he will explain the God-appointed role of rulers for maintaining justice, and in 1 Cor 6:1–8 he urges believers to seek settlement of their disputes from the church leadership. There is no suggestion that we have to abandon justice within the church in order to bless. Indeed, a characteristic of the early church was its anxiety to uphold the laws of the state. By asking the Roman believers to bless their enemies, Paul was effectively saying that they should pray for them—not seeking their humiliation or destruction (Matt 5:44).

The object of all discipline must be that the offender is restored to fellowship and welcomed back with all the forgiveness that God gives to repentant sinners. The Scriptures do not ask us to do anything more than what God would do himself. He forgives only when there is genuine repentance, and when he has to punish never delights in its implementation. Likewise, Christians can only forgive those who have wronged them when there is genuine repentance. Where there is no repentance, there can be no forgiveness, and the resulting pain can be hard to bear for the Christian who has been wronged. Clearly the Christian should always want reconciliation and be ready to forgive. If the law has been broken and due process, as described by Paul in 1 Corinthians 6, has failed to resolve the issue, a Christian must feel empowered to seek legal advice.[22] However, in the pursuit of justice, he must pray for his brother and not delight in his downfall.[23]

12:15 Rejoice with those who rejoice; mourn with those who mourn. It may be that Paul is referring to the normal events in life when he invites the believers to rejoice with fellow believers, events such as births and marriages within the church. However, he usually uses the term "rejoice" in the context of suffering and hope—suffering for Christ and hoping in him (cf. Phil 2:17–18; 4:4–7; Col 1:24). This reflects the teaching that Jesus gave to his disciples in the Sermon on the Mount (Matt 5:10–12; Luke 6:22–23) and is in agreement with Peter's teaching (1 Pet 1:6–9; 4:12–16 where Peter uses a term meaning "rejoice/exult").

22. 1 Cor 6:1–11 deals with injustice that is done by a believer against another believer. The good of the witness of the community has to be seriously considered.

23. Yinger, "Nonretaliation," 74–96, argues that while Rom 12:9–13 is commonly understood to speak of congregational insiders, Rom 12:14–21 speaks of outsiders. More likely, the persecutors (Rom 12:14) and the enemy (Rom 12:20) are hostile insiders (as in Jewish community-literature contemporary to Paul). Yinger claims that this interpretation provides a stronger theological backdrop for Paul's pointed admonitions in Rom 14:1—15:13.

When writing to the Philippians, Paul contemplated the possibility of martyrdom and invited the believers to rejoice with him: ". . . I am glad and rejoice with all of you. So you too should be glad and rejoice with me" (Phil 2:17b–18). This passage reflects his exhortation to the believers in Rome to rejoice with each other.

How could this work out in practice in the local church? Perhaps Paul was exhorting the Christians to rejoice with those who, despite the sufferings that they were experiencing, were rejoicing in the Lord. The believers are not being advised to draw alongside those who are suffering as "Job's comforters" but as encouragers, pointing the sufferers to the great hope that awaits them all. "Let us rejoice and be glad and give him glory! For the wedding of the Lamb has come, and his bride has made herself ready" (Rev 19:7).

Paul then writes that the believers should "weep" κλαιω (klaiō) with those who weep. This is a true mark of sincere love for a fellow believer. The tears are not the fabricated ones of the mourners in the home of Jairus's daughter in Luke 8, or of the professional mourners who followed Jesus to Golgotha (Luke 23:27–31). They come from a spirit that has been deeply troubled and moved at the suffering of another (John 11:33–36, 38).

In today's culture, weeping as an expression of emotion was not often witnessed until recently. There have been incidents covered by TV news and other media that have shown men weeping over events ranging from tragedies in their families to the failure of their football team to succeed in the competition they had thought would be theirs. Paul was unashamed at showing his emotions (2 Cor 2:4; Phil 3:18). He recalls the tears he had shed while with the church in Ephesus (Acts 20:17–19, 31). On bidding the elders of the church a final goodbye before going to Jerusalem, he and the elders wept (Acts 20:36–38). When writing to Timothy, the author recalled Timothy's tears (2 Tim 1:4), and the writer to the Hebrews records the tears that Jesus shed throughout his life as he prayed (Heb 5:7).

What Paul asks of the believers in Rome is that they do not rush to comfort and encourage the broken-hearted with words alone, but that they show their deep sorrow by entering into the pain of their fellow believers. Then, words such as Isaiah 61:1–3 can have their place.

12:16 Live in harmony with one another. Do not be proud, but be willing to associate with people of low position. Do not be conceited. The NIV translation "live in harmony with each other" leads us to assume that Paul is commenting on the previous verse. Unfortunately, this is a misleading translation of φρονοῦντες (phronountes). It means "be of the same mind" (literally, 'think the same thing') as one another." This appeal underscores the importance of the believers meeting together to hear the Scriptures explained.

The related term "being of one mind" φρονεομι (phroneomai) has identical roots with φρονοῦντες noted above, "mind" and "mindset" appearing often in Scripture. Paul has already written in his letter about the importance of a right mind. He has mentioned the "depraved mind" of unredeemed humanity (Rom 1:28–32; 8:6–7) and has reflected on his pre-conversion experience (Rom 7:21–25). Elsewhere, he has written about having the mind of the Spirit (Rom 8:6). Matthew records the rebuke of Peter by Jesus who discerned that Peter did not, at this that stage, have in mind the things of God (Matt 16:23).

However, it appears that after conversion the renewed mind can become corrupt again, especially when exposed to false teachings. So Paul warns the church in Ephesus about some of its community with unspiritual minds wreaking havoc in the church (Acts 20:28–31).

The sanctification of the mind in this way is not an option for believers. In replying to a question posed by a Pharisee, Jesus answered: "'Love the Lord your God with all your heart and with all your soul and with all your mind.' This is the first and greatest commandment" (Matt 22:37–38).

Paul then addresses the matter of pride and conceit in the church. There was clearly much evidence of this—Jews looking down on uncircumcised Gentiles, circumcised Gentiles (who called themselves Jews) looking down on uncircumcised Gentiles, and believing Gentiles looking down on unconverted Jews as discarded branches of the olive tree. The mind of Christ was not much in evidence, and the issues of pride and conceit had to be addressed if the church was to be a light to the nations.

These two sins do more to damage the fellowship of God's people than almost any other. The tragedy is that those who commit them are often unaware of the damage that they are doing, and when approached are deeply offended. The proud and conceited have normally achieved success in life and feel it is their right to pass judgment on others, especially when they perceive them to be hindering the progress of the work into which they themselves invest resources and time (3 John 9–10). In other words, pride and conceit is a particular danger to those who have been promoted to leadership within the Christian community. How dangerous this is. The very ones who should be examples of the grace of Christ can so easily be the cause of offence to new, struggling believers.

12:17 Do not repay anyone evil for evil. Be careful to do what is right in the eyes of everybody. Paul is emphatic in excluding revengeful acts of evil within the church in Rome. He encourages following OT commands where God demanded that the welfare of enemies had to be upheld. The law of Moses commanded that if someone found his neighbor's animal out of its confines and in danger of getting hurt, the animal had to be delivered safely back to its owner even though he might have previously harmed the one who found the animal (Deut 22:1–3). The Scriptures are realistic in recognizing how feuding—which results from taking revenge—incalculably damages the parties involved as well as other members of the community.

Paul urges the Roman believers to appreciate the danger of doing things that are lawful but that give a wrong impression. In saying that they must do what is right in the eyes of everyone, he is effectively saying that their actions must be open to scrutiny. Paul is not so naive as to suggest that we can please everyone or do what everyone considers right. After all, he was criticized by many for what they saw as his radical acceptance of uncircumcised Gentiles.

Many of the world's leading social reformers have had to stand against what their societies considered right because of the flaws they discerned. If we find ourselves in conflict with prevailing values that are morally wrong, we must make sure that we are not open to the accusation of doing wrong to achieve right. For Paul—and the other NT writers—the end never justifies the means. The means we employ to take our stand have to be ones that God himself would own.

12:18 If it is possible, as far as it depends on you, live at peace with everyone. Strain in relationships—even between believers—is recognized in this verse. Paul knows that despite all of his exhortations, tensions do occur within the Christian community as well as outside (Phil 4:2–3). Here, he urges his readers to do all they can to ensure that they are not responsible for the breakdown of peace.

12:19 Do not take revenge, my friends, but leave room for God's wrath, for it is written: "It is mine to avenge; I will repay," says the Lord. The danger in being wronged is of becoming a double victim. If we respond by taking revenge we have taken our case out of the hands of God in order to exercise our own authority. While it is a natural instinct, it is one that must be brought into subjection to Christ. He was wronged more than any, yet did not take matters into his own hands. He committed himself to his Father and suffered the just for the unjust. Once we take matters into our own hands, we cease to be God's servants and people through whom he can reveal himself. His power is never revealed through his people's sin but through his people's weakness.

Paul writes to the believers in Rome that they are to leave revenge to God. He quotes "It is mine to avenge; I will repay, says the Lord" from Deut 32:35 (see also Lev 19:18). The Roman Christians can be confident in the knowledge that the judge of all the earth will do justly. Before God acts on their behalf, he will offer the same mercy to those who offended them as he did to the believers before they responded to his mercy. If this mercy is rejected, he will act in judgment at the time of his choosing (Rom 2:5, 8; 1 Thess 1:10).[24]

12:20 On the contrary: "If your enemy is hungry, feed him; if he is thirsty, give him something to drink. In doing this, you will heap burning coals on his head." The believers are not only to leave their case in the hands of God (who will avenge and repay as he sees fit) but are to do good to those who do evil to them. While responding in like manner justifies the behavior of those who have done wrong, acts of kindness disarm them, leaving them confused and vulnerable. For such people, this is more painful than revenge. The quotation is from Prov 25:21ff. (LXX).

Some find conflict in Paul's teaching. He urges the Romans not to take revenge into their own hands, and yet says that by doing good to their enemies burning coals are heaped on their heads. There need not be any conflict. If Paul means that their kindness will make their enemies extremely uncomfortable, the same meaning is upheld. In other words, Paul is counseling the believers to recognize that revenge will only confirm the attitude and not change the character. By kindness, their enemies can be made so uncomfortable that they can no longer bear it.

---

24. The same ideas are found in the DSS. See 1QS, 10:17ff.; CD, 9:2–3.

However, there is a possible alternative meaning within this text and that echoes the OT. Live coals are a symbol of purging (Isa 6:6–7), and were part of Isaiah's preparation for the service God was calling him to. Perhaps there is an echo of this purging in the passage. It is possible that Paul is saying the outcome of the kindness of the believers is the salvation of their enemies who will then be brought into God's service and counted among his redeemed.

12:21 Do not be overcome by evil, but overcome evil with good. Paul's concern is that the church's testimony is not lost. The church is to overcome evil with good. This is the way God has conquered us and disarmed our hostility toward him.[25]

CONCLUSION OF ROMANS 12

Just as Moses urged Israel to live out her calling as a priestly people, so Paul exhorts the church. She is to live to please her great high priest to whom she is betrothed by living a priestly life, making her God known to the nations. The emphasis is not about obeying the Torah but fulfilling the law of love by encouraging others and being patient in the face of hostility.

---

25. Johnson, *Reading*, 196, summarizes the prevailing view of the ancient worlds of Judaism and Hellenism regarding the validity of taking revenge against those who harm loved ones.

ROMANS 13

THE MESSIAH KING AND HIS DELEGATED REPRESENTATIVES

EVERYONE MUST SUBMIT himself to the governing authorities, for there is no authority except that which God has established. The authorities that exist have been established by God. Consequently, he who rebels against the authority is rebelling against what God has instituted, and those who do so will bring judgment on themselves. For rulers hold no terror for those who do right, but for those who do wrong. Do you want to be free from fear of the one in authority? Then do what is right and he will commend you.

For he is God's servant to do you good. But if you do wrong, be afraid, for he does not bear the sword for nothing. He is God's servant, an agent of wrath to bring punishment on the wrongdoer.

Therefore, it is necessary to submit to the authorities, not only because of possible punishment but also because of conscience.

This is also why you pay taxes, for the authorities are God's servants, who give their full time to governing. Give everyone what you owe him: If you owe taxes, pay taxes; if revenue, then revenue; if respect, then respect; if honor, then honor. Let no debt remain outstanding, except the continuing debt to love one another, for he who loves his fellow-man has fulfilled the law. The commandments, "Do not commit adultery," "Do not murder," "Do not steal," "Do not covet," and whatever other commandment there may be, are summed up in this one rule: "Love your neighbor as yourself." Love does no harm to its neighbor. Therefore love is the fulfillment of the law. And do this, understanding the present time. The hour has come for you to wake up from your slumber, because our salvation is nearer now than when we first believed. The night is nearly over; the day is almost here. So let us put aside the deeds of darkness and put on the armor of light. Let us behave decently, as in the daytime, not in orgies and drunkenness, not in sexual immorality and debauchery, not in dissension and jealousy. Rather, clothe yourselves with the Lord Jesus Christ, and do not think about how to gratify the desires of the sinful nature. (Rom 13:1–14)

INTRODUCTION

Having instructed the Romans in the preceding section about their priestly calling (Rom 12:1–2) and the need to maintain their zeal (Rom 12:11), Paul turns to the issue of earthly rule. There has always been a tendency throughout the church's history to claim authority for herself that exceeds what God intends her to have. Here Paul, clearly aware of the danger, instructs the church in Rome regarding her duties to assist the servants of the state in their God-given calling to promote the good of the people of the empire and to maintain law and order.

Despite the trend to see Paul, and indeed, Jesus himself as political activists, this key passage shows us that Paul never had such ambitions. In fact Paul valued his own Roman citizenship and used the privileges it gave him to ensure that he had a fair trial by appealing to Caesar (Acts 25:10–11). No doubt there were other motives in operation when he made his appeal to Caesar than solely his own survival. He had been told (Acts 9:15) that he was to carry Christ's name "before the Gentiles and their kings," and this knowledge was clearly a driving force for his whole ministry.

Paul not only calls the Roman believers to respect the state and its servants, but to live pure and good lives that mark them out as the people of Christ in a dark and failing society.

13:1 Everyone must submit himself to the governing authorities, for there is no authority except that which God has established. The authorities that exist have been established by God. In saying that "everyone must submit," πασα ψυχη (*pasa psuchē*), Paul emphasizes the importance of willing acceptance of the rulers' claim to authority over the Roman believers. The authorities are not to be obeyed because they have the power to punish but because their authority has been conferred on them by God. They are his appointed agents to govern.

Paul uses the term "authority/ies" in different ways in his writings. He applies it to men such as the chief priests (Acts 26:12; 1 Cor 9:12 [translated "right of support"]; 2 Cor 10:8) and to spiritual powers (Acts 26:18 [translated "power"]; Eph 1:21; 2:2 [translated "kingdom"] 3:10; 6:12; Col 1:13 [translated "dominion"); 2:10; 2:15).While Paul rarely applies the term to the state, this is generally accepted to be his application in Rom 13, the authorities being civil rulers who hold the sword on God's behalf.[1]

If we accept that "authority/ies" in Rom 13 refers to such rulers, we can assume that Paul draws his understanding from the OT Scriptures. It was Yahweh who appointed Saul (1 Sam 9:16) and David (1 Sam 16:1) as Israel's kings. Indeed, the coronation psalms show that the king was the servant (son) of God (Ps 2:7). Importantly, it was not only the Jewish kings who were seen to be Yahweh's agents but also pagan kings. Cyrus, the Persian king, was referred to as "his anointed" and his "chosen," whom God summoned, exalted, and strengthened (Isa 45:1–5). Paul would thus be staying within the OT perspective that, no matter how evil the world, Yahweh controls the nations.[2]

This OT background would provide the reason for Paul's appeal to Christians to recognize that a regime soaked in paganism and violence (with ensuing moral consequences) was, nevertheless, the God-appointed government in Rome. When its laws did not conflict with their calling as Christians, the Roman believers were to give it due honor and homage.[3]

---

1. See Cullmann, *State*.

2. Wright, *Romans*, 721–22, notes: "being" able to respect the office while at least reserving judgment about the holder is part of social and civic maturity."

3. Denova, "Romans 13:1–7," 201–29, claims that an analysis of the authorship, the religious/political context, and the content of early Christian moral teaching shows that this passage is not a systematic political theory nor a Christian blueprint for the state. It is merely an attempt to help Gentile Christians adjust to their new circumstances. For a discussion on the authorship of the section, see Witherington, *Romans*, 304.

Recently, an alternative understanding of "authority/ies" in Rom 13 has been put forward. It is argued that local churches did not always separate from the local synagogues perhaps because they afforded protection to the believers, and that this was the situation in Rome. This meant that Jewish worshippers and Jewish believers in Jesus mixed with each other when they came to the synagogues for worship.[4] Such a situation was not unknown in Judaism as Jews themselves embraced different messiahs and actively sought to persuade their countrymen of the credentials of their chosen "anointed" ones. This relative openness witnesses to the diversity of the Jewish synagogue system as does the fact that visitors were encouraged to share with the congregation messages of exhortation, of news, or some other matter (Acts 13:5, 15; 14:1; 17:10–12; 18:4; 19:8).

However, a major cause of friction in many synagogues was that the followers of Jesus were bringing the message of a crucified Messiah to the congregations. In addition, they were introducing uncircumcised Gentiles as men with equal rights as the orthodox Jews. Indeed, not only did these Jewish followers of Jesus argue for the inclusion of uncircumcised Gentiles into the covenant community, they argued that, unless law-observing Jews believed in Jesus, *they* were excluded from the covenant community! This historical setting has been used to argue that the "governing authorities" of v. 1 are not representatives of the Roman state but of the synagogue.[5]

This recently argued understanding has Paul pleading for the Gentile believers to accept the authority of the Jewish leadership of the synagogue because God has appointed it. If this is the setting of the exhortation, the problem is no longer how the believers relate to the state but to the religious leadership. Paul is appealing for respect, but not at the cost of compromise.[6]

13:2 Consequently, he who rebels against the authority is rebelling against what God has instituted, and those who do so will bring judgment on themselves. The outcome of Paul's reasoning is predictable. If the governments (civil or religious) are the appointed agents of God, to rebel against them is to rebel against the God who appointed them. This is a remarkable position to take if Paul is referring to civil authorities, as many of the believers in Rome were slaves. Their distressing conditions were often due to the greed, ambition and ruthlessness of the mighty Roman Empire, so it would be more than understandable if some of them bitterly resented their masters. As with the earlier exhortation not to take revenge (Rom 12:19), this exhortation would have cut right across their instincts for justice.

---

4. See Nanos, *Mystery*.

5. There are some points that support this position of Nanos, but the main difficulty is that Paul describes the authorities as bearing the sword. This description is too severe a portrayal of the legal authority that the Roman Empire allowed the synagogue to wield. Any capital punishment had to be ordered by the state, as is evident in the sentence carried out on Jesus. Rome would not tolerate anything that challenged her right to order the death penalty. It was a matter of Roman law and order. The reference to paying taxes to the authority in v.6 is thought by most to refer to state taxes–a tax most Jews resented. Nanos claims that it is a reference to synagogue taxes

6. Talbert, *Romans*, 296, comments: "All that is asked of the believers is that they 'do good,' 'pay taxes,' and 'honor and respect those in power.' What is legitimately ascribed to the authorities is the punishment of evil and the reward of good. This limited homage is far from an enthusiastic endorsement of the empire."

Paul is as clear on this issue as he was about revenge: Rebellion would leave the believers open to judgment. Such judgment might be meted out by the authority using its might and power in suppression, or it might be meted out by God for rejecting the authority he had ordained. While this latter suggestion is a possibility, the argument that follows suggests that Paul has the judgment of the former in mind.

13:3 For rulers hold no terror for those who do right, but for those who do wrong. Do you want to be free from fear of the one in authority? Then do what is right and he will commend you. Paul was not idealizing rulers as men who always acted with the purest of motives. He was not naive. He knew the intrigues of political maneuvering in the synagogue and in the state, and how the innocent were often victims of miscarriages of justice, suffering because their legitimate grievances were ignored. How should the Roman Christians respond should these be the prevailing circumstances? While Paul does not address *this* here, it is hard to believe that he would urge his readers to give blind obedience. On such occasions, they will have to take a stand that may prove very costly.

The questions must be asked: "When a ruling authority is corrupt, does it cease to be God's instrument? Moreover, do Christians have a responsibility to join with others to bring such a tyranny to an end?" These are questions that Paul does not address and their answers must be sought by examining Scripture to see what principles it provides. Paul had the same attitude to these matters as Jesus. We are to "give to Caesar what is Caesar's and to God what is God's."(Matt 22:15–22, cf. Rom 13:6).

13:4 For he is God's servant to do you good. But if you do wrong, be afraid, for he does not bear the sword for nothing. He is God's servant, an agent of wrath to bring punishment on the wrongdoer. The one in authority—be he the leader of the synagogue or the head of the state—is God's servant; and his responsibility is to seek the good of the citizens in his care. Of course, authorities should not only punish wrongdoers in order to protect the weak, but should commend and nurture those who do good.[7]

If Paul had the Roman civil authorities in mind, then the believers who lived within their jurisdiction ought to be grateful for how much Rome (God's servant) had bequeathed on them in terms of legal and religious privilege. However, they had to be aware that any civil authority could also punish wrongdoing. Paul warns his readers that if they do wrong they must not think that they will be exempt from punishment.[8]

If Paul meant that the synagogue rulers were God's servant, then he would have in mind the good done by them in, for example, religious, moral, legal and educational matters. The reference to the synagogue ruler bearing the sword is not a problem in this context as the synagogue was the legal center of the Jewish community and the place where punishment was meted out on those who violated its laws. Paul himself had represented such a ruling authority, brandishing the sword on behalf of the high priest

---

7. Winter, *Welfare*, 26–38, suggests that Paul is exhorting his readers to become benefactors who will receive recognition from the state. By this, they will promote the cause of the Gospel as unbelievers watch on.

8. Furnish, *Moral*, 115–41, understands the "sword" to refer to that of the tax police who use it to protect tax collectors. The weakness of this view is that vv. 3–5 clearly refers to higher officials than tax collectors.

(Acts 9:1–2; Gal 1:13–14). Indeed, after his conversion on the Damascus road he became the recipient of its judgment; however such an interpretation is not likely to be correct if it sees the synagogue eldership as having the right to take life as discussed above (fn 5).

The reference to the sword is possibly from Deut 32:41, where Yahweh threatens to take his sword and wreak vengeance on his adversaries. This is supported by the fact that Paul has already quoted from the chapter. He quotes Deut 32:21 in Rom 10:19 and v.35 in Rom 12:19. The threat of Yahweh taking the sword against his enemies suggests that Paul sees that the danger of those who profess faith and disobey is that they are enemies of the Lord. This is not a new perception for Paul—he has spoken of Israel as a nation of unbelievers and having become, effectively, Yahweh's enemy and suffering judgment by his hand. He warned the Corinthians of this danger of coming under their Lord's discipline in 1 Cor 10:1–10, and threatened it in 1 Cor 5–6.9

13:5 Therefore, it is necessary to submit to the authorities, not only because of possible punishment but also because of conscience. Paul underlines two reasons for obeying the authorities. The first is the fear of punishment and the second is because conscience, or religious duty requires it (Exod 22:28; Acts 23:5).[10]

It might seem strange that Paul mentions fear as a motive. Indeed, he not only lists it but puts it before conscience. We live in an age when psychologists tell us never to use fear as a motive. The fact is that society, having yielded to such advice, is returning to the dark ages in terms of much social behavior. Scripture has no hesitation in spelling things out as they are; and for most, including Christians, fear of punishment in this life and the next affects them deeply. We should not be afraid of an emotion that is part of human experience and which can save us from harm.

13:6 This is also why you pay taxes, for the authorities are God's servants, who give their full time to governing. As has been mentioned, Paul asserts the principle taught by Jesus: "Give to Caesar what is Caesar's and to God what is God's" (Matt 22:21b). Because the authorities are God's servants, he has ordained that people should support them.[11] If Paul sees the authorities as the state, then those who work full time in the up-holding of social order should be provided for by means of taxation. Paying taxes would then be as much an act of giving to God as paying "tithes." The former would be for the administration of society's needs, the latter for the administration of the Gospel.

Paul sees nothing wrong in officials being paid fairly for the work they do–theirs is a high calling, ensuring the smooth and just running of affairs. They should be paid

---

9. See Holland, *Contours*, chapter 6.

10. Rancine, "Romains," 187–205, argues that the use of συνείδηεις (*suneidēsis*) "conscience" and ὑποτάσσεσθαι (*hupotassesthai*) "to be in subjection" suggest that Paul was promoting an intelligent and critical respect for the social order. They contributed to the church's faith rather than to a blind obedience towards the civil authorities.

11. Kroger, "Authorities," 344–66, argues against those who claim that vv. 1–7 are a non-Pauline interpolation. He thinks that Paul was aware that taxation was a vexing issue for the Roman Christians. He says that Paul counters the problems this could cause by urging them to adopt a practical attitude of obedience and submission to the governing authorities.

appropriately to avoid corruption. Poorly paid officials might be tempted to accept bribes to supplement their wages if their families' needs could not be met.

13:7 Give everyone what you owe him: If you owe taxes, pay taxes; if revenue, then revenue; if respect, then respect; if honor, then honor. Paul extends the principle of what is owed to governing officials to what is owed to those in daily life.[12] He tells the Romans that they are to settle all their debts–no matter to whom they are indebted.

Debt can cripple the conscience. Moreover, when left unpaid it can cause devastation to those who depend on its repayment. All too often, those who live in abundance hold on to what is not theirs, leaving the ones who are owed with the problem of coping with the unpaid debts. While it is not right at a commercial level, it is especially inappropriate for Christians not to settle debts (Jas 5:4–5). The OT has much to say about this (Deut 24:10–13; Job 24:3; Prov 20:16; Ezek 33:15), and there is no doubt that it is from this source that Paul draws his ethical principles.[13]

Debts are owed by the Roman believers in monetary and non-monetary terms. Paul writes to them that they are to pay appropriate debts of respect and honor to all in authority. If those who have been given responsibilities by God fulfill them in a way honoring to him, they deserve due recognition. Paul would expect the Roman believers to apply this principle to their civil, synagogue, and church lives, recognizing and respecting the work done in the latter by its prophets, evangelists, teachers, pastors, elders and deacons (1 Tim 3:8; Tit 1:7 & 3:2; Heb 13:7, 17; 1 Pet 5:5).

This debt of gratitude owed by the Roman believers to their officialdom could be usefully heeded by churches today. We live in an age of criticism and cynicism, where expression of gratitude is of less importance than demand to entitlement. Many churches would be transformed if members of their congregations took to heart Paul's exhortation to the believers in Rome and paid debts of gratitude to those who, often voluntarily, seek to care for their souls.

13:8 Let no debt remain outstanding, except the continuing debt to love one another, for he who loves his fellow-man has fulfilled the law. The exception to the rule regarding the repayment of debts is the debt of love, which can never be settled. The mention of love is probably a reference to the love of God about which Paul has spoken movingly in Rom 5:8. In saying "he who loves his fellow-man has fulfilled the law," Paul is not suggesting that we can keep the law. Indeed, this is his point. This debt cannot be met because we can never satisfy the law's demands. It is a debt that only Christ has met.

12. Coleman, "Binding," 307–27, discusses the terms "tribute," "tax," "reverence," and "honor" in relation to the Greco-Roman semantic field of political obligation. He divides them into the categories of tangible and intangible obligations. He also examines Rom 13:7 in light of the social context of the Neronian era in which there was an increasing burden of taxation and the introduction of legal penalties for failure to show due reverence and honor to those in authority.

13. See Rosner, *Scripture*.

13:9 The commandments, "Do not commit adultery," "Do not murder," "Do not steal," "Do not covet," and whatever other commandment there may be, are summed up in this one rule: "Love your neighbor as yourself." Paul reminds the believers of the commandments that relate to the treatment of others, reinforcing the permanence of these laws. They express the bottom line for behavior. If a believer loves someone, he cannot sin against that person in ways the commandments forbid. Love is a higher principle than law. What the law commands is the beginning of the expression of love, not its limit.

The commandment "Do not commit adultery" continues to be the key to every stable marriage. While the world treats sexual morality as a private affair, it recognizes that the betrayal of a partner is inexcusable and the immediate grounds for divorce. In this case, natural justice reflects divine justice. Adultery not only sins against God and the partner, but the extended family (especially the children). Scripture is uncompromising in speaking out against sexual immorality because it destroys the fabric of lives. It robs families of security, trust, and dignity, and casts them into a darkness with which little can compare.

Jesus extended this commandment to attitudes of the heart. He warned that whoever looked upon a woman and lusted after her had already committed adultery with her as far as God was concerned (Matt 5:27–28). Such high standards are not out of touch with the pain that women feel when they see their husbands' lingering glances at other women. Such glances attack their security and self-worth.

Murder is another act that is universally recognized as wrong. Many will argue their right to steal and covet, but few would argue that murder is acceptable. While there are grounds for a state taking a life to protect its population against an aggressor, reason can become warped, justifying executions for the wrong cause. The Jesuits, in their South American mission, put people to death on the pretext that their souls would be saved. The Crusaders did the same thing in the Islamic states during the Middle Ages. Jesus gave the commandment against murder a spiritual dimension (Matt 5:21–22). He said that hating a person is as bad as physically harming him. Peoples, characters, and reputations can be put to death just as much as the body can, and Jesus justly applied the commandment beyond the limits of the Mosaic law.

The command "Do not steal" is clear. We are not to take from individuals, companies, or governments. Stealing does not only involve tangible things. It can be taking time from an employer as well as stealing a man's good reputation through gossip and slander.

Coveting is the desire to have what belongs to someone else. This does not mean that we are forbidden to admire a possession of another person and resolve to acquire the same through legitimate means. It means that jealousy—the twin sister of covetousness—must never be in our hearts. We ought to be glad that others have been blessed with possessions that we are not able to own. This is not a hopelessly impossible ideal. Its attainment begins with valuing spiritual blessings above material ones.

Paul writes that these and other commandments are summed up in the principle of loving our neighbor as ourselves. It is one of the great commandments that Jesus gave in response to the scribes' attempt to catch him out. The other is that we love God with all our hearts (Mark 12:29–30). While Paul cites the command to love from Lev 19:18b (a command relating specifically to loving fellow Jews), he is not restricting his command to ethnic Israel. For Paul, as for Jesus, his neighbor is all humanity.

13:10 Love does no harm to its neighbor. Therefore love is the fulfillment of the law. When Paul writes that "love does no harm to its neighbor,"[14] it seems that anything causing pain or sadness cannot spring from love. However, Paul often said offensive and hurtful things (2 Cor 6:14–18; Gal 2:14; Phil 3:2), indicating that there are times when keeping quiet harms a person more than the initial distress caused by speaking out. In other words, there are times when we have to see the long term good of our neighbor and act with that in mind. There can be no greater good than a person's acceptance into heaven. Incalculable harm can be done by believers keeping silent on the remedy for sin for fear of causing their neighbors any distress.

The same principle applies when someone steals from us, attacks our property, or violates us in any way. Paul is not saying that we should disregard the law's support or protection. Indeed, a Christian should hope that the moral welfare of the guilty party will be served by facing the seriousness of what he has done. In other words, Paul's injunction not to harm a neighbor is about dealing justly with him. There should be no thought of stealing from him, slandering, or hurting him in any way. Regardless of his color, creed, or status, he is to be treated with respect and dignity at all times. This concern for equality and justice comes from the OT, where Israel was told to protect the vulnerable. They not only included orphans and widows but strangers (immigrants) and economic casualties (Exod 22:21–27). They were to be accepted as those made in the image of God and those for whom the Lord would plead the cause if they were violated.

This sort of reasoning can be extended to other areas of Christian living. The principle Paul is emphasizing is that we have no right to judge one whom God has accepted. The moment we think that we are more acceptable to God is the moment we cease to appreciate his free grace. To grade Christians in terms of favor is to fall into serious error. We are all accepted on exactly the same grounds, i.e., God's free grace and mercy.

The purposes of the law are that people give to God the love and honor he deserves and that they give to others—who are made in God's image—the love and respect they deserve. Love means dealing with others in the way that God deals with us. This is the fulfillment of the law.

13:11 And do this, understanding the present time. The hour has come for you to wake up from your slumber, because our salvation is nearer now than when we first believed. By writing "And do this," Paul emphasizes that faith in Christ is not only expressed in ideals and doctrines but in the life the Roman believers lead (Rom 12:1–21; 13:9–10). Jesus often stressed what men had to *do*. Faith in him does not take away the Roman believers' personal responsibility but provides them with the resources for living the Christian life (Gal 5:16–26).

14. See the discussion in Witherington, *Romans*, 316, for the meaning of "neighbor." He demonstrates that while it can refer to members of the same community, it can apply to a "fellow human being."

Their actions must flow from an understanding of their current situation in Rome. They must not be content with comfort but alert to the fact that others in the city are in mortal danger and in need of rescuing from God's coming judgment. Paul urges the believers to wake from slumber and buy up the opportunities of serving Christ in the city (cf. Eph 5:8–20). The call to "wake up from slumber" is a direct quote from Isa 60:1, where the people were told that Yahweh was coming to bring them salvation. It is, of course, a text that has new exodus significance. The original context was Yahweh's call to Israel to prepare herself for her return pilgrimage to Jerusalem.[15]

Peter speaks of the coming of Christ as the new dawn (2 Pet 1:19). Until that breaks, unredeemed humanity dwells in darkness; but it is a condition from which he can be rescued. As Christ will come in judgment, those who have declined to be rescued will be left in the darkness they have preferred (Matt 6:23; Eph 5:8; Col 1:13; 1 Pet 2:9) and will be sent into an eternal outer darkness (Matt 8:12; 22:13). It is imperative that the believers in Rome spread the knowledge of God so that it shines in the hearts of those in the city who will believe, bringing them forgiveness and salvation (Acts 26:18). This task demands that they put aside "deeds of darkness" (v. 12) as unbelievers will take the Gospel seriously when they see it being lived out with integrity by the believers.

13:12 The night is nearly over; the day is almost here. So let us put aside the deeds of darkness and put on the armor of light. Elsewhere, Paul has written that the Christian needs to put on the full armor of God in order to bear a good witness (Eph 6:11). This is an echo of Isa 59:16–17 where Isaiah records the coming of the Redeemer to Zion, fully armed and equipped for his saving work. Because of this divine intervention, the remnant was released to make its journey to the promised inheritance—the city of Zion.

The OT citations (and especially Isa 60:1, which was considered in Rom 13:11) suggest that Paul sees believers to be involved in a pilgrimage (see also Rom 5:1ff.; 8:32ff.; 10:14–15). They can only progress on their pilgrimage as they fulfill the responsibility of living as children of light. This understanding supports the case made that Paul constructed his letter to the Romans around Israel's experience of coming out of bondage and shame. This type—this visual aid from the history of Israel—is fulfilled in the church, the true inheritor of the promises of God (Gal 6:16).

The exhortation to put on the armor of God was originally spoken to Israel; while the individual Christian applies it to himself, it is, nevertheless, an exhortation to the community.

Isaiah 59:9–10 speaks of captive Israel being in darkness and knowing nothing of justice. Paul follows this theme in Rom 13:12–13. He urges his readers not to fall into the same sins that Israel fell into on her pilgrimage (Isa 59:2–8, 12–15; cf. 1 Cor 10:1–13), when she involved herself in orgies, drunkenness, sexual immorality, debauchery, dissension and jealousy. Paul used very similar language in 1 Cor 10:6ff., when he warned the Corinthians that God could act to discipline them as he had disciplined the children of Israel. The setting of the exhortation in the Corinthian letter was the wilderness wander-

---

15. Käsemann, *Romans*, 362, considers that the passage reflects the exhortations given at baptism.

ings. We have seen that Paul is able to use material from the Egyptian and Babylonian exoduses to illustrate what God has done for his people through the death of Christ, "our Passover." Typology continues to be the key to interpreting Paul.

13:13 Let us behave decently, as in the daytime, not in orgies and drunkenness, not in sexual immorality and debauchery, not in dissension and jealousy. When Paul writes "Let us behave decently, as in the daytime," he is saying that he and the Roman believers must be open to public scrutiny. He identifies with them, saying that he and they should live transparent lives, doing nothing of which they would be ashamed. For example, the Roman Christians should not be involved in "orgies." The term refers to secret rites and rituals in the worship of pagan gods, especially Bacchus.

Repeated "drunkenness" is also forbidden (cf. 1 Cor 5:11). In 1 Cor 6:10, Paul lists drunkards as people who will not inherit the kingdom of God. This is a warning to believers in an age when alcohol is readily available and much consumed. While it cannot be denied that wine was the accepted refreshment of the NT world, we must recognize Scripture's warning of its misuse; it can bring the strongest man to destruction (Gen 9:21; Prov 20:1; 1 Tim 3:3; Titus 2:3). In the Greek text, the phrase translated "orgies and drunkenness" may suggest an act of drunken revelry rather than two distinct practices.

Paul urges the Roman believers not to be involved in sexual immorality. Again, this is a sin that is as prevalent in modern society as it was in the ancient world. Sex, which is powerful and beautiful, is God's gift to mankind. It brings incredible joy and comfort when contained within the realm of a true and permanent relationship between a man and a woman. We live in an age when traditional forms of morality have largely been abandoned. Indeed, the pain from broken relationships with the psychological and emotional damage they wreak has not yet reached its high water mark. This is not how God intended it to be as he wants sex to be the evidence of genuine love and total trust. If these are present in a relationship, it is difficult to see why anyone should deny the partner the protection that the legal status of marriage gives.

"Debauchery" refers to perverted virtue or morality, and extends the bounds of sexual immorality. As with orgies and drunkenness, the use of the phrase "sexual immorality and debauchery" may be intended to suggest one composite idea or practice. The nouns are plural, suggesting frequent repetition.

"Dissension" refers to attempts to overthrow the prevailing opinion. There are times when it is right to question the status quo; indeed, it is essential for this to take place if there is going to be reform. Paul is not against such freedom. He was, after all, guilty of dissention when he proclaimed the Gospel of Christ in the synagogues. When people embraced "the Way," it meant a shift of power from Jewish leaders to those who were often Gentile (i.e., the God-fearing) and with little official training.

Paul is not concerned in this particular passage about attempts to bring down corrupt leaders. He is concerned, rather, with the overthrow of a person who was disliked because of differences over legitimate alternative policies. Sadly, we find dissension in churches when people think the pastor's ministry is over and they seek to influence others in support of his removal. This has happened throughout history, and no less in biblical history. It is even more tragic when people who were once used by God become the center of dissension. Such examples are Miriam and Aaron, who tried to replace—or, at the very least, share leadership with—Moses, their brother (Num 12). Whether in a civil or a church context, believers should not be involved in dissension unless it is to remove corrupt officials.

"Jealousy" is a state of heart and mind that causes much suffering. It is often hidden under a veneer of respectability. It ruins relationships, twists truth, and excuses gross injustices. To succumb to jealousy's enticements is to be a prisoner of a ruthless mistress. "Dissension and jealousy" is the third pair of nouns in the list and is often the result of drunken revelry and debauchery.

13:14 Rather, clothe yourselves with the Lord Jesus Christ, and do not think about how to gratify the sinful nature. The lifestyle of the people of God is to be different from that of the world. While there are notable exceptions, the sins Paul has listed, which gratify the "sinful nature," are typical of unredeemed humankind. If their application to twenty-first century Western society is denied, the huge sale of news stand and video shop material—pandering to basic instincts and values—stands as witness. Paul gives explicit instructions as to how to deal with such temptations when they attack the believer (1 Cor 10:1–13; Gal 5:16–26; Phil 4:8–9). He should give them no place in his thinking. Appetites must not become the stooges of Satan, who seeks to control people by intoxicating their lives with base passions.

When Paul speaks about gratifying the "sinful nature," he uses the term σαρξ (*sarx*) "flesh." In using *sarx,* Paul has not necessarily referred to the sinful nature of people as the NIV suggests. As we have seen, *sarx* "flesh" has a range of meanings reflecting the weakness of humanity.[16] Paul refers to Christians as continuing in their fallen creaturely weakness. While this does not necessarily equate to sinning, it probably does in this verse. Paul is exhorting the Roman Christians not to gratify the *sarx* as they wait for the completion of their redemption when Christ returns.

In exhorting the Roman believers to "clothe" themselves (ἀλλὰ ἐνδύσασθε τὸν κύριον Ἰησοῦν Χριστὸν), Paul appeals to the church community to live a Christ-like life. This is always corporate language (see Eph 4:24; Col 3:10). The language of clothing is found throughout the OT. It refers to preparation for doing evil (Ps 73:6) or good (Ps 45:3; Isa 51:9) as well as the transformation of people through life events (Job 8:22; Ps 30:11; 35:26; 109:29; 132:16; Isa 52:1; 61:10).

CONCLUSION OF ROMANS 13

Paul continues his exhortation that the church should live a holy life. This is not a call to mysticism but to practical godly living where truth is upheld and ruling authorities are honored.

God's people are to clothe themselves with Christ Jesus. The scriptural basis of this appeal is taken from Isa 60:1, where Israel was commanded to awake from her sleep and

---

16. See Excursus F: Sin in the Theology of Paul, pages 201–24.

prepare for her second exodus. This OT text echoes in the background as Paul warns the church to awake from slumber because her salvation is nearer now than when she first believed (v. 11). Thus, new exodus imagery continues to drive the argument and appeal. The church is to live in such a way to be fit for the coming of the divine bridegroom—an event that Isa 62:1–5 foretold.

ROMANS 14

THE MESSIAH KING AND HIS PEOPLE'S DIFFERENCES

ACCEPT HIM WHOSE faith is weak, without passing judgment on disputable matters. One man's faith allows him to eat everything, but another man, whose faith is weak, eats only vegetables. The man who eats everything must not look down on him who does not, and the man who does not eat everything must not condemn the man who does, for God has accepted him. Who are you to judge someone else's servant? To his own master he stands or falls. And he will stand, for the Lord is able to make him stand. One man considers one day more sacred than another; another man considers every day alike. Each one should be fully convinced in his own mind. He who regards one day as special, does so to the Lord. He who eats meat, eats to the Lord, for he gives thanks to God; and he who abstains, does so to the Lord and gives thanks to God. For none of us lives to himself alone and none of us dies to himself alone. If we live, we live to the Lord; and if we die, we die to the Lord. So, whether we live or die, we belong to the Lord. For this very reason, Christ died and returned to life so that he might be the Lord of both the dead and the living. You, then, why do you judge your brother? Or why do you look down on your brother? For we will all stand before God's judgment seat. It is written: "'As surely as I live,' says the Lord, 'every knee will bow before me; every tongue will confess to God.'" So then, each of us will give an account of himself to God. Therefore let us stop passing judgment on one another. Instead, make up your mind not to put any stumbling-block or obstacle in your brother's way. As one who is in the Lord Jesus, I am fully convinced that no food is unclean in itself. But if anyone regards something as unclean, then for him it is unclean. If your brother is distressed because of what you eat, you are no longer acting in love. Do not by your eating destroy your brother for whom Christ died. Do not allow what you consider good to be spoken of as evil. For the kingdom of God is not a matter of eating and drinking, but of righteousness, peace and joy in the Holy Spirit, because anyone who serves Christ in this way is pleasing to God and approved by men. Let us therefore make every effort to do what leads to peace and to mutual edification. Do not destroy the work of God for the sake of food. All food is clean, but it is wrong for a man to eat anything that causes someone else to stumble. It is better not to eat meat or drink wine or to do anything else that will cause your brother to fall.

So whatever you believe about these things keep between yourself and God. Blessed is the man who does not condemn himself by what he approves. But the man who has doubts is condemned if he eats, because his eating is not from faith; and everything that does not come from faith is sin. (Rom 14:1–23)

INTRODUCTION

Paul begins this section in appealing for the weak and the strong to accept each other. In view of the discussion he had earlier of the division between Jews and Gentiles in chapter 9–11, it is likely that this is the division that is referred to in this section. This is made even more likely by the mention of difficulty of making allowance for food and holy days, the very issues that supported the two sectors of the church that was represented by Jewish and Gentile interests.

Paul stresses that we are all accepted because Christ has died (Rom 14:9, 15) and that no one should be quick to judge because we are yet to be judged by God (Rom 14:10–12). Paul makes the startling claim that if one causes another to stumble because of his attitude, he sins against Christ himself (Rom 14:20). The principle that Paul says must be applied is whether a person does not condemn him/herself in what they do. If they don't, and it is not clearly forbidden nor harming other believers, they are free to continue their chosen course. Thus Paul put down a mark for the importance of Christian freedom.

14:1 Accept him whose faith is weak, without passing judgment on disputable matters. In Christian congregations there are people from different backgrounds and with different experiences. At this point in the letter, Paul writes to the Roman believers about his concern for their differences in faith and the attitudes they adopt towards each other as a result. Exactly who Paul has in mind when addressing this exhortation is not clear[1] as the definition of those with weak faith (or, by implication, strong faith) does not necessarily fall along ethnic lines.[2] He clearly sees himself as one of the strong,[3] but argues that such as he must follow the example of Jesus (Rom 1:3; cf. Phil 2:5–9).

In any community there are those who are full of confidence and opinion. Others are far less robust and hesitant to the point of causing themselves pain in their uncertainties. The "weak" are not necessarily ignorant of Christian doctrine but struggle to work out its consequences and implications.[4] It is all too easy for those who are "strong" to become frustrated with those who do not share their self-confidence. In a community where all must be taken seriously and their opinions respected, there is always tension.

---

1. For a detailed discussion, see Reasoner, *Strong*. Nanos, *Mystery*, argues that the weak are non-Christian Jews, while Gagnon, "Weak," 64–82, argues that the term refers to Gentile Christians. Käsemann, *Romans*, 374, thinks that the strong are Gentile believers who think the Jews are over scrupulous. See also Fitzmyer, *Romans*, 687, and Witherington, *Romans*, 395. Keck, "What," 18, notes: "It is no less obscure why, if the (Jewish) 'root' supports the (Gentile) graftee, it is the strong Gentile who is urged to 'bear with the failings of the weak' (Jewish Christian). Does one not expect Paul to ask the scrupulous 'root' to be patient with the freewheeling Gentile until the graft is 'set'?"

2. See also Wright, *Romans*, 731, who says: "The best reading of this problem, I think, is that the divisions Paul knew to exist within the Roman church have at least a strong element about them of the Jew/Gentile tension that has been underneath so much of the letter. This is by no means to say that 'the weak' are Jewish Christians and 'the strong' are Gentile Christians. Paul is himself a Jewish Christian who sees himself as one of the 'strong.'" Moo, *Romans*, 837, thinks that the term "the strong" suggests dominance and posses questions as to the examples that Paul gives, for they represent both groups.

3. See Rom 15:1.

4. See Fitzmyer, *Romans*, 689; Cranfield, *Romans*, 698, 700.

Paul speaks into such a situation, for differences of opinion and conviction can cause rift and division.

He urges those who are strong in faith to make sure their confidence does not damage weak believers. They are to do this by not passing judgment on them. Paul is anxious that respect for the consciences of other Christians is given and that things are not pressed on them of which they are unsure. What a model Paul is presenting! God does not want a church full of successful and confident people. He wants a church to be full of believers with different natures and characters so that, as they care for each other's needs, the world sees how they love one another. This love is not to be like that of the tax collectors (Matt 5:46) but like the love of God who, in his infinite power and wisdom, comes alongside frail and uncertain believers, working to help them grow and embrace certainties. Imposing stronger "faith" on a weak believer results in a false discipleship where the belief system of others are held without understanding their foundations. The divine example must be the guide as the letter to the Philippians demonstrates. In that letter, Paul used a beautiful piece of poetry—probably adapted as a hymn—to speak of the example of Christ (Phil 2:6–11). This understanding of who the strong are is contrary to what most scholars hold, seeing the description as a reference to numerical superiority. However Paul will go on to say:

> Accept one another, then, just as Christ accepted you, in order to bring praise to God. For I tell you that Christ has become a servant of the Jews on behalf of God's truth, to confirm the promises made to the patriarchs so that the Gentiles may glorify God for his mercy, as it is written: "Therefore I will praise you among the Gentiles; I will sing hymns to your name." Again, it says, "Rejoice, O Gentiles, with his people." And again, "Praise the Lord, all you Gentiles, and sing praises to him, all you peoples." And again, Isaiah says, "The Root of Jesse will spring up, one who will arise to rule over the nations; the Gentiles will hope in him."
>
> May the God of hope fill you with all joy and peace as you trust in him, so that you may overflow with hope by the power of the Holy Spirit. I myself am convinced, my brothers, that you yourselves are full of goodness, complete in knowledge and competent to instruct one another. I have written you quite boldly on some points, as if to remind you of them again, because of the grace God gave me to be a minister of Christ Jesus to the Gentiles with the priestly duty of proclaiming the gospel of God, so that the Gentiles might become an offering acceptable to God, sanctified by the Holy Spirit. (Rom 15:7–16)

Clearly the exhortation is that the Jewish believers welcome the Gentile believers who Christ himself has welcomed and whose welcome has been made possible by the ministry that Paul has fulfilled. Paul has written to the Gentiles to assure them that they are "full of goodness, complete in knowledge and competent to instruct one another,"[5] and that they should be full of joy and peace because God has welcomed them.

---

5. Particularly relevant for a Gentile community in danger of succumbing to the claim that they are not holy if they refuse to become Jews.

14:2 One man's faith allows him to eat everything, but another man, whose faith is weak, eats only vegetables. Paul presents two extremes of faith. One is of a Christian who has no conscience about what he eats. The other belongs to one who is deeply distressed over issues relating to meat and who, therefore, is vegetarian. There is no suggestion in the Scripture that vegetarianism was an issue, so it is probable that Paul has believers in mind, like the ones in Corinth, who are deeply concerned with the meat's origin (1 Cor 10:23–32). In Rome, it appears that some of the believers are taking the rather extreme measure of only eating vegetables in order to ensure that they do not unknowingly eat meat that had been offered to idols.

14:3 The man who eats everything must not look down on him who does not, and the man who does not eat everything must not condemn the man who does, for God has accepted him. Paul raises an issue that was a common problem in the early church. The Christians lived in societies where pagan gods were worshiped daily, the meat of the sacrificed animals being sold on to market traders. Consequently, it was almost impossible to be certain that meat bought in the marketplace was free from association with idol worship. Those who converted to Christ from idolatry knew the significance of such offerings. They were the means of celebrating fellowship with the forces of darkness and the meat of such sacrificed animals was the property of the deities who had been worshiped. "How," such Christians asked, "could any believer eat such food?" They reasoned that it could only be by sinful compromise, offending God and rupturing fellowship with him.

While Paul believes that idols have no objective reality or existence (1 Cor 8:1–8), he realizes, nevertheless, that eating meat sacrificed to them is a cause of great difficulty for some. He explains that there is a reality of demons exploiting idols and enslaving those who worship them.

Here, in Rom 14:3, Paul lays down an important principle of Christian tolerance. It is all too easy to see one's own position as superior. The matter under consideration was the eating of or abstaining from certain meats. Those who ate them saw themselves as more robust and stronger in faith than those who abstained; those who abstained saw themselves as more spiritual and sensitive to the will of God than those who ate. Both believed that they were the ones concerned for the glory of God.

14:4 Who are you to judge someone else's servant? To his own master he stands or falls. And he will stand, for the Lord is able to make him stand. Paul stresses the inappropriateness of intruding into somebody else's relationship with God. His argument is clear: "What right have you got to judge someone whom God has accepted?" If some of the Roman believers were to claim that they knew things about another believer of which God was ignorant, it would be the height of arrogance in the face of his omniscience, for he knows all things. Paul's point is that when God accepts a believer, he becomes God's responsibility.[6] Judgment in such matters is not for his fellow believers to exercise—for

6. Käsemann, *Romans*, 370, says: "Paul is announcing his confidence that the Lord of the community, having once received a member, can cause him to stand again when he falls. Grace is stronger than human frailty."

God has never assigned such authority to them. A pressing reason for Paul writing this letter was because such a presumption was in danger of ripping the church apart.

14:5 One man considers one day more sacred than another; another man considers every day alike. Each one should be fully convinced in his own mind. Paul moves from the issue of meat-eating and applies the same principle to another matter that was straining the relationship between Jewish and Gentile believers in Rome. Some believed that certain days were more holy than others and ought to be observed by following rules that had developed around them. Others did not see any intrinsic sacredness in these days, for God was with them in all their affairs of life and not just in "holy affairs." Such Christians could not see why they should be forced to keep days as holy when the whole of life was holy.

The subtle thing about the choice Paul made in raising these examples is that the eating of meat distressed the Gentile believers[7] but the non-observance of certain days distressed the Jewish believers. He carefully selected issues that gave both parties an insight into the pain of being abused, misunderstood, or rejected. It is this contrast of experiences—highlighted in the following verse—that suggests it is the Gentile believers who are referred to as the weaker in the matter of the eating of meat. If this is not so, then both examples would be about Jewish offense, and this would not serve the greater purpose of both parties learning to accept each other.

14:6 He who regards one day as special, does so to the Lord. He who eats meat, eats to the Lord, for he gives thanks to God; and he who abstains, does so to the Lord and gives thanks to God. As is Paul's practice, he restates the essence of the argument. The attitude of the believers' hearts is the real issue. The argument Paul is making is similar to that found in 1 Cor 8–10, but there are significant differences between the two situations and their associated problems.

In Corinth, some were exercising their freedom by eating idol meat in the pagan temple itself. To "weaker brethren," this suggested a participation in fellowship with the demons that hid behind the idols. However, in Rome the issue does not appear as complicated. Possibly the situation is different because, with a strong Jewish community (estimated between 20,000 and 50,000 at the time of Claudius' edict[8]), kosher butchers were

---

7. Snodgrass "Kingdom," 521–25, argues that the weak are Jewish believers who consider that the food laws of the OT continue to apply. See also Witherington, *Romans*, 330–37, who confuses numerical strength with theological strength, see also Käsemann, *Romans*, 366, who considers the reference to "the strong" to be about numerical strength and sees it to be the Christian Gentile majority. The different opinions on the identity of the weak and the strong reflect how each group viewed itself and its behavior. Both groups were convinced that their attitude and behavior was what God wanted, and saw themselves as strong. It is true that the Gentiles had the numerical strength in the Roman church, but minorities are often stronger in their convictions—especially if driven by an orthodoxy that sustains their sense of superiority.

8. In ca. AD 49, Emperor Claudius expelled Jews from Rome (probably because Christianity had caused unrest within the Jewish community). There is some debate about what actually happened. It is reported by Suetonius that it was a result of some disturbances "at the instigation of Chrestos." This was probably due to some Jewish-Christian missionaries encountering opposition from Jews in Rome when they preached that Jesus was the Christ (see also Acts 18:2). Cassius Dio minimizes the event, and Josephus—who was reporting on Jewish events—does not mention it at all. Some scholars hold that the expulsion did not hap-

well established and provided the assurance that the meat on sale had not had contact with temple worship. Obviously, we have no idea how many such butchers survived the edict—possibly the majority were expelled. Nevertheless, it is reasonable to suggest that if there was ongoing trade from Gentile converts who preferred kosher meat because of its unpolluted source, some businesses would have been taken over to meet the demand.

14:7 For none of us lives to himself alone and none of us dies to himself alone. Paul stresses that no one is a free agent. We all have responsibilities to someone else—a husband has responsibilities to his wife and the wife has responsibilities to her husband, a father to his children and the children to their father, an employee to his employer and the employer to his employee, etc. This said, all are responsible to God, and their lives and deaths are significant to him. Christ has died to save us, and our death is the means by which we enter into his immediate presence. Both life and death serve the purposes of God for his children. We are, therefore, responsible to him in both life and death. To use the psalmist's words: "Where shall I flee from your presence?" (Ps 139:7).

14:8 If we live, we live to the Lord; and if we die, we die to the Lord. So, whether we live or die, we belong to the Lord. No matter what experiences life brings to Paul and the believers in Rome, he reminds them that they are kept by Christ. There may be things that happen that are the opposite of what they want, but Paul encourages them that their status cannot be threatened for they "belong to the Lord."

Paul is saying that God uses the whole range of human experience to teach us about his faithfulness and bring believers to maturity in Christ (see comments on Rom 5:1–8; 8:35ff.). In viewing life from this perspective, distressing experiences become part of the teaching process by means of which God prepares his people for heaven.

The experience of the community is prominent in Paul's thinking–evidenced by the repeated use of the pronoun "we." Theirs is a corporate experience that comes from sharing in the death of Christ (see comments on Rom 6:1–5), and exists because of membership of the covenant community. It is essentially covenantal and corporate, flowing from the work of the Messiah and his Spirit.[9]

14:9 For this very reason, Christ died and returned to life so that he might be the Lord of both the dead and the living. The reason for Christ's death, resurrection, and ascension was the restoration of creation—especially humankind—to its original position of subjection to his Lordship. Through Adam's sin, the cosmos had not merely come under the curse of God's judgment but had passed into the "control" of Satan. However, the death and resurrection of Jesus terminated that relationship just as Adam's disobedience had ruptured the relationship between creation and God.

---

pen, while others have only a few missionaries expelled for the short term. The silence about the edict in official records is hardly surprising as Claudius was obsessed with making edicts, and this one was minor compared to others he had made.

9. Contra, Jewett, *Romans*, 848, who says: "This passage is a clear example of collective mysticism." It is, rather, a clear example of covenantal oneness.

The restoration of all things to their pre-fallen condition is known by theologians as "recapitulation," when the control of all things—created and uncreated—will be handed back to Christ. Sadly, not all people will know this return to blessedness. Humankind, made in the image of God, has been given extraordinary dignity in that God's salvation is not forced upon it; salvation is offered but not imposed. Humankind is invited to exercise their right to respond. Without that right and responsibility being exercised they remain in the kingdom of darkness and outside of the transformation, i.e., outside of the recapitulation. They have denied salvation for one simple reason: they have chosen to remain in the kingdom of darkness—the body of sin. They remain in Adam, and they are responsible for the consequences that flow from the state of alienation.[10]

The declaration that Jesus is Lord would have been seen as an affront to the Emperor. Caesar not only claimed absolute rights over his subjects, he claimed to be the son of God. This claim of divinity impacted many in the empire, especially those in the state's direct employment. They demonstrated their allegiance to him by offering sacrifices. There were times that this practice of honoring Caesar as the incarnate god was demanded of all citizens of the empire. Consequently, submission to the Lordship of Christ placed the Roman Christians in real danger of rousing the state's anger and experiencing its punishment.

Paul is not declaring a political manifesto in this statement—he is declaring a theological truth. Nevertheless, such truth inevitably has implications in many aspects of life including its political dimension.

14:10 You, then, why do you judge your brother? Or why do you look down on your brother? For we will all stand before God's judgment seat. Paul introduces his question to the believers with the words "You, then," making the charge personal. He does not write a generalization such as "we ought not to judge," but addresses the conscience of the believers who gathered to hear the letter read to them.

The issues raised are the judging of and the looking down on brothers. Paul stresses that they are not only undesirable actions, they are sinful. Judgment usurps God's authority. This will become clear on the day of judgment when all will stand before him—not only those who have been condemned by judgmental spirits[11] but also those who have exercised such judgment. The implication seems to be that the one who was unjustly judged will become the accuser and the one who was the self-righteous accuser will be the one charged.

Of course, in writing this, Paul would not want to imply that Christians should not express concern when people are behaving badly but that concern should be expressed in a spirit of love. Christ made it clear that, when believers sin, those in close contact ought to encourage them to repent (Matt 18:15). When this fails, it is the church's respon-

---

10. Käsemann, *Romans*, 372, says: "Christ has gone through life and death and now has power over both. The contour of the cosmocreator becomes visible, who leaves no one in a private sphere and who orients all things to himself. Belonging to him or not becomes the eschatological criterion of all humanity and thus characterizes all activity, transcending our criteria."

11. Some Greek MSS (א^c, C^2, Ψ, 048, 0209, and the *Koinē* text-tradition) read *Chrisou* instead of *theou*, which is the reading of the majority of the best MSS (א*, A, B, C*, D, F, G, 630, 1506, 1739).

sibility to bring discipline (Matt 18:16–17; 1 Cor 5:2–5). What is different in these cases from the ones dealt with in Rom 14 is that Paul is dealing with matters of conscience regarding ceremonial law. The discipline of believers takes place when the moral law has been broken.

14:11 It is written: "'As surely as I live' says the Lord, 'Every knee will bow before me; every tongue will confess to God.'" Paul concludes his argument with a quotation from Isa 45:23. The way he uses this Scripture to support his argument demonstrates how the Scripture determined his worldview. Isaiah had said these words in Yahweh's name and Paul was able to bring the principles behind them to bear on the problems that existed in the Roman church. Paul is anxious that his converts develop this biblical mindset, and that they learn to put all of the issues of life—whether personal and trivial, or international and crucial—into the framework of biblical revelation and thinking (cf. Rom 12:1–2). When Israel failed to do this in the OT (negotiating her place among the nations instead) she was swallowed up with compromise (Isa 31:1–3). However, when she embraced the worldview proclaimed by the prophets, she triumphed and God's name was glorified (Isa 66:10–22).

Paul has also used Isa 45:23 in Phil 2:1–12, where he applied it to all bowing before Christ. However, here in Romans he retains the original Isaianic context of bowing before Yahweh. This ability to move between "God" and "Christ" (i.e., applying the Scripture about Yahweh to Christ) is strong evidence that Paul understood and taught that Jesus is God (this would be developed by the fathers into Trinitarianism). Here, Paul supports his contention by blending Isa 49:18 and Isa 45:23, quoting the latter with minor changes to the word order. The use of Isa 49:18 is of interest to our theme, for the remnant benefits from the subjection of the nations. They are provided as an inheritance and become the attire for the remnant's marriage to Yahweh: "'As surely as I live,' declares the LORD, 'you will wear them all as ornaments; you will put them on, like a bride'" (Isa 49:18).[12]

14:12 So then, each of us will give an account of himself to God. At this point, Paul stresses personal responsibility. As we have seen earlier, we have to be careful not to apply to the individual what is only true of the church. However, while it is true that the church has a corporate responsibility, Paul unequivocally speaks to the individual members of the Roman congregation. He makes it clear that each believer has to put into action what he has been taught. If he fails to do so, he will bear his own guilt on the day of judgment. This shows that Paul expects a judgment for the believer (2 Cor 5:10). This does not relate to salvation but to his life following conversion to Christ. The particular case Paul has in mind at this point is the damage done to other believers.

This is not an isolated passage. It is clear that there was an ongoing concern in church leadership over this issue (Acts 15:5–21; 21:20–21). The church of the twenty-first century also needs to heed this warning. All too often, sensitive believers avoid fellowship with professing local churches because they, or others they know, have been dealt with harshly and uncaringly within them. Christ does not deal with them in such a way.

---

12. See Käsemann, *Romans*, 372–73.

He is the good good shepherd who gives his life for his sheep (John 10:11). When church ideals are in conflict with the compassion and love of Christ, they must be questioned. This is not suggesting that churches abandon standards but that they must hold them in the context of Christ's compelling love rather than destructive legalism which promotes self-righteousness and self-satisfaction.

14:13 Therefore let us stop passing judgment on one another. Instead, make up your mind not to put any stumbling-block or obstacle in your brother's way. We should not pass judgment on others over matters that are not crucial to our relationship with God. Not only is judgment negative but it puts a stumbling-block in the way of those who are being criticized. Such hindrance to their progress is no small thing as the Christian life is likened to a pilgrimage towards our spiritual home. Such criticism discourages others on their pilgrimage, deflecting them from the road that Christ has called them to walk along. For that reason it is sin.

14:14 As one who is in the Lord Jesus, I am fully convinced that no food is unclean in itself. But if anyone regards something as unclean, then for him it is unclean. Paul states his position clearly. He describes himself as one who is "in the Lord Jesus." In doing this, he identifies himself with the status of every other believer.[13] He is not seeking to lord it over the believers, but appeals to them on equal terms.

This conciliatory posture was not always adopted by Paul. When the objective truth of the Gospel was at stake, he was very assertive (Gal 2:14). However, he does not take this confrontational position with the Roman believers for good reason. This was not an issue of Gospel truth or apostolic authority.

Paul's position remains true to the one taken in the earlier part of the chapter. No food is intrinsically unclean. God has given all food as a gift—even food offered in sacrifice to demons is intrinsically clean. However, if a believer is unable to thank God for providing such food—believing it to be unclean—he ought not to eat it. In writing this, Paul was handling the "weaker" believers in Rome with great sensitivity. The eating of meat was a serious issue for them, causing them (they thought) to become psychologically and spiritually "unclean."

In this example, Paul demonstrates his love for Christ and the people of God. He not only tells the weaker in faith not to eat meat but, in his letter to the Corinthians, he says that if in the eating of meat a brother is offended, the stronger in faith should stop eating, even though it was his God-given right to enjoy (1 Cor 8:13). Here is a demonstration of the pastoral heart. In his tenderness, Paul thinks of others above himself. He stands with the weaker brothers, and even though his theological reasoning dismisses their arguments, his love and respect for them does not allow him to march away from the argument as the victor and indulge himself in his legitimate freedoms.

How different churches would be if they recognized the legitimate diversity of views as well as the folly of imposing their views on others who have not been persuaded of

---

13. Contra, Morris, *Romans*, 486, who understands the statement to be based on Paul's union with Christ, citing the GNB: "My union with the Lord Jesus makes me certain."

their perspective. When people are pressurized to conform to expressions of personal preferences rather than the clear directives of Scripture, their growth is inevitably stunted. There are many things that are good but are not the essence of the Gospel—such practices as keeping certain days as holy, upholding good and sensible health principles, and other social norms that societies throw up as "best practice." It is amazing how Christians can confuse their cultural heritage with "Christian norms" and assume that it is an essential non-negotiable part of the Gospel.

14:15 If your brother is distressed because of what you eat, you are no longer acting in love. Do not by your eating destroy your brother for whom Christ died. Paul takes his advice a step further. Earlier, he had been concerned about the weaker brother and his difficulty in eating meat previously offered to idols. Now he widens the issue. He tells those with robust consciences that if their eating of meat causes others to stumble, they affect the faith of those who see danger and defilement in eating in such a way.[14] Paul writes that they are no longer acting in love for, in insisting on their rights, they are in danger of destroying the ones for whom Christ has died.

This is an amazing assertion. These "stronger" believers had seen themselves as mature and liberated members of the church. Paul is effectively saying "If you are mature, then behave as such. Put the needs of the weaker brother as a priority in your lives. It has cost Christ his life to bring this brother into fellowship with himself. Do you dare drive him away as a consequence of demanding your right to practice your freedom?" Such a perspective seriously challenges what most of us understand as Christian maturity. Rather than being strong and arguing for one's own point of view, Christian maturity is about servanthood and following Christ in his self-denial (Phil 2:1–15).

14:16 Do not allow what you consider good to be spoken of as evil. What does Paul refer to when he writes that they should not let what they "consider as good to be spoken of as evil?"[15] It could be argued that it refers to their freedom to eat meat. That certainly has been the flow of the argument. However, it could also be argued that it is a preparatory statement, for in the following verse, he pleads that the members of the church recognize that there is something much bigger than their own interests—the kingdom of God. Indeed, he goes on to show how these contentious issues fall into their proper place when seen in the context of the reign of God.

This exhortation needs to be heard and obeyed by the people of God in the twenty-first century. Christian communities can be divided over matters that are of little significance when seen in light of the issues about which God is concerned. Personal preferences and prejudices can be dressed up as the most spiritual of arguments to justify pressurizing others into accepting them. Such attempts to "defend the truth" demonstrate a lack of spirituality, for the love that pervaded Paul's appeal is missing. The absence of

14. Murray, *Romans*, vol. 2:190, points out that more than grief is involved as there is hurt from the violation of a religious principle.

15. Gagnon, "Meaning," 675–89 argues that despite the widespread disagreement over the meaning of "your good (thing)" in Rom 14:16, the "charism" interpretation of this phrase as "the faith of you, the strong, to eat all things" should be regarded as secure.

love is not rectified by blind devotion to a doctrinal system, no matter how correct and orthodox it might be (1 Cor 13:1–13).

14:17 For the kingdom of God is not a matter of eating and drinking, but of righteousness, peace and joy in the Holy Spirit. The kingdom of God has not been explicitly mentioned until now,[16] despite the fact that the whole of the letter has been dealing with the subject. The Son of David was predicted to be the inaugurator of the kingdom, and he had come in the person of Jesus (Rom 1:3). The letter is centered on the ethnicity of the kingdom.[17] It is composed of Jews and Gentiles, and the letter deals with the problems that this "new man" experiences. Paul is clearly distressed that the church is caught up with matters that divide. The apostles met to give authoritative guidance to the Gentiles (Acts 15:6–29), but the evidence suggests that the instructions fell on many Jewish believers' deaf ears (Acts 21:20–21).

14:18 Because anyone who serves Christ in this way is pleasing to God and approved by men. The definite article with "Chirst" indicates that the term is being used titularly. This confirms that Paul's use has this Messianic significance and that it had not been lost in the Gentile mission. This confirms the correctness of reading the letter in light of the OT expectations regarding Israel's long promised Messiah king, who is the Christ. Thus references throughout the letter to the term "Christ" are correctly read as Messianic in meaning and significance.

It is typical of Paul to write that serving the preference of others serves Christ. It is pleasing to God (Phil 2:1–15) as Christian living should not fight for rights but strive for unity. It respects the uncertainties and fears of others, and is concerned to see them grow into Christ. It is all too easy to think we are serving Christ when motivated by the prejudices of our own hearts and not by his Spirit. How easy it is to confuse the two. How many dreadful mistakes have been made by people who have claimed they were doing God's will while causing the name of Christ to be brought into disrepute? When we serve Christ out of the motive of caring for others, we bring delight to the heart of God and an acknowledgment by others that we are not motivated by bigotry or the like.

14:19 Let us therefore make every effort to do what leads to peace and to mutual edification. The term εἰρήνης "peace" is used earlier in the letter where Paul refers to "peace with God" (Rom 5:1; 8:6). Those who are at peace with him are obliged to be at peace with other believers as this promotes "mutual edification."[18] This clearly suggests that imposing one's view on another is not to be tolerated.

---

16. See Jewett, *Romans*, 863, who points out that while the kingdom of God is rare in Paul's letters, the way it is used here suggests he assumes that the church in Rome has a clear understanding of its theological significance.

17. While some commentators (See Turner, "Interim," 323–42) say that the "kingdom of God" refers to a future kingdom, the following statement clearly presents the kingdom as present in the church.

18. The uses of οἰκοδομή for congregational edification are found elsewhere in Paul (1 Cor 3:9–10; 14:3, 5, 12, 26; 2 Cor 10:8; 12:19; 13:10), and they are used in the LXX as a metaphor to describe the work of God in building Israel as a congregation for himself (Jer 12:16; 38:4, 28; 40:7; 49:10; 45:4; 51:34).

Great effort is needed to enter into the thinking and fears of other people. If we do not take the trouble to appreciate where they come from in terms of the experiences and traditions that mold their understanding, we have little hope of treating them with respect. Without such effort, we are effectively saying that others have to be made in our image—something that is not only dangerous but blasphemous. The only one who has the right to someone in his own image is God himself.

Without understanding how our differences have come into existence, we can never be instruments of peace and attain mutual edification. Demanding conformity to our own particular understanding of secondary issues divides rather than unites. Indeed, it is important that we understand why we hold *our* own views lest we canonize the tradition into which we were converted or which we have adopted.

14:20 Do not destroy the work of God for the sake of food. All food is clean, but it is wrong for a man to eat anything that causes someone else to stumble. Paul returns to the issue of eating meats. He has no difficulty in upholding the Jewish view that all prescribed food is clean, for it is the provision of the gracious Creator God. However, he is not limiting himself to prescribed food. Paul is saying that all food is clean—something with which Peter had to come to terms (Acts 9:9–16). But Paul is equally clear that what God has declared clean can easily become the instrument of Satan, for the insistence of "true understanding" and the practice of one's own rights can lead to the destruction of a weaker brother's faith.[19]

What is sinful is not the eating of meat but the arrogant manner in which it is eaten. It reveals that the freedom demonstrated is irresponsible and nothing to do with the truth and love of God but rather the arrogant rights of the offender. How easily that which is good divides and offends, causing the work of God to be destroyed in a sensitive soul. No amount of arguing about the lack of "spirituality" or about the sovereign grace of God to care for his own will diminish the responsibility that we carry for causing others to stumble. No one defended such doctrines more than the Apostle Paul; yet here he is, pleading for the unity that Christ prayed for, and making it clear that there is no compromise in the giving of high regard and attention to those who are in need of sympathy and support.

14:21 It is better not to eat meat or drink wine or to do anything else that will cause your brother to fall. Not only is it better but it is necessary! The motive of love for fellow believers makes abstinence from what is legitimate something that is God-honoring and glorifying. It is not the other way around as is often argued by advocates of so-called biblical freedom. Freedom is not given so that we may suit ourselves; rather, freedom is given so that we can share in the immense privilege of advancing the kingdom of God—making his love known to his people and to those who are outside of the covenants of promise. It is to be used so that it reveals the tenderness of the one who

---

19. The Greek leaves it unclear who the person is that is eating. In v. 14, the reference was to the "weaker" brother and the same argument may continue. However, the grammar and immediate context suggest that the reference is to the "stronger" brother. For support, Moo, *Application*, 462; Käsemann, *Romans*, 378; Cranfield, *Romans*, 723–24.

is the good shepherd. Freedom is to be restrained for the sake of those who would feel trampled upon and despised by those who consider themselves to be the stronger. By forgoing their freedom to eat meat, the Roman believers will show how much they love their brothers and sisters.

Unexpectedly, Paul raises the issue of drinking wine. In light of the fact that drinking wine was widespread and only drunkenness is condemned in the Scriptures, many assume that the reference points to a pagan ritual that took place in the temple.[20] However, in light of what Paul has written to the believers, it seems probable that he was advising the believers to consider the effect of wine on fellow believers. As today, some will have enjoyed drinking to excess and will have tried to curb their dependence on wine since their conversion. Paul's advice is to abstain from drinking wine lest others, who struggle with a history of personal abuse, hear about or see your enjoyment of it.

14:22 So whatever you believe about these things keep between yourself and God. Blessed is the man who does not condemn himself by what he approves. Paul clearly sees that theological correctness can be morally deficient if it is used to score points. However, there are issues that a believer can keep in his heart. According to the text, certain things can be pondered without being published.

There is clearly a pastoral dimension to teaching. One of the elements is the ability to judge how different Christian truths should be presented and when their implications, as far as Christian living is concerned, should be pressed. Just as there are stages in human development from infancy to adulthood, so there is progression for the Christian. This does not deny that some people develop more rapidly than others, but it does mean that a wise believer should take this into account when dealing with a young Christian.

Does the phrase "Blessed is the man" refer to God's blessing on those who behave in accordance with their conscience, or is it merely Paul's approval of those who act in such a way? Its close proximity to the statement about keeping truth private ought to guide our understanding. It would seem that Paul is saying that the ones who are blessed are those who know that they have struck the right balance. They know that they are not condemned by their conscience. It would, therefore, seem that the blessedness is that of a clear conscience.[21]

14:23 But the man who has doubts is condemned if he eats, because his eating is not from faith; and everything that does not come from faith is sin. In contrast to the man who has a clear conscience and is blessed, the one who goes against his conscience is condemned. It follows that in this case, being condemned is not referring to God's condemnation but the condemnation of the conscience.[22] However, such self-condemnation leads to God's condemnation, for action "that does not come from faith is sin."

---

20. See Morris, *Romans*, 491; Moo, *Romans*, 861.

21. Jewett, *Romans*, 871, says: "The blessing in this case comes to everyone who maintains integrity with the faith as they have received it from God, whether it is consistent with the preferences of other groups or not."

22. There is possibly an echo of the argument in Rom 4, where Paul wrote about Abraham not wavering through unbelief. See Wright, *Romans*, 742.

CONCLUSION OF ROMANS 14

The new community in Rome is in danger of division—worse than that, it is in danger of civil war. The issue centers on the observance of the law and the keeping of its ceremonial requirements. Paul is concerned that this division between Jew and Gentile believers could be the bridgehead that Satan will use to destroy this "new creation" in the capital city.

The key to the whole issue is that Christ is the Lord. It is not for others to judge; rather, they should recognize that Christ has called believers from different backgrounds and with these backgrounds come problems that the Gospel has to address. Paul quotes from the writing of Isaiah to support his argument: Every knee will bow and every tongue will confess the Lordship of Christ [God] (Isa 45:23). Once again, second exodus material is used to make the case for the new exodus. In considering how people are accepted into the kingdom of God, Paul makes it clear that it is not about eating or drinking but righteousness, peace and joy in the Holy Spirit.

ROMANS 15

THE MESSIAH KING AND HIS SERVANT'S WORK

WE WHO ARE strong ought to bear with the failings of the weak and not to please ourselves. Each of us should please his neighbor for his good, to build him up. For even Christ did not please himself but, as it is written: "The insults of those who insult you have fallen on me." For everything that was written in the past was written to teach us, so that through endurance and the encouragement of the Scriptures we might have hope. May the God who gives endurance and encouragement give you a spirit of unity among yourselves as you follow Christ Jesus, so that with one heart and mouth you may glorify the God and Father of our Lord Jesus Christ. Accept one another, then, just as Christ accepted you, in order to bring praise to God. For I tell you that Christ has become a servant of the Jews on behalf of God's truth, to confirm the promises made to the patriarchs so that the Gentiles may glorify God for his mercy, as it is written: "Therefore I will praise you among the Gentiles; I will sing hymns to your name."

Again, it says, "Rejoice, O Gentiles, with his people." And again, "Praise the Lord, all you Gentiles, and sing praises to him, all you peoples." And again, Isaiah says, "The Root of Jesse will spring up, one who will arise to rule over the nations; the Gentiles will hope in him." May the God of hope fill you with all joy and peace as you trust in him, so that you may overflow with hope by the power of the Holy Spirit. I myself am convinced, my brothers, that you yourselves are full of goodness, complete in knowledge and competent to instruct one another. I have written to you quite boldly on some points, as if to remind you of them again, because of the grace God gave me to be a minister of Christ Jesus to the Gentiles with the priestly duty of proclaiming the gospel of God, so that the Gentiles might become an offering acceptable to God, sanctified by the Holy Spirit. Therefore I glory in Christ Jesus in my service to God. I will not venture to speak of anything except what Christ has accomplished through me in leading the Gentiles to obey God by what I have said and done— by the power of signs and miracles, through the power of the Spirit. So from Jerusalem all the way around to Illyricum, I have fully proclaimed the gospel of Christ.

It has always been my ambition to preach the gospel where Christ was not known, so that I would not be building on someone else's foundation. Rather, as it is written: "Those who were not told about him will see, and those who have not heard will understand." This is why I have often been hindered from coming to you. But now that there is no more place for me to work in these regions, and since I have been longing for many years to see you, I plan to do so when I go to Spain. I hope to visit you while passing through and to have you assist me on my journey there, after I have enjoyed your company for a while. Now, however, I am on my way to Jerusalem in the service of the saints there. For Macedonia and Achaia were pleased to make a contribution for the poor among the saints in Jerusalem. They were pleased to do it, and indeed they owe it to them. For if the Gentiles have shared in the Jews' spiritual blessings, they owe it to the Jews to share with them their material blessings. So after I have completed this task and have made sure that they have received this fruit, I will go to Spain and visit you on the way. I know that when I come to you, I will come in the full measure of the blessing of Christ. I urge you, brothers, by our Lord Jesus Christ and by the love of the Spirit, to join me in my struggle by praying to God for me. Pray that I may be rescued from the unbelievers in Judea and that my service in Jerusalem may be acceptable to the saints there, so that by God's will I may come to you with joy and together with you be refreshed. The God of peace be with you all. Amen. (Rom 15:1–33)

INTRODUCTION

THE CHAPTER CONTINUES THE theme followed in the preceding chapter. Believers should not fight for their rights but consider the needs of others, especially the needs of those who are weak in their faith. In doing this they are following the example of the one they say they serve (Rom 15:3–4).

Paul goes on to show that this acceptance was foretold by the prophets, a fact that suggests that those who are the strong, who need to be urged to accept the weaker brethren, are the Jews, for such a citation is especially suited to them in their reluctance to give up their Jewish understanding of what God requires, which tended to be mostly about ritual participation. Their mutual acceptance was to be of the same kind as they have received from Christ who had every right to reject us all because of our uncleanness.

Paul reflects on his ministry, which is not one of salvage to a second rate status but of the restoration of humanity to the privileged position of being priests unto God. He sees his own ministry to be priestly (Rom 15:16) and it is into this ministry that the Gentiles have been brought.

Paul expresses the desire that he will be able to visit them on his way to Spain where he desires to plan the church of Christ (Rom 15:28). He tells of his plans to visit Jerusalem with the gift provided by the Gentile churches. He solicits prayer for this endeavor that he knows is dangerous because of the hatred some hold towards him for defending Gentile freedom (15:31).

15:1 We who are strong ought to bear with the failings of the weak and not to please ourselves. Most scholars consider that Paul is now making an appeal to the Jewish believers for they know there is only one God and that idols are nothing.[1] But has Paul swung from appealing to the Gentiles in chapter 14 to appealing to the Jews in this chapter? I have argued that Paul was addressing the Jewish believers in Rom 14:22–23; therefore, this verse is not a change of argument but an application of what he was say-

---

1. "Under the gospel, the strong—those who, because of the inner freedom which has been given to them, have plenty of room in which to manoeuvre, have an inescapable obligation to help carry the infirmities, disabilities, embarrassments and encumbrances of their brothers who are having to live without that inner freedom which they themselves enjoy." Cranfield, *Shorter*, 353. Cranfield also suggests the strong are the believing Gentile majority, 341. See also, Fitzmyer, *Romans*, 687.

ing. If this is so, then the one who is not eating out of faith is not the Gentile who is going beyond what his conscience allows, but the Jew who is going beyond what love allows.

15:2 Each of us should please his neighbor for his good, to build him up. The pastoral heart of Paul shines through again as he appeals to the believers. He is anxious that they learn to be more concerned for the needs of others rather than their own rights and freedoms.

The respect and love believers give each other complement the teaching ministry of the church in strengthening them in their faith. Indeed, formal teaching can be undone if the members of the congregation do not live out the realities to which they have been exposed, grieving the Holy Spirit as well as "weaker" brethren. While the translators of the NRSV and the NIV understand "building up" in v.2 to apply to the individual, the term regularly refers to the community in Paul's other writings (1 Cor 14:5; Eph 4:12, 29).

In the introduction to the commentary, I suggested Paul's reason for writing the letter was to give the Romans guidance over the issues that were causing divisions in other churches. The Jewish-Gentile relationship was at the center of most of the early church's problems. This suggestion seems to be confirmed in this penultimate chapter. Paul is constantly appealing to his countrymen to accept the Gentiles, showing the Jews that, as the Lord's servant, they have been appointed to bring the light of the good news to the nations. They are to be servants to the Gentiles–not preferring themselves over the ones they serve (Phil 2:2-4).

15:3 For even Christ did not please himself but, as it is written: "The insults of those who insult you have fallen on me." Paul appeals to the great example of Christ in accordance with the apostles' teaching (2 Cor 8:9–15; Phil 2:1–11; Heb 12:1–3; 1 Pet 2:21–25), for when arguments fail, examples often triumph. The example of the Son of God, who offered up his life for those who hated and killed him, has transformed more lives than arguments have ever done. Christ was not only an example because he relinquished his own will but because he subjected himself to the violence and rejection of humankind in all of its ugly brutality. Very soon, those authorities that crucified Jesus would turn on the Roman believers themselves. They will become another example of a vessel chosen for privilege becoming a vessel fitted for wrath.

Paul's point is clear—we have an obligation to follow Christ's example if we dare to call ourselves his disciples. He put others before himself. The citation from the OT is Ps 69:9 (LXX) and it is used elsewhere in the NT (Mark 15:36; Luke 23:36; John 19:29; Rev 13:8). It is significant that, rather than alluding to the actual events in the life of Christ that demonstrate his self-giving, Paul goes back to the OT Scriptures for his support. There can be little doubt that the suffering referred to in the psalm is seen by Paul to speak prophetically of the passion of Christ. We can only speculate about why he avoided making direct reference to the life of Jesus. It is not that he rejected any desire to know anything about the earthly Jesus (as some have argued from 2 Cor 5:16). The reference to not wanting to know Christ after the flesh probably means that he did not want to interpret his life from any nationalistic Messianic perspective as he would have done before his conversion.

15:4 For everything that was written in the past was written to teach us, so that through endurance and the encouragement of the Scriptures we might have hope. The importance of the Jewish Scriptures for the fledgling church cannot be exaggerated. The Jewish believers and the God-fearers were saturated with them because they had no other sacred writings (the NT only existed as an emerging collection). The OT gave them the theological framework by which they interpreted the significance of the life, death and resurrection of Jesus. However, it was not only the life of Jesus that was interpreted through the lens of OT expectation, their experiences were as well.

We have seen in the introduction to the commentary how widespread Paul's use of the Scriptures was in his thinking and writing. He was not unique. The same OT perspective permeated the thinking of the entire church. This is evident from the argument being presented as his readers were expected to understand the context of references and significance of echoes. If our presentation of Romans has been correct, the whole of this Epistle exemplifies this undergirding dependence.

The reference to having hope is significant, for Paul has written in Rom 5:1–5 that hope is the fruit of the gift of the Spirit to the church. Without the outworking of the Word and Spirit, the early church's living hope cannot be experienced. It was the Spirit who applied the promise of the OT to the fledgling church and it is he who continues to apply the same, with its NT fulfillment, to the church of today. Any Christian community which does not keep the Word and the Spirit in balance is in danger of having a deficient understanding and experience of God's grace.

15:5 May the God who gives endurance and encouragement give you a spirit of unity among yourselves as you follow Christ Jesus, Paul prays out of personal experience (2 Cor 1:3–11). The prayer is not a platitude uttered from the safety of a distant administrative center. It was written by a man who is in the heat of battle and desires for the church in Rome to share in what he knows of God's sustaining grace and encouragement.

He prays not only for endurance but also for God's encouragement. As these two blessings flow into the believers' lives, they become united in heart and mind and together gladly submit to Christ. This unity will lead them to serve one another as Paul has encouraged them to do in Rom 15:1.

15:6 So that with one heart and mouth you may glorify the God and Father of our Lord Jesus Christ. This is the goal of the Gospel. The ultimate purpose of God in saving people for himself is that they might corporately demonstrate the character and wisdom of their Savior (Eph 3:10–13). It is no more wrong of God to desire to be acknowledged by those he has saved than for parents to want to hear expressions of love and joy from the children they bore. It is not a selfish obsession, because God is the God of love who rejoices in the overthrow of evil and the recovery of his creation from Sin's captivity. According to the Westminster Catechism, man's chief end is to love God and enjoy him forever.

15:7 Accept one another, then, just as Christ accepted you, in order to bring praise to God. The statement in the Greek begins with the conjunction Διὸ (*dio*) "wherefore." Paul's appeal is based on the preceding verses where he explained the goal and effects of the Gospel and the example set by Christ.

Christian relationships are not an optional extra to discipleship. They are an essential part of the Christian life for, when lived out as God intends, they bring him praise. For the believer, there can be no greater reason for pursuing Christian reconciliation and mutual encouragement than this. As this reason was given in the previous verse, its repetition indicates the importance of accepting one another.

I have claimed that the letter to the Romans is a pastoral letter about Jewish/Gentile relationships. Here, in this verse, Paul makes his final appeal for the acceptance of the Jew by the Gentile community and the Gentile by the Jewish Christian community.[2] His appeal sums up his plea made since Rom 14:1 and has been based on the theological argument of Jewish and Gentile equality as discussed in chapters 1–12. This understanding is endorsed by the next verse, which emphasizes the Gentiles' acceptance into the new covenant community.

However, it must be noted that it is wrong to consider Paul's appeal as a demand to overlook sinful actions in the quest for peace. When a man took his father's wife in the Corinthian church (1 Cor 5:1–13), Paul did not urge the congregation to accept him–he threatened that he would discipline any who behaved in such a way. He made it clear that such behavior violated the commands of God; even the pagans drew the line at such behavior. Respecting the weak did not mean tolerating issues that violated the moral law of the Torah. Roman believers are to accept one another in the way that Christ accepted them, i.e., with no reservation and out of immeasurable grace. The example of Christ is a far greater influence than a theoretical discussion of acceptance and has inspired the reconciliation of people over the centuries who would never have known the restoration of relationship.

15:8 For I tell you that Christ has become a servant of the Jews on behalf of God's truth, to confirm the promises made to the patriarchs The phrase "I tell you," introduces a solemn doctrinal pronouncement.[3] In this verse, there is an echo of Isa 42:1–9, where the servant establishes justice on the earth (v. 4) and is made a light for the Gentiles (v.6). As a result, the blind are given their sight, captives are delivered (v. 7), and idols are exposed as valueless (v. 8).

Servanthood had been Israel's calling, but she failed to fulfill her role.[4] Now the servant church has been called to fulfill the task that Israel refused to do by bringing good news to those in darkness. Paul clearly sees Jesus, the Christ, to be the one who

---

2. Sass, "Römerbriefs," 510–27, argues that vv. 7–13 are a summary of the whole letter. He claims that Rom 15:9b–12, Paul uses OT quotations as evidence for his Gospel.

3. Cranfield, *Shorter*, 356.

4. Williams, "Righteousness," 288, says that Rom 15:8–9a should be translated: "Christ has become a servant from the Jews for the sake of God's truthfulness." If this is correct, then the idea is that God has stayed faithful to his original promise and blessed the Gentiles through the seed of Abraham.

would bless the Gentiles, fulfilling the promise made to Abraham, Isaac, and Jacob (Gen 22:18; 26:4; 28:14).[5]

15:9 So that the Gentiles may glorify God for his mercy, as it is written: "Therefore I will praise you among the Gentiles; I will sing hymns to your name." The reason for the Gentiles being evangelized is that God will be glorified as a result of his saving mercy towards them. In other words, the whole of creation is to acknowledge that God is a merciful and gracious God.[6] Man, who had long been in the clutches of Satan and deceived regarding God's nature, will see that he had believed the lie.

While the purpose of the Gospel is to bring salvation and not judgment, those who reject its message will suffer the consequence of turning away from the Savior. Those who welcome the news of God's grace will be transformed, becoming the instruments by which his grace is magnified. Paul demonstrates this has been God's purpose throughout history and cites Ps 18:49 to illustrate its biblical basis.

15:10 Again, it says, "Rejoice, O Gentiles, with his people." Further evidence is given for the welcome the Gentiles are to receive. Paul quotes from the song of Moses (Deut 32:43), which was composed in the closing days of his life as he prepared to bless the tribes of Israel. The song warned the Jews of the character of God—he would punish their rebellion and be vindicated among the nations. The passage Paul quotes is a call to the nations to recognize that Yahweh is just and righteous in all his dealings, not allowing even his elect to be excused for their wrongdoing.

Although the original song did not explicitly state that the Gentiles would be brought into the covenant community, this is the logical deduction. Moses' song does not finish with the judgment of the Jews and the praise of the Gentiles but with the promise that Yahweh will take vengeance on his enemies and make atonement for his land and his people. Yahweh's call to the nations to rejoice suggests they are going to share in the blessing of Israel's restoration. Those who oppose his people, however, will come under judgment: "Rejoice, O ye nations, with his people; for he will avenge the blood of his servants, and will render vengeance to his adversaries, and will be merciful unto his land, *and* to his people (Deut 32:43). The song is, in effect, a summary of the history that Paul has been outlining in the letter, showing how Israel missed the purpose of her calling and how the Gentiles have been brought in to bring glory to God. The choice of the text is clearly no coincidence, especially as its conclusion is that Israel will be saved.

---

5. See Keck, "Soteriology," 86. Wagner, "Servant," 475, points out that Paul clinches his argument concerning Gentiles' acceptance by appealing to the Torah (Deut 32:43), the Prophets (Isa 11:10), and the Psalms (Ps 17:50; 116:1 [LXX]) as witnesses that the divine goal of the Messiah's ministry is the creation of a community of Jews and Gentiles glorifying God together. Wagner, op cit 477, says that: "Christ is envisioned as God's servant, ministering on behalf of God's faithfulness to his promises."

6. Du Toit, "Römerbrief," 69–77, notes that the beginning of the letter has the Gentiles turning from God, refusing to acknowledge him, and coming under his judgment. By the conclusion of the letter, all this has changed as a result of the Gospel. Out of those who were "by nature children of wrath," God has brought into existence a new humanity—made up of Jews and Gentiles—which loves and serves him.

15:11 And again, "Praise the Lord, all you Gentiles, and sing praises to him, all you peoples." Paul adds a further OT text to his catena. This time it is Ps 117:1. The two-verse psalm is a summons to the nations to worship the Lord in praise of his love and faithfulness. At face value, it is a plea from the Jewish community to the Gentiles to join in the worship of Yahweh. It presupposes—in line with Paul's reasoning—that there is no priority among them: "Praise the Lord . . . all you people."

15:12 And again, Isaiah says, "The Root of Jesse will spring up, one who will arise to rule over the nations; the Gentiles will hope in him." Most modern scholars divide the prophecy of Isaiah into sections composed by different authors. However, as far as NT authors were concerned the prophecy had only one author, and they developed their arguments from that perspective.

Paul quotes from Isa 11:1, 10, which predicts the conversion of the Gentiles. This text was understood by the early church to anticipate the later second exodus' texts, which are prolific in the book of Isaiah. So, once again, we find Paul's use of the OT has strict regard for the original setting of the texts. His use of the OT is mostly confined to demonstrating how they have been spiritually fulfilled through the exodus that Christ has achieved for his people.[7] In saying that Jesus was to rule over the nations, Paul is making a significant political statement. Many in Rome must have hoped desperately that no representative of the Imperial household was present when this statement was read out. It was a direct challenge to the power of the state to say that God would raise his Christ above the nations and all would bow to him. The verse illustrates how the Gospel can clash with the political realm because what fallen leaders seek can be diametrically opposed to what God desires—the establishment of righteousness.

15:13 May the God of hope fill you with all joy and peace as you trust in him, so that you may overflow with hope by the power of the Holy Spirit. Paul adds his own prayer to the Scriptures that he has quoted. It is a beautifully crafted prayer that expresses the most important need of the believers in Rome. He calls God the "God of hope," echoing the previous verse. He does not change the prospects of life so that they become less gloomy but giving hope to man in Sin when, humanly speaking, there is no hope (Eph 2:14–18).

When Paul asks God to fill believers with "all joy and peace" as they trust in him, there is no doubt that he saw emotion to be a key factor in Christian experience and development. He was not looking to produce intellectual know-it-alls in Rome but a community of believers with a loving heartfelt appreciation of the God who had saved them. Unless our intellectual understanding is transformed into overwhelming joy and

---

7. Cranfield, *Shorter*, 358, says: "In the quotation of the promise that the Gentiles shall hope in the coming scion of Jesse, the Messiah of the Jews, a promise now already being fulfilled in the lives of the Gentile Christians in Rome, there is an implicit appeal to the strong (many of them Gentile Christians) to receive (compare v. 7) and show consideration to those weak brothers (most, if not all of them, Jewish Christians), according them special honour for the sake of their Kinsman, the Messiah of the Jews, who is the Gentiles' only true hope." This interpretation of the "strong" has been challenged by this commentary. It finds the "strong" to refer always to the Jews.

peace, we must question the nature of our spiritual understanding. Joy and peace are not the products of intellectual attainment but come from trusting in God. Here is the beautiful simplicity and profoundness of the Gospel. While it has engaged some of the finest minds in attempts to penetrate its truths, its treasures and benefits are offered even to children—for God is a God who meets all who respond to him in simple faith.

Paul desires for the believers to overflow with hope by the power of the Holy Spirit, reflecting the hope of the Gentiles (v. 12). Its abundance in their lives will be the result of the Spirit's work. Already he has written to them about the Holy Spirit pouring love into their hearts (Rom 5:5), inspiring a hope which does not disappoint. Because of this powerful work of God by his Spirit, Paul dares to pray that they will overflow with hope.

Since hope affects the way they live and confront the problems of life, they will need an abundance of it in the years ahead, for Nero—driven by his evil and deranged mind—will turn the capital into a burning inferno. He will blame the city's destruction on the infant church, and the believers—the scapegoat of a madman—will suffer unspeakable cruelty for their faith in Christ.

15:14 I myself am convinced, my brothers, that you yourselves are full of goodness, complete in knowledge and competent to instruct one another. Some see vv. 14–16 as key to the exhortatory discourse of Romans.[8] Paul encourages the members of the church by praising the quality of their lives. His praise of the Roman church is not with an ulterior motive. He is not like those public speakers of the ancient world who praised their audience with an eye on the rewards they would receive for their flattery. Paul is realistic about their moral achievements and knows that they are far from perfect. The point is that he sees that the Romans would allow the Spirit to fulfill his ministry in their lives. If they are full of goodness, they will behave towards each other with love and respect. If they have true knowledge, they will understand how knowledge without love counts for nothing (1 Cor 13:2).

The believers in Rome were equipped to instruct each other; this would mean that Gentiles would teach Jews as well as vice versa. It was this ministry of teaching that the Jews believed was their unique calling, but it had led to pride and arrogance. The Gentiles were not as competent in teaching as their Jewish brethren because they had less knowledge of the OT promises. However, well-instructed Gentiles would acquire this theological perspective and would be competent to address Jewish pride. Gentiles would exhort Jewish believers, and this would not be because they had usurped the Jew's historic role but because they had been called to such a ministry by Abraham's God.

15:15 I have written to you quite boldly on some points, as if to remind you of them again, because of the grace God gave me. The apostles believed their responsibility was to keep reminding the church of her inheritance in Christ (2 Pet 3:2; 1 John 5:13; Heb 12:1–3) and Paul acknowledges that he has written "quite boldly on some points." This may indicate his awareness of the sensitive nature of the issues he has raised. He is certain that problems will not go away unless they are confronted and resolved by a

---

8. See Longacre and Wallis, "Eschatology," 367–82.

clear understanding of the history of salvation. By making a comparison between the ways God has accepted the Jews he has been able to demonstrate that the calling of the Gentiles is not a distortion of the law but its very principle.[9]

15:16 To be a minister of Christ Jesus to the Gentiles with the priestly duty of proclaiming the gospel of God, so that the Gentiles might become an offering acceptable to God, sanctified by the Holy Spirit. Paul describes his ministry in terms of it being a priestly duty. We have noted in Rom 12:1 that the priests in the OT were appointed to represent the firstborn, taking their place in the ministry based on the tabernacle. Yahweh claimed all of Israel's firstborn for himself, the sons being designated to be Yahweh's priests. The term λειτουργὸς (*leitourgos*) "minister"[10] is often used of the Levite in the LXX. Paul has not been released from the obligation to serve God; rather he, like all other redeemed people, is obliged to serve God with his whole life. Indeed, it is because Jesus–God's firstborn–has been delivered up to death that Paul is required to serve as a priest. It is the only response he can make to the God who has spared him through the giving up of his own Son as the Passover sacrifice (1 Cor 5:7b: "For Christ, our Passover lamb, has been sacrificed").[11]

The Jewish nation's priestly duty had been to bring the light of the knowledge of God to the nations, but she failed miserably. Paul sees himself as called to fulfill this work so that the Gentiles are brought into the blessings of the covenant. Their conversion is, therefore, the goal of his ministry. He knew it would happen because the Scriptures predicted it (Gen 12:3; Isa 2:2–3; 11:10; 19:21–25) and he had been commissioned to the task by the risen Christ (Acts 26:17–18).

The Holy Spirit must sanctify the Gentiles to make them acceptable. Paul is not speaking of individual Gentiles being brought into the covenant through personal response and faith; he is viewing them as an entity (προσφορὰ [*prosphora*]) "sacrifice" is singular). This parallels Israel's sanctification when she was brought out of bondage (Isa 50:8; 53:11).

While this new exodus of God's people has been achieved through the cross, it is the Holy Spirit who brought about their unity with Christ.[12] The same Spirit applies this saving work to individuals as he circumcises their hearts and gives them the existential status required for membership in the new covenant community. By this circumcision they are brought into their already-secured inheritance, and can make offerings that are acceptable to God.

---

9. Bryn, "Boldly," 83–96, thinks that Paul is seeking to bring the Roman church under his apostolic authority and into a place where it accepts that the law could not bring justification at the coming judgment. Thus, Paul seeks to fulfill his apostolic calling to the Gentiles, endeavoring to help them understand the wider vision of God's eschatological people.

10. Fitzmyer, *Romans*, 711, acknowledges the term can have a secular meaning but argues that it takes a religious nuance from the context in which Paul has used it.

11. The Greek does not have "lamb." Christ is the firstborn sacrifice in Paul's understanding, see Holland, *Contours*, 237–74.

12. See Excursus E: Baptism into Christ, pages 168–77.

The phrase "the Gentiles might become an offering acceptable to God," suggests they are being brought into the same ministry as the believing Jews. They are also part of the holy nation, the NT priesthood, and it is their responsibility to share the good news with those they meet. In the NT, all those who have been redeemed through Christ, their Passover, are priests unto their God.[13]

It has been pointed out that, while Paul uses priestly terminology for his work of evangelism,[14] he never uses this terminology when speaking of those who preside in worship or lead in the celebration of the Eucharist (the Lord's Table). It was later generations of Christians who reintroduced the OT order, despite the fact that the NT had clearly seen this to have been fulfilled in Christ (Heb 10:11–18). Indeed, the institution of the "Lord's Supper" was nothing more than the Christian version of the Passover, when "Christ, our Passover lamb, has been sacrificed" (1 Cor 5:7).[15] Any later developments of "real presence" or other "sacramental significance" would not have been in the minds of Jesus or the apostles. This is made clear when we question the widely-held view of Hellenism as a key for interpreting the NT, and read, instead, the NT out of the OT. As there is *no* evidence of sacramentalism in the OT sacrificial system, we need to question claims to its presence in the NT. Once the inauguration of the Lord's Supper was removed from its original setting of the Passover, the parameters of its significance were lost and the door was opened to an understanding that was not part of the original celebration.

15:17 Therefore I glory in Christ Jesus in my service to God. For Paul, there could be no greater privilege than being a servant of God. He glorified God for the honor of being called into his service. This was not being said by a man who had lived a life of ease because of privilege, but by one who had experienced immense suffering because of his loyalty to Jesus Christ.

15:18 I will not venture to speak of anything except what Christ has accomplished through me in leading the Gentiles to obey God by what I have said and done. In saying that he "will not venture to speak," Paul can be understood in one of two ways. He may be saying that he is not competent to speak beyond his own experience of ministry, so purposely limiting himself to this. Alternatively, he might be stressing that he has nothing about which to boast. It is God alone who can take glory for what has been achieved. In light of the context, it is probably the latter interpretation that expresses Paul's intention.

---

13. Cranfield, *Romans*, 755, has shown that Paul's frame of reference for designating himself as a priest is the Levites. This observation supports the claim that the ministry of Paul and the believers is rooted in their redemption through the death of their firstborn–Christ, our Passover (1 Cor 5:7). See Holland, *Contours*, chapters 11 and 12.

14. Dillon, "Priesthood," 156–68.

15. For a discussion on the significance of John 6:54, "unless you eat the flesh of the Son of Man . . . ," see Excursus F: Sin in the Theology of Paul pages 201–24. Note that the discussion is in the context of the Passover, which both OT and NT see to be the occasion of Yahweh's marriage to his people. The imagery is matrimonial, i.e., covenantal, not sacramental or mystical.

15:19 By the power of signs and miracles, through the power of the Spirit. So from Jerusalem all the way around to Illyricum, I have fully proclaimed the gospel of Christ. While Paul rarely speaks of involvement in miraculous ministry (2 Cor 12:12), his companion, Luke, reported on it more freely (Acts 13:4–12; 14:8–10; 16:16–18; 25–34; 19:11–20). It is much wiser to let others report on the blessings God has given to our service rather than getting caught up in the cult of self-promotion. Such a cult robs Christ of his glory.

Paul writes: "So from Jerusalem all the way around to Illyricum." Illyricum is part of the Balkan region, which was known as Yugoslavia. This statement creates a problem because there is no record of Paul ministering in this region. Some have concluded that Illyricum is intended to represent the western limit of the eastern part of the Roman Empire. If this is so, then Paul is claiming that he has evangelized the whole of the empire apart from Italy and the west. This interpretation, however, presents its own problem. It was not physically possible for Paul to have preached everywhere in such a vast area. The most plausible understanding is that Paul has preached in its chief centers, confident in the knowledge that others have radiated out from them with the Gospel message.

A better translation of the phrase τὸ εὐαγγέλιον τοῦ Χριστοῦ (to euangelion tou Christou) "the gospel of Christ" is "the gospel about Christ." This has been the thrust of exposition throughout this commentary, for the letter is about Jesus, the Son of David (Rom 1:3) who is the Christ.[16]

15:20 It has always been my ambition to preach the gospel where Christ was not known, so that I would not be building on someone else's foundation. Paul sought to evangelize regions where no one had gone. One such region was to the west of Italy, i.e., Spain. While his intended visit to Italy would serve to strengthen the church in Rome as he shared fellowship with them (Rom 1:11–12), his main purpose was to make the visit a stepping-stone to the west (cf. Rom 15:24). Even though he avoided building on other people's foundations, it would seem that he saw no reason not to exercise an evangelistic ministry while passing through regions on his way to his intended field of ministry (Rom 1:15).

15:21 Rather, as it is written: "Those who were not told about him will see, and those who have not heard will understand." In citing Isa 52:15 (LXX), Paul is not justifying his efforts to take the Gospel to the unreached but his view of himself as part of the servant ministry.[17] Here, it is sufficient to note that he deliberately applies a text that speaks of the suffering Servant to Jesus. For Paul, there is no doubt that Christ fulfills this ministry to the nations, bringing about their forgiveness and reconciliation to God.

Nevertheless, as comments on Rom 1:1 suggest, the application of Servant passages was not limited to Christ by the early church. She saw herself as continuing this ministry—overwhelmed with the privilege and responsibility of making the Gospel known.

---

16. Fitzmyer, *Romans*, 714.

17. See Holland, *Contours*, chapter 4, for a more detailed discussion.

15:22 **This is why I have often been hindered from coming to you.** If we go outside Paul's letter to the Romans, we find examples of him acknowledging how Satan hindered him at times (e.g., 1 Thess 2:18). However, in this verse, Paul is not suggesting that Satan had prevented him from visiting Rome. The reasons for the delay must have been the various ministries in which he was involved (vv. 19–20) for he was constantly stretched. In light of his principles and goals, it was vital for him to identify his priorities (Rom 1:14–16; 15:23–33). He had to be sensible and plan his work ahead, endeavoring (though not always succeeding) to keep to time schedules (cf. Acts 20:16; 2 Cor 1:15ff.; Titus 1:5). Thus, "This is why" indicates that Paul has given an account of the Gentile mission (see Rom 15:1–22) he has been involved in so that those in Rome could understand what had occupied his time and energies. It was these noble activities that had delayed his long desired visit to Rome.

15:23 **But now that there is no more place for me to work in these regions, and since I have been longing for many years to see you,** It is evident Paul had not evangelized all the regions of Asia, so what does he mean by such a statement? It can only be that he saw his ministry to be pioneering–preparing ground and establishing congregations that would take the Gospel to the unevangelized regions of Asia. As a result of this strategy, there were no more places for him to go.

Paul wants to move into Spain and employ the same "relay" strategy there, setting up congregations with the expectation that the Gospel would diffuse throughout the nation by means of the believers' testimonies. With this strategy, the infant church expanded rapidly—and it still does where such a plan of action is implemented! Too often in the West, we lack Paul's missionary vision—we major on his doctrine but ignore his practice. As a result, the transforming gospel is not heard and people are left in darkness. The church cannot call herself apostolic if she does not practice the actions of the apostles. Upholding the apostles' doctrine is essential, but it's equally important to follow their practice too.

15:24 **I plan to do so when I go to Spain. I hope to visit you while passing through and to have you assist me on my journey there, after I have enjoyed your company for a while.** It is unlikely that Paul was able to achieve his goal of ministering in Spain as we know he was arrested in Jerusalem after writing this letter (Rom 15:25). From Jerusalem, he was taken to Rome at his insistence that he be tried under Roman law in front of Caesar (Acts 25:11; 28:16). He chose this in order to thwart the malicious intentions of the Jews who plotted his death (Acts 23:12–30).

While there is no evidence that Paul fulfilled his plan to evangelize Spain, some argue that he was released from house-arrest in Rome and continued on to Spain, being rearrested sometime later. Subsequently, he was brought back to Rome where, according to Christian tradition, he was beheaded at Tre Fontane Abbey (i.e., Three Fountains Abbey), during the reign of Nero (about 65 AD).

When Paul writes: "to have you assist me on my journey," he uses the verb προπεμ- φθῆναι (*propemphthēnai*, aorist passive infin.), which is often translated "escorted by."

It has been suggested that he is looking for more than financial or material support; Paul hopes the Roman believers will share with him in the mission he plans in Spain by sending representatives to work with him. This was not so that he would have company on the journey but that his practice of involving established churches in reaching unevangelized areas could be put into action (Acts 13:1–3; 2 Cor 8:22ff.; Phil 2:25–30; 2 Tim 4:9–13). By this strategy, Paul gives us the model for training Christian workers. Like Jesus, he discipled them by means of his own example (1 Tim 1:15–16; 2 Tim 2:2–3; 3:10—4:2).

15:25 Now, however, I am on my way to Jerusalem in the service of the saints there. Some say Paul does not appeal to the believers in Rome for funds to support the suffering believers in Jerusalem because he wished the gift to be from churches he had established. This is hardly likely to be the reason as, at the time of writing, he was traveling in the opposite direction to Rome, en route for Jerusalem. It would have been unrealistic for Paul to invite the Roman believers to contribute to the gift. His letter—written in Corinth—would have to be delivered speedily to Rome in order for a collection to be made. This would then have be transported quickly across or around the Mediterranean and given to Paul and his party who were on their way to Jerusalem. It is more realistic to think that Paul was asking the Roman believers to pray that the gift would be acceptable to the Jews. This was important because of the strain between the Jewish and Gentile sections of the Jerusalem church for, despite the immense suffering of their brethren, the Judaizers would be tempted to press for the gift to be rejected, fearing it would defile the community.

The suggestion that Paul sought to "buy" legitimacy for his Gentile mission through the presentation of the gift is not acceptable. The proposal misses the fact that the Jerusalem Council had already endorsed his mission (Acts 15). What Paul's action does is to remind us of the practical ways in which the unity of the church can be promoted. His theological knowledge was being given expression; by means of this tangible display of concern Paul was able to underscore the unity that Christ had brought about through his death.[18]

The gift for the poor saints in Jerusalem was a priority for Paul. This was no ordinary gift. If it had been, he would have entrusted it to others and made his way to Rome and then Spain without such a detour. Paul saw the gift as a vital expression of the unity of Jews and Gentiles in the Gospel. Establishing this principle was so important that it took priority over his consuming passion of making Christ known in regions beyond.

Some have seen the delegation that Paul led to Jerusalem to be an expression of the prophetic promise that the nations would come to Jerusalem to worship the Lord (Isa 2:1–5).[19]

---

18. See also Wright, *Romans*, 756, who says: "For Gentiles to give money for Jewish Christians was a sign that the Gentiles regarded them as members of the same family; for Jewish Christians to accept it would be a sign that they in turn accepted the Gentiles as part of their family. The collection was designed to accomplish, *mutatis mutandis*, the same thing that Paul had been urging in 14:1—15:3."

19. See Munck, *Salvation*.

15:26 For Macedonia and Achaia were pleased to make a contribution for the poor among the saints in Jerusalem. The term "the poor" [οἱ πτωχοι (*hoi ptōchoi*)] became a technical term for the pious who were often oppressed and economically deprived (1 Cor 16:3; 2 Cor 8:19). However, there is no reason to see it being used here in this technical sense as Paul says that the contribution is for the poor *among* the saints.

Some believe the Jerusalem church was vulnerable to famine conditions. It has been argued that its members had used their resources to support those believers who had stayed on in Jerusalem after Pentecost. They remained in the city in order to take advantage of apostolic instruction before returning to their homes throughout the empire. While there was clearly great generosity, it is probably claiming too much to say that it left the church members impoverished and without the means of coping with famine. The poor are found in every society, and the church in Jerusalem would not have been exempt.

Following the council of Jerusalem (Acts 15), the apostles urged Paul not to forget the poor, and this request brought ready agreement (Gal 2:10). 2 Cor 8:8–15—a passage referring to the same collection as mentioned in Galatians—shows his ability to manage this important project and his lack of embarrassment in asking for money in order to care for those in need. (While he was unabashed in seeking support for others, he was reluctant to seek it for himself [Phil 4:10–20], preferring to "tentmake" rather than be misunderstood [1 Cor 9:1–18]). The mention of Macedonia and Achaia indicates how far from Jerusalem the contributors lived and how Paul taught the Gentile churches of their debt to the Jewish believers as the ones who brought them the good news.

It is clear from the request made by the apostles at Jerusalem and the willing practice of Paul that caring for the physical needs of people is not to be seen as a deviation from Gospel ministry but a vital expression of it. It is a sad situation when professing Christians are reluctant to support the practical relief of the destitute while priding themselves on being disciples of Christ. It should be noted that Paul's efforts are directed toward the poor among the saints. That does not exclude compassion toward the unbelieving poor, but it is nevertheless a priority toward the believing poor who are often suffering because they are believers.

15:27 They were pleased to do it, and indeed they owe it to them. For if the Gentiles have shared in the Jews' spiritual blessings, they owe it to the Jews to share with them their material blessings. The willing response of the Gentile churches must have been a great encouragement to Paul in his desire to see the two sections of the church learn to respect and accept each other. Their response flowed from the sense of debt they had to the Jewish believing community.[20] Paul spells out what that debt is: they have shared in the spiritual blessings of the old covenant community. This is not to say, of course, that the Jewish nation had, in turn, delighted in the way God had blessed the Gentiles through the Gospel of Christ–most Jews deeply resented them for claiming to be the true inheritors of the Abrahamic blessings.

---

20. Contra Munck, *Mankind*, who claims that the reason for the gift was to provoke the Jews to jealousy (Rom 10:19; 11:13–14). Munck's view has been embraced and modified by others.

The name "the Jews" could refer to the nation of Israel or to the remnant community (the Jewish church). The nation had been given the promises and borne the hope of their fulfillment throughout long years of suffering. Tragically, she had rejected the one to whom these promises pointed. The remnant, however, recognized and welcomed the bringer of salvation (Luke 2:25–38) and accepted its mission to make his salvation known to the nations. However, while the Gentiles owed a great debt to the Jewish remnant there are good grounds for saying they also owed one to the entire Jewish nation for it was used by God as an "incubator" for the Gospel promises. Without Jewish history and the theology that grew out of it, it is impossible to understand the message of Yahweh's redeeming activity for his creation.

15:28 So after I have completed this task and have made sure that they have received this fruit, I will go to Spain and visit you on the way. The language of receiving the fruit is unusual, some suggesting that it had ceremonial roots. If this is correct, it suggests that Paul anticipated a formal handing over of the gift for the poor in Jerusalem. This fulfilled the promise he had made to the Jerusalem Council as recorded in Gal 2:10. No doubt Paul hoped the gift would be presented in a community setting, with the consequent public recognition in Jerusalem of the care and concern of distant Gentile brethren. Paul was prepared to use every means to get across the message of unity between believing Jews and Gentiles. This gave the gift a higher priority, which is probably why he wanted to take it himself rather than send it with an embassy.

As we have seen, Paul expected to follow the visit to Jerusalem with a visit to Rome on his way to Spain, where he planned to start church-planting. We know from the Acts of the Apostles that his pathway was going to be anything but straightforward. (In Jerusalem, he was beaten and almost lynched, then put on trial before the high priest and successive Roman governors. He endured a dangerous and eventful voyage to Rome where he was detained under house-arrest for two years, awaiting his appeal to Caesar.) Did Paul have any inkling of what was going to happen to him as he approached Jerusalem? Certainly he was aware of dangers facing him there (Rom 15:31), and would soon be warned by Agabus of his impending imprisonment (Acts 20–21). How different the cause of the Gospel would have been if the early believers had risk-assessed their missionary endeavors and not accepted the challenge to take the Gospel to the furthest corners of the earth.

15:29 I know that when I come to you, I will come in the full measure of the blessing of Christ. Paul's assurance that he would visit the Roman church in the full measure of the blessing of Christ could express one of the following understandings.

First, Paul did not consider himself to be unique, bringing to the believers something they did not already have. He anticipated he would receive from them the same Gospel fellowship he would bring. He expresses his confidence that believers experience the presence of Christ when they meet together (Matt 18:20). He had verbalized the same expectation of Christ's presence in another setting when he instructed the Corinthians to gather in the name of Jesus in order to deliver one of their members over to Satan (1 Cor 5:4). As Paul would not be with them, it is clear that he did not see his presence to be necessary for Christ to be with them. The heritage of believers meeting together with their Lord is still the privilege and inheritance of the church today.

A second possible understanding of the verse is that Paul thought he was bringing blessings that only an apostle could impart. Clearly, the apostles had a unique authority in the early church, and the visit from such a representative of Christ would inevitably be anticipated with excitement over the blessing that would accompany such a visit.

15:30 I urge you, brothers, by our Lord Jesus Christ and by the love of the Spirit, to join me in my struggle by praying to God for me. Here, we have mention of the three members of the Godhead who the church would later describe as "The Trinity." Just how Paul intended this statement to be understood is not clear. What is generally agreed by scholars is that the understanding of God as triune developed slowly in the thinking of the early church and that too much weight must not be placed on early texts.

However, despite the prevailing opinion, a case can be made that the church used Trinitarian language earlier than is supposed. It has been argued that the Christology of the NT is not titular (understanding who Christ is by analyzing his titles such as Son of Man, Last Adam, Messiah, etc.) as previous generations had supposed, but functional (understanding Christ's person by focusing on what he has achieved).[21] If this is correct, there is reason to believe the church grasped the uniqueness of Christ early in her existence. She certainly recognized his death as the means by which Yahweh had redeemed his creation which is something no creature could do! (Rom 8:18–25).

Paul's request for prayer gives some insight into the agony he went through in his attempts to reconcile the two wings of the church. His appeal to συναγωνίσασθαί (*sunagōnisasthai*) "strive together" indicates his concern. He knew his life was in constant danger because of the intense hatred some Jews had towards him. He covets the prayers of the Roman believers that the visit he is about to make might achieve the goal for which he longed. The danger Paul was willing to face in going up to Jerusalem shows his concern for the Jewish believers and the unity of the church. This concern, no doubt, expresses his knowledge that Christ had specifically prayed for the unity of his people (John 17:11). Divisions amongst believers ought to be the very last option, not the first knee-jerk reaction, to disagreements.

15:31 Pray that I may be rescued from the unbelievers in Judea and that my service in Jerusalem may be acceptable to the saints there. We can only imagine the intensity of feeling that built up as Paul approached Jerusalem. He was urged by Christians on his journey not to put himself in danger (Acts 21:7–14). The prophecy given by Agabus (Acts 21:10–11) would have taken all hope of a peaceful outcome from his heart, but he still continued with his visit. Paul was putting his life on the line for the sake of achieving a better understanding and acceptance of the Gentile believers by the Jewish church. There can only be one reason for such commitment: Paul believed that what he was doing was of vital importance for the work of the Gospel. Such an example must surely condemn us for taking our unity in Christ so lightly!

---

21. See Holland, *Contours*, chapters 11 and 12.

Despite the fact that this was such an important issue for Paul, the book of Acts says very little about whether he achieved his goal. He appears to have presented the collection, or been in the act of presenting it, when Jews from Asia caused a riot and dragged him from the temple (Acts 24:17; 21:27). The relative silence on this point in Acts suggests this aspect of the visit was not successful (possibly Luke chose to avoid mentioning it in case it caused distress).[22] If this is so, Paul had again experienced what many pastors repeatedly encounter: God's people, while claiming to have the highest ideals as their motives, undo the work of the God they say they love by showing intolerance to other believers. Of course Paul also expresses the opposite concern. He is aware how leaders can become dictatorial and harsh in their role as leaders (Acts 20:26–27).

15:32 So that by God's will I may come to you with joy and together with you be refreshed. Paul was to visit them soon but in circumstances he did not envisage when writing these words. A short time later, he was arrested (Acts 24–27), detained in prison and went through several trials in Judea and Caesarea. Having asserted his legal rights as a Roman citizen, Paul was taken to Rome under escort. Here, he was given great opportunities to witness while under house arrest, awaiting Caesar's pleasure to try him (Acts 28:16–31).

15:33 The God of peace be with you all. Amen. The simplicity of the words do not relate the profoundness of the reality. Paul prays for the Roman believers to share in what he has experienced for himself (Phil 4:9). Soon, these very people were going to need to know the God of peace as a living reality. Some would be burned to death as human torches in the gardens of Nero for his amusement, while others were to entertain the depraved Roman crowds by having their limbs ripped apart by lions in the Coliseum. This small Christian community had no idea that its testimony would inspire countless millions of Christians to be faithful to Christ, some even unto death.

There has been ongoing debate among scholars as to whether Paul actually concluded his letter at this point—they see chapter 16 as not being part of the original letter to the Romans but added at a later date.[23] Those who favor this displacement theory claim the doxology at the end of chapter 16 was originally at the end of chapter 15. This is supported by a manuscript dated around 200 AD.[24] Other MSS have the doxology after Rom 15:33 and Rom 14:23, while two ninth century MSS and a derivative one from the fourteenth century omit it entirely. One of these MSS does, however, leave a space at the end of chapter 14, suggesting there may have been something that the copyist intended

---

22. See Dunn, *Diversity*, 256ff.

23. Manson, "Others," 225–41, suggested that Rom 16 was added as a cover letter to make it easy for a copy of the letter to be sent to Ephesus where Paul knew many people. Witherington, *Romans*, 351, sees the chapter to be part of the original letter and argues that its purpose was to encourage the Gentile majority—the "strong" in Witherington's understanding—to accept the returning Jews (the "weak") who Paul met during their Diaspora from the capital. This, in Witherington's thinking, explains why so many are mentioned at the conclusion of this letter in comparison to other letters.

24. P46.

to insert. However, not all scholars accept this interpretation. Indeed, there is a growing minority that accepts the location of chapter 16 as it is in most manuscripts.[25]

CONCLUSION OF ROMANS 15

Paul urges unity, and refers to himself and Christ as examples of those who did not pass judgment on non-essentials. He has shown how Christ has fulfilled the promises made to Abraham and how they intrinsically included the Gentiles. He has also demonstrated how Jesus was fulfilling the mission Israel had failed to perform. Paul, using a series of OT citations which predicted the outcome of the new exodus, demonstrates that believing Gentiles have the right to be within the new covenant community. He showed the believing Jewish community how they were obliged to welcome them.

Paul describes his own ministry in priestly terms. His ministry fulfills what Israel failed to achieve, for she was called to be a priestly people who would take the knowledge of God to the nations. Paul is living in the way he has exhorted others to live in chapter 12, and that includes accepting one another and putting aside any concept of national superiority.

Paul's account of the signs which have accompanied the preaching of the Gospel is further evidence that he sees his ministry in terms of the new exodus (Rom 15:19). They are the same signs that marked the exodus from Egypt and the same ones Scripture also said would take place under the leadership of David's descendant. Christ, the true Son of David, has secured the new exodus of his people.

---

25. See Wright, *Romans*, 758.

Romans 16

THE MESSIAH KING AND HIS PEOPLE IN ROME

I COMMEND TO you our sister Phoebe, a servant of the church in Cenchrea. I ask you to receive her in the Lord in a way worthy of the saints and to give her any help she may need from you, for she has been a great help to many people, including me. Greet Priscilla and Aquila, my fellow-workers in Christ Jesus. They risked their lives for me. Not only I but all the churches of the Gentiles are grateful to them. Greet also the church that meets at their house. Greet my dear friend Epenetus, who was the first convert to Christ in the province of Asia.

Greet Mary, who worked very hard for you. Greet Andronicus and Junias, my relatives who have been in prison with me. They are outstanding among the apostles, and they were in Christ before I was. Greet Ampliatus, whom I love in the Lord. Greet Urbanus, our fellow worker in Christ, and my dear friend Stachys. Greet Apelles, tested and approved in Christ. Greet those who belong to the household of Aristobulus. Greet Herodion, my relative. Greet those in the household of Narcissus who are in the Lord. Greet Tryphena and Tryphosa, those women who work hard in the Lord. Greet my dear friend Persis, another woman who has worked very hard in the Lord. Greet Rufus, chosen in the Lord, and his mother, who has been a mother to me, too. Greet Asyncritus, Phlegon, Hermes, Patrobas, Hermas and the brothers with them. Greet Philologus, Julia, Nereus and his sister, and Olympas and all the saints with them. Greet one another with a holy kiss. All the churches of Christ send greetings. I urge you, brothers, to watch out for those who cause divisions and put obstacles in your way that are contrary to the teaching you have learned. Keep away from them.

For such people are not serving our Lord Christ, but their own appetites. By smooth talk and flattery they deceive the minds of naive people. Everyone has heard about your obedience, so I am full of joy over you; but I want you to be wise about what is good, and innocent about what is evil. The God of peace will soon crush Satan under your feet. The grace of our Lord Jesus be with you.

Timothy, my fellow-worker, sends his greetings to you, as do Lucius, Jason and Sosipater, my relatives. I, Tertius, who wrote down this letter, greet you in the Lord. Gaius, whose hospitality I and the whole church here enjoy, sends you his greetings. Erastus, who is the city's director of public works, and our brother Quartus send you their greetings. Now to him who is able to establish you by my gospel and the proclamation of Jesus Christ, according to the revelation of the mystery hidden for long ages past, but now revealed and made known through the prophetic writings by the command of the eternal God, so that all nations might believe and obey him—to the only wise God be glory forever through Jesus Christ! Amen. (Rom 16:1–27)

INTRODUCTION

THE PROBLEMS POSED BY chapter 16 have been discussed elsewhere.[1] They include a list of Roman believers to whom Paul wishes to send greetings. As it is thought by most that he had not founded or visited the church in Rome, there are many who doubt that this chapter concluded the letter. Some have suggested the chapter belongs to another letter that had been sent to a church whose members were well known to Paul.[2] There is, however, evidence suggesting that its location is misplaced.

When writing to churches he had founded, it was unusual for Paul to mention people by name. For example, there is a notable absence of names in letters to the Corinthian, Galatian, Philippian, and Thessalonian churches, ones which Paul had planted on his missionary journeys. The nearest passage that is similar to the ending of the letter to the Romans is Col 4:15, 17. These are verses in the concluding chapter of a letter written to a church Paul had not founded (Col 1:6–8). A possible pattern Paul adopts is that he does not give personalized greetings to churches he planted but gives them to churches founded by others. If this evidence is reliable, it would be fair to conclude that Paul did not found the church in Rome because he greeted almost thirty named believers at the close of his letter.

What does he hope to achieve with this familiarity? Perhaps he wants to establish a relationship with them that would profit his mission to Spain, or perhaps he has the well-being of the congregation in mind. The names suggest that most of the believers greeted by Paul are Jews. Indeed, some of them have been key workers with him in past missionary endeavors. In writing to a church which was in danger of rejecting its Jewish roots, Paul may be anxious for the Gentile believers to welcome and honor his kinsmen; after all, some of them had come to Christ before him and had ministered to his needs with dedication and kindness (one is described as "a mother" to him). A positive response to the commendations would help to prevent the threatened rift between the two sections of the Roman congregation.

His appeal is similar to the one made to the Gentile churches to provide for the needs of the saints in Jerusalem. In Rome, however, the need among the Jews is not merely practical but emotional, social, and spiritual. The Roman Gentiles are to care for these worthy representatives of the Jewish believing community, and, as an expression of their compassion, they are to share their material prosperity with those who had shared their spiritual heritage (hinted at in Rom 15:26–27).

Since it is acknowledged by most that Paul had yet to visit Rome, how did he know the people he greeted in Rom 16:3–16? We know that Claudius, the Roman Emperor, had expelled the Jews from the city in 49 or 50 AD. This was the reason Priscilla and Aquila were absent from Rome and for meeting Paul in Corinth (Acts 18:1–3). They were able to go back to Rome after the death of Claudius. No doubt before their return, Priscilla

---

1. See Donfried, "Romans," 44–52.

2. Jewett, "Ecumenical," 93, previously treated chapter 16 as belonging to a letter written to Ephesus. He came to reject this, accepting that it was part of the original letter to the Romans.

and Aquila would have talked with Paul about the key believers in Rome as well as the problems they faced within and outside their congregations.

If we accept this reasoning about Priscilla and Aquila, we must accept the possibility that Paul met other believing Jews from Rome in his travels, drawing close to many of them. Many of these would have returned to Rome—along with Priscilla and Aquila—when the way became clear.

Others known by Paul would have gone to Rome for different reasons. Phoebe, from the church in Cenchrea, seems to have had financial independence and was able to travel for personal or business reasons. It is possible that she was the one entrusted to deliver Paul's letter to the Roman believers.

Another possible explanation for Paul's knowledge of the congregation is that his parents lived in Rome before moving to Tarsus, leaving behind family in the city.[3] If this is what happened, Paul's wider family would be a source of information about the church in Rome.

16:1 I commend to you our sister Phoebe, a servant of the church in Cenchrea. Phoebe is from Cenchrea.[4] This is one of the two ports of Corinth, the capital city of Southern Greece (the Roman province of Achaia). As Corinth is thought by many to be the place where Paul wrote his letter (see commentary on Rom 16:23), it is likely that Phoebe is its bearer. The following verse suggests she was a wealthy woman, so it is possible that she was visiting Rome for business reasons and agreed to carry the letter for him. Her background—indicated by her pagan name—was not Jewish. Possibly, she was one of those converted through Paul's Corinthian mission.

While some translate διάκονος (*diakonos*) as "deaconess," many doubt Paul intended to suggest that Phoebe held an office in the Cenchrean church. It is possible the term was used to denote a function rather than an office. If this is correct, then the term indicates that she functioned as a servant of the church, giving support to those in need. Such a functional significance of *diakonon* must equally apply to male deacons, their description not being that of an office they hold but a ministry they exercise.

16:2 I ask you to receive her in the Lord in a way worthy of the saints and to give her any help she may need from you, for she has been a great help to many people, including me. Paul's commendation of Phoebe is a model of diplomacy. He reminds the Romans of their status. They are saints, i.e., people of God. Just as God welcomes people into his family, they are to welcome Phoebe. Paul asks them to help her in whatever way she needs while she fulfills the reason for her visit to Rome. This could be by giving spiritual support as well as the practical help of hospitality—something Paul has already exhorted the believers to do (Rom 12:13).

---

3. See Little, *Mission*.

4. There are six places known in antiquity with the name of Cenchrea. The most likely home of Phoebe is the one near Corinth, which was one of the city's two ports. It was situated seven kilometers southeast of Corinth on the Saronic Gulf. It served the trade route with Asia and was an important commercial center.

The affection shown to Phoebe by her home church in Cenchrea is obvious from Paul's commendation. She had helped many, including Paul himself.[5] Such selfless people are vital for the life of the church for they exercise an essential pastoral gift for the Christian community. Pastoral ministry is not the exclusive ministry of the "pastor" as the Spirit gives this gift more widely in the church for the blessing of God's people.

16:3 Greet Priscilla and Aquila, my fellow workers in Christ Jesus. Like Paul, Priscilla and Aquila were Jews with Roman names. They had settled in Corinth after being expelled from Rome under the edict made by the Emperor Claudius. This affected all the resident Jews in the city.[6] In Corinth, Priscilla and Aquila met Paul, who worked with them for eighteen months. It was during this time that he established the Corinthian church (Acts 18:1–3).

After this, Priscilla and Aquila moved with Paul to Ephesus (Acts 18:18). Here, they used their gift of hospitality in opening up their home to Apollos, who had come to the city. They exercised a pastoral gift too, taking time to help him have a clearer understanding of the way of God (Acts 18:24–26).

In time, they returned to Rome where they opened up their home to believers again. If it is true that Paul had never visited the city, Priscilla and Aquila would have been incredibly important to him as ambassadors, telling of all they had observed of the apostle as they worked alongside him. No doubt, having returned to Rome, they continued in their trade of tentmaking.[7]

(After living in Rome for a period of time, the couple traveled back to Ephesus, opening up their home to all the believers. The Ephesian church met there under the oversight of Timothy [1 Cor 16:19; 2 Tim 4:19].)

Whenever the couple are named, Priscilla is often mentioned before her husband (Acts 18:18, 26; 2 Tim 4:19 [for reverse order, see Acts 18:2; 1 Cor 16:19]). This order is unusual in ancient writings, perhaps implying her greater contribution to Christian work or her higher social status.

---

5. Whelan, "Phoebe," 67–85, points out that under Roman law, women could acquire wealth and freely dispose of it. He says there is evidence in voluntary associations—especially religious ones—that women served as patrons and gained positions of leadership. Whelan suggests this was Phoebe's status, and that Paul, in introducing her, was returning favor to her in response for all that she had done for him and his co-workers. This is, of course, highly speculative. However, whatever Phoebe's role in her church, there have been godly women of other generations who have used their resources for the sake of the Gospel. In England, a notable example was the Countess of Huntingdon, who supported many of the leading preachers of the eighteenth-century revival. Witherington, *Romans*, 383, suggests that Phoebe was Paul's benefactor, and had been sent ahead of him to Rome—as his representative—to prepare for his coming.

6. Acts 18:2 records the event. There is some debate about what actually happened. It is reported by Suetonius, and Cassius Dio minimizes the event. Josephus, who was reporting on Jewish events, does not mention it at all. Some scholars hold that it didn't happen; others record that only a few missionaries were expelled for the short term.

7. Barr, "Tentmakers," 98–113, claims that Priscilla and Aquila were involved in the importation of cilicium (haircloth) to Rome and the manufacture of tents for the Roman army. Barr argues that Paul knows so many people in the city he has yet to visit because of the many contacts he had through the tentmaking trade. Such people were highly mobile.

🙰16:4 **They risked their lives for me. Not only I but all the churches of the Gentiles are grateful to them.** We have partial knowledge of the sufferings Paul experienced in Corinth and Ephesus—the two cities where we know he worked alongside Priscilla and Aquila. Indeed, most of them are mentioned incidentally when Paul felt the need to give his credentials as an apostle (Acts 19:29–40; 1 Cor 15:30; 2 Cor 11:23b–33). We have no details of how Priscilla and Aquila risked their lives, but it is evident from what Paul writes that their devotion to him and to other believers was widely known and highly valued.

The reference to "the churches of the Gentiles" has been seen to suggest that there were Gentile churches meeting separately from Jewish churches.[8] However, in the light of Paul's insistence on the acceptance of each group by the other, it does not seem likely that he would encourage separate congregations.

🙰16:5 **Greet also the church that meets at their house. Greet my dear friend Epenetus, who was the first convert to Christ in the province of Asia.** Again, we find Priscilla and Aquila giving hospitality, for a church meets in their home in Rome as it will in Ephesus (1 Cor 16:19). There was probably a number of "house churches" scattered throughout Rome (Rom 16:14–15), in keeping with the common practice of the early church (Col 4:15; Philemon 2). Church buildings did not become common until the fourth century. It is quite possible that the believers in Rome continued to meet in the synagogue as well, but their unique identity as followers of Christ would eventually bring this relationship to an end.[9]

Epenetus is greeted with warm affection. Paul describes him literally as "the first-fruits of Asia." Again, Paul uses Paschal (Passover) imagery—the firstfruits being brought from the fields three days after the sacrifice of the Passover lamb (Lev 23:11). It was not the harvest crop that Paul had in mind but the Levitical priesthood (evidenced by references to priestly ministry [Rom 12:1–2; 15:16]), which was given as a token that Yahweh claimed not only the firstborn but the whole nation. Epenetus was the first from that region who had become a priest of the new covenant.

🙰16:6 **Greet Mary, who worked very hard for you.** Mary is an unknown member of the Roman church. We don't know if she was Jewish or Gentile, for her name was common in both communities. She is representative of the millions whose devotion and service are the backbones of the churches to which they belong. The reference to her having worked very hard for the Roman believers suggests she had labored with Paul and had rendered a service to the apostolic team on behalf of the Roman church (cf. Phil 2:25–30).

🙰16:7 **Greet Andronicus and Junia, my relatives who have been in prison with me. They are outstanding among the apostles, and they were in Christ before I was.** Andronicus and Junia appear to have been a married couple, the latter name being a

---

8. Oster, "Congregations," 39–52.

9. Nanos, *Mystery*; Dunn, *Parting*.

common Roman name for women.[10] The term συγγενεῖς (*sungeneis*) "relatives" can be translated "kinsmen," so the couple were either part of Paul's extended family or unrelated fellow Jews whom he knew well.

While it is normally accepted that the "relatives" mentioned in chapter 16 (vv. 7, 11, 21) are Paul's kinsmen or countrymen, it is of interest to see how the term is used in the rest of the NT. Its plural form is used in Mark 6:4; Luke 1:58, 61; 2:44; 14:12; 21:16 and Acts 10:24, most translators giving "relatives." When Paul uses the plural form of the term in his letter to the Romans, however, the translation "kindred" is favored (except NIV).

The singular form of the term is found in Luke 1:36 and John 18:26. In most cases, it is translated "relative." However, when it appears in Rom 16:11, the same Greek word is translated "kinsman" or "countryman" (except NIV). Translators appear to be reluctant to concede that Paul may have had relatives in Rome, possibly due to the prevailing opinion that Paul had neither visited nor founded its church. He certainly had family who were sympathetic to him as a Christian (Acts 23:12-22), and while it is true that he was from Tarsus (in modern Turkey), there is no reason why Christian members of his family could not have traveled west to settle in Rome. Indeed, as has been mentioned, his immediate family may well have been citizens of the city of Rome, leaving the wider family in order to settle in Tarsus where Paul was raised.

Andronicus and Junia are referred to as "outstanding among the apostles." This use of the term "apostles" does not mean they were among the twelve, for the term was used in a wider sense in the early church (Acts 14:4, 14; 2 Cor 11:13-15; 12:11ff.). The term ἀπόστολος (*apostolos*) "apostle" means "sent." The writer to the Hebrews describes Jesus as an apostle because he was sent by God the Father, to make known the good news. In his letter to the Galatians, Paul wrote that he was sent by "Jesus Christ and God the Father" (Gal 1:1) by the will and command of God (1 Cor 1:1). This is a description that Andronicus and Junia could apply to themselves. As apostles, their ministry would have been accompanied by supernatural events (2 Cor 12:12) as Christ's, Paul's and the other apostles' had been; and their role would have been to encourage faith in God's elect, imparting knowledge (teaching) that would lead to Godliness (Titus 1:1).

It is of interest that Junia was called an apostle. This begs the question as to whether apostles' wives who believed and accompanied their husbands on their missions were apostles by dint of their marriage (1 Cor 9:5). Alternatively, it may be that Junia was an apostle in her own right. Of course, if this is so, then God's calling, equipping and use of married women in the church may need to be revisited by some.

Andronicus and Junia were "in Christ" before Paul. They were part of the original Jewish church, taking the Gospel to the Gentiles as they worked and suffered alongside him.[11] We have seen throughout the letter that Paul regularly uses the expressions "in the

---

10. Cervin, "Note," 464–70, has established that Junia is a feminine name by studying the method of transcribing Latin names into Greek.

11. Of course, Peter had "opened the door to the Gentiles" (Acts 15:7), but that had not been the result of a planned mission to them. It was imposed by the Spirit and was a mission with which the church had to come to terms.

Lord" or "in Christ." These phrases speak of membership of the Messianic community, which exists because the Spirit has united believers with Christ in his death.[12]

The mention of a second couple to whom Paul sends greetings hints at the importance of married couples to the early church's missionary endeavors. It was not only that they gave each other support (1 Cor 9:5)—no doubt compensating for each other's weaknesses—but they were able to work in situations where a single person, such as Paul, could not operate or would have difficulty.[13] Of course there are also ministries that single people can do that married people would find equally very difficult. Sadly, some married believers neglect what they are commanded first to give, i.e., themselves to their family responsibilities. In failing to do this they dishonor Christ rather than glorify him. Single people don't have this particular restriction and distraction and are able to engage in work that married people should not even consider (1 Cor 7:32–35). Thus both the married and the single have their own special gifting that expresses the will of the same Lord who gives gifts to his people as he wills.

16:8 Greet Ampliatus, whom I love in the Lord. Ampliatus is a slave name. We can only guess how Paul knew a slave living in Rome. It is possible that his master, along with his household, had moved to Rome, or that his freedom had been gained through a process of manumission, leaving him free to travel. Paul's affection for Ampliatus is unashamedly expressed! It must have been a great encouragement to slaves in the early church to know they were valued by their Christian brothers and sisters. Loving people for their own sakes rather than for their status or influence is an important testimony to the power of the Gospel and the love of Christ.

16:9 Greet Urbanus, our fellow-worker in Christ, and my dear friend Stachys. Urbanus is another member of the Roman congregation with a slave name. The status of being a fellow-worker in Christ must have given dignity and self-respect to one who Virgil referred to as nothing other than a talking tool. It would seem that Urbanus worked alongside Paul in his missionary endeavors.

We know nothing of Stachys other than that Paul regarded him with affection. Indeed, Paul describes him as "beloved" (translated "dear friend" by the NIV), suggesting that he knows Stachys very well.

16:10 Greet Apelles, tested and approved in Christ. Greet those who belong to the household of Aristobulus. The reference to Apelles's testing suggests that he has endured something beyond the normal. We have no other reference to him, but no doubt such a commendation must have encouraged him greatly.

Aristobulus might be the grandson of Herod the Great, who was a friend of the Emperor, Claudius. While Paul makes no mention that Aristobulus had become a Christian, the reference suggests that a number of his household had become believers.

---

12. See commentary on Rom 6:1ff.

13. For a discussion on the various ministries women might have exercised in the early church, see Witherington, *Romans*, 390–93.

16:11 Greet Herodion, my relative. Greet those in the household of Narcissus who are in the Lord. Again, we have Paul referring to a relative or kinsman (see comment on v. 7). The greeting gives little away about Herodion. Indeed, the virtual silence supports the view that he was a blood relative as there seems little point in Paul isolating one of his many countrymen in Rome in order to send such a brief greeting.

Narcissus is not greeted personally, so he is probably head of a household with believing members. It is of interest that Narcissus was the name of a famous person in Rome in the middle of first century CE. He was a freed man who had risen to an exalted position under Claudius. This aroused great jealousy in many Romans citizens, to the point that, after Claudius' death, he was provoked to commit suicide. If this Narcissus is the man referred to in this verse (and many assume he is), his untimely death would have put the Christians in his household in a very dangerous position through association.

16:12 Greet Tryphena and Tryphosa, those women who work hard in the Lord. Greet my dear friend Persis, another woman who has worked very hard in the Lord. The warmth and appreciation of these greetings cannot be ignored by those who claim that Paul was a misogynist. Whatever one thinks about Paul's statements concerning the subjection of women to their husbands, it is clear that he had a high regard for his female colleagues. Sadly, many women carry far too many responsibilities in churches and the mission field because men have not been willing to respond to the challenge.

16:13 Greet Rufus, chosen in the Lord, and his mother, who has been a mother to me, too. Rufus is a Latin name. Since it is possible that the Gospel of Mark was written for the Roman church, the Rufus mentioned in Mark 15:21—a son of Simon of Cyrene—may be the same person.[14] Simon was clearly a Jew, visiting Jerusalem for the Passover.

The greeting gives us an insight into the support that Paul received from the mother of Rufus. Possibly, his recollection goes back to when Rufus and his mother joined his apostolic band. Perhaps she met his needs as a mother would have done, caring for her own son at the same time. This would have been very important to Paul as, unlike other apostles, he did not have a wife to help him. Being welcomed into a Christian family is the source of joy and comfort for thousands of unmarried Christian workers. Such hospitality is a ministry that enriches many single people (Acts 18:1–3).

If the identification of Rufus as a son of Simon of Cyrene is correct, it follows that his mother was from Cyrene. It seems likely that, following the death of Simon, Rufus and his mother left Cyrene and served Paul's apostolic band in its missionary work. (Notice the presence of Lucius from Cyrene in the fledgling church in Antioch [Acts 13:1]). At some point after the death of Claudius, Rufus and his mother (who were Jews) moved to Rome, where they became part of the body of believers.

16:14 Greet Asyncritus, Phlegon, Hermes, Patrobas, Hermas and the brothers with them. Again, we have a list of unknown acquaintances. Both Origen[15] and Eusebius[16]

---

14. See Witherington, *Romans*, 394.

15. Comm. *In. ep. ad Romanos*, 10.31 (PG 14.1282).

16. Historia *Ecclesiastica*, 3.3.6.

link Hermes with the early Christian writing, "The Shepherd." This identification has been contested by modern scholarship.[17]

16:15 Greet Philologus, Julia, Nereus and his sister, and Olympas and all the saints with them. Extending the greeting to "all the saints with them" suggests that the named believers are the heads of Christian households. Perhaps they are the leaders of house-church groups in Rome.[18]

16:16 Greet one another with a holy kiss. All the churches of Christ send greetings. A kiss had long been a form of greeting by men in the ancient world (Luke 7:45). Paul's exhortation to the believers in Rome was that it should be a holy kiss. This probably means that they should greet one another as holy in the Lord, as fellow members of the new covenant community. They were to welcome one another, extending the acceptance that Christ had given them. When Paul wrote to believers in Corinth and Thessalonika, he exhorted the believers similarly (1 Cor 16:20; 2 Cor 13:12; 1 Thess 5:26), while Peter urged the Jews of the dispersion to greet each other with a kiss of love (1 Pet 5:14).

Paul sends the greetings of the churches to the believers. As the recognized apostle to the Gentiles, he was able to represent churches even though he had not founded or had contact with them all.

16:17 I urge you, brothers, to watch out for those who cause divisions and put obstacles in your way that are contrary to the teaching you have learned. Keep away from them. This sudden denunciation of some of the congregation seems odd in view of the appeal Paul has made in chapter 14 that the Roman believers accept one another. As a result, some have claimed the chapter does not belong to the original Roman letter but is part of another letter written by Paul.

However, such a closing exhortation to believers to be on their guard is found in some of Paul's other letters (cf. 1 Cor 16:22; Gal 6:12ff.; Phil 3:18ff.), suggesting that contention for the Gospel went on within congregations as well as outside. It is not clear what specific problem among the Roman believers Paul had in mind—perhaps he was thinking of Jews who were trying to persuade the Gentiles the needed to be circumcised or of other groups who were rejecting his exhortation to accept one another. If the latter case is true, Paul urges the church to reject those who are jeopardizing the unity of the believing community. A similar exhortation is found in 2 Cor 6:14–18. Traditionally, this passage has been seen to instruct believers not to marry unbelievers. However, in recent years it has been recognized that Paul is telling the Roman Christians to keep separate from those who seek to usurp authority in the church and nullify his influence.

16:18 For such people are not serving our Lord Christ, but their own appetites. By smooth talk and flattery they deceive the minds of naive people. It is better to translate κοιλία (*koilia*) as "bellies" rather than "appetites." It would seem from such a direct

17. See Fitzmyer, *Romans*, 742, for details.

18. Finger, "Julia," 36–39, strains the text to suggest that Julia was a racist, Paul urging her to put away her prejudices and welcome others of different ethnic backgrounds.

reference to food that the agitators are those who are contending for their right to eat what they wish. If this is correct, they could be the Jews who see no harm in eating meat sacrificed to idols, or in putting their freedom ahead of serving the weaker brethren. Their teaching is right theologically, but it has been taken outside of the dimension of love and it has become motivated by a desire to exercise rights.

The problem with identifying "such people" as Judaizers is there is no suggestion they used flattery. Their belief that they conformed to the law would suggest that their argument would be direct and confrontational. However, it might be that they had developed a more tactful approach to win over the Gentiles—this seems to have been happening in Colossae (Col 2:8, 16–18). The identification of the various groups that Paul contended with is an ongoing problem for scholarship.[19]

16:19 Everyone has heard about your obedience, so I am full of joy over you; but I want you to be wise about what is good, and innocent about what is evil. The news of the Roman believers' obedience was spoken of in other churches. It must have been a real encouragement to others to know there was such a congregation of believers in the capital city of the empire.

The response of the faithful in Rome is not described as belief but obedience (Rom 1:5). This does not deny that the message received was about faith in God, but obedience to the message believed was considered by Paul to be a hallmark of faith. As a result of their response, Paul experienced overflowing joy that God's word was transforming lives in Rome.

However, despite his joy, Paul writes that he wants the believers to be spiritually mature, i.e., wise and innocent. He wants them to recognize instinctively what God is doing; in other words, he wants them to be wise about what is good. Rather than having personal experience of evil, he wants them to be ignorant of it. (Paul writes a similar thing to the Philippians in Phil 4:8). This desired innocence is underlined in the next verse, where reference is made to the serpent who beguiled Adam and Eve. Paul is concerned that the innocence of the Roman believers might leave them vulnerable to smooth talkers. Being taken in by such people can be disastrous.

16:20 The God of peace will soon crush Satan under your feet. The grace of our Lord Jesus be with you. The use of the definite article with Satan τὸν σατανᾶν (*ton satanan*) found elsewhere in the NT (Matt 12:26; Luke 10:18),suggests this is a description or title rather than a name. It is "the Satan." But what does Paul mean by this? He could be referring to those he sees as the servants of Satan, who seek to undermine the work of God among the Romans. If this is correct, then Paul expects these troublemakers to come under some form of judgment.

---

19. North, "Words," 600–614, argues that *eulogia* and *chresto logia* are used disparagingly to describe a means of deception; *chresto logia* is an unusual word and includes an allusion to the plant chreston ("wild endive") that some charlatans used to ensure their popularity and success. Paul presents his opponents as being no better than those who used magic to woo those who had responded to Paul's Gospel from their faith in Christ.

In Rev 3:9, the apostle John records the words of Jesus to the church in Philadelphia: "I will make those who are of the synagogue of Satan, who claim to be Jews though they are not, but are liars—I will make them come and fall down at your feet and acknowledge that I have loved you." Paul has already compared the unbelieving Jewish community with Pharaoh (Rom 9:17–18). The picture given in Revelation is of the apostate Jewish nation serving the will of the state as it persecuted the church.[20] This situation could be reflected here, and if so, then the fall of Jerusalem in AD 70 would have been a significant blow to this unholy alliance.

The expression: "the grace of our Lord Jesus Christ" is used regularly by Paul. It denotes the outpouring of God's free love through his Son upon his people. Grace is more than love. It speaks of the love between those in a covenant relationship—one in which they have vowed to protect and care for each other. It is best illustrated by the love between a husband and wife, which excludes all others and sacrificially strives for each other's blessing and happiness. Paul is praying the Roman believers will be conscious of this unconditional love with which God has blessed them. It is a love that burns in a believer's heart, transforming everything.

16:21 Timothy, my fellow-worker, sends his greetings to you, as do Lucius, Jason and Sosipater, my relatives. Paul concludes his own greetings so that he might convey those of his companions. Timothy had worked with Paul from his earliest days in the faith (Acts 16:1–4; 17:14ff.; 18:5; 19:22; 20:4ff.; 1 Cor 16:10ff.; Phil 2:19–24; 1 Thess 3:2, 6). He was clearly a key worker and is regularly mentioned by Paul in his letters.

For comment on Paul's "relatives," see the discussion on Rom 16:7. While Lucius may be a variant of Luke, the name does not refer to the Gentile physician as Lucius was a Jew, being a kinsman or relative of Paul. It is possible that he is Lucius of Cyrene, who worked alongside Paul as one of the band of prophets and teachers in the church in Antioch (Acts 13:1). This Lucius had come to Antioch as a result of the persecution following Stephen's death, and had spoken to the Jews and Greeks in the city about the Lord Jesus. Despite this serious situation, Lucius and those with him knew great blessing on their ministries and the church expanded significantly; as a result, Paul was brought to Antioch to help Barnabas teach the new believers (Acts 11:19–26).

Jason may be the resident of Thessalonica who gave hospitality to Paul when he stayed there for three weeks. Because Paul took the opportunity each Sabbath day to explain the Scriptures regarding Jesus in the synagogue, jealous Jews precipitated a riot, subjecting Jason to frightening harassment (Acts 17:1–9).

16:22 I, Tertius, who wrote down this letter, greet you in the Lord. It appears that at this point in the dictation of the letter, Paul allowed Tertius to send his own greeting to the believers in Rome. He regularly used a secretary like Tertius, or even an amanuensis.[21] While this may have been necessitated by failing eyesight or another condition that

---

20. See Smolarz, *Covenant*; and Wright, *Perspectives*.

21. Such a person was given a high degree of freedom to write on behalf of the person who engaged him. (The modern equivalent would be a ghost writer.) A secretary would not have that liberty but would take a letter down verbatim.

made writing difficult (Gal 6:11; Philemon 19), this may not have been the case, for many in Paul's day commonly enjoyed the support of a secretary or an amanuensis.

16:23-24 Gaius, whose hospitality I and the whole church here enjoy, sends you his greetings. Erastus, who is the city's director of public works, and our brother Quartus send you their greetings. Not only did Gaius give hospitality to Paul but his home seems to have been used by the church for its gatherings. His name was Roman and he was obviously wealthy, having a home large enough for the "whole church" to meet in and "enjoy."

As it is normally accepted that Paul's letter was written in Corinth, it is assumed this was Gaius's home city. It is of interest that, in the letter to Timothy, the writer mentions "Erastus stayed (or remained) in Corinth" (2 Tim 4:22). This lends support to the idea that the letter to the Romans was written there as greetings were sent from Erastus to the Roman believers (Rom 16:24). Since Gaius is named alongside him, it would be fair to conclude that Gaius was living in Corinth also.

While there is no mention of him in the account of the Corinthian church's founding in Acts 18, Paul does record that he baptized a Gaius from the congregation (1 Cor 1:14) and he is assumed to be the Gaius of Rom 16:23 (LXX). If he is the same man, it is possible he was converted as a result of Paul's ministry in Corinth (Acts 18:8), being baptized by him along with Crispus, the synagogue ruler, and the household of Stephanus (1 Cor 1:14,16). As has been mentioned, Gaius was clearly a man of means, being able to purchase a property large enough to comfortably house the Corinthian congregation. He was also hospitable, extending his kindness to Paul during his time in Corinth.

(There is a reference to a Gaius in Acts 20:4. He was from Derbe, which is about 100 miles from Paul's birthplace in Tarsus. Paul and Barnabas visited Derbe early in their missionary endeavors [Acts 14:6–7, 20b–21a] and a large number of people from the city became disciples–indeed, Gaius of Derbe became one of Paul's traveling companions [Acts 20:4]. It is not known if he is the same Gaius who lived in Corinth, having moved there to further his business interests. Finally, the Apostle John wrote to a church elder called Gaius, commending him for his adherence to the truth as well as his hospitality and support to traveling Christian workers [3 John 1–6]. This is of interest as the Gaius of Corinth gave hospitality to the Apostle Paul and supported the work of the Gospel by allowing the church to meet in his home. These similarities open up the interesting possibility that Gaius of Rom 16 became an elder of a church and the Apostle John's "dear friend.")

Erastus, the city's treasurer or steward, also sends greetings to the Roman church. His position as the city's treasurer ("director of public works") suggests that he enjoyed a comfortable standard of living.[22] Clearly, there were some in the Corinthian church who were among the "elite" of society (implied by 1 Cor 1:26).

---

22. Disputed by Meggitt, "Erastus," 218–23, who argues that his socioeconomic situation was most likely indistinguishable from that of his fellow believers. If correct, his conversion, therefore, is not evidence of the spread of the Gospel among the powerful of the city.

There is another reference to an Erastus. He is described as one of Paul's helpers who was sent by Paul to Macedonia with Timothy (Acts 19:22). These two helpers were sent ahead to prepare the churches' collections for the needy saints in Jerusalem. If this Erastus is the Erastus of Rom 16, he would fulfill this role superbly, being the treasurer of Corinth!

Quartus is someone about whom we have no other information. One can assume he was a believer, perhaps known to the Roman believers.

Having greeted those he knows or has heard of in Rome, Paul concludes his letter by reminding his readers that the message keeping them is the same as that preached to the Old Testament covenant community. It has, at last, been brought to completion, for the message of God's grace is being preached to all nations. This was Israel's calling and service. She was to bring the nations into the community that was set apart to be the bride of Yahweh.

16:25 Now to him who is able to establish you by my gospel and the proclamation of Jesus Christ, according to the revelation of the mystery hidden for long ages past. This verse begins with what is known as the closing formula. The conclusions found throughout Paul's letters have been carefully studied and found to reflect the theology found earlier in the letter.[23] In this conclusion, Paul speaks of the Gospel having gone to the nations. This is a clear reflection of the theme is argued for in chapter 4—that Abraham is the father of many nations.[24]

Since the Gospel is not only about saving people from God's judgment but also about making them into the people God wants them to be, the term στηρίξω (stērixō) "establish" is used. The goal of the Gospel is to bring people into the kingdom of God where they will love and serve him as they live holy lives. Just as the Jews were to be established in their inheritance, so Paul wants the Roman believers to be established in theirs.

When Paul says "by my Gospel," he is not suggesting that his Gospel is any different from that of the other apostles. All of the indications are that he received the content of his gospel from those who had gone before. He was never hesitant to acknowledge his dependency. By referring to "my Gospel," he echoes his calling to apply the good news to the Gentiles. Paul had worked hard to keep them from having to accept the normal Jewish initiation rites of circumcision and dietary laws, etc. In doing this, he had insisted the Gentiles were not obliged to become Jews in order to be reconciled with God. This defense of Gentile liberty made many Jews—even believers—suspicious of him. Some hated Paul so much for what they considered was betrayal of true faith that they sought to kill him. It is this distinctive application of the good news that enables Paul to speak of "my Gospel." Thus his reference to not having received his Gospel from men (Gal 1:12) probably means that he came to see, without any human aid, that the Gentile believers

---

23. Weima, "Closings," 177–97.

24. Not all think the doxology is Pauline or part of the original letter. For discussion, see Elliott, "Language," 124–30; Wright, "Romans," 758.

were not to be circumcised and that on this issue hung the essence of the Gospel, i.e., it is acceptance without the works of the law.

The proclamation of the Gospel revealed the "mystery." This technical term denotes that the purposes of God cannot be known other than when God reveals them. God's purpose is to bring his creation back under his control, having redeemed it through the death of his Son. In this new creation there is no longer a division between Jew and Gentile as both are united in Christ to form one new man. This act of redemption glorifies God before the whole of his creation, and extends his honor. In turn, this leads to the chief end of man—the worship of his Creator.

16:26 But now revealed and made known through the prophetic writings by the command of the eternal God, so that all nations might believe and obey him. Paul cannot separate the preaching of the Gospel and, by implication, its content from the prophetic writings. This was not the result of man's planning but of the command of God. It is no wonder that the Gospel is sometimes called "the Gospel of God."

16:27 To the only wise God be glory forever through Jesus Christ! Amen. It is fitting that Paul finishes his letter in this way, for it was the purpose of his life. He sought through everything he did to honor God and bring others to love and serve him. This is what the letter to the Roman believers is about. He has shown them they are a redeemed people with an obligation to live no longer for their own pleasure or enjoyment. Indeed, they were not even to live as model citizens of the Roman Empire but as members of the kingdom of God. Their calling was to submit themselves to what God required and to seek his glory.

Paul says that God is glorified through Christ Jesus. This is not only saying that Christ has glorified God, but that God is honored and glorified as we embrace what he has done through Christ's death and resurrection and to live in light of the claims made by his Son.

CONCLUSION TO ROMANS 16

This closing section gathers together the themes from the earlier part of the letter and brings them to a glorious conclusion.

Paul's purposes have been to encourage the Roman church and to persuade her believers of the certainty concerning their future. This will prove to be essential, for days will soon unfold when the might and pride of the Roman Empire will be unleashed against her in an attempt to wipe the Christian community from the face of the earth. Recalling Paul's words will bring unspeakable comfort to thousands of Christians in the city and empire of Rome. Yet, while many will lose their lives, others will be attracted to the Christ as a result of witnessing willing deaths. Instead of the church dying, it will grow, and eventually see the demise of the decadent state.

The historic realities of suffering and the seemingly meaningless triumph of evil over good must make us wary of interpreting Paul's statements about suffering in too simplistic a way. Paul did not write these words to assure those who are at ease in this life that God would look after their interests. He wrote to those who were about to be deprived of the most basic human rights and who knew they could lose everything they owned, including life itself. For these Roman believers—whose testimony in the face of appalling suffering will win the admiration of the most skeptical of historians—Paul's words will prove to be the comfort that enables them to see a far greater treasure and to strive for a far more glorious citizenship. They will, indeed, prove the promise that God has given them "all things" (Rom 9:28–39).

Conclusion to the Letter

L IKE MANY OTHER COMMENTATORS, I have sought to follow the teaching of Paul, the apostle to the Gentiles. Some have come to recognize the weight of OT evidence that Paul carried with his arguments, causing a range of scholars to seek to identify the scope of its influence on his theology. However, it has been my contention that, despite moving towards a reading of Paul that takes his Jewishness seriously, many have not appreciated how much Hellenistic baggage they carry, depositing it unconsciously into Paul's arguments. It is my contention that until the OT heritage is properly identified and evaluated; we will not get to the heart of what Paul has said to the church. In trying to accomplish this, much has had to be examined.

We have found that Paul rarely spoke to individuals in his letters; rather, he addressed churches. At all points, his theology was affected by the corporate perspective. This is not only important for a correct understanding of Paul but of the entire NT. As reading corporately was natural for Jewish people, converts from among them who were appointed to teach the Gentiles would have been able to expound the apostles' letters correctly. It must be remembered that the Hellenistic individualism of the early Gentile converts was light years away from the extreme forms spawned by the Enlightenment. As a result, even without Jewish help, Gentile believers in the first century would have had far less difficulty in embracing a corporate reading than members of our extremely individualistic western societies of today, including, sadly, our Christian churches. Tragically, these churches are mostly taught by leaders who have unwittingly read the NT through a predominantly individualistic lens and who have made no serious attempt to recover the lost heritage.

In the first chapter, we saw how Paul rooted his gospel in the promises God had made, particularly to David. So we read that Jesus is of the seed of David (Rom 1:3) and the one who brings the righteousness of God to completion (Rom 1:16–18). This saving activity is desperately needed because of the rebellion of humanity towards its Creator (Rom 1:19–32).

In chapter 2, Paul remonstrated with those who thought they were excluded from the just condemnation that he said, in chapter1, would come upon the ungodly (the Gentiles). The apostle explained that circumcision was not a guarantee that Jews will be saved—what mattered was the circumcision of their hearts. We also noted in Romans 2 that Paul's reference to justification in this particular text is limited to the Jewish understanding of being included in the eschatological community. Paul was saying that only those who strive after righteousness will qualify for this limited experience of justification. This matches the requirements of the Baptist, to repent and be baptized. It is unwise and problematic to read Paul's fully developed Christian theology into this discussion with the representative of the Children of Abraham.

The opening of chapter 3 is made up of a citation of OT texts, all of which have links with the exodus theme. The accumulative force of these texts–that man is in exile from God–results in the incredible statement of Rom 3:21–26, in which Paul described the death of Christ. The exilic theme of the previous verses continued as Paul built his argument on a possible earlier confession of the church that represented Christ as the atoning Passover sacrifice. In Rom 3:27–32, he stressed that, in this new covenant arrangement which the eschatological Passover has inaugurated, there is no special status for Jews or Gentiles. Both call on the same Creator, who is faithful to his covenant promises.

Chapter 4 focused on the issues of justification and membership of the new covenant community. Abraham's justification was considered in terms of the requirements God made upon him. Paul demonstrated that they had nothing to do with Abraham's circumcision, for he was uncircumcised when justified. By contrast, David—another key figure in Jewish history—was circumcised but not justified. By means of this evidence, Paul established that the Jewish community, whose members had undergone circumcision, could not assume covenant membership. They stood in the same state of need as the Gentiles, who they so often despised.

The discussion on justification in chapter 4 established there has been a failure in understanding aspects of Pauline theology. Justification as covenant-making is the primary meaning behind the statement that "Abraham believed God, and it was counted to him as righteousness." We also found that for Paul, the event that showed Abraham as a justified man was his obedience to Yahweh, when he went to offer his son as a sacrifice on Mount Moriah. It was not the act that justified him, but the faith that made his obedience possible. He knew that Yahweh would keep his promise to give seed through Isaac, and would, therefore, raise his son from the dead. Paul's point was that this is the same faith NT believers exercise, for they believe God has raised Jesus from the dead and has raised up a spiritual family as a result.

In chapter 5, we found that Paul continued the theme of the new exodus through his use of pilgrim and paschal language. The discourse on the fall of man in Adam explained humankind's plight, which had previously been discussed in terms of its consequences rather than its origin. By explaining the cause of humanity's predicament, Paul has set the stage for his subsequent discussion of how God brought about a new humanity through the representative death of his Son. Paul's analysis of the consequence of the fall was that it was devastating; all, without exception, could only be saved by participation in the death of Christ.

In chapter 6, Paul expanded the theme of man's solidarity in Adam, which he introduced in chapter 5 (though it is implicitly present in the earlier chapters). His case was that Adam's disastrous representative role can be compensated for by the last Adam. Like the Adam of Genesis, the last Adam's actions will have far-reaching consequences for those who are part of the people he represents. While Adam's sin in the garden brought all under condemnation, Christ's death on the cross brought many into and under righteousness. Throughout chapter 6, Paul continued to use exodus language. He paralleled the baptism into Christ with the baptism into Moses (1 Cor 10:1–4), and so his understanding of baptism into Christ is found to be corporate. The glory of God being displayed in the new exodus is with a far-greater intensity than in the original exodus. The believers are freed from slavery to Sin in order to be servants (not slaves) of righteousness–a title that carries all of the OT connotations of Israel's call to be the servant of the Lord.

We found that chapter 7 exhibited all the signs of a typical piece of Jewish literature, with Paul reviewing the history of the human family. He used many pictures in his collage: Adam, Abraham, Moses, the Gentiles, himself, and the rest of the believing community. Paul began this part of his letter with a reference to marriage. This is the key to the corporate dimension of his argument since divine marriage symbolism is never used in scripture to describe an individual's relationship with God. This appreciation enabled us to see that the passage was not an illustration but an actual description of covenantal reality. The point that Paul established was that salvation depends on Christ; for through his death, the covenantal relationship binding humanity to Satan was cancelled. Christ severed Satan's authority, which had been given to him by the law. (The law was obliged, because of its covenantal nature [i.e., expressing the will of the covenantal God] to respect relationships which were entered into freely and, therefore, had to respect the right of the husband, in this case Satan.) Now, the believing community was in a position to marry another. She was pledged to Christ, her redeemer, whose death delivered her from Sin.

Chapter 8 continued the theme of the exodus, with Paul drawing from its imagery. He described the believing community as the son of God who is lead by the Spirit. This leading is reminiscent of the cloud and pillar of fire—symbols of the Spirit—that lead the children of Israel to the promised land. He picked up on the promise of the new creation, which was predicted by the prophets, saying that the church, along with creation, groan for this fulfillment. He said that this will be accomplished when the "birth pangs" have been completed. The final display of the sons of God (the ones redeemed by their first-born brother [Rom 8:29]) will bring to completion the redemption of creation.

Throughout the chapter, Paul used pilgrimage language. This was especially true in the "who shall separate us" acclamation, for no forces that Satan can array will separate the covenant community from the love of God. Its members are assured of their eventual safe arrival in Zion.

In chapter 9, Paul highlighted the tension that implicitly existed in his letter thus far. The question had to be asked, "Where are the Jewish people in this new exodus salvation?" Paul began by asserting that he valued the blessed heritage that he share with every other Jew, reiterating the key features of those blessings.

In order to explain the status of the Jewish people, Paul reviewed salvation history. He showed that God often bypassed lawful inheritance rights to favor people with no rights. Paul discussed these matters at a corporate level, for when individuals were referred to they were in relation to the people they represented.

Paul's discussion on the hardening of Pharaoh's heart was explored in some detail, my conclusion being that the passage was not about election to salvation but Yahweh's right to elect to privilege and service. Paul's warning was that those who turn from this high calling will become vessels of wrath and come under God's judgment. His lesson was that the hardening (i.e., judgment) of Israel was not an exception—it reflected the pattern of God's dealings with the nations. Disobedient Israel had no divine right to avoid this consequence, even though she had been the one chosen above all other nations to be the instrument of their blessing.

In chapter 10, Paul sought to show his kinsfolk that the gospel is not a departure from the law but what the law pointed to and was intended to serve. Drawing on a familiar passage in Deut 30:11–14, he showed Moses was anxious that the people understood the law to be the benchmark for revelation. It was by this code that all claims to represent God were to be judged. He also showed that Christ is the end of the law for all who believe. I challenged the widespread reliance on intertestamental literature to unlock Paul's teaching and hopefully demonstrated that his discussion is not about the incarnation of Christ but about his ascension and his sending of the Spirit to dwell among his people. Paul saturated his passage with new exodus imagery and OT quotes (as he did with chapters 9 and 11), framing his argument with them.

In the eleventh chapter, Paul discussed the status of his people, the nation of Israel. He reviewed salvation history and recalled the times when it seemed that Yahweh had abandoned his people. He was able to show through the experience of Elijah that Yahweh had always been faithful to the remnant, even when apostate.

However, what was different in the period of apostasy when Paul lived was the fulfillment of the promise that the Gentiles would be brought into the blessings of Israel. Paul explained the Jewish root still remained, but the Gentiles have been grafted into this root (which is the covenant Yahweh made with Abraham). As a result, this hardening was like no other hardening in redemptive history. It changed the "game plan" once and for all. Israel can no longer claim her unique status.

Despite this major shift away from exclusivity, Paul insisted that Yahweh did not cast Israel off. He prophesied that Israel will be saved (i.e., people who have the faith of Abraham), sharing with the Gentiles in the covenant blessings promised to their father, Abraham.

At this point in his letter (chapter 12), Paul turned to apply his teaching to the life of the believing community in Rome. He reminded the Christians that, together, they were called to a priestly ministry, to be holy and pleasing to God and transformed in its thinking so that his will could be discerned. Because of their interdependence, they were to recognize that their gifting was not haphazard but the result of God's will and, as such, their gifts were to be exercised for the sake of the entire community.

Paul exhorted the community to be characterized by sincere and devoted love, a hatred of evil, and humility. The church was to be zealous in service, joyful in hope, patient in affliction, prayerful, and generous. Her members were to live in harmony, and to resist snobbishness. The church also had to resist taking revenge against those who had wronged her, confident that God would eventually settle all accounts.

In chapter 13, Paul discussed the role of authorities and the respect and support the believers were to give them because they served the purposes of God. The believers were to display the character of God by loving their fellowmen and by keeping the commandments–indeed, by going beyond them in living their spirit. He instructed the church to recognize the urgency of the times they lived in and to be fully committed to the Lord.

Paul urged the church to care for the weak (chapter 14)—the "weak" being those believers who did not have strong faith. They were to do this without passing judgment upon them in any way. Although they confused peripheral matters of faith with ones that were more essential, Paul appealed to the church to love and respect rather than reject such people.. Paul's case was clear, these were men and women for whom Christ had died; they had value and worth, and any type of judgment of them would be wrong. The "strong" were exhorted to go out of their way not to cause these believers to stumble. Issues related to eating and drinking were not at the heart of the message of the kingdom of God, and, therefore, were not at the forefront of the church's concerns but weak brothers and sisters were!

In chapter 15, we find that Paul continued his discussion on the relationship between strong and weak believers, for accepting one another was essential if the Roman church was to be healthy. The importance of this matter was demonstrated by Christ, who became a servant of the Jews on behalf of God's truth. His servanthood confirmed the promises made to the patriarchs, resulting in the Gentiles glorifying God for his mercy. Paul supported his argument with an array of OT texts which show that the Gentiles are to be accepted. The acceptance of one another is the evidence of the work of God and this openness brings them joy and peace along with the overflow of hope given by the Holy Spirit.

Finally, in the closing section of his letter, Paul sought to give his understanding of his own ministry—a service in which he gloried. He was "a minister of Christ Jesus to the Gentiles, with the priestly duty of proclaiming the gospel of God." His goal was that the Gentiles would live holy lives, offering themselves to God as an acceptable sacrifice. In recalling the signs and miracles, through the power of the Spirit, that accompanied his preaching, Paul described his ministry as fulfilling the long-anticipated new exodus, and cited a new exodus text from Isaiah (Isa 52:15).

Paul saw his ministry in the east to be complete; after visiting Jerusalem with the collection for the poor, he planned to travel to Rome in preparation for his ministry in Spain. He was aware of the dangers that faced him in returning to Jerusalem and Judea, and elicited the prayers of the Roman believers for his acceptance and protection while he was there.

In closing his letter, which he had dictated to Tertius and, likely, entrusted to Phoebe as its carrier, Paul wrote a series of greetings to people he knew (chapter 16). These greetings were often accompanied by warm commendations. He concluded with a warning to the church—to beware of those who would cause divisions—and a summary of all that he had sought to impart to the believers in Rome:

Now to him who is able to establish you by my gospel and the proclamation of Jesus Christ, according to the revelation of the mystery hidden for long ages past, but now revealed and made known through the prophetic writings by the command of the eternal God, so that all nations might believe and obey him—to the only wise God be glory forever through Jesus Christ! Amen.

And so we come to an end of commenting on the letter to the Romans. While it is a letter to a particular church, written two thousand years ago, the church of today needs its message no less. May we be helped to live it out in the twenty first century, for God's honor and his glory.

Bibliography

Agersnap, S. *Baptism and the New Life. A Study of Romans 6.1–14.* Oakville, CT: Aarhus University Press, 1999.

Albright, W. F., and C. S. Mann. *Matthew.* Garden City, NY: Doubleday, 1971.

Aletti, J. N. "L'argumentation Paulinienne en Rm. 9." *Bib* 68 (1987) 41–56.

———. "Rm. 7:7–25 encore une fois: enjeux et propositions." *NTS* 48:3 (2002) 358–76.

Allison, D. C., Jr. "Jesus and the Covenant." *JSNT* 29 (1987) 57–78.

Anderson, B. W. *The Eighth Century Prophets: Amos, Hosea, Isaiah, Micah, Proclamation Commentaries.* Philadelphia: Fortress Press, 1978.

Anderson, C. "Romans 1:1–4 and the Occasion of the Letter: The Solution to the Two Congregation Problem in Rome." *TJ* 14 (1993) 2–40.

Ashton, J. *The Religion of Paul the Apostle.* New Haven; London: Yale University Press, 2000.

Aune, D. "Human Nature and Ethics in Hellenistic Philosophical Traditions and Paul: Some Issues and Problems." In *Paul in His Hellenistic Context,* edited by T. E. Pedersen, 291–312. Minneapolis: Fortress, 1995.

Badke, W. B. "Baptised into Moses—Baptised into Christ: A Study in Doctrinal Development." *EvQ* 60 (1988) 23–29.

Bailey, K. E. "St Paul's Understanding of the Territorial Promise of God to Abraham. Romans 4:13 in its Historical and Theological Context." *NESTTheolRev* 15 (1994) 59–69.

Ballentine, "G. L. Death of Jesus as a New Exodus." *RevExp* 30 (1962) 27–41.

Balsdon, J. P. V. D. *Roman Women: their History and Habits.* London: Bodley Head, 1963.

Barclay, J. M. G. "Paul and Philo on Circumcision: Romans 2:25–29 in Social and Cultural Context." *NTS* 44:4 (1998) 536–56.

Barr, G. K. "Romans 16 and the Tentmakers." *IBS* 20:3 (1998) 98–113.

Barrett, C. K. *A Commentary on the Epistle to the Romans.* London: A. & C. Black, 1957.

———. *From First Adam to Last: a study in Pauline theology.* London: A. & C. Black, 1962.

Barth, M. *Ephesians, The Anchor Bible.* Garden City, N.Y: Doubleday, 1974.

Bauckham, R. *The Climax of Prophecy,* Edinburgh: T. & T. Clark, 2000.

Baxter, A. G., and J. A. Ziesler. "Paul and Arboriculture: Romans 11:17–24." *JSNT* 24 (1985) 25–32.

Beale, G. K. *The Book of Revelation: A Commentary on the Greek Text: The New International Greek Testament Commentary.* Grand Rapids: Eerdmans, 1999.

———. "Did Jesus and His Followers Preach the Right Doctrine from the Wrong Texts?: An Examination of the Presuppositions of Jesus' and the Apostles' Exegetical Method." *Them* 14:3 (1989) 89–96.

Bechtler, S. R. "Christ, the *Telos* of the Law: The Goal of Romans 10:4." *CBQ* 56:2 (1994) 288–308.

Beet, J. A. *Commentary on St. Paul's Epistles to the Corinthians.* New York: Macmillan, *1882.*

Bekken, Per Jarl. "The Word is Near You: A Study of Deuteronomy 30:12–14." In *Paul's Letter to the Romans in a Jewish Context.* Beihefte zur Zeitschrift fur die Neutestamentliche. Berlin: New York: Walter de Gruyter, 2007.

Bell, R. H. "Rom. 5:18–19 and Universal Salvation." *NTS* 48:3 (2002) 417–32.

Belli, F. "Un'allusione a Is. 50:8–9 in Rm. 8:31–39." *RBB* 50:2 (2002) 153–84.

Berkley, T. W. *From a Broken Covenant to Circumcision of the Heart. Pauline Intertextual Exegesis in Romans 2:17–29.* SBL Dissertation Series 175. Atlanta: Society of Biblical Literature, 2000.

Best, E. *A Commentary on the First and Second Epistles to the Thessalonians.* London: Black. 1977.

———. *A Critical and Exegetical Commentary on Ephesians, The International Critical Commentary*. Edinburgh: T. & T. Clark, 1998.

———. *The Letter of Paul to the Romans*. The Cambridge Bible Commentary: New English Bible. Cambridge: Cambridge University Press, 1967.

———. *One Body in Christ: A Study in the Relationship of the Church to Christ in the Epistles of the Apostle Paul*. London: SPCK, 1955.

Betz, H. D. *Galatians: A Commentary on Paul's Letter to the Churches in Galatia*. Philadelphia: Fortress, 1979.

———. "Transferring a Ritual: Paul's Interpretation of Baptism in Romans 6." In *Paul in His Hellenistic Context*, edited by Troels Engberg-Pedersen, 84–118. Minneapolis: Fortress, 1995.

Bird, M. F. *The Saving Righteousness of God: Studies on Paul, Justification and the New Perspective*. Paternoster Biblical Monographs. Eugene, OR: Wipf & Stock, 2007.

Bird, M. F., and M. P. Preston. *The Faith of Jesus Christ: Exegetical, Biblical, and Theological Studies*. Peabody: Hendrickson, 2009.

Black, M. "The Pauline Doctrine of the Second Adam." *SJT* 7 (1954) 170–79.

———. *Romans, New Century Bible*. London: Oliphants, 1973.

———. "The 'Son of Man' in the Old Biblical Literature." *ExpTim* 60 (1948–1949) 11–15.

Blauw, J. "Paul as a Pioneer of Inter-Religious Thinking." *Studies in SID* [Kampen] 7 (1997) 66–75.

Bligh, J. "Baptismal Transformation of the Gentile World." *HeyJ* 37:3 (1996) 371–81.

Blocher, H. *Original Sin: Illuminating the Riddle, New Studies in Biblical Theology*. Leicester: Inter-Varsity Press, 1997.

Bockmuehl, M. "1QS and Salvation in Qumran." In *Justification and Variegated Nomism*, vol. 2. Wissenschaftliche Untersuchungen zum Neuen Testament, edited by D. A. Carson, P. T. O'Brien, and M. A. Seifrid, 343–59. Grand Rapids: Baker Academic, 2001.

Boers, H. "Jesus and the Christian Faith: New Testament Christology since Bousset's Kyrios Christos." *JBL* 89 (1970) 450–56.

———. "The Structure and Meaning of Romans 6:1–14." *CBQ* 63:4 (2001) 664–82.

Bornkamm, G. *Paul*. Trans. by D. M. G. Stalker. London: Hodder & Stoughton, 1971.

———. "The Revelation of Christ to Paul on the Damascus Road and Paul's Doctrine of Justification and Reconciliation: A Study in Galatians 1." In *Reconciliation and Hope: New Testament Essays on Atonement and Eschatology Presented to L. L. Morris on His 60th Birthday*, edited by R. Banks, 90–103. Exeter: Paternoster, 1974.

Bowker, J. "The Son of Man." *JTS* 28 (1977) 19–48.

Braaten, C. E. "Romans 12:14–21." *Int* 38:3 (1984) 291–96.

Brewer, D. I. "The Use of Rabbinic Sources in Gospel Studies." *TynBul* 50 (1999) 281–98.

Broyles, C. C. *Psalms*. Peabody: Hendrickson, 1999.

Bruce, F. F. *The Epistle of Paul to the Romans: An Introduction and Commentary*. London: Tyndale, 1963.

Buchsel, F. art "θυμός." In *TDNT* 3:168.

Budd, P. J. *Numbers, Word Biblical Commentary*. Waco: Word Books, 1984.

Bultmann, R. *Neueste Paulusforschung*. Tru (1936) Tubingen.

———. *Theology of the New Testament*. London: SCM, 1952.

———."Ursprung und Sinn der Typologie als hermeneutischer Methode." *TLZ* 75 (1950) 205–12.

Burke, T. J. *Adopted into God's family: Exploring a Pauline Metaphor*. Downers Grove, IL: InterVarsity, 2006.

Byrne, B. "Rather Boldly (Rom 15:15): Paul's Prophetic Bid to Win the Allegiance of the Christians in Rome." *Biblica* 74 (1993) 83–96.

———. *Sons of God—Seed of Abraham: A Study of the idea of the Sonship of God of all Christians in Paul against the Jewish Background*. Ana Bib 83. Rome: Biblical Institute, 1979.

Caird, G. F. B. "The Descent of Christ in Ephesians 4:7–11." *SE* 2. Berlin: Akademia (1964) 535–45.

———. *New Testament Theology*. Oxford: Oxford University Press, 1994.

Calvin, J. *Romans*. Edinburgh: The Calvin Society, 1850.

Campbell, D. A. "The Atonement in Paul." *Anvil* 11:3 (1994) 237–50.

———. *The Deliverance of God: An Apocalyptic Rereading of Justification in Paul*. Grand Rapids: Eerdmans, 2009.

———. "Romans 1:17—A Crux Interpretation for the ΠΙΣΤΙΣ ΧΡΙΤΟΥ Debate." *JBL* 113:2 (1994) 265–85.

Campbell, W. S. "The Freedom and Faithfulness of God in Relation to Israel." *JSNT* 13 (1981) 27–45.

———. *Paul and the Creation of Christian Identity* (Library of New Testament Studies). Edinburgh: T. & T. Clark, 2006.

———. "The Rule of Faith in Romans 12:1—15:13." In *Pauline Theology Vol. 3 Romans*, 259–86. Minneapolis: Fortress, 1995 .

Carbone, S. "Israele nella Lettera ai Romanai." *RivistBib* 41:2 (1993) 139–70.

Carson, D. A. "Christological Ambiguities in the Gospel of Matthew." In *Christ the Lord: Studies in Christology presented to Donald Guthrie*, edited by H. H. Rowdon, 97–114. Leicester: InterVarsity, 1982.

———. *The Gospel According to John*. Downers Grove, IL: InterVarsity, 1991.

Casey, M. *From Jewish Prophet to Gentile God: The Origins and Development of New Testament Christology*. Cambridge: Clarke, 1991.

Casey, R. P. "The Earliest Christologies." *JTS* 9 (1958) 253–77.

Cervin, R. S. "A Note Regarding the Name 'Junia(s)' in Romans 16:7." *NTS* 40:3 (1994) 464–70.

Chadwick, H. "All Things to All Men (1 Cor. IX:22)." *NTS* 1 (1955) 261–75.

Charlesworth, J. H. "A Caveat on Textual Transmission and the Meaning of Abba: A Study of the Lord's Prayer." In *The Lord's Prayer and Other Prayer Texts from the Greco-Roman Era*, edited by J. H. Charlesworth, M. Harding, and M. Kiley, 1–14. Valley Forge, PA: Trinity, 1994.

Chilton, B. "Romans 9–11 as Scriptural Interpretation and Dialogue with Judaism." *ExAud* 4 (1988) 27–37.

Chilton, B., and P. Davies. "The Aqedah: A Revised Tradition History." *CBQ* 40 (1978) 514–46.

Coleman, T. M. "Binding Obligations in Romans 13:7: A Semantic Field and Social Context." *TynBul* 48 (1997) 307–27.

Court, J. M. "Paul and the Apocalyptic Pattern." In *Paul and Paulinism: Essays in Honour of C. K. Barrett*, edited by M. D. Hooker and S. G. Wilson, 57–66. London: SPCK, 1982.

Cousar, C. P. "Paul and the Death of Jesus." *Int* 52 (1998) 38–52.

Coxon, P. "The Paschal New Exodus in John: An Interpretive Key with Particular Reference to John 5–10." Unpublished PhD thesis submitted to the University of Wales, St. David's College, 2010.

Cozart, R., "An Investigation Into the Significance of the Promise of a New Exodus of Israel in the Letter to the Ephesians." Unpublished PhD thesis submitted to the University of Wales, Trinity Saint David's College, 2011.

Cranfield, C. E. B. *The Epistle to the Romans*, vols. 1 & 2. ICC Series. Edinburgh: T. & T. Clark, 1975, 1979.

———. "Has the Old Testament Law a Place in the Christian Life? A Response to Professor Westerholm." *IBS* 15:2 (1993) 50–64.

———. *Romans: A Shorter Commentary*. Grand Rapids: Eerdmans,1985.

———. "Some Observations on Romans 8:19–21." In *Reconciliation and Hope*, edited by R. Banks, 224–30. Exeter: Paternoster, 1974.

Cullmann, O. *Baptism in the New Testament*. Translated by J. K. S. Reid. London: SCM, 1950.

———. *The Christology of the New Testament*. Translated by S. C. Guthrie and A. N. Hall. London: SCM, 1959.

———. *The State in the New Testament*. London: SCM, 1957.

Dahl, N.A. "The *Atonement*: An Adequate Reward for the Akedah? (Ro 8:32)." In Neotestamentica et Semitica, ed. E. Earle Ellis and Max Wilcox, 15 27, Edinburgh: T. & T. Clark, 1969), 15.

Davies, R. E. "Christ in Our Place: The Contribution of the Prepositions." *TynBul* 21 (1970) 71–91.

Davies, R. P. "Passover and the Dating of the Aqedah." *JJS* 30 (1979) 59–67.

Davies, W. D. *Jewish and Pauline Studies*. Philadelphia: Fortress, 1955.

———. "Paul and the People of Israel." *NTS* 24 (1977) 4–39.

———. *Paul and Rabbinic Judaism*. 2nd ed. London: SPCK, 1955.

Davila, J. R. "The Old Testament as Background to the New Testament." *ExpTimes* 117:2 (2005) 53–57.

———. *The Provenance of the Pseudepigrapha: Jewish, Christian, or Other?* Supplements to the Journal for the Study of Judaism. Leiden: Brill, 2005.

De Jonge, M. "The Earliest Christian Use of Christos: Some Suggestions." *NTS* 32:3 (1986) 321–43.

De Lacey, D. R. "Image and Incarnation in Pauline Christology: A Search for Origins." *TynBul* 30 (1979) 3–28.

DeMaris, R. E. "Funerals and Baptisms, Ordinary and Otherwise: Ritual Criticism and Corinthian Rites." *BibToday* 29 (1999) 23–34.

Bibliography

Denova, R. I. "Paul's Letter to the Romans 13:1–7: The Gentile-Christian Response to Civil Authority." *Enc* 53:3 (1992) 201–29.

Derrett, J. D. M. *Law in the New Testament*. London: Darton, Longman & Todd, 1970.

———. "You Abominate False Gods; But Do You Rob Shrines? (Rom. 2:22b)." *NTS* 40:4 (1994) 558–71.

Dillon, J. R. "The Priesthood of St Paul, Romans 15:15–16." *Worship* 74:2 (2000) 156–68.

Dodd, C. H. *According to the Scriptures: The Substructure of New Testament Theology*. London: Nisbet, 1952.

———. *Essays in New Testament Studies*. Manchester: Manchester University Press, 1953.

———. *The Interpretation of the Fourth Gospel*. Cambridge: Cambridge University Press, 1953.

Donaldson, T. L. "The Curse of the Law and the Inclusion of the Gentiles: Galatians 3:13–14." *NTS* 32 (1986) 94–112.

———. *Paul and the Gentiles: Remapping the Apostle's Convictional World*. Minneapolis: Fortress, 1997.

———. "Riches for the Gentiles (Rom. 11:12): Israel's Rejection and Paul's Gentile Mission." *JBL* 112 (1993) 81–98.

Donfried, K. P. "A Short Note on Romans 16." In *The Romans Debate*, edited by K. P. Donfried, 44–52. Edinburgh: T. & T. Clark, 1991.

Donne, B. K. *Christ Ascended*. Exeter: Paternoster, 1983.

Downing, J. "Jesus and Martyrdom." *JTS* 14 (1963) 279–93.

Dozeman, T.B. *God at War: Power in the Exodus Tradition*. New York: OUP, 1996.

Driver, J. *Understanding the Atonement for the Mission of the Church*. Scottdale, PA: Herald, 1986.

Dunn, J. D. G. "1 Corinthians 15.45. Last Adam, Life Giving Spirit." In *Christ and Spirit in the NT, Studies in honour of C. F. D. Moule*, edited by Lindars. B. and Smalley SS, 127–46. Cambridge: Cambridge University Press, 1973.

———. *Baptism in the Holy Spirit*. London: SCM, 1970.

———. *Christology in the Making. An Inquiry into the Origins of the Doctrine of the Incarnation*. 2nd ed. London: SCM, 1989.

———. *The Epistle to the Galatians*, Black`s New Testament Commentary Series. Peabody: Hendrickson,1993.

———. *Jesus and the Spirit: A Study of the Religious and Charismatic Experience of Jesus and the First Christians as Reflected in the New Testament*. London: SCM,1975.

———, editor. *Jews and Christians: The Parting of the Ways, AD70 to 135; the Second Durham Tubingen Research Symposium on Earliest Christianity and Judaism (September 1989)*, Wissenschaftliche Untersuchungen Zum Neuen Testament: Vol. 66, Tubingen: Mohr,1992.

———. *The New Perspective on Paul: Collected Essays*. Wissenschaftliche Untersuchungen zum Neuen Testame. Tubingen: Mohr Siebeck, 2005.

———. "Paul's Understanding of the Death of Jesus." In *Reconciliation and Hope*, essays presented to L. L. Morris on his 60th birthday, edited by R. Banks, 125–41. Exeter: Paternoster Press, 1974.

———. *Romans 916*. Waco: Word, 1988.

———. *The Theology of Paul the Apostle*. Edinburgh: T. & T. Clark, 1998.

———. *Unity and Diversity in the New Testament: An Inquiry into the Character of Earliest Christianity*. 2nd ed. London: SCM, 1990.

———. "Who Did Paul Think He Was? A Study of Jewish-Christian Identity." *NTS* 45:2 (1999) 174–93.

Durham, J. I. *Exodus*. Waco: Word Books,1987.

Du Toit, A. B. "Die Kirche als doxologische Gemeinschaft im Romerbrief." *Neot* 27 (1993) 69–77.

Earnshaw, J. D. "Reconsidering Paul's Marriage Analogy in Romans 7:1–4," *NTS* 40 (1994) 68–88.

Edwards, J. R. *Romans*. Peabody: Hendrickson, 1992.

Elliott, J. K. "The Language and Style of the Concluding Doxology to the Epistle to the Romans." *ZNW* 72 (1981) 124–30.

Ellis, E. E. "11 Cor V.1–10 in Pauline Eschatology." *JNTS* 111 (1959) 211–24.

———. "A note on 1 Cor. 10:4." *JBL* 76 (1957) 53–56.

———. *Paul and His Recent Interpreters*, Grand Rapids: Eerdmans, 1967.

———. *Paul's Use of the Old Testament*, Edinburgh: Oliver & Boyd, 1957.

———. *Prophecy and Hermeneutic in Early Christianity*, Grand Rapids: Eerdmans, 1978.

———. "Traditions in 1 Corinthians." *NTS* 32:4 (1986) 481–502.

Emerton, J. A. "The Origin of the Son of Man Imagery." *JTS* 9 (1958) 225–42.

Engberg-Pedersen, T. *Paul and the Stoics*. Louisville, KY: Westminster John Knox, 2000.

Eskola, T. "Paul, Predestination and 'Covenantal Nomism'—Re-assessing Paul and Palestinian Judaism." *JSJ* 28 (1997) 390–412.

Esler, P. "Ancient Oleiculture and Ethnic Differentiation: the Meaning of the Olive-Tree Image in Romans 11." *JSNT* 26 (2003) 103–24.

Espy, J. M. "Paul's 'Robust Conscience' Re-Examined." *NTS* 31 (1985) 161–88.

Fee, G. D. "Christology and Pneumatology in Romans 8:9–11." In *Jesus of Nazareth, Lord and Christ: Essays on the Historical Jesus and New Testament Christology,* edited by J. B. Green and M. Turner, 312–31. Grand Rapids: Eerdmans, 1994.

———. *God's Empowering Presence: The Holy Spirit in the Letters of Paul* Peabody: Hendrickson, 1994.

Finger, R. H. "Was Julia a Racist? Cultural Diversity in the Book of Romans." *DS* Chicago 19:3 (1993) 36–39.

Fitzmyer, J. A. "The Consecutive Meaning of ΕΦ' Ω in Romans 5:12." *NTS* Vol. 39:3 (1993) 321–39.

———. *Romans: A New Translation with Introduction and Commentary*. Anchor Bible. New York: Chapman, 1993.

Foerster, W. "εἰρήνη," *TDNT* 2:400–420.

Ford, D. "What about the Trinity?" In *Meaning and Truth in 2 Corinthians,* edited by F. Young and D. Ford, 255–60. Grand Rapids: Eerdmans,1987.

Ford, J. M. "The Son of Man Euphemism?" *JBL* 87 (1969) 189–96.

Fretheim, T. E. *Exodus*, Louisville: Westminster John Knox, 1991.

Friedbert, N, *Indicators of Typology within the Old Testament: The Exodus Motif.* Frankfurt/M., Berlin, Bern, Bruxelles, New York, Oxford, Wien, 2001

Friesen, G., and J. R. Maxson. *Decision Making and the Will of God: A Biblical Alternative to the Traditional View*. Portland, OR: Multnomah, 1980.

Fuller, R. H. *The Foundations of New Testament Christology*, London: Lutterworth, 1965.

Furnish, V. P. *The Moral Teaching of Paul*, Nashville: Abingdon, 1979.

Gager, J. G. "Functional Diversity in Paul's Use of End Time Language." *JBL* 84 (1970) 325–37.

Gagnon, R. A. J. "The Meaning of ὑμῶν τὸ ἀγαθόν in Romans 14:16." *JBL* 117:4 (1998) 675–89.

———. "Why the 'Weak' at Rome Cannot be Non-Christian Jews." *CBQ* 62 (2000) 64–82.

Garlington, D. B. "The Obedience of Faith in the Letter to the Romans. Part III: The Obedience of Christ and the Obedience of the Christian." *WTJ* 55 (1993) 87–112.

———. "Romans 7:14–25 and the Creation Theology of Paul." *TJ* 11:2 (1990) 197–235.

Garnet, P. "Atonement Constructions in the Old Testament and the Qumran Scrolls," *EvQ* 46 (1974)131-63.

Gaston, L. "Israel's Enemies in Pauline Theology." *NTS* 28:3 (1982) 400–423.

Gathercole, S. J. "A Law unto Themselves: The Gentiles in Romans 2:14–15 Revisited." *JSNT* 23:3 (2002) 27–49.

———. *Where is Boasting? Early Jewish Soteriology and Paul's Response in Romans 1–5*. Grand Rapids: Eerdmans, 2002.

Getty, M. A. "Paul and the Salvation of Israel: A Perspective on Romans 9–11." *CBQ* 50:3 (1988) 456–69.

Giblin, C. H. "Three Monotheistic Texts in Paul." *CBQ* (1975) 527–47.

Ginzberg, L. *The Legends of the Jews,* Philadelphia: Jewish Publication Society of America,1925.

Given, M. D. "Restoring the Inheritance in Romans 11:1." *JBL* 118 (1999) 89–96.

Glancy, J. "Israel vs. Israel in Romans 11:25–32" *USQR* 45:3/4 (1991) 191–203.

Goldingay, J. *Psalms vol 2:42–89*. Grand Rapids: Baker Academic, 2007.

Goppelt, L. *Typos. The Typological Interpretation of The Old Testament in the New*. Translated by D. H. Madvig. Grand Rapids: Eedermans, 1982.

Goulder, M.D. *The Psalms of the Return (Book 5, Psalms 107-150): Studies in the Psalter, 4, Journal for the Study of the Old Testament Supplem*. Sheffield: Sheffield, 1998.

Gray, G.B. *A Critical and Exegetical Commentary on Numbers, International Critical Commentary ICC*. Edinburgh: T. & T. Clark, 1903.

Grech, P. "The Old Testament as a Christological Source in the Apostolic Age." *BibToday* 2 (1975) 127–45.

Green, G. L. *Jude and 2 Peter*. Grand Rapids:Baker, 2008.

———. *The Letters to the Thessalonians*. Grand Rapids: Eerdemans. 2002.

Gulley, N. R. "Ascension of Christ." In *ABD* 1:472–74.

Hahn, F. *The Titles of Jesus in Christology, their History in Early Christianity*. New York: World Publishing, 1969.

Hall, D. R. "Romans 3:1–8 Reconsidered." *NTS* 29 (1983) 183–97.

Hamerton-Kelly, R. G. "Sacred Violence and the Curse of the Law (Galatians 3.13). The Death of Christ as a Sacrificial Travesty." *NTS* 36 (1990) 98–116.

Hanson A. T. *New Testament Interpretation of Scripture.* London: SPCK, 1980.

Harman, Alan. *Psalms.* Fearn: Christian Focus, 1998.

Harris, M. J. *Jesus as God: the New Testament use of Theos in Reference to Jesus.* Grand Rapids: Baker, 1992.

Harris, W. Hall III. *The Descent of Christ: Ephesians 4:7–11 and Traditional Hebrew Imagery*, Arbeiten zur Geschichte des Antiken Judentums und. Leiden: E. J. Brill, 1996.

Hays, R. B. "Adam, Israel, Christ." In *Pauline Theology, Vol. III, Romans*, Edited by Hay, D. M. and Johnson, E. E. Minneapolis, Minn: Fortress, 1995.

———. *The Conversion of the Imagination: Paul as Interpreter of Israel's Scripture.* Grand Rapids: Eerdmans, 2005.

———. *Echoes of Scripture in the Letters of Paul.* New Haven, CT: Yale University Press. 1989.

———. "Have we found Abraham to be our Father According to the Flesh? A Reconsideration of Rom 4:1." *Nov T* (1985) 76–98.

———. "ΠΙΣΙΣ and Pauline Christology: What is at Stake?" in SBL Seminar Papers, edited by E. H. Lovering Jr., 714–29. Atlanta: Scholars Press, (1991).

———. "'Who Has Believed Our Message': Paul's Reading of Isaiah" In *New Testament Writers and the Old Testament: An Introduction*, edited by J. M. Court. London: SPCK, 2002.

Hellholm, D. "Die argumentative Funktion von Romer 7:1–6." *NTS* 43:3 (1997) 385–411.

Hendriksen, W. *Exposition of Paul's Epistle to the Romans: Vol.1: Chapters 1–8.* Grand Rapids: Baker, 1981.

Hengel, M. *The Atonement: The Origins of the Doctrine in the New Testament.* Philadelphia: Fortress, 1981.

———. *The Son of God, The Origin of Christology and the History of Jewish-Hellenistic Religion.* Translated by J. Bowden. London: SCM, 1976.

Herrmann, J. art "ἱλασμός" *TDNT* 3: 301-310.

Hester, J. D. *Paul's Concept of Inheritance: A Contribution to the Understanding of Heilsgeschichte.* Scottish Journal of Theology, occasional papers: 14. London: Oliver & Boyd, 1968.

Hill, D. *Greek Words and Hebrew Meanings. Studies in the Semantics of Soteriological Terms.* London: Cambridge University Press, 1967.

Hills, J. V. "Christ was the Goal of the Law: Romans 10:4." *JTS* 44:2 (1993) 585–92.

Hodge, C. *A Commentary on Romans.* Grand Rapids: Eerdmans, 1886.

Hoehner, H. W. *Ephesians: An Exegetical Commentary.* Grand Rapids: Baker Academic, 2002.

Holland. T. "A Case of Mistaken Identity: The Harlot and the Church (1 Corinthians 5–6)." *ATI* 1 (2008) 56–68. Online: http://atijournal.org/ATI_Vol1_No1.pdf.

———. *Contours of Pauline Theology.* Fearn, Scotland: Christian Focus, 2004.

———. *The Paschal New Exodus Motif in Paul's Letter to the Romans with Special Reference to its Christological Significance.* PhD diss., University of Wales, 1996.

Hooker, M. D. "Adam in Romans 1." *NTS* 6:3 (1960) 297–306.

———. "Further Notes on Romans 1." *NTS* 13 (1967) 297–306.

———. "Interchange in Christ." *JTS* 22:2 (1971) 349–61.

———. *Paul: Apostle to the Gentiles,* St Paul's Lecture given at St Botolph's, Aldgate on November 16th 1989.

———. "Paul and 'Covenantal Nomism.'" In *Paul and Paulinism: Essays in Honour of C. K. Barrett*, edited by M. D. Hooker and S. G. Wilson, 47–56. London: SPCK, 1982.

Horst, J. "μελη." *TDNT* 4:555–68.

Howard, J. K. "Into Christ: a Study of the Pauline Concept of Baptismal Union." *ExpTim* 79 (1968) 147–51.

———. "Passover and Eucharist in the Fourth Gospel." *SJT* 20 (1967) 329–37.

Jansen, F. J. "The Ascension, the Church and Theology." *TToday* 16 (1959) 17–29.

Jeremias, J. *New Testament Theology.* London:SCM, 1971.

———. *The Prayers of Jesus.* Philadelphia: Fortress, 1967.

Jewett, R. "Ecumenical Theology For the Sake of Mission." In *Pauline Theology*, vol. 3, edited by D. M Hay and E. E. Johnson, 80–108. Minneapolis: Fortress, 1995.

———. *Paul's Anthropological Terms: A Study of their Use in Conflict Settings.* Arbeiten zur Geschichte des Antiken Judentums und. Leiden: Brill, 1971.

——— *Romans: A Commentary.* A Critical and Historical Commentary. Minneapolis: Fortress, 2006.

Johnson, A. R. *Sacral Kingship in Ancient Israel*. Cardiff: University of Wales Press, 1967.

Johnson, B. C. "Tongues: A Sign for Unbelievers?—a Structural and Exegetical Study of 1 Corinthians XIV 20–25." *NTS* 25 (1978/79) 180–203.

Johnson, D. G. "The Structure and Meaning of Romans 11." *CBQ* 46 (1984) 91–103.

Johnson, L. T. *Reading Romans: A Literary and Theological Commentary*. New York: Crossroads, 1997.

Karlberg, M. W. "Israel's History Personified: Romans 7:7–13 in Relation to Paul's Teaching on the Old Man." *TrinJ* 7 (1986) 68–69.

Karris, R. J. "Romans 14:1—15:13 and the Occasion of Romans." In *The Romans Debate*, edited by K. P. Donfried, 65–84. Peabody: Hendriksen, 1991.

Kasemann, E. *Exegetische Versuche und Besinnungen I*. Gottingen: Vandenhoeck & Ruprecht, 1965.

———. *Romans*. Grand Rapids: Eerdmans,1980.

Kay, B. N. *The Thought Structure of Romans with Special Reference to Chapter 6*. Austin, TX: Scholar Press, 1979.

Keck, L. E. "Christology, Soteriology, and the Praise of God (Romans 15:7–13)." In *The Conversation Continues: Studies in Paul and John in Honour of J. Louis Martyn*, edited by R. T. Fortna and B. R. Gaventa, 85–97. Nashville: Abingdon, 1990.

———. "Towards the Renewal of New Testament Christology." *NTS* 32 (1986) 362–77.

———. (1995) "What Makes Romans Tick?" In *Pauline Theology*, vol. 3, edited by D. M. Hay and E. E. Johnson, 3–29. Minneapolis: Fortress, 1995.

Kee, H. C. "Christology and Ecclesiology. Titles of Christ and Models of Community." *SBL* Seminar Papers, 227–42.

Keesmaat, S. C. "Exodus and the Intertextual Transformation of Traditions in Romans 8:14–30." *JSNT* 54 (1994) 29–56.

———. "*Paul and His Story: Exodus and Tradition in Galatians*." *Horizons in Biblical Theology* 18.2 (1996) 133–68.

Kelly, J. N. D. *The Epistles of Peter and of Jude*. Black: London, 1990.

Kennedy, A. A. *Saint Paul's Conception of the Last Things*. London: Hodder and Stoughton, 1904.

Kidner, D. *Genesis*. Leicester: InterVarsity, 1967.

———. "Sacrifice—Metaphors and Meaning." *TynB* (1982) 119–36.

Kim, S. "The Mystery of Rom. 11:25–26 Once More." *NTS* 43:3 (1997) 412–29.

Kirby, J. C. *Ephesians: Baptism and Pentecost—An Inquiry into the Structure and Purpose of the Epistle to the Ephesians*. London: SPCK, 1968.

Kirkpatrick, A. F. *The Book of Psalms*. Cambridge: Cambridge University Press, 1910

Klein, W. W. *The New Chosen People: A Corporate View of Election*. Eugene, OR: Wipf & Stock, 2001.

Klijn, A. F. J. "The Study of Jewish Christianity." *NTS* 20 (1974) 119–31.

Kline, M. G. "The Old Testament Origins of the Gospel Genre." *WTJ* 1.38 (1975) 1–27.

Knox, J. *Life in Christ: Reflections on Romans 5–8*. Greenwich, CT. Seabury, 1961.

Knox, W. L. *St. Paul and the Church of the Gentiles*. Cambridge: Cambridge University Press, 1939.

Kosmala, H. "The Bloody Husband." *VT* 12 (1962) 14–28.

Kramer, W. *Christ, Lord, Son of God*, London: SCM. 1966.

Kraus, Hans-Joachim. *Psalms 60–150*. Minneapolis: Fortress, 1993.

Kreuzer, S. "Der den Gotlosen rechtfertigt (Rom. 4:5). Die fruhjudische Einordnung von Gen. 15 als Hintergrund fur das Abrahambild und die Rechtfertigungslehre des Paulus." *TheolBeitr* 33:4 (2002) 208–19.

Krimmer, H. *Romer-Brief*. Stuttgart: Hanssler, 1983.

Kroger, D. "Paul and the Civil Authorities: An Exegesis of Romans 13:1–7." *AsiaJournTheol* 7:2 (1993) 344–66.

Kummel, W. G. *The Theology of the New Testament according to its Major Witnesses: Jesus—Paul—John*. London: SCM, 1974.

Kuss, O. *Der Römerbrief*. Regensburg: F. Pustet, 1963-1978.

Laato, T. "Paul's Anthroplogical Considerations: Two Problems." In *Justification and Variegated Nomism*, vol. 2. Wissenschaftliche Untersuchungen Zum Neuen Testamet, edited by D. A. Carson, P. T. O'Brien, and M. A. Seifrid, 343–59. Grand Rapids: Baker Academic, 2001.

Lagrange, P. M.-J. *Saint Paul. Epitre aux Romains*. Paris: Gabalda, 1950.

Lambrecht, J. "Paul's Christological Use of Scripture in 1 Cor. 15:20–28." *NTS* 28:4 (1982) 502–27.

Landy, F. *Hosea, Readings: A New Biblical Commentary*. Sheffield: Sheffield Academic Press, 1995.

Lane, W. L. "Covenant, the Key to Paul's Conflict with Corinth." *TB* 33 (1982) 3–29.

Laurer, S. "Traces of a Gospel Writing in 1 Corinthians 1 to 7: Rediscovery and Development of Origen's Understanding of 1 Corinthians 4:6b." PhD diss., University of Wales, 2010.

Leaney, A. R. C. "1 Peter and the Passover: An Interpretation." *NTS* 10 (1963/64) 238–51.

Lee, Y. L. *Pilgrimage and the Knowledge of God*. Unpublished PhD diss., University of Wales, Lampeter, 2007.

Leenhardt, F. J. *L'epitre de Saint Paul aux Romains*. Geneva: Labor et Fides, 1981.

Lemico, E. "The Unifying Kerygma of the New Testament." *JSNT* 33 (1998) 3–17.

Levinson, J. D. *The Death and Resurrection of the Beloved Son. The Transformation of Child Sacrifice in Judaism and Christianity*. New Haven: Yale University Press, 1993.

Lincoln, A. *Ephesians*. Dallas: Word, 1990.

———. "From Wrath to Justification" In *Pauline Theology*, vol. 3, edited by David M. Hay and E. Elizabeth Johnson, 130–59. Minneapolis: Fortress, 1995.

Little, R. C. *Mission in the Way of Paul: Biblical Mission for the Church in the Twenty-First Century*. New York: Peter Lange, 2005.

Longacre, R. E., and W. B. Wallis. "Soteriology and Eschatology in Romans." *JETS* 41:3 (1998) 367–82.

Longenecker, B. W. "Pistis in Romans 3:25—Neglected Evidence for the 'Faithfulness of Christ'?" *NTS* 39:3 (1993) 478–80.

Longenecker, R. N. *Galatians*. Waco: Word, 1990.

———. "Prolegomena to Paul's Use of Scripture in Romans." *BBR* 7 (1997) 145–68.

Lyall, F. "Roman Law in the Writings of Paul—Adoption." *JBL* 88 (1969) 458–66.

Maartens, P. J. "The Relevance of 'Context' and 'Interpretation' to the Semiotic Relations of Romans 5:1–11." *Neot* 29 (1995) 75–108.

———. "The Vindication of the Righteous in Romans 8:31–39: Inference and Relevance." *HvTSt* 51:4 (1995) 1046–87.

MacGregor, G. H. C. "Principalities and Powers: The Cosmic Background of Paul's Thought." *NTS* 1:2 (1954/55) 17–28.

Macintosh, A. A. *A Critical and Exegetical Commentary on Hosea*, ICC. Edinburgh: T. & T. Clark, 1997.

Mackay, J. L. *Exodus: A Mentor Commentary*. Fearn, UK: Christian Focus, 2001.

Maddox, R. "The Function of the Son of Man according to the Synoptic Gospels." *NTS* 15 (1968–1969) 45–74.

Maddox, R. "The Function of the Son of Man in the Gospel of John." In *Reconciliation and Hope, New Testament Essays on Atonement and Eschatology, Presented to L. L. Morris on His 60th Birthday*, edited by R. Banks, 186–204. Exeter: Paternoster, 1974.

Maile, J. F. "The Ascension in Luke-Acts." *TynB* 37 (1986) 29–59.

Maillot, A. *L'epitre aux Romains: epitre de l'oecumenisme et theologie de l'histoire*. Paris: Centurion, 1984.

Malherbe, A. J. *The Letters to the Thessalonians*. New York: Doubleday, 2000.

Malick, D. E. "The Condemnation of Homosexuality in Romans 1:26–27." *BibSac* 150:599 (1993) 327–40.

Manek, J. "The New Exodus in the Book of Luke." *NovT* (1955) 8–23.

Manson, T. W. "Romans," *PCB*, 940–53.

———. "St. Paul's Letter to the Romans—and Others." In *The Romans Debate*, edited by K. Donfried, 1–16. Minneapolis: Augsburg, 1977.

———. *The Teaching of Jesus: Studies of Its Form and Content*. 2nd ed. Cambridge: Cambridge University Press, 1935.

Marsh, J. *The Fullness of Time*. London: No Publisher, 1952.

Marshall, I. H. "Living in the 'Flesh.'" *BibSac* 159:636 (2002) 387–403.

———. *The Origins of New Testament Christology*. Leicester: InterVarsity, 1976.

———. "Palestinian and Hellenistic Christianity: Some Critical Comments." *NTS* 19:2 (1973) 271–87.

Martin, J. P. "Kerygma of Romans." *Int* 25:2 (1971) 308–28.

Martin, R. P. *Colossians: The Church's Lord and the Christian's Liberty*. Exeter: Paternoster, 1972.

Mays, J. L. *Psalms, Interpretation, a Bible Commentary for Teaching and Preaching*. Louisville: Westminster John Knox, 1994.

McKay, C. "Ezekiel in the NT." *CQR* 162 (1961) 4–16.

McKelvey, R. T. *The New Temple: The Church in the New Testament*. London: Oxford, 1969.

McNeile, A.H. *The book of Numbers*. Cambridge: University Press, 1911.

McKnight. S. *A New Vision for Israel: The Teachings of Jesus in National Context*. Grand Rapids: Eerdmans, 1999.

McWhirter, J. *The Bridegroom Messiah and the People of God: Marriage in the Fourth Gospel*. Society for New Testament Studies Monograph Series. Cambridge: Cambridge University Press, 2006.

Meggitt, J. J. "The Social Status of Erastus (Rom. 16:23)." *Nov Test* 38:3 (1996) 218–23.

Meissner, S. "Paulinische Soteriologie und die 'Aqedat Jitzchaq." *Jud* 51 (1995) 33–49.

Metzger, B. M. "The Punctuation of Rom. 9:5." In *Christ and Spirit in the New Testament: In Honour of Charles Francis Digby Moule*, editors B. Lindars and S. Smalley, 95–112. Cambridge: Cambridge University Press, 1973.

———. *The Text of the New Testament*. 3rd ed. New York: Oxford University Press, 1992.

Meyer, B. F. "The Pre-Pauline Formula in Rom. 3:25–26a." *NTS* 29 (1983) 198–208.

Michael, O. *KEK*. Gottingen: Vandenhoeck & Ruprecht, 1957.

Millard, A. R. "Covenant and Communion in First Corinthians." In *Apostolic History and the Gospel: Essays Presented to F. F. Bruce on His Sixtieth Birthday,* edited by W. Gasque and R. P. Martin, 242–48. Exeter: Paternoster, 1970.

Miller, J. C. *The Obedience of Faith, the Eschatological People of God, and the Purpose of Romans*. SBL Dissertation Series, 177. Atlanta: SBL, 2000.

Mitton, L. C. *Ephesians*, New Century Bible Commentary, ed. Matthew Black. London: Marshall, Morgan, and Scott, 1973

Molland, E. *Das Paulinische Evangelion: Das Wort und die Sache*. Oslo: Jacob Dybwad, 1934.

Monte, W. D. "The Place of Jesus' Death and Resurrection in Pauline Soteriology." *SBT* 16 (1988) 39–97.

Moo, D. J. *The Epistle to the Romans*. Grand Rapids: Eerdmans, 1996.

———. "'Law,' 'Works of the Law' and legalism in Paul." *WTJ* 45 (1983) 73–100.

Morris, L. L. *The Apostolic Preaching of the Cross*. London: Tyndale, 1955.

———. *The Atonement: Its Meaning and Significance*. Leicester: InterVarsity, 1963.

———. *The Epistle to the Romans*. Leicester: InterVarsity, 1988.

———. "The Meaning of *Hilasterion* in Romans 3:25." *NTS* 2 (1955) 33–43.

———. "The Passover in Rabbinic Literature." *AusBR* 4 (1954/55) 57–76.

Moule, C. F. D. *An Idiom Book of New Testament Greek*. Cambridge: Cambridge University Press, 1979.

———. "The Influence of Circumstances on the use of Christological Terms." *JTS* 10 (1960) 247–64.

———. *The Origin of Christology*. Cambridge: Cambridge University Press, 1977.

———. *The Sacrifice of Christ*. London: Hodder & Stoughton, 1956.

Moule, H. C. G. *The Epistle of Paul the Apostle to the Romans with Introduction and Notes*. Cambridge: Cambridge University Press, 1903.

Muilenburg, J. "The Son of Man in Daniel and the Ethiopic Apocalypse of Enoch." *JBL* 79 (1960) 197–209.

Muddiman, J. *A Commentary on the Epistle to the Ephesians, Black's New Testament Commentaries*. London: Continuum, 2001.

Munck, J. *Christ and Israel: An Interpretation of Romans 9–11*. Philadelphia: Fortress, 1967.

———. "Jewish Christianity in Post-Apostolic Times." *NTS* 6:2 (1959) 103–16.

———. *Paul and the Salvation of Mankind*. London: SCM, 1959.

Murray, J. *The Collected Writings of John Murray, Vol 2: Lectures in Systematic Theology*. Edinburgh: Banner of Truth, 1977.

———. *The Epistle to the Romans*, vols. 1 & 2. London: Marshall, Morgan & Scott, 1967.

Nanos, M. D. "The Jewish Context of the Gentile Audience Addressed in Paul's Letter to the Romans." *CBQ* 61:2 (1999) 283–304.

———. *The Mystery of Romans: the Jewish Context of Paul's Letter*. Minneapolis: Fortress, 1996.

Nida, Eugene A., and Johannes P. Louw. *Lexical Semantics of the Greek New Testament: A Supplement to the Greek-English Lexicon of the New Testament Based on Semantic Domains*. Atlanta: Scholars, 1992.

Ninow, F. *Indicators of Typology within the Old Testament: The Exodus Motif*. Friedensauer Schriftenreihe—Reihe A Theologie. Frankfurt-am-Main: Peter Lang, 2001.

Nixon, R. E. *The Exodus in the New Testament*. London: Tyndale, 1963.

North, J. L. "'Good Words and Faire Speeches' (Rom. 16:18 AV): More Materials and a Pauline Pun." *NTS* 42:4 (1996) 600–614.

Noordtzij, A. *Numbers, Bible student's commentary*. Grand Rapids, Mich: Zondervan Pub. House, 1983.

Nwachukwu, M. S. C. *Creation-Covenant Scheme and Justification by Faith: A Canonical Study of the God-Human Drama in the Pentateuch and the Letter to the Romans*. Rome: Editrice Pontifica Universita Gregoriana, 2002.

Nygren, A. *Commentary on Romans*. London: SCM, 1958.

Olyott, S. *The Gospel as It Really Is: Paul's Epistle to the Romans Simply Explained*. Darlington: Evangelical, 1979.

O'Neill, J. C. *Paul's Letter to the Romans*. Harmondsworth: Penguin, 1975.

Oster, R. E. "Congregations of the Gentiles (Rom 16:4): A Culture-Based Ecclesiology in the Letters of Paul." *ResQuar* 40 (1998) 39–52.

Owen, J. *Temptation and Sin*. Indiana: Sovereign Grace, 1958.

Pamment, M. "The Kingdom of Heaven according to the First Gospel." *NTS* 27 (1981) 211–32.

Pate, C. M. *Adam Christology as Exegetical and Theological Substructure of II Corinthians 4:7—5:21*. Lanham, MD: University Press of America, 1991.

Perrin, N. *A Modern Pilgrimage in New Testament Christology*. Philadelphia: Fortress, 1974.

Petersen, N. R. *Rediscovering Paul: Philemon and the Sociology of Paul's Narrative World*. Philadelphia: Fortress, 1985.

Peterson, A. K. "Shedding new light on Paul's Understanding of Baptism: A Ritual-Theological Approach to Romans 6." *StudTheol* 52 (1998) 3–28.

Peterson, D. "Worship and Ethics in Romans 12." *TynBul* 44:2 (1993) 271–88.

Pierce, C. A. *Conscience in the New Testament*. London: SCM, 1955.

Piper, J. *The Future of Justification: A Response to N. T. Wright*. Nottingham: InterVarsity, 2008.

Powers, D. G. *Salvation through Participation. An Examination of the Notion of the Believers' Corporate Unity with Christ in Early Christian Soteriology*. Leuven: Peeters, 2001.

Procksch, O., art "λύω" *TDNT* 4 : 328-335

Punt, J. Paul, "Hermeneutics and the Scriptures of Israel." *Neot* 30:2 (1996) 377–426.

Ra, K. U. "An Investigation of the Influence of the Paschal—New Exodus Motif on the Description of Christ and His Work in the Gospel of John (chapters One to Four)." Unpublished PhD thesis submitted to the University of Wales, St. David's College, 2009.

Raisanen, H. "Paul's Conversion and the Development of His View of the Law." *NTS* 33 (1987) 404–19.

Rancine, J. F. "Romains 13:1-7: Simple Preservation de l'ordre Social?" *EstBib* 51:2 (1993) 187–205.

Rapinchuk, M. "Universal Sin and Salvation in Romans 5:12–21." *JETS* 42:3 (1999) 427–41.

Reasoner, M. *The Strong and the Weak: Romans 14:1—15:13 in Context*. Cambridge: Cambridge University Press, 1999.

Reumann, J. "The Gospel of the Righteousness of God: Pauline Reinterpretation in Rom. 3:21–31." *Int* 20 (1966) 432–52.

Richardson, A. *An Introduction to the Theology of the New Testament*. London: SCM, 1958.

Ridderbos, H. "The Earliest Confession of the Atonement in Paul (1 Cor. 15:3)." In *Reconciliation and Hope: Essays Presented to L. L. Morris on His Sixtieth Birthday*, edited by R. Banks, 76–89. Exeter: Paternoster, 1974.

Ridderbos, H. *Paul: An Outline of His Theology*. Grand Rapids: Eerdmans, 1975.

Riesenfeld,.H. art "ὑπερ." In *TDNT* 8:507–16.

Robichaux, K. S. "Christ the Firstborn." *AffCr* 2 (1997) 30–38.

Robinson, D. W. B. "Towards a Definition of Baptism." *RTR* 34 (1975) 1–15.

Robinson, J. A. T. *Wrestling with Romans*. London: SCM, 1979.

Rogerson, J. W. "Corporate Personality." In *ADB* 1:1156–157.

———. "The Hebrew Conception of Corporate Personality: A Re-examination." *JTS* 21 (1970) 1–16.

Rosenberg, R. A. "Jesus, Isaac and the Suffering Servant." *JBL* 84:4 (1965) 381–88.

Rosner, R. S. *Paul, Scripture & Ethics: A Study of 1 Cor. 5-7*. Leiden: Brill, 1994.

Rosen-Zvi, I. "The school of R. Ishmael and the origins of the concept of Yeser hara' (The Evil Inclination)", *Tarbiz*, 76 (2006-2007)1-2

Rowley, H. H. *The Faith of Israel: Aspects of Old Testament Thought, Sprunt Lectures*. London: SCM Press, 1956.

Russell, W. "The Apostle Paul's Redemptive-Historical Argumentation in Galatians 5:13–26." *WTJ* 57:2 (1995) 333–57.

Ryan, J. M. "God's Fidelity to Israel and Mercy to All." *TBT* 35:2 (1997) 89–93.

Sahlin, H. "The New Exodus of Salvation according to St. Paul." In *The Root of the Vine: Essays in Biblical Theology*, edited by A. Fridrichsen, 81–95. Westminster: Dacre, 1953.

Sahlin, H. "Adam-Christologie im Neuen Testament." *ST* 41 (1987) 11–32.

Sampley, J. P. *Paul in the Greco-Romans World*. Harrisburg: Trinity, 2003.

Sanday, W. and A. Headlam. *A Critical and Exegetical Commentary on the Epistle to the Romans*. Edinburgh: T. & T. Clark, 1902.

Sanders, E. P. *Paul*. Oxford: Oxford University Press, 1991.

———. *Paul and Palestinian Judaism*. London: SCM, 1977.

Sandnes, K. O. "'Justification by Faith'—An Outdated Doctrine? The 'New Perspective' on Paul—A Presentation and Appraisal." *Theology & Life* 17–19 (1996) 127–46.

Sandy, W and A. Headlam. *A Critical and Exegetical Commentary of the Epistle to the Romans*. Edinburgh: T. & T. Clark, 1902.

Sass, G. "Rom 15:7–13—als Summe des Romerbriefs gelesen." *EvT* 53 (1993) 510–27.

Schaefer, J. R. "The Relationship between Priestly and Servant Messianism in the Epistle to the Hebrews." *CBQ* 30 (1968) 359–85.

Schillebeeckx, E. *Jesus: An Experiment in Christology*. Translated by H. Hoskins. New York: Seabury, 1979.

Schnackenburg, R. *Baptism in the Thought of St. Paul: A Study in Pauline Theology*. Translated by G. R. Beasley-Murray. Oxford: Basil Blackwell, 1964.

Schneider, B. "The Corporate Meaning and Background of 1 Cor. 15:45b—O Eschatos Adam eis Pneuma Zōiopoioun." *CBQ* 29 (1967) 450–67.

Schoeps, H. J. *Paul: The Theology of the Apostle Paul in the Light of Jewish Religious History*. London: Lutterworth, 1961.

———. "The Sacrifice of Jesus in Paul's Theology." *JBL* 65 (1946) 385–92.

Schrange, W. *Der erste Brief an die Korinthen 1*. Teilband, 1 Kor. 1:1—6:11. Benziger: Neukirchener, 1991.

———. *Der erste Brief an die Korinthen 2*. Teilband, 1 Kor. 6:12—11: 16. Benziger: Neukirchener, 1995.

Schreiner, T. R. *Circumcision: An Entree into 'Newness' in Pauline Thought*. PhD diss., Fuller Theological Seminary, 1983.

———. "Did Paul Believe in Justification by Works?: Another Look at Romans 2." *BullBibRes* 3 (1993) 131–55.

———. "Does Romans 9 Teach Individual Election unto Salvation? Some Exegetical and Theological Reflec-tions." *JETS* 36 (1993) 25–40.

———. "Paul's View of the Law in Romans 10:4–5." *WTJ* 55 (1993) 113–35.

———. *Romans*, Grand Rapids: Baker, 1998.

Schweizer, E. *Lordship and Discipleship*. Naperville: Allenson, 1960.

———. "πνεῦμα." *TDNT* 4, 435.

———. "The Son of Man." *JBL* 79 (1960) 119–29.

Scott, J. M. "Adoption, Sonship." In *DPL*, 15 18.

———. *Adoption as Sons of God: An Exegetical Investigation into the Background of* ΫΙΟΘΕΣΙΑ *in the Pauline Corpus*. Tubingen: Mohr-Siebeck, 1992.

Scroggs, R *The Last Adam: A Study in Pauline Anthropology*. Oxford: Blackwell, 1966.

Seifrid, M. "Romans." In *Commentary on the New Testament Use of the Old Testament*, edited by G. K. Beale and D. A. Carson, 607–94. Grand Rapids: Baker Academic, 2007.

Shepherd, M. H. *The Paschal Liturgy and the Apocalypse*. London: Lutterworth, 1960.

Sherlock, C. *The Doctrine of Humanity*. Leicester: InterVarsity, 1996.

Shin, C. S. "New Exodus Motif in the Letter to the Hebrews." PhD diss., University of Wales, Lampeter, 2007.

Shogren, G. S. "Presently Entering the Kingdom of Christ: the Background and Purpose of Col. 1:12–14." *JETS* 31 (1988) 173–80.

Shum, Shiu-Lun. *Paul's Use of Isaiah in Romans: A Comparative Study of Paul's Letter to the Romans and the Sibylline and Qumran Sectarian Texts*. Wissenschaftliche Untersuchungen zum Neuen Testament. Tubingen: Mohr Siebeck, 2002.

Bibliography

Siegert, F. *Argumentation Bei Paulus, Gezeigt an Rom. 9–11*. Wissenschaftliche Untersuchungen Zum Neuen Testament 34. Tubingen: Mohr, 1985.

Skehan, P. W. *Studies in Israelite Wisdom and Poetry*. Washington, DC: Catholic Biblical Association, 1971.

Smiles, V. M. "The Concept of 'Zeal' in Second Temple Judaism and Paul's Critique of it in Romans 10:2." *CBQ* 64:2 (2002) 282–99.

Smith, G. "The Function of 'Likewise' (ΩΣΑΥΤΩΣ) Romans 8:26." *TynBul* 49 (1998) 29–38.

Smolarz, S. R. *Covenant and the Metaphor of Divine Marriage in Biblical Thought: A Study with Special Reference to the Book of Revelation*. Eugene, OR: Wipf & Stock, 2010.

Snodgrass, S. G. "Is the Kingdom of God about Eating and Drinking or Isn't It? Romans 14:17." *NovTest* 42:3 (2000) 521–25.

Song, Y. M., and J. S. Du Rand. "The Story of the Red Sea as a Theological Framework of Interpretation." *VE* 30(2), Art. 337, 5 pages. DOI: 10.4102/ve.v30i2.337.

Stahlin, G. "απαξ." *TDNT* 1:381–84.

Stanley, Christopher D. *Arguing with Scripture: The Rhetoric of Quotations in the Letters of Paul*. London: T. & T. Clark, 2004.

Strauss, M.L. *The Davidic Messiah in Luke-Acts: The Promise and its Fulfillment in Lukan Christology, Journal for the Study of the New Testament Supplem*. Sheffield: Sheffield Academic Press, 1995. Stendahl, K. "The Apostle Paul and the Introspective Conscience of the West." *HTR* (1963) 199–215.

Stott, J. R. W. *The Message of Ephesians: God's New Society*. Leicester: InterVarsity, 1979.

Stowers, S. K. "Paul's Dialogue with a Fellow Jew in Romans 3:1–9." *CBQ* 46 (1984) 707–22.

———. *A Rereading of Romans*. New Haven: Yale University Press, 1994.

Strickland, W., Jr., W. C. Kaiser, D. J. Moo, W. A. Van Gemeren, and S. N. Grundy. *Five Views on Law and Gospel*. Grand Rapids: Zondervan, 1996.

Strom, M. *Reframing Paul: Conversations in Grace and Community*. Downers Grove, IL: InterVarsity, 2000.

Stuart, D. K. *Hosea-Jonah, Word Biblical Themes*. Dallas: Word Books, 1989.

Stuhlmacher, P. *Paul's Letter to the Romans: A Commentary*. Louisville, KY: Westminster John Knox, 1994.

———. "The Theme of Romans." *ABR* 36 (1988) 31–44.

Stuhlmacher, P., and E. R. Kalin. *Reconciliation Law and Righteousness: Essays in Biblical Theology*. Philadelphia: Fortress, 1986.

Talbert, C. H. "Non-Pauline fragment at Romans 3:24–26." *JBL* 85:3 (1966) 287–96.

———. *Romans*. Macon, GA: Smyth & Helwys, 2002.

Taylor, V. *The Atonement in the New Testament Teaching*. 2nd ed. London: Epworth, 1954.

———. *The Epistle to the Romans*. London: Epworth, 1955.

Thielman, F. "The Story of Israel and the Theology of Romans 5–8." In *Pauline Theology*, vol. 3, editor by David M. Hay and E. Elizabeth Johnson, 169–96. Minneapolis: Fortress, 1995.

Thiselton, A. T. *Hermeneutics: An Introduction*. Grand Rapids: Eerdmans, 2009.

———. *The Hermeneutics of Christian Doctrine*. Grand Rapids: Eerdmans, 2007.

———. *The Living Paul: An Introduction to the Apostles Life and Thought*. Downers Grove, IL: InterVarsity, 2009.

Tobin, T. H. "What Shall We Say That Abraham Found?: The Controversy behind Romans 4." *Dia* 35:3 (1996) 193–98.

Torrance, T. F. *Theology in Reconstruction*. London: SCM, 1965.

Trumper T. J. R. "From Slaves to Sons!" *Foundations* 55 (2006) 17–19.

Tsumura, D. T. "An OT Background to Romans 8:22." *NTS* 40:4 (1994) 620–21.

Turner, M. *The Holy Spirit and Spiritual Gifts Then and Now*. Carlisle: Paternoster, 1996.

Turner, N. *Grammatical Insights into the New Testament*. Edinburgh: T. & T. Clark, 1965.

Turner, S. "The Interim, Earthly Messianic Kingdom in Paul." *JSNT* 25:3 (2003) 323–42.

Udoeyop, E. A. "The New People of God and Kingdom Fruitfulness: An Exegetical and Theological Study of the Parable of the Wicked Tenants in Matthew 21:33–46 and its Significance for a Corporate Hermeneutic." PhD diss., Queen's University Belfast, 2006.

Van der Horst, P. W. "Only then will All Israel be Saved: A Short Note on the Meaning of καὶ οὕτως in Romans 11:26." *JBL* 119:3 (2006) 521–25.

Vaughan, C. J. *St Paul's Epistle to the Romans*. London, 1885.

Vermes, G. "Redemption & Genesis XXII. The Binding of Isaac and the Sacrifice of Jesus." In *Scripture and Tradition in Judaism*, 193–227. Leiden: Brill, 1961.

Vleugels, G. "The Jewish Scriptures in Galatians and Romans." Brussels: *Analecta Bruxellensia*, vol. 7 (2002) 156–63.

Wagner, J. R. "The Christ, Servant of the Jews and Gentiles: A Fresh Approach to Romans 15:8–9." *JBL* 116:3 (1997) 473–85.

———. *Heralds of the Good News: Isaiah and Paul 'In Concert' in the Letter to the Romans*. (Supplements to Novum Testamentum, 101.) Leiden: Brill, 2002.

Wanamaker, C. A. *The Epistle to the Thessalonians: A Commentary on the Greek Text*. Grand Rapids: Eedermans. 1990.

Warnack, V. "Taufe und Heilsgeschehen nach Rom. 6." *ALW* 111:2 (1954) 259.

———. "Die Tauflehre des Romerbriefes in der neueren Theologischen Diskussion." *ALW* 2 (1958) 274–332

Watts, R. E. *Isaiah's New Exodus and Mark, Wissenschaftliche Untersuchungen Zum Neuen Testame*. Tübingen: Mohr, 1997.

Webb, W. J. *Returning Home; New Covenant and Second Exodus as the Context for 2 Corinthians 6:14—7:1*. JSNTSupp 85. Sheffield: JSOT Press, 1993.

Wedderburn, A. J. M. "Adam and Christ: An Investigation into the Background of 1 Corinthians XV and Romans V:12–21." PhD diss., Cambridge University, 1970.

———. "The Theological Structure of Romans 5:12." *NTS* 19 (1973) 339–54.

Weima, J. A. D. "The Pauline Letter Closings: Analysis and Hermeneutical Significance." *BullBibRes* 5 (1995) 177–97.

Westerholm, S. *Israel's Law and the Church's Faith*. Grand Rapids: Eerdmans, 1988.

———. *Perspectives Old and New on Paul: The "Lutheran Paul" and his Critics*. Grand Rapids: Eedermans, 2004.

Whelan, C. F. "Amica Pauli: The Role of Phoebe in the Early Church." *JSNT* 49 (1993) 67–85.

Whiteley, D. E. H. "St. Paul's Thought on the Atonement." *JTS* 8 (1957) 240–55.

———. *The Theology of St. Paul*. Oxford: Oxford University Press, 1964.

Whitsett, C. G. "Son of God, Seed of David: Paul's Messianic Exegesis on Romans 1:3–4." *JBL* 119:4 (2000) 661–81.

Wifall, W., "Son of Man—A PreDavidic Social Class?", CBQ 37 (1975)331-40.

Wilckens, U. *Der Brief an die Romer*, 3 vols. Benziger/Neukirchener, 1978, 1980, 1982.

Wilder W. N. *Echoes of the Exodus Narrative in the Context and Background of Galatians 5:18* (Studies in Biblical Literature, Vol. 23) New York: Peter Lang, 2001.

Williams, S. M. "The 'Righteousness of God' in Romans." *JBL* 99 (1980) 241–90.

Winger, M. "The Law of Christ." *NTS* 46:4 (2000) 537–46.

Winter, B. *Seek the Welfare of the City: Christians as Benefactors and Citizens*. Grand Rapids: Eerdmans, 1994.

Witherington, B., III. *Grace in Galatia: A Commentary on St. Paul's Letter to the Galatians*. Grand Rapids: Eerdmans, 1998.

———. *Paul's Letter to the Romans: A Socio-Rhetorical Commentary*. Grand Rapids: Eerdmans, 2004.

Wood, J "The Purpose of Romans." *EvQ* 40:4 (1968) 211–19.

Wright, N. T. "Adam in Pauline Christology." In *SBL Seminar Papers*, edited by K. H. Richards. Chico, CA (1983) 359–89.

———. *The Climax of the Covenant: Christ and the Law in Pauline Theology*. Edinburgh: T. & T. Clark, 1991.

———. *The Epistles of Paul to Colossians and Philemon: An Introduction and Commentary*. Leicester: InterVarsity, 1986.

———. *Jesus and the Victory of God*. London: SPCK, 1996.

———. "The Letter to the Romans: Introduction, Commentary, and Reflections." In *The New Interpreter's Bible, Volume X, Acts–1 Corinthians*, edited by L. E. Keck, 359–770. Nashville: Abingdon, 2002.

———. "The Messiah and the People of God." PhD diss., Oxford University, 1980.

———. *The New Testament and the People of God*. London: SPCK, 1992.

———. "The Paul of History and the Apostle of Faith." *TB* 29 (1978) 61–88.

———. "Redemption from the New Perspective? Towards a Multi-Layered Pauline Theology of the Cross." In *Redemption*, edited by S. T. Davies, D. Kendall, and G. O. O'Collins, 69–100. Oxford: Oxford University Press, 2006.

Bibliography

————. "Romans and the Theology of Paul." In *Pauline Theology*, vol. 3, edited by David M. Hay and E. Elizabeth Johnson, 30–67. Minneapolis: Fortress, 1995.

————. *What Saint Paul Really Said*. Oxford: Lion, 1997.

Yinger, K. L. "Romans 12:14–21 and Nonretaliation in Second Temple Judaism: addressing persecution within the community." *CBQ* 60 (1998) 74–96.

Young, N. H. "C. H. Dodd, 'Hilaskesthai' and His Critics." *EQ* Vol. 48:2 (1976) 67–78.

————. "Did St. Paul Compose Romans 3:24f.?" *ABR* 22 (1974) 23–32.

Zeller, D. *Der Brief an die Romer*. Regensburg: Friedrich Pustet, 1985.

Ziesler, J. *The Meaning of Righteousness in Paul: A Linguistic and Theological Enquiry*. London: Cambridge University Press, 1972.

————. *Paul's Letter to the Romans*. London: SCM, 1989.

————. "Soma in the Septuagint." *NovT* 25.2 (1983) 133–45.

Zorn, W. D. "The Messianic Use of Habbakkuk 2:4a in Romans." *Stone-Campbell Journal* 1:2 (1998) 213–30.

Zwiep, A. W. *The Ascension of the Messiah in Lukan Christology*. Leiden: Brill, 1997.

Index of Authors[*]

Agesnap, S., 168
Albright, W. F., 58
Aletti, J. N., 241, 299
Allison, D. C., 237, 386
Anderson, C., 17, 438
Arnold, C., 347
Ashton, J., 2
Aune, D., 64, 203

Badke, W. B., 171
Bailey, K. E., 137
Ballentine, G. L., 10
Balsdon, J. P. V. D., 240
Barclay, J. M. G., 71
Barr, G. K., 471
Barth, M., 209, 347
Barrett, C. K., 28, 48, 68, 85, 289, 313, 410
Bauckham, R., 311
Baxter, A. G., 379
Beale, G. K., 6, 91, 322, 311
Bechtler, S. R., 341
Beet, J. A., 158
Bekken, P. J., 344
Bell, R. H., 165
Belli, F., 288
Berkley, T. W., 65
Best, E., 64, 94, 175, 187, 285
Bird, M. F., 97
Black, M., 85, 88, 163, 284
Blauw, J., 3
Bligh, J., 169
Blocher, H., 213
Bockmuehl, M., 230
Boers, H., 2, 168
Bornkamm, G., 15, 32, 91, 356
Bowker, J., 88

* Because theological discussion is reserved to the footnotes all references refer to the footnotes found on the particualar page.

Braaten, C.E., 418
Brewer, D. I., 24
Broyles, C. C., 205
Bruce, F. F., 15, 35, 189, 266, 272, 274, 376, 397
Buchsel, F., 284
Budd, P., 96
Bultmann, R., 83, 88, 163
Burke, T., 272, 302
Byrne, B., 260, 273

Caird, G. F. B., 32, 270, 312, 347
Calvin, J., 122, 384, 385, 387
Campbell, D. A., 43, 84, 97, 98, 190
Campbell, W. S., 18, 300, 327
Carbone, S., 384
Carson, D. A., 32, 88, 109,
Casey, M., 4, 209
Casey, R. P., 32, 89, 91
Cervin, R. S., 473
Chadwick, H., 2, 277
Charlesworth, J. H., 270
Chilton, B., 230, 286, 375.
Coleman, T. M., 429
Court, J. M., 28
Cousar, C. P., 88
Coxon, P., 10, 83
Cozart, R., 10, 83, 121, 322
Cranfield, C. E. B., 63, 68, 83, 89, 102, 106, 200, 274, 280, 286, 308, 313, 340, 384, 437, 447, 451, 454, 456
Cullmann, O., 32, 163, 170, 304

Dahl, N. A., 145
Davies, R. E., 88
Davies, R. P., 24, 230, 288
Davies, W. D., 2, 32, 89, 155, 163, 181, 187, 217, 260, 300, 345, 385, 386
Davila, J. R., 24
De Lacey., 32

Index of Subjects

Index of Ancient Sources

~

New Testament

∼